FOCAL PROBLEMS IN GEOGRAPHY SERIES

# RECREATION IN THE COUNTRYSIDE

*Focal Problems in Geography Series*

*Published*

DAVID GRIGG:                    The Harsh Lands A Study in Agricultural Development

ALAN HAY:                       Transport for the Space Economy A Geographical Study

MICHAEL F. THOMAS:              Tropical Geomorphology A Study of Weathering and
                                Landform Development in Warm Climates

J. T. COPPOCK and               Recreation in the Countryside A Spatial Analysis
B. S. DUFFIELD:

*Titles in preparation include*

BARRY J. GARNER:                Linkage Within Cities

H. ROBINSON:                    Population and Resources

D. C. D. POCOCK and             Images of the Urban Environment
R. HUDSON

# Recreation in the Countryside
## A Spatial Analysis

**J. T. Coppock**

and

**B. S. Duffield**

*Department of Geography, University of Edinburgh*

*First published 1975 by*
THE MACMILLAN PRESS LTD
*London and Basingstoke*
*Associated companies in New York Dublin*
*Melbourne Johannesburg and Madras*

SBN 333 15110 0  (hard cover)
333 15170 4 (paper cover)

Text set in 10/11 pt  Press Roman by
Reproduction Drawings Ltd

Printed and bound in Great Britain by
REDWOOD BURN LIMITED
Trowbridge & Esher

# Contents

# List of Figures

# Acknowledgements

It is impossible to do justice to all those who have contributed to this volume. In one sense it is a tribute to all who have worked in the Tourism and Recreation Research Unit and whose contributions are acknowledged in the various publications on page 240. Pride of place, however, must go to Mrs Sharyn Reilly for the part she has played in the production of this book. Mrs Reilly has done a vast amount of preparatory work in checking references and locating and abstracting publications; she has received, checked and made intelligible the authors' manuscripts; prepared and checked tables and illustrations; acted as intermediary between the authors and provided the spur that has brought the book from rough draft to finished manuscript.

Another major contribution has been made by Mrs Mona Robertson, the Unit's secretary, who has typed or co-ordinated the typing of many drafts and coped with typical academic scrawls. Mrs Robertson has had the capable assistance of Caroline Czoski and Monica Barry who have both helped with the typing. In addition, the authors are most grateful to those outside the Unit who have helped the book forward, notably the staff of the Regional Computing Centre, especially Mr W. Gordon, Assistant Service Manager, Mr Colin Davies, Mr Dave Sturgess and the operating staffs of the IBM 360/50 and ICL 4/75; the staff of the Department of Geography, especially Mrs S. Allan, Mrs P. Paterson and Mrs P. Robertson, secretaries, and Messrs A. Carson Clark, A. Bradley and R. Harris of the cartographic and reprographic unit; and the staff of the Research Centre for the Social Sciences, under Mr J. Nimmo. Essential, too, has been the work of others in this field, on whose publications the authors have drawn extensively, notably Professor H.B. Rodgers, Professor J. Allan Patmore, Mr K.K. Sillitoe, Dr M. Young and Professor P. Willmott, the North West Sports Council and the North Regional Planning Committee.

The authors also wish to acknowledge with gratitude the financial support provided by a number of bodies, for without this neither the book nor the studies on which it is based would have been possible: the Natural Environment and Social Science Research Councils; the Countryside Commission for Scotland; the Forestry Commission; the Highlands and Islands Development Board; the Scottish Tourist Board; the local authorities that participated in the studies; and the University of Edinburgh, which has provided a home for the Unit, much indirect support and access to a range of facilities. Many of the staffs of these different organisations have contributed in various ways and their help is gratefully acknowledged.

We would wish to record our appreciation of the work of our colleague Mike Owen, who has shared with us the joys and tribulations of the extensive research programme that the Unit has implemented over the last six years, and Steve Dowers, the Unit's Systems Analyst, who has undertaken most of the computing. Our sincere thanks are also due to Sheila Coppock who has contributed to the book in various ways, especially by casting a critical eye on professional jargon and ambiguity, so helping to make the text more readable and comprehensible. Lastly our thanks are due to our families for tolerating the neglect which that spare-time occupation, academic authorship, inevitably brings. No doubt they are all too well aware of the paradox that research in leisure and recreation leaves no time for recreation and leisure for the researchers.

# Preface

Although extensive reference is made in this book to studies undertaken elsewhere, particularly in the United Kingdom, its writing stems primarily from the work of the Tourism and Recreation Research Unit in the Geography Department of the University of Edinburgh.

This unit began its existence in embryo form in 1967 when the Natural Environment Research Council gave a grant in support of a reconnaissance study of the impact of outdoor recreation on the countryside of central Scotland, though it had a precursor in a small study of tourism in the Borders, undertaken by students of the Geography Department for the Scottish Tourist Board in the summer of 1966. This reconnaissance study was envisaged in two stages. The first was to be essentially a desk study in which a general picture of recreational use of the countryside in central Scotland was to be constructed, largely by inquiry among local authorities, associations of recreationists and of land-users, and the like. The second was to be a detailed investigation of a number of sites, selected to illustrate a range of problems identified at the first stage.

The research team at that time consisted of the two authors, but they were soon joined, on a voluntary basis, by M.L. Owen, a Senior Assistant in the Department of Physical Education who was studying for a higher degree in outdoor recreation. In the course of these reconnaisance inquiries, contact was made with staff of the Planning Department of Lanarkshire County Council who were then beginning to prepare plans for recreation and tourism, as requested by the Secretary of State for Scotland. It became clear that it would be mutually advantageous if the embryo Unit undertook the necessary surveys — additional resources would become available for the reconnaissance study and the local authority would have the services of a research team at little cost. Such a survey was therefore undertaken in the summer of 1969 and the results published the following year (Duffield and Owen, 1970). It provided the Unit with valuable experience and with data (especially on recreational travel and participation) of a kind that could be acquired only by direct survey, and laid the foundations for the local authority's plans.

As the desk study proceeded, it became clear that the impact of outdoor recreation in central Scotland could be conveniently considered in relation to three types of areas. There were those, such as the middle Clyde valley, where large numbers of potential recreationists lived but where recreational resources were only meagre (by Scottish standards). The second type, represented by the Greater Edinburgh area, also had large populations but had a wealth of recreational resources, so that supply and demand were roughly in balance. Thirdly, there were areas, mostly on the margins of central Scotland, which were rich in recreational

resources but were within easy motoring range of only small populations. It seemed
to the staff of the Unit that there was a great deal to be gained by a comparative
study of three such areas, of which the Lanarkshire survey provided an example of
the first type. Approaches were therefore made to local authorities and to the
Countryside Commission for Scotland. In conjunction with a consortium of local
authorities (Edinburgh Corporation and the County Councils of East and West
Lothian, Midlothian and Peebles), the Countryside Commission agreed to support
such a study of Greater Edinburgh, and this was undertaken at the same time as
the Lanarkshire survey, the results being published shortly after the report on the
latter survey (Duffield and Owen, 1971). Approaches to those authorities responsible for areas in the third group, which were not then under pressure, were
unsuccessful, the chief argument against any such investigation being that they
did not wish to encourage recreation and tourism in their counties. For one
authority at least, the futility of such a policy was soon amply demonstrated
when the opening of a motorway made the county immediately vulnerable to a
rapid increase in recreational pressures.

The study of individual sites was also put in hand, though on a less ambitious
scale than had previously been intended; for it had become apparent that the
effects of recreational pressures could be established with any degree of certainty
only over a longer time span than had been originally expected. Coastal sites in
East Lothian, in the care of the County Council and at varying distances from
Edinburgh, were selected for investigation and, with the help of ecologists from
the Department of Forestry and Natural Resources in Edinburgh University and
Napier College, detailed vegetation and topographic surveys were made of each site,
the former in relation to a permanent 100-m grid so that samples could be
compared in the future. These surveys were complemented by the monitoring of
recreational use and movement throughout the sites on sample days, chosen to
explore the effects of different factors. It is intended to repeat these surveys at
regular intervals and so obtain some measure of recreational pressures.

From this point the Unit grew both in strength and in the range of studies
undertaken. M.L. Owen had become a full-time member of the team in 1969, a
geographer–planner, R.L. Brown, was recruited in 1970, a systems analyst, S. Dowers,
in 1971, a sociologist, S. Reilly, in the same year and an agricultural economist,
R.L. Cousins, and a geographer–statistician, P. Forer, in 1973; this was recognition of
the fact that, although the Unit's work has always had a strong geographical flavour,
with an emphasis on spatial and environmental aspects of recreation, the study of
outdoor recreation is necessarily multi-disciplinary. In addition, the Unit has
received extensive advice from computer scientists, ecologists, economists,
sociologists and statisticians in the two universities in Edinburgh and has
employed up to 200 temporary workers during the summer seasons as interviewers
and coders and in a variety of other capacities.

Since the successful completion of the Lanarkshire and Greater Edinburgh
surveys, the Unit has undertaken a number of studies of recreational travel in
Scotland for the Countryside Commission and the Scottish Tourist Board (Owen
and Duffield, 1971, 1972), and a grant from the Social Science Research Council
has enabled a more extensive examination of the nature of recreational travel to
be undertaken (Duffield, 1973). Studies have also been completed of recreational

accommodation (Owen and Duffield, 1973) and the Unit, which was formally recognised by the University in 1972, is currently engaged on three major investi-gations, namely, a study of recreational demand by residents and visitors through-out Scotland; a methodological study of the economic and social impact of tourism on a region; and the design and operation of an information system on resources for tourism and recreation in Scotland. In all, the Unit has received contracts and grants to the value of more than £120 000 and published sixteen reports as well as a number of papers.

During this period, parallel investigations have been undertaken in other parts of the United Kingdom and there is a vast literature on recreation and tourism in North America, though comparatively little is explicitly geographical. In view of the very different balance between man and land in Great Britain and the different social and economic conditions, there seemed to be a place for a book which, while using North American material where relevant, would attempt to bring together the various studies that have been undertaken in this island. The resulting book draws heavily on the work of the Unit and is written by geographers primarily for geographers, though it is intended also to be useful to planners, ecologists and all who use and manage recreational resources in the countryside, whether for the resident population or for visitors. It is hoped, too, that it will be of interest to administrators, conservationists, recreationists and others who are concerned to achieve a prosperous and healthy countryside; for only by understanding the forces at work will it be possible to devise sensible policies. The book is not intended to be a compendium about recreation in the British countryside, though, in defining the key parameters that govern recreational activity, it will inevitably throw a good deal of light on patterns of outdoor recreation. Instead, it is selective in its coverage, seeking rather to evaluate the findings and approaches of those surveys that have been specifically undertaken to illuminate the many dark areas of British policy for outdoor recreation in the countryside. Underlying this evaluation is a concern for method and for organising concepts; while these are firmly based on empirical studies, the authors are all too well aware of the needs for further research in a field where well-founded facts are hard to come by and where fundamental thinking is necessary on the nature of these recreational activities and their geographical manifestations.

One important theme in this book is the key role of the motor car in outdoor recreation in the countryside. In the short term, estimates of future levels of recreational activity are being called into question by rapid increases in the prices of petroleum products and by the prospects of shortfalls in supply. Crises have arisen before and it is difficult to know at the present time whether this crisis is different in nature. It can certainly be expected that it will lead to renewed searches for alternative supplies, whether of oil or of other fuels; the scale of potential supplies in the North Sea would hardly have been predicted in the mid-1950s. Whatever the outcome, it seems unlikely that, once people have experienced the freedom of personal mobility that the motor car provides, they will willingly forgo it. If they do, a new model of rural living and countryside recreation will be necessary.

# 1 Aims and Concepts

Although the use of the countryside for recreation by those living there is a long-established feature of rural life and the provision of opportunities for access to open space by an increasingly urban and industrial population was a matter of growing concern during the nineteenth century, the need to make provision for outdoor recreation has been curiously neglected by both academics and policy-makers. Even in North America, with its abundant land resources and long tradition of national parks, it was possible for a leading authority to write in 1964 that 'little more than a decade ago, the literature on outdoor recreation was relatively meagre, and the geography of the subject had scarcely been touched' (Wolfe, 1964), and he went on to note the contrast at the time he was writing between the voluminous publications on recreation which had then appeared from other sources (notably the 27 study reports of the Outdoor Recreation Resources Review Commission) and the continued dearth of published geographical studies. In the United Kingdom, apart from a concern with scenic quality and a number of papers on tourism, there was a similar dearth of either official or academic publications; the development of both official and academic interest came later, the former expressed particularly in the creation of the Countryside Commissions. The first paper to be concerned specifically with the geography of outdoor recreation in the countryside appeared in 1966 (Coppock) and the first book on this theme in 1970 (Patmore), but there has been a rapid increase in interest in the last decade, a fact reflected in the appointment of two geographers, J.A. Patmore and H.B. Rodgers, as specialist advisors to the Select Committee of the House of Lords on Sport and Leisure (itself an indication of growing public interest) and the appointment of geographers as Director and Assistant Directors of the Countryside Commission (R. Hookway, J.M. Davidson and A.A.C. Phillips). The present volume also reflects this growing interest and springs in large measure from the work of the Tourism and Recreation Research Unit over the six years from 1967 to 1973.

This apparent lack of geographical concern (as measured by geographical publications) is the more surprising in view of the fact that recreation, especially outdoor recreation in the countryside, exhibits to a marked degree many of the characteristics of human activity which have interested geographers. Yet recreation was not recorded as a use of land on the maps of the first Land Utilisation Survey and there is hardly any reference to it in the published reports; only 'Open Space, tended but unproductive land' is recorded on the maps of the Second Land Use Survey (Coleman and Maggs, 1965). The standard texts on economic and human geography similarly ignore it, and, although there has been a growing interest in aspects of economic activity other than production, notably marketing, retailing and transport, and in other tertiary occupations, leisure is rarely mentioned. These gaps are understandable, for recreation is not often the primary use of land and a distinctive feature of outdoor recreation, at least in the United Kingdom, has been the paucity of information about it. Yet the study of outdoor recreation, like that of geography itself, embraces both physical and human aspects of the subject, for such recreation depends not only on the natural environment, which provides the recreational resources, but also on the social, demographic and economic characteristics of the population which uses it. Moreover, the relationships between user and resources are markedly influenced by their respective distributions. Outdoor recreation thus exhibits those distinctive features of man's relationship with his environment and of spatial patterning which have long been the primary concerns of geographers, and it is particularly appropriate that, at a time when the quality of life and the conservation of the natural environment have become matters of major concern in developed countries, geographers should turn in increasing numbers to the study of leisure and its effects on the countryside.

This book focuses on the application of geographical methods to the study of such recreational use and on the modifications that are necessary to existing concepts to accommodate the distinctive features of outdoor recreational activities. It is concerned with both method and analysis, and concludes that a systems approach provides the best method of understanding the observed characteristics and relationships of outdoor recreation in the countryside. It should be noted that the subject matter is confined to outdoor recreation in the countryside, which, though it shares many characteristics with outdoor recreation as a whole, notably its seasonal character and its dependence on the weather, is only part of outdoor recreation. This in turn, as chapter 2 shows, is only a small part of all leisure activities. Nevertheless, participation in outdoor recreation is thought to be expanding faster than leisure as a whole and has been estimated by the Countryside Commission as rising at a compound rate of between 10 and 15 per cent (Select Committee, 1973); such recreation may also have an impact on the environment and on other land users out of all proportion to the numbers involved. Outdoor recreation thus merits special attention.


THE OPERATIONAL CONCEPT: THE DEMAND/SUPPLY MODEL

The success of any study of outdoor recreation depends on the synthesis of two contrasting elements:

(1) the sociological phenomenon of leisure or, for this book, that part of leisure time which an individual spends on outdoor recreation; and
(2) the physical resources that are necessary for the particular recreational activities.

In this book the working hypothesis that can best give some coherence to these disparate elements is the classic economic model of supply and demand. Outdoor recreation is one aspect of man's relationship with his environment which still retains, to a large degree, the basic structure of a market economy. Although many other aspects of man's daily life, such as work, urban living and transport, are planned to a greater or lesser degree, outdoor recreation in the countryside is, in many ways still free to obey the basic market laws of supply and demand and, until recently, has remained largely unaffected either by public control or by public provision. There are two basic reasons for this situation:

(1) Recreational activities are part of man's leisure time and, within certain restraints, he can dispose of this time as he wishes. Although it is possible to isolate several motives in the use of leisure time, it cannot be directed or controlled openly except by the provision of facilities. Thus *recreational demand* is still free to respond to the prevailing market forces.

(2) The other element in the equation, the *supply of recreational resources,* has also been largely outside planning control. Public authorities have seldom acquired and managed land for outdoor recreation which has thus, in large measure, been parasitic on other uses, such as agriculture, forestry and water management.

This book examines the changes in this relationship between demand and supply that have been brought about in recent years by changes in leisure time itself, by the growing impact of recreation on the countryside and also by the passing of recent legislation, particularly the Countryside Acts, under which the two Countryside Commissions were established. These developments, together with other legislation and a growing awareness among local authorities that recreation should have a more important place in planning strategies, will encourage a more ordered development of recreational land use in the future. Nevertheless, the resolution of the relationships between supply and demand still offers a valid basis for the design of research in this field.

## Demand for Recreation

The concept of demand used in this model of recreation has many similarities to that used in discussions of the production of consumer goods, but there are some important differences which this investigation will endeavour to illuminate. In economic terms, demand describes the relationship between the quantities of a product that people will purchase and the prices they will pay; that is, it refers to a desire which is backed by ability and willingness to pay for the product that is desired. The amount of demand at some given price indicates the amount of *consumption* of the product which will occur at that price.

In recreation, many more complex influences bear on the consumption of an activity than the price paid to participate in it, and this is obviously the case with those many forms of outdoor recreation for which no payment is made. The consumer must spend some amount of time performing the activity. He may have to purchase market goods, such as boats and trailers, he must usually expend time and money in travelling before and after participating, and he may have to pay for participating. Qualitative differences in the environments in which the activities are performed also play a significant role in his choice, even to the extent that apparently identical activities may, in effect, be several different 'goods' performed in different environments — for example, swimming in a public pool as opposed to swimming at the seaside. As far as countryside recreation is concerned, the term *demand* refers to the amounts of various recreational activities in which a population will be willing and able to participate, given that access to facilities is very easy, that these facilities are all of high quality and that the limits of their capacity have not been reached. If demand is defined in this way, it is then dependent solely on the specific characteristics of the population, such as their income, age, family structure, occupation and psychological parameters, and not on their location, the quality of the facilities actually available or the means of access to them.

In most circumstances these perfect market conditions do not exist, for problems of information about and access to recreational resources and their uneven distribution in relation to population will combine to constrain the full expression of demand for an activity. It is in these conditions that confusion arises between concepts of demand and concepts of *consumption* (or *participation*).

Participation and consumption are closely allied concepts, but there is an important distinction between them. *Participation* should be used only with reference to areas of residence, so that participation levels will define, for a given community, the numbers of people participating in particular activities. *Consumption*, on the other hand, relates to the recreational use of a particular area and denotes the level of use of that area by the activity under consideration. *Consumption* is thus a measure of use at a particular destination, while *participation* is a measure of use as generated at a particular origin. In the whole system, total consumption (at site) must equal total participation (at origin), since they represent complementary views of the same recreational event. Demand, therefore, does not necessarily equal participation (or consumption) and will seldom do so. This difference between demand and participation, which is due to imperfect access, imperfect information and/or lower quality of facilities, will normally mean that participation is lower than demand. This will be so because most of the population resides in urban areas which are generally remote from recreational areas of the highest quality. This difference between demand and participation is called 'latent' demand, and represents an unsatisfied element of demand which would be converted to participation if access to facilities and the quality of those facilities were brought to ideal levels (Snaith, 1973). This concept of latent demand is a fundamental consideration in planning the immediate provision of recreational facilities. It also highlights the fact that interaction between recreationists and the demands they make on resources is the key to the understanding of countryside recreation. A further aspect of interest to planners is that of 'potential' demand, that is, the level of demand at some future date, which may depend on economic, social and technological changes. Predicting this demand is a major problem of long-term recreational planning.

The difference between demand and participation can also be such that participation in some activities exceeds the expected levels of demand in some locations. In such cases 'excess' participation exists and may occur, for example, in areas where the recreational resources for, and access to, some activities are superb and for others poor, thus resulting in the 'substitution' of demand for one activity by that for another, so that participation rates exceed normal demands.

These descriptions of recreational demand make it clear that in many respects such concepts of demand differ fundamentally from those of economic demand, particularly in their intimate relationship with a supply of facilities which is spatially dispersed. Three other concepts must therefore be considered.

## (a) Time budgets

Because outdoor recreation takes place in that portion of people's lives in which they are free (within constraints) to choose their activities, that is, their leisure time, how they spend their time (their time budgets) is of paramount importance in any attempt to establish recreational demand, since it determines where recreational activities are possible. This concept is further examined in chapter 2.

## (b) Life space

In the same way that people's leisure activities are constrained by the time available to them, participation in outdoor recreation is also influenced by their 'life space', that is, an area with a radius that is a function of their resistance to travel (which varies with their time budget and so represents the normal radius within which activities take place during a leisure period of defined length). Obviously the supply of recreational facilities within the daily life space of a particular group will influence the repertoire of activities in which they will be able to participate and will therefore be reflected in actual rates of participation.

## (c) Motivation

There obviously exist within a community marked differences in the propensity of individuals to participate in recreational activities. If levels of demand are calculated for the community at large, it is important to assess the degree of motivation of individuals within the community. Such motivation is a product of social, economic and psychological attributes which result in a particular propensity to undertake recreational activities. Another factor in motivation will be the response of individuals to the actual opportunities to participate in recreational activities within their individual life spaces.

These preliminary thoughts give some indication of the nature of recreational participation. It is explored in greater depth in chapters 3 and 4 in which passive and active recreation are examined.

## Supply of Resources for Recreation

Recreational resources are not to be seen simply as an inventory of identifiable physical elements but rather as dynamic elements which are defined culturally by the nature of activities. While the physical environment will necessarily dictate the *absolute level of supply*, resources should be seen within this total constraint as 'expanding and contracting in response to human effort and behaviour' (Zimmerman, 1951).

## (a) Total potential supply

As with the demand for recreational resources, the supply is both potential and actual. Recreational activities make a variety of physical demands upon the environment. These demands are essentially static for, while levels of consumption may change, the characteristics of activities remain relatively stable. When changes in the characteristics of recreational activities do occur, for instance, because of some technological advance, as with the development of artificial ski slopes, it could be argued that, rather than the old activity changing, a new (if related) activity has been created. This relatively stable relationship between activities and land and water resources provides a basis for assessing the potential of such physical resources to support recreational activities. It is thus possible to locate, identify and grade areas which, because of their physical characteristics, are suitable for recreational activities, and the areal extent and distribution of these resources provides an indicator of the countryside's potential for outdoor recreation. Clearly, the proportion of these potential resources suitable for recreation at any given time will vary with the characteristics of the activities themselves and of their participants, but by identifying potential resources, a stable basis can be provided against which changes over time can be measured. Moreover, the concept of 'potential' supply enables the planner to compare present and potential use of resources. This concept is further examined at some length in chapter 6.

## (b) Available supply

The relationship of the concept of available supply to potential supply is similar to that of participation (consumption) to demand. Available supply indicates that proportion of the potential supply which is available to recreationists under a given set of constraints. As Linton (1968) has observed in discussing scenery as a natural resource, 'scenery that charms, thrills or inspires is a potential asset to the land in which it is found. But like other natural resources it is a potential asset that becomes actual only when valued and exploited by a society that has reached a particular cultural and economic level.' It will be clear that the availability of such resources will vary over time with increased knowledge, improved technology and changing individual wants and social objectives. This 'available' supply of resources, too, will likewise reflect at any one time the contemporary relationships of these dynamic elements.

## (c) Constraints on supply

Just as participation depends upon an individual's time budget, life space and motivation, so various constraints on supply affect the use of those resources suitable for outdoor recreation. These factors may be of regional or local significance, for example, the distance between resources and urban centres, the network of roads, the extent of individual properties and the attitudes of their owners, and the policies of water boards and other authorities controlling resources. Some of these attitudes are considered in chapter 7. Other cultural and economic factors also exert a strong influence upon the use of resources. For example, recreational · developments must be considered alongside other claims on rural resources such as those of industry, housing and shopping facilities, and it has been suggested that local authorities have hitherto given them very low priority. Furthermore, it is often the case that resources which can serve the needs of recreationists are also suitable for other uses and in such circumstances recreation must compete with agriculture, forestry or water supplies. In addition, local factors such as land ownership, the availability of local finance, the infrastructure of communications and other services may affect the recreational use of different localities.

A key consideration in the assessment of opportunities for outdoor recreation is the relative accessibility to recreationists of suitable resources, a point considered in some detail in chapter 8. This accessibility comprises both the time and the costs of journeys and is related in many ways to the total leisure time available to individuals; for the amount of time they are prepared to spend travelling increases in proportion to their available leisure time. Another key factor in an individual's assessment of recreational resources revolves around his awareness of resources, namely his level of knowledge about the availability and characteristics of a facility. Clearly, many factors will influence an individual's assessment of a potential resource and these individual 'mental maps' will vary to a greater or lesser extent from the 'real potential' as indicated by objective physical assessment. Given that a considerable degree of choice still remains in the use of rural resources for leisure, these perceptual differences can be of great importance to those responsible for managing and planning facilities for outdoor recreation.

It will be seen that the recreational demand/supply model has several fundamental characteristics in common with those used in economic evaluation. Nevertheless, the concepts discussed in this chapter make it clear that important modifications need to be made in the interpretation of the model, the most significant of which is the intimate relationship between the components of both demand and supply. This relationship will vary with the scale of the area under study and the primary importance of this interaction, particularly as it finds expression in the spatial distribution of resources and the homes of recreationists, is a recurring theme in this book and is discussed in particular in chapters 8 and 9.

# 2 The Leisure Budget and Passive Recreation

Recreation in the countryside can be seen in perspective only if it is placed in the context of the leisure patterns of the British people. The movement of people from their homes into the countryside for recreation creates spatial patterns of activity which must be understood clearly if suitable provision is to be made, but these complex spatial patterns are further complicated by the variations in leisure time which occur throughout the day, the week and the year. Leisure, as an integral part of the life of the British people, has to take its place alongside other human activities, some of which (especially work) command higher priority in an individual's time budget. This chapter will examine briefly patterns of life in Great Britain and the extent to which leisure and, more particularly, the recreational use of leisure time, fit into these patterns. Unfortunately, this topic has not been the subject of any detailed comprehensive surveys, but since the mid-1960s the national and regional recreation studies outlined in the Appendix have investigated and thrown some light on respondents' leisure and recreation in the context of a 'normal' week.

## TIME BUDGETS

### Weekly Time Budget

The *Pilot National Recreation Survey*, the first of these national studies, did not undertake a detailed analysis of the time budgets of respondents, but it did seek to determine, by direct evidence from the questionnaire and by inference, just how much time the British people were able to devote, on average, to leisure and to recreation in that leisure time. On the assumption that particular activities, such as work, sleep, housework and eating, had to be undertaken, it was possible to deduce just how much of the 168 hours available each week was 'disposable time' and therefore available for leisure.

For analytical purposes the *Pilot National Recreation Survey* assumed that the average individual spent a standard 8 hours in bed. For those in full-time employment the survey established that an average 39 hours per week were spent at work, 3 hours on overtime and 6 hours in travelling to work (on the basis of a five-day week) and therefore, on average, 48 hours were committed to work and associated activities. Thus, the average British citizen in full-time work spent 104 hours on work and sleep each week, leaving 64 hours (38 per cent of the total) available for activities less fundamental to existence and survival. Survival, however, means more than work and sleep, and the *Pilot National Recreation Survey* estimated that a further 15–20 hours per week were devoted to the 'mechanics of living', including eating, cooking and housework (though it is clear that hard and fast times cannot be drawn and that what is work to one person—for example, cooking—may be pleasure to another). The *Pilot National Recreation Survey* defined the 45–50 hours left as 'disposable time', that is, time which the individual may spend as he chooses; it is in no way synonymous with leisure and a large proportion of the British population uses it to increase the time devoted to sleep, work and the mechanics of living, or to undertake other activities, such as a second job or casual spare-time work, which are more correctly seen as adjuncts of committed time rather than of leisure pursuits. The complexity of decisions about the composition and definition of individual activities can be seen from table 2.1, which is based on the 'Leisure Model' constructed by Maw (1969).

## TABLE 2.1

### COMMITTED AND LEISURE TIME

| | *Fully committed* *Essential* | *Partly committed* *Optional* | |
| --- | --- | --- | --- |
| | | Highly committed | Leisure |
| Sleeping | Essential sleep | | Relaxing |
| Personal care and exercise | Health and hygiene | | Sport and active play |
| Eating | Eating | | Dining and drinking out |
| Shopping | Essential shopping | Optional shopping | |
| Work | Primary work | Overtime and secondary work | |
| Housework | Essential housework and cooking | House repairs and car maintenance | Do-it-yourself gardening |
| Education | Schooling | Further education and homework | |
| Culture and communication (non-travel) | | | TV, radio, reading, theatre, hobbies and passive play |
| Social activities | | Child-raising, religion and politics | Talking, parties, etc. |
| Travel | Travel to work/ school | | Walking, driving for pleasure |

Source:    Maw (1969), p. 924.

# TABLE 2.2

## LENGTH OF THE OFFICIAL WORKING WEEK IN GREAT BRITAIN

(Percent of working sample)

| Hours | All adults | Sex | | Occupational group | | | Income level | | Educational status | |
|---|---|---|---|---|---|---|---|---|---|---|
| | | Men | Women | Manual | Executive | Other | £650–849 | £1200–1949 | Secondary | University |
| Under 35 | 17 | 7 | 43 | 13 | 18 | 27 | 14 | 18 | 16 | 32 |
| 35–9 | 10 | 10 | 15 | 5 | 16 | 18 | 7 | 14 | 9 | 20 |
| 40 | 14 | 14 | 12 | 14 | 8 | 15 | 12 | 14 | 14 | 5 |
| 40–5 | 16 | 15 | 15 | 17 | 10 | 14 | 19 | 14 | 18 | 5 |
| 45+ | 35 | 45 | 9 | 45 | 30 | 17 | 40 | 32 | 39 | 10 |
| Average | 42 | 46 | 34 | 44 | 41* | 37 | 43 | 42 | 43 | 36* |

* 32 per cent of the Executive sample reported no fixed/normal hours of work, as did 28 per cent of the University trained sample.

Source: British Travel Association–University of Keele (1967), p. 30.

The ways in which people use their available time vary greatly according to a number of social criteria; the housewife, student and the old age pensioner have patterns of living which are quite different from those in full-time paid employment. Even among those who are employed, there will be differences arising from the type of employment and other social criteria (table 2.2). Contrasts between occupational groups were not very pronounced, for although executives did have a shorter 'official' working week, they frequently worked several hours of overtime. Similarly, the contrast between income groups was slight; the *Pilot National Recreation Survey* found no evidence to suggest that those with higher incomes benefited from shorter working weeks. The only clear contrast between groups that did emerge was that based on educational status: employees with only secondary education had a considerably longer working week (43 hours) than those who had received a university education (36 hours).

The survey carried out recently in north-west England also investigated the breakdown of the time budget in much the same way. The average working week of 44·6 hours for residents in the North-west Region was considerably longer than that revealed by the *Pilot National Recreation Survey* for Great Britain as a whole; as the report itself concludes, 'these values scarcely suggest that an age of leisure has yet dawned in the north-west' (North West Sports Council, 1972, p. 22). The contrast in the North-west Region between the working week and socio-economic parameters echoed the findings of the national study; marital status was found to have a considerable effect on the length of the working week, perhaps because overtime is necessary to increase income. The survey established that the number of children in the household had little influence on the working week, nor were there great differences between the various socio-economic groups. Skilled workers had the longest week, and non-manual and non-skilled workers the shortest; however, the differences were very small and had little effect on the time available for recreational activities. The survey also established that, on average, over 16 hours per week were devoted by individuals to domestic housework; this commitment varies considerably, for the young and the single can often avoid domestic drudgery, while both the old and those with children had an abundance of such duties.

On the evidence of this survey, the population of north-west England had approximately 33 hours available for leisure activities each week (table 2.3); there was very little difference in available leisure time between men and women. The most interesting finding was that high socio-economic status was not necessarily associated with greater leisure, though it will be demonstrated later that participation in recreational activities is generally more common among the higher socio-economic groups. This seeming paradox should not be overlooked, as it shows clearly that the creation of a leisured class (as measured by time available) does not necessarily create a corresponding increase in the recreational use of that leisure time.

The North-west study also revealed that the group with the least leisure comprised married couples with children; their available leisure time averaged less than 26 hours per week, and many young people must find that the acquisition of a young family is accompanied by a sharp reduction in available leisure time.

The study of work and leisure in the Metropolitan Region undertaken by Young and Willmott, which was designed to reveal the contrast between different social groups, displays a similar pattern in time budgets. Table 2.4 translates the hours

## TABLE 2.3

### HOURS OF AVAILABLE LEISURE IN NORTH-WEST ENGLAND

*Hours of available leisure*

| | |
|---|---|
| *Age* | |
| 12–29 | 35 |
| 30–44 | 27 |
| 60+ | 44 |
| *Marital status* | |
| Single | 33 |
| *Children* | |
| With children | 26 |
| *Socio-economic status* | |
| Group A | 31 |
| Group F | 36 |
| Average | 33 |

Source:   North West Sports Council (1972), p.24.

## TABLE 2.4

### AVERAGE WEEKLY AND ANNUAL WORKING HOURS IN THE METROPOLITAN REGION

| | Professional and managerial | Clerical | Skilled | Semi-skilled and unskilled | All |
|---|---|---|---|---|---|
| Total hours at work in week | 48·2 | 44·7 | 47·8 | 47·6 | 47·5 |
| Hours worked at home | 2·2 | 0·8 | 0·1 | 0·0 | 1·0 |
| Hours on second job | 0·4 | 0·3 | 0·3 | 0·3 | 0·3 |
| Hours spent on journey to and from work | 6·1 | 5·6 | 4·1 | 3·5 | 4·7 |
| Total hours working and travelling to and from work in week | 56·9 | 51·4 | 52·3 | 51·4 | 53·5 |
| Bank holidays per year (in weeks) | 1·2 | 1·2 | 1·2 | 1·2 | 1·2 |
| Paid holidays per year (in weeks) | 3·4 | 2·6 | 2·5 | 2·1 | 2·6 |
| Total weeks worked in year | 47·4 | 48·2 | 48·3 | 48·7 | 48·2 |
| Total hours working and travelling to and from work in year (weekly hours × weeks) | 2697 | 2477 | 2562 | 2503 | 2564 |

Source:   Young and Willmott (1973), p. 139.

worked during the week into annual totals, which take holidays into account. Once overtime, hours worked at home and hours spent on the journey to and from work are included, semi- and unskilled workers have a total work commitment of 51·4 hours per week, or over 5 hours less than professional and managerial workers. As Young and Willmott conclude, 'whatever things may have been like in the past of Britain the highest-status people are for the most part no longer, as they were in the nineteenth century, the leisure class. In 1970 they appeared to have less leisure time than anyone else' (Young and Willmott, 1973, p.141). It should, however, be noted that the distinction between work and leisure is much more difficult to draw for professional and managerial work, in which the work itself may be intrinsically interesting.

TABLE 2.5

AVERAGE WEEKLY TIME BUDGET (IN HOURS)
IN THE METROPOLITAN REGION

| | Men | Women working full-time | Women working part-time | Women not in paid work |
|---|---|---|---|---|
| Paid work and travel to work | 49·5 | 40·2 | 26·3 | — |
| Household tasks | 9·9 | 25·1 | 35·3 | 45·5 |
| Subsistence | 73·9 | 76·1 | 72·5 | 73·7 |
| Leisure | 31·7 | 25·7 | 31·2 | 44·4 |
| Non-work travel | 3·0 | 2·9 | 2·7 | 4·4 |

Source:   Young and Willmott (1973), p. 113.

When necessary tasks are taken into account, the amount of leisure available to those living in the Metropolitan Region is very similar to that available to residents of north-west England. Average leisure time per week was slightly less for men in full-time employment than for women as a whole, whose leisure time is much more variable (table 2.5). Although the working week of women in full-time employment was more than 9 hours shorter than that of their male equivalents, their commitment to household duties more than offset this short-fall and greatly reduced their available leisure time; in fact, even part-time working women had less leisure time than males after household duties were taken into account. Only full-time housewives, with an average leisure budget of over 44 hours per week, have more available leisure time than men.

Although the weekly time budgets established for the Metropolitan and North-west Regions are not necessarily typical of the whole of Great Britain, they suggest that there are major variations in available leisure time which depend primarily upon employment status. Moreover, while the time available for leisure varied from 25 to 45 hours per week, it is not merely this total which determines the amount of time devoted to recreation; for the distribution of leisure time throughout the week and, indeed, throughout the day, will play a large part in determining what can be done with the time available.

## The Daily Time Budget

Although the weeks of the year generally have a regular pattern, there are considerable variations in leisure time within the week. In particular, the character of the daily time budget and the amount of time available for leisure differ considerably at weekends and week days, and there are quite different patterns on Saturdays and Sundays. The study by Young and Willmott clearly revealed that the contrasts between the different days were greater than the differences between males and females (table 2.6). On an average weekday, the total work commitment of an individual was approximately 6 hours, except for full-time housewives, who averaged 7 hours. Although the workload diminished on Saturday, overtime for men and household chores for women resulted in an average commitment of 6 hours. Sunday was still, in relative terms, a 'day of rest', particularly for men whose work duties accounted for only a third of their average weekday workload; housewives, on the other hand, reduced their workload by only 30 per cent. The weekend thus represents a large increase in the time that can be committed to leisure pursuits, which in turn affects the weekend daily time budget.

TABLE 2.6

### AVERAGE HOURS OF PAID AND UNPAID WORK IN THE METROPOLITAN REGION

|  | Men | Women working full-time | Women working part-time | Women not in paid work |
|---|---|---|---|---|
|  | (188) | (46) | (55) | (61) |
| *Weekday* |  |  |  |  |
| Paid work and travel to work | 9·1 | 7·7 | 5·0 | 0·0 |
| Household tasks | 0·9 | 2·7 | 4·9 | 7·0 |
| Total work | 10·0 | 10·4 | 9·9 | 7·0 |
| *Saturday* |  |  |  |  |
| Paid work and travel to work | 3·0 | 1·6 | 0·8 | 0·0 |
| Household tasks | 3·0 | 4·9 | 6·1 | 5·7 |
| Total work | 6·0 | 6·5 | 6·9 | 5·7 |
| *Sunday* |  |  |  |  |
| Paid work and travel to work | 1·0 | 0·1 | 0·5 | 0·0 |
| Household tasks | 2·4 | 4·7 | 4·7 | 4·8 |
| Total work | 3·4 | 4·8 | 5·2 | 4·8 |
| *Total for week* Paid work, travel to work and household tasks | 59·4 | 63·3 | 61·6 | 45·5 |

Source:   Young and Willmott (1973), p. 111.

Respondents in north-west England were asked to indicate the hours spent on particular activities on weekdays, Saturdays and Sundays. A large and fairly constant proportion (approximately 30 per cent) of leisure time was occupied by television viewing, perhaps the most passive of all leisure activities, and in sharp contrast to the very small proportion of time committed to physical activities, particularly on Saturdays and weekdays (North West Sports Council, 1972, p. 26).

Although much detailed research work is necessary on time budgets in the United Kingdom (Burton, 1971), and the information at present available is limited and does not permit detailed analysis, it is nevertheless possible to give a general picture of the availability of leisure time to the British people and its distribution throughout the week. The recreational use of this leisure time will be as variable and subject to as many influences as leisure time itself and, as the amount of time committed to leisure varies from day to day and from person to person, so too will that devoted to recreation.

It is important to remember that, although there has been a remarkable growth in leisure activities and outdoor recreation in recent years, the British people appear to retain an ambivalent attitude towards leisure and the recreational use of leisure time. It would be quite wrong to assume that individuals necessarily wish to use available leisure time for recreation or indeed to increase the amount of leisure each day or week. The *Pilot National Recreation Survey* revealed that over 50 per cent of the British population felt that their present leisure time was adequate. Not surprisingly, this view was most strongly held by retired people, although many of those on lower incomes and those with only secondary education also felt that they had sufficient leisure time; it is probable, however, that the two latter groups in particular reduce their leisure time in favour of overtime and other income-generating activities (table 2.7); groups in manual occupations and those with lower incomes are characterised by a high proportion of people who would like the opportunity to work more overtime.

It has been argued that there are limits to the amount of leisure time which people can use before serious social problems arise (Select Committee, 1973.) Available evidence from British surveys clearly indicates that these problems remain for the future and it is likely that present attitudes are forced upon the population more by economic needs than by the fear of a 'brave new world' of

TABLE 2.7

ATTITUDES TO OVERTIME AND LEISURE IN GREAT BRITAIN

| | All adults | Age group | | | Occupational group | | | Income | |
|---|---|---|---|---|---|---|---|---|---|
| | | 17–24 | 35–44 | 65+ | Manual | Executive | Other | £650–889 | £1950+ |
| | (percentage of sample who would like more overtime) | | | | | | | | |
| More overtime | 14 | 22 | 10 | 0 | 18 | 3 | 10 | 19 | 11 |
| Less overtime | 67 | 60 | 72 | 66 | 65 | 71 | 72 | 56 | 67 |
| More leisure | 45 | 46 | 59 | 14 | 53 | 59 | 53 | 42 | 52 |
| Less leisure | 4 | 2 | 1 | 14 | 1 | 1 | 1 | 3 | 2 |

Source:    British Travel Association–University of Keele (1967), p. 33.

leisure. This view is corroborated by evidence from the *Pilot National Recreation Survey* which established that only 14 per cent of the national sample were prepared to admit that they were 'at a loss for something to do' in their leisure time (British Travel Association–University of Keele, 1967).

A knowledge of leisure budgets is essential in any evaluation of patterns of recreational activity; but all the evidence currently available supports the conclusion of the North West Sports Council (1972, p. 24), that

> while the amount of leisure available is one of the factors that determine recreational preferences it may not be the most significant . . . active participants in time-consuming activities often have less leisure time than non-participants. Clearly other factors such as income level and educational experience are more important determinants of participation in activities such as sailing and golf. In this sense the general increase in the leisure of the population at large is perhaps less significant in influencing the future growth of recreational demand than a rise in material wealth would be.

### Recreational Use of Leisure Time

Once the amount of time committed to leisure has been established, the next step is to determine what activities are undertaken during these periods of leisure. The most detailed breakdown of leisure activities on a national basis is provided by Sillitoe's *Planning for Leisure* (1969) which established, for a sample of English and Welsh residents, the most time-consuming activities during leisure time (table 2.8). The dominant leisure activity was watching television and 23 per cent

TABLE 2.8

PARTICIPATION IN LEISURE ACTIVITIES IN ENGLAND AND WALES

| Activity | Percentage of leisure time when activity was cited as chief pursuit |
|---|---|
| Television | 23 |
| Reading | 7 |
| Crafts and hobbies | 11 |
| Decorating and house/vehicle maintenance | 5 |
| Gardening | 11 |
| Social activities | 6 |
| Drinking | 2 |
| Cinema and theatre | 1 |
| Non-physical games | 5 |
| Physical recreation: | |
| (i)  as participant | 8 |
| (ii)  as spectator | 2 |
| Excursions to countryside and seaside | 7 |
| Park visits and walks (intra-urban) | 5 |
| Anything else | 7 |
| No answer or don't know | 4 |

Source:    Sillitoe (1969), p. 41.

of the total sample cited it as the most time-consuming pastime. Gardening, crafts and hobbies were the next most popular activities, although each accounted for only 11 per cent of available leisure. On the evidence of this survey, activities carried out in and around the home accounted for 57 per cent of leisure time; a further 14 per cent of leisure time was devoted to social activities that take place indoors but away from home. Only 22 per cent of leisure time (excluding gardening) was spent out-of-doors; 5 per cent was devoted to walks in the town and visits to urban parks and a proportion (perhaps a majority) of the time spent on physical recreation was probably also spent within urban areas. Thus, it is unlikely that more than 15 per cent of leisure time was devoted to activities that took their participants into the countryside. Moreover, since *Planning for Leisure* did not provide an accurate estimate of the time spent on individual activities, it might well be that the overall share of the total leisure budget devoted to 'countryside' activities is even smaller.

Young and Willmott's study in the Metropolitan Region confirms these results from Sillitoe's investigation (Young and Willmott, 1973, p. 218). Over half the leisure budget was committed to home-based activities, while only a small proportion of the activities outside the home took participants away from towns. One quarter of the active pursuits considered took place indoors, for example, table tennis, badminton and squash; another 30 per cent were outdoor sports requiring facilities that are usually found in towns, for example, cricket, tennis and association football. In total, less than 50 per cent of the activities required a countryside location and only 4 of the 16 'non-home' activities examined by the survey could possibly take their participants into the countryside. The average resident of the Metropolitan Region thus spent only 12 to 15 per cent of his leisure time in the countryside, a figure comparable to that given in *Planning for Leisure* and a salutary reminder of the urban nature of most leisure activities in the United Kingdom.

### The Effect of Weather and the Seasons on the Use of Leisure Time

The amount of leisure available each day and its occurrence within the day obviously affects the timing of recreational activity, particularly outdoor recreation in the countryside. Unlike indoor activities, such recreation must generally be pursued in daylight and this fact, together with seasonal variations in British weather, has a marked influence on the temporal distribution of outdoor recreation. This seasonality must obviously be taken into account, for it affects not only the provision and management of facilities but also the possible contribution of recreation in the countryside to the year-round pattern of leisure of the British people. Table 2.9 demonstrates the great variation throughout the year in four categories of outdoor recreation. Not surprisingly, the level of trips to the countryside and coast is nearly 400 per cent higher in summer than in winter; there is also a marked difference between visits on a weekday and those on weekends. In contrast, active recreation for both participant and spectator shows much less variation.

These major variations in numbers of visitors at recreational sites throughout the year are undoubtedly due to seasonal differences in weather conditions, but the relationship is not simple. An exploratory investigation of the relationships

## TABLE 2.9

### SEASONAL PARTICIPATION IN OUTDOOR RECREATION IN ENGLAND AND WALES

|  | Summer weekends | Summer weekdays | Winter weekends | Winter weekdays |
|---|---|---|---|---|
| | (average percentage of leisure periods when each activity was cited as chief pursuit) | | | |
| *Active recreation* | | | | |
| Participant | 11 | 7 | 9 | 4 |
| Spectator | 2 | 1 | 4 | 1 |
| *Passive recreation* | | | | |
| Trips to the countryside and coast | 19 | 5 | 5 | 1 |
| Park visits and walks | 9 | 8 | 3 | 2 |

Source:   Sillitoe (1969), p. 41.

between numbers of visitors and weather has been undertaken in central Scotland, using data from the three coastal sites in East Lothian. For several years it has been the policy of the East Lothian County Council to charge a nominal sum for parking at these sites and, as a result, statistics of the number of cars at each of the three sites are available for summer months (May to September inclusive) since 1967; it is thus possible to examine in detail the variations in day visits over the summer. Unfortunately, the quality of these statistics is not matched by information on local weather but, with the help of information from Edinburgh, North Berwick and Dunbar, it was possible to estimate wind speed, maximum temperature, rainfall and the amount of sunshine for each day.

The contribution of weather to variations in numbers of visitors to the three coastal sites was estimated by multiple regression, treating daily numbers of visitors

## TABLE 2.10

### WEATHER AND VISITORS AT EAST LOTHIAN COASTAL SITES: 1968–71

|  | Gullane | Longniddry | Yellowcraig | All Sites |
|---|---|---|---|---|
| Total daily visitors | 123 | 108 | 53 | 289 |
| Weekday visitors | 69 | 59 | 31 | 162 |
| Weekend visitors | 195 | 173 | 82 | 453 |
| Wind speed (knots) | 9·2 | 9·2 | 9·1 | 9·1 |
| Maximum temperature ($^\circ$F) | 60·8 | 60·8 | 60·9 | 60·9 |
| Rainfall (in.) | 0·07 | 0·06 | 0·07 | 0·07 |
| Sunshine (h.) | 5·8 | 5·7 | 5·7 | 5·8 |

Source:      North Berwick District Council; Prestonpans District Council; Meteorological Office.

as the dependent variable and weather factors as the independent variables. The analysis was carried out in two stages; first, visitors at weekends were separated from those on weekdays, and secondly, statistics of visitors for each year were examined to eliminate the effect of underlying trends on the results of the survey. Table 2.10 provides a breakdown of the visitor and weather variables over the period 1968–71 and table 2.11 indicates the correlation between the two sets of statistics. The relationships are what might be expected, although it is interesting to note that the 'positive' factors of maximum temperature and daily sunshine have a stronger correlation with numbers of visitors than the 'negative' factors of wind speed and rainfall. The 'explanation' of the variation in the number of visitors provided by the multiple regression equation is shown in table 2.12. More detailed work, with more reliable statistics, is required before definite links between numbers of visitors and weather factors can be established; however, this preliminary investigation does confirm the effect of seasonal factors on outdoor recreation in the countryside.

## TABLE 2.11

### EAST LOTHIAN COASTAL SITES: CORRELATION OF WEATHER STATISTICS AND VISITORS

|  | Gullane | | | Longniddry | | | Yellowcraig | | | All sites | | |
|---|---|---|---|---|---|---|---|---|---|---|---|---|
|  | All | Wd | We | All | Wd | We | All | Wd | We | All | Wd | We |
| Wind | − |  | − | − | − |  |  |  |  | − |  |  |
| Temperature | + | + | + | + | + | + | + | + |  | + | + | + |
| Rainfall | − |  | − |  |  |  |  |  |  | − |  | − |
| Sunshine | + | + | + | + | + | + | + |  | + | + | + | + |

All  Totals of daily trips for the summers 1968–71 inclusive
Wd  Totals of weekday trips for the summers 1968–71 inclusive
We  Totals of weekend and statutory holiday trips for the summers 1968–71 inclusive
+  Positive correlations significant at the 0·1 per cent level and above
−  Negative correlations significant at the 0·1 per cent level and above

Source:   North Berwick District Council; Prestonpans District Council; Meteorological Office.

## TABLE 2.12

### WEATHER AND VISITORS AT EAST LOTHIAN COASTAL SITES: PERCENTAGE OF VARIANCE EXPLAINED BY MULTIPLE REGRESSION EQUATIONS

|  | Gullane | | | Longniddry | | | Yellowcraig | | | All sites | | |
|---|---|---|---|---|---|---|---|---|---|---|---|---|
|  | All | Wd | We | All | Wd | We | All | Wd | We | All | Wd | We |
| 1968 | 23 | 21 | 41 | 18 | 21 | 31 | 11 | 8 | 26 | 19 | 21 | 36 |
| 1969 | 39 | 43 | 43 | 23 | 33 | 24 | 8 | 13 | 10 | 28 | 40 | 31 |
| 1970 | 34 | 39 | 46 | 21 | 34 | 26 | 3 | 7 | 1 | 30 | 35 | 35 |
| 1971 | 36 | 34 | 54 | 30 | 33 | 45 | 20 | 31 | 29 | 32 | 36 | 47 |

Wd  Weekday
We  Weekend

Source:   North Berwick District Council; Prestonpans District Council; Meteorological Office.

### The Role of the Weekend in Leisure Budgets

A further complicating factor in the pattern of recreation is that variations over the week disturb the pattern of seasonal variations. In the Government Social Survey the level of visits at weekends in winter was as high as it was during weekdays in summer, which in turn were little more than one-quarter of that at summer weekends (Sillitoe, 1969, p. 41). This pattern is confirmed by the statistics for the coastal sites where the contrast between weekday and weekend visitor levels is marked; numbers of visitors at weekends were nearly three times as high as during the week, despite broadly comparable weather conditions. Contrasts within the week are undoubtedly due to the greater availability of leisure time at weekends, much of which occurs during hours of daylight.

Most of the recreational studies undertaken in Great Britain have attempted to analyse the differences in leisure patterns during the week and at weekends; several have recognised the dominance of the 'weekend' by undertaking detailed examinations of time budgets and of recreational activities pursued on Saturdays and Sundays. Thus the *Pilot National Recreation Survey* examined the popularity of different activities over the weekend by dividing Saturday and Sunday into three periods, morning, afternoon and evening. For the vast majority of the British people recreational activity, even at a weekend, is centred around the home (table 2.13). In all the six periods considered, at least 60 per cent of the population had undertaken at least one leisure activity within the home, compared with 35 per cent who had undertaken an activity away from home during the same periods.

TABLE 2.13

PARTICIPATION AT WEEKENDS IN AWAY-FROM-HOME ACTIVITIES
IN GREAT BRITAIN

|  | Morning | Afternoon | Evening |
|---|---|---|---|
| (percentage of respondents reporting participation in one or more activities) | | | |
| *Active recreation* | 3 | 6 | 1 |
| Walk (of 3 miles or more) | 2 | 4 | 1 |
| Played active game | 0 | 1 | 0 |
| Other outdoor sport or pursuits | 0 | 0 | 0 |
| Water sports | 1 | 1 | 0 |
| *Passive recreation* | 2 | 9 | 2 |
| Drive (2 hours or more) | 2 | 5 | 2 |
| Had picnic | 0 | 1 | 0 |
| Watched live sport | 0 | 3 | 0 |
| *Social Recreation* | 6 | 12 | 16 |
| To party of friends | 6 | 12 | 14 |
| Went dancing | 0 | 0 | 2 |
| *Cultural Recreation* | 0 | 1 | 3 |
| To cinema/theatre or concert | 0 | 1 | 3 |

Source:   British Travel Association–University of Keele (1967), p. 47.

Moreover, this latter figure relates to the afternoon and is significantly higher than figures for the morning (15 per cent) and evening (25 per cent). It is interesting to note that active recreation dominated during the mornings, but the proportion of people involved in both passive and active recreation was so small (3 per cent and and 2 per cent respectively) that they would hardly be able to exert any pressures on the countryside.

Although the incidence of recreational activity outside the home increased to 22 per cent in the evening, recreation in the countryside is even less likely at that time. In the afternoon one in three of the national sample took part in a leisure activity out-of-doors and those activities which might be expected to take place in the countryside accounted for a significant proportion of all participation; although passive recreation was predominant, active pursuits were also popular. Young and Willmott (1973) correlated participation in outdoor pursuits during weekend periods with socio-economic characteristics; their findings confirmed the evidence of the *Pilot National Recreation Survey*, that participation in away-from-home activities by those in the higher social groups is greater than that by manual workers.

TABLE 2.14

PARTICIPATION IN OUTDOOR RECREATION ON SUMMER WEEKENDS
IN CENTRAL SCOTLAND

| *Activity* | *Percentage of total interviewed* |
|---|---|
| Went for a walk for 1 hour or more | 23.2 |
| Drove for pleasure for 2 hours or more | 20.9 |
| Had a picnic in the countryside | 7.9 |
| Played a game: e.g., football, cricket, golf | 5.7 |
| Water sports: e.g., swimming, sailing, fishing | 3.9 |
| Countryside activity: e.g., riding, cycling, camping | 1.8 |
| None of these activities | 42.8 |

Source:    Duffield and Owen (1970), p. 50; Duffield and Owen (1971), p. 51.

Recreation patterns over the weekend were also investigated in the studies carried out in central Scotland. Respondents were asked whether they had spent any of their leisure time during the previous weekend on outdoor recreation (table 2.14). Perhaps the most interesting fact to emerge from this table is that nearly 43 per cent of those interviewed had not participated in any of the pursuits listed despite the inclusion of the more popular forms of passive recreation. Most of those participating followed passive pursuits; walking and driving for pleasure were the most popular, with more than one person in every five taking part, compared with less than one in ten who were involved in active recreation. The survey carried out in the Northern Region confirmed these general trends and also provided more detailed statistics for individual activities (table 2.15). As the report itself concluded, 'the most popular activities, although of undoubted importance in the context of urban planning problems, are of relatively small consequence when considering planning for outdoor recreational pursuits. Visiting friends, pubs

TABLE 2.15

PARTICIPATION AT WEEKENDS IN AWAY-FROM-HOME ACTIVITIES
IN NORTHERN ENGLAND

| Activity | Average Saturday | Average Sunday |
|---|---|---|
| | (percentage of those interviewed) | |
| Visiting pub/club | 18 | 14 |
| Visiting friends | 12 | 13 |
| Films/theatre/dancing/bingo | 8 | 3 |
| Going for walks (not using transport) | 5 | 9 |
| Trip to coast | 4 | 7 |
| Trip to country | 2 | 5 |
| Trip(neither to coast nor country) | 2 | 2 |
| Going for walks (using transport) | 1 | 2 |
| Church/Sunday School | 1 | 11 |

Source:    North Regional Planning Committee (1969), p. 6.

or clubs, going to places of entertainment and going to church on Sunday account
for 65 per cent of all reported activities on an average Saturday and for 57 per cent
on an average Sunday' (North Regional Planning Committee, 1969).

   Passive recreation of a kind likely to take participants into the countryside
tended to be more important on Sundays than on Saturdays, a finding which
confirmed that from other studies; trips to the seaside and the coast were twice
as frequent on Sundays as on Saturdays.

## Time–Space Circle

Although much more fundamental research is necessary before the patterns of
recreational activities and their variations over time are understood, the sketchy
evidence available at present demonstrates the dominance of the weekend in recreation in the countryside and points to factors which are of fundamental importance.
The greater availability of leisure time at the weekend does not increase participation in countryside recreation merely by allowing individuals to participate in a
greater range of activities; it also provides time for people to travel from their
homes into the countryside. In chapter 8 the time, energy and financial resources
spent on such journeys and the patterns of recreational travel which emerge will
be studied in detail, but it is appropriate at this point to indicate the key factor
responsible for the distinctive features of recreation in the countryside, particularly
passive recreation. On weekdays, when the time available for leisure is limited, the
individual recreationist who wishes to undertake recreation in the countryside,
particularly that of an informal, passive kind, has to decide whether to use a substantial proportion of his leisure time in travelling from his home into the countryside, and it is not surprising, therefore, that leisure time during the week should be
devoted mainly to pursuits within the home or in towns. At the weekends the loss
of time in recreational journeys is less important in relation to the time available
for leisure, though the individual recreationist still faces a dilemma posed by the
desire to limit the loss of leisure time which is spent in travelling and, at the same

time, to maximise the recreational opportunities which are available to him in the countryside. Fortunately for those engaged in passive recreation, the journey may itself be part of the recreational experience, as chapter 8 demonstrates.

Each recreationist can thus be viewed as working within a fixed time–space circle which dictates his pattern of leisure and within which he must decide his priorities. The more time a recreationist seeks to spend on a particular activity, the more restricted will be the area that he can use, for journeys from home to place of participation must be kept to a minimum. If, on the other hand, he seeks to enjoy a particular recreational facility located many miles from his home, he must reconcile himself to the fact that his time there must be limited by the requirements of the journey itself. It is possible, therefore, to delimit an area around each individual's home which circumscribes his recreational activities and within which (from his point of view) the development of recreational facilities should take place; its dimensions will depend upon the time he is willing to devote to travelling. The nature of each individual's time–space circle is thus both central to any understanding of recreational activity in the countryside and a valuable tool for planning the development of countryside recreation.

These time–space circles are not only a function of the time available for travel; they must also reflect the mobility of the individual concerned and the mode of transport which he selects for his journey. For example, an individual prepared to devote one hour to an average journey from home has a choice of three modes of transport, walking, public transport and private car. The pedestrian could expect to travel approximately 4 miles (6·4 km) within the hour and thus operates within a time–space circle of approximately 50 square miles (130 km$^2$). Those using public transport within the same period could expect to reach destinations approximately 20 miles (32 km) from their homes, and their outward journeys would be approximately five times those of pedestrians; however, the time–space circle which results from this greater distance is 1200 square miles (3100 km$^2$), that is, twenty times as large. Similarly, a private car could be expected to take the motorist some 30 miles (48 km) from his home within the hour, and the resulting time–space circle would cover approximately 2700 square miles (7000 km$^2$). This simple example shows how the countryside 'at risk' from recreationists increases geometrically with the speed at which they can travel from their homes.

CONCLUSION

This chapter began with a consideration of time budgets and of factors affecting the allocation of leisure time and its distribution throughout the day, the week and the year, and has linked this concept to that of travel time, which is part of the leisure budget and determines the radius within which outdoor recreation can take place. The changing nature of both the leisure budget and the means of transport available to recreationists must clearly affect the size of time–space circles in the future. Further aspects of the recreational time–space continuum will be explored in subsequent chapters; that which follows will consider one aspect, the role of the motor car in passive outdoor recreation in the countryside.

# 3 Passive Recreation and the Role of the Motor Car

The preceding chapter has demonstrated that outdoor recreation in the country-side accounts for only a small part of leisure time, and that the opportunities for such recreation are most abundant at weekends, particularly Sundays. Superim-posed on this weekly pattern are both irregular fluctuations, which reflect the change-able weather of these islands, and variations throughout the year in response to the march of the seasons. It has also been shown that there are important distinctions within recreation in the countryside between active recreation (the subject of chapter 4) and passive recreation, and that, in terms of numbers participating, the latter is far more important. Nevertheless, by its nature, it is in many ways more difficult to study: it is both diffuse and unorganised.

There are three ways in which participation in passive recreation in the country-side can be studied: by interviews in respondents' homes, as in the surveys described in the Appendix; by traffic surveys, especially near the origins of recreational journeys into the countryside, as in the cordon surveys described in chapter 8; and by interviews at recreational sites in the countryside. The first two suffer from obvious disadvantages of recall and anticipation respectively, for the diffuse nature of much passive recreation is likely to make recall difficult (especially if journeys have multiple destinations), while changes of plan may result in information given at the point of departure subsequently being incorrect. Yet site surveys present equally difficult problems. At large sites, where visitors are continually arriving and leaving, possibly by several entrances and exits, it is difficult to achieve either a random or a systematic sample. Furthermore, an unknown proportion of recreational traffic disperses into the countryside at large and is missed by such surveys. To over-come the latter problem a technique of rural traverses was devised for the studies in central Scotland, whereby teams of an interviewer and driver toured the country-side at intervals throughout the day, questioning such recreationists as they encountered. Yet, while this approach does provide information on an aspect of passive recreation in the countryside which has largely been ignored in other surveys (though site surveys as such have been one of the commonest forms of recreational surveys), it was not possible to relate the information gathered in this way quantitatively to that gathered on larger sites or to assess the relative import-ance of such dispersed recreation. A more satisfactory solution was achieved in a recreational survey of the Pentland Hills, a major recreational area near Edinburgh containing a number of sites that attract those driving into the countryside for enjoyment (Duffield and Owen, 1971b), but in general, the quantitative study of passive recreation in the countryside must await better data.

## TABLE 3.1

PLACES VISITED ON THE LAST DAY OR HALF-DAY OUTING IN GREAT BRITAIN

| Type of place | Age | | Occupation | | Education | | |
|---|---|---|---|---|---|---|---|
| | 17–24 | 45–64 | Manual | Executive | Secondary | University | All |
| | | | (percentage of those making trips) | | | | |
| Town | 18 | 22 | 26 | 25 | 26 | 22 | 24 |
| Countryside | 27 | 37 | 33 | 37 | 39 | 30 | 34 |
| Seaside | 33 | 26 | 30 | 23 | 30 | 26 | 28 |

Source:    British Travel Association–University of Keele (1967), p.84

What is clear is that the motor car plays a major role in passive recreation, for most of those participating in such recreation in the countryside travel by car; by far the most important kind of passive recreation is the 'trip out' into the countryside or the seaside (table 3.1). As Law and Perry (1971) have shown in the context of Greater London, access to a car may not only determine the distance that can be travelled on a recreational outing but even whether such a journey is possible. They examined the recreational facilities in the countryside within a 30-mile (48-km) radius of central London, constructing matrices of travel time and accessibility cartograms for both public transport and private transport by road. This study showed that, while 'almost all of the region within 30 miles of central London can be reached by car in less than an hour, using standard travel times', it was 'almost impossible to reach the countryside from London in less than one hour's travelling time by public transport and large areas beyond 15–18 miles out are attainable only after more than 1½ hours travel' (Law and Perry, 1971, 20–1). Those whose personal mobility is restricted to public transport also tend to belong to lower socio–economic groups, and Law and Perry concluded that 'non-car owners relying on public transport had very little opportunities for countryside recreation. These limitations are apparent not only in terms of the leisure time eaten into by long journeys by public transport but also in the relatively heavy money costs involved, especially when families are large' (Law and Perry, 1971, 23).

The effectiveness of constraints on travel was confirmed by Sillitoe in *Planning for Leisure* in which the average number of excursions to country or seaside made by those with a car was compared with excursions made by those without a vehicle of any kind. Over the summer people with access to a motor vehicle made an average of 8 excursions to the countryside or seaside, compared with an average of 3 excursions by those without a vehicle of any kind (Sillitoe, 1969).

The study in the Northern Region confirmed the effect of car ownership on participation in countryside recreation, for although only 40 per cent of the sample were from car-owning households, 73 per cent of those making a trip to the countryside on an average weekend came from households with access to a motor vehicle; only 53 per cent from households without access to a motor vehicle made such trips to the countryside (North Regional Planning Committee,

1969). Indeed, the *Pilot National Recreation Survey* stated, 'if there is one truism in recreational research which is more obvious than any other, it is that the complete personal mobility, conferred by the ownership of a car, has revolutionised our use of leisure time' (British Travel Association–University of Keele, 1967, p. 69). Not only does the car provide greater opportunities for recreation in the countryside and widen the horizons of those wishing to participate, but, on the evidence of this survey, it also heightens the expectations of the recreationists themselves. When the *Pilot National Recreation Survey* sought to establish the desires of the population for greater leisure time, they found that 52 per cent of car-owners would like more leisure compared with only 39 per cent of those without access to a motor vehicle. Similarly, while only 9 per cent of car–owners admitted to 'being at a loss for something to do', 20 per cent of those without cars placed themselves in that category (British Travel Association–University of Keele, 1967, p. 43).

### The Recreational Use of the Motor Car

The influence of the motor car is now so much part of daily life that it is easy to forget how recent the rapid rise in car ownership has been. Over the first half of the century numbers of motor vehicles increased slowly and it was not until the early 1950s that growth began to accelerate. Since that time, the number of cars has grown at a rate of nearly 10 per cent per annum. The *Pilot National Recreation Survey* sought to establish the degree to which people take this opportunity to reach the countryside. Only 11 per cent of those who owned cars stated that they never used their motor vehicle for half-day or full-day trips and a further 45 per cent had not made any trips in the previous month. In all, 44 per cent of car owners had made pleasure outings within the previous month. The frequency of trips in this period was, however, fairly limited and, of those car owners making trips, 56 per cent made only one or two trips within the month, a further 32 per cent took three or four trips and only 12 per cent made more than four trips (British Travel Association–University of Keele, 1967, p. 81). These figures confirm Sillitoe's estimates of an average of eight such excursions to the countryside or seaside during the summer. In the studies of central Scotland evidence was collected on leisure trips by motor vehicle lasting over two hours within the four weeks preceding the interview. This definition was less restrictive than that adopted in the national studies and the frequency of trips was therefore considerably higher. Of the sample of car owners 82 per cent had taken at least one trip during the four-week period and the average number of trips for the whole sample was 3·6; however, individual figures varied greatly and over 60 per cent had made up to five trips (Duffield and Owen, 1970, p. 62).

Both half-day and full-day trips were examined in the North-west study. In the year before the interview, 71 per cent of the sample (that is, irrespective of car-ownership) had been on at least one full-day trip and 60 per cent had taken at least one half-day trip. When more detailed attention was paid to the four weeks before the interview, 38 per cent of those owning motor vehicles had taken at least one full-day and a further 26 per cent had taken a half-day trip. These figures were at least twice as high as those for respondents not owning cars. Although such trips are clearly popular in north-west England, the survey established (as other studies had done) that such trips were not very frequent, with an average of two full-day trips in four weeks, and that half-day trips averaged less than two and a half. Only 4 per cent of those taking full-day trips and 10 per cent of those taking half-day trips took more than four trips over the four weeks. Another interesting point to emerge from the North-west study was that there was surprisingly little overlap between those taking full-day and those taking half-day trips; 66 per cent of the former and 57 per cent of the latter took one kind of trip only (North West Sports Council, 1972, pp. 33–4). Such statistics help to explain the high frequency of trips established by the Scottish studies where all trips were considered together.

Unlike public transport, which has prescribed routes and destinations, the private car is restricted only (and not always then) by suitably surfaced roads. Moreover, the greater part of Great Britain is characterised by a dense and complex network of roads and the individual motorist has therefore a wide variety of choice. According to the *Pilot National Recreation Survey,* the destinations of most motorists are likely to be either the countryside or the seaside, which accounted for 62 per cent of the places visited on the last trip specified by the respondents to that survey (table 3.1). The appeal of these locations varies for different groups; the countryside was generally more popular than urban locations for pleasure outings and 34 per cent of all respondents, particularly the middle–aged, elderly and those in executive occupations, had gone to the countryside on their last trip. The traditional type of pleasure outing to the seaside was slightly less popular than trips to the countryside; in all, 28 per cent of those making trips had a seaside locality as their last destination. Visits to the seaside were most popular among the young, those in manual occupations and those with only secondary education, and appealed least to those in executive occupations.

A similar pattern emerged from the studies in central Scotland, in which an indication was sought from those taking trips of the types of places which had been visited on the last excursion (table 3.2). The statistics are not exactly comparable to those obtained by the *Pilot National Recreation Survey*, because it was recognised that an individual excursion might contain visits to more than one type of location, so that the totals in table 3.2 exceed 100 per cent. The ranking of places visited confirms the general findings of the previous survey. Perhaps the most interesting fact to emerge was the popularity of the small town among car-borne visitors; it appears that one role of these small settlements, often in a rural setting, is to provide a focus for the visits of many recreationists to the countryside. In considering the popularity of the countryside it is appropriate to combine two categories, namely the countryside in general and beauty spots; when this is done, the countryside ranks first in order of popularity, with nearly 50 per cent of last trips including a visit to a location in the countryside. The seaside ranked second in the list of places visited and was included as a destination in over a third of most recent rips. It is also noteworthy that a large proportion of respondents (17 per cent of the sample) indicated that their last trip had no specific destination or purpose in mind.

As might be expected, the availability of particular resources in the countryside affects the types of places visited by those taking trips; the levels of visits to coastal locations recorded in the North-west study were well above those indicated by the *Pilot National Recreation Survey* or by the studies in central Scotland. On full-day

## TABLE 3.2

CENTRAL SCOTLAND: PLACES VISITED ON THE LAST TRIP

| Type of place | Percent of all trips involving visit to location |
|---|---|
| Small town | 40·5 |
| Seaside | 34·6 |
| Countryside in general | 31·4 |
| Beauty spot | 22·8 |
| Large town or city | 17·6 |
| Just for a ride, nowhere in particular with friends, relatives, etc. | 17·0 |
| Stately home, historic house, etc. | 6·3 |
| Site of sporting event | 5·9 |

Source:   Duffield and Owen (1970), p. 52; Duffield and Owen (1971a), p. 52.

excursions, 52 per cent of those taking trips in the North-west Region visited the coast, compared with 31 per cent visiting countryside locations; the corresponding figures for half-day trips were 35 and 29 per cent respectively. Another interesting contrast emerged from the North-west study: while only 12 per cent of full-day trips had destinations in urban areas, the comparative figure for half-day excursions was 31 per cent (North West Sport Council, 1972, p. 64), a clear indication of the unwillingness of those taking half-day trips to waste valuable leisure time on long journeys.

To establish the purposes of journeys a detailed examination was undertaken by roadside interview surveys in central Scotland and this confirmed the evidence collected during the home interview surveys. Despite a wide variety of replies, journeys undertaken for specific active recreational pursuits accounted for only a small proportion of the total. For some activities, such as golf and swimming, these figures were underestimates since they did not include the short journeys undertaken entirely within the cordon, which the home interview survey has shown to be characteristic of these activities. Even allowing for considerable underestimates, there can be little doubt that active pursuits are of minor significance in the pattern of recreational traffic as a whole. Traffic in the category 'countryside trips' accounted for over 60 per cent of all journeys for outdoor recreation in Lanarkshire and for over 55 per cent of those in Greater Edinburgh (table 3.3); this group of journeys includes all those where the main aim was an informal drive in the countryside. 'Just touring round', 'just out for a drive', 'trip out' were the answers most commonly given to the question on the purpose of the journey. This category of countryside trips probably contains many journeys which included more specific activities, such as picnics and visits to parks or the seaside, but which were primarily motivated by a wish to 'go for a drive', with a loosely defined destination in mind. The results from a cordon survey thrown around the city of Dundee in 1971 confirm these figures, for 53 per cent of recreational trips into the countryside on a Saturday and 75 per cent of those on a Sunday represented pleasure trips for informal activities such as sight-seeing, picnicking, or merely driving around with no specific destination in mind (Beaty, Pearson-Kirk, Cal and Greig, 1973, p. 6). Information from interviews undertaken at various recreational sites in central Scotland further confirms these observations. Visitors to a range of countryside and seaside locations were asked whether they had planned to visit the particular site at which interviewing took place or were 'just passing'. Although the proportion varied from site to site, from 20 to 40 per cent of visitors indicated that their visit was unplanned.

TABLE 3.3

CENTRAL SCOTLAND: PURPOSE OF JOURNEY

| Purpose of journey | Percentage of all outdoor recreation traffic | |
| --- | --- | --- |
| | Lanarkshire | Greater Edinburgh |
| Countryside trip | 61·6 | 56·8 |
| Holiday | 24·1 | 16·3 |
| Picnic | 1·8 | 8·6 |
| Seaside | 2·2 | 6·4 |
| Golf | 2·7 | 3·8 |
| Stately homes, etc. | 0·6 | 2·1 |
| Competition | 1·9 | 1·9 |
| Fishing | 1·6 | 1·0 |
| Climbing | 0·2 | 1·0 |
| Swimming | 1·6 | 0·7 |
| Sailing | 0·5 | 0·6 |
| Riding, pony-trekking | 0·2 | 0·2 |
| Skiing | — | 0·2 |
| Water-skiing | — | 0·1 |
| Naturalist activities | — | 0·1 |
| Flying, gliding | 0·1 | 0·1 |
| Hunting, shooting | 0·1 | 0·1 |
| Visit to a park | 0·6 | 0·1 |
| Organised outing | 0·3 | — |
| Total outdoor recreation travel | 100 | 100 |

Source:    Duffield and Owen (1970), p. 90; Duffield and Owen (1971a), p.94.

Apart from information on general objectives of the kind listed in tables 3.1, 3.2 and 3.3, relatively little is known about the use made of such trips for passive recreation in the countryside, though aspects of the recreational journey itself are explored further in chapter 8. There is scattered evidence, confirmed by general observation, that those who visit the countryside for passive recreation (the great majority of whom travel by car) seldom stray far from their vehicles (Patmore, 1970) and picnicking, strolling about or walking, and playing games seem to be most important activities (Lindsey County Council, 1967; Wager, 1967).

Some additional evidence is available from the site surveys undertaken as part of the studies of central Scotland. A number of sites, together with general recrea-

## TABLE 3.4

### CENTRAL SCOTLAND: RECREATIONAL ACTIVITIES AT COUNTRYSIDE SITES

| Activities | Lanarkshire countryside sites | Lothian countryside sites | East Lothian coastal sites | Parks near small urban centres | Edinburgh parks |
|---|---|---|---|---|---|
| | | (percentage of total visitors) | | | |
| Informal outdoor activities | 25·1 | 33·8 | 31·2 | 71·9 | 41·3 |
| Informal indoor activities | 4·9 | 2·7 | 14·9 | 1·5 | 4·3 |
| Watched children play | 3·8 | 12·7 | 11·9 | 9·2 | 4·7 |
| Sunbathing | 2·2 | 4·5 | 6·5 | 2·6 | 5·3 |
| Picnic | 31·2 | 22·9 | 19·0 | 10·3 | 7·8 |
| Sat in car | 3·7 | 2·0 | 1·3 | — | 1·4 |
| Spectating | — | 0·6 | 0·6 | — | 4·6 |
| Photography | 0·6 | 0·5 | 0·3 | — | 1·5 |
| Exploration | 1·0 | 0·7 | 1·0 | 0·5 | 0·6 |
| Visiting historic sites | 2·8 | 4·0 | 1·1 | — | — |
| Naturalist activities | 2·1 | 1·1 | 2·0 | — | 4·2 |
| Fishing | 13·1 | 4·6 | 1·5 | — | 0·7 |
| Hiking | 5·1 | 4·7 | 2·4 | — | 11·2 |
| Climbing | 4·5 | 2·8 | 0·1 | 0·5 | 4·6 |
| Sailing | 4·5 | 0·1 | 0·5 | 0·5 | 0·4 |
| Skiing | — | — | — | — | 3·7 |

Source: Duffield and Owen (1970), p.119; Duffield and Owen (1971a), p.126.

tional areas were monitored by the technique of rural traverses (p. 24) and used a simple questionnaire, which sought information on origins, length of stay, reasons and frequency of visits; other information about method of travel and composition of parties was gathered by observation. Respondents (who were selected at random as far as this was possible) were asked an open-ended question, 'What have you been doing since you have been here, and what do you plan to do during the rest of your stay?' and the results are given in table 3.4.

The three most important categories in these answers were informal activities, picnicking and watching children play (a response which emphasised the family character of many parties). Additionally, there were forms of active recreation, such as fishing, though these were, on average, very much in the minority. Nevertheless, they do serve as a reminder that, while the broad distinction between passive and active recreation is useful, it is often not possible to classify trips into the countryside as one or the other, for many such trips combine both active and passive recreation.

The motor car has so far been considered only in relation to individuals, but the recreational journey by car is, more than any other recreational activity, a group pursuit. The tendency for recreational trips into the countryside to be undertaken in groups is confirmed by data from the studies of central Scotland (table 3.5). The average occupancy of cars used for recreational journeys was just over three persons and only 7 per cent of vehicles used for such journeys contained a single occupant; indeed, 19 per cent of all cars carried more than four people.

TABLE 3.5

RECREATIONAL TRAFFIC IN CENTRAL SCOTLAND: VEHICLE OCCUPANCY

| Number of occupants | Percentage of vehicles in each category |
|---|---|
| 1 | 7·1 |
| 2 | 31·9 |
| 3 | 19·4 |
| 4 | 22·8 |
| 5+ | 19·0 |
| Average number of occupants per car | 3·1 |

Source:   Duffield and Owen (1970), p. 93; Duffield and Owen (1971a), p. 98.

A very similar figure was recorded in the study carried out around Dundee, with an average of 3·1 persons per vehicle on Sunday pleasure trips, though parties on Saturdays were somewhat smaller (2·7 persons). On the evidence of this survey more than 50 per cent of all cars on pleasure trips were occupied by three or more people (Beaty, Pearson-Kirk, Cal and Greig, 1973, p. 12). Further confirmation is provided by the North-west survey, which established that 64 per cent of full-day trips and 69 per cent of half-day trips were in groups containing members of the family (North West Sports Council, 1972, p. 40). The most detailed information was obtained by the *Pilot National Recreation Survey* (table 3.6), which showed that such groups most commonly consisted either of adults alone (51 per cent) or adults with children (38 per cent), and that the proportion of teenagers visiting the countryside was low (14 per cent of groups). Not surprisingly, the adult-only groups were more common among the middle-aged (45–64 age group, 74 per cent) and among younger adults with children (25–34 age group, 61 per cent), but there was little variation with either income or occupation.

## TABLE 3.6

### RECREATIONAL OUTINGS IN GREAT BRITAIN: COMPOSITION OF GROUPS
(percentage of those interviewed)

|  | Age | | Income | | Occupation | | |
|---|---|---|---|---|---|---|---|
|  | 25–34 | 45–64 | £850–£1199 | over £1950 | Manual | Executive | All |
| Self only | 3 | 4 | 3 | 6 | 4 | 5 | 3 |
| Husband and wife | 23 | 48 | 35 | 27 | 30 | 33 | 34 |
| Husband, wife and other adults | 10 | 26 | 17 | 31 | 22 | 21 | 17 |
| Teenagers in party | 0 | 7 | 3 | 10 | 7 | 7 | 7 |
| Children under 16 in party | 56 | 11 | 38 | 20 | 30 | 26 | 31 |
| Teenagers and children in party | 5 | 4 | 7 | 6 | 7 | 11 | 7 |

Source:    British Travel Association–University of Keele (1967), p. 86.

## Length of Trip

Consideration has so far been confined to the total number of recreational trips undertaken by samples of the British population, but the impact of these journeys on the countryside and the recreational use made of the countryside will be affected by the distribution of these journeys over time. Just as the distribution of recreational journeys varies markedly throughout the year and the week, so too does the pattern within each day; there is a distinctive sequence of departures of recreationists from their homes and a corresponding pattern of return journeys. As part of the roadside survey undertaken in the studies of central Scotland (chapter 8), information was gathered on the times when people began their recreational journeys and also on their intended time of return. The analysis of this information provides a great deal of background information on the density of traffic throughout the day on the major roads that carry people into the countryside and also on the time when the recreational areas are likely to feel the greatest pressures. The general pattern was much as expected (table 3.7). Most people set out during the morning, 50 per cent of all recreational journeys having begun before midday. Between noon and 13.00 hours there was a drop in the number of departures, which rose again as those who set out after lunch were recorded; between 13.00 and 16.00 hours a further 37 per cent began their journeys. Only a few of those interviewed (11

TABLE 3.7

TIMES OF DEPARTURE AND RETURN ON
RECREATIONAL JOURNEYS IN CENTRAL SCOTLAND

|  | Time of departure | Estimated time of return |
|---|---|---|
|  | (percentage of those interviewed) | |
| Before 10.00 | 19·1 | 0·2 |
| 10.00–10.59 | 16·4 | 0·8 |
| 11.00–11.59 | 14·1 | 1·1 |
| 12.00–12.59 | 8·2 | 1·5 |
| 13.00–13.59 | 12·7 | 2·9 |
| 14.00–14.59 | 13·6 | 2·7 |
| 15.00–15.59 | 11·3 | 2·9 |
| 16.00–16.59* | 9·6 | 7·1 |
| 17.00–17.59 | – | 15·5 |
| 18.00–18.59 | – | 21·3 |
| 19.00–19.59 | – | 17·4 |
| After 20.00 | – | 27·7 |

* Interviewing terminated at 17.00 hours

Source:   Duffield and Owen (1970), p. 94; Duffield and
Owen (1971a), p. 99.

per cent) intended to return home before 16.00 hours, but a rapid build-up was
expected after that time, with over 54 per cent planning to return between
17.00 and 20.00 hours, when there is a peak of recreational traffic returning
home. Like the journey to work, the 'journey to play' has its rush hours when
the concentration of traffic causes far greater difficulties than data on total
traffic would suggest.

The period over which people were away from home was computed from
these statistics (table 3.8). Apart from very short journeys of less than two

TABLE 3.8

RECREATIONAL JOURNEYS IN CENTRAL SCOTLAND:
TOTAL TIME IN HOURS

| Time taken on journey | Percentage of all recreational journeys |
|---|---|
| Less than 2 | 12·0 |
| 2–4 | 22·3 |
| 4–6 | 25·2 |
| 6–8 | 19·7 |
| Over 8 | 20·8 |

Source:   Duffield and Owen (1970), p. 96; Duffield and Owen
(1971a), p. 100.

hours, the duration of journeys was fairly evenly spread and, on the evidence of these studies, there seems to be no clear division between half-day and full-day trips adopted in the questionnaires (North West Sports Council, 1972). It is also noteworthy that, on the evidence of the Dundee study, the vast majority of weekend leisure trips (90 per cent) are completed on the same day on which they begin, with nearly three-quarters of leisure trips on Saturday and Sunday having a duration of six hours or less (Beaty, Pearson-Kirk, Cal and Grieg, 1973, p. 7).

This discussion of the recreational role of the motor vehicle in the country-side illustrates the evolution of what is virtually a new recreational activity; the popularity of the 'trip out' has grown rapidly in the last decade and its development requires more attention than it has received. At the same time, the conclusions drawn are necessarily tentative and, to some extent, temporary. The motor car is both a vehicle that enables the individual to participate in particular chosen pursuits in the countryside and also an integral part of the recreational experience. Passive recreation that is dependent on the motor car makes a broad-based yet distinctive appeal to particular social groups within the community, and in this respect seems very much of a piece with the evolving society of the twentieth century, drawing participants from a broad section of society and a wide range of age groups. At present, car ownership is an indicator of social class and to that extent is correlated with socio-economic variables such as occupation, education and income. Yet as car ownership itself becomes more broadly-based, it can be expected that, for the first time, there will emerge a recreational activity in the countryside that is not the perquisite of a particular social group.

## Provision of Facilities for Passive Recreation in the Countryside

In the same way that the advent of widespread car ownership has transformed, in a qualitative way, the recreational aspirations of the British population and their opportunities for recreation in the countryside, these new opportunities have created pressures on the countryside and have brought a growing demand for the provision of facilities to cater for these needs; for while passive recreation in the countryside has characteristically taken place on open land (much of it in private ownership) and to a lesser extent on enclosed farmland, such use is often without legal justification and has been tolerated in the past only because pressures have been light (chapter 7). With the establishment of the Countryside Commission in England and Wales and of the Countryside Commission for Scotland attempts have been made to alleviate these pressures partly through Access Agreements (chapter 7) and partly through the creation of picnic sites and Country Parks (Zetter, 1971). The Government White Paper *Leisure in the Countryside* (Ministry of Land and Natural Resources, 1966) envisaged such parks as having three objectives:

(1) to make it easier for those seeking recreation to enjoy their leisure in the open without travelling too far and adding to congestion on the roads;
(2) to ease the pressure on the more remote and solitary places;
(3) to reduce the risk of damage to the countryside, aesthetic as well as physical,

which often comes about when people simply settle down for an hour or a day when it suits them somewhere 'in the countryside' to the inconvenience and expense of those who live and work in the locality.

It was in this spirit that the concept of the Country Park was included in the Countryside Acts of 1967 and 1968. As the policy on Country Parks evolved, it became clear that they were primarily intended to provide informal facilities and were not envisaged as providing opportunities for organised sports; it was also expected that only a small proportion of a Country Park would be covered by buildings. This policy repeated the largely intuitive feelings of those responsible for planning facilities for outdoor recreation. In fact, very few practical standards of provision for recreation were available, although certain general principles did exist—for example, the National Playing Fields Association's guideline of 6 acres (2·4 ha) of usable playing space per thousand persons, developed primarily in respect of urban land. It is not surprising, therefore, that uncertainties still surround the concept of Country Parks, particularly about what constitutes a Country Park, what function it should serve and what facilities it should contain.

There are three considerations which ought to be borne in mind in the creation of Country Parks: their location in relation to centres of population, a topic which will be considered more fully in chapters 8 and 9, in the context of recreational travel; the character of the land and its suitability for outdoor recreation on a continuing basis, a topic that is explored in chapter 6; and the facilities which should be provided in such parks. There are at least three ways of approaching the last problem: to seek objective standards of provision of recreational facilities; to analyse the kinds of things that recreationists in the countryside seek to do; and to ask members of the public what facilities they would like to see in Country Parks. The first approach has been shown earlier to be able to contribute little at present (though work on standards of provision is clearly needed), but some information is available upon both the second and third.

As part of the site surveys undertaken in central Scotland, respondents were asked, in an open-ended question, why they had gone to particular sites (table 3.9). The reasons offered varied widely from site to site, as might be expected, from the attractiveness of the site, its suitability for children, a particular resource and, most important, the general appeal of the countryside (Duffield and Owen, 1970, p. 118; 1971a, p. 125). For many visistors the visit to the particular site had been planned, and over three-quarters had been there before (Duffield and Owen, 1970, p. 115; 1971a, p. 122). Studies of sample forest areas show a similar variety of motives; for example, the people whose main motive was to have a picnic ranged from 5 per cent in Glen More to 39 per cent in Cannock Chase (Mutch, 1968).

Those facilities and activities which now attract visitors to the countryside must be found in newly created Country Parks. The facilities provided in these Parks, however, should be a balance of proven attractions and those facilities that can support the recreational aspirations of the public. In many ways the absence of an adequate working definition of a Country Park probably stems partly from a lack of appreciation of what the 'customer' wants. Although public demand need not necessarily dictate decisions in recreational planning, evidence on public attitudes in a field which is subject to such rapid and continuing change is necessary if planners are to avoid creating Country Parks of a kind which nobody wants.

## TABLE 3.9

### CENTRAL SCOTLAND: REASONS FOR VISITING COUNTRYSIDE SITES

| Reason for visit | Lanarkshire countryside sites | Lothian countryside sites | East Lothian coastal sites | Parks near small urban centres | Edinburgh parks |
|---|---|---|---|---|---|
| | (percentage of all reasons given) | | | | |
| Attractive site | 0·6 | 16·4 | 13·0 | 14·5 | 12·8 |
| Suitable for children | 5·2 | 9·9 | 7·2 | 24·8 | 5·8 |
| Visited before | 3·4 | 4·6 | 4·9 | 0·9 | 6·2 |
| Recommended | 1·2 | 2·0 | 3·9 | 1·7 | 1·6 |
| Take photos | 0·6 | 0·3 | 0·1 | – | 0·1 |
| Met friends | 3·7 | 2·0 | 2·5 | 1·7 | 2·3 |
| Exploration | 2·5 | 3·3 | 3·3 | – | 3·7 |
| Easy accessibility | 2·4 | 3·8 | 7·0 | 10·3 | 2·3 |
| Just for a trip out | 5·9 | 1·6 | 1·6 | 1·7 | 1·5 |
| Car-parking facilities | 0·4 | 0·8 | 5·2 | 0·9 | 0·2 |
| Plenty of open space | 1·2 | 3·1 | 3·4 | 3·4 | 0·9 |
| Just passing through | 2·9 | 0·5 | 0·5 | – | 0·2 |
| Nice weather | 2·7 | 2·9 | 6·8 | – | 3·8 |
| For a picnic | 2·1 | 3·8 | 2·5 | 5·1 | 2·1 |
| Natural history | 1·4 | 0·9 | 1·3 | – | 3·3 |
| Historic interest | 2·7 | 2·6 | 1·4 | – | 0·4 |
| To take part in: | | | | | |
| Passive outdoor activities | 20·8 | 26·1 | 14·3 | 31·6 | 33·8 |
| Passive water activities | 6·1 | 4·5 | 15·5 | 1·7 | 5·0 |
| Fishing | 12·9 | 4·2 | 1·1 | – | 0·9 |
| Hiking/walking | 4·9 | 3·8 | 0·6 | – | 7·4 |
| Sailing | 5·3 | 0·3 | 0·7 | 1·7 | 0·5 |
| Water-skiing | 1·1 | – | – | – | – |
| Skiing | – | – | – | – | 3·3 |
| Climbing | 0·6 | 1·0 | 0·1 | – | 1·7 |

Source:   Duffield and Owen (1970), p. 118; Duffield and Owen (1971a), p. 125.

Some light is shed on what the public wants by questions in the home interview surveys in central Scotland on the provision of facilities for outdoor recreation in general and for Country Parks in particular. Spontaneous replies were sought and questions were therefore 'open-ended'. No guidance was given to respondents, so that more than 140 different facilities were mentioned; these were then grouped to give a more manageable total (table 3.10). In addition to the wide variety of suggestions, a further point of interest was the urban nature of many of the facilities suggested. Although it would not be wholly true to say that the people of central Scotland framed their suggestions in the light of existing facilities, it appears that many responses were conditioned by the fact that most provision for outdoor recreation is in urban locations. This is clearly demonstrated in the facilities sugges-

## TABLE 3.10

### CENTRAL SCOTLAND:
### PROVISION OF FACILITIES FOR OUTDOOR RECREATION

| Facility | General | Country Parks |
|---|---|---|
| | (percentage of all choices) | |
| Children's amusements | 12·4 | 15·2 |
| Indoor games | 11·1 | 3·1 |
| Swimming pool | 10·3 | 5·1 |
| Tennis | 6·9 | 5·7 |
| Football | 6·6 | 4·7 |
| Golf | 5·2 | 8·2 |
| Parks | 4·4 | 0·7 |
| Bowls (outdoor) | 4·4 | 2·2 |
| Sports (stadium) | 3·2 | 2·3 |
| Youth hostels | 3·0 | 0·6 |
| Boating | 2·6 | 8·9 |
| Gardens | 2·3 | 5·6 |
| Walks | 2·0 | 2·7 |
| Ice rink | 1·7 | 0·4 |
| Sports (coach) | 1·6 | 0·6 |
| Fishing | 1·6 | 1·6 |
| Riding | 1·3 | 1·8 |
| Skiing | 1·2 | 0·7 |
| Cafe/hotel | 1·2 | 4·5 |
| Nature reserves | 1·0 | 1·8 |

Source:   Duffield and Owen (1970), p. 58; Duffield and Owen (1971a),
p. 58.

ted, which have been grouped and categorised in table 3.11; in general, respondents asked for facilities that might be found in urban parks, although the scale and variety are larger, including for example, 'pitch' facilities (that is, defined and enclosed recreational areas usually restricted to one activity), which are normally located near their homes in urban areas.

Clearly the concept of a Country Park has had little influence on public thinking about the provision of facilities for recreation, although there was slightly less emphasis on specific facilities and pitches in response to a question on Country Parks. Even so, only one person in four named facilities that call for a location in the countryside and even some of these, such as walks and boating facilities, could equally well be sited in urban parks. The 'natural' elements of the countryside, which are seen as essential ingredients by all those responsible for the planning of Country Parks, were mentioned by only 4 per cent of all those interviewed. The interpretation of these data poses a fundamental dilemma for planners, whether such preferences should have a marked influence on the development of policies for Country Parks or whether they merely reflect the conditioning of past experience. In the light of these findings, it seems desirable that Country Parks should be complemented by urban-based facilities, a conclusion that is given added

## TABLE 3.11

CENTRAL SCOTLAND: FACILITIES DESIRED FOR OUTDOOR RECREATION

|  | Specific facilities* | Pitch facilities* | Countryside facilities* | The Countryside* |
|---|---|---|---|---|
|  | (percentage of total choices) | | | |
| General | 55·6 | 25·0 | 17·0 | 2·2 |
| Country Parks | 46·1 | 43·2 | 25·6 | 4·0 |

*Including:

| Specific facilities | |
|---|---|
| Indoor games | Hockey |
| Children's amusements | Netball |
| Swimming pool | Rugby |
| Sports track | |
| Ice rink | Countryside facilities |
| Cafe/hotel | Youth hostels |
| Seats | Walks |
| Motorcycling | Gardens |
| Cycle track | Boating |
| Roller-skating | Fishing |
| Marina | Caravan/camping |
| Zoo | Shooting |
| | Picnic sites |
| Pitch facilities | Riding |
| Football | |
| Tennis | The Countryside |
| Golf | Nature reserves |
| Bowls | Natural countryside |
| Cricket | Trees |
| | Unpolluted rivers |
| | Bird sanctuary |

Source:    Duffield and Owen, 1970, p. 59; Duffield and Owen, 1971a, p. 59.

strength when it is related to the minority role that even passive recreation in the countryside plays in the leisure budget of the British people.

## THE FUTURE

The future growth and popularity of passive recreation and its place in the development of recreation in the countryside has not been a subject of detailed study; investigations and forecasts of such recreation have tended to concentrate on active pursuits, a tendency even reflected in the inquiries of the Select Committee of the House of Lords on Sport and Leisure (1973). Yet there are sound reasons for believing that the growth in passive informal recreation in the countryside may be more rapid than in any other activity (assuming trends are not substantially affected by the energy crisis); the basis of participation is very much broader and one of the key factors in participation, namely the ownership of a motor vehicle, is known to be still growing and spreading more evenly throughout the community. It has been estimated that, as early as 1985, there will be an average of one car per household in Great Britain, and there can be little doubt that the coming decade will see an increasingly broader social spectrum of people seeking opportunities for passive recreation in the countryside. A tentative glance into the future has been undertaken by the Institute of Community Studies on behalf of the General Post Office. They predict that, over the next 30 years, the popularity of passive pursuits, particularly going for a 'drive in the car for pleasure' is expected to increase by approximately 10–20 per cent (Young and Willmott, 1973). This forecast seems very cautious and the predictions given to the Select Committee on Sport and Leisure on the growth in recreation activities in the countryside seem more realistic; the Countryside Commission suggested that there is 'something like a 10–15 per cent compound increase in the rate of recreational activity in the countryside' (Select Committee, 1973). The Select Committee believe that the present rate of growth may not continue until the year 2000 in that it owes much to the release of 'latent demand' for facilities and is therefore in some part a measure of present deficiencies. Since the Committee reported, the validity of such projections has been challenged by growing uncertainty about the future supplies and prices of petrol, though past experience suggests that, except in times of crisis, motorists are not highly sensitive to the cost of fuel. Irrespective of the actual pattern of growth over the next thirty years, it can be expected that ever-continuing pressure will be exerted on rural resources in the British countryside by an army of recreationists whose desire for these resources is conditioned more by a general wish to get away from an urban environment than by a particular desire to enjoy a specific kind of recreation. Catering for this broad-based group of recreationists offers both the greatest challenge in resolving the relationship between demand and supply and the greatest opportunities for imaginative development.

# 4 The Demand for Active Recreation

Active recreation in the countryside differs from passive recreation in a number of ways. Not only are participants a minority of those visiting the countryside for outdoor recreation, but they are generally younger and differ in respect of a number of socio-economic characteristics; they often depend on particular (and sometimes scarce) recreational resources in the countryside; and they are frequently organised in clubs or other kinds of associations. Yet, as with passive recreation, information about such activities is scanty, and the main purpose of this chapter is to examine some of the available evidence.

In the mid-1960s, when geographers in Great Britain first began to investigate the ways in which land is used for outdoor recreation, few official (or officially financed) surveys of active recreation had been undertaken. Academic researchers were therefore driven to sift through available sources for both direct and indirect evidence of the recreational use of the countryside. This data-dredging approach was used in a pioneer paper, in which information of varying reliability was collected on various forms of active recreation (Coppock, 1966).

Although much of the information acquired by this approach has now been superseded by data supplied by specially designed surveys, the method still has several advantages at the national level and has recently been used by Tanner (1973) in his survey of water recreation. Much of the information obtained indirectly casts light on minority activities, on which it has proved singularly difficult to obtain adequate information through sample surveys, owing to low rates of participation and the small size of samples. Moreover, data-dredging offers a continual source of information, which has proved invaluable in updating that gained by more expensive surveys. Such surveys, on the other hand, provide quantitative information that permits comparisons between different parts of the country and can be used to estimate future levels of demand. In this chapter the contribution of both approaches towards the assessment of demand for various kinds of active recreation is considered. An attempt will first be made to update the findings of the 1966 paper, both to provide insights on activities which other national surveys have neglected and to illustrate the approach.

## INFORMATION ON ACTIVE RECREATION IN RURAL BRITAIN

In 1966 the use of land and water in Great Britain for active recreation had been divided into four types on the basis of demands on land and other resources: in-

formal activities, such as walking, which need access to the countryside at large;
traditional rural sports, such as grouse-shooting and fox-hunting, which generally
involve either game or land management; sports such as cricket or motor racing,
for which a pitch or other specially constructed facilities are required; and aquatic
sports, such as fishing and canoeing, which are practised in both coastal and inland
waters and make only limited (though very localised) demands on land.

## Informal Active Recreation

Those participating in a more informal kind of active recreation in the countryside
have a variety of interests. The study of natural history has become increasingly
popular and, under the provisions of the Countryside Acts, the Countryside Commissions encourage and support such ventures as the new residential study centre
in the Peak District National Park (*Recreation News*, 1972). However, most of
those seeking access to the countryside for informal active recreation are cyclists,
riders and walkers, though canoeing and skiing are of growing importance.
Cycling represents one of the few forms of outdoor recreation to show a decline;
membership of the Cyclists Touring Club fell from 60 000 in its hey-day in 1889
to 17 727 in its nadir in 1971 (Cyclists Touring Club, 1972). It seems likely that
this decline is due to the impact of the motor car, but the number of those seeking a more leisurely and inexpensive form of transport is increasing again and may
well do so markedly in the face of sharp increases in the price of petrol; membership
of the CTC reached 20 053 in 1972, and pleasure cycling has also been expanding
in North America. Numbers of riders of horses and ponies are increasing at an
estimated 20 per cent per year (British Horse Society, 1972). Walkers are probably
the most numerous participants in this kind of recreation, although the 25 818
members of the Ramblers Association (Ramblers Association, 1972) and the
265 700 belonging to the Youth Hostels Assocations (Youth Hostels Association,
1972; Scottish Youth Hostels Association, 1972) represent only the hard core.
Membership of these clubs has increased considerably since the Second World War,
for the Ramblers Association had only 3778 members in 1950 and Youth Hostels
Association 201 863 in 1946, but it is now fairly stable. Interest in sports such as
canoeing, climbing and skiing may overlap with that in walking and cycling, but its
growth has been much more rapid and these sports can be undertaken only in
suitable localities. An estimated 100 000 people canoe in Great Britain, 2000 of
them competing in races (British Canoeing Union, 1972); participation in mountaineering is estimated to be doubling every 10 years (British Mountaineering Council,
1972); and the 60 000 affiliated to the National Ski Federation, whose membership
is growing at 15 per cent per annum, are only the minority of the estimated
200 000 Britons who ski regularly each year (British Ski Federation, 1972).

## Traditional Field Sports

These are long-established activities, and it is generally held that hunting and
shooting are less widespread than before the First World War. In recent years,
however, there has been a considerable revival, part of which appears to be due
to commercial and industrial interests, part to the increasing affluence and leisure
of the population at large and part to growing interest among foreign visitors.

Information on the use of the countryside for field sports is scanty, since these activities take place chiefly on privately-owned land, of which the main use is agriculture or forestry, and many of the participants are landowners or their tenants (see chapter 7); it is probably for this reason that hunting and shooting are often ignored or treated only summarily in discussions of outdoor recreation. Much land is used for recreation of this kind, although only from time to time as these activities are markedly seasonal, being restricted for much of the year by the requirements of other land users or by the existence of close seasons to ensure the survival of the hunted animals or birds.

Fox-hunting is a long-established sport that still retains its popularity (British Field Sports Society, 1972). Some 250 000 people follow the hounds at least one day a week (Masters of the Fox Hounds Association, 1972) and there are 206 fox-hound packs in Great Britain, numbers which have remained stable since 1966. Stag, otter and hare are also hunted, though there are only four packs of stag-hounds, and the sport is confined to Devon and Somerset. Otter are followed on foot and there are 15 packs of otterhound, but hares are more widely hunted and there are 120 packs of basset hounds, beagles and harriers. There are also six packs of draghounds, which follow artificially laid scents, a popular sport in the Lake District (British Field Sports Society, 1972).

Even less is known about shooting because so much is informal and kept in private hands, but numbers of holders of gun licences and of gamekeepers provide some indication of its extent. At present some 600 000 people hold shotgun licences and an estimated 70 000 of these shoot game (Wildfowlers' Association of Great Britain and Ireland, 1972); the number of gamekeepers has remained stable at about 6000 since 1946, although it was 13 416 in 1921 (Gamekeepers Association, 1972). Shooting is of several kinds and includes the shooting of game birds, chiefly partridge, pheasant and grouse, deer-stalking, wildfowling, the shooting of hares and rabbits and the extermination of vermin. The shooting of game birds, which are protected by law and may not be killed in the close season, is widespread. The acreage of partridge and pheasant-shooting has been estimated at about 20 million acres (8 million ha), and the number of pheasants shot annually is thought to be about 6 million; the chief areas are found in the eastern half of Great Britain from Morayshire southwards. Grouse–shooting is largely confined to about 4 million acres (1·6 million ha) of heather moors, which are mainly located on the drier uplands on the eastern side of Great Britain from Derbyshire northwards. Shooting rights over grouse moors proper, which are usually grazed by sheep as well, are often let and the cost per brace of birds killed can be as high as £7.10. The period before the First World War was the hey-day for grouse-shooting, which has since been hit by the break-up of estates and by falling numbers of grouse; thus, whereas one and three-quarter million grouse were shot in Scotland in 1911, it is estimated at present that between $\frac{1}{2}$–1 million are shot annually (Game Conservancy, 1972). Yet, with other forms of shooting, there has been a revival in recent years.

Although the hunting of deer was once widespread, the shooting of red deer, or deer-stalking, is now virtually confined to north-west Scotland. It, too, has declined from a peak before the First World War, when there were an estimated 3 850 000 acres (1 460 000 ha) of deer forests, compared with approximately 3·5 million acres (1·4 million ha) in 1972. The Red Deer Commission has estimated that red deer range over some 7 million acres (2·8 million ha) of Scotland, for there is a large acreage of marginal ground where deer winter and they are also found from time to time on farmland (Red Deer Commission, 1972a). The total population of deer is only some 185 000 but, even so, the land is overstocked and the 22 067 carcases purchased by dealers in 1971, together with unrecorded killing by poachers, are inadequate to keep numbers stable (Red Deer Commission, 1972b). Deer-stalking is thought barely to pay its way, but provides revenue and supplementary employment for some of the most sparsely populated parts of the Scottish Highlands (Wynne Edwards, Jenkins and Watson, 1960). Like other forms of game shooting, it can never be other than a minority interest.

There is increasing interest in the shooting of wildfowl, which is both less organised and less expensive. In 1972 there were over 24 000 acres (9600 ha) under the management of the Wildfowlers' Association of Great Britain and Ireland and its 270 affiliated clubs, together with 340 000 acres (146 000 ha) under their direct control, including 60 miles (97 km) of foreshore (Wildfowlers' Association of Great Britain and Ireland, 1972). Other shooting is even less organised. Hares are shot over a wide area of cultivated land and moorland, but the numbers of rabbits, which once made a valuable contribution to rural incomes in some poorer parts of the country, have been greatly reduced by myxomatosis; it is also official policy to encourage their extermination and a number of areas have been declared free of rabbits (Warden, 1956), although there has been some recovery in recent years. Other animals are also shot because of the damage they cause, notably rooks, pigeons, stoats and squirrels.

By comparison with other forms of recreation that need large areas of land, the number of people engaged in most kinds of field sports (except wildfowling) is comparatively small. Although the area used for field sports is large, their contribution should not be exaggerated; the Forestry Commission received only £64 000 in shooting revenue in respect of an estate of nearly 3 million acres (1 200 000 ha), although shooting is not let on much of this land, or it has been reserved to former owners (*Forestry Policy*, 1972). Nonetheless, field sports provide a valuable supplement to rural revenues in some poorer areas, since they differ from many other forms of recreational use in being directly productive, yielding an annual harvest worth several million pounds, a figure that is capable of considerable expansion (Phillips, 1972).

## Organised Recreational Uses of Land

The location of land used for formal recreation, in organised sports or activities that need specially constructed facilities, is determined chiefly by considerations of accessibility from the main centres of population and, although the nature of the terrain may be important, the quality of the scenery is not. Despite the intensive nature of such use and the fact that most land is owned or rented by clubs or local authorities, even the supply and location of this land is not well-known statistically. It is safe to say that, with the exception of sports such as gliding and motor-racing, most lies in or on the margin of towns; unfortunately no satisfactory data exist on the respective shares of town and country.

Football is the most important winter sport and there are 36 404 amateur association football clubs (Football Association, 1972). Cricket and tennis are probably the most widely practised summer sports; there are approximately 20 000 cricket clubs in Great Britain with an estimated 500 000 participants (National Cricket Association, 1972), whilst tennis clubs number 2905 and a further 1748 schools are affiliated (Lawn Tennis Association, 1972). Athletics are increasing in popularity; the number of clubs is approximately 2000 and cinder tracks (including synthetic tracks) total more than 300, whereas there were only 50 arenas before the Second World War (British Amateur Athletic Board, 1972).

Sports requiring more extensive areas of land are to be found mainly in the rural areas. There are some 1800 golf courses in Great Britain, covering nearly 200 000 acres (80 000 ha) (Golf Development Council, 1972). The distribution of golf courses corresponds broadly to that of population, but they are most abundant near coastal resorts and in Scotland, where golf is popular at all social levels. Because of high land values within the built-up area, most golf courses lie near, rather than in, towns. Other kinds of recreation demanding special facilities and space include gliding, flying, motor and motorcycle racing, horse-racing and horse-riding. Gliding has increased rapidly in popularity and there are now 83 clubs compared with 21 in 1951, and launching sites are widely scattered throughout the countryside (British Gliding Association, 1972). Flying is also popular and a proportion of the land used for some 120 private airfields also ought to be counted as recreational land (British Light Aviation Centre, 1972). Motor and motorcycle racing range from formal race meetings at one of the 16 motor race circuits (British Automobile Club, 1972) or the motorcycle circuits (Auto Cycle Union, 1972), through sprint meetings, often on airfields, to hill climbs and motorcycle scrambles on rough country, and much of the land used is in rural areas. Most of the 63 courses for horse-racing are on the periphery of towns although their numbers are declining; they are widely scattered, but major courses are concentrated around London and in Yorkshire (Horserace Betting Levy Board, 1972). Most of the 3500 riding establishments are also to be found on rural land on the periphery of towns (British Horse Society, 1972).

## The Recreational Use of Inland and Coastal Waters

The Outdoor Recreation Resources Review Commission's observation that 'water is often the focal point of much outdoor recreation' is equally valid in Great Britain and applies to coastal and inland water and to both passive and active recreation (Dower, 1964). There are some 605 953 acres (244 000 ha) of inland water in Great Britain, including reservoirs but excluding small patches of water and the lesser rivers; and nearly 65 per cent of this is in Scotland, much of it in areas which are quite remote from the main centres of population. As a result much activity on inland waters is concentrated in a relatively small part of the area potentially available.

None of the many kinds of aquatic recreation requires much land; indeed, their chief impact on land use is their contribution towards congestion in certain popular areas, notably the Lake District. The principal recreational use of inland waters is fishing. There were almost 3 million anglers, including those who engage

in sea–fishing, in England and Wales in 1970 (Natural Environment Research
Council, 1971). Most inland waters provide some fishing although reduction of
flow by water abstraction and pollution from urban and industrial areas have
greatly reduced the fishing potential of some stretches of river. Fishing varies
greatly in character and intensity, although it is everywhere in demand. Coarse
fishing in publicly owned waters near towns attracts large numbers of people who
fish at little or no cost; the National Angling Survey in 1970 estimated that 67
per cent of anglers went coarse fishing at an average cost of £1 per outing (Natural
Environment Research Council, 1971, p. 1). At the other extreme, comparatively
small numbers of anglers fish for trout and salmon on privately owned lakes and
rivers, especially in the more sparsely populated areas, such as the Scottish
Highlands; between these extremes, much fishing is let to angling clubs, many of
which belong to the National Federation of Anglers, or to casual visitors. In 1972
the Scottish Tourist Board listed nearly 200 hotels, as well as 220 rivers and over
800 lochs, where fishing could be had, either free, or at charges ranging from 20
pence a day to over £100 per week on exclusive rivers (Scottish Tourist Board,
1972). Fishing everywhere is increasing in popularity and, as it does so, the
distinction between exclusive fishing for the few and coarse fishing for the many
is tending to break down (Baring and Goodhead, 1964).

The second major use of inland waters is for boating and related activities,
which range from commercial pleasure craft on the larger rivers and lakes,
through sailing on lakes and reservoirs, rowing and canoeing (the latter, in part,
on the swifter flowing streams around the uplands), to speed-boat-racing and
water-skiing. It is estimated that two million people participated in recreational
boating on coastal or inland waters more than once or twice during 1971 and that
there were some 470 000 pleasure craft in the United Kingdom (Sports Council,
1972). Interest in many of these activities has been growing rapidly; thus the
number of boats in the British Waterways Board's system has increased from
12 724 in 1967 to 18 050 in 1971 (Select Committee, 1973).

There are 950 yacht clubs in Great Britain at present, 60 per cent of which are
based on inland waters (Royal Yachting Association, 1972). The larger stretches
of inland water are increasingly in demand, but the law controlling their use for
recreation is far from clear and there are varying restrictions on different classes of
use on different categories of inland water (see chapter 7). Natural lakes, reservoirs,
rivers, canals, disused wet gravel pits and ornamental lakes all provide facilities, but
most natural lakes are too remote to be intensively used and recreation in lakes is
concentrated in the more accessible Scottish lochs, the Lake District and the
Broads. Reservoirs and wet gravel pits are particularly important in England and
Wales because of the growing demand for recreational water from the large urban
population (Tanner, 1973, p. 21). In 1971 sailing was allowed on more than 50
reservoirs compared with only six direct-supply reservoirs and four compensation
reservoirs in 1962. Canoeing is allowed on three compensation and two direct-
supply reservoirs (Institution of Water Engineers, 1972). The Thames is the focus
of most inland rowing and nearly half the regattas held on inland waters take place
there; the Severn and Trent are also important.

The use of coastal waters, Britain's Blue Belt, is closely connected with the
holiday industry; some 75 per cent of those British residents who take their annual

holidays in Great Britain do so at the coast, at least in part (British Travel Association, 1969). It is not surprising that the coast is also the focus of much weekend
recreation, for no part of Great Britain is more than 75 miles (120 km) from the
sea or an estuary. There are some 2750 miles (4400 km) of coastline in England
and Wales and a further 5300 miles (8500 km) in Scotland (including the islands),
giving an average allotment of less than a foot per head of population. Much
coastal recreation is passive or is unconnected with either the sea or the surrounding countryside, but 40 per cent of all yacht clubs are based on coastal waters, and
a considerable part of the rowing, cruising and fishing also takes place there. Most
swimming, other than in artificial pools and swimming baths, and activities such
as aqua-planing also take place at the coast. Sub-aqua has become an increasingly popular coastal activity, with an 80 per cent increase in the number of clubs
since 1956 (British Sub-Aqua Club, 1972). As with other kinds of recreation,
coastal recreation is very unevenly distributed; much is concentrated at more than
150 holiday resorts, most of which are in the southern part of the country,
especially where there are sandy beaches, as at Weston-Super-Mare, or sheltered
natural harbours, as at Looe.

## Strengths and Weaknesses of Data-Dredging

This summary of evidence on active recreation in Great Britain demonstrates both
the strengths and weaknesses of data-dredging at a national level. Although the
majority of recreational pursuits, particularly those of an active kind, have
nationally constituted organisations, there is wide variation in their ability to
provide data on the nature and volume of participants and on the facilities they
use and, hence, on the reliability of information obtained in this way. Thus, while
the majority of dinghy sailors belong to a club or organisation, some national
sporting organisations represent only a small minority of the participants; for
example, the Ramblers Association contains only a small, though committed, part
of the vast number of people who enjoy walking in the countryside. Nevertheless,
despite these deficiencies, this technique will continue to be needed to describe
patterns and numbers in different sports, alongside other techniques which are
potentially more efficient but also more difficult to administer and costly to implement. Moreover, unless a very large number of home interviews is undertaken,
the information they provide, especially on active recreation, will be sketchy
compared with that which can be compiled by data-dredging. Several examples of
such surveys will now be considered.


## HOME INTERVIEW SURVEYS


### Pilot National Recreation Survey

The *Pilot National Recreation Survey,* which is discussed in the Appendix, was
the first attempt to acquire data on patterns of recreation in Great Britain and
illustrates the problems of gaining valid, reliable data on those recreational
activities pursued by minorities; it was undertaken jointly by the British Travel
Association and the University of Keele.

## TABLE 4.1
### ACTIVITIES EVER EXPERIENCED AND WHEN THEY WERE
### LAST EXPERIENCED (Adults 17+)

|  | Ever experienced | In 1965 | In 1960–4 | Before 1960 excluding school/college | At school/ college |
|---|---|---|---|---|---|
| | (percentage of all respondents) | | | | |
| Team games | 56 | 4 | 4 | 18 | 30 |
| Swimming, diving | 50 | 11 | 10 | 15 | 14 |
| Cycling for pleasure | 47 | 2 | 5 | 26 | 15 |
| Athletics | 36 | 1 | 2 | 9 | 25 |
| Tennis | 36 | 4 | 5 | 16 | 11 |
| Camping | 31 | 4 | 6 | 11 | 10 |
| Hiking (5 miles or more) | 30 | 5 | 5 | 15 | 5 |
| Skating — ice or roller | 23 | 1 | 4 | 11 | 7 |
| Fishing, angling — fresh or sea water | 21 | 5 | 6 | 8 | 3 |
| Bowls (outdoors) | 13 | 2 | 5 | 4 | 1 |
| Golf | 12 | 3 | 4 | 5 | 1 |
| Horse-riding, hunting, show-jumping | 11 | 1 | 2 | 6 | 2 |
| Hill and fell-walking, climbing | 10 | 1 | 2 | 5 | 1 |
| Natural history activities | 10 | 2 | 2 | 2 | 6 |
| Youth hostelling | 8 | 0 | 1 | 4 | 2 |
| Motor/motorcycle-racing, rallies, scrambles | 7 | 1 | 2 | 3 | 0 |
| Inland water sailing, boating, rowing, etc. | | | | | |
|    powered boats | 4 | 1 | 2 | 1 | 0 |
|    sail boats | 4 | 1 | 3 | 4 | 1 |
|    canoe and other boats | 9 | 1 | 3 | 4 | 1 |
| Sea-sailing, boating, rowing, etc. | | | | | |
|    powered boats | 5 | 1 | 2 | 2 | 0 |
|    sail boats | 6 | 1 | 2 | 2 | 0 |
|    canoe and other boats | 5 | 1 | 1 | 3 | 1 |
| Underwater swimming, skin-diving | 4 | 0 | 1 | 1 | 1 |
| Archery | 3 | 0 | 1 | 1 | 1 |
| Skiing, winter sports | 3 | 0 | 1 | 1 | 0 |
| Go-karting | 3 | 0 | 1 | 1 | 0 |
| Pony-trekking | 1 | 0 | 1 | 0 | 0 |
| Climbing | 1 | 0 | 1 | 0 | 0 |
| Water-skiing | 1 | 0 | 0 | 0 | 0 |

Source:   British Travel Association–University of Keele (1967), p. 9.

## TABLE 4.2

LIST OF THE SPORTS AND GAMES IN THE GOVERNMENT SOCIAL SURVEY

| | |
|---|---|
| Dancing (inc. recreational and competitive ballroom, folk and ballet) | Canoeing |
| | Boating |
| Soccer | Pleasure craft cruising |
| Rugger | Boxing |
| Cricket | Wrestling |
| Hockey | Judo or Karate |
| Basketball | 'Keep fit' classes |
| Netball | Gymnastics |
| Baseball | Athletics (track or field) |
| Lacrosse | Cross-country running |
| Tennis | Mountaineering |
| Squash | Rock-climbing |
| Badminton | Potholing |
| Table tennis | Organised rambles |
| Golf | Bird-watching |
| Croquet | Horse-riding |
| Bowling (on a green) | Pony-trekking |
| Bowling (ten-pin) | Hunting (all kinds) |
| Shooting (indoor) | Polo |
| Shooting (outdoor—all kinds) | Horse-racing |
| Archery | Greyhound-racing |
| Fencing | Motor-racing |
| Ice skating | Motorcycle-racing |
| Roller skating | Stock-car-racing |
| Fishing | Go-kart-racing |
| Swimming (in swimming pools) | Bicycle-racing |
| Swimming (in the sea or rivers) | Scrambles |
| Surfing | Rallies |
| Water-skiing | Hill-climbing events |
| Aqua-lung diving | Winter sports |
| Sailing | Amateur flying |
| Rowing | Gliding |

Source:   Sillitoe (1969), p. 255

    Each contact was asked whether he or she had ever participated in thirty active pursuits, ranging from the more popular team games such as cricket and hockey to minority pursuits such as go-karting and gliding. Despite this wide range, half the pursuits had participation rates of less than 10 per cent over the whole life span of those interviewed. When a more recent period was considered (within five years before the interview), participation was considerably less and in only two activities, swimming and diving, and fishing, had more than 10 per cent of respondents participated. Indeed, 19 of the activities considered had participation rates of less than 5 per cent over the previous five years; they include not only the acknowledged minority pursuits, but also popular activities such as youth hostelling, hill and fell-walking, all forms of sailing, skiing and pony-trekking. Accordingly, the detailed analysis of approximately two-thirds of the pursuits was based on a sub-sample of less than 150 and, for most pursuits, samples were considerably smaller. The organisers of this study have acknowledged the weakness of an analysis based on an inadequate sample, but the implications for future studies were clear; very large samples of at least 30 000 interviews would be necessary to permit analysis of participation in the majority of active pursuits.

The major contribution of the *Pilot National Recreation Survey* was to establish for the first time the levels of participation in outdoor recreational pursuits (table 4·1). It was ironic that this primary finding should, at the same time, create the need for such caution in the interpretation and analysis of participation in individual pursuits.

## The Government Social Survey

The Government Social Survey, undertaken on behalf of the Department of Education and Science and directed by K. K. Sillitoe, was made between September 1965 and March 1966; the report, *Planning for Leisure,* was published in 1969. The survey was intended to provide data on participation in outdoor and physical recreation, that is, all forms of organised sport and games of a physical or outdoor character; in all, 63 activities were covered (table 4.2).

The statistics on these sports and games played or watched regularly (that is, once a month for at least part of the preceding year), confirm the conclusion of the *Pilot National Recreation Survey* and other surveys on the minority character of participation in active recreation. In the national sample only two activities — swimming (in pools) and ballroom dancing — had participation levels greater than 10 per cent, and a further four activities — soccer, table tennis, ten-pin bowling and tennis — had levels of participation of between 5 and 10 per cent. Thus, over 90 per cent of the activities considered had levels of recent participation of less than 5 per cent.

Despite differences in the definitions of activities, it is possible to compare some of the statistics reported in the *Pilot National Recreation Survey* and *Planning for Leisure,* though it will be recalled that great care is necessary in such comparisons owing to the different bases of the two surveys. The recorded rates for recent participation (that is, in the year before interview) are given in table 4.3.

Two major conclusions emerge from an examination of these statistics. First, several of these activities depend primarily upon 'countryside' facilities — for example, fishing, horse-riding and sailing. Secondly, the levels of participation observed in the *Pilot National Recreation Survey,* which included town and countryside dwellers, are comparable to or greater than those established from the sample used in *Planning for Leisure,* which was confined to urban areas. Con-

## TABLE 4.3

### COMPARISON OF CURRENT PARTICIPATION LEVELS AS RECORDED BY THE 'PILOT NATIONAL RECREATION SURVEY' AND 'PLANNING FOR LEISURE'

|  | *Pilot National Recreation Survey* | *Planning for Leisure* |
|---|---|---|
|  | (percentage of participants) | |
| Swimming | 11 | 12·5 (in pools) |
| Athletics | 1 | 2 |
| Bowls | 2 | 3·5 |
| Fishing | 5 | 4·5 |
| Tennis | 4 | 5 |
| Golf | 3 | 3·5 |
| Horse-riding | 1 | 1 |
| Skating | 1 | 1 |
| Sailing | 3 | 1 |

Source:   British Travel Association–University of Keele (1967), p. 9; Sillitoe (1969), p. 235.

versely, activities which are usually located within urban areas, particularly athletics, bowls, swimming and tennis, had higher levels of participation in the urban-based sample used in *Planning for Leisure* than did those in the *Pilot National Recreation Survey*. Although the differences between the two surveys may in part be attributed to sampling errors, they provide a clear indication that the abundance of recreational facilities in urban areas permits participation in pursuits for which demand remains latent among those living in more rural areas.

### Opinion Research Centre

In September 1972, the Opinion Research Centre obtained data on twenty-one sports (some of them indoor) from a nationally representative sample of adults (see Appendix). In this survey, too, there is some confusion about the figures for participation in outdoor activities; for example, statistics on participation in greyhound and horse-racing clearly relate to spectators, but those for association football appear to relate to both participants and spectators. As a result, it is possible to compare the statistics for only six activities surveyed by the Opinion Research Centre and the *Pilot National Recreation Survey* and even these comparisons are complicated by differences of definitions in the two surveys.

The six activities for which national levels of participation can be directly compared are golf, athletics, outdoor bowling, cycling, sailing and tennis. No clear trends emerge and recent participation in all these pursuits never exceeds 6 per cent. The differences in the estimates from the two surveys might be attributable to sampling errors, arising from the small sub-samples used in both, rather than to real changes in levels of participation between 1965 and 1972, although changes undoubtedly will have occurred. There are further difficulties in regional levels of participation; for example, the Scottish sub-sample even for the most popular activity, golf, numbered only 14 people. These statistics must therefore be seen as providing only a general guide to participation and interest in these activities. If all activities are considered, irrespective of whether other comparable statistics exist, it is still noteworthy that of the 21 sports only 6 (darts 10 per cent, snooker 6 per cent, tennis 6 per cent, association football 5 per cent, golf 4 per cent and cricket 3 per cent) had levels of participation greater than 2 per cent, another striking reminder of the minority character of active recreation.

### TABLE 4.4

#### REGIONAL CONTRASTS IN PARTICIPATION IN ACTIVE RECREATION

| | National average | | North | | Midlands | | Metropolitan England | | South and West | | Wales | | Scotland | |
|---|---|---|---|---|---|---|---|---|---|---|---|---|---|---|
| Sample size | (3167) | | (929) | | (468) | | (564) | | (583) | | (299) | | (324) | |
| | *a* | *b* | *a* | *b* | *a* | *b* | *a* | *b* | *a* | *b* | *a* | *b* | *a* | *b* |
| Athletics | 36 | 1 | 32 | 1 | 34 | 1 | 42 | 2 | 42 | 1 | 28 | 1 | 32 | 0 |
| Bowls | 13 | 2 | 15 | 4 | 12 | 2 | 11 | 2 | 7 | 1 | 6 | 1 | 18 | 5 |
| Camping | 31 | 4 | 28 | 5 | 31 | 4 | 33 | 4 | 34 | 5 | 19 | 1 | 29 | 2 |
| Cycling | 47 | 2 | 43 | 1 | 49 | 1 | 52 | 4 | 50 | 4 | 37 | 3 | 49 | 1 |
| Fishing | 21 | 5 | 17 | 3 | 22 | 7 | 26 | 6 | 27 | 7 | 11 | 3 | 17 | 5 |
| Golf | 12 | 3 | 11 | 4 | 13 | 3 | 12 | 3 | 11 | 4 | 5 | 1 | 21 | 6 |
| Hiking | 30 | 5 | 35 | 5 | 25 | 4 | 33 | 6 | 30 | 4 | 18 | 4 | 22 | 3 |
| Hill-walking, climbing | 10 | 1 | 12 | 3 | 8 | 1 | 12 | 0 | 8 | 1 | 3 | 1 | 8 | 1 |
| Riding | 11 | 1 | 8 | 1 | 10 | 0 | 14 | 1 | 15 | 1 | 5 | 1 | 8 | 1 |
| Skating | 23 | 1 | 22 | 1 | 24 | 2 | 24 | 1 | 22 | 2 | 6 | 0 | 28 | 2 |
| Sea sailing | 16 | 3 | 7 | 1 | 12 | 0 | 21 | 5 | 29 | 5 | 9 | 1 | 11 | 1 |
| Inland sailing | 17 | 3 | 18 | 4 | 15 | 3 | 23 | 3 | 21 | 0 | 4 | 1 | 8 | 2 |
| Team games | 56 | 4 | 52 | 4 | 59 | 5 | 59 | 4 | 61 | 6 | 40 | 3 | 51 | 3 |
| Swimming | 50 | 11 | 47 | 10 | 49 | 11 | 56 | 12 | 56 | 18 | 29 | 7 | 47 | 7 |
| Tennis | 36 | 4 | 33 | 3 | 38 | 4 | 41 | 6 | 39 | 6 | 23 | 2 | 32 | 5 |
| Natural history, etc. | 10 | 2 | 9 | 2 | 10 | 2 | 12 | 2 | 14 | 3 | 6 | 1 | 7 | 0 |

(percentage of adult sample reporting)

*a*  at any time in the past
*b*  current participation (1965)

Source:   British Travel Association–University of Keele (1969), p. 6.

## Regional Studies

These low levels of participation present many problems of both interpretation and validity when attempts are being made to analyse the results of these surveys. Home-interview surveys at a national scale are expensive, tedious and time-consuming, especially if they are large enough to provide valid statistics for minority pursuits. To allow a reasonable breakdown of these statistics, samples of at least 50 000 would be desirable. It is unlikely that many surveys of this kind can be mounted and it is not surprising that this experience has led to a number of regional investigations, which attempt, within a more restricted area, to overcome the limitations of sample design which have confronted those carrying out national surveys (see Appendix). Some perspective on these regional studies is provided by Report No. 2 of the *Pilot National Recreation Survey*, though, as has been noted, the samples are small and the results should be treated as broad indicators only (table 4.4 and p. 49). There are obvious and expected features, such as the high rate of participation in golf in Scotland, but no firm conclusion can be drawn from this table (see Appendix).

## Outdoor Leisure Activities in the Northern Region

This survey, the first of the regional surveys proper was carried out in June and July 1967 and attempted to overcome the problem of establishing levels of participation in minority pursuits by having a much larger sample for the region. The questionnaire used in this survey sought to establish levels of 'normal' participation, defined as those participants who take part in a particular activity at least once every three months. These latter statistics provide the closest comparison with data from the *Pilot National Recreation Survey*, which defined recent participation as 'that within the year of interview', namely 1965. In all, twenty-four active pursuits were considered, the majority of them spectator sports requiring a formal structure (table 4.5). Only three informal pursuits were included.

TABLE 4.5

OUTDOOR LEISURE ACTIVITIES IN NORTHERN ENGLAND

| | |
|---|---|
| Swimming | Athletics |
| Sailing | Horse racing |
| Pleasure boating | Horse-riding/hunting |
| Rowing/canoeing | Pony-trekking |
| Fishing | Rambling |
| Water-skiing | Nature/field study |
| Sub-aquatics | Climbing/caving |
| Cricket | Camping/caravanning |
| Golf | Gliding/flying |
| Bowls | Cycling |
| Tennis | Motorcycle/car rally |
| Archery | Motorcycle/car-racing |

Source:    North Regional Planning Committee (1969), p. 154.

This survey, too, revealed the minority nature of informal active pursuits and the difficulty of analysing them. Participation in all active pursuits was less than 7 per cent on both an average summer Saturday and an average Sunday. The remaining 93 per cent of the population were not involved, either as players or spectators, in any of the pursuits considered. Moreover, such pursuits accounted for only 9 per cent of all away-from-home activities reported on an average Saturday and only 12 per cent on an average Sunday. The second important conclusion drawn by the authors of this report was that, while the most popular activities were important in the context of urban planning, they were of relatively minor consequence for the planning of outdoor recreation in the countryside. On both Saturday and Sunday, at least twice as many people visited pubs or clubs as took part in all outdoor sports or games. On Saturdays, ten times as many people visited friends as went swimming ( the most popular individual sport); on Sundays the ratio was 8 to 1.

For this regional study of particular activities it was necessary to analyse participation over a period of three months prior to interview in order to provide subsamples large enough to warrant correlation with social, economic and demographic variables. Participation levels over this period are shown in table 4.6 and were used to examine the correlation between participation and the characteristics of the participants, and also to provide a basis for forecasting future levels of participation.

## TABLE 4.6

### PARTICIPATION IN ACTIVITIES IN NORTHERN ENGLAND

| Activities | Current participation (percentage of respondents) |
|---|---|
| Small pitches | 13 |
| Tennis | 6 |
| Bowls | 2 |
| Large pitches | 13 |
| Cricket | 5 |
| Athletics | 33 |
| Large courses | 7 |
| Horse-racing | 3 |
| Golf | 2 |
| Motor sports | 2 |
| County sites | 7 |
| Camping/caravanning | 5 |
| Open country | 11 |
| Cycling | 7 |
| Fishing | 5 |

Source:  North Regional Planning Committee (1969), p. 27.

*Leisure in the North-west*

Information in this survey, undertaken in the summer of 1969, was collected for a standard list of sixty-one sports and active pastimes, which proved to be fairly comprehensive since only 4 per cent of the sample claimed to take part in other pursuits. The survey established that a substantial minority (37 per cent) of all respondents aged twelve and over in north-west England had played one or more sports at least once in the twelve months before the interview. Of the 8 per cent of the sample population over twelve who were still at school or college, 97 per cent claimed to have played a sport in the last twelve months, but much of this participation took place involuntarily on school premises and cannot be treated at face value as a sector of demand. In contrast, of the 92 per cent not at school or college, only 31 per cent had played a sport during this period. Only twenty-two of the sixty-one active pursuits had been undertaken by more than 2 per cent of the sample (table 4.7).

One interesting point to which the designers of the survey drew attention was the effect of the choice of minimum age on levels of participation. The lower age limit of twelve years was the same as in other studies, but while younger children could not be expected to complete a questionnaire of this kind successfully, it is important to ensure that such a decision does not result in considerable under-estimates of participation levels in many sports. This problem is well illustrated by swimming, where the proportion of those under twelve participating in the sport is so large that a survey limited to those aged twelve and over would produce misleading results. This view was confirmed by a turnstile survey that was carried out by the Institute of Baths Management in the Northern Region and demonstrated that approximately 50 per cent of swimmers in north-west England were

## TABLE 4.7

### POPULARITY OF SPORTS IN NORTH-WEST ENGLAND

| Sports (in order of popularity) | Percentage of sample playing | Frequency rates and rank order | |
|---|---|---|---|
| Swimming | 15 | 83 | 1 |
| Soccer | 6 | 48 | 2 |
| Tennis | 6 | 41 | 4 |
| Table tennis | 5 | 34 | 5 |
| Bowls | 5 | 44 | 3 |
| Fishing | 5 | 25 | 9 |
| Ten-pin bowling | 4 | 10 | 16 |
| Putting | 4 | 11 | 15 |
| Cricket | 3 | 25 | 9 |
| Athletics | 3 | 26 | 8 |
| Gymnastics | 3 | 24 | 12 |
| Netball | 3 | 27 | 7 |
| Golf | 3 | 30 | 6 |
| Badminton | 3 | 21 | 13 |
| Rambling | 3 | 10 | 16 |
| Camping | 3 | 4 | 21 |
| Rounders | 3 | 25 | 9 |
| Fell-walking | 3 | 4 | 21 |
| Hockey | 2 | 17 | 14 |
| Five-a-side football | 2 | 10 | 16 |
| Basketball | 2 | 10 | 16 |
| Keep fit | 2 | 10 | 16 |

Source:   North West Sports Council (1972), p. 91.

under twelve years old. Although swimming is probably an extreme example, it seems likely that the survey might have under-estimated the demand for other sports which have a large proportion of young participants.

As the authors of the report make clear, it is not easy to assess the relative popularity of sports, for the frequency of participation must also be taken into account. The report quoted the example of golf, which ranked only thirteen in terms of the number of people who had played during the last twelve months, but was sixth in order of frequency of participation. The organisers of the North-west study found it appropriate to group together the twenty-two most popular recreation activities in order to warrant more detailed analysis; as in the study of the Northern Region, the grouping of activities reflected their nature and the type of resources they used. On the basis of this grouping, the report was able to indicate the demand generated by the twenty-two sports (table 4.8). One of the interesting facts to emerge from this grouping is that the greatest demand was for indoor urban facilities and, to a lesser degree, for urban outdoor 'compact sites', for which provision is made in most urban centres. Indeed, over 85 per cent of the demand for active recreational pursuits in north-west England was contained within urban areas, and formal outdoor recreational activities in the countryside made a contribution that the authors of the report correctly describe as 'quite trivial'. Although this analysis of demand is based on the most popular activities, the general picture would have changed little if other minority pursuits had been included, though those in the countryside may well have a disproportionately large impact. This near self-sufficiency of urban centres in catering for the existing demand for active recreation emphasises the inadvisability of making separate plans for the development of recreational facilities in town and countryside.

TABLE 4.8

FREQUENCY OF PARTICIPATION IN PURSUITS IN NORTH-WEST ENGLAND

| Groups of pursuits | Based on 'best estimates' person–games/week/1000 population |
|---|---|
| Urban indoor (swimming, table tennis, ten-pin bowling, gymnastics, badminton, five-a-side, basketball, keep fit) | 202 |
| Urban outdoor, small-space demands (tennis, bowls, putting, netball, rounders) | 148 |
| Urban outdoor, large-space demands (soccer, cricket, athletics, hockey) | 116 |
| Urban fringe (fishing, golf) | 55 |
| Countryside (rambling, camping, fell-walking) | 18 |
| Total | 539 |

Source:   North West Sports Council (1972), p.92.

## TABLE 4.9

### CONTRASTS IN RECREATIONAL PARTICIPATION IN NORTHERN ENGLAND

| Activities | North (at any time) (17+ yrs) | Northern Region (12+ yrs) | North (last 12 months) (17+ yrs) | Northern Region (last 3 months) (12+ yrs) | North-west (last 12 months) (12+ yrs) |
|---|---|---|---|---|---|
| | | (percentage of sample participating) | | | |
| Athletics | 32 | 11 | 1 | 3 | 3 |
| Bowls | 15 | 6 | 4 | 3 | 5 |
| Camping | 28 | 18 | 5 | 10 | 3 |
| Cycling | 43 | 30 | 1 | 6 | 1 |
| Fishing | 17 | 13 | 3 | 6 | 5 |
| Golf | 11 | 4 | 4 | 2 | 5 |
| Hiking | 35 | 11 | 5 | 4 | 3 |
| Hill-walking/climbing | 12 | 3 | 3 | 1 | 1 |
| Riding | 8 | 5 | 1 | 1 | 1 |
| Inland sailing | 18 | | 4 | | |
| Swimming | 47 | 40 | 10 | 20 | 15 |
| Tennis | 33 | 21 | 3 | 7 | 6 |
| Natural history | 9 | 3 | 2 | 1 | – |

Northern Region – Cumberland, Westmorland, Durham, Northumberland, Yorkshire (North Riding)

North-west – Lancashire, Cheshire, Derbyshire (part)

North – Northern Region, North-west and East and West Ridings

Source: British Travel Association–University of Keele (1969), p.6; Northern Regional Planning Committee (1969), p.27; North West Sports Council (1972), p.93.

*Recreation in Northern England*

The fact that the two regional studies just discussed were both undertaken in
Northern England and that the *Pilot National Recreation Survey's* definition of
the North embraced the two standard regions of the North-west and North provides an opportunity to compare participation rates in active recreational activities
in this part of Great Britain. Table 4.9 records the range of comparative statistics
that can be assembled and clearly shows that this statistical information is confined
to the more popular activities; sampling errors for those with participation rates
of less than 2 per cent are so large that such comparisons would be virtually
meaningless.

Closer investigation of table 4.9 reveals that the comparison is less one of
statistics of participation than of the nature and structure of the surveys, the
definitions they adopted and the way in which they were implemented. Only the
*Pilot National Recreation Survey* and the survey in the Northern Region established
participation rates over the full life-span of those interviewed. In the North-west
study attention was confined to the twelve months prior to interview. Comparison
of the estimates of participation at any time from the *Pilot National Recreation
Survey* and the Northern Region survey highlights the remarkable contrasts between the two sets of statistics; the *Pilot National Recreation Survey's* estimates
are considerably higher than those provided from the survey of the Northern
Region. Although a few of these differences could be explained by differences in
definition, the contrasts are marked for every pursuit and some estimates from the
*Pilot National Recreation Survey* are as much as 300 per cent higher than those
from the Northern Region study. At first glance such striking differences are very
puzzling, but further investigation reveals a possible explanation. The survey of
the Northern Region established whether the respondent participated in any of
the activities named in a checklist. When these current levels of participation had
been established, the respondent was then asked to re-examine the list and to
answer the question (Q.18): 'Are there any activities on this list that you used to
do but have now given up?' This provided an estimate of levels of current participation and of participation over the whole life-span. The procedure followed in
the *Pilot National Recreation Survey* was exactly the reverse; the respondent was
presented with a list of activities and the first question related to long-term participation (Q.39): 'Which, if any, of these activities have you ever taken part in –
I mean done it yourself, even if only once, not just watched them? It doesn't
matter how long ago it was.' Having established involvement over the respondent's
life-span, the interviewer then sought to determine participation over more recent
periods. There can be little doubt that the order of the questions in the two
surveys and more particularly, the format of the questions themselves, contributed
to the marked differences in the estimates of participation shown in table 4.9. The
*Pilot National Recreation Survey*, both by establishing participation over the life-
span as a first priority and by the emphatic nature of the question itself, tended to
elicit a more accurate record of the respondents' participation, whereas in the
Northern Region survey initial attention was concentrated on more recent participation, and this was followed by a less emphatic question, leading to marked
underestimates of respondents' participation levels over their lifetime.

Contrasts in the statistical information provided by surveys that seem to share a common structure and similar methodology, are a valuable reminder of the care that must be taken both in the design of surveys and, equally, in assessing the validity and accuracy of information gained. It may be argued that inaccuracies in estimates of past participation are of limited relevance because the second part of table 4.9 reveals that there is a greater consistency between the three surveys when more recent participation in active pursuits is considered. Unfortunately, such arguments avoid the major issue; these surveys usually serve a utilitarian purpose in the planning and development of facilities for recreational activities and it must be acknowledged that differences in their structure, the format of the questionnaire, the wording of questions and the definitions adopted will all influence the nature of the results obtained. Research into recreation would benefit greatly from a standard survey, for greater weight could be placed on comparative statistics as true indicators of distinctive, regional differences in participation, which may now be attributable to the particular survey techniques used.

## TABLE 4.10

### RECREATIONAL ACTIVITIES OVER THE WHOLE LIFE-SPAN IN CENTRAL SCOTLAND

| Activity | Greater Edinburgh + Lanarkshire | Pilot National Recreation Survey | |
|---|---|---|---|
| | | Great Britain | Scotland |
| | (percentage of those interviewed) | | |
| Team games | 48 | 56 | 51 |
| Swimming | 41 | 50 | 47 |
| Cycling | 39 | 47 | 49 |
| Camping | 32 | 31 | 29 |
| Hiking or walking | 28 | 30 | 22 |
| Golf | 21 | 12 | 21 |
| Angling | 15 | 21 | 17 |
| Pleasure boating | 13 | — | — |
| Sea fishing | 11 | — | — |
| Youth hostelling | 10 | 8 | — |
| Cricket | 8 | — | — |
| Horse-riding, etc. | 8 | 11 | 8 |
| Nature studies | 8 | 10 | 7 |
| Sailing | 7 | — | — |
| Field sports | 5 | — | — |
| Skiing | 5 | 3 | — |
| Rock-climbing | 5 | — | — |
| Canoeing | 3 | — | — |
| Motor-racing | 3 | — | — |
| Rallying | 3 | — | — |
| Power-boating | 2 | 5 | — |
| Orienteering | 2 | — | — |
| Flying, gliding | 2 | 1 | — |
| Scrambling | 1 | — | — |

Source:   Duffield and Owen (1970), p.39; Duffield and Owen (1971), p.39; British Travel Association–University of Keele (1969), p. 26.

*Outdoor Recreation in Central Scotland*

In the two surveys in central Scotland, undertaken in 1969 by the Tourism and
Recreation Research Unit, attempts were also made to obtain information on
active recreation and, as far as possible, a comparable approach to that used in
the *Pilot National Recreation Survey* was adopted, so that valid comparisons
might be made with that survey and other regional investigations which might
pursue the same objective.

The first question in the household interview survey was designed to provide
basic information on the recreational habits of the residents of the study areas,
which would be amplified and supplemented by later questions. The respondent
was asked to indicate whether he or she had ever taken part in any of twenty-four
outdoor recreational activities. The answers gave a picture of the recreational
experience of the sample population and provided a basis for comparison with
levels of subsequent participation and with levels of participation in Great Britain
as a whole (for the question was very similar to one used in the *Pilot National
Recreation Survey*); see table 4.10.

Over 24 per cent of those interviewed claimed that they had never participated
in any of the activities mentioned; this figure is probably an over-estimate, reflecting difficulties of recollection, especially among the elderly. Nevertheless, the
figure indicates the irrelevance of outdoor recreation to a large section of the
population, a conclusion confirmed later when data on recent levels of participation were examined (table 4.11).

As far as participation over the whole life-span is concerned, it is the similarities
rather than the differences between the results of the *Pilot National Recreation
Survey* and those for central Scotland which are the most striking feature of table
4.10. Both the relative popularity of activities and the levels of participation are
similar; the major exception is golf where the Scottish figure (20·5 per cent) is
very much higher than that for Great Britain (12 per cent), reflecting both the
popularity of this sport in Scotland and the abundant facilities, particularly in
the Edinburgh area. The disparity between the popular and the minority activities
is also clear. Although most of the sample had acquired recreational skills at some
time, these were largely confined to a small number of popular activities. Thus,
the largest number (48 per cent) had participated in team games, which play a
large part in physical education at school, followed by swimming, cycling, camping,
hiking and walking, all activities that can be undertaken at a wide range of ages
and need not make heavy demands on equipment, skills or physical resources. The
twelve activities that claimed less than 10 per cent of the total response can be
classed as minority activities. On the basis of the available evidence, it would be
fair to conclude that, with the exceptions already noted, the residents of central
Scotland are fairly typical in their recreational experience of residents of Great
Britain as a whole.

When more recent participation levels are considered, the first impression is
again of the general similarity of results for Great Britain and the study areas,
with the sole exception of golf (see table 4.11). There is, however, a significant
contrast between levels of participation during the year prior to interview. In
nearly every instance where direct comparisons were possible, the levels of participation in central Scotland were higher than the average for Great Britain. Two

## TABLE 4.11

### POPULARITY OF ACTIVITIES OVER WHOLE LIFE-SPAN (*BY PERIODS*)

| Activity | Last Year E+L | G.B. | 1–5 years E+L | G.B. | 5 years+ E+L | G.B. | At school E+L | G.B. |
|---|---|---|---|---|---|---|---|---|
| | | | (percentage of those interviewed) | | | | | |
| Swimming | 17·6 | 11 | 8·1 | 10 | 12·6 | 15 | 2·0 | 14 |
| Golf | 8·4 | 3 | 4·3 | 4 | 7·3 | 5 | 0·5 | 1 |
| Hiking, walking | 7·8 | 5 | 5·9 | 5 | 12·0 | 15 | 1·9 | 5 |
| Team games | 7·5 | 4 | 6·1 | 4 | 21·6 | 18 | 12·0 | 30 |
| Camping | 5·8 | 4 | 7·5 | 6 | 15·2 | 11 | 2·5 | 10 |
| Angling | 5·3 | 5 | 3·8 | 6 | 5·2 | 8 | 0·4 | 3 |
| Sea fishing | 3·4 | – | 2·6 | – | 4·3 | – | 0·3 | – |
| Nature studies | 2·9 | 2 | 1·3 | 2 | 2·6 | 2 | 1·0 | 6 |
| Pleasure boating | 2·9 | – | 3·9 | – | 5·5 | – | 0·4 | – |
| Cycling | 2·4 | 2 | 6·8 | 5 | 25·2 | 26 | 4·4 | 15 |
| Sailing | 1·6 | – | 1·7 | – | 3.23 | – | 0·3 | – |
| Horse-riding, etc. | 1·2 | 1 | 1·8 | 2 | 3·8 | 6 | 0·4 | 2 |
| Field sports | 1·4 | – | 1·1 | – | 2·0 | – | 0·2 | 0 |
| Skiing | 0·9 | 0 | 1·9 | 1 | 1·4 | 1 | 0·2 | 0 |
| Youth hostelling | 0·8 | 0 | 2·0 | 1 | 6·1 | 4 | 0·8 | 2 |
| Motor-racing | 0·7 | – | 0·8 | – | 1·2 | – | 0·1 | – |
| Rock-climbing | 0·7 | – | 1·1 | – | 2·3 | – | 0·2 | – |
| Cricket | 0·7 | – | 1·3 | – | 4·3 | – | 1·7 | – |
| Canoeing | 0·6 | 1 | 0·8 | 2 | 1·0 | 4 | 0·2 | 1 |
| Flying, gliding | 0·3 | 0 | 0·2 | 1 | 0·8 | 0 | 0·1 | 0 |
| Rallying | 0·6 | – | – | – | 1·1 | – | 0·2 | – |
| Orienteering | 0·4 | – | 0·6 | – | 0·6 | – | 0·2 | – |
| Power-boating | 0·4 | 1 | 0·7 | 2 | 0·8 | 2 | 0·2 | 0 |
| Scrambling | 0·1 | – | 1·5 | – | 0·4 | – | 0·1 | – |

E    Greater Edinburgh
L    Lanarkshire

Source:    Duffield and Owen (1970), p.41; Duffield and Owen (1971), p.41; British Travel Association–University of Keele (1967), p. 9.

factors must be noted before great significance is attached to these results. First, respondents in the *Pilot National Recreation Survey* were asked if they had taken part in activities during the summer of 1965 and figures are therefore lower than for the Scottish surveys which referred to participation over the twelve months before the interview. Secondly, levels of participation in outdoor activities had probably risen during the four years between the *Pilot National Recreation Survey* and the Scottish studies. Nevertheless, despite these considerations, it appears that recent rates of participation for central Scotland are as high as, if not higher than, those for Great Britain as a whole.

Further examination of these figures reinforces the conclusion that active recreational pursuits play a minor role in the population's use of leisure. Even in swimming, which is twice as popular as any other activity, less than 20 per cent of those interviewed had participated in the previous year. Indeed, participation levels were greater than 5 per cent in only six instances, while for eleven others the proportion was less than 1 per cent. These studies in central Scotland thus confirm the findings of the *Pilot National Recreation Survey* and the other regional studies, that a large majority of the population is not interested in active recreational pursuits.

## DATA-DREDGING AT A REGIONAL SCALE

The role of data-dredging as a means of providing information on recreational activities at a national scale has been discussed earlier in this chapter. A very similar approach was used in the surveys of central Scotland to provide detailed information on the local distribution of active recreation. All the regional studies have highlighted the inability of surveys based on direct interviews to provide information on minority activities, for all showed that recent participation in many active pursuits was very low. Of the twenty-four activities considered in the studies in central Scotland, nearly 50 per cent had a participation level in the last 12 months of less than 1 per cent of the sample population. It is tempting to ignore the lack of data relating to minority activities on the grounds that it would be reasonable to expect pursuits that attract more general interest to be given priority in planning and development, but such activities often make a disproportionate use of resources in the countryside. For this reason data-dredging was also undertaken at a regional scale.

At some stage in their history, most forms of active recreation develop some kind of organisation, usually based on a club or association. The nature of the organisation depends partly on the activity; in some, such as rowing and cross-country running, there is a complex organisation, while in others, such as hill-walking and most field sports, clubs are much less important. These organisations provide repositories of information, varying in reliability and depth, on a wide range of recreational activities, and, with the co-operation of the relevant clubs and associations, an investigation could provide valuable evidence on the scale and character of participation and on the location and nature of the resources used.

Such an investigation was undertaken in central Scotland in two stages; first, the parent associations for each activity were asked to provide basic information, including the names and addresses of secretaries of affiliated clubs and associations and, secondly, questionnaires and personal letters explaining the aims of the survey were sent to all clubs based in the study areas, as well as to others whose members might use resources in the study areas. A questionnaire was used to obtain comparable replies from all clubs, but as might be expected, the replies, which span a range of twenty activities, varied greatly in both coverage and quality. The information obtained should thus be treated with caution, for it is neither fully representative of the clubs themselves, owing to different response rates, nor of the activities, since the proportion of participants who are members of clubs varies greatly. Nevertheless, despite these limitations, the results provide a useful supplement to the statistically imperfect data obtained by the home-interview surveys (table 4.12). This information was supplemented by data obtained from other sources, in the study areas, such as local authorities; planning officers were particularly helpful in this respect. Moreover, the local authorities themselves had

TABLE 4.12

ACTIVITIES ON WHICH DATA WERE COLLECTED IN CENTRAL SCOTLAND

| | |
|---|---|
| Auto sports | Mountaineering, rock-climbing |
| Canoeing | Orienteering |
| Caravanning, camping | Rambling |
| Cross-country running | Riding |
| Cycling | Rowing |
| Field archery | Sailing |
| Freshwater angling | Shooting |
| Gliding, flying | Skiing |
| Golf | Water-skiing |
| Motorcycling | Youth hostelling |

Source:     Duffield and Owen, (1970), p. 76.

statutory responsibilities, which often led to the collection of valuable information on recreational activities. For example, under the provisions of the Horse Riding Establishments Act 1964, all riding stables must be registered with local authorities, who know not only the names and addresses of such establishments, but also the number of horses and ponies registered there. All caravanning and camping sites must similarly be registered with the Public Health Authorities. Another indirect source is provided by the valuation rolls which exist for all Scottish local authorities. Not only formal recreational facilities such as bowling greens and golf courses, but also other less specific but no less important recreational resources, are also subject to rates; detailed information on the location and value of 'shootings' and 'fishings' can be obtained in this way.

Some kinds of active recreation, notably golf and freshwater fishing, cannot in any sense be termed 'minority activities', for their participation rates are among the highest of all the activities considered. Nevertheless, the organisation of these sports made an investigation based on clubs rather than on individual participants very worthwhile. Much valuable information was gathered about the distribution of angling, and valuable insight was obtained into the growth of interest in golf over the last two decades and the pressures that currently exist on resources. In both sports, such investigations depended on the particular role of the 'club' and the administrative structure supporting the activity concerned.

Figure 4.1 shows the kind of detailed information that can be obtained in this way though it does not provide a comprehensive picture of the distribution of recreational resources; for it reflects the weaknesses and deficiencies of the data. Nevertheless, it is possible to discern certain underlying features: the major point of interest is the difference between resource and demand-oriented activities. Some activities, such as fishing, hill-walking and sailing, are intimately linked with the natural resource on which they depend and their development is closely related to its location, a relationship that places a severe constraint on their development. Other activities, such as riding, auto sports and golf, are much less dependent on resources. Although they require access to rural land, their demands are less specific and can be satisfied in many more locations; such activities therefore tend to be located around the towns where most participants live, and this

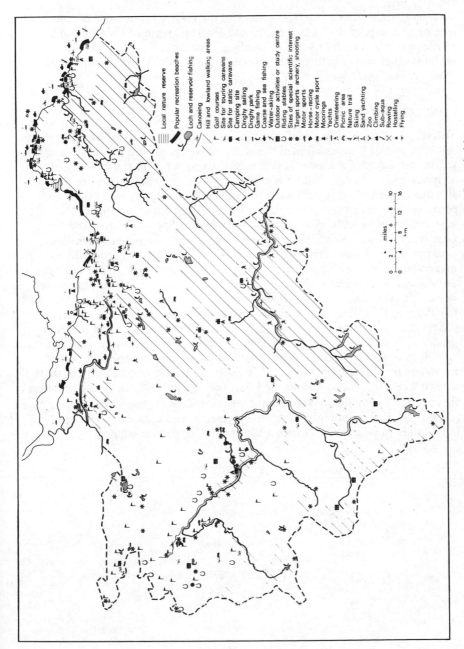

Figure 4.1 Recreational resources: Greater Edinburgh and Lanarkshire

responsiveness to urban-generated demand will also facilitate their provision in Country Parks.

The uneven response rate from clubs and the varying importance of club membership implies that data-dredging at a local and regional scale cannot alone provide a comprehensive picture of outdoor recreation. Nevertheless, it does offer useful insights into the distribution of recreational activities and complements other types of investigation.

## CONCLUSION

This review of the sources of information on active recreation in Great Britain or any large part of it has confirmed the uneven coverage in time and space and the varying reliability of the data. In part this situation is due to the diversity of activities and to the fact that rates of participation are generally low; but it is also due to the lack of any adequate machinery for collecting such information, comparable to the Office of Population Censuses and Surveys or the census branches of the agricultural ministries. Although the Sports Councils and the Countryside Commissions have a general responsibility for recreation in the countryside, they lack both the machinery and the power to collect such information (although the Countryside Commission produces a valuable compendium of information). Similarly, the clubs and associations are of varying importance in the different kinds of active recreations and this is affected in the coverage and reliability of the information they do provide. The government's decision to collect statistics of leisure on a regular basis as part of the household survey is greatly to be welcomed, though the small number of questions cannot provide reliable information on active recreation. For the strategic planning of outdoor recreation the gaps are less important, since it can be shown that many of these activities can be grouped together and that they are linked both by the resources they require and by the socio-economic characteristics of their participants (chapter 5). These relationships between recreation and socio-economic attributes can in turn be used to forecast future levels of participation.

# 5 Recreation, Participants and Future Levels of Demand

Although the description of individual activities, their levels of participation and the characteristic profiles of demand associated with them are of considerable intrinsic interest and a very valuable guide to planners and managers in the development of recreational facilities, they do not provide a complete picture of recreation in the countryside. Academic researchers will wish to look beyond the individual activities and to examine the relationships between them and participants, while those responsible for the strategic planning of recreational facilities require an understanding of likely future trends and developments in this field. This chapter will examine these relationships and evaluate the contribution that different statistical techniques can make to their projection into the future.

The purpose of examining the relationships between activities and their participants is to establish whether there are links between particular kinds of activities and thus whether it is possible to substitute the development of one activity for that of another. The characteristics of the participants themselves will then be examined in greater detail to determine whether people from different social, economic and cultural backgrounds have greater or lesser propensities to participate in recreation in the countryside. Finally, the relationships between recreationists and their pursuits will be used to indicate the changing patterns of recreation in the countryside over the next decade through a variety of techniques, both subjective and statistical, though throughout these explorations into the future it will be necessary to bear in mind Wolfe's comment, that 'in reporting on outdoor recreation, past, present and future, imprecision is the only wisdom' (1969).

## RECREATION TYPES

While recreational activities in the countryside have been divided for convenience into two groups—active and passive—they could have been grouped in other ways. Geographers have tended to argue that, for many purposes, an appropriate subdivision of recreational activities is one based on the resources used by particular activities and, in the previous chapter, information from clubs and associations was used to demonstrate a contrast between those activities that depended on the nature of the resources used (resource-based) and others whose location was more closely related to the demand from urban centres (user demand-oriented) (see figure 4.1). To test the validity of this visual impression, data on active pursuits

## TABLE 5.1
### STATISTICAL CORRELATIONS BETWEEN OUTDOOR ACTIVITIES IN CENTRAL SCOTLAND

| | Team games | Swimming | Cricket | Golf | Cycling | Hiking | Camping | Climbing | Hostelling | Field sports | Orienteering | Riding | Nature studies | Skiing | Pleasure-boating | Sailing | Power-boating | Canoeing | Angling | Sea-fishing | Motor-racing | Scrambling | Rallying | Flying |
|---|---|---|---|---|---|---|---|---|---|---|---|---|---|---|---|---|---|---|---|---|---|---|---|---|
| Team games | | | | | | | | | | | | | | | | | | | | | | | | |
| Swimming | + | | | | | | | | | | | | | | | | | | | | | | | |
| Cricket | + | | | | | | | | | | | | | | | | | | | | | | | |
| Golf | | + | + | | | | | | | | | | | | | | | | | | | | | |
| Cycling | | + | + | + | | | | | | | | | | | | | | | | | | | | |
| Hiking | | + | + | | + | | | | | | | | | | | | | | | | | | | |
| Camping | | + | + | + | + | + | | | | | | | | | | | | | | | | | | |
| Climbing | | | | | | + | + | | | | | | | | | | | | | | | | | |
| Hostelling | | | | | + | + | + | + | | | | | | | | | | | | | | | | |
| Field sports | | | | | | | | | | | | | | | | | | | | | | | | |
| Orienteering | | | | | | | | + | | | | | | | | | | | | | | | | |
| Riding | | | | | | | | | | | | | | | | | | | | | | | | |
| Nature studies | | | | | + | | | | | | | | | | | | | | | | | | | |
| Skiing | | | | | | | | | | | | | | | | | | | | | | | | |
| Pleasure-boating | + | + | + | + | + | + | | | | | | | | | | | | | | | | | | |
| Sailing | + | | | | | | | + | | | | | | + | + | | | | | | | | | |
| Power-boating | | | | | | | | | | | | | | | | + | | | | | | | | |
| Canoeing | | | | | | | | + | | | | | | | + | + | + | | | | | | | |
| Angling | | | | | | | + | | | + | | | + | | | | | | | | | | | |
| Sea-fishing | | | | | + | + | | | | | | | | + | + | | | | + | | | | | |
| Motor-racing | | | | | | | | | | | | | | | | | | | | | | | | |
| Scrambling | | | | | | | | | | | | | | | | | | | | | | | | |
| Rallying | | | | | | | | | | | | | | | | | | | | | | + | | |
| Flying | | | | | | | | | | | | | | | | | | | | | | | | |

+ Positive correlation significant at the 0·1 level of confidence

Source:   Duffield and Owen (1970); Duffield and Owen (1971).

from the surveys undertaken in central Scotland were analysed statistically. Correlation coefficients for pairs of activities were calculated to indicate the degree to which participants in one activity also participated in the other (table 5.1), and so to establish whether participants in one activity have statistical links with those in other activities. The activities in table 5.1 were loosely grouped according to the resources they use and the correlation coefficients computed from these data confirm the validity of such groupings, showing strong relationships between activities within groups; thus demand-oriented activities, such as team games, swimming, cricket and golf, have strong relationships with each other while many of the land-based countryside activities, such as hiking, camping, climbing and youth hostelling, are closely related; as might be expected, the various water sports are also strongly related. Such relationships do not occur only within groups, for certain activities in one group are positively correlated with participation in activities in other groups; there appear, therefore, to be links between demand-oriented activities and resource-based activities, particularly cycling and hiking. It may be that such activities have an important bridging role to play between different groups of activities, leading participants in one to a knowledge of, and participation in, activities in different groups. Similar links exist between the activities in the resource-based groups, as is shown in the correlation between land- and water-dependent activities. However, such correlations are not necessarily resource-based; for example, there are positive relationships between those activities that are expensive to pursue, such as skiing and sailing, and between those that are arduous and require a high level of skill, such as canoeing, climbing, sailing and skiing.

Such economic and social determinants and their influence on recreational activity will be examined in more detail later, but it may be noted here that, although relationships between participants and the nature of activities do provide other bases on which classifications can be made, this analysis has again confirmed the fundamental dichotomy between user demand-oriented activities and resource-based activities. These correlations between activities are crucial to the development and planning of recreation in the countryside. The ability to 'substitute' the development of one activity for that of another, where a particular resource is scarce, can be of great help to those responsible for the planning of recreational facilities. If the determination of types of activity is linked to an examination of compatibility of resources between one activity and another, it also provides a more stable basis for forecasting recreational demand and for planning alternative yet compatible recreational developments. Burton (1971) has pursued the correlation of activities even further using multivariate analysis. He adopted the concept of recreation types hypothesised by Proctor (1962), who argued that people are more likely to take part in several activities within a given group of activities than to take part in those that fall into different groups. Proctor's analysis was based on an examination of fifteen outdoor recreation activities and used factor analysis to establish the recreation types. Burton carried out a more rigorous examination of this concept, for he tested the relationships between 71, 59 and 40 recreational activities using two multivariate techniques, cluster and factor analysis. The data on which the analysis was undertaken were generated by a home interview survey of 1056 persons over the age of twelve years within the city of Birmingham.

Cluster analysis, as its name suggests, is a statistical technique designed to group together particular variables on the basis of a known attribute of those variables. In this analysis the variables were recreational activities and the classifying attribute was whether a respondent had participated in the activity or not. The technique adopted by Burton calculates correlation coefficients between activities similar to those illustrated in figure 4.1. On the basis of these inter-correlations the technique proceeds systematically to discover the grouping of activities which produces highest possible average correlations between the activities within the groups and the lowest coefficients with activities outside the group (Burton, 1971, p. 186). The seventy-one activities that formed the basis of the initial analysis were reduced to forty as individual activities were demonstrated, for one reason or another, to be unsuitable for inclusion in the final analysis (Burton, 1971, p.189).

TABLE 5.2

ACTIVITY GROUPS IDENTIFIED BY CLUSTER ANALYSIS (40 ACTIVITIES)

*Group A*

Soccer
Cricket
Tennis
Golf
Table tennis
Fishing
Hobbies/do-it-yourself
Other activities

*Group B*

Rugby
Netball
Athletics
Basketball
Badminton
Keep fit
Cycling
Amateur dramatics/music

*Group C*

Outdoor bowls
Ten-pin bowling
Swimming

*Group D*

Ice-skating
Roller-skating
Horse-riding
Youth club

*Group E*

Rowing
Motor-boat cruising
Pleasure-boating

*Group F*

Hill-walking
Rambling
Camping/youth hostelling/caravanning
Walking

*Group G*

Picnicking
Driving in the countryside
Gardening
Dining out
Visit to a pub or club
Visit to a community or church centre
Bingo

*Group H*

Visit to a cinema
Visit to a theatre/concert
Dancing

Source:   Burton (1971), p. 200

Cluster analysis of forty activities led to the identification of eight groups that, on examination, appeared to be generally homogeneous in respect of their activities.

The interpretation of such analyses is not always straightforward, but cluster analysis does reveal features common to activities within groups; these are partly related to the type of resource and partly to the facilities that the activities demand, thus confirming statistically the relationships outlined earlier.

Apart from fishing, group A comprises popular activities in which at least two participants are required and includes active, competitive sports, undertaken at little cost to participants (except in golf). Group B brings together a group of active pursuits, though amateur dramatics and music are exceptions. Participation in these activities, too, is relatively cheap and they are mainly group activities, which are usually undertaken as members of a team or club; moreover, apart from cycling, all these activities are urban-based and, as with group A, are demand-oriented. Group C contains only three activities and these, too, are usually provided within an urban setting. Group D is a heterogenous group, except that the four activities are all dominated by young participants. Group E comprises water-based activities and confirms that participation in different activities is governed by the resources used as well as by the social and economic characteristics of participants. This view is also confirmed by Group F which is similarly resource-based, but comprises countryside activities which require access to rural areas. Group G brings together forms of recreation which are linked by their essentially social character; they include many of the passive recreational activities that characterise the lives of most British people, making few, if any, physical demands and having a broad-based appeal to all ages and social groups. Finally, Group H comprises three kinds of urban recreation, which are also social in character and are undertaken indoors.

Factor analysis is a more complex statistical method than cluster analysis. Unlike cluster analysis, which is based on the strength of individual correlation coefficients between pairs of activities, factor analysis takes into account the interrelationships between all activities. The method generates 'factors' with which the activities will show a degree of relationship, indicated by the 'factor score'. Each activity is related to each factor in turn and the size of the factor score indicates the factor with which the activity is best identified. In this way the nature of the factors can be assessed by their identification with particular activities, and activity groups can thereby be defined (Burton, 1971, p. 188). Burton undertook factor analysis on forty activities and identified five factors that accounted for 38·6 per cent of the variance observed in the activity variables. (Table 5.3)

Because of the smaller number of groupings defined by this factor analysis, groups are more general in composition than those generated by cluster analysis. Nevertheless, several features of interest emerged. Group I, based on the first factor, consists of types of active recreation that, with a few exceptions such as fishing and cycling, are demand-oriented and thus usually located in or around urban communities. The second factor comprises a broad-based group of types of passive recreation in which participation takes place both in towns and in the countryside; this group accounts for the greater part of the leisure time available outside the home to the British population. Factor 3 is a group of much more

## TABLE 5.3

### ACTIVITY GROUPS IDENTIFIED BY FACTOR ANALYSIS (40 ACTIVITIES)

| Factor 1 (Group I) | Factor score | Factor 3 (Group III) | Factor score |
|---|---|---|---|
| Soccer | 0·753 | Netball | 0·526 |
| Rugby | 0·649 | Ice-skating | 0·608 |
| Cricket | 0·654 | Roller-skating | 0·566 |
| Tennis | 0·488 | Horse-riding | 0·516 |
| Athletics | 0·751 | Youth club | 0·430 |
| Basketball | 0·726 | | |
| Badminton | 0·478 | Factor 4 (Group IV) | |
| Table tennis | 0·569 | | |
| Keep fit | 0·557 | Visit to pub or club | 0·338 |
| Swimming | 0·345 | Bingo | 0·280 |
| Fishing | 0·339 | Dancing | 0·205 |
| Cycling | 0·529 | | |
| Amateur dramatics/music | 0·250 | Factor 5 (Group V) | |
| Other activities | 0·192 | | |
| | | Golf | 0·449 |
| | | Outdoor bowls | 0·418 |
| Factor 2 (Group II) | | Ten-pin bowling | 0·602 |
| | | Rowing | 0·490 |
| Picnicking | 0·689 | Motor-boat cruising | 0·441 |
| Driving in the countryside | 0·667 | Pleasure-boating | 0·441 |
| Gardening | 0·3522 | Hill-walking | 0·278 |
| Dining out | 0·671 | Rambling | 0·283 |
| Visit to a community or | | Camping/youth hostelling/ | |
| church centre | 0·166 | caravanning | 0·280 |
| Visit to a cinema | 0·473 | Hobbies/do-it-yourself | 0·070 |
| Visit to a theatre/concert | 0·509 | | |
| Walking | 0·001 | | |

Source: Burton (1971), p. 206.

specialised active pursuits that seem to be dominated by young participants and, in this sense, is very similar to the Group D generated by cluster analysis; indeed, all four activities identified in Group D are found in this group, together with netball. The fourth factor comprises only three pursuits but these have very distinctive social characteristics, all being group activities and usually taking place during the evening. The last factor is a strongly identifiable group of activities based on resources in the countryside. This group corresponds with the activities based on land resources discussed earlier and, with the exception of ten-pin bowling, all make demands on both land and water resources and take place out of doors, usually in the countryside.

These results from cluster and factor analysis provide a very useful insight into the structure of recreational activities and confirm the complexity of their relationships. Although strong links can be discerned within particular groups, the relationships observed are based on a range of parameters, namely, the social characteristics of the participants, the economics of participation, the social framework within which the activity is set and the nature and scale of the facilities that the activities demand.

The cluster analysis and factor analysis undertaken by Burton are based on quite different mathematical and statistical procedures, although they exploit similar relationships between activities, and it is therefore of considerable interest that the groups of activities identified by the two techniques are similar in many ways. Much work on the analysis of types of activity remains to be done, but this preliminary investigation by Burton, while not statistically conclusive, nevertheless provides encouragement for further research in this field.

## THE INFLUENCE OF SOCIO-ECONOMIC CHARACTERISTICS ON RECREATIONAL ACTIVITIES

Although the preceding analysis has facilitated discussion of the grouping of particular activities, it revealed that neither the linkages between activities nor the structure of activity groups were necessarily related to the nature of the resource used, for they also reflected the characteristics of their participants. In some kinds of recreation the distinctive profile of participants is governed by the nature of the activity itself, notably in many active pursuits where the physical demands on participants tend to restrict involvement to younger age groups or where the need for expensive equipment implies a high income. The demands of other activities are less restrictive, but relationships with socio-economic characteristics nevertheless exist and the various activities appeal to different sections of the population. All pursuits, whether active or passive, thus have distinctive 'customer' profiles, defined by the social, economic and demographic characteristics of their participants. Moreover, an examination of these characteristics not only gives a perspective on the recreational habits of the British people, but also facilitates the making of forecasts about changing levels of participation during the next decade; for as society itself changes, participation in recreational activities can be expected to adapt itself to the nature of the emerging society. These conclusions are confirmed by Sillitoe's study (1969), where the influence of socio-economic characteristics was investigated in depth (table 5.4); yet the most telling point to emerge from this analysis is that, while socio-economic characteristics influence participation in physical recreation, there is less variation in participation between different social and demographic groups in the more passive forms of recreation. If participation in active pursuits is influenced by social forces, this does not seem to be true of the spectators who follow such pursuits; for while males dominate this group also, the influence of age, car ownership and socio-economic status is negligible. The ownership of a motor vehicle obviously has a marked influence on participation in trips to the countryside and seaside, the most important kinds of passive recreation, but, although socio-economic group 5 is under-represented, there are few significant differences in the other social characteristics shown in this table. Similarly, such characteristics appear to have little influence on urban-based passive recreation, although walks from home and visits to urban parks are not unexpectedly dominated by the elderly and those without access to a motor vehicle. These findings are confirmed by evidence from the Metropolitan Region (table 5.5), which reveals that, although participation in all recreational activities is higher among professional and managerial staff, the rate of decline with increasing age is most strongly evident in active sports, while forms of passive

## TABLE 5.4
### RECREATIONAL ACTIVITIES:
### INFLUENCE OF SOCIO-ECONOMIC CHARACTERISTICS

| Socio-economic characteristics | Physical Recreation As participant | As spectator | Trips to the countryside and seaside | Visits to urban parks and walks |
|---|---|---|---|---|
| | (percentage of leisure periods where each activity was cited as chief pursuit) | | | |
| *Sex* | | | | |
| Male | 11 | 3 | 7 | 5 |
| Female | 4 | 1 | 7 | 5 |
| *Age* | | | | |
| 15–18 | 15 | 2 | 8 | 4 |
| 19–22 | 16 | 1 | 8 | 3 |
| 23–30 | 9 | 3 | 8 | 6 |
| 31–45 | 5 | 2 | 9 | 4 |
| 45–60 | 3 | 2 | 9 | 4 |
| 61+ | 1 | 1 | 4 | 7 |
| *Car ownership* | | | | |
| With access to motor vehicle | 10 | 2 | 12 | 3 |
| Without access to motor vehicle | 5 | 2 | 3 | 6 |
| *Socio-economic group* | | | | |
| 1 Employers, managers of large establishments, professionals | 9 | 2 | 7 | 4 |
| 2 Employers, managers of small establishments, intermediate non-manual workers | 7 | 2 | 11 | 6 |
| 3 Supervisors and foremen (manual), skilled manual workers | 7 | 2 | 8 | 5 |
| 4 Junior non-manual workers | 10 | 2 | 8 | 4 |
| 5 Semi-skilled and unskilled manual workers | 5 | 2 | 5 | 6 |

Source:    Sillitoe (1969), pp. 42, 43, 46, 47, 50.

recreation show a much more gradual decline in rates of participation. It would be quite erroneous, therefore, to treat outdoor recreation as homogeneous, making similar demands and involving similar participants. Differences in the relative popularity of active and passive recreation, in their incidence in time and space and in the profiles of their participants indicate that a clear distinction may be drawn between them.

**Passive Recreation**

As chapter 3 has shown, passive recreation in the countryside is dominated by casual informal trips, usually undertaken in a motor vehicle, and several surveys pay particular attention to those undertaking such trips and have examined those

## TABLE 5.5

### AVERAGE NUMBERS OF LEISURE ACTIVITIES IN THE METROPOLITAN REGION

| | Professional and managerial | Clerical | Skilled | Semi-skilled and unskilled | All |
|---|---|---|---|---|---|
| | (average number of activities) | | | | |
| **Participated once or more in previous year** | | | | | |
| Home-based* | 7·3 | 7·3 | 6·6 | 5·6 | 6·7 |
| Active sports | 2·2 | 1·3 | 1·2 | 0·7 | 1·3 |
| Spectator sports | 1·3 | 1·1 | 1·2 | 0·8 | 1·1 |
| Other non-home activities | 7·5 | 6·7 | 5·7 | 5·0 | 6·2 |
| Total | 18·3 | 16·4 | 14·7 | 12·2 | 15·3 |
| **Participation twelve times or more in previous year** | | | | | |
| Home-based* | 5·7 | 5·9 | 5·2 | 4·2 | 5·3 |
| Active sports | 1·1 | 0·8 | 0·6 | 0·3 | 0·7 |
| Spectator sports | 0·4 | 0·3 | 0·5 | 0·3 | 0·4 |
| Other non-home activities | 3·5 | 3·3 | 2·8 | 2·5 | 3·0 |
| Total | 10·7 | 10·3 | 9·1 | 7·3 | 9·4 |

*Excluding watching T.V.

Source:   Young and Willmott (1973), p. 218.

social factors that appeared to underlie the demand for this particular form of passive recreation. The most comprehensive attempt to define the social profile of those taking such trips was that undertaken as part of the survey in north-west England, which defined the percentages of a range of social and economic sub-samples of those who took a trip out for recreation in the four weeks before the interview (table 5.6). Although, as has been noted, the effect of age on partici-pation in passive recreation is much less than in active recreation, there is never-theless a general tendency for trip-taking to decline with age. It is relatively low in the 20–24 age group probably because this group is dominated by young married couples with small children, who have been shown by all surveys to be a handicap to the use of leisure time for recreation in the countryside. This con-clusion receives some confirmation from the fact that households containing children less than five years old had participation levels significantly lower than those of households with older children (25 per cent taking full-day trips as against 31 per cent). In general, however, family size itself does not seem to be a deterrent, and there is evidence to suggest that passive recreation is very much a family pursuit, for levels of participation were highest for medium-sized house-holds (three–five persons), declining somewhat with larger families. Groups of only one or two persons, on the other hand, took somewhat fewer trips than the average for the sample as a whole. The broader appeal of passive recreation compared with

## TABLE 5.6

### PROFILE OF THOSE MAKING TRIPS IN NORTH-WEST ENGLAND

|  | Percentage of sub-sample taking day-trip in last 4 weeks | Percentage of sub-sample taking ½ day-trip in last 4 weeks |
| --- | --- | --- |
| *Age* | | |
| 12–14 | 39 | 33 |
| 15–19 | 35 | 24 |
| 20–4 | 30 | 30 |
| 25–9 | 33 | 24 |
| 30–44 | 31 | 24 |
| 45–59 | 26 | 20 |
| 60–4 | 27 | 21 |
| Over 64 | 22 | 12 |
| *Household size* | | |
| 1 | 26 | 10 |
| 2 | 24 | 18 |
| 3 | 30 | 23 |
| 4 | 32 | 25 |
| 5 | 34 | 28 |
| 6+ | 22 | 20 |
| *Marital status* | | |
| Married | 28 | 22 |
| Single | 33 | 25 |
| Other | 20 | 17 |
| *Educational status* | | |
| Elementary | 23 | 16 |
| Secondary | 31 | 24 |
| Further | 32 | 33 |
| *Socio-economic group* | | |
| A Professional | 34 | 30 |
| B Managerial | 35 | 28 |
| C Skilled manual | 29 | 23 |
| D Clerical | 30 | 22 |
| E Semi-skilled manual | 27 | 19 |
| F Unskilled manual | 19 | 17 |
| G Unclassified | 15 | 9 |
| *Car ownership* | | |
| Access to vehicle | 38 | 30 |
| No access to vehicle | 14 | 18 |
| Overall average | 28 | 18 |

Source:   North West Sports Council (1972), pp. 36–41.

active recreation is also confirmed by the lack of any difference in rates of trip-taking by males and females in the North-west; other studies have similarly demonstrated that there is little difference between the sexes in participation in either full-day or half-day trips. The statistics on marital status indicate that single people were more likely to take trips than those who were married, an apparent contradiction of conclusions already reached.

Further examination of the statistics, however, reveals that only in the 12–29 age range did single people make more outings than married people with children; indeed, above the age of thirty years, single people appeared to have much less inclination to go on excursions than married people.

The impact of educational status on trip-making probably reflects not only greater interest in what is seen on such trips, developed by attendance at institutions of secondary or further education, but also the relationship between this variable and occupation and income, which themselves influence participation in recreational trips to the countryside. Those with elementary education had participation levels well below average, while those with secondary and further education had above-average levels. Socio-economic groupings provided a more reliable indicator of the influence of social factors; it is clear that there is a general link between participation in trips into the countryside and socio-economic status, with levels of participation declining with position on the socio-economic scale. Those in professional and managerial groups had participation levels of 25 per cent higher than the average of the whole sample, while those in the unskilled manual groups had levels only two-thirds of the average. The importance of the motor car is also confirmed by table 5.6, which shows the marked influence that access to a motor vehicle had on rates of participation in trips; for those with access to a motor vehicle, the likelihood of making a trip into the countryside in the four weeks before the interview was nearly three times higher than for those without access to a motor vehicle. The table also demonstrates the broad appeal of passive recreation in the countryside in the community at large, for while there are variations between different social groups in rates of participation, they are slight, and all groups are represented in the 'market' for this kind of recreation.

## Active Recreation

As table 5.4 has shown, this broad appeal of passive recreation does not extend to active recreation; not only does participation in active pursuits generally tend to be restricted to particular and distinct groups in society, but there are also strong contrasts between the individual pursuits that arise from various constraints on participation. It is nevertheless possible to identify a distinctive profile of participants in active pursuits. The surveys in central Scotland (see table 5.7) demonstrated that those in canoeing, cricket, skiing, motor-racing, youth hostelling and horse-riding all had an average age of less than thirty, and this youthful profile is confirmed by other national and regional studies. The North-west study found that 44 per cent of participants in active pursuits were aged between twelve and twenty-five years old compared with the 21 per cent of the total population in this age group. The Northern Region study established that in two groups of activities, swimming and activities in the open country (horse-riding, hunting, pony-trekking, rambling, cycling and motor-rallying), the majority of participants are

## TABLE 5.7

INFLUENCE OF SOCIAL AND DEMOGRAPHIC CHARACTERISTICS ON
PARTICIPATION IN RECREATIONAL ACTIVITIES IN CENTRAL SCOTLAND: 1970–1

| Activity | Average age | Average net income weekly £ | Average age finished full-time education | Per cent married | Per cent Male |
|---|---|---|---|---|---|
| Swimming | 33 | 22 | 16 | 71 | 53 |
| Hiking | 39 | 21 | 16 | 66 | 56 |
| Golf | 38 | 26 | 16 | 79 | 78 |
| Team games | 29 | 19 | 16 | 30 | 81 |
| Camping | 35 | 22 | 15 | 71 | 56 |
| Angling | 39 | 25 | 15 | 76 | 82 |
| Sea-fishing | 36 | 23 | 15 | 77 | 82 |
| Nature studies | 45 | 25 | 16 | 75 | 62 |
| Cycling | 29 | 18 | 16 | 42 | 60 |
| Pleasure-boating | 38 | 24 | 16 | 77 | 63 |
| Horse-riding | 28 | 25 | 16 | 50 | 55 |
| Sailing | 34 | 26 | 17 | 76 | 59 |
| Skiing | 26 | 24 | 18 | 16 | 58 |
| Field sports | 33 | 25 | 16 | 64 | 85 |
| Youth hostelling | 28 | 27 | 18 | 29 | 76 |
| *Rallying | 40 | 31 | 16 | 73 | 64 |
| †Motor-racing | 27 | 22 | 16 | 47 | 60 |
| †Flying and gliding | 31 | 29 | 17 | 56 | 89 |
| Rock-climbing | 29 | 21 | 16 | 42 | 71 |
| Cricket | 27 | 27 | 17 | 56 | 100 |
| Canoeing | 26 | 27 | 18 | 47 | 78 |

* Lanark only
† Edinburgh only

Source: Duffield and Owen (1970), p. 47 Duffield and Owen (1971), p. 47

teenagers. In contrast, only one activity can claim to be dominated by the older age groups, namely nature studies. In the surveys in central Scotland, the average age of participants in pleasure-boating, angling, walking and golf all exceeded thirty-eight, reflecting the more leisurely and less strenuous nature of these activities.

Active pursuits are also dominated by males. In every activity considered in central Scotland there were more male than female participants and in some, such as cricket, field sports, youth hostelling, fishing and team games, participants were almost exclusively male, a reflection of both tradition and the physical demands of the activity. Similar findings were established by the *Pilot National Recreation Survey* and by the other regional studies. Over the full range of activities considered in the North-west study the ratio of men to women among active sports players was 61:39, although women outnumbered men 54:46 in the sample population. Activities where this imbalance is less marked are those such as swimming, pleasure-boating and camping, in which the whole family can participate.

Married people are less likely to take part in active pursuits than the unmarried. It is likely that this factor does not act in isolation, but partly reflects the dominance of young people in active pursuits. Despite this general rule, certain activities do tend to be associated with those who are married (sailing, golf, fishing and swimming), while others seem to be the prerogative of single people (skiing, youth hostelling, cycling and team games). These tendencies must be viewed with caution, for a high degree of association with marital status need not be reflected in participation in the activity itself. For example, the studies in central Scotland showed that, although 82 per cent of those playing golf in the year before the interview were married, 76 per cent played their last game before the interview either alone or in the company of friends, and only 20 per cent played with members of their family.

The influence of education on participation in active pursuits is not as direct as some other social factors, but attendance at school beyond the compulsory minimum age or at particular types of school and at university or college, provides a range of recreational opportunities which may be denied to those leaving school earlier. Statistics from the North-west study demonstrate that, while 40 per cent of the region's population had only an elementary education (that is, to age 13 or 14), this group accounted for 18 per cent of participants in active recreation. The studies in central Scotland showed that certain activities, such as youth hostelling, canoeing, cricket and skiing, were associated with a high average school-leaving age; but that others, such as camping, fishing and swimming, had little association with age of school-leaving. These findings suggest that the raising of the school-leaving age from 15 to 16 and the growth in further and higher education are likely to have a marked influence on future levels of demand for recreation, for a longer period of education will probably lead to increased participation. This tendency will be strengthened by the great expansion in the place of outdoor recreation in school curricula that has accompanied the raising of the school leaving age.

Income greatly affects recreational habits, for the need to purchase costly equipment, to travel long distances and to pay club membership fees can markedly influence participation. The *Pilot National Recreation Survey* demonstrated that 'among those with family incomes below £650 (1965 levels), predominantly from the older age groups, a quarter had never attempted any activity on the list and seemed almost to be recreationally inert. In almost every pursuit, particular participation increases with income. In this sense it is difficult to identify any genuinely low-income recreations' (British Travel Association–University of Keele, 1967, p. 6). The studies in central Scotland showed that field sports, pleasure-boating, golf and nature studies were all characterised by participants with an average weekly net income of over £25 (1969 levels). The studies in England demonstrated that golf was the game most characteristic of those with high incomes; according to the Northern Region study, 40 per cent of recent participants in activities on large courses (golf, horse–riding and motor and motorcycle-racing) were from households with an annual income of over £2000. The characteristic activities for those with lower incomes were cycling, team games, camping and swimming, none of which make heavy financial demands.

Society is now characterised by great social mobility, especially in relation to income distribution and educational attainment, and the *Pilot National Recreation Survey* examined the implications of these trends for the land-use planner:

In general 'low income/low educational category' recreations require modest facilities (cycling and fishing) or very modest space allocations (swimming, team games) and few generate serious transport demands. A local bath, a few acres of football pitch, a length of canal bank meet these needs. In contrast many 'high income groups/high education category' recreations generate enormous land demands (golf, riding) or require the provision of very specific facilities localised to a particular site (sailing, camping, water-skiing). And, in almost every case, these are activities more likely to be some distance from home, generating large and often localised traffic flows.

(British Travel Association–University of Keele, 1967, p. 6).

The *Pilot National Recreation Survey* found quite strong correlations between respondents' occupation and social class, and the likelihood of their participating in recreation. The contrasts that emerged between three broad occupational groups –'executives', 'clerical workers' and manual workers' –are interesting in that they did not follow an entirely expected course. The *Pilot National Recreation Survey* found that the higher occupational groups had a much wider range of recreational experience than the lower; thus 20 per cent of manual workers, but only 2 per cent of executives, had never taken part in any pursuit listed in the questionnaire, and even recreations normally associated with manual workers—for example, fishing—were as often reported by executives. The regional studies did not demonstrate a clear division between occupational and social groups in general participation and in some activities, such as golf, there was a distinct likelihood that participation was correlated with social class groups A, B or C, but imbalance was generally much less marked.

Further light on the role of economic and social factors is shed by the survey undertaken by Young and Willmott (1973) in the Metropolitan Region. This had, as one of its primary objectives, an investigation of work and leisure in different social classes. Although the findings of this survey are limited to the Metropolitan Region they confirm the more general findings of the *Pilot National Recreation Survey*. The authors examined twenty active sports and participation rates in four occupational groups – professional and managerial, clerical, skilled, and semi-skilled and unskilled workers. Distinct differences were observed and participation among those in the sub-sample of semi-skilled and unskilled exceeded average participation rates only in outdoor bowls. In nearly all other pursuits levels of participation were positively correlated with the occupational status; participation, particularly in the minority activities, such as motor-cruising, motor sports, boating, water-skiing and sailing, seems to be confined mainly to white-collar workers. Indeed, the semi-skilled and unskilled groups of workers did not participate in twelve of the twenty activities; in only three pursuits (swimming, fishing and association football) were levels of participation in this occupational group 5 per cent or more, whereas levels of participation among the professional and managerial group exceeded 5 per cent in 9 different sports (table 5.8).

Car ownership and the ability to drive are both stimuli to participation in active recreation. In the North-west study, only 32 per cent of the population over the age of 12 held driving licences, but 45 per cent of the sportsmen fell in this category. With the exception of such sports as rallying, the motor vehicle is generally a means of transport rather than an essential part of active recreation.

## TABLE 5.8

### INFLUENCE OF OCCUPATIONAL STATUS ON ACTIVITY IN SPORTS IN THE METROPOLITAN REGION

| | Professional and managerial | Clerical | Skilled | Semi-skilled and unskilled | All |
|---|---|---|---|---|---|
| | (percentage of respondents taking part in each sport 12 times a year or more in the previous year) | | | | |
| Swimming | 34 | 25 | 20 | 8 | 22 |
| Fishing (all kinds) | 9 | 3 | 9 | 5 | 8 |
| Association football | 6 | 6 | 8 | 5 | 7 |
| Golf | 9 | 11 | 4 | 2 | 6 |
| Table tennis | 10 | 10 | 4 | 2 | 6 |
| Cricket | 8 | 0 | 6 | 4 | 5 |
| Tennis | 8 | 7 | 2 | 0 | 4 |
| Badminton or squash | 7 | 6 | 2 | 0 | 4 |
| Sailing | 6 | 0 | 1 | 0 | 2 |
| Bowls | 2 | 3 | 2 | 3 | 2 |
| Ten-pin bowling | 2 | 0 | 2 | 1 | 2 |
| Athletics | 2 | 0 | 1 | 0 | 1 |
| Rugby, football | 2 | 3 | 0 | 0 | 1 |
| Horse-riding | 0 | 3 | 1 | 0 | 1 |
| Motor-cruising | 2 | 0 | 0 | 0 | 1 |
| Boxing, judo, karate, wrestling | 1 | 0 | 1 | 0 | 1 |
| Fencing, archery, shooting | 1 | 1 | 0 | 0 | 0 |
| Motor sports | 2 | 0 | 0 | 0 | 1 |
| Boating | 1 | 0 | 0 | 0 | 0 |
| Water-skiing | 1 | 0 | 0 | 0 | 0 |
| Average number of pursuits undertaken 12 times or more in previous year | 1·1 | 0·8 | 0·6 | 0·3 | 0·7 |

Source:    Young and Willmott (1973), p. 214.

Nevertheless, because many activities are pursued at some distance from home in areas that are often difficult to reach by public transport, ownership or access to a car can have a marked influence on the levels of participation. This is confirmed by table 5.9, which demonstrates that levels of car ownership among recent participants in central Scotland are generally greater than in the sample as a whole. The table demonstrates, first, the supporting role played by the motor vehicle in such sports as sailing and angling, although vehicle ownership is not a prerequisite of involvement; secondly, that the need to convey the necessary equipment makes access to a motor vehicle a necessity in such activities as golf and, increasingly, camping; thirdly, that cycling and team games, which are normally associated with lower income groups, not unexpectedly occupy the bottom two places.

An examination of levels of participation, factor by factor, makes it possible to compile a generalised profile of those who participate in active outdoor recreation. According to the North-west study, they are likely to be young (below 30), single and male; to be able to drive, to be drawn from all social groups except the lowest 3, to have stayed at school beyond the minimum leaving age, to be in employment, and to live in either the smaller settlement units or the suburbs of large units. Conversely those who engage in no active physical recreation are most likely to be over 44 years old, to be women and especially housewives, drawn from the lower social group, and to have left school early, to be a non-driver living within the inner areas of the cities and conurbations.

(North West Sports Council, 1972, p. 98)

TABLE 5.9

CAR OWNERSHIP AND PARTICIPATION IN ACTIVE RECREATION
IN CENTRAL SCOTLAND

| Activity* | Percentage of participants with access to a motor vehicle† |
|---|---|
| Sailing | 87·5 |
| Field sports | 85·3 |
| Golf | 74·9 |
| Angling | 71·6 |
| Pleasure-boating | 69·1 |
| Horse-riding | 66·7 |
| Sea-fishing | 62·1 |
| Nature studies | 60·6 |
| Swimming | 60·5 |
| Camping | 60·4 |
| Hiking, walking | 55·8 |
| Team games | 45·5 |
| Cycling | 36·3 |

* Only activities with levels of recent participation over 1 per cent have been included in the table.

† Of all those interviewed, 46·2 per cent had access to a motor vehicle.

Source:   Duffield and Owen (1970), p. 62.

## FORECASTING LEVELS OF PARTICIPATION IN ACTIVE RECREATION

To those planning the development of recreation facilities it is essential to know the pattern of participation in the future, particularly which activities will show the highest rates of growth and which will show a relative decline. Establishing statistical links between the nature of participants and their propensity to participate in outdoor recreation provides one means of forecasting future trends, and these links have been exploited in all the regional studies. Yet the principal difficulty in forecasting is the lack of knowledge of the forces that govern recreational behaviour. While there is overwhelming evidence that social and economic factors do influence participation in certain activities, use of these factors for forecasting is less a reflection of their proven validity than of the present lack of knowledge. It must be recognised that other factors, both psychological and environmental, also have a profound influence on recreational habits.

It would be much easier to estimate future trends in participation if reliable data existed for past years, since their absence transforms simple arithmetic into a complex statistical task. Because statistical relationships between recreational behaviour and certain socio-economic variables can be demonstrated, it has seemed reasonable to use this relationship for forecasting, but such a procedure requires the dubious assumption that existing relationships will continue in the future. The 'leisure revolution' has been accompanied by, and to some extent has fostered, great social changes, and it seems inevitable that the relationship between social variables and leisure habits will continue to be transformed. Changes in the pattern of marriage and in the nature of the family, the new social roles of the young and of women, and new technological and educational advances are all contributing to a fundamental restructuring of society. In these circumstances it has been suggested (Rodgers, 1969) that socio-economic parameters are a feeble tool for predicting the changing shape of recreational demand. The total demand for recreation is never fully realised and at any time there is a latent demand, untapped because of a scarcity of resources or for other reasons; it could be argued, therefore, that future effective demand will be conditioned more by the available supply and capacity of resources for recreation than by the demand generated by changes in social and economic factors.

There are those who feel that the difficulties of forecasting are so great that planners would be better advised to confine their attention to present problems. They may take the view that, since affluence and demand are expected to increase in step, supply would be hard put to keep pace with demand and the intensive use of all resources will result; facilities should therefore be provided only when specific demands for new or growing activities become evident. The authors, while not fully accepting this pessimistic viewpoint, are nevertheless aware of the major obstacles to forecasting in such a rapidly changing field. Forecasts must be continually revised and should be allied to an evaluation of resources. In this way the provision of facilities can keep pace with the expected growth of desire for recreation where and when it becomes evident. If the planner is to identify priorities and choose between conflicting options, he must have the most reliable forecasts that can be given; a haphazard approach could lead to either inadequate or wasteful provision of facilities.

The simplest way to obtain an indication of the changing popularity of activities is to ask people. Respondents in the *Pilot National Recreation Survey* were asked whether, if they had the opportunity, they would like to participate in any of the activities considered. Although estimates for some of the more glamorous activities are clearly unrealistic, most respondents seem to have taken these questions seriously. Since the future plans of people will largely follow the present pattern of popularity, the *Pilot National Recreation Survey* compared the rank order of present participation with that of intended participation to establish which activities showed the greatest potential for growth (table 5.10). In the Northern Region study respondents were asked a similar question and identified seven activities that seemed to show the greatest potential demand, namely, water-skiing, swimming, horse-riding/hunting, sailing, camping/caravanning, gliding/flying, and pony-trekking. Of these activities, swimming and camping or caravanning are quite popular at present and feature prominently in the list of pursuits in which people have ever participated, but the others are all activities

## TABLE 5.10

### RECREATIONS RANKED BY PAST AND EXPECTED PARTICIPATION

| | Rank order of past participation | Rank order of expected participation* | Rank difference |
|---|---|---|---|
| Team games | 1 | 13 | −12 |
| Swimming | 2 | 3 | − 1 |
| Cycling | 3 | 16 | −13 |
| Tennis | 4 | 11 | − 7 |
| Athletics | 4 | 19 | −15 |
| Camping | 6 | 8 | − 2 |
| Hiking | 7 | 13 | − 6 |
| Skating | 8 | 8 | 0 |
| Fishing | 9 | 4 | + 5 |
| Bowls | 10 | 11 | − 1 |
| Golf | 11 | 12 | + 9 |
| Riding | 12 | 4 | + 8 |
| Hill-walking/climbing | 13 | 16 | − 3 |
| Natural history | 13 | 13 | 0 |
| Youth hostelling | 16 | 20 | − 4 |
| Motor sports | 17 | 8 | + 9 |
| Sub-aqua sports | 18 | 16 | + 2 |
| Winter sports | 19 | 4 | +15 |
| Archery | 19 | 8 | +11 |
| † Sea sailing | (10) | 1 | + 9 |
| † Inland sailing | (10) | 4 | + 6 |

* The ranks refer to the averages of the responses to the questions 'What would you like to do?' and 'What have you firm plans for doing?'

† Sea and inland sailing are listed separately, but the rank of present participation is the average for both types of sailing.

Source:   British Travel Association–University of Keele (1967), p. 19.

in which the proportion who would like to take part is greater than the proportion who have ever participated in the past. The North-west study posed identical questions to those asked in the *Pilot National Recreation Survey* (table 5.11), but the organisers of the studies in central Scotland had serious doubts about the validity of such an approach, particularly the 'credibility gap' between aspiration and actual participation. They decided, therefore, to use both an objective statistical technique and the subjective evidence acquired during the home-interview survey and so avoid complete dependence on a single approach. It was also hoped that comparisons of the results from the two techniques would prove useful.

Although the home-interview survey did not yield precise numerical data it was capable of indicating levels of interest and future participation. For example, answers to one question established the last occasion on which respondents had participated in an active pursuit, in order to gauge any change of interest, and

## TABLE 5.11

### RESPONDENTS IN NORTH-WEST ENGLAND WHO WOULD 'LIKE TO' TAKE UP SPORTS

| Sport | Percentage of those interested |
|---|---|
| Golf | 5 |
| Swimming | 4 |
| Ice-skating | 3 |
| Water-skiing | 3 |
| Riding | 3 |
| Tennis | 3 |
| Sailing | 3 |
| Shooting | 3 |
| Ten-pin bowling | 3 |
| Keep fit | 2 |
| Judo | 2 |
| Bowls | 2 |
| Auto cross | 2 |
| Gliding | 2 |
| Soccer | 2 |
| Skin-diving | 2 |
| Skiing | 2 |
| Archery | 2 |

Source:    North West Sports Council (1972), p. 95.

others provided information on respondents' involvement in activities over their whole life-span, during the previous five years and during the previous twelve months. These details gave a good indication of present popularity, the 'wastage' of participants over the long term and the ability of specific activities to sustain interest over the short term. This historical perspective can help to measure the likelihood that an activity will grow in importance in the near future.

Recent participants were also asked whether their interest in that activity has increased, decreased or remained the same in the twelve months before the interview. Analyses of responses to this question identified those activities that are most popular and those that appear to be in decline. On the basis of answers to these questions, a subjective 'index of growth potential' was established for a range of activities (table 5.12). The index of growth potential does not provide a quantitative forecast and thus cannot be used to calculate future numbers of participants in any activity. It does, however, identify those activities most subject to changing levels of interest. Nature studies, swimming, sailing, golf and sea-fishing all achieved a high score. Further examination of the table shows that certain minority activities such as skiing, though commanding keen interest from their adherents, are also characterised by high wastage rates in both the short and long term, so that, while their demands for resources in the countryside may be expected to increase, such sports are unlikely to challenge the more popular activities. In contrast, participation in swimming and angling is fairly stable and their wastage rates are much lower, so that, while a rapid increase in interest is

## TABLE 5.12

### RECREATIONAL ACTIVITIES IN CENTRAL SCOTLAND: INDICES OF GROWTH POTENTIAL

|  | Index A | | Index B | | Index C | | Index D | | Index E | |
|---|---|---|---|---|---|---|---|---|---|---|
|  | % | Rank | % | Rank | % | Rank | % | Rank | Total Score | Rank |
| Swimming | 45 | 1 | 60 | 3 | 27 | 9 | 14 | 9 | 22 | 5 |
| Golf | 43 | 2 | 70 | 1 | 37 | 6 | 12 | 8 | 17 | 3 |
| Team games | 15 | 12 | 51 | 8 | 27 | 8 | 19 | 12 | 40 | 10 |
| Angling | 39 | 3 | 60 | 5 | 33 | 7 | 14 | 10 | 25 | 7 |
| Hiking, walking | 25 | 9 | 51 | 9 | 26 | 11 | 19 | 13 | 42 | 12 |
| Camping | 19 | 11 | 43 | 12 | 40 | 4 | 10 | 6 | 33 | 9 |
| Sea-fishing | 37 | 4 | 56 | 7 | 39 | 5 | 7 | 3 | 19 | 4 |
| Pleasure-boating | 27 | 8 | 45 | 11 | 9 | 14 | 12 | 7 | 40 | 10 |
| Nature studies | 37 | 5 | 69 | 2 | 45 | 2 | 8 | 4 | 13 | 1 |
| Cycling | 6 | 15 | 26 | 15 | 4 | 15 | 20 | 14 | 59 | 15 |
| Field sports | 34 | 6 | 64 | 4 | 21 | 13 | 6 | 1 | 24 | 6 |
| Sailing | 29 | 7 | 58 | 6 | 54 | 1 | 7 | 2 | 16 | 2 |
| Horse-riding | 14 | 13 | 35 | 13 | 23 | 12 | 15 | 11 | 49 | 13 |
| Skiing | 20 | 10 | 33 | 14 | 42 | 3 | 8 | 5 | 32 | 8 |
| Cricket | 10 | 14 | 46 | 10 | 17 | 10 | 36 | 15 | 49 | 13 |

Index A   Number of people participating within last year divided by the number of those ever participating, multiplied by 100.

Index B   Number of people participating within last year divided by number of people participating within the last five years, multiplied by 100.

Index C   Percentage of recent participants who claimed that their interest had increased in the twelve months prior to interview.

Index D   Percentage of recent participants who claimed that their interest had decreased in the twelve months prior to interview.

Index E   Summation of rank scores for indices A, B, C and D.

Source:   Duffield and Owen (1970), p. 68; Duffield and Owen (1971), p. 68.

unlikely, demands on resources and facilities can be expected to grow. Some of the activities listed were popular in the past but appear to be losing their attraction. The decreasing interest in cycling and youth hostelling has been well documented and their decline among the population of central Scotland is clear from table 5.12.

Interesting and informative as such subjective measures may be, they cannot stand alone. All the British regional studies have acknowledged the need for a more objective analysis that could add statistical and quantitative support to such subjective indices. Two techniques have been used: multiple regression (in the studies of north-west England and of central Scotland) and discriminant analysis (in the Northern Region study).

Multiple regression is a statistical technique that postulates that variation in one variable can be 'explained' by variations in other variables (for example, age, sex, income and vehicle ownership). The first step in multiple regression is to measure the degree of correlation between the range of socio-economic variables collected

## TABLE 5.13

### STATISTICAL RELATIONSHIP BETWEEN PARTICIPATION IN RECREATIONAL ACTIVITIES AND SELECTED SOCIO-ECONOMIC VARIABLES IN CENTRAL SCOTLAND

| Activity | Ownership of motor vehicle | Age of terminal education | | Sex (male) | Marital status (single) | Age | | | | Occupation | | Weekly income | | |
|---|---|---|---|---|---|---|---|---|---|---|---|---|---|---|
| | | less than 16 | over 17 | | | less than 20 | 20–39 | 40–59 | 60+ | manual | non-manual | £0–14 | £15–29 | £30+ |
| Golf | + | − | | + | | | | − | | | + | − | + | + |
| Hiking, hill-walking | | | + | | + | + | | | | | + | | | + |
| Skiing | | | + | | + | + | + | | | | + | | + | |
| Cycling | | | − | | + | + | | − | | | | | | |
| Field sports | + | | | + | | | | | | | | | + | + |
| Sea-fishing | + | | + | + | | | | − | − | | + | | + | + |
| Sailing | + | | | + | | | | | | | + | | | + |
| Power-boating | | | | | | | | | | | | | | |
| Motor-racing | + | | | + | | | | | | | | | | |
| Rallying | + | | + | | | | | | | | | | | |
| Orienteering | | | + | | | + | | | | | + | | | |
| Team games | + | | + | + | + | + | + | − | − | | + | | | + |
| Camping | + | | + | + | + | + | + | | | | + | | | |
| Rock-climbing | | | + | | | + | | | | | + | | + | + |
| Youth hostelling | + | | + | | | + | | | | | + | | | |
| Horse-riding | + | | | + | | | | | | + | + | | | |
| Fresh water fishing | + | − | + | + | | + | + | − | − | + | | | + | + |
| Swimming | + | | + | + | | + | + | | | | + | | + | + |
| Canoeing | | − | | | | | | | | | + | | | |
| Scrambling | | − | | | | | | | | | + | | | |
| Naturalist activities | | | + | | | | | | | | + | | + | |
| Cricket | + | − | | + | + | | | | | | | | | |
| Pleasure boating | + | − | + | | | | | | | | | | | |
| Flying, gliding | | − | | | | | | | | | | | | |

Table indicates the positive (+) and negative (−) correlations between recreational activities and certain socio-economic variables. All correlations are significant at 0·01 level of confidence.

Source: Duffield and Owen (1970), p. 191; Duffield and Owen (1971), p. 191.

for each respondent and participation in an activity. Although all these variables can be expected to have some influence on participation in recreational activities, they do not all have the same predictive value. Table 5.13 shows, for the surveys undertaken in central Scotland, the direction and strength of the relationships between participation in recreational activities and selected socio-economic variables. The power of each variable to act as an indicator of changing levels of participation depends on its own susceptibility to change over the period of the forecast. For example, there is no point in using the sex of the respondents as a variable in the estimation of future levels of participation because, although this factor has a marked influence on participation in certain activities, it is unlikely that the sex structure of the population will change greatly in the next decade; for the same reasons, marital status and employment status are also not appropriate. Occupation and education do influence present participation and are likely to undergo marked changes over the coming decade, but they could not be included in these regressions because adequate projections were not available. As a result only three variables, age, income and car ownership, were used.

The next step is to establish the relationships between those variables and

TABLE 5.14

COMPARISON OF ACTUAL AND ESTIMATED LEVEL OF
PARTICIPATION IN RECREATIONAL ACTIVITIES IN CENTRAL SCOTLAND

|  | Levels of participation over the previous 5 yrs (1965–9) | | Levels of participation over last year (1968–9) | |
|  | Actual* | Estimated† | Actual* | Estimated† |
|---|---|---|---|---|
| Swimming | 24·8 | 28·8 | 17·1 | 19·9 |
| Team games | 14·0 | 14·3 | 7·1 | 7·3 |
| Camping | 13·4 | 14·0 | 5·7 | 6·0 |
| Hiking, walking | 11·6 | 12·4 | 5·9 | 6·3 |
| Golf | 11·3 | 14·4 | 7·9 | 10·1 |
| Angling | 10·4 | 12·5 | 6·2 | 7·3 |
| Cycling | 9·1 | 9·8 | 2·4 | 2·5 |
| Pleasure-boating | 8·2 | 9·9 | 3·7 | 4·5 |
| Sea-fishing | 6·6 | 8·5 | 3·7 | 4·8 |
| Nature studies | 3·9 | 4·5 | 2·7 | 3·1 |
| Field sports | 2·8 | 3·7 | 1·8 | 2·4 |
| Sailing | 2·6 | 2·7 | 1·5 | 1·6 |
| Horse-riding | 2·0 | 2·0 | 0·7 | 0·7 |
| Skiing | 1·8 | 2·1 | 0·6 | 1·0 |
| Cricket | 1·3 | 1·6 | 0·6 | 0·7 |

* Based on the results of the household-interview survey
† Based on the multiple regression equations

Source:    Duffield and Owen (1970), p. 71; Duffield and Owen (1971), p. 71.

present levels of participation, and a series of multiple regression equations was calculated showing the relationship between each of the activities and levels of participation. To check their reliability, present levels of participation were calculated by means of these equations and compared with the actual levels of participation as indicated by the home-interview survey. As table 5.14 shows, there is a close correspondence between the 'estimated' and the true values.

Forecasts of values for the three socio-economic variables, provided by the research section of the Scottish Development Department, were then substituted in the equations for present values to establish participation levels in 1981 (table 5.15). The results of this analysis are presented in table 5.16. The forecast refers to levels of participation for a five-year period before 1981 and, in order to relate these estimates to current levels of participation, further calculations were undertaken to estimate levels of participation in the twelve months before 1981. These calculations assumed that the relationship between recent and five-yearly levels of participation in 1981 was the same as in 1969 for each activity. Table 5.16 shows the present rank order of participation to provide a comparison with the forecast.

Forecasts for the five-year period before 1981 indicate that different rates of growth in activities will lead to some changes in rank; for example, golf and freshwater angling both improved their rank at the expense of team games, camping and hiking and walking. Forecasts of levels of participation in 1981 (that is, over a twelve-month period, 1980-1) show that, despite major differences in the growth rates of particular activities, the ranking is very similar to present ranking; according to the forecasts, swimming will clearly still be the most popular activity, although golf should achieve nearly double its level of recent participation over the forecast period.

TABLE 5.15

PREDICTOR VARIABLES USED IN THE MULTIPLE
REGRESSION ANALYSIS ON DATA FOR CENTRAL SCOTLAND

|  | | *1969* *Values* | *1981†* *Values* |
|---|---|---|---|
|  | | (percentage of those interviewed) | |
| A. | Ownership of motor vehicle | 45·0 | 61·5 |
| B. | Age 16–19 years | 9·0 | 8·0 |
| C. | Age 20–39 years | 37·4 | 39·6 |
| D. | Age 40–59 years | 34·2 | 27·7 |
| E. | Age 60 years and over | 19·4 | 24·7 |
| F. | Net income less than £15 | 49·8 | 37·0 |
| G. | Net income £15–29 | 40·0 | 41·1 |
| H. | Net income £30 and over | 7·1 | 18·9 |

* Based on the household-interview survey

† Forecast values based on information supplied by the Scottish Development Department (Research Section).

Source:    Duffield and Owen (1970), p. 192.

RECREATION IN THE COUNTRYSIDE

TABLE 5.16

RECREATIONAL ACTIVITIES IN CENTRAL SCOTLAND:
FORECAST AND PRESENT LEVELS OF PARTICIPATION

|  | Participation over the previous 5 yrs | | Participation over the last year | | |
|---|---|---|---|---|---|
|  | 1977–81 level estimated* | Rank 1965–9 | 1980–1 level estimated* | Rank 1980–1 | Rank 1968–9 |
| Swimming | 32·3 | 1 | 22·3 | 1 | 1 |
| Golf | 20·2 | 5 | 14·1 | 2 | 22 |
| Angling | 17·5 | 6 | 10·2 | 3 | 4 |
| Team games | 15·5 | 2 | 7·9 | 4 | 3 |
| Camping | 15·3 | 3 | 6·6 | 7 | 6 |
| Hiking, walking | 14·5 | 4 | 7·4 | 5 | 5 |
| Pleasure-boating | 12·4 | 8 | 5·6 | 8 | 8 |
| Sea-fishing | 11·9 | 9 | 6·7 | 6 | 7 |
| Cycling | 9·8 | 7 | 2·5 | 11 | 10 |
| Nature studies | 5·5 | 10 | 3·8 | 9 | 9 |
| Field sports | 5·2 | 11 | 3·3 | 10 | 11 |
| Sailing | 4·2 | 12 | 2·4 | 12 | 12 |
| Horse-riding | 2·5 | 13 | 0·9 | 14 | 13 |
| Skiing | 2·5 | 14 | 1·3 | 13 | 14 |
| Cricket | 1·5 | 15 | 0·7 | 15 | 15 |

* Percentage of total population aged 16 and over having participated in the period stated.

Source:    Duffield and Owen (1970), pp. 71, 73.

Table 5.17 lists each of the activities in descending order of the rate of growth
between 1969 and 1981 as forecast by the multiple regression equation, and
shows a marked contrast between the high growth rates of the more popular
activities (sailing, angling, golf and sea-fishing) and the zero growth rates of
activities now in decline (cycling and cricket). Table 5.17 also shows the ranking
of each activity against the subjective indices of 'growth potential' discussed earlier,
to provide a direct comparison between the 'subjective' and 'objective' techniques
of forecasting future levels of participation in active pursuits. It is interesting to
note that the two techniques, using the same data (the home-interview survey)
but very different methods, provide very similar assessments of growth potential,
a result that gives confidence in the ability of both to indicate future patterns of
outdoor recreation in central Scotland. They both predict zero growth for cycling
and cricket and slow rates of growth for team games and camping; in contrast,
sailing, golf, sea-fishing and angling all achieved high scores from both techniques,
with growth rates exceeding 40 per cent for the twelve-year period covered by the
forecast. This close agreement gives greater confidence in the forecast than could
be placed in the results from any one technique, and although it cannot be
claimed that these forecasts are completely accurate, they do provide a reliable
and valuable guide for long-term recreation planning, when taken together.
    Multiple regression analysis was used in the North-west study in a similar way.

## TABLE 5.17

### RECREATIONAL ACTIVITIES IN CENTRAL SCOTLAND:
### ASSESSMENT OF GROWTH POTENTIAL

|  | Forecast growth rate (%) 1969–81* | Index of growth potential rank |
|---|---|---|
| Sailing | 50 | 1 |
| Angling | 40 | 7 |
| Golf | 40 | 3 |
| Sea-fishing | 40 | 4 |
| Field sports | 38 | 6 |
| Skiing | 30 | 8 |
| Horse-riding | 29 | 13 |
| Pleasure-boating | 24 | 10 |
| Nature studies | 23 | 1 |
| Hiking, walking | 17 | 12 |
| Swimming | 12 | 5 |
| Team games | 8 | 10 |
| Camping | 5 | 9 |
| Cycling | 0 | 15 |
| Cricket | 0 | 13 |

\* Based on a comparison of regression estimates for 1969 and 1981 data.

Source:    Duffield and Owen (1970), p. 73.

Relationships were established between eleven groups of outdoor recreation activities and a set of fifteen possible explanatory variables, but these were used largely as an exploratory test of methodology. Future levels of participation were forecast for only one activity, angling, and much more work relating forecast values to the socio-economic variables would have been necessary before levels of participation in 1981 could have been calculated for other activities. National Opinion Polls used another multivariate statistical technique, discriminant analysis, in the Northern Region study. In many ways discriminant analysis has a very similar statistical basis to multiple–regression analysis (North West Sports Council, 1972, chap. 10); both techniques exploit the statistical relationship between participation in an activity and certain demographic characteristics. The form of discriminant analysis used by the Northern Region selects those socio-economic variables that best 'discriminate' between participants and non-participants in the activity under consideration; on the basis of these variables, participation rates were calculated for different sub-groups of the total population. The social profile of the population in 1980 was then estimated, using the combinations of characteristics; forecasts of participation rates in activities were made by relating the levels of participation in 1967 from the various groups to the 1980 forecast of the population in respect of these same characteristics (table 5.18).

In the Northern Region study discriminant analysis was performed on twelve

## TABLE 5.18

### THE USE OF DISCRIMINANT ANALYSIS IN FORECASTING LEVELS OF PARTICIPATION IN ACTIVE RECREATION FOR NORTHERN ENGLAND: A THEORETICAL EXAMPLE

Step 1    Isolate for the activity under study the variables that are found to be capable of discriminating between participants and non-participants. For this activity, say, two variables only (sex and car ownership) are found to be sufficient for this purpose.

Step 2    Produce for the population of the study area two-way (or in some cases one multi-way) tables using the selected variables:

Table A: Profiles of Respondents 1967

| Car Ownership | Male (%) | Female (%) | All (%) |
|---|---|---|---|
| Yes | 40 | 10 | 50 |
| No | 20 | 30 | 50 |
| All | 60 | 40 | 100 |

Step 3    From the survey data establish participation levels for these sub-groups:

Table B: Participation Levels in Stated Activity

| Car Ownership | Male (%) | Female (%) |
|---|---|---|
| Yes | 20 | 30 |
| No | 10 | 10 |

Step 4    Multiply each of the four cells in table A by its equivalent cell in table B, summing the four products, and dividing by 100, to give the overall participation level (%) for the whole sample relating to the survey year (1967). Thus

$$\text{Participation } 1969 = \frac{(40 \times 20) + (10 \times 30) + (20 \times 10) + (30 \times 10)}{100} = 16\%$$

Step 5    Establish for the forecast year (1980) the breakdown of population into the sub-groups concerned (as in table A):

Table C: Profiles of Population 1980

| Car Ownership | Male (%) | Female (%) | All (%) |
|---|---|---|---|
| Yes | 50 | 20 | 70 |
| No | 5 | 25 | 30 |
| All | 55 | 45 | 100 |

Step 6    Apply the 1967 participation levels to table C and repeat step 4, multiplying tables C and B. Thus

$$\text{Participation } 1980 = \frac{(50 \times 20) + (20 \times 30) + (5 \times 10) + (25 \times 10)}{100} = 19\%$$

Source:    North Regional Planning Committee 1969, p. 131.

TABLE 5.19

FORECAST OF PARTICIPATION IN NORTHERN ENGLAND: 1967–80*

| | Changes in percentage levels of participation (%) | Changes in absolute levels of participation (%) | Proportion of population normally participating (%) | |
|---|---|---|---|---|
| | 1967–80 | 1967–80 | 1967 | 1980 |
| Golf | +54·9 | +74·3 | 3·0 | 5·0 |
| Camping/caravanning | +55·4 | +64·0 | 4·2 | 6·5 |
| Motor sports | +45·4 | +52·5 | 2·9 | 4·3 |
| Bowls | − 0·9 | + 3·0 | 2·3 | 2·3 |
| Climbing | − 1·3 | + 3·7 | 5·4 | 5·3 |
| Rambling | − 2·1 | + 1·9 | 3·9 | 3·8 |
| Cycling | − 2·4 | + 2·9 | 6·6 | 6·4 |
| Athletics | − 2·6 | + 2·3 | 5·0 | 4·9 |
| Fishing | − 3·8 | + 1·5 | 5·1 | 4·9 |
| Swimming | − 5·1 | 0·0 | 17·8 | 16·9 |
| Cricket | − 6·0 | − 0·8 | 5·1 | 4·8 |
| Tennis | − 7·2 | − 3·3 | 5·8 | 5·3 |

* Taking into account change in population structures and population increase.

Source:   North Regional Planning Committee (1969), p.81.

active pursuits, namely, swimming, fishing, cricket, golf, bowls, tennis, athletics, rambling, camping/caravanning, cycling, flying and motor sports. Participation in these activities was related to eleven demographic characteristics that were used to predict participation in 1980: age, sex, marital status, social class, car ownership, householding, working status, terminal education age, with/without children, Saturday working and Sunday working (table 5.19). Only three of the twelve activities showed substantial growth rates, namely, golf, camping/caravanning and motor sports, all of which had growth rates of over 45 per cent over the thirteen-year period. All other individual activities showed a decline in percentage rates of participation, though if regional changes in population structure over the forecast period are taken into account, only three activities did not demonstrate a regional growth in demand, namely, tennis and cricket, which showed a decline, and swimming, which exhibited a zero growth rate. At first sight the increases forecast seemed remarkably low, but it is probably wise to treat the forecasts as indicators of propensity to grow rather than as an accurate estimate of the actual rate of growth that might be achieved.

The most recent forecasts of leisure activities were those undertaken on behalf of the Post Office by the Institute of Community Studies and reported in Young and Willmott's survey of work and leisure in the Metropolitan Region (1973, appendix 5). The technique was similar to that used in the Northern Region: participation rates for the different activities and for various social groups in the 1970 population were applied to the projected social profile of the population in 2001 to produce forecasts of levels of participation in that year. Forecasts were made for twenty-two active pursuits. The participation rates for 1970 were those established by Young and Willmott for the Metropolitan Region, with adjustments to compensate for the differences in the composition of the population of the United Kingdom as a whole. 'The London Region population was higher in class, richer, more educated and had more cars, that is, contained more of the people who were most active in leisure— and so the U.K. estimates came out as lower than the actual participation rates in the London region sample—5 per cent lower on average' (Young and Willmott, 1973, p. 366). Regional differences in participation rates were also taken into account.

The next step was to isolate those socio-economic characteristics which would best serve as 'predictor' variables. The basis of this choice was a multiple regression analysis from which five variables were chosen as contributing most to observed

TABLE 5.20

**FORECASTS OF CHANGES IN FIVE POPULATION VARIABLES
IN THE UNITED KINGDOM**

|  |  | *1970* | *2001* |
|---|---|---|---|
| *Age* | 18–24 | 15 | 15 |
|  | 25–29 | 9 | 10 |
|  | 30–39 | 16 | 19 |
|  | 40–49 | 17 | 17 |
|  | 50–59 | 17 | 16 |
|  | 60 or over | 26 | 23 |
| *Income* (2001 incomes at 1970 prices) | Under £1000 a year | 44 | 3 |
|  | £1000 or more but less than £2000 | 44 | 28 |
|  | £2000 or more but less than £3000 | 8 | 27 |
|  | £3000 or more but less than £4000 | 2 | 23 |
|  | £4000 or more but less than £5000 | 1 | 6 |
|  | £5000 or more | 1 | 8 |
| *Occupational class* | Professional | 5 | 19 |
|  | Managerial | 17 | 14 |
|  | Clerical | 10 | 7 |
|  | Skilled | 41 | 44 |
|  | Semi-skilled | 19 | 11 |
|  | Unskilled | 8 | 5 |
| *Age of finishing full-time education* | 16 or under | 84 | 55 |
|  | 17–19 | 9 | 29 |
|  | 20 or over | 7 | 16 |
| *Car ownership (in household)* | No car | 50 | 18 |
|  | One car | 42 | 58 |
|  | Two or more cars | 8 | 24 |

Source:   Young and Willmott (1973), p. 367.

variations in participation in leisure activities. These variables were: (1) age, (2) car ownership, (3) occupational class, (4) annual income, and (5) terminal educational age. The forecast socio-economic distribution of the population of the United Kingdom in 2001 was established using these predictor variables (table 5.20). On the basis of the socio-economic variables the population in 1970 was divided into different social groups and participation rates for each of the twenty-two activities were calculated for each sub-group. The forecasts of participation rates in 2001 were made by applying the participation rates in 1970, sub-group by sub-group, to the estimated population in 2001 (table 5.21).

TABLE 5.21

FORECASTS OF CHANGES IN ACTIVE SPORTS IN THE UNITED KINGDOM

|  | *Percentage doing the activity 1970* | *Percentage doing the activity 2001* | *Participation Growth rate 1970* | *2001* |
|---|---|---|---|---|
| Swimming | 29 | 37 | 20 | 30 |
| Sailing | 3 | 4·5 | 40 | 50 |
| Golf | 7 | 10 | 35 | 45 |
| Fishing (all kinds) | 9 | 10 | 10 | 20 |
| Association football | 6 | 7 | 5 | 15 |
| Cricket | 4·5 | 5 | 5 | 15 |
| Tennis | 8 | 10 | 23 | 35 |
| Table tennis | 11 | 13 | 10 | 20 |
| Bowls | 2 | 2 | 0 | 10 |
| Ten-pin bowling | 9 | 10 | 5 | 15 |
| Athletics | 2 | 2 | − 1 | 5 |
| Badminton and squash | 3 | 4·5 | 50 | 60 |
| Rugby football | — | 1 | 10 | 20 |
| Boating | 1·5 | 1·5 | 0 | 10 |
| Motor-cruising | — | — | −15 | −20 |
| Water-skiing | — | — | 35 | 45 |
| Skating | 1·5 | 1·5 | 0 | 10 |
| Boxing, judo, karate, wrestling | — | — | −10 | 0 |
| Fencing, archery, shooting | — | — | −10 | 0 |
| Hiking, climbing, rambling | — | — | − 5 | 5 |
| Horse-riding, pony-trekking, hunting | 1 | 1·5 | 15 | 25 |
| Motor sports | — | — | 5 | 15 |
| Any sport | 44 | 52 | 15 | 25 |

Source:   Young and Willmott (1973), p. 369.

A first impression from these results is the modest rate of growth in the majority of active pursuits over the thirty-year period of the forecast; of the twenty-two activities considered, twelve had forecast levels of growth of less than 20 per cent. The activities with the most rapid rates of growth were badminton and squash, water-skiing, sailing and golf, but even these activities exhibited extremely modest growth rates and are hardly indicative of an age termed the 'leisure revolution'.

TABLE 5.22

ESTIMATES OF GROWTH POTENTIAL FOR ACTIVE RECREATION PURSUITS
(SIX ACTIVITIES WITH HIGHEST GROWTH RATE)

| Pilot National Recreational Survey Estimates* | Northern Region (Subjective†) | Northern Region (Discriminant Analysis) | North-West Region (Subjective‡) | Central Scotland (Subjective) | Central Scotland (Multiple Regression) | United Kingdom (Objective∮) |
|---|---|---|---|---|---|---|
| Winter sports | Water-skiing | Golf | Golf | Sailing | Sailing | Badminton and squash |
| Archery | Swimming | Camping | Swimming | Golf | Angling | Sailing |
| Sailing | Horse-riding | Motor sports | Ice-skating | Sea-fishing | Golf | Golf |
| Golf | Sailing | Bowls | Water-skiing | Swimming | Sea-fishing | Water-skiing |
| Motor sports | Gaming | Climbing | Horse-riding | Field sports | Field sports | Tennis |
| Horse-riding | Gliding/Flying | Rambling | Tennis | Angling | Skiing | Swimming |

\* Based on the comparison between:

(a) past participation levels for each activity and
(b) desire to participate in the future, as indicated by answers to 2 questions:

   (i) 'If you had the opportunity, are there any of these activities that you would *like* to take up seriously, even if you have not done so as yet?'

   (ii) 'Are there any of these activities which you are not doing at present, but which you are definately *planning* to take up seriously?'

† Based on replies to question:

   'Are there any (activities) that you would like to do if you had the opportunity?'

‡ Based on replies to question:

   'If you had the opportunity, would you like to take up any of these activities, even if you have not done so as yet?'

∮ Based on a technique described in Young and Willmott (1973), Appendix 5.

Source:   British Travel Association–University of Keele, (1967), p. 19; North Regional Planning Committee (1969), p. 81; North West Sports Council (1972), p. 95; Duffield and Owen (1970), p. 73.

Those involved in the planning and development of recreational facilities may find it difficult to know which technique provides the most reliable forecasts of future growth in recreational pursuits, but it is encouraging to note that, despite the varying natures of the techniques, there is a large measure of agreement about which sports are likely to show the most vigorous growth over the next decade. The various surveys considered somewhat different activities but, as table 5.22 illustrates, when the six activities identified by each of those with the highest growth rates are considered, some common trends emerge. There seems little doubt that participation in golf will grow vigorously during the 1970s, since all studies except that of the Northern Region included golf among the six leading sports. Similarly, sailing, winter sports, horse-riding and swimming are identified by at least three of the approaches adopted in the various surveys. In view of this evidence, recreational planners throughout Great Britain would be wise to examine the existing provision for these activities, the pressures on present facilities and the desirability of planning new facilities.

## CONCLUSION

In this context of future changes in levels of participation, it is interesting to consider the views of the Select Committee of the House of Lords, appointed in 1972 to 'consider the demand for facilities for participation in sports and in the enjoyment of leisure out of doors and to examine what impediments may exist to the fuller use of existing facilities or the development of new ones and how they might be removed'. In the Committee's view, the population of Great Britain changes its leisure habits only under definite stimuli, the major stimuli being income, mobility, education and fashion, changes in which would combine to produce a redistribution of leisure time and so encourage participation in sport and outdoor recreation. However, despite the expected changes in leisure habits, the Committee concluded that 'the Nation's tastes in recreation cannot be expected to change suddenly nor the distribution in leisure time between different types of activity. Sport and outdoor recreation are still subject, as they always have been, to the forces of inertia and the weather. The Committee consider that the current rate of growth and the apparent change in leisure habits must owe much to the release of "latent demand" for facilities. It is therefore a measure of "present under-provision" ' (Select Committee, 1973). The Committee concluded that present growth rates in active recreation are abnormally high and that the energetic provision of facilities to satisfy latent demand in the coming decade will reduce the rate of demand for new facilities over the whole field of recreation; thus, 'when the backlog of latent demand has been satisfied the growth rate of demand will fall. The Committee believe that the graph of demand which is rising steeply at present can flatten out provided that latent demand is met'.

Whether the views of the Select Committee are correct or not remains to be seen, but it is appropriate that they should identify as important the relationship between demand for recreation and the supply of resources available to meet this demand. It will be argued in chapter 9 that there is an intimate spatial relationship between these two basic elements, which determines the balance of the supply/demand equation at any one time.

# 6 Recreation Resources: Towards an Evaluation

So far in this discussion the emphasis has been placed mainly on the demand for and participation in outdoor recreation in the countryside. Yet such recreation does not take place in a vacuum; the various kinds of recreation depend for their continuance on the availability of physical resources which can both support and sustain the demands they make. An objective measure of the 'supply' of natural resources available within an area is necessary, therefore, if the present relationships between recreationists and the countryside are to be assessed and if proper provision is to be made for the future. The main aim of such an evaluation of resources should be to locate and identify those areas which, because of their physical characteristics, are suitable for recreational activities. The areal extent and distribution of these resources will indicate the potential capacity of the countryside to support such activities, and will aid the planning and provision of opportunities and facilities for outdoor recreation.

## RESOURCES CURRENTLY USED FOR OUTDOOR RECREATION

In principle, establishing what resources are actually used for outdoor recreation should be a simple matter of survey, but, as the discussion on data-dredging in chapter 4 has shown, this is not so in practice. Major difficulties arise from the wide variability of recreation in time and space, for intensities of use differ greatly over quite short distances and throughout the year, the week and even the day (chapter 2). These difficulties are aggravated by the fact that the most common form of outdoor recreation, informal passive recreation, shows these characteristics to a marked degree; for by its very nature it is both unorganised and widespread. Furthermore, very little attempt has been made to record levels of recreational use, even for those activities that are clearly defined and occur within discrete areas. The only firm data relate to places for which there is a charge for admission or for the use of facilities, as in country houses open to the public, car parks or golf courses, and even these data are normally confined to numbers participating, sometimes for each day, but more commonly on a weekly, monthly or even annual basis. Rarely is there any other indication of intensity of use, such as length of stay; indeed, for most forms of outdoor recreation, it is not easy to obtain such information.

There is thus a need for techniques and procedures by which resources already used for outdoor recreation can be readily identified. Remote sensing, whether by conventional vertical air photography or, as has more commonly been the case in the United Kingdom, by observation and oblique photography from light aircraft (Sidaway, 1972; Bungay, 1972), offers one obvious possibility, although there are considerable practical problems, particularly the critical timing of flights and the difficulties of penetrating tree cover, a matter of some importance in view of the well-known 'edge' effect (the tendency for recreationists to concentrate at the boundaries between different land uses, such as woodland and open space). The method devised to identify levels of activity in areas of extensive recreational use in central Scotland, was to have two observers patrolling an area by car at frequent intervals, recording and interviewing such recreationists as they encountered (Duffield and Owen, 1971a, p. 113). The name 'rural traverse' was given to this method. Apart from these methods, aimed at acquiring the facts by direct observation, there remains, as chapter 4 has shown, a variety of techniques for collecting data, which can be used to complement each other: consultation with the police, local authorities, motoring organisations, tourist and amenity bodies; surveys of households to identify those areas that respondents use; and surveys of clubs and associations (both local and national) concerned with, or responsible for, particular forms of outdoor recreation, such as angling associations, natural history clubs and bodies such as the Ramblers Association. These clubs are not only a source of information, but also have an important role to play in the proper management of countryside resources for recreation.

## Levels of Use

Identifying the areas used is only a first step, for it is probable that any reasonably comprehensive survey would show that most rural land is used for outdoor recreation at some time and to some degree. What is needed is greater insight into the nature of these activities, a measure of the level of use and, if outdoor recreation is to be adequately planned, how nearly that level of use matches capacity. Though little progress has been made with assessing either levels of use or capacity, the former is essentially a matter of technique, whereas capacity is a concept that those researching in the field of outdoor recreation have neither adequately clarified nor discovered how to measure satisfactorily.

Several approaches have been adopted towards the measurement of levels of use, notably automatic counting devices, remote sensing and direct observation. Vehicle counters are a standard feature of traffic censuses and attempts have been made to count pedestrians by similar devices such as trample meters (Coker and Coker, 1972), photoelectric cells linked to counters and the like (Bayfield and Picknell, 1971: Bayfield and Moyes, 1972), though there are obvious problems of securing equipment against theft or vandalism. Counts of visitors using the footpath to the summit of Arthur's Seat in Holyrood Park, Edinburgh, have been made from photographs taken at intervals with a hand-operated camera from a vantage point (Huxley and Pratt, 1966). Experiments have also been undertaken using cameras suspended from balloons and controlled from the ground by means of a nylon line or fixed to the struts of light aircraft and operated by clockwork motors (Duffield and Forsyth, 1972). A technique used to estimate caravan traffic, employing a battery-operated cine camera mounted at a vantage point to take single shots at frequent intervals, has potential application at high-density sites, provided that security can be assured (Duffield and Owen, 1971b; chapter 8 of present volume). Perhaps the most comprehensive attempt to record levels of use on recreation sites has been undertaken at two beaches in East Lothian — Yellow-craig, to the west of North Berwick, and Whitesands, to the east of Dunbar—where teams of observers recorded at frequent intervals the numbers of visitors using each link of a network of footpaths and sections of beach (Coppock, 1973a). Such an approach is expensive in terms of labour but, provided that sufficient resources are available, there appear to be no insuperable difficulties in measuring levels of use.

## Capacity

The term 'capacity' is widely used in a recreational context, but there is little firm knowledge of the degree to which recreational areas differ in this respect. Furthermore, while capacity has been defined by the Countryside Recreation Research Advisory Group as 'the level of recreation use an area can sustain without an unacceptable degree of deterioration of the character and quality of the resource or of the recreation experience' (Countryside Recreation Research Advisory Group, 1970-2), this definition can be interpreted in a variety of ways—physical, ecological, economic and psychological—each of which is likely to produce a different measure of capacity. The most commonly used interpretation is the ecological one, that is, the capacity of the vegetative cover to support recreational use without deterioration, although a change in the vegetation that makes an area more attractive for recreation might nevertheless be regarded as retrograde by an ecologist (see, for example, Nature Conservancy, 1967). Furthermore, while it is not difficult to show that a site is being over-used once the vegetative cover has become discontinuous and accelerated soil erosion has begun, it is much more difficult to establish the point at which changes in soil and vegetation begin. Many factors other than recreational pressure are involved and it is not easy to isolate those effects that are due to variations in weather or to biotic factors, such as changes in the rabbit population, from those that are due to recreational pressure; long-term programmes of research and careful monitoring will be necessary. Such considerations will be particularly important where the ecological balance is delicate, as in coastal sand-dunes, but in more robust areas, such as downland, the important threshold may be psychological; that is, it may be the point at which people feel themselves crowded out and go elsewhere (see, for example, Outdoor Recreation Resources Review Commission, 1962a). Such thresholds may be quite low; in a study of canoeing in Algonquin Park, Ontario, it was found that an area was thought to be crowded if more than six other canoeists were seen on a lake (Priddle, Clark and Douglas, 1973). It is apparent that capacity not only involves value judgments, but can also be modified by appropriate management (An Foras Forbatha, 1966; Buchanan and Partners, 1971).

## POTENTIAL RESOURCES FOR OUTDOOR RECREATION

This ignorance of capacity clearly presents a problem to those planning for future requirements, for they have no reliable indication of the extent to which additional resources will be needed as a result of over-use of existing sites. Nevertheless, it is generally agreed that additional recreation land will be required and that both planners and those who control rural resources will need some comparative measure of the suitability of the countryside to support sustained recreational use, although there are important gaps in information that need to be filled before recreational potential can be adequately assessed. These concern not only the capacity of different types of land and vegetation, but also a knowledge of what the recreationist seeks from different kinds of outdoor recreation, how far these desires are likely to change over time and even what constitutes suitability (in a technical sense) for different kinds of recreation. Recreational standards, both optimal and minimal, arc rudimentary or non-existent. Even in the much longer established field of recreational planning in urban areas, one of the few firm standards used, that of 6 acres (2·4 ha) of playing fields and open space per 1000 population, is derived from circumstances that have changed since it was devised in 1925. The National Playing Fields Association has recently reviewed this figure and sees no present basis for departing from it (National Playing Fields Association, 1971). Current prescriptions of the resource requirements of different forms of outdoor recreation arc at best based on the cumulative experience of practitioners and instructors and at worst are little more than inspired guesses.

While the various forms of outdoor recreation differ in the physical resources they require, they can be conveniently divided into 'user-oriented' and 'resource-based', those that are located primarily with reference to the residences of users and those that depend on the location of scarce resources (Clawson and Knetsch, 1966; see also chapters 4 and 8 of present volume). Many recreational activities are catholic in their requirements; provided that a sufficient area of land is available, its physical characteristics do not matter greatly so long as they arc not extreme, for example, steep and rocky, or liable to frequent flooding. Playing fields and golf courses can be established on most of the land surrounding towns, although heavy costs may be involved in using earth-moving equipment to mould the topography. As with most man-made structures, a fairly level, well-drained site is preferable, but some investment can be justified if land is to be used intensively, and ease of access for large numbers of people may be more important than physical attributes. Recreation may also be an appropriate use for derelict land that has been rehabilitated, and substantial grants of up to 85 per cent of the cost of restoration are awarded for such purposes; many playing fields in industrial areas are on land formerly used for industrial or mineral workings.

Resource-based outdoor recreation, on the other hand, is dependent on the availability of specific natural resources, and recreationists are often prepared to travel long distances to reach those of high quality. Some activities, of which pot-holing is an obvious example, are possible only in the very few locations where a particular resource occurs; but more commonly, a range of sites can be used, differing chiefly in the quality of the recreational experience they can provide. Skiing is possible at some time during the winter in quite a large number of places in Scotland, but there are only a few with the prospect of sufficient snow each year to warrant investment in ski lifts and other facilities. Even for these activities, any generally agreed and soundly based criteria for selection are lacking.

## PROBLEMS OF RESOURCE EVALUATION

If the surveyor can satisfactorily resolve the conceptual problems of evaluation of resources for recreation activities, he still faces a number of difficulties that must be overcome before a suitable procedure for classification can be devised, the basic difficulty being that of scale. Criteria that would be relevant in a broad regional assessment designed to provide information for strategic planning and to indicate areas needing further study, are quite different from those appropriate to the selection and planning of a specific site. In the latter case, questions of ownership and availability of land will be involved, major capital investment to alter accessibility may be justified and specific management techniques will be required. In a broad survey many of these considerations can be disregarded and attention focused on the intrinsic qualities of land and water. Most assessments of the suitability of natural resources for outdoor recreation have been attempted at the regional scale, notably the survey of land capability for recreation, undertaken for the Canada Land Inventory (1969), which classified approximately one million square miles (2·6 million $km^2$) (Burbridge, 1971). Indeed, a reconnaissance evaluation of this kind is an essential prerequisite to a more detailed examination at a larger scale. It is appropriate therefore to recommend an evaluation in two stages. At the first stage resources are examined by means of a 'coarse sieve', thus identifying areas worthy of more thorough examination at the second stage. This chapter is primarily concerned with the first stage.

A two-stage evaluation is consistent with the planning legislation embodied in the Town and Country Planning Acts (1968, England and Wales, and 1969, Scotland), under which structure plans for urban and rural areas will provide the broad policy framework within which local action plans can be made. All planning studies of regional recreation that have been completed, or are under way, are either financed directly by local authorities or are intended to serve their needs. The two-stage evaluation has another practical advantage: the initial appraisal would eliminate areas unsuitable for recreation, thus permitting the available finance, effort and time to be directed towards those areas where the greatest benefits are likely to accrue.

The surveyor has a further critical decision concerning the geographical scale at which he is working—the unit of assessment. This choice can influence, and has done so, the technique of assessment used. Ideally it should be possible to quantify data so that distributions identified in different studies can be compared directly, but the choice of the basic unit of assessment continues to divide those working in this field. The South Hampshire Plan, prepared for three local planning authorities and covering over 300 square miles (483 $km^2$), was considered in its entirety as a single unit. This was necessarily a very general approach to resource analysis; there was a categoric decision not to classify resources arbitrarily, although the analysis identified the zones and major landscape elements of which the existing landscape is composed (South Hampshire Plan Advisory Committee, 1969). In contrast, other investigators have usually divided their study area into smaller geographical units, although the basis of this division has varied considerably. Thus, Clark (1970), in a scenic appraisal of Hertfordshire, adopted the 'tract' as his unit of assessment; this was a visually self-contained unit, homogeneous in character, which he regarded as both meaningful in terms of landscape and simple in terms of analysis. Using contoured and geological maps, he identified 96 tracts (average size 7·7 square miles (20 km²)), which were then checked and adjusted as necessary in the field. He rejected the use of the grid square, a regular geometric unit, on the grounds that, although it would nevertheless ensure units of uniform size, it cannot readily be identified in the field, involves more complex decisions and does not reduce the subjectivity of those decisions. Yet irregular units, which inevitably vary in size, are themselves open to criticism, particularly with regard to the definition of boundaries. Landforms do not consist of units that can be defined by discrete boundaries, and, while the use of watersheds may permit more exact definition of landform units, it is clear that those surveying recreational resources require more than a geomorphological definition of tracts. Moreover, if characteristics of the landform are to be considered, it hardly seems logical to ignore land use. To avoid this dichotomy other surveyors have attempted to define 'visually self-contained tracts' as the framework for their evaluation, particularly whère landscape has been seen as an important component; but visual tracts are even more difficult to locate than landform tracts and the possibilities for inconsistency are numerous. Obviously the area seen from a high ridge will be vastly different from that seen from a valley floor, and even relatively small movements by a surveyor may greatly affect his field of vision because of intervening obstacles such as shelter belts. In addition, such factors as the surveyor's eyesight, seasonal changes in the landscape and the effect of weather on visibility may all cause variations in the results. The fundamental objection, however, to the use of such tracts is that any one landscape area, however defined, includes a variety of scenery. Furthermore, in attempting to delimit landscape tracts, the surveyor has an unenviable task of interpretation which, in practice, cannot be standardised from individual to individual.

The principal alternative to a geographical or visual unit is a standard geometric unit, usually a grid square. A reticule of these units is usually placed arbitrarily over the area under study, subdividing it into a number of well-defined, equal and regular areas. Jean Forbes (1969), who used grid squares in a study of developable land in the west of Scotland, contended that they had two main advantages when applied to planning:first, the squares permit the easy calculation of densities, and second, such units can be defined in terms of co-ordinates, thus facilitating both statistical analysis and mapping by computer. Moreover, the use of predetermined boundaries of regular units avoids dependence on the surveyor's subjective judgement, makes data collection easier, is independent of administrative changes and facilitates comparison between units and between data sets. It also removes any misapprehension in those who use the classification that the boundaries shown have any precise significance.

Discussion on the correct unit to adopt will inevitably continue, but it is unlikely that the compromise between the two schools of thought suggested by Land Use Consultants (1971) in their proposals to the Countryside Commission for Scotland for the evaluation of Scotland's landscape will be acceptable. They proposed that visually self-contained areas should first be defined and that their boundaries should then be generalised to correspond with one grid squares; data would be collected for a variety of criteria, either for the tract as a whole or for a sample within it. Thus the main advantage of the grid square would be lost as the visual tracts would have first to be defined according to the subjective judgement of the surveyor. The authors of this book believe that the balance of advantage at present remains with the grid square and their studies in central Scotland utilised this unit.

Once it has been decided to use a grid square as the basic unit, it is important to define the dimensions of the squares to be used. Clearly no definitive ruling can be given on this question, for decisions will be affected by local circumstances, the size of the area to be studied, the methods of data collection and the detail required in the final evaluation. Some studies, such as Blacksell's (1971) study of recreation and land use on Dartmoor, have been based on a one-kilometre grid. Those responsible for studies of larger areas have adopted a larger unit; for example, the study of recreation in south-east England (South-East Joint Planning Study, Informal Working Party, 1971), covering the whole of the South-east Economic Planning Region (including Greater London and eleven counties), is based on a five-kilometre grid. The studies in central Scotland, intermediate in scale between these two examples, employed a two-kilometre grid. The decision on unit size remains controversial and must be based on the sensitive judgement of those evaluating a study area.

## TECHNIQUES OF EVALUATION

As all classification procedures should reflect the aims of the assessor, so techniques should be evaluated, not on some constant criteria, but rather by their success in meeting the required objectives. However, there is a danger that, in meeting these objectives, lack of knowledge of the nature of recreation itself and of its relationship to resources may lead to the creation of artificial divisions within a complex system through the examination of individual aspects where, in fact, the interaction of all parts itself has a profound effect. Resources are often seen as identifiable, physical elements, a view that is misleading since it gives the impression that they are necessarily finite (Zobler, 1962). Similarly, preoccupation with physical aspects at the expense of human and cultural factors can prevent a true understanding of the nature of resources in a variety of contexts, including that of outdoor recreation. This limited view of resources leaves the researcher with little to do beyond preparing an inventory of resources able to serve the needs of recreation; such a procedure is not without its merits, but it is unlikely to provide effective measures of extent or capability. The An Foras Forbatha manual (1970), designed to aid planning authorities in Ireland, is based on a comprehensive range of significant items relating to tourism and amenity, arrayed under four broad categories: recreation and tourism; historic, scientific and other cultural values; landscape and the natural environment; and good design in the man-made environment. This technique of inventory-making is inadequate for outdoor recreation, which depends not only on the availability of physical resources but also on their capacity to support recreational activities on a continuing basis. Resource-capability, in the context of outdoor recreation, is dictated by the type of resource in relation to the relevant activities. In this sense, resources are not absolute but dynamic, defined by the nature of the range of possible uses. Recreational resources, therefore, are defined culturally by the nature of activities, although the physical environment will dictate the absolute level of supply. Furthermore, it is important to remember that resources must be continually reassessed in the light of increased knowledge and improved technology and also of changing individual wants and social objectives.

Since resources for recreation are effectively defined as those capable of sustaining recreational activities, the procedure for evaluation should reflect the needs of the community, and several local authorities in Great Britain have attempted to assess rural resources as an aid to the formulation of policies for the future. For example, the Hertfordshire countryside appraisal (Kitching, 1969) aimed at evaluating the visual quality, physical value and accessibility of the countryside in a way that would facilitate comparison between different areas. The countryside was divided into 'visual entities', or areas of single overall character and quality (for example, river valleys or plateaux). Three aspects were considered in the evaluation: (1) visual assessment; (2) leisure assessment; (3) physical assessment. Although the survey has certain operational weaknesses, it does indicate an awareness that recreational resources must be viewed as having several dimensions if future planning is to be effective.

The technique devised and used in the Clyde Sub-Region in Scotland (Scottish Tourist Board, 1970) took this awareness further. The study was undertaken in two phases: the objective of the first was to produce an analysis and inventory of existing recreational facilities in the region, while that of the second was to prepare alternative development strategies. The authors of this report recognised that, in terms of development, it was important to be able to assess the ability of different types of resource to withstand differing intensities of recreational use. They adapted the Outdoor Recreation Resources Review Commission's (1962b) classification to suit conditions in Great Britain and endeavoured to define resources within the following groups (Scottish Tourist Board, 1970, 1.6):

Type A    Developed or proposed resorts: urban, indoor and outdoor recreation resources
Type B    Country Parks and pocket resources: major scenic routes with facilities; linear route resources
Type C    National Water Parks; National Forest Parks and areas of national park-type
Type D    Special Conservation Areas: rural action for conservation
Type E    Wilderness Management Areas
Type F    Heritage Sites
Type G    Transport routes and interchange points
Type H    Economic Activity

This classification of recreational resources in the Clyde makes a distinct advance in that it takes account of the ability of the resources to withstand development; and although it is less general than the American classification from which it is derived, the grouping is still not sufficiently precise to evaluate fully the use of countryside resources for many forms of recreation.

A technique of evaluation suggested by Vedenin and Miroshnichenko (1971), and undertaken for the whole of the U.S.S.R., represents further development; it not only takes account of the ability of resources to withstand development, but also identifies natural factors that favour or hinder the organisation of large recreational zones both for summer and winter. For each 'natural province' of the U.S.S.R. the selected climatic and physiographic factors were evaluated on a five-point scale. The grades were then combined to produce 'environment evaluation maps' for summer and winter recreation and tourism; the maps, based on earlier research that emphasised differences in the significance of particular natural factors for recreational purposes, indicate large regions of the U.S.S.R. that are suitable for prolonged recreation (Lopatina and Nazarevskiy, 1967).

The Canada Land Inventory (1969), which began in 1963, represents a more functional appraisal of the recreational potential of countryside resources. Des-pite its title, it is in fact, a comprehensive survey of land capability and use, des-igned to provide a basis for resource and land-use planning at the municipal, provincial and federal levels of government. It provides land capability maps of four alternative uses (agriculture, forestry, recreation and wild life) for the settled parts of the provinces of Canada. The vast amount of information collected re-quired computer methods for data storage and mapping and these in turn offered compactness and consciseness, thereby facilitating comparison both within and between the four sectors, correlation of socio-economic or other data for selected areas, and analyses in map or statistical form. The land's suitability for recreation was determined by acquiring a reliable estimate of the quality, quantity, type and distribution of outdoor recreation resources. The basis of the classification is the quantity of recreation that may be generated and sustained per unit area of land per year under perfect market conditions; that is, a high class unit has a very high index of attraction in terms of popular preferences and a 'use tolerance' which permits intensive use without undue degradation of the resource. Although the form of the classification used may be criticised, it is apparent that the Canada Land Inventory is more than a simple listing of countryside resources. Rather it attempts to provide an assessment of the ability of resources, not only to withstand use, but also to sustain recreational or other activities over time; indeed, a similar approach underlies the technique utilised in the studies of central Scotland.

The use of sieve maps has provided another step forward in the evaluation of recreational resources. A good example is provided by Forbes' (1969) study of the supply of potentially developable land in the west of Scotland, in which areal data were collected for one-kilometre grid squares. A series of maps was prepared for different criteria and, by overlaying these maps (or surfaces), potential re-sources could be highlighted and different development strategies assessed by combining a series of surfaces for individual factors (for example, measures of land use, access, landscape value and provision of services), thus permitting the impli-cations for planning and development to emerge.

Recent recreational studies have adopted a similar approach, for example, the development-potential technique (Coventry County Council, Solihull Borough Council, Warwickshire County Council, 1971), the potential surface technique (Standing Conference on Regional Planning in South Wales and Monmouthshire, 1971) and potential surface analysis (Zetter and Benyon, 1971). In the Coventry-

Solihull–Warwickshire Study, ten different 'factor surfaces' were compiled to generate alternative strategies for the sub-region covering all aspects of development. The statistics for each surface were then weighted to provide a composite potential surface. In all, forty-two such surfaces were produced (combining the ten elements in different ways), and these were then considered in devising a preferred development strategy. In this example, the technique was designed to deal not only with recreation but also with other elements in planning and has mainly been used in this broader planning context. The Standing Conference on Regional Planning in South Wales and Monmouthshire, on the other hand, used potential surfaces to develop a strategy for informal recreation in the countryside (Standing Conference on Regional Planning in South Wales and Monmouthshire. 1973, chapter 5). When devising their strategy the Standing Conference defined two main goals:

(1)    to minimise harm to the landscape and to the architectural, archaeological, historic, scientific or educational interest of the region;
(2)    to maximise opportunities for informal recreation in the countryside and, as far as natural resources permit, to provide similar opportunities in number, type and convenience for everybody.

In order to achieve these two general goals, six specific objectives were defined against which alternative strategies could be assessed. Seven non-recreational objectives were also defined, on the grounds that it would have been unrealistic to produce a strategy for recreational development without reference to non-recreational objectives; these other areas of investigation were: (1) nature conservation; (2) landscape conservation; (3) minerals; (4) agriculture; (5) forestry; (6) residential development; (7) industrial development. The Standing Conference devised four indices to define the recreational potential of the study area:

(1)    the catchment population of a given recreational site;
(2)    the ease of access from a defined road network;
(3)    the spatial distribution and quantification of notable countryside features, namely, the coast, dunes, deciduous and coniferous woodlands, rivers, lakes and canals, available relief, conservation areas, listed buildings and other special attractions;
(4)    the degree to which these combine in a given spatial unit (one-kilometre grid square) to produce an attractive and varied potential recreational environment.

These indices were then combined in six ways using various weightings to produce 'preferred' strategies. The potential surface technique permits a full description of the various resources likely to affect the development and the distribution of rural recreational facilities to be brought together in a unified whole, but it is open to one fundamental criticism: although it permits the ready and speedy integration of numerous factors, it combines not only a potential analysis of resources but also the constraints on their development. For example, factors of accessibility are themselves subject to marked changes (for example, the opening of motorways or the closures of railway lines) and integrating them with the primary assessment will require constant updating and reformulation of the procedure of assessment.

The authors of this book would argue that a more appropriate formulation of development strategy would arise from a primary evaluation of potential resources before present (possibly temporary) links are considered.

Whereas previous techniques for assessing recreational resources had been designed to evaluate specifically defined alternatives for development, the potential surface technique can take full account of the multiple uses of different resources and has therefore been particularly welcomed by planners because it allows them to generate alternative strategies. In this way it forms an important link in the conventional planning process by providing a systematic means of progress from survey to recommended plan.

## RECREATION ENVIRONMENTS IN CENTRAL SCOTLAND

The technique of resource evaluation used as part of the investigations in central Scotland was similarly linked to the planning processes that arose from the Countryside (Scotland) Act, 1967. These assessments, undertaken as part of recreation surveys in Lanarkshire and Greater Edinburgh, were constrained by the small budget available for surveys of areas covering 1 241 759 acres (502 522 ha) and were, therefore, primarily desk studies, amplified by field work where this seemed necessary. The aim was to identify 'recreation environments', areas intermediate in scale between the local and regional, with a similar capacity to support various forms of outdoor recreation on a continuing basis. The results were intended to provide the sponsoring local authorities with a broad comparative evaluation of the study area and were not a plan for outdoor recreation, although, on the basis of this assessment and other surveys, recommendations were made and those for Lanarkshire accepted by the local planning authority.

Recreation environments were identified on the basis of the functional connections between different recreational activities, that is, the significance of any one activity depends on its relationship with others, in terms of both the resources it uses and the kind of participants. Experience in the field and evidence from local planning authorities, clubs and associations concerned with outdoor recreation, has confirmed the range and interdependence of the various activities supported by the countryside, for an area seldom supports only one kind of recreation and complex relationships exist between recreation and other land uses.

In view of these considerations, it is more realistic to consider activities not singly, but in groups. This approach, which is based on the premise that, in outdoor recreation, the 'whole is greater than the sum of the parts', is better suited to observed reality and conforms to planning concepts, particularly that of the Country Park as outlined in the Countryside (Scotland) Act and amplified in an information sheet (Countryside Commission for Scotland, 1973). It is clear that conscious efforts will be made to provide facilities within such parks for a range of pursuits, formal and informal, active and passive. The identification of recreation environments will thus assist the choice of suitable areas for Country Parks, particularly where cells of high recreational potential are juxtaposed. In addition, the concept of recreation environments can play an important role in conserving the countryside itself; for recreational developments grouped into specific areas would be more amenable to planning control, thus lessening the risk of indiscriminate, haphazard and possibly harmful use of the countryside.

The method adopted was to make four separate, independent assessments of the components of land capability for outdoor recreation, and then to combine these into one single assessment. The four categories selected were: suitability for land-based recreation, suitability for water-based recreation, scenic quality and ecological significance. The basic spatial unit for all assessments was a two-kilometre square of the National Grid, and a total of 1312 such squares covered the area. This choice was in part conditioned by the size of the area to be studied and the degree of resolution that was thought desirable, and partly by the meagre financial resources that were available for the assessment.

The distinctive feature of the technique was that it sought to identify those resources with suitable potential for recreation, and contemporary constraints on the realisation of this potential therefore were not considered at this stage. Recreational activities may make a variety of physical demands on the environment. As chapter 1 has shown, these demands are essentially static, except in so far as the characteristics of recreational activities themselves are subject to change, when it can be argued that, rather than the old activity changing, a new, albeit related, activity has been created. This relatively stable relationship between activities and land and water resources provided the basis for the first stage of evaluation. The aim was to locate and identify areas that, because of their physical characteristics, were suitable for recreational activities; the areal extent and distribution of these resources would be an indication of the countryside's potential for outdoor recreation. Clearly, the proportion of these potential resources suitable for recreation at any given time would vary with the dynamic characteristics of activities and their participants; but, by identifying potential resources, it was hoped to provide a stable basis for comparison of changes over time. Moreover, the ability to compare present use and potential supply of resources would provide a useful tool for those responsible for the development and planning of recreational facilities.

Another major aim of the method of assessment was to identify resources that could support each activity both now and in the long term. The measure was, therefore, not one of minimum requirements but of a level at which development would warrant the involvement of local authority planners. The standards used were determined subjectively, but they were based on the results of a questionnaire survey of the national bodies concerned and of every relevant club and association in the study area, and on an assessment of the physical characteristics of the facilities used by these clubs.

## Suitability for Land-Based Recreation

Any comprehensive analysis of resources for recreation must include an assessment of capability to support recreational activities. It has been demonstrated that, although recreational activities on land and water are undertaken by relatively few people, they can make demands on resources that are quite disproportionate to the numbers of participants involved. In addition, participation rates are not necessarily a true reflection of general interest, for large numbers may attend as spectators. Furthermore, as was suggested in the previous chapter, low levels of participation in some activities may not continue, for levels of demand are generally rising and changes in relative importance may occur.

This analysis of capability to support active recreation was divided into separate assessments for land-based activities and water-based activities. Such a division rests not only on distinct differences in the resources used but also on contrasting features of the activities themselves. Nine kinds of land-based recreation were considered in the first stage of this assessment: camping, caravanning, picnicking, pony-trekking, walking, hiking, game-shooting, rock-climbing and skiing. It was recognised that many forms of outdoor recreation were excluded from consideration, but these were either user-oriented, such as golf, or the concern of a small minority of recreationists, for example scrambling, or made demands on resources similar to one of the nine chosen, for example, orienteering. These activities were then grouped into six sets of activities with similar characteristics and, for each of these, several criteria were identified which indicated levels at which recreational development would be warranted; if these criteria were satisfied within a square, a point was scored for that square, so that a maximum of six points could be recorded in any square. The criteria used were:

(1) Camping, caravanning and picnicking: all countryside within 1220 ft (400 m) of a metalled road.
(2) Pony-trekking: all upland areas above 985 ft (300 m) in altitude and with rights of way, or established footpaths and bridleways.
(3) Walking and hiking: all upland areas above 1475 ft (450 m) with rights of way, or established footpaths and bridleways.
(4) Game-shooting: all areas assessed as shooting on valuation rolls.
(5) Rock-climbing: all cliff faces over 99 ft (30 m) in height.
(6) Skiing: available relief of over 915 ft (280 m) with an average snowholding period of more than three months.

For all activities suitability was judged in relation to present accessibility and without regard for rights of access. These criteria are admittedly arbitrary, but they were devised from the known characteristics of the different activities and after consultation with experts in the different fields. Their range was restricted to enable scores to be established by inspection of maps and aerial photographs, supplemented where necessary by field observation. The least satisfactory criterion is probably that for shooting, partly because only rateable shootings (that is, mainly game shootings) were considered and these generally provided an assessment of present rather than potential use. Unfortunately, no method of estimating shooting potential was readily available, though it can be argued that the potential for expanding this kind of recreation lies in better management of areas already used in this way rather than in the identification of new areas.

Figure 6.1 shows the distribution of squares shaded according to their scores and has been produced by computer, as have other maps in this chapter, using the CAMAP program devised at Edinburgh University by J. McG. Hotson. CAMAP is a system of automated cartography which uses a lineprinter attached to computers as standard equipment for printing the results of compilations, and is particularly suitable when areal data are to be represented, especially if these have been assembled by squares.

It is clear from figure 6.1 that land resources for outdoor recreation provide two contrasting recreational environments, upland and lowland. The uplands are

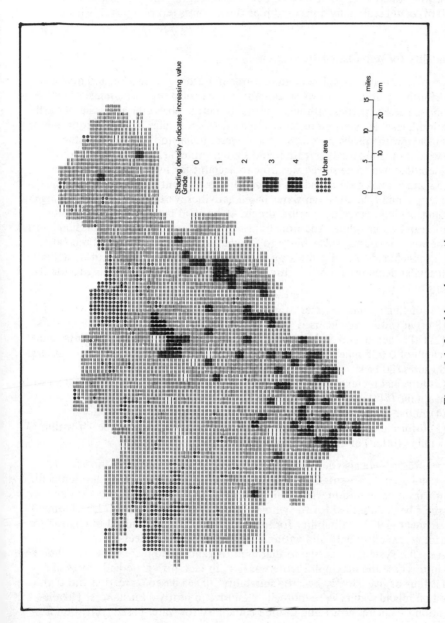

Figure 6.1 Land-based recreation

generally able to support a wider range of activities than the lowlands, since there
is less conflict with other land uses than in the more intensively used lowlands;
thus, when areas were graded for land-based recreation, those below 1000 ft
(300 m) could score only a maximum of three points out of a possible total of
six.

## Suitability for Water-based Recreation

Water plays a major, possibly dominant role in outdoor recreation and not only
contributes significantly to visual amenity but can also support a range of active
pursuits. These activities, although quite different in character and scale of participation, make demands on resources that are often similar in scale. From this
point of view the problems of assessment were similar to those faced in the
assessment of land-based recreation and similar principles were applied. Another
problem that had to be solved was how to account for the differing character of
inland and coastal waters, and the criteria for assessment were chosen with this
problem in mind. In all, seven water-based activities were identified: swimming and
bathing, angling, canoeing, rowing, dinghy-sailing and pleasure-boating, motor-
boating and water-skiing. Additionally, since water acts as the focus of many visits
to the coast or countryside, ability to attract water-oriented informal recreation
was also included. As with the assessment of land-based recreation those activities
with similar demands in both nature and scale were grouped according to the following criteria:

(1) Angling on inland water: unpolluted rivers, streams and canals over 26 ft
(8 m) in width and enclosed water bodies over 12·4 acres (5 ha) in area.
(2) Other active pursuits on inland water: unpolluted waters with a minimum
length of 0·625 mile (1 km) and width of $\frac{1}{8}$ mile (200 m) or an area of at least
50 acres (20 ha).
(3) Informal recreation oriented towards inland waters: unpolluted waters within $\frac{1}{4}$ mile (400 m) of a metalled road.
(4) Active sea-based pursuits: the presence of coastline.
(5) Informal recreation oriented to the coast: sandy or shingle beach within
$\frac{1}{4}$ mile (400 m) of a metalled road.

These criteria were also devised after consultation with experts in the various
fields and again represented the requirements necessary to warrant development.
Information on pollution was obtained from the river purification boards and
has since been published for the whole of Scotland by the Scottish Development
Department (1972). Suitability for informal recreation was judged in relation to
present accessibility only and without regard for rights of access.
    A similar system of scoring to that used for land-based recreation was employed,
but in this case the maximum score was five. In fact, no square had scores of
either four or five, chiefly because suitability for sea-based recreation and that
based on inland waters were mutually exclusive in nearly all instances. The distribution of squares according to their suitability for water-based recreation is
inevitably very different from that shown in figure 6.1 for many squares contain
no water and no points (figure 6.2). The distribution of squares is essentially
linear, picking out the main river systems and the coast, although there are

Figure 6.2 Water-based recreation

noticeable gaps in North Lanarkshire, reflecting the urbanised and industrial nature of that area. The highest values are in squares containing major bodies of inland water, all of which are reservoirs. This fact highlights the nature of the assessment, which is concerned solely with suitability, for these areas would rank low with respect to present use because it is generally the policy of water authorities in Scotland to forbid water sports other than angling on direct supply reservoirs under their control.

## Scenery

Although the methods and criteria used to assess the ability of the countryside to support active recreation may, and indeed should, be criticised, it is unlikely that any critic would dispute the necessity of including such assessments in any scheme for the identification of areas suitable for outdoor recreation. The inclusion of scenery, on the other hand, is more debatable, for the assumption is made that it is the principal resource in the countryside for informal outdoor recreation. What is not in doubt is that informal recreation, particularly the drive into the countryside or to the coast, is overwhelmingly the most important form of outdoor recreation, at least judged by the number of participants and the frequency of their trips (British Travel Association–University of Keele, 1967; chapter 2 of present volume). All active forms of recreation are undertaken by minorities and, although these proportions are likely to change with rising levels of education and affluence, the dominance of passive recreation, confirmed by all surveys undertaken in Great Britain, seems likely to persist for the foreseeable future. There is, therefore, a strong case for giving particular weight to informal passive recreation in any assessment of suitability. Some consideration has already been given to aspects of informal recreation by the inclusion of picnic sites and of accessible coastline and water bodies in the assessments of land- and water-based recreation, but the weight given to scenery in this method for assessment accords with the Countryside Commission's decision on its priorities, namely, that the appearance and perception of landscape is the most important common denominator in the public enjoyment of countryside (Select Committee on Scottish Affairs, 1972). This view receives some confirmation from the household surveys of recreational demand conducted in conjunction with this assessment, in that 'countryside' and 'coast' were the kinds of place that 80·9 per cent of respondents liked to visit on a day out; but it is important to recognise that it is an assumption that has not been tested adequately (chapter 3). The assessment of scenic quality is in its infancy, though several approaches have been suggested and tested. These range from wholly subjective judgements, as in Murray's *Highland Landscape* (1962), through the matching of photographs of views against an international scale (Fines, 1968), to the prescription of sets of criteria—the approach employed here. The choice was again determined in part by the limited financial resources available, but the major reason was the success of D.L. Linton's (1968) classification of Scottish scenery. His method has been adapted for this assessment. The main modifications are that, whereas Linton identified tracts, used a system of scoring and drew on very extensive first-hand knowledge of Scottish scenery to moderate judgements where they appeared inappropriate, this assessment is based on a simple ranking of each grid square and has relied entirely on the prescribed criteria.

113

Figure 6.3 Scenery

Linton identified two elements in the scenic resources of any area: 'One is the form of the ground, not as defined by the contour of the topographic surveyor, but rather by the landform categories of the geomorphologist. The other is the mantle of forests and moorlands, farms and factories, natural vegetation and human arti-facts, by which the hard rock body of the landscape is clothed' (Linton, 1968, p. 223). To these elements he gave the names 'landform' and 'land-use' landscapes, terms that have been retained in this assessment.

## Landform Landscapes

Two criteria are used in the ranking of landform landscapes, absolute relief (the maximum height above sea level) and relative relief (the difference in altitude between the highest and lowest points in each square), and these have been com-bined to identify six classes of landform, which have been ranked according to a subjective judgement of scenic attractiveness, particular weight being given to boldness and contrast of relief (see figure 6.3). In ascending order of importance, these are:

(1) Lowlands: below 500 ft (150 m) in height.
(2) Rolling countryside: between 500 ft (150 m) and 1500 ft (450 m) in height, with available relief of less than 400 ft (120 m).
(3) Upland plateau: exceeding 1500 ft (450 m) in height, but with less than 400 ft (120 m) available relief.
(4) Hill country: either between 500 ft (150 m) and 1500 ft (450 m) in height and with available relief exceeding 400 ft (120 m), or between 500 ft (150 m) and 2000 ft (600 m), with available relief between 400 ft (120 m) and 800 ft (250 m).
(5) Bold hills: either exceeding 2000 ft (600 m) in height, with an available relief of between 400 ft (120 m) and 800 ft (250 m) or between 1500 ft (450 m) and 200 ft (60 m), with available relief exceeding 600 ft (180 m).
(6) High hills: exceeding 2000 ft (600 m) in height and with more than 800 ft (250 m) of available relief.

These classes were given ranks from 0 (lowlands) to 5 (high hills). Linton's system included two other categories (low uplands and mountains), but they were not included in this classification.

## Land-use Landscapes

Land-use landscapes were similarly divided into six categories and also ranked in ascending order of their contribution to scenic quality. This assessment was based on two untested but plausible assumptions: that people prefer 'natural' or 'semi-natural' landscapes to those where man's influence is more evident, and that diversity of use is more attractive than uniformity. These judgements in Linton's view are 'not so much personal as the judgements of our own society in a particular day and age' (1968, p. 230). Diversity was measured by a statistical technique involving the computation of least squares (Weaver, 1954; Thomas, 1963), so that the decision on diversity is made objectively. Those squares in which only one use is identified by this method are first ranked, and the squares in which two or three of the categories, improved farmland (crops and grass), moorland and woodland, are identified (that is, diverse landscapes), are ranked above them. The highest category is represented by those squares where there is a sufficient area of inland water for this to appear as a significant element (as measured by the least squares method). The six categories in ascending order of importance are:

(1) Urban areas: all built-up land and land within 1 mile (1·5 km) of such land—that is, the urban shadow zone.
(2) Agricultural land: crops and grass are the dominant use and no other use is significant.
(3) Woodland: woodland is the dominant use and no other use is significant.
(4) Moorland: moorland is the dominant use and no other use is significant.
(5) Diversified use: at least two of the categories, crops and grass, woodland and moorland, make significant contributions.
(6) Water: squares where water makes a significant contribution.

As with landform landscapes, these ranks are equated with scores from 0 (urban) to 5 (water).

These two aspects of landscape were then synthesised by adding the rank scores for landform and land-use landscapes to achieve scores on a scale from 0 to 10, and then dividing these into five classes of scenery. The contrasts that emerge in figure 6.3 confirm the underlying validity of the hypotheses adopted, with the striking scenic contrasts of east central Scotland clearly evident; the Pentland Hills are a conspicuous feature of the map, while the lower grades of scenery are to be found in the north and west of the study area reflecting an association of mainly low relief and diversified agricultural landscapes. The most extensive areas in the higher grades are to be found where high ground coincides with diverse land use. Parts of the coast are rated relatively high, as are isolated hill features that interrupt the uniformity of the agricultural lowlands.

## Ecological Significance

The inclusion of a fourth element in the assessment of recreational resources, ecological significance, is the most contentious and has been the subject of considerable debate among members of the research team that carried out the Edinburgh and Lanark surveys. The justification for including this element is that areas of high ecological significance represent part of the attraction of the countryside, as is shown by the increasing numbers of visitors to nature reserves and the growing interest in activities such as natural history.

The method used was adapted from one devised by D.R. Helliwell for the rapid assessment of the conservation value of large areas. No attempt was made by Helliwell to assess the quality of individual plant communities; instead, he relied on the diversity of habitats and ranked these in order of biological richness, his scoring reflecting 'the consensus of opinion among a number of conservation staff [of the Nature Conservancy] as to the relative weighting to be given to the different habitat types' (1969). In this assessment the basic unit and the various types of habitat were simplified so that they could readily be identified from the available information. Seven types were recognised: water, broad-leaved woodland, marsh or bog, dunes, moorland, coniferous woodland and improved farmland. These were ranked according to the following rules, though an exception was made in respect of any square that contained a nature reserve or Site of Special Scientific Interest (S.S.S.I.), for this was automatically placed in the highest class. Five grades of habitat were identified, in order of ascending ecological significance:

(1) Grade 0: urban areas, with no other habitat occupying 10 per cent of each square.
(2) Grade 1: improved agricultural land accounting for at least 10 per cent of each square.
(3) Grade 2: over 10 per cent of each square in either moorland or coniferous woodland.
(4) Grade 3: over 10 per cent of each square in either broad-leaved woodland, or marsh or bog, or dunes or water.
(5) Grade 4: over 10 per cent of each square in any two of broad-leaved woodland, marsh or bog, dunes and water.

Clearly squares could be classified under a number of grades and each was given the highest possible score.

The resulting map provides a relative grading of ecological habitats (figure 6.4). It is more fragmented than those of the previous three assessments, a feature that is partly due to the widespread scatter of S.S.S.I.s.

## Recreation Environments

These four assessments were then synthesised to identify recreation environments. Each assessment was given the same weight, 100, representing the highest score that could be (but rarely was) attained. There was thus a theoretical maximum of 400 points, but this was nowhere approached, and any score exceeding 250 represents an area with a high capacity to support outdoor recreation on a continuing basis. Areas with a score of less than 100 have only a very limited capacity for outdoor recreation as defined in this survey, though they might be suitable for user-oriented activities that are not very exacting in their physical requirements. It will be noted that urban areas were given a score of zero and the remaining scores were then divided into five grades.

Figure 6.5 shows the quality and distribution of recreation environments in the study area; although the assessment of recreational resources undertaken in this way does not provide a plan for their development, it does provide a systematic and objective assessment of resource potential, which can then be used as the necessary foundation for a development strategy.

Clearly the system adopted has weaknesses and these centre largely around the criteria of evaluation and the way in which they have been related. Because of the limited evidence available at present, it was inevitable that the individual surfaces themselves, and the detailed criteria used, should have been chosen somewhat

117

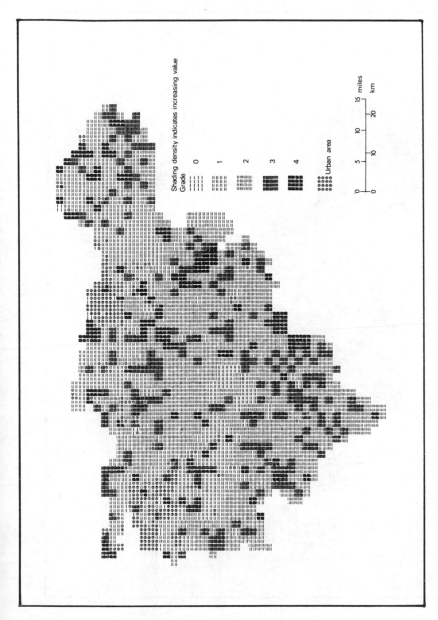

Figure 6.4 Ecological habitats

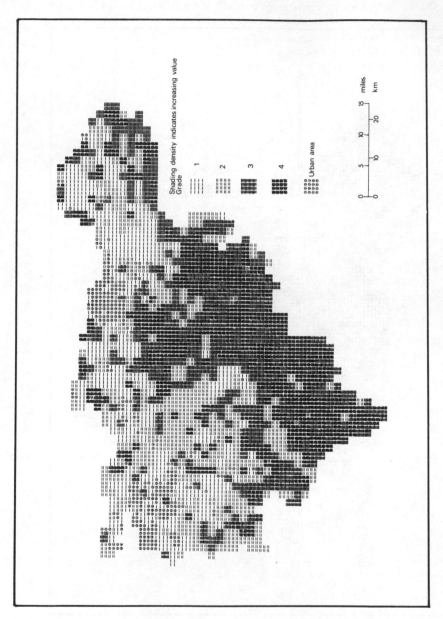

Figure 6.5 Recreation environments

arbitrarily, although it can be claimed that, while selection was subjective, it was objectively derived from such evidence as was available. A further criticism could be that the system makes no attempt to assess the relative contribution of the individual surfaces to the countryside's capability to support recreation. As a consequence, inevitable distortions have occurred; for example, it could be argued that the failure to weight criteria has allowed active sporting and minority uses of the countryside to make a disproportionate contribution to the final index of recreation environments. It is appropriate in this connection to recall Jean Forbes' comments on the effects of similar weaknesses in her own work: 'The map is only as valid as the premises built into it and as secure as the input data from which it was derived' (1969, p. 194).

## THE FUTURE

This procedure for assessing the recreational potential of countryside resources in Lanarkshire and Greater Edinburgh has inevitably been experimental, for it represented one of the first attempts to evaluate comprehensively and systematically any large tract of Great Britain for this purpose. Many of its deficiencies, particularly those arising from the necessity of devising what was in essence a desk study, were due to very limited financial resources. Yet there are more fundamental difficulties. Research is urgently needed to identify much more precisely the space standards and other resource requirements of the different kinds of outdoor recreation, to test the reactions of visitors to different landscapes and to assess the extent to which the quality of scenery, however measured, is a major factor in the location of passive, informal recreation.

Both the values given to some of the elements and the choice of activities included in the assessments are debatable. It could be argued, for example, that ancient monuments and other features that attract visitors to the countryside should have been included in the scenic assessment as specific foci of attraction. It might also have been desirable to have incorporated other forms of outdoor recreation — for example, those that are user-oriented. But the limited knowledge available at the time made inevitable a somewhat arbitrary choice of the components of the classification and of the detailed criteria, although it was made in good faith on the basis of available evidence. The decision to give equal weight to the four assessments and to the individual components could also be challenged, but it seemed logical in the absence of any firm evidence to the contrary. Any subsequent evaluations can profit from this and other experience, and their organisers should seek in advance some more firmly based indicators of the values that should be attached.

It is also important to stress that, although significant in its own right, this evaluation of the recreational potential of resources was only one stage in the formulation of a regional strategy for recreational development. The procedure for assessment fulfils the first objective, namely, that of providing a comparative evaluation of resources by which it would be possible to locate and identify all areas suitable for recreational activities on the basis of their physical characteristics.

To make the transition from evaluation to the second stage of formulating a strategy for development, the research team was aided by the fact that all material was suitable for handling by computer and could be analysed by means of a computer mapping system. Nevertheless, the selection of criteria by which a more detailed classification can be made of the potential resources that have been identified at the first stage is even more difficult, for such criteria will often be subjective and are as likely to change as the human values from which they are derived. Furthermore, developmental strategy will be influenced by factors of regional and local significance — for instance, the distance between resources and urban centres, the network of roads, the pattern of land ownership and the policies of water boards and other major resource owners. It is also necessary to consider recreational development alongside other priorities, such as new industry, housing and shopping facilities, and other claimants for land, notably those with interests in agriculture, forestry or water supply. In addition, there are factors of a more local kind, such as land ownership, availability of local finance and the infra-structure of communications and other services that are relevant to those with responsibility for planning outdoor recreation, although their relative import-ance may change with time.

The programme of development by which the potential of countryside resources is released for recreational use, will also be governed by developments in the recreational field itself. In the period of the 'leisure revolution' changing levels of participation in outdoor recreation will affect the quantity of resources that will be needed, although the scale of participation in outdoor recreation is only one of the factors influencing the choice of resources to be made available for development; others include the character of participants, the nature of the resources used and the spatial relationships between recreationists and resources. Inevitably, relative accessibility to centres of population will play a major part in determining whether or not the potential of a resource is ever realised. As chapter 9 shows, research in central Scotland has proved that there are distinct and constant relationships in recreational travel between the user and his resource, and that this is true not only of active pursuits but also of informal and passive recreation.

It is at this second stage of resource assessment that management constraints can be incorporated into the evaluation of resources. It may, for example, be appropriate to include the negative attitude of Scottish water authorities as a factor, or to take account of the changing policies of the Forestry Commission towards the recreational use of their woodlands. Similarly, it would be possible to devise management policies based on the argument that areas of high ecological significance should be protected against recreational development and so should have a negative score. The effect of treating ecological significance as a negative factor, so that areas of high ecological value are ranked low as recreation environ-ments, is shown in figure 6.6. Other possibilities would be to change the weighting of the different elements in the assessment as more accurate and reliable information on the relevant importance of different recreation pursuits becomes available. In this way, the computer provides a flexible tool by which to model a range of alternatives, and the technique is ideally suited to this field of study where the variables are so closely interrelated, although much work remains to be done on the development of this tool. This technique of environmental mapping has

Shading density indicates increasing value
ecological evaluation scored negative

Grade

1
2
3
4

Urban area

15 miles
20 km

0   5   10   15
0   10   20

Figure 6.6  Recreation environments: ecological factor negative

recently been used in a closely related field in an attempt to define possible
locations for an open-air museum in Scotland (Coppock, 1973b). On the assumptions that certain resources would provide the most suitable locations and that
the relationships to centres of population could be specified, it was possible to
obtain a broad indication of areas where a further search for a suitable site would
be justified.

Despite its admitted deficiencies, this assessment of physical potential offers a
sounder basis for recreational planning than wholly subjective assessments. Furthermore, the method has the added advantage that, since the steps are clearly identified and the original data retained, any evaluation can easily be modified as and
when firmer guide lines become available. The techniques devised also permit the
data to be used and manipulated to indicate appropriate development strategies
in the light of known or specified constraints. The exploitation of these techniques
is still in its infancy, but there can be little doubt that they constitute a powerful
tool both for the scholar investigating the use of physical resources and for the
planner whose aim is the wise use of those resources.

# 7 Government Policies and the Attitudes of Other Land Users

The previous chapter focused attention on the potential resources of the country-side. Whether these are in fact so used will depend both on their accessibility from large centres of population and the awareness of potential users of the existence of such resources, and also on the attitudes and decisions of those who own or other-wise control the use of land. This latter consideration is of special significance in Great Britain where there is relatively little publicly-owned or managed land available for outdoor recreation, and where much recreation in the countryside consequently takes place, with or without permission, on private land used pri-marily for other purposes. Much recreation is thus, in a sense, parasitic on pro-ductive uses of the countryside, especially farming and forestry. These attitudes are in part shaped by public policies, and government agencies, both national and local, have an increasingly important role to play in providing recreational oppor-tunities for members of the public on land they control. Unfortunately, although there is pioneer work, especially in North America, on perceptions and attitudes, little systematic work has been done in Great Britain or elsewhere on the attitudes of those who determine policies for the recreational use of land, whether publicly or privately owned. Nor is it easy to assemble these policies partly because of the range of official agencies involved and the frequent lack of explicit information. This chapter will attempt to review what is known, in the context of Great Britain, about the nature of public policies that bear on the recreational use of land and of the attitudes of owners and occupiers towards the recreational use of land they control.

The ratio of man to land in Great Britain is one of the least favourable of all the developed countries and is worsening as the population grows and the proportion of land devoted to rural uses declines. As a result, virtually all land is used (at least nominally) for some purpose and, unlike North America, there are not vast areas of public land which have been little modified by human activity and are available or potentially available for outdoor recreation. Moreover, rising values for urban land are likely to result in much new recreational space being found beyond the urban fence, a move away from parks embedded in towns to the towns embedded in parkland (Dower, 1965). The growing number of outdoor recreationists must therefore be accommodated either on land acquired from other users or on land used primarily for other purposes. The balance between these alternatives will largely depend on public policies and on the attitudes of both public and private landholders.

## GOVERNMENT POLICY ON THE COUNTRYSIDE

Understandably, there is no single policy for the countryside, but rather a collection of policies, devised by the various agencies of central government with responsibilities for different sectors of the rural economy. In an ideal world these plans and policies would be comprehensive and mutually compatible, but in practice they are not; there are gaps, as with field sports, which are the responsibility of no agency, and inconsistencies, as where the agricultural departments provide grants for the improvement of heather moor, which those agencies responsible for tourism and informal outdoor recreation would prefer to retain (Select Committee on Scottish Affairs, 1972, 3, 422; hereafter referred to as Select Committee, 1972). Specific policies for recreation in the countryside first appeared in the National Parks and Access to the Countryside Act of 1949, which established an official agency, the National Parks Commission, with responsibilities in this field; but other government policies may have effects on outdoor recreation that were not specifically intended or are a by-product of the attainment of some other objective. For example, it is by no means clear whether the tax reliefs given to owners of private woodlands in the late 1940s were intended to promote the large increase of afforestation by investment groups that took place in the 1960s (which some critics regard as adversely affecting amenity), or whether the decision to construct the M6 motorway was in any way influenced by the potential recreational consequences for the Lake District and south Scotland. Although the Countryside Acts, under which the Countryside Commission (with responsibility for England and Wales) and the Countryside Commission for Scotland were established, contain clauses requiring public bodies, in the execution of their duties, 'to have regard for the desirability of conserving the natural beauty and amenity of the countryside', there is evidence that this injunction is generally regarded as purely exhortatory and does not greatly influence the policies of other departments or their implementation outside areas of statutory control (Select Committee, 1972, 3, 529). While the government has a general policy of encouraging the use of the countryside for outdoor recreation, public bodies outside the recreational sector may also affect the attractiveness of the countryside to recreationists, the ease with which potential areas for recreation can be reached, and the willingness or otherwise of those who occupy private land to encourage, allow or even tolerate recreational use of their land.

## LOCAL AUTHORITY PLANNING

If there is no national plan, and often no clear national policy for the countryside, there are at least local plans and policies. Since the Town and Country Planning Acts of 1947 and 1948, it has been the responsibility of local planning authorities to prepare 'development plans' showing how they propose that the land in their area of jurisdiction (whether administrative county, county borough or large burgh) should be used, and to exercise control over changes of use through the granting of planning consent, generally in conformity with such plans. There can be no doubt that such powers have affected the recreational use of the countryside, especially by constraining urban expansion and by preventing the building of dwellings in the countryside, whether for permanent occupation or as second homes; the contrast in this latter respect between Great Britain and continental Europe (notably France and Scandinavia) and North America, where holiday homes and summer cottages are widespread, is striking. Nevertheless, there have been notable imperfections in such planning, particularly its urban orientation (understandable in the light of its origins) and its negative character; for planning has been much better at preventing undesirable developments occurring than in promoting those which are desirable. Furthermore, the two major uses of the countryside, agriculture and forestry, are exempted from planning control, as are, in effect, those recreational developments that are ancillary to other uses and do not require structures of any kind. Indeed, until the 1960s, outdoor recreation did not have a significant part in statutory planning over large parts of the countryside.

The major exception to this statement was in respect of the conservation of visual amenity, whether in the National Parks and Areas of Outstanding Natural Beauty, which were designated in England and Wales under the National Parks and Access to the Countryside Act, or in the National Park Direction Areas in Scotland, designated under the Town and Country Planning General Development (Scotland) Order 1948 (see figure 7.1). In the ten National Parks, which are located mainly in the uplands and cover some 5000 square miles (12 950 km$^2$), or nearly 10 per cent of England and Wales, there are rather stricter controls over development and limited powers to enhance amenity; Areas of Outstanding Natural Beauty, numbering 28 and covering more that 4500 square miles (11 655 km$^2$), tend to be smaller and to include a higher proportion of improved farm land. Together they identify the most attractive countryside in England and Wales and so, on the reasoning of chapter 6, those areas potentially most attractive for informal outdoor recreation. Other areas have been designated as Areas of Great Landscape Value on county development plans, but the criteria for doing so have been variable and the additional protection afforded the landscape by such designation has been of limited value. The five National Park Direction Areas in Scotland were those suggested by the National Parks Committee; they cover 1530 square miles (3960 km$^2$) and it can be argued that they provide a better protection for Scotland's finest scenery than does designation as a National Park in England and Wales, since all proposals for development must be referred to the Secretary of State. Areas of Great Landscape Value have also been identified in Scotland, though the criteria for their selection seem to have been even more variable (Coppock, 1968). Although not intended to preserve amenity as such, the Green Belts designated around London and recognised, since 1955, around other major cities, can be regarded as contributing in a lesser way to the conservation of visual amenity in those areas where recreational pressures are greatest.

The recognition of such areas of fine scenery has been made on the basis of informed opinion rather than of objective survey, and it is interesting to compare those chosen in Scotland with Linton's (1968) assessment of scenic quality. Their designation constitutes one element in a recreational strategy for the whole country, although, owing to the fact that the National Parks Commission's remit did not extend to Scotland, the formulation of a comprehensive strategy for Scotland is still in an early stage (Select Committee, 1972, 5, 54-7). Yet, while the National Parks and Access to the Countryside Act was also concerned with the promotion of public enjoyment of the countryside, neither the National Parks

Commission nor the local planning authorities had any power to promote such enjoyment outside National Parks, and little was done within them. It is only since the Countryside Acts that more comprehensive national strategies for recreation have begun to emerge; but there are still notable gaps, as with second homes, on which the Countryside Commission has received recommendations on the policies that might be adopted (Downing and Dower, 1973). Even before 1967, local authorities in Scotland had been instructed to make proposals for tourist development and, under the stimulus of the Countryside Acts, local authorities had begun to prepare recreational strategies for the countryside, though many have not yet done so and the necessary survey work is often lacking. The strategies that either exist or are being developed are concerned primarily with public provision for informal outdoor recreation, chiefly in Country Parks, picnic sites, caravan sites and the like, although attempts are also made to identify areas where private recreational developments should be encouraged and those where they should be discouraged. At the same time, under the Town and Country Planning Act 1968 and the Town and Country Planning (Scotland) Act 1969, the nature of statutory planning is being altered (though a date for implementation of 'new planning' in Scotland has yet to be decided), with the replacement of development plans by broad structure plans, which are intended to indicate the main policies, and by detailed local action plans, which will implement these policies. As part of this process a much wider view of the countryside will be taken than in the past, including consideration of all government policies that bear on the countryside (Select Committee, 1972, 1, 11 and 12). The new authorities will often combine rural and urban areas, a desirable development in recreational planning, for most demand for recreation is generated in urban areas and recreational journeys characteristically ignore administrative boundaries (see chapter 8). As yet it is too early to say how effective this new approach to rural planning will be, but it is clear that recreation and tourism must have a much larger part in statutory planning than in the past.


## GOVERNMENT BODIES WITH DIRECT RESPONSIBILITIES FOR COUNTRYSIDE RECREATION

Although there is no explicit national strategy and only embryonic regional strategies for the countryside as a whole, there are (as reference to the Countryside Commissions has indicated) several government agencies with responsibilities for outdoor recreation, which have devised policies for recreational use of the countryside in amplification either of more general government policies or of their remits as provided by the legislation under which they were established. The principal bodies under this head are the Countryside Commissions, the statutory Sports Councils and the statutory Tourist Boards; the divisions of responsibility between them are not wholly clear, but it can broadly be said that, while the Countryside Commissions are primarily concerned with informal recreation in the countryside, the main responsibilities of the Sports Councils are for active recreation (whether in town or country) and those of the Tourist Boards are for those aspects of both formal and informal recreation that involve holidaymakers, whether from overseas or (the great majority) from other parts of Great Britain.

## Countryside Commissions

The two Countryside Commissions differ in detail, but are broadly similar in their functions and policies. Both are essentially advisory, executive action being taken by local planning authorities, provided their proposals are recommended by the Commissions and approved by the appropriate minister (the Secretary of State for the Environment, the Secretary of State for Scotland or the Secretary of State for Wales). Both Commissions have a dual function of facilitating the conservation of natural beauty and promoting public enjoyment of the countryside, objectives that are sometimes seen as conflicting but can, in fact, be complementary. Both seek to influence standards of recreational provision by research and example and by providing advice to local authorities. The Countryside Acts of 1967 and 1968 have placed more emphasis on enjoyment of the countryside than did the National Parks Act and have given both local authorities and private bodies powers to propose and, if approved by the government on the recommendations of the Commissions, to operate Country Parks and picnic sites (figure 7.1), and have granted additional powers to the Forestry Commission and to statutory agencies to make provision for outdoor recreation. Both Countryside Commissions have powers to recommend the designation of areas of high scenic quality for special protection and to recommend proposals originating from local authorities for Access Agreements or (where agreement is not possible), Access Orders to open country, which would facilitate public recreational use of moor, heath or woodland in private ownership; in fact, very few Access Agreements have been made in England and Wales and none in Scotland, probably because local authorities do not see any reason to pay for what they think they can get for nothing. There are minor differences in structure and powers, reflecting in part the different origins of the two Commissions; for example, the Countryside Commission may recommend approval of a Country Park anywhere in the countryside, whereas the Countryside Commission for Scotland can give such approval only for sites near urban areas. Conversely, in Scotland any private individual can be grant-aided, whereas in England and Wales such support can be given only where public provision is impossible.

## Sports Councils

The Sports Council, the separate Sports Councils for Scotland and Wales, and the Regional Sports Councils in England, were established in 1972 with the object of fostering knowledge of and facilities for sport and physical recreation. The Sports Councils operate by means of grants-in-aid to local authorities, to other public bodies such as Water Boards and to private bodies to help them provide sports and recreational facilities of a regional or sub-regional nature, while themselves providing national sports centres. Like the Countryside Commissions, they can also finance experimental and prototype schemes. It seems probable that many of these facilities will be in towns, particularly in the provision of multi-sports centres, but the Sports Council has already contributed grants towards facilities for water sports on reservoirs and lakes and towards a ski complex.

## Tourist Boards

The role of the tourist authorities is more diverse. Under the 1969 Development

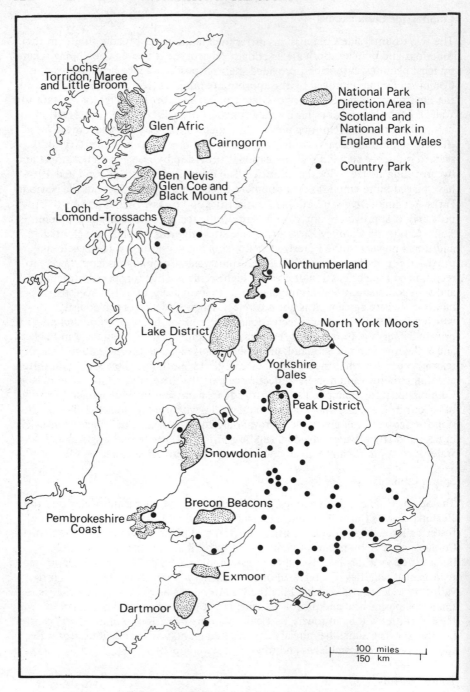

Figure 7.1  National parks and country parks

of Tourism Act the British Tourist Authority is responsible for attracting overseas visitors and for encouraging British citizens to take their holidays in Great Britain, while the English, Scottish and Wales Tourist Boards share with it the task of encouraging the provision and improvement of tourist amenities, to which they can give financial assistance; their concern is thus primarily with development rather than with protection. It is clearly impossible to make a distinction between those facilities and amenities enjoyed by tourists from those enjoyed by local residents, especially since more than four-fifths of the tourists are British citizens. Furthermore, many visitors are attracted by the same features that encourage British residents to seek outdoor recreation in the countryside, whether for informal recreation or for such activities as fishing and shooting. The chief differences arise from the need to provide accommodation for visitors and from the greater seasonal but less marked weekly variation in their demand for facilities; the different distribution of the holiday population compared with that of the resident population is likely to affect seasonal variations in recreational pressures, as in the Lake District. One beneficial consequence is that recreational facilities may be provided of a kind or on a scale that could not be justified by the needs of the resident population alone; but it is equally clear that uncontrolled pressure by visitors may have adverse effects on the quality of the recreational experience that they and others have come to enjoy, a consideration of which the Tourist Boards are aware. The Boards are not, however, primarily concerned with the countryside, although information from the British Travel Association (1969) shows that the greatest rate of growth among different kinds of holidays is in those for outdoor recreation, the Scottish Tourist Board recognises active holidays in the countryside as a particular attraction of Scotland (Select Committee, 1972, 3, 412) and the Wales Tourist Board has issued an advisory leaflet for farmers on farm tourism as a means of supplementing income.

## OTHER GOVERNMENT DEPARTMENTS AND AGENCIES

Although their policies differ somewhat in the emphasis given to protection or development, to informal or organised recreation, and to the contribution of town or country, the bodies that have already been discussed are all concerned specifically with recreation, and it is to them that government departments, local authorities and others may be expected to turn for advice and guidance. Nevertheless, to confine a discussion of the impact of official policies on outdoor recreation to these bodies alone would be to provide a very incomplete view. Other departments and agencies also play a part, whether because they are major owners or occupiers of rural land or because their policies affect, directly or indirectly, the suitability of the countryside for outdoor recreation. Since 80 per cent of the land area of Great Britain is used for agricultural purposes, pride of place will be given to the agricultural departments, the Ministry of Agriculture, Fisheries and Food, which has responsibility for agricultural matters in England and Wales, and the Department of Agriculture and Fisheries for Scotland, although in many ways the most important body from the viewpoint of outdoor recreation is the Forestry Commission.

## Ministry of Agriculture, Fisheries and Food and the Department of Agriculture and Fisheries for Scotland

Unlike the United States Department of Agriculture, which has specifically recognised outdoor recreation as a potential contributor to farm income and has provided training, advice and grants-in-aid (Ironside, 1971), the Ministry of Agriculture and the Department of Agriculture for Scotland have no direct policies in respect of recreation, despite the fact that farm holidays are of growing import- ance and farmers increasingly affected by recreational pressures of various kinds. Nevertheless, agricultural policy concerns outdoor recreation in two main ways: by encouraging the intensification of agricultural use, especially on the upland margins, which may affect both the visual amenity of the countryside and access by the public to open land; and by influencing the size of the agricultural population, which may in turn affect the viability of rural communities and hence their ability to support recreation, especially that which depends on tourists. The agricultural departments are also substantial land-holders.

How far current pressures on farmers to maximise incomes can be attributed to agricultural policy is debatable; but whatever the causes of such pressures, there can be little doubt that rationalisation of field patterns, the removal of hedgerows and hedgerow timber, the reclamation of patches of waste land and the conversion of rough grazing into improved pasture affect the character of scenery and hence, by inference, the attractiveness of the countryside to recreationists. Improvement of rough grazings not only changes the texture and colour of the landscape; it is often accompanied by fencing with post and wire, and thus both diminishes visual amenity and prevents access to what was formerly open land. Such changes can even take place in National Parks and other areas of high amenity; and while agricultural advisers in England and Wales now draw the attention of applicants for grants to the amenity aspects of proposed reclamation, grants cannot be refused on grounds of amenity (Verney, 1972, p. 13). The removal of hedgerows, until recently encouraged by grants from the agricultural departments, has similarly had profound effects on lowland scenery.

The role of agricultural policy in respect of the level of rural population is also both debatable and paradoxical, for it is not clear how far policies, such as the support of sheep and cattle breeding on the uplands through the Hill Sheep and Hill Cattle Subsidies and the Winter Keep Scheme, have a social rather than an economic purpose. It seems reasonable to suppose that, without such support, the amalgamation of farms and the withdrawal of land from effective agricultural use would have gone much further than they have. On the other hand, it should also be noted that it has been government policy since 1958 to encourage the trend to- wards farm enlargement, notably through the grants authorised by the 1967 Agriculture Act to those who make non-viable holdings available for amalgamation, though the effects of this policy have been much less than had been expected. It is probably true that the recreational use of areas outside the range of daily travel from the main urban centres must depend to some extent on the existence of a range of services that it is often uneconomic to provide for a diminishing agricul- tural population. In this connection there is some conflict between the govern- ment's agricultural policy in general and that for the crofting areas in particular (see p. 136).

The role of the agricultural departments in respect of the land they control is primarily that of a generous landlord and no special provision is made for outdoor recreation. In so far as these agricultural estates consist mainly of small holdings or experimental farms, they are not readily compatible with public recreation and the departments' remits do not encourage them to take a wider view of the use of their estates, although the Department of Agriculture for Scotland is undertaking limited developments on some of its estates to increase their recreational use (Select Committee, 1972, 1, 82). Research stations are clearly unsuitable for general recreational use, though they might play a role in the growing market for recreational education, providing townspeople with insight into countryside activities, as is done at the Flevohof on the Flevoland polder in the Netherlands.

## Forestry Commission

While the main role of the agricultural departments is in formulating and implementing agricultural policy, and their function as landowner is relatively unimportant and little different from that of a large private landowner, the Forestry Commission plays a major part in formulating and implementing forest policy, in its role as Forest Authority, and is the largest landowner in Great Britain, managing, in its role as Forest Enterprise, one-third of all woodland and adopting a very different attitude to public recreational use from that prevailing in the private sector (see figure 7.2).

Until 1972 government policy towards private woodlands was primarily concerned with their rehabilitation, and with making good decades of neglect and the devastation of two world wars. Grants were available to private owners in the 1920s and 1930s to encourage the rehabilitation of woodland and, since the Second World War, almost one million acres (404 700 ha) of woodland have been brought under the Dedicated and Approved Woodland Schemes; under the former (by far the more important), planting and maintenance grants were payable to those who dedicated their woodland to long-term forestry and managed it in accordance with a plan approved by the Forestry Commission. Since the late 1950s there has also been an increasing area of land afforested by private owners, especially through the agency of investment groups, and although such afforestation is encouraged by the Dedicated Woodland Scheme, it appears to be due primarily to concessions in respect of both income tax and estate duty. Such planting and replanting may have a profound effect on the landscape and the suitability of land for outdoor recreation. Replanting of derelict woodland can lead to the fencing of woodland and the exclusion of the public from areas where recreational use was tolerated if not allowed; it may also lead to visual changes, as where conifers replace broad-leaved trees. Afforestation can similarly lead to the exclusion of the public and to changes in the landscape, especially the replacement of moorland by plantations of conifers. The Forestry Commission does attempt to influence grant-aided private planting in the spirit of the amenity clauses in the Countryside Acts, by discouraging planting schemes that would harm amenity, and has even been prepared to withhold grants in some instances (Select Committee, 1972, 3, 104). Changes in forest policy in the private sector, as envisaged in the consultative document, *Forestry Policy* (1972), and subsequently elaborated by ministers, will abolish the Dedicated and Approved Woodland Schemes and replace them by a

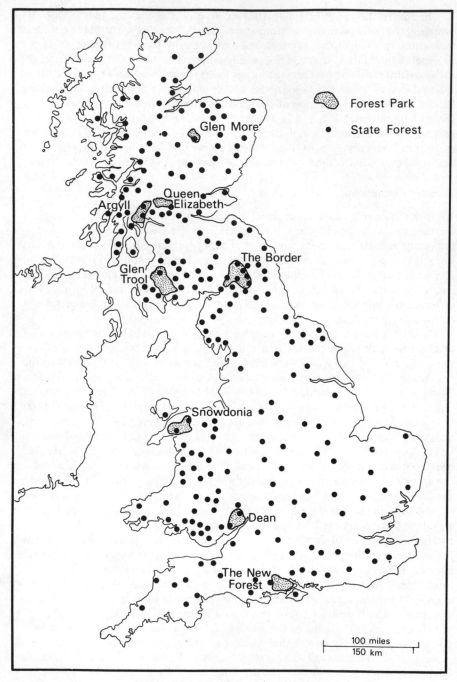

Figure 7.2  Forest parks and forests

grant, in return for which owners would manage woodland 'to secure sound forestry practice, effective integration with agriculture and environmental safeguards, together with such opportunities for recreation as may be appropriate' (*Parliamentary Debates*, 1973).

In respect of its own woodlands, the Forestry Commission has long played a major part in the provision of outdoor recreation and its contribution in this respect is growing. The Commission permits access to its own woodlands to members of the public on foot, subject to necessary constraints of management and of fire control and to obligations to previous owners or tenants; thus, there may be restrictions on access to young plantations (which are not in any case very attractive to recreationists), or when fire risks are high during a dry spell, where the Commission is itself a tenant, or where there are shooting tenants. In the last context, it is now Commission policy to acquire the shooting or fishing rights to its woods wherever this is possible, to make these available to members of the public at cost, and to give priority to the general public where there is a conflict of interest between public and private recreation (Select Committee on Sport and Leisure, 1973, *Evidence*, p. 158).

The Commission occupies four categories of land. Of these, land under plantations is by far the largest, totalling 1·8 million acres (749 000 ha) or 60 per cent of the Commission's holdings (Forestry Commission, 1972). The Commission also holds agricultural land that is awaiting planting, for it is desirable to have at least four years plantable land in reserve; it also holds agricultural land that is either too good to be planted, given current government policy towards agricultural land, or too poor because of exposure, elevation, rockiness or other reasons, and a small acreage in forestry small-holdings. It is policy to dispose of land that cannot be planted, but this is not always possible and in Scotland such land is managed by the Department of Agriculture until it can be sold. The Commission also has a small acreage of nurseries and other working land. In respect of its agricultural holdings, the Commission, like the agricultural departments, does not differ greatly from any private landowner whose land is tenanted; its plantations, on the other hand, make a major contribution to the resources available for outdoor recreation in Great Britain.

As with all woodlands, the Commission's recreational role in respect of its forests has been twofold: the contribution to visual amenity and the provision of land for outdoor recreation of various kinds. Between the two world wars the Commission was severely criticised for the adverse effect of its plantations on visual amenity, especially in the uplands, and as early as 1936 it reached an agreement with the Friends of the Lake District to undertake no further planting in the 300 square miles (777 km$^2$) of the central Lake District (National Parks Commission, 1955). In the post-war period it reached a similar agreement with the National Parks Commission to consult that Commission over its proposals for planting in National Parks (Best and Coppock, 1962), though it was under no statutory obligation to do so, and appointed a distinguished landscape architect as its consultant on those aspects of planting that affect landscape. Moreover, modification of the management of woodland in the interests of amenity can be expensive and the Commission estimates that the maintenance of amenity woods in the New Forest costs approximately £ 50 000 per annum (Select Committee, 1972, Appendix, 3, 106). Under the government's new policy, as outlined in

*Forestry Policy* (1972), amenity will be one of the two major considerations governing future planting.

Long before any National or Country Park was designated, the Forestry Commission also took the initiative of establishing National Forest Parks, of which the first, Argyll Forest Park, was formed in 1936 (Select Committee on Sport and Leisure, 1973, *Evidence,* p. 157); there are now seven such parks, covering an area of 600 000 acres (242 820 ha) (figure 7.2). In these parks recreation is encouraged through the provision of camp and caravan sites, forest walks and the like. The Commission has been gradually extending its recreational role in the remainder of its forests, subject to constraints of con-servation and good forestry, and is now being encouraged by the government to do so; it is particularly conscious of further recreational needs within motoring distance of the main conurbations and holiday areas and sees the principal demand for outdoor recreation as arising from day visitors (Select Committee, 1972, 2, 90 and 109). Motor cars are generally forbidden in the Commission's woods except for access to car parks, camping sites and the like, which are generally expected to be financially self-supporting (Select Committee on Sport and Leisure, 1973, *Evidence,* p. 158); access on foot, on the other hand, is free, and is being encouraged through the provision of nature trails and forest walks. In the Lake District the Commission is undertaking pioneer work at Grizedale Forest in integrating various forms of outdoor recreation with forestry. Apart from the provision of a camp site, nature trail and wildlife museum, artificial ponds have been created to attract wildlife, observation posts have been constructed, and shooting of roe deer is also let to visitors. The revenue from such activities now constitutes a substantial part of the total revenue from the forest.

The Commission's forests now make a major contribution to outdoor recreation, with 134 car parks, 177 picnic places and more than 200 forest trails (Forestry Commission, 1972; Select Committee on Sport and Leisure, 1973, *Evidence,* p. 158). They provided about a million camper nights in 1971, and were estimated to have received nearly 9 million day-visits in three months in the summer of 1969 (Forestry Commission, 1972). The Commission is now preparing regional recreational plans for its forests in consultation with the Countryside Commissions, Sports Councils and local authorities, and has established local committees to advise it on questions of amenity (Select Committee on Sport and Leisure, 1973, *Evidence*, p. 157).

## The Nature Conservancy Council

The Nature Conservancy or, as renamed in 1973, the Nature Conservancy Council, has two main functions: to maintain a nationally representative series of natural and semi-natural habitats, with their characteristic floras and faunas, and to pro-vide advice to public bodies on issues that affect or are likely to affect the conser-vation of natural flora and fauna or features of geological or physiographic interest (though it has no standing in the countryside outside statutorily pro-tected areas). Protection is chiefly afforded through designation as National Nature Reserve, of which there are 135, occupying some 279 000 acres (112 900 ha), though only 26 per cent of this land is owned by the Nature Conservancy, the remainder being under long lease or under Nature Reserve Agreements, whereby

the landowner undertakes to manage the land in question in the interests of conservation (Natural Environment Research Council, 1973). Such National Nature
Reserves are managed according to a management plan and, while their main purpose is conservation, the Conservancy welcomes visitors where this is possible.
Access may, however, be restricted for scientific reasons or because the land is
leased or held under Nature Reserves Agreements and the needs of the landowner or others with an interest in the land must be safeguarded. Opportunities
are offered for specialist pursuits, such as rock-climbing, skiing, caving and wildfowling, provided that this can be done without adversely affecting the conservation interest; the Conservancy prefers to deal with organisations rather than
with individuals because of the greater control that this provides (Select Committee on Sport and Leisure, 1973, *Evidence*, p. 548).

In addition to National Nature Reserves, there are also twenty-one National
Wildfowl Refuges, which are generally coastal, and more than 3400 Sites of
Special Scientific Interest (S.S.S.I.s); but these latter remain in private ownership
and the public has no rights of access to them unless these are provided by other
means (Nature Conservancy, 1973).

## The Ministry of Defence and other Large Government Land-Holders

Other government departments and agencies that affect the use of the countryside
for recreation do so primarily by virtue of their ownership or occupation of land,
excepting those with responsibilities for water bodies (which are discussed
below). Probably the most important in this respect is the Ministry of Defence,
which holds about 662 000 acres (267 900 ha) (Ministry of Defence, 1973) — compared with over eleven million (4·5 million ha) during the Second World War. A
large part of this consists of training areas and firing ranges, and many of these
are in remote areas of attractive scenery, notably in Dartmoor, which is a National
Park and an important area for summer visitors. The public will generally be
excluded from such areas, and even from roads crossing them when firing is taking
place, although limited agricultural use is often possible. A recent review of the
Ministry's land holdings has recommended the release of 32 700 acres (13 200 ha),
including some areas important, or potentially important, for outdoor recreation,
such as the northern end of the Pentland Hills on the outskirts of Edinburgh (Ministry of Defence, 1973). Other large users include the nationalised industries,
notably the National Coal Board, with 209 000 acres (84 580 ha); much of this
land is unsuitable for outdoor recreation and for such land as is suitable, the
nationalised industries will not differ greatly from other landowners (Denman,
1963). The chief exception is abandoned railway lines, for which an active
recreational role has been suggested as recreational routes (Appleton, 1970), but
these are generally being transferred in fragmented ownership to private owners of
adjacent property.

## Regional Agencies

In addition to policies that affect the whole country, there are also regional
policies and agencies for giving effect to these, notably the Crofters Commission
and the Highlands and Islands Development Board. The former, established in

1955, is responsible for holdings in crofting tenure in the seven crofting counties (Argyll, Caithness, Inverness, Orkney, Ross, Sutherland and Zetland) and has as its prime task the well-being of the crofting communities. But while its role was conceived primarily in agricultural terms, so that other economic activities can be encouraged only where they are subsidiary to agriculture, it is now clear that agriculture can no longer play this primary role on many crofts; the Commission thus sees tourism and outdoor recreation as playing a much more important part in providing crofters with a livelihood (Select Committee, 1972, 3, pp. 291 and 326). Already there is assistance for the erection of accommodation for visitors and for the operation of unlicensed caravan sites on croft land, though under present law the position about non-agricultural improvements on crofts is uncertain, and legislation to give crofters the freehold of their croft sites has been proposed by the government.

The Highlands and Islands Development Board, established in 1965, has a wider remit and is able to encourage a much greater range of economic activities by grants, loans or by joint participation. Yet it, too, sees recreation and tourism as being major props of a revived, Highland economy (Select Committee, 1972, 5, Appendix, p. 225). While the Board does not itself own land, it has played an active part in promoting Highland holidays and has given grants for the construction of accommodation and recreational facilities: for example, it has promoted the building of hotels in areas where they were lacking and is a shareholder in the Cairngorm Development Co. Ltd, which constructed and operates the ski lifts that have greatly extended the skiing potential of the Cairngorms. It has also undertaken a review of the game resources of the Highlands to see how far their recreational potential might be developed (Select Committee, 1972, 5, Appendix, p. 225).

An interesting development of this kind, the rural development board, was authorised by the 1967 Agriculture Act to provide a means of helping problem rural areas in the uplands, particularly by the integration of agriculture, forestry and recreation. The concept had a mixed reception, primarily because of powers given to boards to control sales of land in the interests of establishing viable holdings, and a board proposed for central Wales encountered strong opposition from local farmers. Only one, the Northern Pennine Rural Development Board, was formed, and this is thought to have played a useful co-ordinating role during its short life (Select Committee, 1972, 5, Appendix, pp. 168-70).

## Local Agencies

Local authorities are not only local planning authorities with responsibility for making provision for public recreation, but they are also major land-holders. Much of this land is held for purposes other than recreation, but local authorities also own land held primarily for amenity and recreational purposes. Even before the Countryside Acts, some local authorities acquired land for its amenity value under the Green Belt Act, and others had acquired recreational land, such as Epping Forest (Essex), Burnham Beeches (Buckinghamshire) and Clumber Park (Nottinghamshire). Under the Countryside Acts, local authorities acquired powers to purchase land to serve as Country Parks, car parks and picnic sites and have used these powers with varying degrees of enthusiasm. Between 1968 and 1972, sixty-six

Country Parks proposed by local authorities were approved by the Department of the Environment and the Welsh Office on the advice of the Countryside Commission; they totalled over 20 000 acres (8090 ha), though twenty-six of them were existing parks that have now been recognised as Country Parks and fifteen were extended or greatly improved parks (Phillips, 1972). On such land recreation is the prime purpose and the land is managed with this aim in mind. A much smaller area, totalling less than 2000 acres (809 ha), consists of picnic sites, which have also been designated under the Countryside Acts. In Scotland, only four parks, totalling 1844 acres (768 ha), have so far been recognised, though many more are in various stages of negotiation (Countryside Commission for Scotland, 1973).

Some 500 000 acres (200 000 ha) of land, mainly rough grazings, are also held by water undertakings as gathering grounds (Natural Resources (Technical) Committee, 1957). Water undertakings generally impose restraints on agricultural use which is largely confined to sheep and, to a lesser extent, cattle grazing. Some authorities also impose restrictions on recreational use, though walking is generally allowed, except in the vicinity of reservoirs.

**Water Authorities**

Policy in respect of the use of water for outdoor recreation is equally complex and a large number of bodies is involved, although the structure of national administration of water resources in England and Wales is being changed to facilitate a more integrated approach to water management. The management and control of water for recreational purposes is the responsibility of a variety of bodies, though most inland waters are privately owned. Owners of some lakes—for example, the National Trust for Scotland (1964)— have forbidden certain activities because they interfere with the enjoyment of others, but planning authorities in National Parks have statutory powers under the Countryside Act to make by-laws controlling recreational use of lakes and the navigation authority may make such by-laws on rivers which are statutory navigation. The British Waterways Board, which is responsible for canals, has a statutory duty in respect of recreational use under the 1968 Transport Act and is advised by an amenity council (Tanner, 1973, p. 63). The Board also allows recreational use of its feeder reservoirs, where this is consistent with operational efficiency, and 70 of its 100 reservoirs are so used. Statutory water undertakings are responsible for water supply reservoirs, which number 183, and have powers to permit recreation on reservoirs owned by them. They have generally become more sympathetic towards recreational use of reservoirs over the past thirty years. In 1966 they were requested to conduct a careful and sympathetic review of their rules and were advised in a memorandum to pay particular attention to the needs of recreationists (Ministry of Land and Natural Resources, 1966). There is usually greater willingness to permit recreation on regulating and compensation reservoirs, and a more liberal attitude is particularly noticeable in respect of new reservoirs opened since 1967 (Institution of Water Engineers, 1972). Game fishing is allowed on more than half the reservoirs, but coarse fishing on only a few; sailing is the only other activity allowed on any scale. The preferred method of permitting recreational use is through clubs and associations. Under the Countryside Acts, local authorities are empowered to facilitate recreational use by creating Country Parks on those reservoirs where water undertakings wish to permit it. Gravel pits, more than half of which are in southern England, where there are few reservoirs and even fewer large natural water bodies, are in private ownership, but conditions on subsequent use may be imposed by local planning authorities when granting planning permission for the gravel to be worked. In the past, operators were often required to fill in workings on completion, but wet pits are increasingly being landscaped and used for water-based recreation and there is a waiting list of organisations wanting to use pits when they cease to be worked. Several large water-sports complexes are in being or in prospect, notably the Cotswold Water Park (created under the provisions of the Countryside Act) and the Holme Pierrepoint National Water Sports Centre. In Scotland, the North of Scotland Hydro-Electric Board (1971) controls some 80 000 acres (32 380 ha) of reservoirs, though most of these have been created from natural lochs by raising the water level; pre-existing recreational activities, notably fishing, have been allowed to continue and the Board is, in fact, advised by Fisheries and Amenity Committees. New recreational resources have also been created, such as the reservoir at Faskally near Pitlochry.

The coast is mainly in private ownership, but the foreshore is Crown property and recreational use of coastal waters within 1000 yards (914 m) of low-water mark can be controlled by local authorities by means of by-laws issued under the authority of the 1961 Public Health Act (Tanner, 1973, p. 64).

**The National Trusts**

Occupying an intermediate position between public authorities and private landowners are the National Trust for England, Wales and Northern Ireland, which was established in 1895, and the National Trust for Scotland, which was formed in 1931; they were created by statute and properties acquired by them are inalienable. Their estates now total some 433 000 acres (175 235 ha) and, like the Countryside Commissions, they have a dual function of preserving amenity and promoting public enjoyment. Their estates comprise mainly woodland and farmland, the latter largely let to tenants, and public access is encouraged where this does not conflict with the interests of conservation. There is a large acreage of Trust land in the Lake District, including common land, and the Trust is unusual among landowners there in adjusting rents of farmland in the light of recreational pressures. In Scotland, where most Trust property is rough hill land, the Trust attempts to meet recreational needs through multiple use where this is possible (Select Committee, 1972, 3, 168).

**Conclusion**

This brief review has indicated something of the variety of public bodies with some concern for the recreational use of the countryside or which affect in some way the availability of rural land for recreation. In general such bodies have usually permitted recreation where this does not conflict with their principal objectives. They have been encouraged in this direction by the provisions of the Countryside Acts, though it would not be true to say that any comprehensive recreational strategy on public land has so far emerged. In general it seems that public ownership has tended to increase the availability of land for recreation, while explicit policies for recreation have sought to ease pressures on private land by controlling them through wardening and Access Agreements and by canalising them through the creation of Country Parks. Whatever the process of decision-making that has led consciously or unconsciously to these policies, it seems likely that this choice has been affected to some degree by the attitudes of these policy makers and their advisers. These policies are perhaps even more important in affecting the decisions of private landowners.

## PRIVATELY OWNED LAND

Although there is frequent comment in the press from landowners, farmers and other users of rural land about the impact of outdoor recreation, there is remarkably little firm information about the extent of recreational use of the nine-tenths of the countryside that is privately owned or about the impact of such recreation. Nor is it easy to generalise, for there is a great variety of both recreational land users and kinds of landholders, and, *a fortiori*, of attitudes to recreation. Furthermore, the different uses of rural land vary greatly in their compatibility with outdoor recreation.

### Recreational Use of Private Land

The recreational use of private land is broadly of four kinds: (1) that undertaken by landholders and their friends; (2) that undertaken with their consent, sometimes with payment and a firm contractual agreement, and sometimes not; (3) use by the public of private land over which the public has some right of access; and (4) use by the public of private land to which there is no such right of access, but which is accepted or tolerated by the landholder. The first two categories are most widely represented by land used for field sports; though there is little firm evidence of the extent to which sporting rights are kept in hand or let to others, at least this choice is one that the individual landowner can make freely.

Fishing is one of the most important resources and may be reserved for the owner's use or may be let to individuals, to a hotel or to an angling association, which, although primarily concerned with securing fishing for its members, may also let fishing on a casual basis to others; alternatively fishing rights may be sold. Game fishing may be a valuable and closely-guarded resource commanding high rents and with a capital value measured in tens of thousands of pounds per mile, though coarse fishing will cost much less and may be free in the more sparsely populated parts of the country. Hunting generally takes place on farmland in winter without payment, but with an obligation on the hunt to make good any damage; before the Second World War, a hunt might pay £1000 or more a year in compensation (Frederick, 1930). The landholders may or may not take part and not all landowners will permit such hunting, though the great majority do. Shooting too, may be kept in hand or let and, like fishing, ranges from an expensive recreation, which may cost participants several hundred pounds a week during the season, to a casual activity for which no payment is made. Shooting of game birds may require some form of land management, notably in the case of grouse, which feed almost entirely on heather and depend for their supply of feed on the careful burning of heather moor to maintain an adequate supply of young shoots

le habitat. Pheasant-shooting also depends on the maintenance of
r and a supplementary supply of food. Deer-stalking, on the other
less dependent on such management, for most of the land regularly
by deer is above 1000 feet (300 m) and includes some of the poorest land
in Great Britain. Most deer forests are large, some extending over tens of
thousands of acres, for the carrying capacity is low and 25 acres (10 ha) per beast
represents the maximum density consistent with good management (Darling and
Morton-Boyd, 1964).

Such activities are long-established features of the countryside and may even
merit the epithet of traditional recreations. Shooting represents part of the capital
value of an estate and may be an important factor in the price it will fetch (and the
kind of person who may buy it), although few purely sporting estates were known
to the Department of Agriculture and Fisheries for Scotland (Select Committee,
1972, 5, 204). Alternatively, the revenue they provide from letting to urban
dwellers or foreign visitors may be an important source of income to landholders,
both in the arable farming areas of the east and on the heather moors of eastern
Scotland, where they may be more valuable than sheep grazing, as measured by rent
per acre. Strangely, field sports are not the responsibility of any governmental
agency, with the exception of the Red Deer Commission, which has responsibilities for the conservation of stock of red deer; and there appears to be no
explicit government policy towards them.

The letting of field sports is not the only kind of contractual relationship between
private landholders and recreationists. There are increasing numbers of examples
of the provision of camping and caravanning facilities and other more scanty
evidence of payments by, or agreements with, clubs and associations for the
exclusive use of recreational resources, such as a lake for water-skiing or a cliff
face for climbing. Little is known about such relationships because, by their
nature, they avoid friction between landholders and recreationists, to their mutual
benefit.

## Rights of Access to Private Land

Access to land is necessary for most kinds of recreation but, despite the widespread
belief that there is public right of access to open land, this is not the case even in
Scotland where this belief is most strongly held. In fact, land over which there are
public rights of access is largely confined to certain categories of common land
in England and Wales (Stamp and Hoskins, 1963) and no such rights exist in
Scotland. There is also right of access, subject to any by-laws, to land over which
an Access Agreement has been made with a local authority or other appropriate
body, either under the National Parks and Access to the Countryside Act or the
Countryside Acts (under which the concept of open country has been extended
to include woodland). Those made under the 1949 Act were largely confined to
the Peak National Park, since other local authorities felt that there was sufficient
provision in their areas to meet existing demand. No Access Agreement has yet
been created in Scotland, though this is partly a reflection of the lower pressures
of population on land, partly of the newness of the procedure, and partly of the
difficulties of reconciling the interests of the two parties to such an agreement.
It is also appropriate to consider under this heading of rights of access both the

complex network of footpaths in the lowlands, many of them inherited from the medieval period and estimated at over 100 000 miles (160 000 km) in England and Wales (Select Committee on Sport and Leisure, 1973, *Evidence*, p. 392) and the new rights of way, notably long-distance footpaths such as the Pennine Way, established under post-war legislation. Not all footpaths are rights of way and the latter have slowly been identified in England and Wales in the post-war period and recorded on definitive maps, though not all counties have yet reached agreement; such a procedure was not thought necessary in Scotland. Such lowland footpaths, which provide access through farms and woods, have sometimes been a source of friction, especially between walkers and farmers who may plough or stop up little-used footpaths.

The very limited success of attempts to secure Access Agreements is an interesting reflection on recreational pressures on the countryside; but it also reflects the suspicions of landowners and the feelings among local authorities that there is no need for legal sanction for what is already enjoyed without it. However, landowners are becoming increasingly aware of the benefits of controlled access.

( In reality )
## De Facto Access to Private Land

The fourth category of private land used for outdoor recreation, that used by members of the public without any right of access, is probably the most widespread and is certainly that which generates most friction between recreationists and landholders. It ranges from intensive use by children of farmland adjoining built-up areas, through a family picnic in a grass field or a woodland clearing adjoining a metalled road, to the lone walker on desolate moorland. Where pressure is light and the main use of land extensive, such illegal use of land for recreation will generally be tolerated. When pressure increases, ditches may be dug or fences erected along roads giving access to such land to discourage the great majority who come by car, as in the Lammermuirs; but it will often be impracticable to exclude recreationists from such extensively used land, since neither fencing nor wardening will be economically justifiable. On land that is intensively used for agriculture or forestry, on the other hand, high fences and locked gates may deter all but the most determined trespassers, though in any case, intensively used farm land will not be very attractive to recreationists. The scale of this problem should not, however, be exaggerated. Widespread evidence shows that most recreationists do not stray far from their cars and visitors to woodland often exhibit the well-known edge effect by concentrating along the woodland margins. It is chiefly in areas where crops or livestock (including game animals and birds) are particularly vulnerable, where recreational pressures are great, as around towns, and where there is inadequate public provision, that the main difficulties occur.

## The Private Landowner

If recreational demands vary widely, so too do the characteristics of those who control the use of privately-owned land, for attitudes are likely to vary with the size of estates, the degree of dependence of the owner or occupier on the land for his livelihood and the personality traits of each individual, as well as with the pressures to which the land is subject. Until the beginning of the twentieth century, the characteristic pattern of rural land-holding was that of an estate, divided into tenanted farms, but with the woodlands and usually a home farm kept in hand. While no satisfactory data exist on the size of estates, some were very large, especially in Scotland where the Duke of Sutherland was believed to hold nearly 1·2 million acres (0·5 million ha) in 1873 (Parliamentary Papers, 1874) whatever their size, they had in common the fact that they were planned as a unit, with agriculture, forestry and often field sports and amenity considered from the viewpoint of the resources of the whole estate. With the break-up of estates and the rise of owner-occupation, which now accounts for more than half of all farmland, such a synoptic view of the land has become less common and there is some evidence that the resulting land units are, in any case, too small for the management of certain activities, such as grouse-shooting (Select Committee, 1972, appendix 5, 221). There is also evidence that owner-occupiers are less likely to take a broad, long-term view of the resources they control. Occupiers of small holdings, on the other hand, may be more willing to accept recreationists and other visitors to the countryside as a potential source of income than may those who occupy much larger economic units; but they may also feel that large numbers of recreationists are a threat to their way of life. Institutional landowners, such as insurance companies, who have invested in large acreages of rural land in the post-war period, are likely to take a longer-term view of the land they control than are individuals, though the owner of a long-established estate was often concerned to hand on his property unimpaired and preferably enhanced to his successor. Status as tenant or owner-occupier will also be a factor, for the former may be discouraged by his landlord from making provision for recreationists and tourists even though he may wish to do so, a situation confirmed by the studies discussed later in this chapter.

An increasingly important category of land-holder comprises those non-traditional occupiers of land who do not depend on their estates for their livelihood but have other sources of income, often as professionals or managers working in nearby cities. Such people may acquire land as a by-product of purchasing an attractive residence and, retaining sufficient to provide a degree of privacy, let or sell the remainder to neighbouring farmers. Others may acquire a farm with the intention of running it as a hobby, either employing a manager or foreman, or working it in their spare time. Such occupiers are important around large cities, especially London, or in areas of attractive countryside within easy access to such cities, as in the chalklands of southern England, and there are indications from several surveys that their importance is growing (Gasson, 1966; Harrison, 1966). It is, of course, debatable whether such people are not themselves more properly regarded as recreationists than landowners, though they are also reputed to be less ready to permit other recreationists to use land they control than traditional landowners. A related development, which has already been noted, is the acquisition of second homes or holiday cottages in the main holiday areas, though these are characteristically acquired with only a small plot of land. The type of land and the nature of the land use are also important determinants, both of the kind of recreational pressure and of the attitudes of land-holders to recreational use of their estates. Land under crops is generally not attractive to recreationists, nor are they welcome on it. Grassland is less susceptible to damage by recreational use, except where it is being kept for mowing, and is also more attractive to recreationists as camping sites or as places for picnics and informal games; but farmers are very conscious of the hazards to stock arising from litter, open gates and broken fences, and of the risks of visitors transmitting animal diseases. Rough grazing is generally less vulnerable to recreational pressure, except at high altitudes, and is also managed at low levels of intensity; recreationists are least welcome at critical times of the year, such as lambing, nesting and the shooting season, but their exclusion is difficult and may be more costly than any damage they cause. The suitability of woodland for recreational use and its vulnerability to damage from such use vary greatly with its age and character and with the extent to which it is also used for shooting or is valued by its owners for its amenity or for the privacy it provides. Young plantations are both vulnerable and unattractive, and young trees at the thicket stage, especially conifers, will generally be unsuitable for any kind of recreation. Light recreational pressure in mature woods will probably be acceptable, unless they are also used for shooting by the owner or by shooting tenants, or are valued chiefly for the privacy they provide to a residence. Heavy recreational pressure may adversely affect tree growth by compacting the soil; it is, however, the margins of such woodlands that are most subject to pressure.

The attitudes of land-holders to the appearance of the countryside is also important. Economic pressures have generally made both farmers and foresters unwilling to take measures to safeguard rural amenity if these involve costs that are not offset by revenue. It is true that woods can be preserved by local planning authorities issuing Tree Preservation Orders, but these are ineffective as a long-term solution, which must recognise that the visual character of the countryside is largely a by-product of its use. There is an increasing awareness among landowners of the importance of visual amenity and the Economic Forestry Group (Select Committee, 1972, 3, 481) is prepared to sacrifice at least 5 per cent of potential income in the interests of amenity and conservation; government proposals for recasting the grants payable to those who manage private woodland envisage the payment of grants to those who plant in the interests of amenity. Farmers and foresters resent the suggestion that they should absorb the costs that would result from operating against their best commercial judgement, and it is interesting to note that the Verney Committee, in its report *Sinews for Survival* (1972, p. 48), envisaged a conservation grant, a proposal over which the Select Committee on Scottish Affairs had reservations, preferring to see whether, as had been alleged, production and conservation would together make good economic sense (Select Committee, 1972, 1, 81).

As with public policies and public land, the attitudes of individual owners towards the recreational use of the land they control limits the actual supply of the potential recreational resources identified in chapter 6. This supply may be increased by a willingness to sell for recreational purposes, to accept a measure of control or to provide facilities for recreation. All these possibilities are increasingly being considered by landowners.

## ATTITUDES OF LANDOWNERS TO RECREATION AND TOURISM: CASE STUDIES

Few studies of the attitudes and policies towards outdoor recreation of those who occupy rural land have been undertaken in Great Britain, although there have been numerous conferences on the use of agricultural and forest land for recreation and many personal opinions have been volunteered; indeed, it was one of the themes considered by the three *Countryside in 1970* conferences in 1963, 1965 and 1970. Some indications can, however, be given by three investigations, two of them concerned with provision for tourists by farmers in south-west England and Denbighshire respectively, and the third with the general experience of landholders in central Scotland.

Tourism, much of it concerned with outdoor recreation in the broadest sense, is of increasing importance in south-west England, the most popular holiday area in Great Britain. For several years, agricultural economists from the University of Exeter have been conducting surveys of those farmers in Devon and Cornwall who have provided accommodation (Davies, 1969, 1971, 1973). These surveys demonstrated that, while farm holidays were originally confined to the coast, they were rapidly extending inland. A survey of eight parishes in the Teign valley showed that, of the 159 farmers who co-operated in the survey, 18 per cent provided for tourists, and that, of the remainder, 12 per cent were opposed, 25 per cent were not interested, 25 per cent had unsuitable accommodation and 16 per cent had other reasons such as old age, ill health and lease restrictions; most of those with unsuitable accommodation would seriously consider catering for tourists when their families had grown up or if capital became available. A high proportion of those opposed to tourism were 'immigrant' farmers who had bought their farms as residence or for semi-retirement. Two groups of reasons were advanced by those who opposed tourism in principle: that farms were meant to be farmed, and that tourists deposited litter, caused damage to crops and were a threat to livestock. Only a third of respondents favoured the development of the valley as a major tourist attraction; to many, tourism was a potential threat to the countryside, to be tolerated but not encouraged. It is interesting to note that only about one tenth of those providing accommodation also made provision for any form of outdoor recreation.

The study of farm tourism in Denbighshire concerned an area that is not itself a major tourist attraction, but adjoins such an area, Snowdonia, and is beginning to experience overspill from it (Jacobs, 1973). Of 889 farmers approached in two districts, one near Snowdonia and the other further away, 524 (66 per cent) responded, and of these only 77 (13 per cent) were in any way concerned in catering for the needs of tourists. This proportion was lowest on the largest farms (in an area of predominantly small farms) and highest in those between 50 and 99 acres in size (20 and 40 ha); proportions were generally higher in the district nearer Snowdonia. Those who took visitors were unanimous in believing that they had no adverse effects on agricultural production, but opinions were also sought from those who did not cater for visitors. 53 per cent said that they had no time to cater for visitors and 49 per cent that they had no space, these being the principal reasons, though some respondents gave more than one; other less important reasons were lack of capital (14 per cent), the poor conditions of buildings

(13 per cent), lease restrictions (12 per cent) and old age or ill health (10 per cent). Only 13 per cent thought that visitors would interfere with farm activities, while 7 per cent thought they would disturb the Welsh way of life. Interference was seen to be more of a problem by those occupying the larger farms. Paradoxically, it was also regarded as a more serious threat by those who did not perceive a demand for tourist accommodation than those who did. Eighty-one per cent of the respondents regarded tourism as profitable and 78 per cent thought that it should be encouraged, though some emphasised the need for proper control. In interpreting the results, it should be noted that farm tourism in Wales has not only been encouraged by the Wales Tourist Board, but is also being assisted by the National Farmers Union of Wales, which runs an accommodation bureau and has recently issued an advisory leaflet to its members.

Both these studies were concerned with only one aspect of recreation, the provision of accommodation on farms for those who wish to stay in the countryside, and both were near major holiday areas and some distance from large centres of population. A more general appraisal of attitudes to recreation by town-based day visitors was provided by a sample survey of occupiers of land in the five counties in central Scotland (Duffield and Owen, 1970, 1971). With the approval of the various organisations, postal questionnaires were sent to all members of the Scottish Landowners Federation and the Scottish Woodland Owners Federation in these counties and to a 25 per cent sample of members of the National Farmers Union of Scotland; 239 usable replies were received. Although this response rate (29 per cent) is low, it is fairly typical of that obtained in postal questionnaires (which were all that available funds would allow) and the replies related to about a fifth of the area of the five counties, approximately 41 per cent of which was under crops and grass, 54 per cent under rough grazing and only 5 per cent under woodland (compared with 50 per cent, 28 per cent and 8 per cent respectively for Great Britain as a whole). Shooting, fishing, picnicking, car-parking, walking, camping and caravanning were the most widely reported recreational activities, a not surprising result in view of the almost universal finding that active pursuits are nearly all undertaken by small minorities of the population. Most of the recreational activities were reported in either woodland or moorland. Respondents were asked, in open-ended questions, to list the problems they saw as arising from recreational use of rural land and the results are shown in table 7.1. Disturbance of stock and the dropping of litter were seen as the two most important problems.

Only a small proportion of land-holders admitted to having any proposals for developing recreational facilities on the estates they controlled, and a quarter of all such proposals related to fishing and shooting; others included parking and picnic space, camp sites and other accommodation, facilities for youth organisations and for the Scottish Wildlife Trust, and sports facilities and pitches. They were also asked for their comments on the recreational use of rural land and table 7.2 gives the proportion of replies given to open-ended questions, though the low response rates to the survey suggest that only a minority of landowners feel strongly about recreational problems. These answers stress particularly the role of education and the need to control access, though a considerable number can be regarded as punitive. They also illustrate the wide range of views and reactions.

## TABLE 7.1

### PROBLEMS ARISING FROM THE RECREATIONAL USE OF RURAL LAND

| | Problems arising from: | | | |
| --- | --- | --- | --- | --- |
| | Use of Rights of Way | Walking | Picnicking | Car-parking |
| | (percentage of all problems notified) | | | |
| Disturbance and damage to stock | 20 | 27 | 28 | 18 |
| Gates left open | 14 | 12 | 7 | 5 |
| Litter/rubbish | 14 | 18 | 27 | 30 |
| Damage to dykes and fences | 9 | 8 | 15 | — |
| Vandalism | 7 | 9 | 2 | — |
| Damage to crops/grazing | 8 | 6 | — | 4 |
| Poaching/theft | 10 | 7 | 4 | 16 |
| Fire and arson | 4 | 8 | 10 | 7 |
| Noise | 3 | — | — | — |
| Trespass | 2 | 2 | 2 | — |
| Damage to trees | 2 | 2 | — | 2 |
| Access roads blocked | 2 | 3 | — | 16 |

Source:   Duffield and Owen (1970), pp. 138, 146.

## TABLE 7.2

### COMMENTS ON RECREATIONAL USE OF RURAL LAND

| Summary of Comment | Percentage of all respondents giving replies |
| --- | --- |
| More education in the use of the countryside | 46 |
| Channel recreation into open land | 29 |
| No objection to well-behaved townspeople | 17 |
| Restrict public access to the countryside | 9 |
| Local authorities should provide facilities | 8 |
| Introduce penalties for trespass | 7 |
| Stiffer penalties for poaching and vandalism | 6 |
| Local authorities should reimburse for damage | 5 |
| Farmers have not time to provide facilities | 4 |
| Recreationists interfere with farming | 4 |
| Protect wildlife habitats and beauty spots | 2 |

Source:   Duffield and Owen (1970), pp. 131, 147.

There is no means of knowing how representative these views are and there is clearly a need for carefully controlled studies of attitudes towards recreation, held by owners and occupiers of rural land. Whatever the present situation, there is no doubt that these attitudes are changing. Of course, the letting of fishing and shooting has a long history. In the agricultural depression of the late nineteenth century, the partridge was said to have been 'the salvation of Norfolk farming' (Rew, 1895) and remains an important, though minor, element in incomes from rural land, and the letting of grouse moors has long contributed to the economy of estates in the eastern Highlands. In the post-war period, catering for visitors to the countryside has grown in importance at opposite ends of the scale. At one end are the increasing numbers of houses and gardens open to the public on payment; at their most extreme, at a Longleat or a Woburn Abbey, such land has become primarily recreational. At the other end, there has been the provisions of accommodation and caravan sites on the smaller farms; in the sample of farms in Devon and Cornwall revenue from tourism contributed more than half of net farm income on farms of less than 50 acres (20 ha).

None of these developments should be exaggerated for, in several studies of tourism, the proportion of farms catering for visitors has not exceeded a third and has generally been less than a fifth. Certainly there has been little sign of the recreational farming (or 'amenity agriculture') that is of growing importance in North America, although this may be due in large measure to the absence of satisfactory data on the numbers of farms offering different kinds of outdoor recreation (Irvine, 1966).

More recently, the Countryside Acts have provided an opportunity for private owners to receive government support for the provision of facilities for outdoor recreation. In Scotland it is possible for any private land-holder to receive Exchequer grants towards both the cost of establishing facilities and their running expenses, chiefly through wardening and the removal of litter; thus a land-holder may propose that part of his land be used as a Country Park or a picnic site or transit caravan site. In England and Wales similar powers exist, but they can be used only where it is not possible to make public provision. As yet, the number of cases in which support has been given is small, but the potential for growth now exists. Similarly, private landowners who make Access Agreements with local authorities can receive financial assistance towards the cost of wardening and to compensate for any loss which such recreational use entails to agricultural or silvicultural production. Landowners are becoming increasingly aware of the opportunities to control the recreational pressures that these measures offer.

There are also signs that commercial initiatives to provide recreational opportunities that are not grant-aided are of increasing importance. An interesting development in south-east England is the Countryside Club, which is open to members of the public for a fee of £10.50, for which they receive a key giving them access to fifty woods. In Scotland a Scottish Recreational Land Association was formed in 1972 to link those landowners interested in using their land for recreational purposes, and there are several instances of owners attempting to develop the recreational potential of their estates. One example is provided by the Kilkerran Estates in Ayrshire, covering some 11 500 acres (4654 ha). Of the agricultural land, 85 per cent is let, but a company, Kilkerran Parklands, has been established to develop the land for sport, leisure, recreational and tourist use, especially through activities that can coexist with agriculture and forestry (Ferguson, 1972). If it does not prove possible to generate sufficient income in this way, semi-rural pursuits such as golf will be developed. Such developments are likely to become increasingly common.

LUSION

Chapter 6 has established that the physical resources in the countryside contribute in varying degrees to the ability of the countryside at large to support and sustain recreational activities of different kinds. Although assessment procedures are still simple and require much greater sophistication, it has been possible to demonstrate that an identifiable range of 'goods' existed in the countryside which were capable of supplying the range of recreational experiences demanded by the British population. This chapter, however, has shown that this simple and theoretical concept of the demand/supply model is complicated by the reality of the multifarious interests, both public and private, which control their use and management of rural land. These interests mould and often impinge on the free workings of the recreational market and it is clear that an evaluation of those resources actually available for recreational use can only be fully appreciated if these constraints are taken into account.

Although some private landowners have developed parts of their holdings for recreational purposes, it is clear that for the foreseeable future such development will take place on only a minority of holdings and estates. Many occupiers lack the skill, interest, temperament or capital to make such ventures a success; others lack the time, while still others lack the opportunity, being too remote from major urban centres or holiday areas, or occupying the kind of rural land, such as intensively managed farmland or young coniferous plantations, which is unattractive to recreationists. Public policies will also be important for those who do not wish to participate or who wish to avoid or minimise recreational pressures. One view of the Country Park is that it should act as a honeypot, attracting visitors, and so relieve pressure on other rural land. Even those who wish to escape urban pressures may find that this can best be done by sacrificing a little land, which can often easily be spared because of its physical characteristics, to provide a picnic or camping site.

A great deal will also depend on public attitudes, particularly on the willingness of the public to pay for recreational opportunities and facilities in the countryside. Many land-holders say that they do not object to well-behaved visitors to the countryside and certainly one of the best hopes for avoiding friction between those seeking recreation in the countryside and those who earn their livelihood from rural land will be through education, particularly of the young. A Committee on Environmental Education, representing a wide range of interests, has been established in England and Wales, and a comparable Committee on Education and the Countryside existed in Scotland until 1974. Increasing numbers of schools at all levels in the educational hierarchy are providing pupils with opportunities to study the countryside, both in formal classes and on field excursions. Many local education authorities now provide field and outdoor centres, capable of satisfying a wide range of recreational needs in the broadest sense; indeed, such centres are now themselves important ingredients of the rural scene in some parts of Great Britain, such as the Welsh Borderland. Though catering for a minority of pupils, they provide an example of far-sighted public policies for the countryside, which will help to make it easier for recreation and rural production to coexist.

In the short run, recreational pressures and conflicts will be eased by well-planned recreational strategies, which zone the countryside according to its suitability to withstand recreational pressures without harming the resource base itself and without interfering with the main business of the countryside, and which provide recreational opportunities, whether in Country Parks and other facilities in the public sector or on those private estates whose owners are anxious to provide such opportunities. For it is clear that public policies, public land-owners and private land-holders at large each have a part to play in meeting a recreational demand that will probably continue to grow at its present rate of about 10 per cent per annum, one of the fastest of any sector of the national economy. Understandably, the decisions that lead to these policies and the attitudes that inform them will be an important area of research. Equally important are the spatial perceptions of those who seek recreation in the countryside; for these help to determine the 'journey to play', which is the subject of the next chapter.

# 8 The Interaction of Recreationists and Resources

The spatial interaction between the homes of recreationists and the resources they use has emerged as a key factor in the analysis of the demand/supply model. In chapter 4 data-dredging at a regional scale revealed a distinctive distribution of recreational activities in the countryside; some were located on the edges of towns and cities, while participants in other activities had to make longer journeys through the countryside to reach particular resources. In chapter 6 the ability of resources in the countryside to support recreational activities was discussed and the actual use of such resources was seen to depend on proximity to towns and cities and on the willingness of people to travel. It is clear that a better under-standing of recreation in the countryside will be found, not in separate studies of either the supply of, or the demand for recreational resources, nor indeed in their abstract analysis, but in an integrated study of their interaction. Because the homes of recreationists and the resources they use are separated in space, the interaction between demand and supply creates patterns of movement, and the distances between origins and destinations influence not only the scale of demand, but also the available supply of resources.

These patterns of movement, which result from the use of the countryside for recreation, are distinctive and contrast markedly with those of people travelling to obtain other goods and services. For example, whereas the individual who travels to work, on business or to shop, is generally involved in a complex pattern of intra-urban movements, the origins and destinations of journeys for outdoor recreation are usually widely separated. The origins, which can readily be defined, are usually the towns and cities of Great Britain, in which the majority of the population lives, whereas the destinations in the countryside are necessarily some distance away. Superimposed on these daily movements from home are complex movements of those on holiday, many of whom will have some temporary holi-day base from which they will make excursions into the surrounding countryside. This chapter will examine the importance of this spatial interaction between the demand for and the supply of recreational resources and will consider the factors that govern its form and nature, namely, the nature of the recreational activities themselves, the type of resources they require and the distances separating re-creationists and resources. The chapter is divided into two parts. In the first, the pattern of journeys from home for both active and passive recreation will be analysed; in the second, attention will be focused on the touring caravan as an important but distinctive form of holiday traffic.

## RECREATIONAL TRAVEL

### User-oriented and Resource-based Activities

Each kind of active recreation requires a distinctive set of physical resources, and the ability of an area to support such activities must obviously depend on the availability of such resources, as chapter 6 has shown. Attempts have therefore been made in most regional studies to define the 'space needs' of recreational activities in some way. Yet, it is not only the amount and kind of land required at this point of consumption that characterises the individual activities, but also the length of journey that recreationists are prepared to make to reach suitable resources. Clearly, these two elements are intimately related, for the more specific (and hence scarcer) the resources required for a particular activity, the further participants may have to travel to find suitable conditions. Conversely, the more general the requirements, the shorter the distance and the greater the probability that recreationists will be able to find resources near their homes.

This contrast between 'resource'-based and 'demand'-oriented activities was noted in North America by Clawson and was also clear from the survey of clubs and associations described in chapter 4, which showed that while some activities, such as fishing, hill-walking and sailing, were wholly dependent on relatively scarce resources, others, such as riding, motor sports and golf, were much less demanding and so had a much greater range of possible locations. Clawson divided recreational areas into three types, user-oriented, resource-based and intermediate (table 8.1), and these, while devised in an American context, also have relevance to outdoor recreation in Great Britain.

Law (1967) has incorporated similar distance relationships in England and Wales in a classification of recreational facilities and resources based on their relative powers of attraction over distance. After examining a series of recreational studies, she suggested a fivefold division of facilities according to whether they have a local, intermediate, sub-regional, regional or national zone of influence. She suggested that local and intermediate facilities would perhaps draw the bulk of their visitors from between 5 and 10 miles (8–16 km), sub-regional from 5–10 to 20–30 miles (32–48 km) and regional from 20–30 to 50 miles (80 km), while there would be no such limitation for facilities of national significance. It was further argued that the first three groups came within the range of half-day visitors while regional facilities would require a day visit.

Such distinctions are fundamental for the planning of outdoor recreation. The distinctive spatial distribution of different types of activities demonstrates that it is more realistic to view active pursuits not singly, but in groups which make similar use of resources and attract similar participants, a view that was given further support in the recognition of recreation types, discussed in chapter 5. Figure 8.1 demonstrates diagrammatically, on the evidence of the surveys of central Scotland, the distances participants travel in pursuit of their leisure activities; so that they can be compared, the results from the Lanark and Edinburgh surveys are shown separately.

The first point revealed by figure 8.1 is the statistical confirmation of the observed contrast between demand- and resource-oriented activities, which is demonstrated in figure 6.1. The activities that are located in the 0–10 mile

## TABLE 8.1

### A GENERAL CLASSIFICATION OF OUTDOOR RECREATIONAL USES AND RESOURCES

| | *Type of recreation area* | | |
|---|---|---|---|
| *Item* | *User-oriented* | *Resource-based* | *Intermediate* |
| General location | Close to users; on whatever resources are available | Where outstanding resources can be found; may be distant from most users | Must not be too remote from users; on best resources available within distance limitation |
| Major types of activity | Games, such as golf and tennis; swimming, picnicking, walks, horse-riding; zoos, etc.; play by children | Major sightseeing, scientific, historical interest; hiking, mountain-climbing, camping, fishing, hunting | Camping, picnicking, hiking, swimming, hunting, fishing |
| When major use occurs | After hours (school or work) | Vacations | Day outings and weekends |
| Typical sizes of areas | One to a hundred or at most to a few hundred acres | Usually some thousands of acres, perhaps many thousands | A hundred to several thousand acres |
| Common types of agency responsibility | City, county, or other local government; private | National parks and national forests primarily; state parks in some cases; private, especially for seashore and major lakes | Federal reservoirs; state parks; private |

Source:    Clawson, Held and Stoddard (1960), p. 136

(0–16 km) zone are largely those with resource needs that can be met in many rural areas; indeed, those required for some activities, such as golf and cricket, could be found in urban parks or in suitable locations on the urban fringe. Within the 10–20 mile (16–32 km) zone the range of activities is greater, but this zone tends to be dominated by those activities that, while requiring particular kinds of resource, make demands that are nevertheless readily met in central Scotland within relatively short distances of the homes of participants — for example, horse-riding, hiking, walking and field sports. At a greater distance the list of activities is dominated by sports and physical pursuits that require very specific resources and often involve long journeys from home — for example, orienteering,

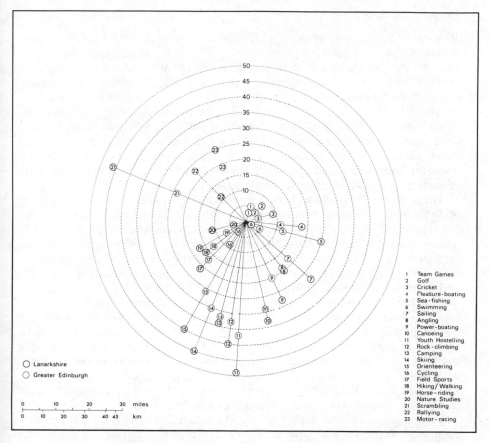

Figure 8.1  Active pursuits: distance relationships

canoeing, skiing and rock-climbing. There is also a fairly high correlation between
the ranking of activities by participation levels and that by distance travelled to
pursue them. While there are exceptions to this generalisation, it appears that,
despite the growing mobility of the population, the most popular sports are still
those that can be conveniently pursued near home.

Comparison of the results from the Edinburgh and Lanark surveys shows that
the distances travelled for demand-oriented activities are more similar than those
of resource-based activities; for the more distinctive the resources required for an
activity, the more likely it is that there will be large variations from one area to
another. This relationship is best demonstrated by a comparison between the
distances travelled for various kinds of water-based activities. Whereas residents of
Edinburgh enjoy unrivalled access to water resources in the Firth of Forth, which
provides good opportunities for a variety of water-based activities, the residents of
Lanarkshire must seek suitable water bodies outside their county, and their
journeys for water-based recreation are inevitably much longer.

## Distance and Resources

If comparable and consistent relationships between recreational resources and the distances that participants are prepared to travel to enjoy these resources can be established, thresholds can be determined beyond which 'suitable' resources will, in effect, be inaccessible. The location of resources thus affects participation; however inclined the residents of particular areas may be to undertake a particular activity, the probability of this desire being transformed into participation will, in part at least, be a measure of the availability of accessible resources. It has already been noted that the more popular activities are generally those that can be pursued near home; this concept, which is termed 'supply-generated demand', is vitally important to an understanding of participation in recreation and to the possibility of developing particular resources within a region.

The Greater Edinburgh and Lanark surveys clearly illustrate the influence of available supply on figures for participation. Although these areas are contiguous, they are very differently endowed with recreational resources, and this in turn influences levels of participation. This relationship is particularly marked in skiing, for although both regions are located many miles from the major skiing centres in the Scottish Highlands, the residents of Greater Edinburgh have ready access to a well-equipped artificial ski-slope at Hillend on the outskirts of the city, a facility that the residents of Lanarkshire do not enjoy. It is not, therefore, surprising that recent levels of participation in skiing in the Edinburgh area should be nearly double those in Lanarkshire. A similar contrast emerges between the proportion of residents of the two areas who participate in the more popular activities of walking and hiking. In Greater Edinburgh, ample and readily accessible opportunities for walking lie close to the city and recent participation in this activity is two-thirds higher than that in Lanarkshire, where areas used for hill-walking are mainly in the south of the county, some distance from the main urban areas.

The importance of such supply-generated demand determining the pattern of countryside recreation was uppermost in the minds of the organisers of the North West Sports Council's survey (1972) of outdoor recreation in north-west England, and an attempt was made to examine the relationship between participation levels and the availability of accessible resources for the activities under consideration. Three hypotheses were proposed to explain the spatial relationship between supply and demand:

(1) For a given sport, the proportion of participants will be greater in a population with a large number of facilities than in one where few facilities are available.
(2) The number of people in a population participating in a sport increases in proportion to the increase in the number of facilities available.
(3) People play a sport at the nearest available facility.

To test these hypotheses, twelve sports were analysed. The number of facilities for each sport that were located between specified radii from a respondent's home was established; the critical distances varied with the sport, but three were common to all sports: 1·2 miles (2 km), 3·1 miles (5 km) and 6·2 miles (10 km). It was considered both unnecessary and inappropriate to relate the total sample to the pro-

TABLE 8.2

DISTANCES AND POPULATION 'AT RISK' IN NORTH-WEST ENGLAND

| Sports | Distances for which analysis performed (km) | | | | | | | | Population 'at risk' and percentage of all players included | |
|---|---|---|---|---|---|---|---|---|---|---|
| Bowls* | ½ | 1 | 2 | 3 | 5 | 7 | 10 | | Whole sample | 100 |
| Cricket* | ½ | 1 | 2 | 3 | 5 | 10 | 20 | | Males 12–59 | 95 |
| Soccer* | ½ | 1 | 2 | 3 | 5 | 10 | 20 | | Males 12–44 | 97 |
| Tennis* | ½ | 1 | 2 | 3 | 5 | 10 | 15 | | All 12–59 | 99 |
| Rugby | | 1 | 2 | 3 | 5 | 10 | 15 | 30 | Males 12–44 | 100 |
| Hockey | | 1 | 2 | 3 | 5 | 10 | 15 | 30 | Females 12–44† | 92 |
| Swimming | | 1 | 2 | 3 | 5 | 10 | 20 | 40 | All 12–64 | 100 |
| Indoor sports‡ | ½ | 2 | 5 | 10 | 15 | 20 | 25 | 30 | All 12–59 | 99 |
| Riding | | 2 | 5 | 10 | 15 | 20 | 30 | 40 | All 12–44 | 97 |
| Golf* | | 2 | 5 | 10 | 15 | 20 | 30 | 50 | Whole sample | 100 |
| Fishing* | | 2 | 4 | 10 | 20 | 30 | 50 | 70 | Whole sample | 100 |
| Sailing | | 2 | 5 | 10 | 25 | 50 | 75 | 99 | All 12–59 | 100 |

*Sports for which sub-samples were large enough to allow breakdown by strata to be attempted.

† Only 8 percent of the hockey players in the sample were male; the rest were women aged between 12–44 and it was for these this exercise was carried out.

‡ This is a diverse group of activities but using one type of facility; it was adopted to ensure a large sub-sample.

Source:   North West Sports Council (1972), p. 153.

vision of facilities in the sports in which participants have distinctive social and
demographic profiles. The survey accordingly established the population 'at risk'
in nine sports, that is, the proportion of the total population who might potentially be expected to participate. Table 8.2 lists the twelve activities studied, the
zones for which the analysis was undertaken and the parameters that define the
population 'at risk' for the sports concerned.

Once the different levels of provision in each of the various zones had been
determined, the results were analysed to test participation in activities against
the supply of facilities. The results of this test were inconclusive; six of the
selected sports – namely, cricket, bowls, soccer, tennis, golf and fishing – supported
the first hypothesis, that is, that the percentage of participants was greater in an
area of high provision than in one of low provision, but this hypothesis was not
borne out by the remaining six activities.

The analysis indicated that increases in the density of facilities were most
effective at short distances; at distances greater than six miles (10 km), participation increased with an increase in facilities in only one of the sports (fishing).
In the remaining eleven sports an increase in participation with an increase in the
number of facilities only occurred within six miles (10 km) of respondents' homes.
The degree of response to this hypothesis could not be measured with sufficient accuracy because of the small size of the sub-samples of participants in
each of the activities concerned.

The third hypothesis, that people generally played at the nearest available
facility, was also only partially confirmed. In some sports, for example, bowls
and golf, a higher proportion of people living near facilities participated than of
those living further away, but the survey identified sports in which, for various
reasons, people were not likely to participate at the nearest facility, for example,
team games and fishing.

It is unfortunate that this analysis was so inconclusive and that only tentative
statements can be made about the effect of supply on demand. As the report
itself states, the supply/demand relationship is a complex one, and the analysis
is a useful pioneer attempt to investigate these relationships. There can be little
doubt that other studies will seek to unravel the effects of the location of resources
on participation. It is necessary to establish how the participants themselves perceive 'available supply' and what factors determine their concept of accessibility
and proximity.

## Passive Recreation and the Journey to Play

As chapters 2 and 3 revealed, outdoor recreation in the countryside is dominated
by passive rather than active recreation. Although participants in active recreation
must undertake journeys from their homes to the resources they require in order
to enjoy their chosen pastime, the relationship between passive recreationists and
the 'journey to play' is much more subtle.

As the home-interview surveys in central Scotland have shown, nearly one in
four respondents had been for a drive for pleasure during the previous weekend,
and 87 per cent of all car owners had taken at least one drive for pleasure lasting
more than two hours during the month before the interview, the average being

four trips. It is evident that the 'trip out' has a wider appeal than any other activity in the countryside. It is also clear that the role of the recreational journey is a much more essential part of the total recreational experience in passive recreation than it is in active recreation.

For passive recreationists, then, 'the medium is the message' and unravelling the nature of the spatial interaction with resources will make a major contribution to understanding the nature of passive recreation in the countryside. However, before the spatial expression of such pursuits is examined, it is best to consider the nature of the 'complete personal mobility' that the motor vehicle provides. While the role of car-borne recreation should not be underestimated, it is important to be aware of its limitations. In the city a vehicle can give easy access to many recreational facilities, but outside the town this is not always the case; for the road network is far less dense and the car can bring only part of the countryside within reach. It is clear that few recreationists overcome these limitations. Cars do provide a superficial air of mobility, but in practice the mobility of individuals is a good deal less than is often claimed; very large areas of attractive countryside in Scotland have an in-built protection against car-borne recreationists. While the central lowlands of Scotland are characterised by a relatively intricate and close-knit pattern of communications, the uplands further south are traversed by only a sparse system of roads and traffic is largely confined to the major roads, which usually skirt the high ground. As a result, several large 'islands' of countryside have been created, generally over 1000 feet (300 m) in height, and these are thus unintentionally protected against the adverse affects of 'people pressure' (figure 8.2). More accessible areas close to roads, on the other hand, are frequently visited by large numbers of people who seek passive recreation but do not stray far from their cars. The open panoramas and the vistas of attractive countryside provide an illusion of freedom from which very few town dwellers ever attempt to escape. The slim corridors of land on either side of metalled roads thus imprison their motor vehicles and represent the effective limits of colonisation by urban recreationists; the rest of the countryside is invaded only by an intrepid minority who take to the hills on foot. This immobility of car-borne recreationists has been confirmed by a large number of surveys (for example, Burton, 1967; Wager, 1967).

Even in the lowlands, where access is easier, the discipline of urban living protects the countryside; the motorist in the town obeys traffic lights, road signs and parking restrictions and responds to similar direction in the countryside. Although he often has no clear knowledge of his final destination he commits himself to the suggested route under the marshalling influence of the sign post. Thus, while the major roads to seaside and beauty spot are congested with ordered convoys, the lanes and tracks of the intervening countryside remain largely undisturbed. Whatever the spatial pattern of recreational journeys, there is little doubt that the dominance of recreational traffic is particularly marked at weekends; a specially designed cordon survey was undertaken in the studies of central Scotland to investigate the geographical patterns of the 'trip out'.

## Cordon Survey in Central Scotland

The justification for a cordon survey is that all kinds of outdoor recreation in the country necessitate a journey. Because most journeys originate in the town, a

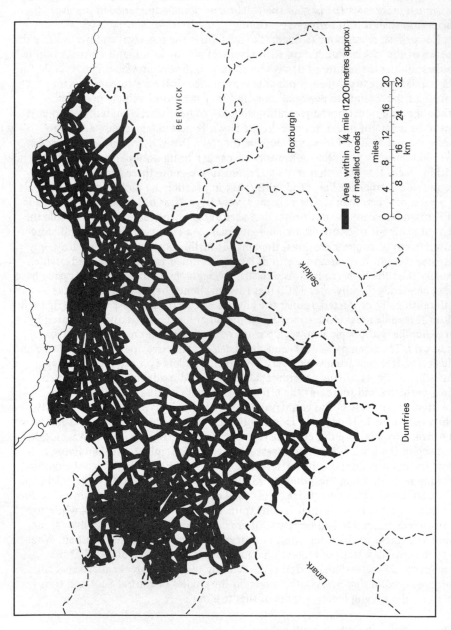

Figure 8.2 Central Scotland: traffic pressures

cordon can be conveniently established at the edge of the town; as recreationists pass through this cordon they can be observed, counted, recorded and interviewed. In the studies of central Scotland, such a survey was made easier by the distinctive pattern of communications and by the distribution of population. In Lanarkshire the population is concentrated in the north and west of the county in a compact area adjoining the city of Glasgow; in Greater Edinburgh most of the population lives in the city and in adjacent settlements, with lesser concentrations in the industrialised parts of the Lothians (figure 8.3). It is primarily these urban agglomerations that generate the recreational traffic, while the resources able to support outdoor recreation are some distance from the centres of population, primarily in the south of Peeblesshire and East Lothian. Recreational traffic from the 'generating' areas in the towns to the rural 'reception' areas could thus be monitored by a network of survey points around the two main urban areas (see also Beaty, Pearson-Kirk, Cal and Greig, 1973).

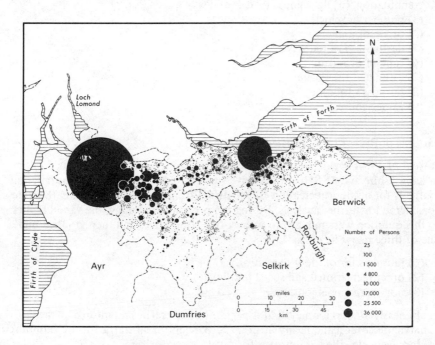

Figure 8.3  Central Scotland: distribution of population

After an examination of the road system, twenty-one survey points were selected in Lanarkshire and twelve in Greater Edinburgh; these cordons enclosed three-quarters of the resident population of both study areas and covered all major routes. The exact location of survey points was chosen after consultation with the Ministry of Transport (which had responsibility for trunk roads) and the police. The volume of weekend traffic for these roads was then examined so that

the number of interviewers could be related to expected volumes of traffic. At
each point a police officer controlled traffic and up to three interviewers were used,
depending on the volume of traffic. A traffic count was taken throughout the
survey by means of automatic counters and cumulative totals were recorded at
half-hourly intervals, so that the sample data in those intervals could be related to
total traffic.

Occupants of vehicles leaving the urban areas were interviewed between 9 a.m.
and 5 p.m. on two Sundays in August and approximately 15 000 interviews were
completed. Traffic was heavy and, to minimise inconvenience, only a short
questionnaire was used taking only one minute to complete; nine items of information were recorded, only six of which required answers to questions, the
remainder being obtained by observation. The questions covered:

(1) time of interview
(2) type of vehicle: (a) car, (b) motorcycle, (c) private omnibus or motorcycle
combination, (d) light goods (van), (e) heavy goods (lorry)
(3) number in vehicle
(4) origin of journey
(5) destination of journey
(6) time of departure
(7) estimated time of return to origin
(8) purpose of journey
(9) garage address

## Patterns of Recreational Traffic in Central Scotland

A total of 39 447 vehicles was recorded at the twenty-one points on the cordon
in Lanarkshire and 35 810 at the twelve survey points in Greater Edinburgh; only
journeys for outdoor recreation (as identified from answers to question (8) were
considered for further analysis. During the preliminary coding, the varied replies
to this question were reduced to twenty-one alternatives and then grouped under
one of three major headings:

(1) journeys for outdoor recreation
(2) other recreational and social journeys
(3) non-recreational journeys.

In all, nearly 17 000 journeys (44·4 per cent of all traffic) monitored at the
Lanarkshire cordon and nearly 20 000 (55 per cent of all traffic) at the Edinburgh
cordon, were classified as journeys for outdoor recreation.

Urban centres generate traffic roughly in proportion to their size and the totals
observed at both cordons were as expected, but the destinations of journeys are
much more difficult to predict, for neither the destination nor the proportion of
traffic can be calculated easily. Although certain major movements are fairly
predictable, the specific destinations depend largely on the whims and fancies of
individuals. Figure 8.4 shows the destinations of journeys monitored at both cordons and indicates clearly the dispersed nature of destinations, with journeys
radiating from the survey cordons to all points of the compass. On closer examination, however, the selection of destinations does not appear to be entirely

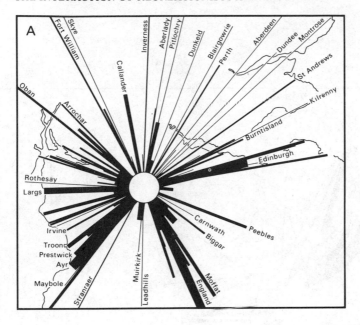

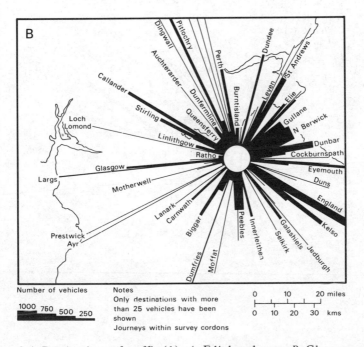

Figure 8.4 Destinations of traffic (1): *A*. Edinburgh area; *B*. Glasgow area

162

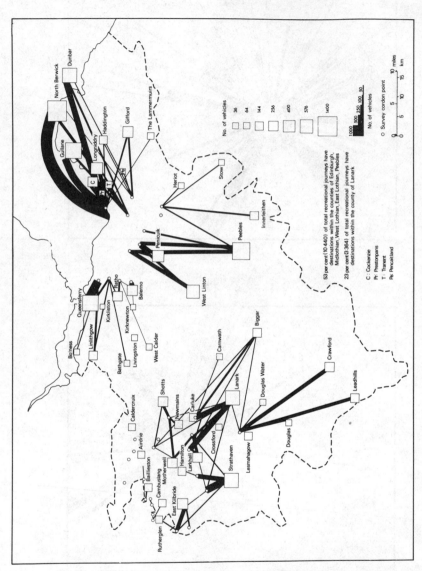

Figure 8.5 Destinations of traffic (2): recreational journeys in central Scotland

random and several general features emerge from both surveys.

Short journeys account for a large proportion of all this recreational traffic, many destinations lying within 10 miles (16 km) of the centre of the survey cordon. Yet, while numbers declined beyond this local zone, an intermediate zone was identified, approximately 25–40 miles (40-64 km) from the centre of the cordoned area, which attracted a large number of day visitors.

A more detailed examination of recreational journeys terminating within each of these two study areas confirms the existence of these 'local' and 'intermediate' zones (figure 8.5). As in active recreation, the distance that pleasure motorists are prepared to travel is crucial in the planning and provision of facilities for them, for the proper siting of developments can ensure that the correct balance is struck between accessibility and use. The distances of all trips for outdoor recreation were therefore computed, using the origins and destinations provided by those interviewed; a graph of the distribution of these journeys is shown for both cordons in figure 8.6.

Since the census points were situated at the edge of the major centres of population in the study areas, many short journeys must have escaped recording, so that journeys between 0 and 10 miles (16 km) have been underestimated at most stations, a fact reflected in the summary histogram. Even so, approximately 20 per cent of all recorded journeys involved an outward movement of less than 10 miles. Within this category are included those journeys for active pursuits, such as golf and swimming, which tend to take place near the homes of participants; also included is a large number of informal trips made either in the morning or in the afternoon.

If travelling is regarded from an economic point of view as a 'disutility' which adds to the cost of the trip out, the histogram of distances travelled should show the characteristic features of the classic demand curve; 'consumption' (the number of recreational journeys) would be inversely related to 'cost' (the length of the journey). Yet, as has been shown, the evidence from the Lanark and Edinburgh surveys does not support this evaluation, for many stations recorded a sharp increase in the number of journeys in the 25–40 mile (40-64 km) range, after a steady decline from the peak at 10 miles (16 km). The incidence of this feature at so many of the census points in both Lanarkshire and Greater Edinburgh cannot be attributed to the accidental siting of interview stations in relation to particular resources for recreation or to the balance between half-day and day trips, and seems to indicate that it is characteristic of recreational journeys.

The most likely explanation is that the journey itself has a positive appeal. Those numerous travellers who were 'just out for a ride' thus acquire a new significance, for it appears that for many of them the ride itself is an important part of the recreational experience. The location of specific resources for recreation will, of course, influence patterns of travel, but it must equally be recognised that, even when the desired facilities exist near home, many will choose to travel further afield so that their wish for a drive in the countryside can be satisfied. An outward journey of about one hour would seem to satisfy the needs of most people and it appears that the controlling factor is the time taken for the journey, rather than the distance travelled. It is thus interesting to note that drivers using the M8 motorway, on which faster travel was possible, were prepared to travel 5-10 miles (8-16

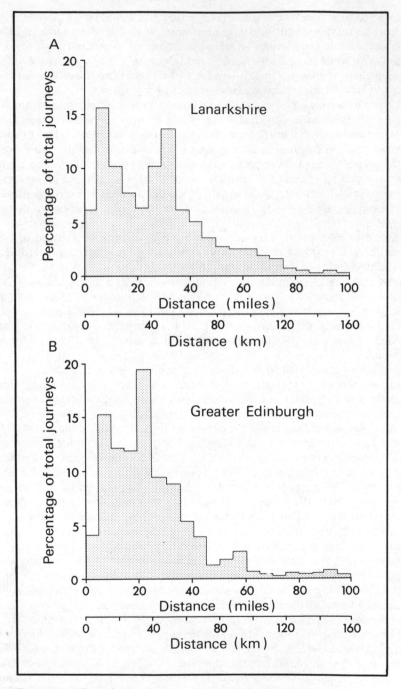

Figure 8.6  Histograms of distances travelled on recreational journeys:
*A*. Lanarkshire; *B*. Greater Edinburgh

km) further than most motorists. At distances above 40 miles (64 km) the number
of journeys decreases as distance increases and the graph approximates more closely
to the classic demand curve. It is true that the data for several stations show further
peaks at distances greater than 40 miles (64 km), but no consistent pattern
emerges, and it is likely that such peaks indicate the presence of particularly
attractive locations, which induce many visitors to make longer journeys.

This examination of recreational traffic thus provided a greater understanding
of the use recreationists make of countryside resources in central Scotland, and
revealed an ordered pattern of both regional and local movements. These patterns
of recreational journeys show both the desire of the motoring public for a particular kind of recreation and the present resources available to meet these demands.
Yet, despite differences in types of scenery and in the provision for recreation
throughout the study area, there are trends common to the majority of journeys,
for their timing, origin, destination and even the distance travelled have conformed
to a pattern.

The highly dispersed nature of recreational journeys also shows the irrelevance
of local authority boundaries to such movements and thus the necessity of planning outdoor recreation on at least a regional scale. In Lanarkshire over 75 per cent
of the journeys for outdoor recreation that were generated within the county were
destined for locations beyond its boundaries. Greater Edinburgh, with its greater
wealth of recreational resources, was better able to meet local demands, but, even
so, nearly 50 per cent of journeys made by recreationists had destinations outside
the study area. Under the present structure of local government, the local authorities in urban areas that 'export' large volumes of recreational traffic, do not
have to accept responsibility for the development of recreational facilities outside their boundaries, while those in 'receiving' areas, where appropriate developments might be expected to take place, are often unable or disinclined to finance
the development of facilities that will cater primarily for recreationists from nearby towns. The provision of such recreational facilities in the countryside will more
easily be achieved under the new structure of local government (Local Government
(Scotland) Act, 1973).

## Passive Recreation in North-West England

The positive value of the passive recreation journey demonstrated by the Scottish
studies was also confirmed in *Leisure in the North West* (North West Sports
Council, 1972), in which the trip from home was also examined. This survey
established that the median one-way distance for full-day trips was between 40 and
50 miles (64–80 km) but, as the report correctly states, such a median figure alone
has little relevance; it is rather the whole range of distance over which demand is
spread that is important. The findings of this report were summarised thus:
'Having ventured forth for the day, the tripper likes at least to make the experience
commensurate with the effort. Destinations close at hand had little favour. Only
18 per cent travelled less than 20 miles; 26 per cent were satisfied with journeys
of between 20 and 40 miles, but more than a third (35 per cent) had ventured
between 40 and 75 miles. Evidence from many other sources underlines this
general finding, that for a majority of trippers a one-way journey of some $1\frac{1}{2}$–2
hours is typical, long enough to give the feeling of "getting away from it all", but

not so long that there is little time or consequence available at the destination'
(North West Sports Council, 1972, p. 53). The longer distances reflect the fact that
this report was concerned with full-day trips only, whereas the Scottish study included all trips. Nevertheless, the major findings are similar and confirm the
consistency of distance and travelling patterns among those engaged in passive
recreation.

### Recreational Journeys in the Northern Region

Those studying recreation in the Northern Region also attempted to examine the
recreational movement of people from their homes. For various reasons, primarily
the structure of the sample used in the home-interview survey, it was impossible
to carry out an exhaustive analysis of movement from one part of northern
England to another, but certain trends did emerge. Recreational travel in summer
was appreciably greater on Sundays than on Saturdays, partly because the time-
budget for journeys from home on Saturday is less (see chapter 2). Secondly, this
survey established that there were substantial variations in the extent to which
people travel outside their home area. For example, while only 7 per cent of those
living on the Northumberland coast leave this area on an average Saturday and only
16 per cent on an average Sunday, the comparable figures for the Tyneside conurbation were 34 per cent and 39 per cent, respectively. It thus appears that even
within regions, there are notable 'exporting' and 'receiving' areas. It also appears
that, despite the complex patterns of movement in the Northern Region, most
people took part in recreational activities quite close to their homes. On an average
Saturday, 73 per cent of all activities took place in the sub-area in which participants lived, and the comparable figure on an average Sunday was 70 per cent.
In agreement with the Scottish studies the most prominent kind of journeys from
home were those for informal recreation.

## THE TOURING CARAVAN

This concept of exporting and receiving areas is equally important in respect of
holiday travel, which has so far largely been disregarded in this discussion. Throughout the home-interview survey and the cordon survey, the main emphasis has been
on travel from home, but recreational travel is influenced, as chapter 2 has shown,
by the time available for leisure. On both short and long holidays, those seeking
outdoor recreation in the countryside can travel much further than on day trips
and will generally operate from some holiday base or bases. For a large proportion of the British residents who take their main holiday in Great Britain (26
million in 1968), this holiday base is somewhere on or near the coast, from which
no part of the country is more than 75 miles (120 km). From such a base, large
numbers of these visitors will tour the surrounding countryside. Evidence from
Wales in 1961 showed that 42 per cent of visitors made excursions of more than
10 miles (16 km) outward from these centres, and surveys in Devonshire have
shown that even on such a tourist attraction as Dartmoor, visitors from outside
the Dartmoor area outnumbered those staying in the area by seven to one (Patmore,
1970). The impact of visitors on recreational resources in the countryside may
thus be far greater than figures of resident population suggest; on Speyside, for

example, visitors at the peak of the season were equivalent to some three-quarters of the resident population (Mackinlay, 1969) and in Anglesey, one of the most popular holiday areas, visitors probably outnumbered residents (Archer, 1973). The growing popularity of second homes is also a factor, though on a much smaller scale than in most countries of western Europe or North America. According to a Wye College study, there were about 200 000 second homes in England and Wales in 1969 (Bielckus, Rogers and Wibberley, 1972), excluding caravans, of which there were probably about 375 000 (Downing and Dower, 1973). Holidays in caravans represented about 16 per cent of main holidays in Great Britain in 1970, a proportion that has been rising fairly steadily over the past twenty-five years (Owen and Duffield, 1971, p.88). Of particular relevance to the present discussion are the touring caravans, which numbered some 221 000 in 1970 (Owen and Duffield, 1971, p. 24); for they provide a mobile holiday home that can bring the recreationist to the resource. The distinctive features of caravan travel are thus worthy of special attention.

Until recently there has been little information about this activity, in part because the mobility of caravanners and the wide dispersal of the sites they use make the acquisition of data particularly difficult. The discussion that follows highlights the distinctive spatial relationships and distributions that characterise this activity and is based upon a survey of touring caravans in Scotland (Owen and Duffield, 1971). It also illustrates the methodologies and procedures that can be used to monitor movements of all kinds of recreational traffic; these same techniques were subsequently used to monitor the movements of summer holiday traffic throughout Scotland.

This survey was undertaken in 1970 for the Scottish Tourist Board, the Countryside Commission for Scotland and the Highlands and Islands Development Board. Its primary objectives were:

(1) to provide estimates of the volume, frequency and distribution of caravan traffic leaving central Scotland for the Scottish Highlands over the summer period;
(2) to estimate the volume of holiday traffic, so that touring by caravan could be examined in the context of tourism and recreation;
(3) to establish the characteristic features of caravanning and caravan holidays in Scotland;
(4) to investigate the travel patterns of caravanners who visit Scotland, including their regions of origin and the areas and sites they visited;
(5) to investigate the experiences of mobile caravanners and their attitudes to caravanning in Scotland.

The surveys designed to meet these objectives contained five elements, all but one involving a cordon survey. They were:

(1) the recording of caravan traffic leaving the Central Belt for the Scottish Highlands in summer, using automatic recorders at three strategic locations;
(2) roadside interviews with occupants of south-bound caravan traffic on the A74, A7, A68 and A1 roads, undertaken at points near the English–Scottish border;

(3) a survey of vehicle registration letters on caravans passing the three
locations at which automatic recorders were sited;

(4) the automatic monitoring of traffic in late autumn at the three survey
points;

(5) a postal survey of approximately 7000 members of the Caravan Club.

## Automatic Recording Survey

The aims of the automatic recording survey fulfilled the first two objectives.
Although those aims were simple in concept, achieving them required either a
large labour force or complex recording apparatus, for statistics were required of
daily caravan traffic for a continuous period for three months. While the data
could have been collected by observers, costs would have been prohibitively high,
and over such a long period expenditure would be greatly reduced by the use of
automatic recorders. The technique designed for this survey combined the use of
automatic road counters and of cine cameras adapted for time-lapse photography.
Such photography, with the camera shutter actuated by a clock mechanism at
regular intervals, has been extensively used to obtain statistics of traffic flow. The
disadvantage of this system is that the sample of photographs taken is not governed
by the volume of traffic, and many photographs are taken when vehicles are not
present; it would, therefore, have been difficult to establish reliable estimates of
the volume, frequency and distribution of caravans. For this project, the cameras
and counters were linked so that photographs were taken at intervals governed by
the frequency of vehicles, thus enabling a known sample of photographs to be
related to the total flow of traffic. A conventional pneumatic detector was fixed
to the road and each vehicle that passed operated the counting mechanism. After
a predetermined number of vehicles had passed, the counter activated the camera
and a photograph was taken of the selected vehicle.

Each cine camera could accommodate 200 feet of 16 mm film to give a total of
8000 photographs and a sample of approximately this size was taken from each site
every week — that is, more than a quarter of a million over the full period. It was
possible, therefore, to record approximately one week's traffic on a single reel. By
relating the sample photographs to figures for total traffic reliable estimates could
be made of the numbers of caravans passing the survey point over a fixed period.
The automatic recording survey began on the 23rd June 1970 and continued until
the 1st October, 100 days later.

In order to estimate the component of holiday traffic in summer, the automatic
traffic counters were re-located at the same sites for four weeks from 16th
November until 14th December 1970; late autumn traffic counts have a stable
pattern unaffected by the seasonal peaks that mark the summer period. On the
assumption that business, social and domestic traffic is relatively stable throughout
the year, it is possible to estimate the proportion of holiday traffic in summer by
subtracting the figures of average autumn traffic.

Sites had first to be selected for the cameras. Most holiday traffic entering
Scotland from the south uses one of four major roads — A74, A7, A68 and A1 —
and diffuses over the more complex network of routes in central Scotland, where
it is joined by that carrying the many other holidaymakers who are resident there
and are also heading for destinations north of the Highland line. Further north,

the road system is again simple and traffic is confined to a few routes by the bold relief of the Highlands. The narrow waist of central Scotland between the Clyde and Forth estuaries similarly channels traffic along a few routes and it was therefore possible to choose three strategic locations, namely, the Forth Road Bridge, the A9 south of Stirling and the A82 north of Dumbarton, at which automatic traffic counters could be located.

Over six million vehicles used the Forth Road Bridge in 1970, and the bulk of tourist traffic entering Scotland on the A7, A68 and A1 routes, as well as traffic generated locally in the Lothians, uses the bridge to reach destinations in north Scotland. The town of Stirling is the main focus for traffic in the northern half of the Central Belt, with two major routes, the A9 and the A80, entering the town from the south, the former bringing traffic from the south and east. A large proportion of the tourist traffic entering Scotland on the A74 moves northward through Motherwell, Airdrie and Cumbernauld to join vehicles from Glasgow and the west, and enter Stirling on the A80 (Duffield and Owen, 1970). This amalgam of tourist and domestic holiday traffic was monitored at a survey station south of the town. Routes to the north-west of the central lowlands are the least used by commercial traffic but nevertheless play a significant role in movements of tourist traffic. Apart from the large numbers of tourists from the Glasgow conurbation itself, there are many others from south of the Border whose main holiday destinations are in north and west Scotland. The A82 carries traffic from Glasgow along the western side of Loch Lomond to destinations in the Western Highlands. The recording station to the north of Dumbarton on the A82 monitored a large proportion of the north-bound holiday traffic. There is little doubt that nearly all the holiday traffic leaving central Scotland for destinations to the north of the Highland Line was monitored at one or other of these stations.

The automatic recording survey was thus able to achieve its objective of providing statistically reliable estimates of the total volume of caravan traffic leaving the Central Belt for the Scottish Highlands throughout the summer period. The analysis of results from the individual stations also provided details on the frequency and geographical distribution of caravan traffic and these records were then linked to results from the roadside interview survey.

### Roadside Interview Survey

The roadside interview survey fulfilled the last three primary objectives of the study. The sponsor wished as many interviews as possible to be obtained with caravanners who had just taken a holiday in Scotland. Accordingly, census points were established on the A6 south of Carlisle (NT 452 492), at which traffic leaving Scotland on the A74, A7 and A75 was monitored, on the A68 at Carter Bar (NT 698 068) and on the A1 in East Lothian (NT 770 723). The survey itself took place on five weekends in August, during which a sample of south-bound caravans, both towed and motor, was stopped at random at each census point and the drivers interviewed, unless they were residents from Scotland on their way south for a holiday. A count of caravans was also taken throughout the survey, so that the sample data could be related to total traffic.

In the cordon surveys undertaken as part of the investigations in Lanarkshire and Greater Edinburgh a very short questionnaire was used because of the need to get the maximum number of interviews with the very small budget available. In the caravan survey, where the volume of traffic was much less, the questionnaire took between five and fifteen minutes to complete and covered three major topics:

(1) the patterns of travel, including questions on home address, point of entry into Scotland, and areas and sites visited;
(2) the characteristics of caravan holidays, including questions on size and composition of groups, duration of holidays, timing of visits and wild camping (that is, camping overnight on the roadside or on private land where no facilities are provided or charges made);
(3) the experiences and attitudes of caravanners, including questions on road conditions, site facilities and costs.

In all, 2688 caravanners were interviewed during the five weeks, and this information, together with the results of the automatic recording survey, provided a detailed picture of the geographical distribution and patterns of travel of caravanners in Scotland. In methodological terms, too, the Caravan Roadside Survey was extremely successful, confirming the feasibility of sampling one component of total holiday traffic, albeit a readily identifiable one, and extracting detailed, complex data from a co-operative and informed band of respondents. Initially there had been considerable doubt about the desirability and feasibility of delaying returning holidaymakers for several minutes and seeking answers to twenty-eight questions on their holiday, including a daily itinerary, but these fears proved groundless. This confidence in the roadside interview laid the foundation for future surveys carried out in the summer of 1973 when holidaymakers at the roadside, in coaches, on trains, on ferries and at airports were asked to devote even more time to complex questioning. Once again these surveys have confirmed that, given a properly structured and well-designed study, respondents will readily provide the necessary information.

## Postal Survey

The aims of the Postal Survey were:

(1) to provide a perspective for the results from the roadside interviews by establishing the patterns of caravanning over the period 1967–70, and by investigating respondents' plans for 1971, so that some tentative forecasts of future developments could be made;
(2) to investigate the popularity of other caravanning areas, both in the United Kingdom and abroad, so that the Scottish data could be seen in a broader context;
(3) to acquire details of caravanning for Great Britain as a whole for comparison with the Scottish data;
(4) to examine the preferences of caravanners for facilities at transit sites and lunch-time stops.

The collection of such data required a survey of caravanners in Great Britain, whether or not they had taken holidays in Scotland. No general list of names and addresses of caravan owners exists and it was decided to approach the national caravan clubs, which were known to represent a large proportion of touring caravanners. All three clubs (the Caravan Club, the Motor Caravanners' Club and the caravan section of the Camping Club of Great Britain and Ireland) agreed to co-operate and their membership lists provided the population from which a sample of 6878 touring caravanners was drawn. Each caravanner in the sample was sent a copy of the questionnaire accompanied by an explanatory letter requesting co-operation with the survey. In all, 3442 questionnaires were returned and these provide a comprehensive picture of caravanning in Great Britain.

It is important to remember, however, that the sample is self-selected, as in all postal surveys, and probably does not represent a statistically valid cross-section of Caravan Club members, let alone caravanners generally. It is probable that those returning completed questionnaires represent the more active club members or, alternatively, the more articulate or socially aware sections of the club. Accordingly, all conclusions drawn from the analysis of questionnaires obtained from postal surveys must be carefully surrounded by caveats, unless firm and reliable information exists on known parameters of the 'population' from which the sample is drawn, and corrective weighting can be undertaken.

## The Distribution of Caravan Traffic in Great Britain

The postal survey established patterns of visiting for both main and second caravan holidays over the period 1967–70 for a sample in Great Britain. Respondents were asked to give details of the locations visited over this period, thus providing a great deal of information on both popular places for holidays and areas used in transit. In order to gauge the regional importance of caravanning, holidays were allocated to twenty-one regions in England and Wales as well as to Scottish destinations and to others in continental Europe. Although many locations attracted some caravanners, a very large proportion went to relatively few holiday areas. Three popular areas each accounted for over 20 per cent of all main holidays and their locations make it unlikely that there was much double counting.

Analysis of the distribution of caravan traffic in Great Britain for both main and additional holidays revealed that accessibility is an important factor influencing these patterns of holidaymaking. When patterns of visiting were examined on a regional basis, they showed that the appeal of the major holiday areas varies over the country; table 8.3, which illustrates regional preferences, makes it clear that average figures for main holidays conceal quite large differences in regional preferences. For example, whereas less than 13 per cent of all caravanners from the south-central region of England visited Scotland in 1970, over 40 per cent of caravanners from Durham came to Scotland. The data from table 8.3 have been used to compile figure 8.7. So that the regional preferences for each of the six main holiday areas can be clearly seen in graphical form, the regions of England and Wales have been shaded to show whether caravanners in these areas have an above-average preference for the holiday area in question.

Caravanning holidays in continental Europe are also growing in importance, but there are variations in popularity which are related to areas of residence. For those in the south and east of England easier access to continental car ferries saves travel time and reduces costs, and it is not surprising that percentages from this area are above average. In 1970 south-west England, which attracted an average of

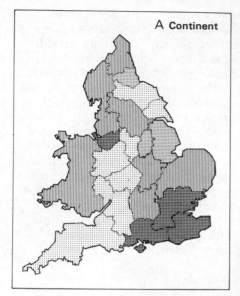
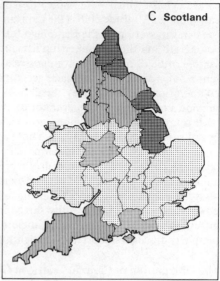
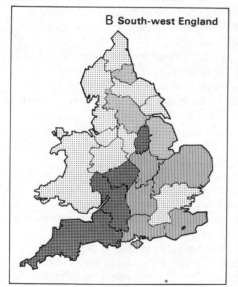
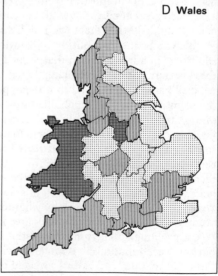

Figure 8.7  Regional preferences for 1970 main holidays

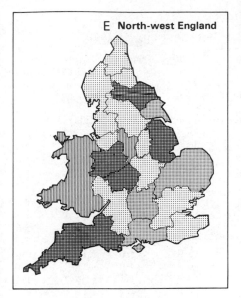

E **North-west England**

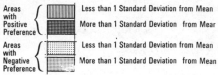

| Areas with Positive Preference | | Less than 1 Standard Deviation from Mean |
| | | More than 1 Standard Deviation from Mean |
| Areas with Negative Preference | | Less than 1 Standard Deviation from Mean |
| | | More than 1 Standard Deviation from Mean |

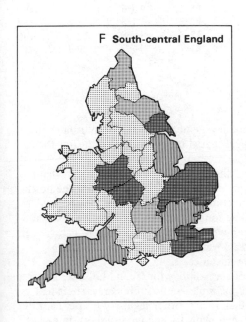

F **South-central England**

## TABLE 8.3

### REGIONAL PREFERENCES FOR MAIN HOLIDAYS 1970

| Region of Origin | Holiday Areas | | | | | |
|---|---|---|---|---|---|---|
| | The Continent | South-west England | Scotland | Wales | North-west England | South-central England |
| | (percentage of caravanners taking holidays) | | | | | |
| Northumberland | 23·1 | 15·4 | 38·5 | 7·7 | 7·7 | 3·9 |
| Durham | 14·8 | 14·8 | 40·7 | 11.1 | 7·4 | 7·4 |
| North Riding | 15·0 | 20·0 | 30·0 | 15·0 | 15·0 | 5·0 |
| East Riding | 17·7 | 17·7 | 35·3 | 11·8 | 5·9 | 11·8 |
| West Riding | 22·7 | 10·7 | 25·3 | 10·7 | 9·3 | 5·3 |
| Lincolnshire | 9·1 | 13·6 | 31·8 | 13·6 | 13·6 | 9·1 |
| Nottinghamshire | 10·7 | 28·6 | 17·9 | 17·9 | 7·1 | 7·1 |
| Derbyshire | 16·7 | 16·7 | 16·7 | 27·7 | 11·1 | 5·6 |
| Cheshire | 28·6 | 17·1 | 20·0 | 22·9 | 8·6 | 5·7 |
| West Midlands | 20·0 | 20·0 | 15·0 | 15·0 | 15·0 | 10·0 |
| East Midlands | 21·1 | 24·6 | 19·3 | 14·0 | 8·8 | 7.0 |
| East Anglia | 22·6 | 22·6 | 17·0 | 15·1 | 5·7 | 11·3 |
| Wales | 21·1 | 21·1 | 15·8 | 36·8 | 10·5 | 5·3 |
| South Midlands | 15·3 | 28·8 | 20·3 | 18·6 | 13·6 | 10·2 |
| Thames Valley | 23·9 | 23·9 | 19·6 | 15·2 | 6·5 | 4·4 |
| Home Counties and London | 25·3 | 20·6 | 15·8 | 18·5 | 8·2 | 8·9 |
| West Country | 18·6 | 30·2 | 20·9 | 14·0 | 9·3 | 7·0 |
| South-east | 25·5 | 21·8 | 18·2 | 14·6 | 9·1 | 10·0 |
| South-central | 27·7 | 23·4 | 12·8 | 21·3 | 6·4 | 6·4 |
| South-west | 19·3 | 31·6 | 22·8 | 17·5 | 12·3 | 8·8 |
| Average | 21·5 | 22·0 | 21·7 | 16·7 | 9·1 | 7·9 |

Source:   Owen and Duffield (1971), p. 50.

22 per cent of all caravanners on main holidays, emerged as the primary area in Great Britain. Here, too, there was a logical spatial order, with areas nearer the South-west having above-average percentages.

The adverse effect of inaccessibility on the incidence of holidays in Scotland is also apparent. Scotland attracted a large number of caravanners from the north of England, particularly the north-eastern counties, while all areas with below-average levels of preference for Scotland lie south of a line from the Wash to the Mersey, the sole exception being the south-west region. Proportions of caravanners visiting the other three major holiday areas, Wales, the north-west and south-central regions, were similarly affected by distance.

As might be expected, the influence of accessibility on second holidays was even stronger than on main holidays. For example, while more caravanners had plans to take a second holiday in Wales than in any other region, 47·8 per cent of those caravanners resident in Wales, who had plans for second holidays, intended to take those holidays in Wales itself — a higher proportion than in any other region. This pattern is common in other areas; each region is favoured by its own residents and by others who live close by. For example, the only regions from which more than the average number of caravanners visited Scotland lie north of the Humber–Mersey line and include the North-west Region, Yorkshire and Northumberland and Durham; the sole exception was Derbyshire.

It has already been shown that the length of journey is a major factor that caravanners consider in choosing their holiday locations. It appears that caravanners tend to choose the nearest holiday area that satisfied their particular requirements, thus keeping their travelling time in transit to a minimum.

### Total Caravan Traffic in Scotland

During the hundred days of the summer survey a total of over 2 700 000 vehicles passed through the three survey points – an average daily flow of some 27 100 vehicles. A large proportion of these totals cannot, of course, be attributed to holidaymakers, but it was possible to provide a more accurate estimate of holiday traffic by using the results of the autumn survey. Just under one-third (32·8 per cent) of all traffic monitored during the summer can be directly attributed to holiday traffic, although this represented an average daily count of nearly 9000 vehicles. Such averages, of course, conceal large daily variations, from a low point of just under 3700 on the last day of the survey (Thursday, 1st October) to a high point of 19 140 at the peak of the summer holiday season (Saturday, 1st August). Since the primary aim of the survey was to examine various aspects of mobile caravanning, such statistics for the volume of holiday traffic were used primarily as background information for the more detailed statistics relating to caravans.

An estimated 50 150 caravans passed through the three survey points during the period of the survey, an average daily rate of over 500 caravans, or nearly 6 per cent of the total holiday traffic (table 8.4). The daily totals showed marked

TABLE 8.4

CARAVAN SURVEY: SUMMARY TRAFFIC STATISTICS

| Traffic | | Dumbarton | Stirling | Forth Road Bridge | Combined |
|---|---|---|---|---|---|
| | | (number of vehicles) | | | |
| *All traffic | Total | 642 630 | 946 160 | 1 121 010 | 2 709 800 |
| (Summer survey) | Daily average | 6 430 | 9 460 | 11 210 | 27 100 |
| †All traffic | Total | 129 060 | 191 390 | 207 850 | 528 310 |
| (Autumn survey) | Daily average | 4 450 | 6 600 | 7 170 | 18 220 |
| *Holiday traffic | Total | 197 630 | 286 160 | 404 010 | 887 800 |
| (Summer survey) | Daily average | 1 980 | 2 860 | 4 040 | 8 880 |
| *Caravan traffic | Total | 15 720 | 13 980 | 20 450 | 50 150 |
| (Summer survey) | Daily average | 160 | 140 | 200 | 500 |

*23 June to 21 October 1970
†16 November to 14 December 1970

Source:   Owen and Duffield (1971), p. 13.

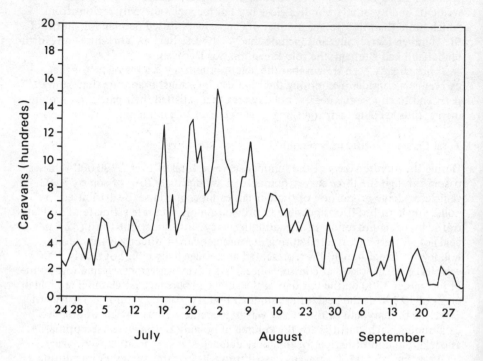

Figure 8.8  Caravan traffic: Daily totals;

fluctuations, both seasonally over the summer period and within the individual weeks (figure 8.8). On Wednesday, 30th September (Day 99), an estimated total of only 81 caravans passed northwards through the cordon, in marked contrast to the maximum of 1546 recorded on Saturday, 1st August. Graphs of the daily totals show numerous peaks, usually coinciding with weekends, which conceal underlying seasonal trends.

To reveal long-term trends, the results of the daily counts have been summarised in figure 8.9 using seven-day moving means (chosen so that each mean would include values for each day of the week). This technique smooths out the sharp irregularities of the graphs while preserving the details of major fluctuations.

The data from individual stations are shown separately in a summary graph (figure 8.10), which gives a concise picture of the major features of the movements of caravans. Over the early part of the survey period, that is the end of June and early July, the estimates of caravan traffic were relatively stable, ranging from 300 to 600 units per day. This was followed by a marked increase in mid-July to high levels that continued throughout the last fortnight of the month, with peak values of between 1000 and 1500 units. This marked increase within two weeks was also characteristic of the pattern of all holiday traffic and, although the rapid decline throughout August was also similar, the fall in caravan traffic in September,

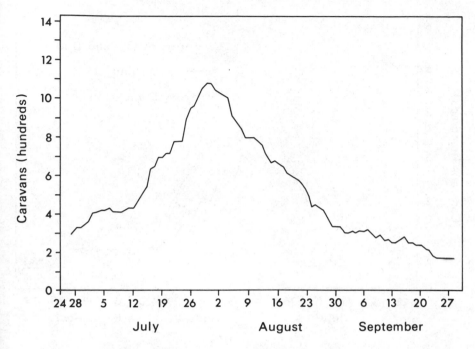

Figure 8.9  Caravan traffic: moving means

though continuous, was less steep than that for holiday traffic as a whole; this seasonal pattern was common to all sites. Caravan traffic at Dumbarton accounted for 31·4 per cent of the total for the survey period, a disproportionately high figure by comparison with both total and holiday traffic flows, which thus emphasises the importance of this route as the western gateway to the Highlands for caravanners travelling from England as well as for the large numbers originating in the Glasgow conurbation. In contrast, less caravan traffic was monitored at Stirling than the statistics for either total or holiday traffic would suggest. The data collected at the survey station on the Forth Road Bridge established that the A90 was the primary route for both holiday and caravan traffic moving north through Scotland; in all, an estimated 40·7 per cent of caravan traffic passed through this survey station in the summer period.

### The Distribution of Caravan Traffic in Scotland

While the review of patterns of caravan holidays in Great Britain has demonstrated the importance of Scotland as a holiday area, the country is not uniformly popular with caravanners from other parts of Great Britain. Furthermore, the regions of Scotland vary in character and in appeal.

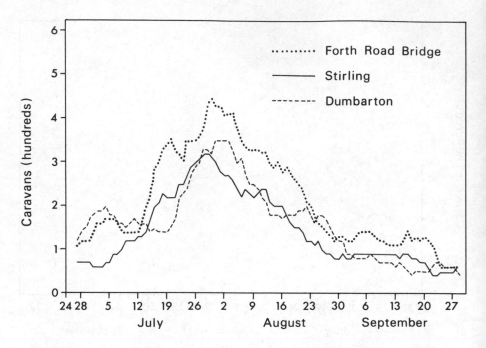

Figure 8.10  Caravan traffic: Moving means: individual survey stations

Table 8.3 showed the preferences for Scotland as a main holiday location among caravanners from the twenty-one English and Welsh regions. When these preferences are related to the caravanning populations of the individual regions, actual numbers of caravanners visiting Scotland can be assessed. Table 8.5 presents these data, identifying those areas that generate most caravan traffic to Scotland.

In order to examine more fully the effects of distance on the geographical patterns of both main and second holidays, regression analysis has been applied to the data in table 8.5 to measure the relationships between two variables, namely, the percentage of caravanners from each region who visit Scotland for a holiday and the distance between that region and Scotland. Although the data were rather crude, the results confirm the influence of distance on caravan holidays to Scotland.

Pairs of values were first plotted against each other on a scattergram. The values used in this analysis were:

(1) the percentage value of the proportion of caravanners who took main holidays in Scotland during 1970, for each of the twenty-one English and Welsh regions;
(2) an estimate of the average distance in miles from the twenty-one regions to the town of Stirling (chosen because of its nodal position in the road pattern of Scotland).

## TABLE 8.5

### ORIGINS OF CARAVANNERS WHO VISIT SCOTLAND

|  | Population of region as a percentage of population for England and Wales | Percentage of all caravanners who visited Scotland for a main holiday in 1970 | Percentage of all caravanners from region who visited Scotland for a main holiday |
|---|---|---|---|
| Northumberland | 1·8 | 4·9 | 38·5 |
| Durham | 3·3 | 5·4 | 40·7 |
| North Riding | 1·2 | 3·0 | 30·0 |
| East Riding | 1·1 | 3·0 | 35·3 |
| West Riding | 7·9 | 9·4 | 25·3 |
| North-west | 11·9 | 10·3 | 24·1 |
| Lincolnshire | 1·6 | 3·4 | 31·8 |
| Nottinghamshire | 2·0 | 2·5 | 17·9 |
| Derbyshire | 1·9 | 1·4 | 16·7 |
| Cheshire | 3·0 | 3·4 | 10·0 |
| West Midlands | 4·4 | 1·4 | 15·0 |
| East Midlands | 2·6 | 5·4 | 19·3 |
| East Anglia | 3·9 | 4·4 | 17·0 |
| Wales | 5·7 | 1·4 | 15·8 |
| South Midlands | 5·6 | 5·9 | 20·3 |
| Thames Valley | 2·8 | 4·4 | 19·6 |
| Home Counties and London | 22·3 | 11·3 | 15·8 |
| West Country | 3·4 | 4·4 | 20·9 |
| South-east | 5·1 | 4·9 | 18·2 |
| South-central | 4·0 | 3·0 | 12·8 |
| South-west | 4·5 | 6·4 | 22·8 |

Source:   Owen and Duffield (1971), p. 52.

The resulting scattergram (figure 8.11A) gives a visual indication of the relationship between the two variables. As was to be expected, the scatter of points suggests a negative correlation between these two variables, that is, that the proportion of visitors decreases as distance increases.

To test the strength of this relationship Pearson's $R$ correlation coefficients were calculated. The coefficient for main holidays to Scotland in 1970 was −0·74 and was significant at the 99 per cent confidence level, indicating a strong negative relationship between the percentage of caravanners in a region who visited Scotland for a main holiday in 1970 and the distance they travelled from home to their holiday destination. On the strength of this relationship, the following regression equation was established for the data for 1970 caravan holidays

$$y = 41·5 - 0·058x$$

where $y$ is the percentage of the total caravanners of a region who visited Scotland for a main holiday in 1970 and $x$ is the length of journey (miles) between the region and Stirling.

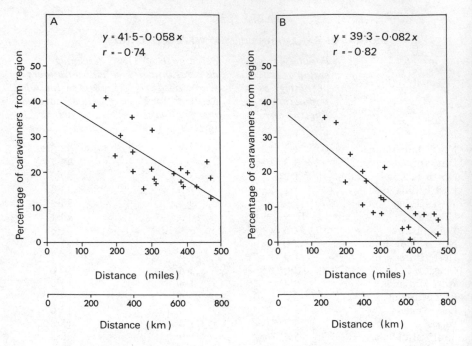

Figure 8.11   Caravan holidays to Scotland: Caravan traffic and distance travelled:
A. Main holidays; B. Second holidays

When the same technique was applied to the 1971 data for second holidays, an even higher correlation coefficient (−0·82) was established. The appropriate scattergram and the form of the regression line are shown in figure 8.11 B and there is a clear visual indication of a negative relationship between the two variables. The resulting regression equation was

$$y = 39·3 - 0·082x$$

where $y$ is the percentage of the total caravanners in a region with plans for a second holiday in 1971 who plan to visit Scotland for that holiday, and $x$ is the length of journey (miles) between that region and Stirling.

The importance of length of journey has already been noted; these calculations confirm this hypothesis and quantify the relationship between the incidence of holidays and length of journey.

## The Attractiveness of Regions Within Scotland

The appeal of Scotland for caravanners has been outlined and the regional distribution of caravan holidays will now be examined to show the relative attractiveness of different parts of Scotland. The regions defined by the Scottish Tourist Board have been used in this analysis, though the Highlands and Islands Region has been further divided into four areas namely, Islands, Northern Highlands, Central Highlands, West Highlands, to give ten regions in all. These regions permit the distribution of caravan traffic within Scotland to be studied in detail, and table 8.6 shows the percentage of caravan visitors who stayed overnight in each region during their holidays. On average, each party stayed overnight in three of the regions. Several regions, especially those in south and central Scotland, act as transit zones for caravanners on their way to destinations further north. This phenomenon is investigated later in greater detail, but it should be noted that these data reflect both the distribution of overnight stops in transit and preferences for regions.

TABLE 8.6

POPULARITY OF REGIONS AND LENGTH OF STAY IN SCOTLAND*

| Region | Percentage of total visitors | | Visitor nights per party per region (average number) |
|---|---|---|---|
| | By party† | By nights | |
| Islands | 4·0 | 1·9 | 5·2 |
| Northern Highlands | 25·5 | 11·4 | 5·3 |
| Central Highlands | 49·6 | 17·5 | 4·1 |
| West Highlands | 30·6 | 12·1 | 4·4 |
| North-east | 17·6 | 5·3 | 3·5 |
| East-central | 55·3 | 18·1 | 3·7 |
| West | 27·5 | 6·5 | 2·5 |
| Edinburgh and the Lothians | 45·2 | 13·7 | 3·3 |
| South-west | 29·5 | 10·6 | 3·4 |
| Borders | 10·6 | 2·9 | 2·0 |

*Data in this table relate to caravanners who were interviewed during August 1970.

†This column totals more than 100 per cent because some caravanners visited more than one region.

Source:  Owen and Duffield (1971), p. 56.

Table 8.7 illustrates more clearly the relative popularity of these regions among caravanners from England and Wales who take holidays in Scotland. Caravanners, like so many other holidaymakers, are attracted to the Highlands and Islands, in which nearly 43 per cent of all visitor nights in Scotland were spent; such caravanners spent over four nights within this region. In contrast, parties who visit the Borders and West regions (both with large proportions of transit traffic) stayed an

## TABLE 8.7

### REGIONAL PREFERENCES FOR CARAVAN HOLIDAYS TO SCOTLAND

*Percentage of Visitors from English and Welsh Regions who stayed in Scottish Regions\**

| Region | Highlands and Islands | North-east | East-central | West | Edinburgh and the Lothians | South-west | Borders |
|---|---|---|---|---|---|---|---|
| Northumberland | 56·5 | 15·8 | 59·9 | 12·4 | 52·5 | 7·9 | 22·3 |
| Durham | 51·9 | 13·6 | 57·0 | 22·4 | 50·5 | 18·2 | 15·9 |
| North Riding | 64·6 | 14·6 | 62·2 | 30·5 | 53·7 | 34·1 | 7·3 |
| East Riding | 78·0 | 22·0 | 62·6 | 27·4 | 44·0 | 25·3 | 16·5 |
| West Riding | 61·6 | 16·8 | 51·7 | 24·6 | 43·8 | 30·3 | 6·9 |
| North-west | 62·4 | 15·7 | 44·2 | 38·0 | 29·7 | 50·0 | 7·1 |
| Lincolnshire | 58·9 | 21·9 | 49·8 | 26·4 | 51·3 | 20·6 | 8·7 |
| Nottinghamshire | 64·4 | 17·4 | 52·1 | 30·1 | 47·9 | 32·9 | 13·7 |
| Derbyshire | 66·7 | 19·0 | 54·0 | 27·0 | 39·7 | 31·7 | 15·9 |
| Cheshire | 62·4 | 15·6 | 41·3 | 26·6 | 39·4 | 54·1 | 3·7 |
| West Midlands | 75·0 | 22·0 | 50·0 | 37·0 | 40·9 | 33·0 | 5·0 |
| East Midlands | 68·3 | 20·0 | 73·4 | 26·7 | 48·3 | 21·7 | 10·0 |
| East Anglia | 72·7 | 20·3 | 58·9 | 29·9 | 49·7 | 24·6 | 11·9 |
| Wales | 69·8 | 23·4 | 47·8 | 39·2 | 51·8 | 45·6 | 6·5 |
| South Midlands | 72·1 | 17·4 | 53·4 | 30·2 | 38·9 | 34·8 | 8·5 |
| Thames | 69·9 | 16·4 | 53·4 | 24·7 | 37·0 | 19·2 | 11·0 |
| Home Counties and London | 70·3 | 18·8 | 60·8 | 21·7 | 43·6 | 24·7 | 14·1 |
| West Country | 70·5 | 13·2 | 56·1 | 31·0 | 41·7 | 40·7 | 8·8 |
| South-east | 71·0 | 17·1 | 63·2 | 25·0 | 34·3 | 23·7 | 7·9 |
| South-central | 69·8 | 15·1 | 63·0 | 34·3 | 39·7 | 23·3 | 13·8 |
| South-west | 81·2 | 18·7 | 75·0 | 28·1 | 53·1 | 25·0 | 6·2 |
| Average | 65·9 | 17·6 | 55·3 | 27·5 | 45·2 | 29·5 | 10·6 |

\*Data in this table refer to caravanners interviewed during August 1970.

Source:   Owen and Duffield (1971), p. 60.

average of two and two and a half nights respectively. The regions of Scotland thus have different roles; the southern and central regions have an individual appeal, but also provide overnight accommodation for those who wish to move on to holiday areas further north. The Highlands and Islands, and to a lesser extent the East-central and Lothians regions, stand out as the areas of greatest attraction. In the perspective of Scotland as a whole the Borders region was of comparatively little significance for caravanning, since the region attracted little more traffic (much of it in transit) than the isolated Islands region.

Differences in the appeal of holiday areas, which are usually linked to distance and physical accessibility, produce a distinctive pattern of caravanning in Great Britain. Within Scotland there are also differences in the appeal of certain areas, although such influences are less easy to discern. Distance may be a factor, but it is likely that other less tangible factors also contribute, reflecting the aspirations and personal preferences of the caravanning public. This relationship is further explored in figure 8.12, which records the preferences of caravanners from England and Wales for the various Scottish regions (see table 8.3).

The map for the Highlands and Islands shows the complexity of factors that motivate the caravanner in his choice of holiday area. It was demonstrated earlier that there was a significant negative correlation between distance and the incidence of caravan holidays in Scotland, but, contrary to this evidence, caravanners who visited the Highlands and Islands were more likely to come from the Midlands and the south of England than from any other part of England and Wales (table 8.7). Correlation with distance cannot explain this pattern and it must therefore be attributed to the personal motivations of caravanners. North-east Scotland has limited appeal for caravanners from England and Wales and preferences for this region also are not easily interpreted, for again average values for those living in the north of England were low. In general, east-central Scotland was more popular among caravanners from eastern England than among those from western England and Wales. Many caravanners undoubtedly stayed in the east-central region be- cause of its individual appeal, but others, particularly from eastern England, spent nights in transit in the region because it is crossed by the major routes to the pop- ular areas in the Highlands; this transit role probably accounted for the below- average values for western England and Wales compared with England and Wales as a whole. In the west of Scotland, too, access routes affect a region's popularity; caravanners from western England and Wales were frequent visitors and, with the exception of Cheshire, all areas with below average preferences for the west region lay in eastern England. A similar relationship existed in the Edinburgh and Lothians region which lies astride the two main routes from the east of England to Scotland, the A1 and A68, and it is not surprising that values in table 8.7 for the eastern areas of England were generally above the average for England and Wales, while values for all the western counties of England were below average. In their pre- ferences for regions visitors to south-west Scotland also reveal a dichotomy be- tween eastern England and western England and Wales, and figures for the latter area were well above average (figure 8.12). The Borders attracted less caravan traffic than any other Scottish region, but has distinctive appeal. The region was popular with caravanners from northern counties of England, namely, Northumber- land, Durham, the East Riding of Yorkshire and Derbyshire, which are within, at the most, two days' journey of the Scottish border. The average length of stay was short, suggesting that the Borders region was used mainly by caravanners in transit.

This survey of the touring caravan in Scotland has shown that each Scottish region has a distinctive appeal, related both to the intrinsic attraction of the region itself and also to distance and location in relation to the major access routes into Scotland. These criteria contribute in varying degrees to the geograph- ical pattern of main caravan holidays in Scotland, and should be taken into account in planning the provision of facilities.

## Balance of Supply and Demand

There were considerable variations in the number of caravans visiting Scotland over the holiday season; but, since the supply of caravan pitches is essentially stable and the demand for caravan sites is constantly changing according to the season,

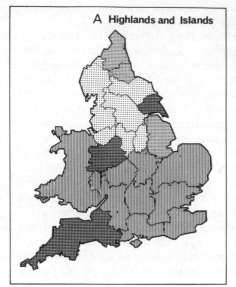

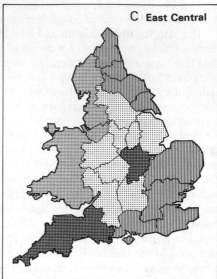

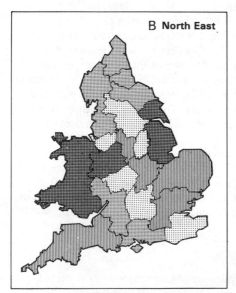

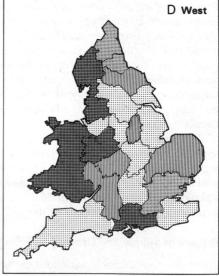

Figure 8.12  Regional preferences for 1970 holidays (seven areas)

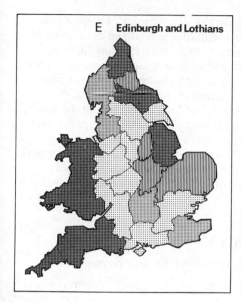

E   **Edinburgh and Lothians**

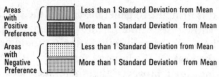

Areas with Positive Preference
- Less than 1 Standard Deviation from Mean
- More than 1 Standard Deviation from Mean

Areas with Negative Preference
- Less than 1 Standard Deviation from Mean
- More than 1 Standard Deviation from Mean

F   **South West**

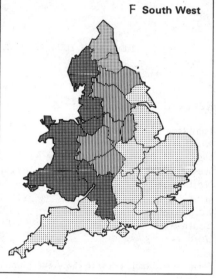

G   **Borders**

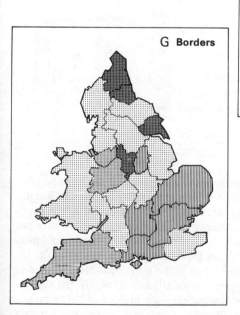

it is difficult to generalise about the needs for the development of caravan sites. Those responsible for the planning of tourist facilities in Scotland are concerned, however, to ensure that supply should generally be adequate, falling short only at the peak of the holiday season, in late July and early August. The caravan survey indicated, however, that there was a lack of balance between supply and demand in many regions over a considerably longer period in the holiday season.

One consequence of this shortage of pitches has been an increase in the numbers of caravanners who camp wild. Facilities on sites are often used to capacity, so that caravanners are forced to camp wherever space can be found, frequently without permission· the roadside survey showed that 34·1 per cent of caravanners camped wild on at least one occasion during their holiday, which was largely attributable to space on caravan sites being unavailable or the location of available space being unknown.

## TABLE 8.8

### REGIONAL DEMAND FOR AND SUPPLY OF SITE PITCHES*

| Region | (percentage of Scottish total) | | Wild nights as a percentage of total visitor nights |
|---|---|---|---|
| | Total visitor nights | Total tourist pitches | |
| Islands | 1·9 | 1·0 | 54·3 |
| Northern Highlands | 11·4 | 9·8 | 23·7 |
| Central Highlands | 17·5 | 16·9 | 14·6 |
| West Highlands | 12·1 | 8·0 | 16·0 |
| North-east | 5·3 | 12·7 | 17·1 |
| West | 18·1 | 18·8 | 12·2 |
| Edinburgh and Lothians | 13·7 | 9·5 | 7·3 |
| South-west | 10·6 | 17·7 | 8·3 |
| Borders | 2·9 | 3·5 | 14·4 |

*Data in this table relate to caravanners interviewed during August 1970.

Source :   Owen and Duffield (1971), p. 66.

Table 8.8 illustrates the relationships between wild camping and the balance of supply and demand in the various regions of Scotland in 1970. Visitors in August exceeded the pitches available for towing caravans in most regions; this was particularly notable in the Highlands and Islands region which accounted for 42·9 per cent of nights in 1970, although it had only 35·7 per cent of the available pitches in Scotland. In such circumstances high totals for wild camping are inevitable. In contrast, caravanners who visited the South-west at the same time had a choice of sites; although accounting for only 10·6 per cent of all caravan nights, the region provided 17·7 per cent of the pitches for towing caravans in Scotland. The proportion of visitors camping wild in the south-west region was consequently nearly half the average figure for Scotland.

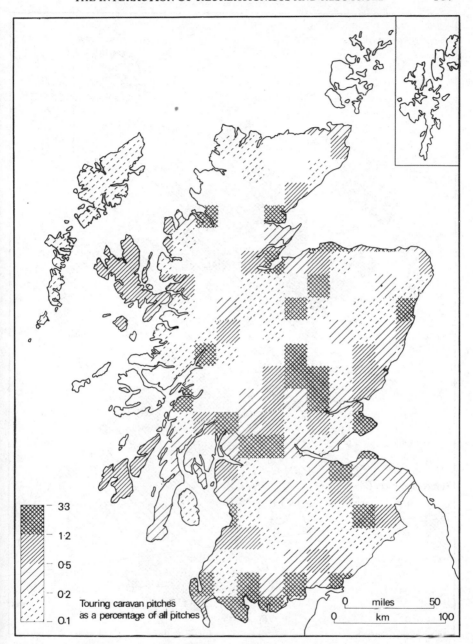

Figure 8.13  Touring caravan pitches

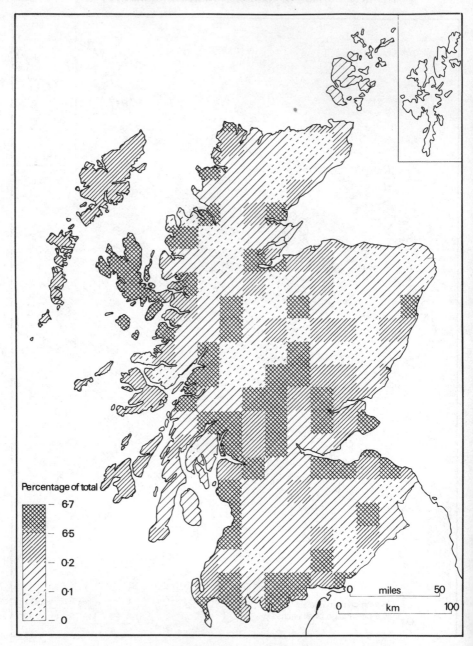

Figure 8.14   Caravan pitch nights

Figure 8.13 shows in more detail the distribution throughout Scotland of the pitches for towed caravans. Highland Scotland was characterised by generally low proportions, usually less than 1 per cent of the total number of pitches, with the exception of some major centres, notably Oban, Fort William and Inverness. The major concentrations of pitches were on coastal sites, especially on the Moray, East Lothian and Ayrshire coasts. There was also a high proportion of pitches in the South-west, which contrasted with lower numbers of sites in the Eastern Borders.

There was a similar sharp contrast between the high proportion in the Edinburgh area and the marked absence of facilities around Glasgow. Indeed, with the exception of coastal areas, the whole of central Scotland south of the Edinburgh/Glasgow line was marked by relatively few sites.

The demand for caravan pitches did not, however, follow the pattern of available supply (figure 8.14). Some marked concentrations of caravan traffic were apparent; nearly 7 per cent of all visitor nights spent by caravanners in Scotland were in the Edinburgh area. Other major centres were Inverness, Fort William, Oban, Pitlochry and Aviemore; some larger areas were also popular and had values much above average, including Loch Lomondside, the Trossachs, Loch Earn, and Strathyre, with Glen Dochart linking this area to Loch Tay and other areas to the north. Despite the relatively difficult access, the west coast of Scotland near Oban attracted a large number of caravanners, as did the Isle of Skye. The Great Glen between Fort William and Inverness also showed high values and was clearly a primary holiday area for caravanners, giving access to the Highlands for those visitors travelling northwards from the west coast. The A9 between Perth and Inverness fulfilled a similar role for traffic moving north from eastern Scotland and values were above average along this route. Other major holiday areas included Aberdeen and its environs, the East Lothian coast, the Renfrew and Ayrshire coast and the coastal areas of Galloway.

To evaluate the relationship of supply and demand at the height of the season, comparisons were made between average levels of demand throughout the months of July and August 1970 and the supply of caravan pitches available at that time. Although this comparison covers only eight weeks of the summer period, it nevertheless accounted for nearly 50 per cent of caravan traffic in Scotland and is therefore an appropriate base against which to evaluate imbalances between supply and demand (figure 8.15). The areas of greatest deficit were in the north and west of Scotland in Sutherland and Wester Ross and in the Ardnamurchan–Moidart–Arisaig areas. These deficiencies probably reflect policies of site development, as much as the popularity of these areas with caravanners. Despite large-scale provision, there was also a deficit of sites in and near the Great Glen between Fort William and Inverness, and further deficits occurred in Perthshire along Glen Dochart and Loch Tay. In central and southern Scotland there tended to be a surplus of sites, with important exceptions, notably the area between and including Glasgow and Edinburgh. Indeed, Edinburgh itself exhibited the second highest deficit in the whole of Scotland, a measure of its appeal and an indication of the difficulties of predicting shortfalls with reference to present supply only. Other areas which had a deficit in the supply of pitches were south of Glasgow along the A74 and the East Lothian coast, where the popularity of existing sites

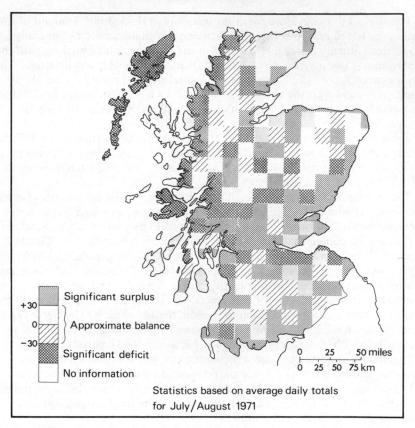

Figure 8.15 Caravan holidays: supply–demand (July/August 1971)

has similarly generated a level of demand that cannot be met by existing facilities.

There was generally a surplus of sites in eastern and southern Scotland. This was true of all the east-coast areas with the exception of East and West Lothian. Equally extensive belts of surplus capacity stretched from Dundee and St Andrews in the east to Loch Lomond in the west, and in the Borders and, indeed, in the whole of southern Scotland apart from central Lanarkshire.

This analysis of caravan traffic in Scotland has shown that holiday traffic, too, demonstrates similar relationships between resource and recreational journeys, though the scale of inquiry has been quite different and destinations have been identified only as broad regions that themselves contain a great variety of recreational resources. It has also demonstrated that the absence of facilities will not necessarily discourage recreationists, a fact of some importance for those who wish to turn a Nelsonian eye on the growing volume of traffic and hope that, by ignoring it, such traffic will go elsewhere. Caravan traffic does, of course, differ from other holiday traffic in its independence of accommodation, and it seems likely that recreational journeys by those staying at holiday resorts will not differ greatly from those making day and half-day trips from home. Nevertheless, the methodology used for the survey of caravan traffic is capable of much wider application to the study of recreational traffic as a whole, particularly that entering and leaving recreational sites (provided that the equipment can be adequately safeguarded).

## CONCLUSION

This analysis of the patterns of movement and the distribution of recreational traffic is of intrinsic interest and has served to demonstrate the relationships that exist between a recreational activity and the resource it uses. The analysis has also shown that recreational activities have not only spatial dimensions, but also a time dimension, for recreation varies in intensity throughout the day, the week and the year. These temporal variations must be taken into account in any attempt to devise a model to describe recreational interaction. And, while neither demand nor supply can be considered except in relation to travel, all three must be viewed together as part of a recreational system.

# 9 Prospects: A Systems Approach

In previous chapters of this book the nature of the use of the countryside for recreation has been examined within the conceptual framework of a supply/demand model. The two basic components of this equation have been studied separately: in chapters 2, 3, 4 and 5 the factors influencing and moulding the demand for recreational activities of many kinds were considered, while in chapters 6 and 7 the supply of resources, the factors that influence their suitability for recreation, and the human, governmental and institutional constraints on their use were discussed. Even when the components of the supply/demand model were examined separately, it became evident that there were intimate relationships between the two components that governed both the levels of consumption of recreational activities and the spatial pattern and distribution of these activities. In chapter 8 the two components were brought together and an examination of the interaction between recreationists and resources confirmed this pattern. The distance between people's homes and the countryside and the separation of demand and supply, the differences between demand-oriented and resource-based activities, the emergence of identifiable and constant patterns of recreational traffic for the whole range of activities—these all serve to emphasise the key role played by spatial interaction in the resolution of the model of recreational supply and demand.

As an interactive economic model, the supply/demand concept has served recreational researchers well in helping them to conceptualise relationships between user and resource. But although it is an interactive model, it is general and does not cater for distinctive forms of spatial interaction, nor does it permit them to be effectively calibrated. Researchers must therefore seek other analogues that will more adequately take account of the true nature of recreational land use.

In observing the key role of spatial interaction, researchers have instinctively looked towards models of transport systems for a solution; but while a good deal of attention has been given to modelling people's movements, particularly patterns of migration and journeys to work, recreational activity has largely been ignored until quite recently. When attempts were made to apply transportation models to recreational journeys, it became clear that parallels did exist between recreational travel and other forms of human interaction. Recreational journeys, like other kinds of travel, have a standard structure: a set of *origins* (population centres) generates *journeys,* which are distributed over a network of routes to a set of *destinations* (recreation sites). It was therefore understandable that social scientists should come to believe that recreational journeys constituted only one of a number of human systems of spatial interaction.

Once this acceptable assumption had been made, it was a small and seemingly logical step to apply existing land-use/transportation models to the study of recreational journeys. In this final chapter the nature of these transportation models and their value to the study of patterns of recreational activity will be examined. If models are to form a basis for future research in the field of countryside recreation, then it is essential that the techniques adopted are both conceptually and operationally compatible with the realities of recreation in the countryside. In order to test the models, particular attention must be paid to the nature of recreational travel itself, rather than to the basic components of supply and demand. If the essential characteristics of the forms of spatial interaction that distinguish recreational activity can be discerned, then suitable modelling procedures can be devised.

## THE NATURE OF RECREATIONAL TRAVEL

### The Gravity Model

For the last four decades, since the early work of Reilly (1929) and Converse and his associates (1930), geographers have tended to favour the gravity model as an appropriate way of describing human spatial interaction. Applied initially to patterns of retailing, the model has since been developed for forecasting the distribution of journeys to business and work, patterns of migration and, belatedly, recreational journeys. These related techniques grew from an awareness that the volume of traffic from a given origin declines with distance, a relationship analogous to that postulated by Newton in his law of universal gravitation. Social scientists have accepted Newton's dictum that 'two bodies in the universe attract each other in proportion to the product of their masses and inversely to the square of their distances apart' (Newton, 1687). Applied to human interaction, this model takes the following mathematical form

$$I_{ij} = K \frac{P_i P_j}{d_{ij}{}^\alpha}$$

where $I_{ij}$ = interaction between points i and j;

$P_i$ and $P_j$ = population of i and j (analogous to the mass variables in Newtons's equations);

$d_{ij}$ = distance between i and j;

$\alpha$ = an exponent;

$K$ = a constant.

The key component in the equation is the nature of the distance variable, as defined by $\alpha$, an exponent that describes the force of distance as an obstacle to the kind of spatial interaction being investigated. This argument, that distance acts as a deterrent to interaction between two phenomena, has attracted great

attention from social scientists. The ensuing debate around this concept has spawn-
ed, like the gravity model itself, a complete lexicon of jargon, where 'distance',
'interaction', 'gravity', 'deterrent' and 'impedance' functions have become mutually exchangeable terms in describing the inbuilt assumptions of these models.
Early studies closely followed Newton's formulation and used the square of
geographical distance to measure the deterrence effect in order to explain the
interaction between the origins and destinations of trips (Steward, 1948; Zipf,
1949).

As the gravity formula became more widely used in different areas of human
interaction, empirical testing led to the employment of various exponents other
than the square of distance, ranging from a power of one-half to over three, and
other forms of measuring 'distance' between the points concerned were adopted,
such as journey time, the cost of travel and, more recently, perceived travel time
and cost. Nevertheless, despite the growing sophistication of the various gravity
formulae used, the basic principle remains the same; that is, human interaction
is brought about by an individual's desire to satisfy a need for a good or service
which is unavailable in one area but available in another; so that acquisition of the
good requires interaction over space. For many goods and services the location
of the 'purchasing' point is geographically discrete: thus, homes, factories, shops
and business all have well-defined locations and there can be no ambiguity
about the destination of the particular journey. Moreover, the journey itself
represents at least part of the costs of the transaction and can be seen purely as a
disutility that the 'customer' will endeavour to minimise in the pursuit of his
good. Since many forms of recreational activity do not demand direct payment from
participants, the costs of journeys have become accepted as a surrogate 'price' for
participation in a given recreational activity. The application of the gravity formula
to recreation has thus taken the form

$$T_{ij} = KO_i A_j F(C_{ij})$$

where

$T_{ij}$     = trips between origin i and recreation area j;
$O_i$     = number of trips generated in origin i;
$A_j$     = the attractiveness of recreation area j;
$F(C_{ij})$ = a function that expresses the 'friction' involved in overcoming
          the distance between $O_i$ and $A_j$;
$K$     = constant.

At first glance, recreational activity appears to conform to these assumptions and,
indeed, a point destination is appropriate for many formal recreational pursuits.
For example, anglers, golfers and yachtsmen all have fixed destinations in mind
when they embark on recreational journeys, and the origin and destination of
such journeys and the spatial interaction between them are similar in nature to
other systems of travel. Yet no generalisations are possible about all recreational
journeys. Table 9.1 demonstrates, for two separate samples used in household-

## TABLE 9.1

OUTDOOR RECREATION ACTIVITIES: DISTANCE AND TRAVEL RELATIONSHIPS

| Name of activity | Car owners | | Travelled by car | | Average length of journey (one way in miles) | |
|---|---|---|---|---|---|---|
| | Edinburgh | Lanark | Edinburgh | Lanark | Edinburgh | Lanark |
| | | | (percentage of participants) | | | |
| Angling | 72·7 | 70·4 | 78·0 | 70·0 | 19 | 20 |
| Camping | 67·0 | 63·8 | 84·0 | 75·0 | 32 | 34 |
| Canoeing | 67·0 | 70·0 | 67·0 | 60·0 | 29 | 33 |
| Cricket | 67·0 | 55·0 | 92·0 | 36·0 | 4 | 9 |
| Cycling | 32·6 | 40·0 | – | – | 3 | 9 |
| Field sports | 88·9 | 81·8 | 78·0 | 54·0 | 17 | 21 |
| Golf | 70·9 | 78·9 | 75·0 | 84·0 | 4 | 7 |
| Hiking, walking | 52·9 | 58·7 | 37·0 | 41·0 | 13 | 16 |
| Horse-riding | 66·7 | 100·0 | 63·0 | 46·0 | 7 | 17 |
| Motor-racing | 80·0 | 86·0 | 93·0 | 86·0 | 19 | 25 |
| Nature studies | 58·5 | 62·8 | 42·0 | 37·0 | 4 | 11 |
| Orienteering | 25·0 | 67·0 | 37·0 | 67·0 | 26 | 40 |
| Pleasure-boating | 70·6 | 67·6 | 68·0 | 53·0 | 11 | 18 |
| Power-boating | 71·0 | 86·0 | 71·0 | 71·0 | 20 | 28 |
| Rallying | 100·0 | 100·0 | 100·0 | 91·0 | 23 | 11 |
| Rock-climbing | 38·0 | 73·0 | 46·0 | 73·0 | 33 | 40 |
| Sailing | 78·6 | 96·4 | 71·0 | 79·0 | 18 | 28 |
| Sea-fishing | 57·4 | 66·7 | 63·0 | 73·0 | 12 | 25 |
| Scrambling | 100·0 | 100·0 | 50·0 | 100·0 | 24 | 46 |
| Skiing | 55·0 | 58·0 | 55·0 | 83·0 | 30 | 45 |
| Swimming | 60·3 | 60·7 | 47·0 | 42·0 | 5 | 2 |
| Team games | 48·2 | 42·8 | 32·0 | 31·0 | 5 | 3 |
| Youth hostelling | 66·7 | 40·0 | 44·0 | 40·0 | 37 | 49 |

Source:   Duffield and Owen (1970), pp. 43, 62; Duffield and Owen (1971), pp. 43, 62.

interview surveys in central Scotland, that, although travel and distance relationships for each activity are similar in both studies, relationships vary for the different activities. Each activity appears to have its own distance function, which depends on the nature of the activity, the characteristics of participation and the spatial distribution of resources and facilities available to meet the demand.

### The Journey for Informal Recreation

The role of the journey for informal recreation is much less certain, and recent studies have indicated that it would be simplistic to consider it merely as a cost to be minimised as in other forms of human interaction (see chapter 8). Indeed, not only can it be hypothesised that the recreational journey contributes, at least in part, to the recreational experience, but also that, for certain kinds of informal recreation, the 'good' is acquired partly from the journey itself. Even if such trips, on which people merely 'tour around', constitute only a small minority of all journeys for recreation (and this does not appear to be the case), they require some re-thinking about the role of the journey for recreation, which cannot be accepted without question merely as an element of cost.

Recent studies have provided further confirmation of this view. Information was sought from weekend motorists in the Lake District on the purpose of their journey (Yapp, 1969); of those on day or half-day trips, 43·5 per cent said they were just driving around, a figure nearly matching the 48 per cent who said they were going to a particular place. This evidence is supported by Mansfield's investigations into pleasure motoring in the Lake District National Park. His results demonstrated that factors other than the quickest journey are considered by those choosing a route in the National Park. Indeed, a substantial number selected a route because of its scenic attraction, an approach most strongly marked among day visitors, 36 per cent of whom gave the highest priority to the scenic or natural attractiveness of their journey. Faced with this and other evidence, Mansfield concluded that '...in an extreme case, the saving on journey time may itself be a disutility to the pleasure motorist, since it reduces the time period over which the primary objective of his journey, the viewing of scenery, can be accomplished' (Mansfield, 1968).

Colenutt also found evidence of the positive contribution of recreational journey to the leisure experience as a whole in his study of recreational motor traffic in the Forest of Dean. More than 70 per cent of visitors from major centres did not take the shortest route to the Forest on either the outward or the return journey. Moreover, most journeys were either partial or complete circuits, rather than direct outward and return trips; on average, visitors duplicated only 45 per cent of their routes (Colenutt, 1969, 45) and only 26 per cent chose the same route on the outward and return journeys (Colenutt, 1970, p. 103). In the light of this evidence Colenutt concluded that 'distance is not a simple disutility as we generally imply when we use a gravity or linear programming model to assign trips' and that the 'objective of the tripper is not to minimise travel time between origin and a single destination but to maximise the recreational benefit he can obtain from both travel time and the time spent at stopping points' (Colenutt, 1969, 45).

More recent evidence has been provided by a study in Hull of the pattern of pleasure trips of car owners, in which a random sample of 500 car owners in the city was interviewed between August and October 1969; 62·6 per cent of these had taken a drive into the countryside with no particular destination in mind. Wall suggests therefore, 'that a change of environment may be as strong a motive in taking a pleasure trip, as the attraction of a specific location and that the enjoyment derived from driving and sightseeing may be as important as the pleasures to be experienced in the final destination' (Wall, 1972, 51).

The cumulative weight of this evidence thus strongly suggests that a motorist on such a journey gains pleasure from parts of his journey. This is not to suggest that all recreational journeys are undertaken as an end in themselves, but rather that the distance travelled has different aspects and acts concurrently as both a utility and a disutility. The positive or negative value of the journeys as a whole is thus determined by the balance of these utilities, which is determined by the nature and stage of the journey. This concept contrasts directly with the assumption of gravity-based interaction models, namely, that the acquisition of benefits takes place at a point destination. Many recreationists make several stops on a journey and, depending on the nature of the areas through which they pass, they can accumulate utilities from the enjoyment of scenery throughout their trip. A recreational journey is therefore a gradual accretion of utilities and disutilities, and a 'stop' is merely a different kind of utility from a 'view'.

## The Spatial Distribution of Recreation Journeys

If distance travelled is considered as part of the cost function, the distribution of journeys over distance would be expected to decline with distance, since recreationists attempted to minimise the distance travelled in selecting a suitable destination; but such a distribution is seldom characteristic of journeys for informal recreation. Of course, this does not imply that recreational journeys are unaffected by distances, for all such journeys must take place within the time available for recreation.

The influence of distance on the distribution of recreational journeys can be illustrated by a number of recent studies. Home-interview surveys carried out in Scotland established that, for leisure trips by car lasting over 2 hours, only 34 per cent exceeded 40 miles (64 km) one way; the average journey was nearly 33 miles (53 km) (Duffield and Owen, 1970, 1971). The *Pilot National Recreation Survey* established that 38 per cent of motorists on recreational trips reported return journeys of less than 50 miles (80 km) and only 27 per cent travelled more than 100 miles (160 km) (British Travel Association–University of Keele, 1967). A study by Burton, who examined the recreational use of Windsor Great Park, revealed that 83 per cent of visitors to the park came from within a radius of 30 miles (48 km) (Burton, 1967). The study, *Leisure in the North West,* established that the median one-way journey for a full-day trip was between 40 and 50 miles (64–80 km), with the majority of recreationists making a one-way journey of between $1\frac{1}{2}$ - 2 hours from their homes (North West Sports Council, 1972, p. 33); and Wall concluded from his study of car owners in Hull that an outward journey by road of 62 miles (100 km) marks the upper limit of the distance that most owners were prepared to travel on pleasure excursions (Wall, 1972, 52). Thus, although results vary from survey to survey, journeys for informal recreation do not generally exceed 100 miles (160 km) and, within the pattern of recreational travel as a whole, motorists clearly do accept a measure of discipline over the distance they travel.

Nevertheless, when the distribution of journeys within this radius is examined, the findings also substantiate the hypothesis that journeys play a positive part in the leisure experience and are, therefore, not distributed according to gravity formulae. For example, only 7·5 per cent of Hull car owners spent their last pleasure trip within 10 miles (16 km) of the city, whereas 12 per cent travelled between 50–60 miles (80–96 km) on their outward journey (Wall, 1972, 52). In explaining this phenomenon, Wall subscribed to Bonsey's conclusion that 'there may be a minimum distance that car owners travel on pleasure excursions, and that at a lower distance they are not sufficiently removed from their accustomed environment to regard themselves as taking a pleasure trip' (Bonsey, 1968). There was a similar under-representation of short trips in the North West study, with only 18 per cent of full-day trips in the 0–20 mile (32 km) zone compared with 26 per cent in the 20–40 mile zone (32–64 km) (North West Sports Council, 1972, p. 53). Scottish data also confirmed this pattern (chapter 8), for outward trips of between 0–10 miles (0–16 km) — 12 per cent of total trips — and the 10–20 miles (16–32 km) — 15 per cent — were under-represented compared with more distant journeys, while 38 per cent of all journeys were equally divided between the 20–30 (32–48 km) and 30–40 (48–64 km) mileage zones (figure 9.1).

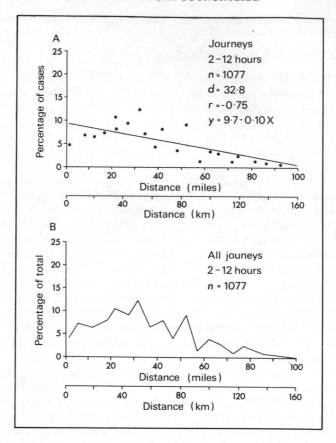

Figure 9.1 Recreational journeys: distance travelled (1)

These distributions of recreational journeys are not compatible with a distance decay function for recreational journeys, particularly those for passive and informal recreation, which earlier evidence has shown to be the dominant form of outdoor recreation for British people. In the light of the distinctive character of the interaction function in recreational journeys and its effect on the distribution of travel over distance, it is now possible to assess how far existing transportation models adequately represent such patterns, or whether formulations that accord better with the observed nature of recreational journeys are necessary.

## Existing Transportation Models

Classic land-use/transportation models are usually divided into four major areas of investigation:

    (1) trip generation: the ability of areas to generate journeys for a particular activity;
    (2) trip attraction: the ability of areas to attract journeys of a particular type;

(3) trip distribution: the establishment of an origin/destination matrix of journeys that represents the resultant of the generation and attraction forces over the system;

(4) trip assignment: the allocation of journeys to particular routes in the network of communications linking the origins and destinations under study.

As far as recreational travel to the countryside is concerned, the other major concern of transportation models, modal split (the distribution of journeys between different forms of transport), is of little significance in that such a large proportion of journeys take place in private cars. The Edinburgh and Lanark studies showed that while on summer Sundays the private car accounted for 91 per cent of total traffic, it was responsible for conveying 95 per cent of recreational traffic into the country-side. Statistics from other studies confirm the dominance of the automobile; only on trips to the seaside does the contribution of public transport become significant and even here, on the evidence of the Northern Region study (North Regional Planning Committee, 1969), the private car still conveys 53 per cent of total recreational traffic.

## Trip Generation

The ability of an area to generate journeys of a particular kind has usually been seen as a function of the resident population in that area. Even if it is accepted that socio-economic parameters effectively define the number of persons likely to undertake a certain journey, it is clear that, if such a model is applied to different areas, it will measure only the potential trip-generating ability of the areas concerned; the actual number of trips generated must necessarily reflect the opportunities that residents of the study area have to undertake their journey. In turn, these opportunities are a function of the ability of other areas to attract journeys of a particular kind and of the costs of acquiring the 'good' in question. Thus, the utilities and disutilities associated with the journey between origin and destination influence the form of the interaction function and thereby the volume of traffic generated from an area.

## Trip Attraction

Planners working on land-use transportation models similarly saw the ability of an area to attract particular journeys as a function of the resources, both human and physical, available within that area. Again, it must be appreciated that such factors define only the potential attractiveness of an area; the real ability to attract journeys of a particular kind will need to take account of its accessibility to zones generating demand for journeys of a particular kind. As with measures of 'opportunity', 'accessibility' reflects real and perceived costs associated with the journey from the area of origin to the area of attraction.

## Trip Distribution

It is in respect of trip distribution that the builders of existing transportation models have seen fit to introduce the interaction variable between trip generating and trip attracting areas. Indeed, the solution of the trip distribution matrix depends wholly on the character of this function, and any variation in it will necessarily be reflected in a variation in the trip patterns between the origins and destinations under consideration.

## Trip Assignment

The final stage of transportation modelling, trip assignment, is also affected by the nature of the interaction function, because its character determines the way journeys are distributed over the network between origins and destinations.

The dominance of this interaction function throughout the modelling of any transportation system is therefore obvious. Should this function fail to represent accurately the factors influencing travel between particular areas, the calibration of the whole transport system would be invalid.

## Recreational Interaction

Classical land-use transportation models introduce the interaction component into trip distribution, and the spatial distribution of trips is determined by the nature of this component. Indeed, the form of the trip-distribution matrix depends entirely on the character of the impedance function; any variation in this function will necessarily be reflected in a variation in the pattern of trips between the origins and destinations being considered. Faced with the distinctive character of the interaction function in recreational journeys and its effect on the distribution of journeys over distance, several research workers have suggested that the answer lay in a reworking of the impedance function. Colenutt's study of the Forest of Dean revealed that recreationists making short journeys differed from those making longer ones in the value they placed on travel time; while distance was a strong predictor for both total and long-distance trips to the Forest, it did not explain local trips. Colenutt concluded that sensitivity to travel distance is not a continuous linear function, but a gentle curve with a sharp increase in slope beyond 15-20 miles (24-32 km) and that 'travel time may, therefore, fail to exert any independent effect on trip generation at all distances below 15-20 miles from the Forest of Dean' (Colenutt, 1970, p. 115). In the face of this and other evidence, Colenutt concluded that '...if visitors to the countryside are actually deriving some benefit from the drive itself, the route choice cannot be solved on the basis of a distance or time/cost criterion. More elusive measures of costs and benefits must be obtained' (Colenutt, 1970, p. 218).

The idea of a variable-distance relationship is not new; many authors, in both the field of recreation and other forms of spatial interaction, have sought greater sophistication in the measurement of travel costs. Carrothers, in his review of the use of gravity techniques in the study of human interaction, observed that the distance factor in the model may itself 'be a variable function relating inversely to distance itself, rather than to population . In this case the interpretation would be that friction per unit of distance against interaction caused by short distances is disproportionately greater than friction per unit of distance caused by longer distances. For instance, friction against movement within an urban area is generally greater than that caused by an equal distance in the less densely developed space between two such areas. Or again, an extra unit of distance added to a long movement is of less importance than an extra unit added to a short movement' (Carrothers, 1956). Within the field of recreation, Ellis and Van Doren tried several exponents in the gravity model, which they used to determine the spatial distribution of state-wide flows of recreational traffic in Michigan. Even the smallest exponent (0·36) did not prevent over-estimation of short distance trips. Their final model not only utilised the smallest exponent, but added one hour travel time to each journey; even so, over-predictions were not completely eliminated (Ellis and Van Doren, 1966, 64).

Further developments are due to Wolfe who, in his first application of the gravity model to recreational travel, found that the distance decay function estimated trip volumes efficiently only over a narrow range of distances and tended to over-estimate the number of long trips. Wolfe correctly hypothesised that this problem arose from the nature of recreational travel itself and argued that an element of inertia was

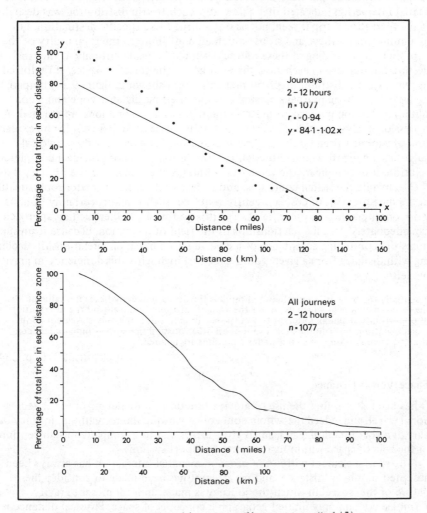

Figure 9.2 Recreational journeys: distance travelled (2)

involved in recreational traffic, an element that the gravity model was not designed to take into account. Thus, 'when trips are very short, the friction of distance is negligible. The number of short trips may, however, be smaller than expected because a great many people may not wish to make a trip of any length, however short; their starting up inertia, as it were, is too great to overcome' (Wolfe, 1966, p. 73). Wolfe devised an inertia model to test this hypothesis, which in effect made the distance exponent itself a function of distance; that is, the interaction function makes the response to distance change as distance itself changes and thus provides a feedback mechanism for the exponent. Although avoiding some deficiencies of the simple gravity formula, the inertia model remains unsatisfactory in many ways, since it preserves the interaction function as a criterion of cost, although in an amended form.

The hypothesis that the recreational journey is different from other forms of spatial interaction indicated that a new approach to trip distribution was desirable. If the recreational trip is seen, not as one journey to a specific destination, but as a bundle of journeys and stops, which all contribute to the total utility of the trip, then the recording of these journeys should be made not only at the final destination but also in each zone through which the traveller passes. If replotted in this way, the distribution graph takes the form shown in figure 9.2 (compare figure 9.1), with all journeys passing through the first distance zone and a continuing reduction in journeys in subsequent zones as destinations are reached. A regression analysis on this curve provides an increase of 30 per cent in the explanation of variance given by the original calculations. The data for these two calculations are identical and, although reformulation does not provide a complete solution, it does indicate the value of re-thinking the analysis of the primary data.

Meanwhile the search continues, and it may well be that a greater sophistication in the measurement of cost is urgently required; such thinking certainly dominates work on interaction in other fields. Yet it is doubtful whether such an approach can adequately describe relationships in the field of recreation, because it presupposes the continuing acceptance of a cost function based on a relationship declining with distance from a given point. Colenutt highlights this deficiency in gravity models:

Essentially the only difference between models for the various activities is the value of the distance exponent which expresses the variable attitude to travel (and the distribution of opportunities) among different trip purposes. In fact, this is the only statement about travel behaviour made in the model so that all other possibilities such as time-budget constraints, scenic routing, or step distance functions are ignored.

(Colenutt, 1970, p. 234)

### Space Versus Distance

It has been shown that the use of gravity functions in modelling outdoor recreational travel, and indeed the whole concept of viewing the recreational journey as part of a cost function, can lead to gross errors and to a complete misconception of the role of space within recreational transport systems.

The spatial element within the process of spatial interaction has always been accepted simply as 'distance' and no attempt has been made to consider the nature of the 'space' in which the journey is made. Indeed, present gravity formulae contain only limited geographic concepts of space. Physical distance is used as a surrogate of 'cost' and geographic space is seen merely as the medium in which transport takes place. Existing transportation models disregard the character of that space and do not allow environmental 'noise' of this kind to affect the process of interaction. Thus, while many workers advocate more suitable measures of impedance, these new functions are still encompassed within Euclidean spatial concepts, which define space merely as a frame of reference within which relationships occur. In this philosophy of 'absolute space' the metric in that space remains isotropic and constant. This is certainly true in the application to transportation problems of gravity concepts, which assume flat surfaces, equal ease of transport in all directions and uniform resources, and thus permit a Euclidean treatment of the problem. Adjustment of the 'mass' variables and of the 'distance' function are made during calibration to take account of the environmental realities of travel space. It is interesting to note that Morrill (1963), in studying migration interaction, sees the failure of existing approaches as due, not to the lack of sophistication in the distance function, but to 'the ignoring of variations in the geographical environment, especially the micro-distribution of population and in addition the failure to admit area itself'.

Within the field of recreation, however, it must be accepted that the spatial disposition of resources and facilities for recreation in relation to the distribution of population has a profound influence on the nature and pattern of travel. Recreational travel space cannot be treated as a random 'noise' in the model, to be adjusted during calibration, but should be contained within the theoretical parameters of the model itself. In recreational interaction the activities and objects themselves define the spatial fields of influence, and the major task of research workers is to select a geometry that can deal with the complexities of these · fields, where 'the recreational system for a given activity presents a spatial pattern resulting from a complex interaction between people, facilities, resources and space' (Ellis and Van Doren, 1966, 57).

## A SYSTEMS APPROACH

Existing land-use transportation studies resolve various analytical stages sequentially and constraints on the volume of traffic are applied from one stage to the next. This sequential approach is unsatisfactory for recreational journeys, because the processes of 'trip generation', 'trip distribution' and 'trip allocation' are more intimately connected; in any model it must be recognised that the distribution of trips between origins and destinations will be affected by the nature of the route network and by the scenic value of the intervening travel space. This relationship is self-evident once it is accepted that travel space can make a positive contribution to the selection of destinations and does not act merely as a medium of transport. Equally, the attractive power of destinations can no longer be resolved in isolation, no matter what progress is made in quantifying the attractiveness of individual sites. Rather, the route taken and the places visited on a recreational journey are a function of origin, destination and travel space combined. The aim of those working within the field of recreational travel must be to cater for these reciprocal relationships.

The most promising area of research at present seems to be in the field of systems modelling. Systems modelling likens the recreational transport system to a physical system (whether electrical, hydraulic or thermal), and Ellis has used this technique with some success in both Michigan and Ontario to model movements of campers to state parks (Ellis, 1966; 1967). He used an electrical analogue in which the origins act like sources of current. 'The current (flow of campers) sees various paths of differing resistance and distributes itself across the network in a minimum-energy fashion, eventually returning to "ground" via the park components. The flow at each park is thus determined by the relative resistances of all parks, all links and the relative strength of all origin sources' (Ellis and Van Doren, 1966, 60).

In the remainder of this chapter it is intended to examine the concepts underlying the systems models and their effect on the modelling of recreational traffic movements. For this purpose models developed by Ellis in a North American context will be used, as well as more recent developments in Great Britain that could lay the groundwork for a similar systems model for recreational traffic.

## A Systems Approach to Recreational Travel in North America

It should be emphasised that, in designing a systems approach to recreational transport systems, Ellis was in no way motivated by the premise that recreational transport systems are in themselves intrinsically different from other transport systems; his starting point was rather that the gravity model inadequately represented traffic movements of any kind. In his view,

the drawbacks of using such a simplified model [namely, the gravity model] in the case of recreational travel are chiefly that the system of alternative destinations available to a given recreational user are highly interdependent. That is, given an improvement in one destination area, recreationists who usually visit other areas will tend to try out the new one. Their frequency of usage may well increase at the same time. Nearby or 'en route' areas may also experience slightly different user pressures than previously. With the gravity model, however, the change in one component affects only that component. Because the formula is applied sequentially to each pair of points, the interactive effects are not represented.

(Ellis, 1967, p.3).

This pragmatic argument alone justifies the adoption of the systems approach, and it should further be recognised that, if the positive contribution that recreational travel space may make to the recreational experience is accepted, the effect of that space can be represented adequately only within the framework of such a model.

Ellis' approach to recreational travel within the systems framework is based on a simple hypothesis:

... every system ... is no more and no less than a collection of parts or components. Each part has certain properties of its own, inherent in its nature. Each system has a specific structure or inter-connection pattern of its own, by which it constrains its parts to perform only in certain ways. A successful systems model must combine a mathematical recipe for the systems structure in order to show how the whole system behaves. Every part affects every other part through the inter-connection.

(Ellis, 1966, p. 31).

The modeller's first task is, therefore, to 'identify' the components of his system, and Ellis recognised three basic elements in his recreational travel system: (1) origin/generating areas; (2) destination areas; and (3) highway links.

*Origin/Generating Areas*

Ellis saw origin areas as sources of specified traffic flows, analogous in hydraulic terms to a set of constant-flow pumps. These 'generators' were the centres of population in the study area. Lacking the means to establish the relationship of population and socio-economic factors to 'trip making propensity', Ellis quantified his component from known survey data — that is, camp site permits, which noted the origin of each camper. This approach has fundamental weaknesses, for actual flows reflect the spatial distribution of recreational facilities and the obstacles facing the recreationists enjoying these facilities; it would therefore have been more appropriate to use a measure of 'potential demand' rather than one of 'consumption', which represents only the realised part of total demand (Countryside Commission, 1970).

The difference between levels of demand and actual levels of consumption is important, for the confusion of these two concepts has bedevilled conventional modelling techniques and still does so. Transportation models usually explain the variation in trip-taking by individuals (or, more usually, by households) by treating the number of trips taken as a function of the socio-economic characteristics of the individuals or households concerned. Such thinking is misconceived, for socio-economic variables can determine only trip-making propensity, or the potential trip-generating ability of the areas concerned. The actual number of trips generated must necessarily reflect this demand. Thus, in different areas with similar social profiles the scale of trip-making may differ considerably according to the location of the supply of resources and facilities relative to residents' homes; a shortfall in supply will result in the creation of 'latent demand', which will be realised only when further facilities are made available. In turn, the key that determines which resources are available is the interaction function itself; as this function varies, so will the level of 'available' resources.

An understanding of differential levels in trip generation will be obtained only when the nature of the interaction function is resolved. Until then, the practice of relating the level of trip-making (as a dependent variable) to selected socio-economic variables in linear-regression models will have doubtful validity, except in areas where the resources are uniform and equally accessible. This view has certainly been confirmed by analysis undertaken on data from the studies in central Scotland. Separate multiple regression analyses were undertaken on the results of interviews in Lanarkshire (1858) and Greater Edinburgh (1779), treating the number of pleasure trips taken in a motor vehicle in the four weeks before the interview as the dependent variable and six socio-economic variables (education, sex, marital status, age, occupation and income) as independent variables. As an attempt to identify the factors responsible for variations in trip generation, the two analyses failed, for the levels of explanation (as revealed by the square of the correlation coefficients of the equations established) were very low. Nevertheless, one interesting explanation of variations in levels of trip generation did emerge. The level of trip-making by residents of Greater Edinburgh was 60 per cent higher than that of Lanarkshire residents; in the four weeks before the interview the car-owning residents of the Greater Edinburgh region took on average 2·4 pleasure trips lasting over 2 hours, compared with 1·5 trips in Lanarkshire. A significant variation of this kind might reasonably be expected to be reflected in major

TABLE 9.2

SOCIO-ECONOMIC VARIABLES: STATISTICAL BREAKDOWN

| Code name of variable | Description | Definition | Greater Edinburgh Mean | Standard deviation | Lanarkshire Mean | Standard deviation | Combined Mean | Standard deviation |
|---|---|---|---|---|---|---|---|---|
| | | | (percentage of car-owning households) | | | | | |
| TAE 1 | Terminal age of education | Less than 16 years | 69 | 46 | 78 | 42 | 74 | 44 |
| TAE 2 | | Over 16 years | 19 | 39 | 12 | 33 | 16 | 37 |
| SEX 1 | Sex | Male | 52 | 50 | 58 | 49 | 55 | 50 |
| MARS | Marital status | Single | 21 | 41 | 22 | 41 | 22 | 41 |
| AGE 1 | Age | Less than 20 years | 06 | 24 | 08 | 28 | 07 | 26 |
| AGE 2 | | 20–39 years | 38 | 49 | 39 | 49 | 38 | 49 |
| AGE 3 | | 40–64 years | 38 | 48 | 39 | 49 | 38 | 49 |
| JOB 1 | Occupation | Manual occupation | 22 | 41 | 29 | 45 | 25 | 44 |
| INC 1 | Income (personal) | Less than £1000 per annum | 52 | 50 | 50 | 50 | 51 | 50 |
| INC 2 | | Between £1000–£1999 per annum | 38 | 48 | 42 | 49 | 40 | 49 |
| No. Trips | Pleasure trips | Integer value indicating number of trips taken in 4 weeks prior to interview | 2·37 | 4·23 | 1·47 | 2·65 | 1·92 | 3·57 |

Source: Duffield (1973), pp. 11–12.

differences in the socio-economic profiles of the populations concerned, but an examination of the socio-economic statistics of the two populations does not show such differences (see table 9.2). Indeed, the two areas are more notable for their similarities and so could be expected to have a similar propensity for trip-making. The differences in actual trips taken, which is a measure of consumption rather than demand, seems to be more strongly related to major differences in the recreational resources of the two areas. These results support earlier contentions that consumption levels of trip-making are inextricably linked to available resources by means of the interaction function.

## Origins and the TRIP Data Bank

Although this finding poses formidable difficulties in the use of standard transportation models, it does not run counter to the underlying principle of the systems model, where each component is modelled separately and where the structure of the model itself caters for the effects of such interaction. Thus, the input into the systems model in respect of areas of origin should not be levels of consumption for those areas, but an indication of their trip-making propensity. In its most straightforward form the generation of this demand, or trip-making propensity, can be seen as some function of population, and attempts have been made to see how a population can be expressed effectively in this way. Data from the 1971 census have been adapted to provide, on a 5 × 5-km square grid, statistics on the distribution and density of population throughout Scotland. These statistics have been entered into the TRIP data bank (Tourism and Recreation Information Package), a system conceived and developed by the Tourism and Recreation Research Unit at Edinburgh University, and are the basis for calculations of 'demand surfaces' at a national level. TRIP is a computer-based information system that comprises the collection, storage and manipulation of data. One of the main attributes of the system is its link with computer mapping. The system of recording data is at present based on a 5 × 5-km grid, compatible with the National Grid and covering the whole of Scotland. Thus, for each of the 3416 squares covering Scotland, individual items of data are identified, recorded and permanently stored within the computer. Data collected may refer to areal, point or linear features and are retained at their lowest level of aggregation within the data bank.

Existing land-use transportation models invariably use a zonal breakdown of their study areas to collect and manipulate data on both trip-generation and trip-attraction, and the TRIP data bank is fully compatible with these needs. Moreover, it can also be used as an interactive tool which is of considerable value in analysing a whole transportation model. The system contains programs that can 'search out' all the locations of a specified type (or types) of resource within any radius of an identifiable point (or points); this allows the integration of inter-action and impedance functions to assess both realised and latent demand for trips and available and potential resources (Tourism and Recreation Research Unit, 1974).

The starting point for the calculation of demand for recreational activity is the map of population density (figure 9.3). The spatial expression of the demand generated from these population centres will vary, however, with the distance

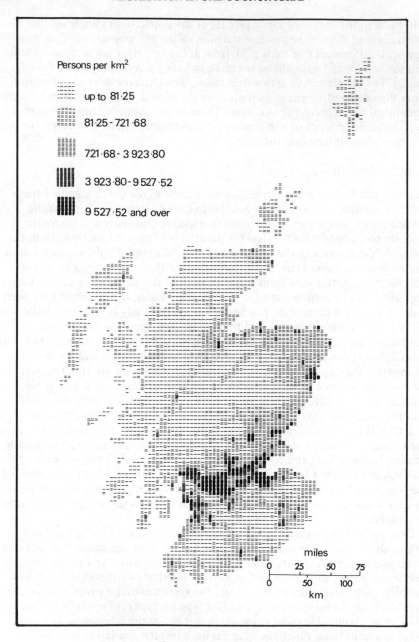

Figure 9.3 Population density in Scotland

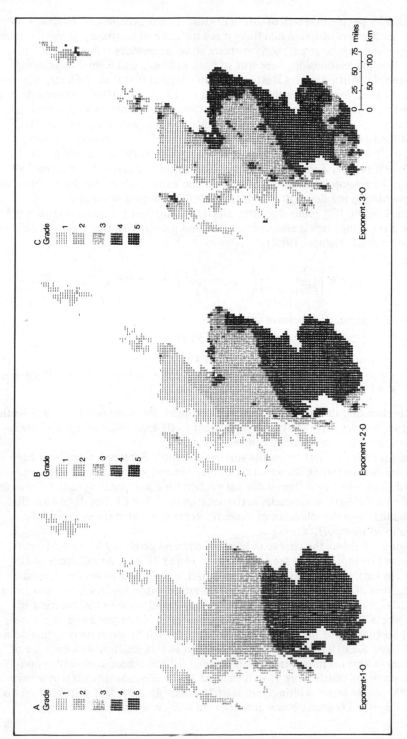

Figure 9.4 Population pressure by exponents. *A*. Exponent = 1·0; *B*. Exponent = 2·0; *C*. Exponent = 3·0

travelled by people in search of different recreational experiences. Evidence presented earlier demonstrated that there was a measure of constancy in the distances that people travel to acquire a given recreational experience (table 9.1) and that these distance relationships were true of both informal and formal recreational activities. In North America Wolfe (1966) has argued that these different patterns of recreational journeys should be reflected in the use of different exponents in a standard gravity model, on the grounds that such exponents are necessary to represent the attitude of recreationists to different recreational activities. He established exponents for three activities: (1) second-home owners, 2·22; (2) campers, 1·45; and (3) commercial resort visitors, 0·95 (Wolfe, 1966, p.18).

While it is necessary to reserve judgement on the exponents he selected and also on the appropriateness of North American experience to the British situation, it is possible to use the TRIP system to show the changing demand surfaces within Scotland that result from the selection of different exponents (figure 9.4). If the gravity approach is adopted, the demand pressure on each square is defined by the formula (Hansen, 1959)

$$A_i = K \left[ \frac{P_1}{D_{i-1}{}^x} + \frac{P_2}{D_{i-2}{}^x} + \frac{P_3}{D_{i-3}{}^x} + \cdots + \frac{P_n}{D_{i-n}{}^x} \right]$$

where $A_i$ = population pressure on square i;

$P_{1-n}$ = resident population of squares $1-n$;

$D_{i-(1-n)}$ = distance from i to squares $i-n$;

$x$ = an exponent describing the effect of travel distance between the zones;

$K$ = a constant.

It is clear that the higher the selected exponent, the more restrictive will be the effect of distance; with the highest exponent (3·0), high levels of demand are restricted to areas close to urban centres.

On the basis of results from the surveys of central Scotland, maps have been prepared demonstrating the variation in this demand surface; they have been produced by selecting different distance functions corresponding to the distances travelled to undertake particular activities (figures 9.5–9.8). The discussion that follows indicates the relevance of these different demand surfaces in a model of recreational transport.

Figure 9.5 shows the change in levels of demand produced by two different distances (10 and 30 miles are equivalent to 16 and 48 km). At a distance of 10 miles (16 km), the heaviest potential population pressure follows the general distribution of population, defining not only the central lowlands, but also towns and cities in north and east Scotland. This map could assist in the selection of areas where the development of demand-oriented facilities, such as golf courses, might take place; for the surveys in 1969 showed that Scottish participants do not travel more than 10 miles (16 km) to take part in this activity. At a distance of 30 miles (48 km), a more generalised demand surface is produced, with population pressures much more closely related to the central lowlands where over 400 000 people reside within a radius of 30 miles (48 km). This distance function is suitable when resource-based activities are being examined — for example,

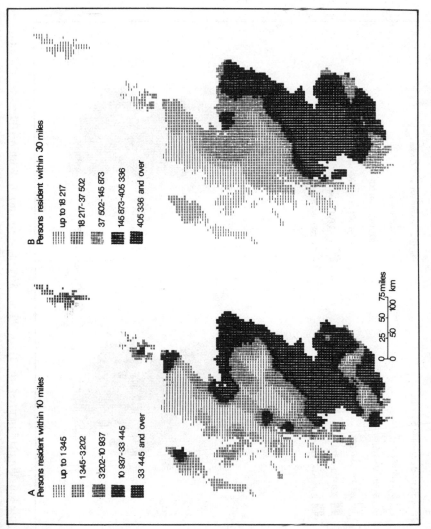

Figure 9.5 Population pressure (1): A. Within 10 miles (16 km); B. Within 30 miles (48 km)

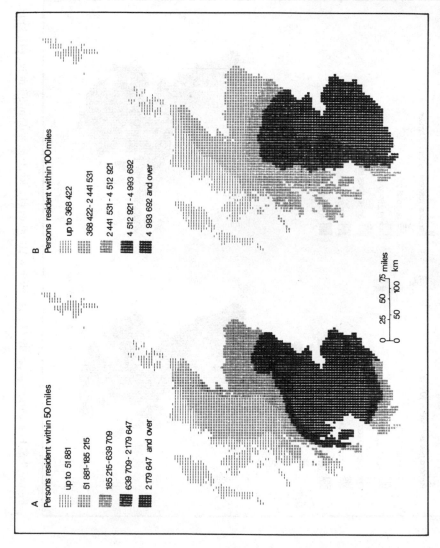

A

Persons resident within 50 miles

up to 51 881

51 881- 185 215

185 215- 639 709

639 709- 2 179 647

2 179 647 and over

B

Persons resident within 100 miles

up to 368 422

368 422- 2 441 531

2 441 531 - 4 512 921

4 512 921 - 4 993 692

4 993 692 and over

0    25    50    75 miles
0    50    100    km

Figure 9.6  Population pressure (2): *A*. Within 50 miles (80 km); *B*. Within 100 miles (160 km)

canoeing, orienteering and sailing — for which participants are prepared to travel greater distances.

Figure 9.6 shows the alteration in the demand surfaces arising when distances are increased to 50 and 100 miles (80 and 160 km). At greater distances the demand surface becomes more generalised and is influenced by the distribution of population in England and Wales. This is particularly true of the map of population within 100 miles (160 km), which shows that the areas of greatest demand are in southern and eastern Scotland, for at this radius the conurbations of northern England affect the results.

It is interesting to note the similarity between figures 9.5 and 9.6 and the exponent demand surfaces in figure 9.4. It may well be that future research in the field of recreational travel can exploit these similarities, particularly in the calibration of transport models.

However, earlier discussion on the nature of informal recreational journeys has shown that it is inappropriate to consider demand surfaces merely as an accumulation of population pressure within a given radius, for evidence has revealed that those on day trips tend to be unconstrained by shorter distances; in Colenutt's view, a friction-free zone of up to 20 miles (32 km) exists for day trips where the impedance effect of distance is very small (Colenutt, 1970, p. 115). Accordingly, maps showing population pressures between specified radii may be more appropriate for both informal half-day and full-day trips than these maps that show the total population enclosed by a given radius.

Demand surfaces produced by adopting the former approach are shown in figures 9.7 and 9.8. The contrast between these surfaces and those produced by cumulative population pressure maps is marked, for at greater distances demand shadow-zones emerge around the major urban areas, features that correspond with the observed distributions of recreational traffic in central Scotland. In figure 9.7, the two maps (10–20 miles is equivalent to 16–32 km; 20–30 miles is equivalent to 32–48 km) correspond respectively with half-day and day journeys from home for those informal activities undertaken close to home, whereas figure 9.8 appears to correspond with the demand for those recreational activities that depend on a particular resource, and hence may be useful in evaluating levels of demand for caravans and second homes or for wilderness areas, where participants wish to be some distance from their permanent residences.

## Destinations

Destinations were considered by Ellis to attract trips in direct proportion to their attractiveness for the desired activity; that is, an area was considered to act as a magnet for recreationists. Accordingly, for a given population pressure that depends on the distribution of population and the nature of the whole network of routes, recreational flows into an area for a given activity will be proportional to the attractiveness of the area for that activity. The form of the equation is

$$\text{flow in the area} = K \times \text{attraction index} \times p$$

where $p$ equals a given level of demand, $K$ is a constant and the attraction index is based on the attributes and quality of the features of the area (Ellis, 1966, p.9).

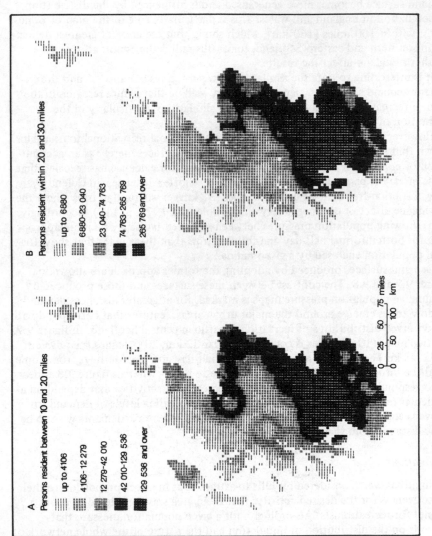

Figure 9.7  Population pressure (3): *A*. Between 10 and 20 miles (16 and 32 km);
*B*. Between 20 and 30 miles (32 and 48 km)

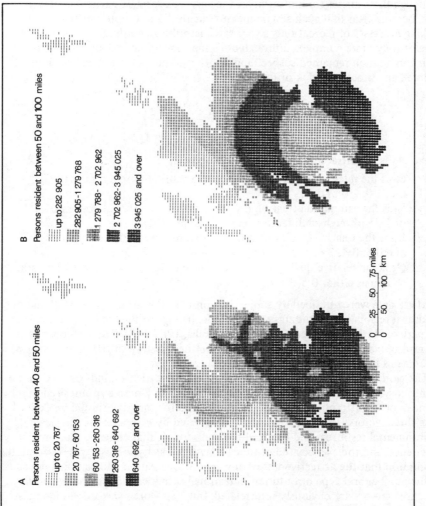

Figure 9.8  Population pressure (4): *A.* Between 40 and 50 miles (64 and 80 km);
*B.* Between 50 and 100 miles (80 and 160 km)

In early work very simple indicators of the attractiveness of individual recreation sites have generally been used. If, for example, a particular activity was being studied, then the index was based on either a simple measure of capacity, such as the number of camp-sites, or a surrogate capacity measurement based on the type of resource, such as the area of a water body (Wennergren and Neilsen, 1970). Although these are useful indicators of the varying appeal of particular sites, it soon became clear that such simple measurements did not represent the decision-making processes of recreationists very satisfactorily. Accordingly, indices became progressively more complex, although both the conceptual and statistical basis of their formulation remained suspect and arbitrary. For his Ontario study, Ellis adopted an attraction index of the form

$$A_d = C_d\,S_d \left( \frac{W_d\ +\ 0 \cdot 5\,Q_d}{1 \cdot 5} \right)$$

where $A_d$ is the attraction of the park for campers;

$C_d$ is the relevant capacity of the park, a value chosen either as $0 \cdot 2$, $0 \cdot 6$, $1 \cdot 0$, $2 \cdot 0$ or $3 \cdot 0$;

$S_d$ is the estimated effect of any special factor, a value chosen as $0 \cdot 75$ or $1 \cdot 25$, though such factors may not be present;

$W_d$ is the relative quality of water-related resources of the park, chosen as either $0 \cdot 2$, $0 \cdot 6$, $1 \cdot 0$, $1 \cdot 5$ or $2 \cdot 0$;

$Q_d$ is the relative quality of the outdoor setting or the locale of the park, chosen as either $0 \cdot 5$, $1 \cdot 0$ or $2 \cdot 0$.

These data were obtained by subjective consideration of the park itself and of its known regional surroundings and also from listings of the facilities available at the park of the kind marked on road maps (Ellis, 1967, p.8). This approach is an interesting example of progressive thinking on the question of site attractiveness, but remains unsatisfactory in that it is highly subjective.

The work of Van Doren (1967), who devised the attraction indices used in the Michigan systems model, avoids such subjectivity. Van Doren hypothesised that an index of the attraction of Michigan State Parks for camping should be derived from three factors: the outdoor activities preferred by campers; the physical and environmental resources and the facilities and services that enhance the camping experience; and their associated outdoor activities. His hypothesis was based on the assumption that the attractiveness of any area for recreation and camping depends on the number and type of outdoor recreational activities that can be undertaken. The three factors are obviously interrelated, but Van Doren was able to identify seventy-two features (natural, cultural, facility and service, activity), which were then quantified for each Michigan State Park. In order to combine this long inventory for each park into a meaningful index of attractiveness to campers, Van Doren used factor analysis to reduce the variables to a smaller and more manageable number. After preliminary work fifty-five of the seventy-two variables were selected as representative of the park's attraction, but these variables did not produce the original three factor groupings. Instead, four factors emerged, which between them explained fifty-four per cent of the total variation in the variables examined. These factors were interpreted by Van Doren as being association with: water (inland lakes), land (physical environment), camping (amenities), water (Great Lakes).

Each of the four factors included variables of natural resources, facilities and services, which, it could be argued, were essential for a good recreational area. The 'camping attraction index' for each Michigan State Park was developed by combining weighted factor loadings of the variables to provide one factor for each park (Van Doren, 1967, p. 106).

While the choice or the evaluation of individual variables is a matter for further debate, Van Doren's approach appears to offer a useful opportunity of quantifying the complex contribution of a large number of variables to an explanation of the attractiveness of recreation sites. Adaptations for particular activities would clearly be necessary and, indeed, this is recognised in Van Doren's concept of attractiveness. The successful incorporation of his indices of attraction in the framework of a systems model suggests that this approach is worthy of consideration for future use.

Although work in Great Britain has been much more limited, indices of the type described in chapter 6 could form useful inputs into a systems model. 'Recreation environments', combining as they do four separate evaluations of an area's suitability to support recreational activity—namely, the ability to support land-based recreational activities, the ability to support water-based recreational activities, scenic quality and ecological quality—could serve as a valuable interim indicator of the attractiveness of a destination, at least until more objectively-based indices have been devised for use within Great Britain.

As was the case with trip generation, the spatial resolution of the attractiveness of destinations is complicated by the interaction function; areas may have the same potential attraction or ability to sustain an activity, but the realisation of that ability will depend on their accessibility to zones generating demand for journeys of a particular kind. If the spatial disposition of suitable resources is related to the interaction function it can reveal different 'supply surfaces', depending on the nature of the distance function used.

Figure 9.9 provides a simple demonstration of such variations in supply surfaces on a Scottish scale. One category of landscape that can be readily identified within Scotland is 'mountain country', a resource that clearly offers great potential for certain types of recreation, but is often found at some distance from the major urban centres. The degree to which the potential of mountain country is used for recreation will depend on the distance that people are prepared to travel to reach the resource, and the Lanark and Edinburgh surveys established that the residents of central Scotland generally did not travel more than 20 miles (32 km) from their homes for walking and hiking. If this distance is adopted, only a limited proportion of Scotland's mountain country is accessible for such recreation by home-based Scots (figure 9.9). Mountain country also supports rock-climbing and the surveys showed that participants in this activity travelled greater distances; figure 9.9 shows mountain country within 50 miles (80 km) of urban centres and clearly demonstrates the much larger proportion of the latent resources that becomes potentially available because of participants' greater willingness to travel further in search of suitable resources for rock-climbing.

218

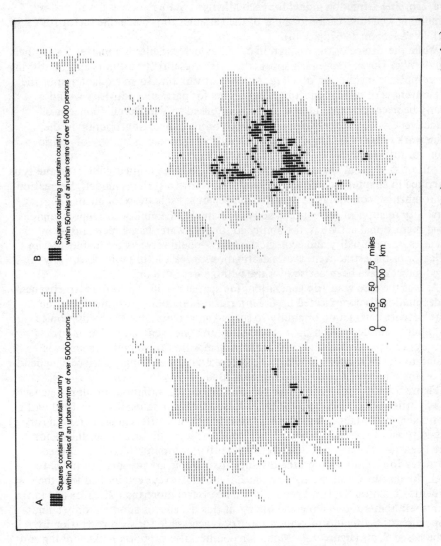

A

Squares containing mountain country
within 20 miles of an urban centre of over 5000 persons

B

Squares containing mountain country
within 50 miles of an urban centre of over 5000 persons

0   25   50   75 miles
0   50   100  km

Figure 9.9  Mountain scenery: *A*. Within 20 miles (32 km); *B*. Within 50 miles (80 km)

The TRIP system can facilitate such evaluation of supply in respect of site attractiveness; that is, sites with the same physical attractiveness (potential) offer different real opportunities for recreational use depending on their accessibility to visitors, as defined by the distribution of population and the nature of the interaction function. The TRIP system will not only permit the calculation of both 'potential' and 'real' supply and demand surfaces, but, by the ability to compare these different surfaces, can also help to identify opportunities for recreational development.

## Highway Links

In his models Ellis argued that, given a set of generating points (population centres) and attraction areas (provincial parks suitable for camping), the flow of recreational traffic will be governed by the links between the two. For the majority of recreationists, barriers of distance, time and money lie between them and their recreational goals, and the selection of the travel component is a key element in a systems model.

In his studies of both Michigan and Ontario, Ellis selected the trunk highway system as his route network. His next task was to represent the barrier that these links offered to potential recreational traffic. Ellis considered the flow along any particular link to be inversely proportional to the friction (resistance) that people perceive when they consider travelling along that link, and directly proportional to the innate pressure (the desire or the propensity for recreation) generated by the population of the area. The key element in the equation was the resistance of the link, since it determines the distribution of trips over the system. Ellis combined both time and distance costs in formulating his resistance function. Although he was aware of the possible benefits acquired by recreationists travelling over scenic routes, Ellis adopted a formula more appropriate to a gravity model, an indication of his pragmatic use of the systems model. The resistance function adopted was

$$\text{resistance} = [K_1 \text{ (distance)} + K_2 \text{ (gasoline + tolls)}]^\alpha$$
(for any link)

where distance     = length of route link;

gasoline     = travel costs in travelling along link (petrol, oil, etc.);

tolls     = any toll charge for travelling along the link;

$\alpha$     = exponent;

$K_1, K_2$     = constants.

A conventional definition of route resistance of this kind is not, however, a prerequisite of the systems approach; indeed, the resistance component can be manipulated in many ways. Firstly, the nature of the cost elements in the resistance formula can be altered to suit particular circumstances; secondly, the exponent within the cost function can be adjusted to take account of possible changes in attitudes to recreational travel, with lower values indicating a reduction in the constraint of travel costs on journeys. Yet the main advantage of the systems approach is that each link can be modelled separately, thus allowing the various links of the transportation system to take account of the characteristics of the surrounding environment (including scenic quality); this information can then be related to road capacity and route length to define the resistance of that link to recreational journeys. In considering alternative forms of the resistance function, Ellis, mindful of the positive appeal of certain routes, proposed a resistance function that would include a bonus of reduced resistance for travel along very attractive routes and a penalty for the use of routes of low scenic quality. The resistance function for each link would then take the form (Ellis, 1966, p. 52)

$$\text{resistance} = K_1 \left[\text{distance/speed} + K_2 \ 0 \cdot 025 \ (\text{distance} + \text{tolls}) - 0 \cdot 1 \ \text{scenic}\right]^\alpha$$

where      distance    = length of route link;

                speed       = the average speed of recreational traffic over the link;

                toll          = any toll charge for travelling along the link;

                scenic     = a measure of the scenic quality of the countryside through which the road link passes;

                $\alpha$           = exponent;

                $K_1, K_2$  = constants.

An index of this kind will certainly be a prerequisite of a systems model in which recreational travellers recognise the appeal of scenery as one factor in their choice of destination. Such a model must both include measures of the scenic attractiveness of areas surrounding road links and acknowledge the positive role of the recreational journey. This fundamental contrast between recreational and other journeys was succinctly put by Colenutt who stated that 'for the pleasure tripper, the objective of the trip, however, is not to minimise travel time between origin and a single destination but to maximise the recreational benefit he can obtain from both the travel time and time spent at stopping points' (Colenutt, 1969, 45).

Any attempt to calculate the enjoyment provided by scenery on a recreational journey must take account of many factors (Appleyard, Lynch and Myer, 1964; Burke, Lewis and Orr, 1968). A satisfactory measure of the scenic appeal of areas adjoining roads would be confined, as far as possible, to those areas that are visible to the motorists and should not include areas obscured from view, either by the alignment of the road or by natural or man-made obstructions. Moreover, Simpson and Zetter (1971), in their work in the Lake District, argued that the faster a driver's speed, the more restricted his view from the road. Although this is patently true, it must be remembered that, on a recreational journey, the passengers in a motor vehicle (who are usually the majority) enjoy a very much less restricted view of the scene. In any case, these attempts are no more than preliminary sorties in what will be a long campaign of research to establish the relationship between the scenic value of areas surrounding roads and the flow of recreational traffic along them. Preliminary pilot work in Scotland (Duffield, 1973) has served only to confirm the operational difficulties in such an approach, although it has proved technically feasible to use the method adopted (multiple regression) by employing the number of journeys along a route as the dependent variable, and three independent variables—namely, (1) the attractiveness of the destination chosen; (2) the travelling distance along the specified route; and (3) the scenic attractiveness of the chosen route.

## Interconnection of the System

Once all the components of the three classes (origins, destinations and links) have been modelled, a systems approach requires the construction and operation of an appropriate model for the activity under study. Unlike the components themselves, which can and will change according to the activity under consideration, the structure of the system does not vary for each activity, since it depends on the spatial arrangement of cities, counties and highways. To solve the interconnecting elements of his system Ellis used a method devised by McLaughlin (1966), derived from linear graph theory.

## The Ontario and Michigan Systems Models

It was within this framework that Ellis incorporated the distinctive feature of the two investigations. Although both studies were concerned with the movements of campers to State Parks, there were some significant differences.

Ontario's highway system was represented in the model by a set of 178 segments of provincial highways and other minor roads. The origins of campers were a set of fifty-four points centred on the larger cities, towns and border points (so as to give a reasonable coverage of the province) and the destinations were seventy-one provincial parks. The nature of the attraction indices used in these studies has already been discussed. The data on flow sources at the origins were derived from a sample survey of park users carried out in 1964. When the model was run with these data, the results were compared with actual attendance, as measured by the number of permits in 1964; the margin of error was found to be 'in the middle to upper 30 per cent range', a figure that, in fact, corresponds with the year to year variation in park attendances (Ellis, 1967, p. 11).

The study undertaken in Michigan using the same systems modelling approach, linked seventy-seven areas of origin to fifty-five camping parks by a road network comprising 208 segments. More reliable data on origins and the use of a more powerful technique for modelling the attractive power of different parks enabled the margin of error in this study to be reduced to approximately 20 per cent (Milstein and Reid, 1966).

Much remains to be done to improve the accuracy of forecasts made by a systems model, but there can be little doubt that, even with the inadequate data available at present, the approach has much to commend it. In a joint article with Van Doren, Ellis compared the systems approach with the standard gravity model, using the same data from the Michigan study; the systems model was significantly more efficient in explaining variations in camping visits than the simple gravity model (Ellis and Van Doren, 1966, 66).

## Advantages of a Systems Approach

The main justification for adopting such an approach is its conceptual soundness. Unlike the gravity model, which survived because of its ability to approximate known distributions, the systems model provides an integrated structure, which successive studies of recreational travel have shown to be the distinctive feature of recreational interaction.

The strengths of this approach are not only conceptual, for it has practical advantages over other approaches. Despite its integrated nature, the modelling of each component within the system is a separate undertaking and the influence of one component does not affect the modelling of any other component. For example, distances from centres of population are not considered in the attraction index, since distance is inherently only a property of the highway links. The mutual influences or interactions of the components are due only to their interconnections and not to their actual nature. Thus interaction is solved only when the entire simultaneous equation of the systems model is solved and not before; this is in direct contrast to the gravity model, whose history is marked by the manipulation of the interaction component to fit observed phenomena.

Once the components have been correctly modelled, the system operates as a whole and there is complete integration of all the travel elements. As has been demonstrated, trip generation is influenced by the spatial disposition of resources and the nature of the interaction function; the potential attractiveness of individual sites is modified by their spatial relationships to centres of population and the impedance function adopted; and trip distribution and assignment are one process, so that the output from the model is capable of indicating not only flows from origins to specific destinations, but also flows along particular road links. Thus, while the main aim of both the Ontario and the Michigan studies was to see how far the systems approach could predict the actual inflow of campers recorded at each park, it is clear that the technique is equally appropriate for calculations of the flows along the road network.

This synthesised calibration of all components in the transportation model has important operational benefits since the system always remains in equilibrium. Any alteration in a component, be it origin, destination or road link, alters the entire system, so that the effects of the change are immediately apparent in the system. This is in direct contrast to the gravity model where the alteration in a particular component affects only those interactions in which it is itself involved and leaves the rest of the system undisturbed.

Furthermore, the interactive nature of the system solves key problems such as the effect of intervening opportunities between an origin and a particular destination. There is no need to define the effect of alternative destinations if all links in the system are modelled correctly. By its nature, a systems model includes the effect of intervening opportunities; that is, travellers select links according to the relative resistance of individual paths and not on an all-or-nothing basis, and they terminate their journeys at any destination along any route in proportion to the relative resistance of the various paths.

More important than its immediate predictive power is the fact that everything known about the system is laid out explicitly, so that the model can easily be modified in the light of experience or when improved data become available. Adaptation can take three forms: firstly, extensive remodelling of individual components; secondly, rethinking of the connections between components; and, finally, the addition of new components.

Certainly one of the most necessary improvements of the model used in Michigan and Ontario is a more appropriate form for modelling behaviour from origin. Numbers of participants cannot be generated by the model on the basis of information from the origins, but have to be supplied as known data. This is a major weakness and indicates the necessity of establishing absolute levels of potential demand and treating existing levels of consumption as only the realised part of the total demand for an activity. Demand should therefore be seen as some function of the population of an area, and earlier discussion on multiple regression work in this field may well provide an appropriate starting point for further modelling of this component.

The application of different indices of attraction within the Michigan and Ontario studies also demonstrates the possibility of work in this field. One major development that may attract researchers is the incorporation in the attraction index of not only absolute attraction but also constraints on capacity, which could have an important effect on the resolution of the demand surface.

Adjustments in the model that involve adding to or adapting components within its structure are particularly useful in any evaluation of the effect of proposed plans or developments. One particularly valuable feature of the systems model is the way in which it can deal with growth in demand or with the provision of new facilities. It is often assumed (and is sometimes inherent in models—for example, the gravity model) that uniform rates of increases in participation over time at all trip origins will lead to uniform increases in the spatial expression of that demand. This assumption is quite erroneous, for the unequal distribution of facilities and people will mean that even uniform growth of participation at each origin will lead to uneven growth in numbers moving into parks or along road links. The systems approach can easily cater for this phenomenon, as was demonstrated in the Michigan study; an increase in participation of 8 per cent per year over a fifteen-year period at all origins was envisaged and incorporated into the systems model. The results showed increases in demand at State Parks (assuming that no new parks were created during the period of the forecast) of between 143 per cent and 329 per cent (Ellis, 1966, p. 49).

More specific developments can also be evaluated using the systems approach. One of the major problems facing recreation managers is deciding where valuable or limited resources can best be used for the greatest benefit to the community, either to permit the largest increase in participation or, conversely, to reduce pressures of demand on particular areas to a more acceptable level. The systems approach can facilitate such a decision by providing quantitative assessments of the likely effect of locating such developments at different points within the system.

In a similar way the projected growth of an existing settlement or the creation of a new one and its subsequent effect on demand at parks or along road links can quickly be assessed. In the Michigan study, several kinds of experiments relating to specific planning problems were performed. Perhaps the most interesting of these was one that assessed the impact of removing tolls on the bridge over the straits of Mackinac, which link Lake Michigan to Lake Huron; this toll was the equivalent, as a deterrent to travel, of 106 miles (171 km) of two-lane highway. This study showed an increase in attendance at parks in the eastern upper peninsula of 13–14 per cent, with much smaller gains in parks in the western upper peninsula, and slight percentage losses in those on the northern lower peninsula. Other experiments included assessing the effect of increases in participation up to 1980, of the addition of parks into the system and of increasing the capacity of existing parks on the distribution of demand (Milstein and Reid, 1966).

## THE FUTURE OF RECREATIONAL MODELLING

The development and application of a systems model to outdoor recreation in North America, its greater efficiency than the gravity model and its ability to cope with both practical and predictable developments in the transportation system, are strong reasons for urging the wider application of a systems approach in the modelling of recreational travel. Although the studies in North America were confined to recreational trips for camping, there is no reason why the systems approach would not be equally rewarding in the study of other kinds of recreational journeys, provided appropriate data were available. Indeed, as was indicated earlier, it may well be that systems modelling is even more appropriate to trips for informal recreation where the gravity model is at its weakest.

It must be acknowledged that the adoption of a systems model poses many problems, particularly in the collection and assembly of basic data. The strength of the system, as outlined above, also provides its basic weakness, in that each individual component must be modelled separately before the full analysis can proceed.

Nevertheless, whatever practical problems the adoption of a systems approach may bring, they are a necessary consequence of the adoption of a valid conceptual approach; for a systems model combines conceptual soundness with an operational approach that would ensure an efficient and valid modelling of recreational journeys over the transportation system. Obviously the technique requires further development and also demands the benefit of research in associated fields of recreation. Nevertheless, as Wolfe has stated, 'it is not enough simply to utilise the techniques that have been found valid for the analysis of traffic flows on urban streets and non-recreational rural highways, for these have traffic patterns that differ fundamentally from those on recreational highways' (Wolfe, 1966, p. 1). If real progress is to be made towards an efficient modelling of recreational transport systems, past techniques must be abandoned.

# Postscript

The research on which this book is based represents only the beginnings of what is necessary if the study of outdoor recreation is to make the contribution of which it is capable both to geography and to public policy. Nevertheless, it is a cause of satisfaction to those in the Tourism and Recreation Research Unit that, while seeking to maintain academic standards in such a programme of work and publications, they have been able to produce studies that have played a significant part in the formulation of official plans and policies; for example, nearly all the recommendations made to Lanark County Council in *Leisure + Countryside =* (Duffield and Owen, 1970) have been accepted as part of the county's recreational strategy, and the report, *The Touring Caravan in Scotland* (Owen and Duffield, 1971), provided a basis for the Scottish Development Department (1972) circular on the subject to local planning authorities. It is true that what has been required by sponsors has sometimes involved a larger element of survey than researchers in a wholly academic environment would voluntarily have sought, though even such studies have provided opportunities for devising new techniques of survey, such as the monitoring of caravan traffic by means of cine cameras linked to traffic counters described in chapter 8, and the data collected in such surveys now provide unrivalled sources of information for more fundamental studies of outdoor recreation and tourism and for the illumination of aspects other than those required by the sponsors in the original survey.

At the same time, other research needs have become increasingly apparent. A major requirement is research into attitudes towards outdoor recreation on the part of both participants (or potential participants) and those who provide recreational opportunities, whether intentionally, as with the creation of Country Parks and picnic sites by local authorities or of leisure complexes by commercial developers, or unintentionally as with landowners whose land is used without permission by members of the public. The supply/demand model used in this book has provided an organising principle for much of the work undertaken by the Unit, but in its present form it is admittedly a rather simple tool; for demand and supply are clearly more complex concepts than has been allowed for. There is already empirical evidence to suggest that participation in outdoor recreation is strongly influenced by kinds of occupation, and that those in jobs with a marked routine tend to carry this experience into their recreational behaviour (Parker, 1971). Again, as Emmett (1973) has indicated, recreation is often a social activity and the reasons for participation or non-participation may be found in people's relationships with others, though this may be overlooked in sampling the recreational preferences of individuals only. Non-participation may thus be related not only to lack of information, particular skills, equipment or access to transport, but also to the attitudes of peer groups; for example, the participation rate for pony-trekking by boys may be low not because they dislike it, but because it is regarded as inappropriate by their friends.

Sociologists will explore these dimensions further in order to understand more fully the complex motives of participants in leisure pursuits, but analysis of the data already collected in these surveys in central Scotland can throw some light on this topic by relating participation not only to social class, but also (where samples are sufficiently large) to occupation.

Two other approaches would seem profitable. Firstly, there is a need for studies in depth, inevitably with small samples, of motivations for pursuing different kinds of recreation, such as that conducted by Sewell and Roston (1970) into sea-angling in British Columbia, in which insights were sought into what participants perceived as the benefits they gained from this pursuit. These preferences and motivations may often be different from those assumed by planners and legislators, and Sewell (1971) has already shown in the environmental field how the discipline of a professional may influence both the problems he sees and the solutions he proposes.
Secondly, there is a need for careful observation of what recreationists actually do, as opposed to what they say they do; for these may differ substantially. Such observation needs careful handling, not only because of the obvious risks of intrusion into privacy, but also because of the possible effects of observation on the recreational activity itself; attempts to monitor recreational movements on coastal dunes, using a camera operated by remote control from a tethered balloon, were in part frustrated by the fact that the balloon itself became an object of interest, disturbing pre-existing recreational patterns!

Such inquiries will throw much needed light on factors affecting the demand for outdoor recreation (both actual and latent), and similar approaches are needed to identify obstacles to the supply of opportunities and facilities for outdoor recreation. Additionally, refinements of the methods outlined in chapter 6 for evaluating potential resources for outdoor recreation are also required. A particular weakness in this approach was the lack of any firmly established bases for determining the requirements of the different kinds of recreation, so that rather crude rules of thumb had to be used. It has been suggested that standards of recreational provision are inappropriate in the countryside (Select Committee, 1973), but while it must be accepted that they cannot be inflexibly applied owing to the great variety of physical conditions throughout the country, it still seems desirable to have some better understanding of at least the minimum desirable dimensions and characteristics of, say, golf courses and ski runs, and of the necessary level of provision in relation to population (with appropriate variation in the light of the distribution of people). Such information is also necessary if any kind of assessment of national need is to be made, and especially if forecasts are required. What is undisputed is the need for further work on the carrying capacity of different kinds of land and for different kinds of recreation. Such studies should not be confined to ecological capacity, but should also attempt to assess psychological capacity, the value of which may vary with different social groups and psychological types. Assessment of physical capacity must rely on long-term research, in view of the complexity and variability of the factors involved, and the surveys undertaken at selected points on the coast of East Lothian now provide datum lines from which vegetation al change can be measured and related to recreational pressure. Parallel investigations will also be needed into the impact of recreation and tourism both on other land users and on the local economy. The Tourism and Recreation Research Unit has recently undertaken a methodological study of the latter on Tayside, but the impact on other land users has largely been neglected; there is urgent need to find ways of minimising the friction between recreationists and the land users on which they so heavily depend.

Two other related aspects of the supply of resources may also repay further work—the location of new recreational facilities and the nature of the recreational journeys on which their viability will largely depend. Little theoretical work has so far been done on the location of different kinds of recreational facilities in the countryside, though staff of the Tourism and Recreation Research Unit have been concerned with preliminary analyses of the location of a national water-sports centre for Scotland and of a national open-air museum (Duffield *et al.*, 1968; Coppock, 1973). Large investments are likely to be made in such facilities in the next decade and, while it must be recognised that they may well create new demands for recreation, the soundness of decisions on location will depend in no small measure on a better understanding of the forces at work. Here, too, a systems approach will be helpful. This is particularly true of recreational travel, and further research on the lines indicated in chapter 9 is needed. In this connection it is important that, despite the present and growing importance of the motor car in recreational travel, the needs of other social groups should not be overlooked, particularly those of the young, whose participation rates in many forms of active recreation are much higher than those of the population as a whole (chapter 4). Their dependence on public transport, a characteristic shared with the old and the underprivileged, suggests that particular attention should be paid to the possibility of locating such facilities on the urban fringe.

All these developments will increase the capability of recreational planners to make adequate and satisfactory provision for outdoor recreation, though they cannot predict those arbitrary changes of fashion that greatly influence recreational choice from time to time. Effective planning will also benefit from recognition of the fact that recreational traffic ignores administrative boundaries, so that recreation must be planned on a regional basis, and that sound planning depends on a flow of adequate and near-contemporary information in a form in which it can be quickly handled and evaluated.

As chapter 9 has shown, the development in Edinburgh of a computer-based information system (TRIP), for a consortium of public authorities with responsibilities for various kinds of recreation and tourism in Scotland, provides an opportunity for such information to be rapidly retrieved and analysed, with the results produced as statements, tables or maps, depending on which form will be most useful to those using the information system. The value of such a system will depend not only on the quality and quantity of the information it contains and on the efficiency with which this can be analysed, but also on the kinds of questions that planners and others ask. This development has further strengthened the case for adopting a systems approach to outdoor recreation, for certain of the linkages in such a system are already implicit in the data structures of the system and others can be added as the information system is developed.

Recreation geography is still in its infancy. A start has been made in increasing understanding of recreation in the countryside, but the equally important questions on urban recreational travel (which may be complicated by the role of social contacts between different groups) and the location of recreational and other leisure facilities likewise require the attention of geographers. If the amount of leisure time grows, it is likely to become one of the major determinants of the location and nature of new settlements in the developed countries. Already there is evidence that decisions about work and homes are influenced by the nature of the recreational opportunities that different localities can provide, so that recreationists can make the best use of their leisure time, a trend that the electronic revolution, by weakening the pull of place of work, may well accentuate (Berry, 1970). In the meantime, inadequate provision, spatial imbalance and conflicts of interests between different users of resources make a better understanding of the geography of leisure an urgent necessity.

# Appendix: National and Regional Recreation Studies in Great Britain

Although reference has been made to work elsewhere, prime attention in this book has been given to a number of studies conducted in Great Britain in the past decade. It will be convenient, therefore, to outline the nature of these surveys so that reference can be made to particular aspects of their findings where these are appropriate. Particular attention will be paid to methods of survey and size of sample, the latter being of special importance in view of the low participation rates in many forms of outdoor recreation.

## NATIONAL RECREATION STUDIES

### Pilot National Recreation Survey

The *Pilot National Recreation Survey* was the first attempt to acquire national data on patterns of recreation and illustrates the problems of gaining valid, reliable data on those recreational activities pursued by minorities. The survey was undertaken jointly in 1967 by the British Travel Association and the University of Keele. It was based on a national sample of 3167 respondents over the age of twelve and was intended to provide reliable data on participation in both active and passive recreation. Information was collected on thirty pursuits, but, despite this wide range, half the pursuits had participation rates of less than 10 per cent over the whole life-span of those interviewed. When a more recent period was considered (within five years prior to interview), participation was considerably less and in only two activities, swimming and diving, and fishing, had more than 10 per cent of respondents participated. Accordingly, the detailed analysis of approximately two-thirds of the pursuits was based on a sub-sample of less than 150 and in most cases samples were considerably smaller. The organisers of this study have always stressed that it was a pilot survey and have acknowledged the weakness of an analysis based on an inadequate sample. Nevertheless, the implications for future studies were clear: detailed analysis of participation in the majority of active pursuits would be possible only with very large samples.

The survey also investigated related fields, including the ownership of recreational equipment, recreational plans for the future, the time budgets of British residents and thus the time available for recreation. More particularly, patterns of leisure at the weekend and the influence of car ownership on recreation were investigated. All these aspects of the recreational use of leisure time were related to socio-economic attributes of the sample population.

One of the aims of the *Pilot National Recreation Survey* was the provision of at least descriptive statistics on regional variations in recreational participation (British Travel Association–University of Keele, 1969, p.2). The Registrar General's nine standard regions of England, together with Wales and Scotland, were considered separate 'regional' areas and provided the eleven basic divisions for the sampling frame. At least twenty sampling points were selected within each region and the regional sub-samples were made approximately equal to ensure that the draw would be large enough to permit simple regional analysis. The objective was not fully realised, however, and the authors of the report concluded that

simple descriptive material derived from the full undivided sample is not likely to be seriously in error. But any analytical and associational work on our sample must involve its division into sub-samples using such parameters as age, income, occupation type and community size; and though this seems to be generally permissible using the full national sample, it becomes hazardous or indeed impossible for regional sub-samples. Even the full sample is too small to give adequate and representative data for the minority sports and pastimes: indeed, it would have to be increased at least ten-fold to pick up large enough numbers of water skiers and riding enthusiasts to draw significant conclusions about their characteristics.

(British Travel Association–University of Keele, 1967, p.93).

The major contribution of the *Pilot National Recreation Survey* was to establish for the first time the levels of participation in outdoor pursuits. It was ironic that this primary finding should at the same time create the need for such caution in the interpretation and analysis of participation in individual pursuits. It is also interesting to note the influence of this survey on the character of subsequent regional investigations, which all included much larger samples of respondents.

## Government Social Survey

The Government Social Survey, undertaken on behalf of the Department of Education and Science, and with the special interests of the Ministry of Housing and Local Government and the Inner London Education Authority in mind, was directed by K.K. Sillitoe, and also threw some light on leisure activities. It was made between September 1965 and March 1966 and the report, *Planning for Leisure,* was published in 1969. The survey had two objectives, namely, to investigate both the present pattern of participation in outdoor and physical recreation among people living in the urban areas of England and Wales, and the frequency and manner of their use of public open spaces. In all, sixty-three activities were covered, ranging from those with very low levels of participation, such as baseball and croquet, to the more popular outdoor pursuits, such as soccer and tennis.

The sample for this study was assembled in three steps to cater for the special interests of the sponsors. Firstly, a national sample was drawn, consisting of 2682 persons aged fifteen and over from the urban areas of England and Wales, excluding Inner London. Secondly, a sample of 1321 persons was drawn from the Inner London area. Finally, a sample of 1732 persons was drawn from the eight New Towns in England and Wales, thus giving an average of 218 persons per town. Altogether 5735 persons were interviewed.

Although the total sample was larger than in the *Pilot National Recreation Survey,* sampling still presented problems. The first difficulty arose from the fact that the national sample covered only the urban areas of England and Wales, an urban area being defined for this purpose as one with a minimum of 6000 households and a minimum density of six persons per acre (fifteen per hectare) according to the 1961 census. The sample was thus restricted to fifty urban areas, and care is required in interpreting some of the statistics derived from the national sample, since levels of participation will doubtless be influenced by facilities that are available only to those living in towns or in the countryside. Evidence from other studies has clearly indicated that the availability of recreational facilities can influence participation in different pursuits and the prime value of this study, therefore, is to those planning for the recreational needs of urban areas. A further problem arises from the fact that the national sample constituted less than 50 per cent of the total persons interviewed and is smaller in scale than the *Pilot National Recreation Survey,* the inadequate size of which has already been noted. When the statistics from the three samples are compared, it is clear that, for statistical purposes, the survey should be seen as three separate sampling frames rather than one of 7535 interviews. The results from this survey add further confirmation to those obtained by the *Pilot National Recreation Survey.*

## Opinion Research Centre Survey

In September 1972 the Opinion Research Centre conducted a survey among a nationally representative sample of adults on the subject of sports and sports sponsorship. This was to be the first of a regular series of surveys and contained information on the following:

(1) the extent of interest in twenty-one different sports;
(2) the frequency of attendance at sports matches and meetings;
(3) unprompted awareness of companies involved in sponsorship of each sport;
(4) attitudes towards sports sponsorship;
(5) the readership and television viewing habits of those who follow each of the twenty-one sports.

The information was obtained through personal interviews with a random sample throughout Great Britain of 2209 adults over the age of sixteen. Not only outdoor activities, but also indoor and informal pursuits, notably darts and snooker, were investigated. The range of information gained through this survey was very limited and it contributes little towards a deeper understanding of the recreational activities considered.

REGIONAL RECREATION STUDIES

**Pilot National Recreation Survey, Report No. 2**

Following the publication of the *Pilot National Recreational Survey,* Report No. 1
and the launching and completion of regional investigations, the authors of the
*Pilot National Recreation Survey* recognised the need for broad indications of the
assumed, distinctive regional variations in recreational participation throughout
Great Britain. They therefore decided to examine further the regional information
that had been collected. The results of this analysis were made available in the
*Pilot National Recreation Survey,* Report No. 2, 1969. To increase the sample size
of the English regions and to overcome the problems posed by regional sub-samples
that are too small to support analysis, seven of the Registrar General's regions
were grouped into four regions; the Welsh and Scottish samples were still analysed
separately (see table A.1.). Grouping the regions improved the reliability of the
data at a regional level, but for larger divisions of the country than was initially
envisaged. It must be acknowledged, however, that even these grouped samples
are small and it would be wise to accept the advice of the authors of the *Pilot
National Recreation Survey,* 'to treat our conclusions about the characteristics of
our regional samples merely as a set of sign-posts to the general direction in which
regional and recreational patterns differ from the national norm' (British Travel
Association–University of Keele, 1969, p.5).

**Outdoor Leisure Activities in the Northern Region**

Partly because of the difficulties of obtaining reliable regional data for the *Pilot
National Recreation Survey,* several regional studies have been undertaken. The

TABLE A.1

STRUCTURE AND SAMPLE OF THE PILOT NATIONAL RECREATION SURVEY

| Grouped regions | Registrar General's regions | Regional sub-sample size | Grouped sub-sample size |
|---|---|---|---|
| | | (number in sample) | |
| | Northern England | 344 | |
| | East and West Ridings | 306 | |
| The North | North West England | 279 | 929 |
| | North Midlands | 243 | |
| The Midlands | Midlands | 225 | 468 |
| Metropolitan | Eastern England | 280 | |
| England | London and the South-east | 284 | 564 |
| | Southern England | 297 | |
| The South and West | South-west England | 286 | 583 |
| Wales | Wales | 299 | 299 |
| Scotland | Scotland | 324 | 324 |

Source:   British Travel Association–University of Keele (1969), p. 3.

first such study was that undertaken by National Opinion Polls on behalf of the North Regional Planning Committee. The survey, carried out in the months of June and July 1967, had two primary objectives: firstly, to examine patterns of current outdoor leisure activities and to discover how people spent their spare time and, secondly, to forecast the extent to which participation in leisure activities would increase or decline during the next decade or so. To a large extent the first objective created an investigation with many parallel features to the *Pilot National Recreation Survey*, with which it shared a primary concern for leisure activities outside the home, particularly outdoor pursuits taking people to the coast and to the countryside.

A further similarity was that the area covered by this survey coincided with the North of England region as defined by the *Pilot National Recreation Survey;* but whereas in the latter survey 344 interviews were conducted in the region, National Opinion Polls interviewed 3828 residents aged twelve and over. The sampling framework consisted of 100 administrative district sampling points, selected on the basis of population size, from each of which forty-four households were drawn from the electoral register. This procedure led to oversampling of adults and children in small households, but the results were weighted to conform with the known distribution of the region's population.

The survey used a standard home-interview questionnaire, which included a form of diary in which detailed information on the two weekends prior to interview could be recorded. In an attempt to overcome the problem of establishing levels of participation in minority pursuits, the questionnaire sought levels of 'normal' participation, defined as those participants who take part in a particular activity at least once every three months. These latter statistics provide the closest comparison with data from the *Pilot National Recreation Survey*, which defined recent participation as within the year of interview (1965). No distinction was made between formal and informal or active and passive pursuits. In all, twenty-four active pursuits were considered, the majority of which are spectator sports, and only three informal pursuits were included.

From the start the problem of minority pursuits was apparent. Although the survey was designed to permit analysis of the geographical characteristics of participants in particular pursuits, 'it was not possible to provide a meaningful demographic analysis of very small numbers of people' (North Regional Planning Committee, 1969, p. 7). It was therefore decided to group activities. The emphasis of this survey was on the use of countryside and coastline and the organisers decided that the best way of grouping was related to land use. Accordingly, the groupings listed below were made to take account of the nature of the resources that the activities require:

(1) Water activities: sailing, pleasure-boating, rowing and canoeing, fishing, water-skiing, sub-aquatics;
(2) Activities on small pitches: playing and watching bowls, playing and watching tennis;
(3) Activities on large pitches: athletics, playing and watching cricket;
(4) Activities on large courses: playing and watching golf, horse-racing, motor-racing, motorcycle-racing;

(5) Activities on sites in the country: climbing, caving, camping, caravanning, gliding, flying, nature study;

(6) Activities in the open country: horse-riding, hunting, pony-trekking, rambling, cycling, motor-rallying.

The only formal active pursuit that could be analysed separately was swimming.

Despite a regional sample larger than the national sample used by the *Pilot National Recreation Survey* and nearly ten times larger than the northern England sub-sample of that survey, this investigation in the Northern Region did not over-come the problems of examining participation in minority activities. As the authors of the study concluded:

> it would have been of considerable interest to have obtained details of leisure activity levels in the various sub-areas of the region and to have described population movements for leisure within and between sub-areas. However, financial limitations on the sample size and design made this impossible. The report is confined in the main to a consideration of activities in the region as a whole. The identification and quantification of minority recreational pur-suits is precluded for the same reason

(North Regional Planning Committee, 1969, p. 2).

### Leisure in the North West

The second major regional survey was the North West Sports Council's survey of recreational patterns in north-west England, undertaken by Mass Observation Limited from May to August 1969. The aim was to assess recreational demand in order to indicate accurately priorities in the provision of recreational facilities. The survey was designed to expand the scanty knowledge of leisure activities in the North-west provided by the *Pilot National Recreation Survey*, in which it had been necessary to submerge the region within a larger North of England region to permit analysis (see p. 232). Moreover, the results were subjected to a more sophisticated analysis than had hitherto been attempted in British recreational surveys; in parti-cular, the relationship between provision of facilities and participation in recreation was explored and, through regression analysis, equations were derived to enable future demand to be predicted.

In all, 8130 people aged twelve and over were approached; 83 per cent (6719) completed the questionnaire and 5078 responses were used in the analysis. The sample was drawn from the electoral register which was then confined to those over twenty-one. As a result, there was some bias against households composed of young adults, a difficulty that was solved by interviewing, where possible, one person aged from twelve to twenty at any adult respondent's house. Those who planned the survey made a deliberate attempt to bias the sample in favour of people under forty-five in order to strengthen the statistics relating to active recreation; only one in every two of those over forty-five was given the complete questionnaire. The statistics in the report, however, have been weighted so that they apply to a population with a normal age distribution. The sample was not geographically random; the designers of the survey felt that participation in recreational activities was more likely to be governed by the size of the community in which people lived rather than by its geographical location, and accordingly the region was split into seven groups based on place of residence. Within these groups a number of wards was sampled in proportion to the total population of the area (table A.2).

## TABLE A.2

COMPOSITION OF SAMPLE INTERVIEWED IN NORTH-WEST ENGLAND

| Strata | Percentage of population | Number of wards sampled |
|---|---|---|
| Liverpool CB | 10·4 | 18 |
| Remainder of Merseyside conurbation | 9·8 | 18 |
| Manchester CB | 9·0 | 17 |
| Remainder of S.E. Lancashire and N.E. Cheshire conurbation | 27·3 | 52 |
| Other urban areas over 50 000 population | 15·9 | 29 |
| Other urban areas under 50 000 population | 18·1 | 33 |
| Rural districts | 9·4 | 19 |
| Total | 99·9 | 186 |

Source:    North West Sports Council (1972), p. 211.

It is interesting to note the influence of previous surveys. When the questionnaire for the North-west study was designed, attention was paid to the wording used in the two national surveys, the *Pilot National Recreation Survey* and *Planning for Leisure.* The designers were also conscious of the advantages, both for the region and for other researchers, of compatability between questions and of using similar wording where the same topic was being investigated.

The questionnaire had five main areas of study:

(1) respondents' use of their time budgets for both the week prior to interview and, in more detail, the day prior to interview;

(2) trips from home, day trips and half-day recreational trips;

(3) participation in sport and physical recreation in the twelve months prior to interview and, in more detail, from those who had played a sport in the previous four weeks;

(4) recreational aspirations, that is, the sports and recreation people planned to do or would like to take up;

(5) socio-economic characteristics of respondents, excluding questions on income.

### The Symmetrical Family

One other regional study, undertaken by Young and Willmott (1973) and rather different in kind, was of particular relevance to this book (especially to the subject matter of chapter 2), and involved a sample of residents in the Metropolitan region. This sample was drawn in two stages: the selection of local authority areas for sampling, and the choosing of samples within the selected areas. Twenty-four local authorities at varying distances from the centre of London were first selected. The region was divided into four zones, namely, Inner London, the remainder of Greater London, the inner part of the Metropolitan region beyond the boundary of Greater London, and the outer part of the Metropolitan region. Each zone was divided into northern and southern zones and the outermost zone was further divided into smaller and larger authorities on the basis of population. From these twelve sectors, two local authorities were selected, one relatively 'high' in class status and one relatively 'low'.

In the second stage, numbers of individuals were selected from each authority in proportion to the total resident adult population; for, unlike earlier surveys, this was not a survey of households. Three thousand names were selected but only 1928 of these were interviewed, representing 63 per cent of the initial sample and 73 per cent of those known to be eligible. The proportions of men and women in the sample were very similar to those given in the population census, though both the young and single persons of both sexes were slightly under-represented; social classes 1 and 2 were over-represented and those in classes 4 and 5 (semi- and un-skilled) under-represented. In addition to these interviews, a sub-sample of those interviewed completed a self-administered diary covering both weekends and one weekday. This sample was drawn from those who were married and between the ages of thirty and forty-nine inclusive. In all, 411 diaries were received. Surveys were also made of active sportsmen and sportswomen, of managing directors and workers in a number of plants.

Although the main aim of Young and Willmott's enquiry into leisure was to assess its effect on the family, they sought information on participation and its variation by class in both home-based and away-from-home and passive and active leisure pursuits.

### Studies in Central Scotland

The only other detailed studies into the demand for recreational activities in the United Kingdom were undertaken by the Tourism and Recreation Research Unit of Edinburgh University, which began a geographical appraisal of countryside recreation in Lanarkshire and Greater Edinburgh in 1969. Although the two areas are contiguous (figure A.1), it was thought desirable to carry out separate investigations because they represent different relationships between the demand for and the supply of outdoor recreation and thus provided an opportunity to test techniques of survey.

In many ways these two surveys were meant to serve aims similar to those of other regional studies, that is, to establish the main features of the demand for recreation as a necessary preliminary to making plans for the use of the recreational resources in each region. Thus the Home Interview Survey was designed, firstly, to provide data on the recreational habits of the residents of the two study areas and secondly, to examine the relationship between socio-economic characteristics and participation in leisure activities, and thus enable tentative plans to be made by providing a guide to levels of participation over the next few years.

Although these were separate surveys, great care was taken to ensure that the methodologies adopted were identical. These surveys therefore provide profiles of demand for outdoor recreation and also an insight into the particular methodological approaches used. As in the North-west study, a comparable approach to the *Pilot National Recreation Survey* was used wherever possible, in the hope of permitting valid comparisons with the latter survey and other regional investigations that might pursue the same objective.

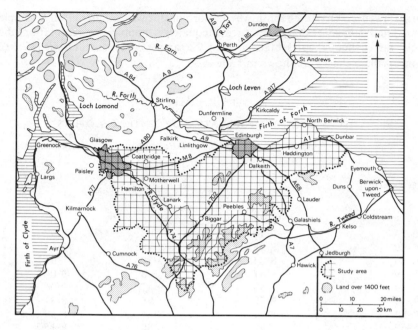

Figure A.1 Location of study area

Whereas in the *Pilot National Recreation Survey* only 324 interviews were conducted in the whole of Scotland, a total of 2300 addresses (1100 from Lanarkshire, 1200 from Greater Edinburgh) was extracted from the valuation rolls at a fixed sampling interval (1 :170 Lanarkshire, 1 :280 Greater Edinburgh), the first address being taken at random. This systematic sample ensured that all inhabited parts of the study areas were represented, thus avoiding the spatial clustering that either a truly random sample or the two-stage sampling used in the *Pilot National Recreation Survey* and in both English regional studies might have given.

A dual system of data collection was used. Interviewers called at the selected addresses and interviewed one person over sixteen in each household; 'self-administered' questionnaires were then left for all other members of the household over sixteen to complete and the interviewer arranged for these to be collected at a later date. This technique served two purposes. Similar surveys have found that young people are usually under-represented in a sample since they are often away from home, and conversely, that those in the older age groups are often over-represented; it was hoped that this problem and the consequent need for 'weighting' the data would be avoided by using the self-administered questionnaire. In addition, a restricted budget made it essential to maximise the number of interviews; the self-administered questionnaire enabled the size of the sample to be increased by an average of 75 per cent while costs of the survey increased by only 35 per cent.

Field work for both studies was carried out from June to September 1969 and a total of 3637 individuals (1779 in Lanarkshire and 1858 in Greater Edinburgh) aged sixteen and over completed questionnaires. After the collection of data it was necessary to establish whether or not this was a representative sample; for, while systematic sampling ensured adequate geographical representation, the social and economic representativeness of the sample data had still to be checked. Some of these checks are shown in table A.3.

TABLE A.3

CHECKS ON SAMPLE POPULATION OF CENTRAL SCOTLAND

| | Those interviewed | Total sample | 1966 Census |
|---|---|---|---|
| | | (percentage) | |
| *Age groups* | | | |
| 16–19 | 2·71 | 7·16 | 9·06 |
| 20–24 | 5·90 | 8·03 | 8·97 |
| 25–29 | 8·35 | 9·18 | 8·68 |
| 30–34 | 8·84 | 9·38 | 8·04 |
| 35–39 | 9·67 | 9·43 | 9·04 |
| 40–44 | 9·58 | 9·47 | 9·06 |
| 44–49 | 9·70 | 8·95 | 8·31 |
| 50–54 | 8·98 | 8·64 | 8·59 |
| 55–59 | 7·90 | 6·80 | 8·15 |
| 60–64 | 9·42 | 8·10 | 7·20 |
| 65+ | 19·49 | 14·77 | 14·48 |
| *Sex* | | | |
| Male | 40·4 | 45·2 | 46·5 |
| Female | 59·6 | 54·8 | 53·5 |
| *Marital status* | | | |
| Married | 70·5 | 68·7 | 65·0 |
| Single | 12·9 | 20·0 | 25·2 |
| Other | 16·4 | 11·3 | 9·8 |

Source:    Duffield and Owen (1970), pp. 170, 178; Duffield and Owen (1971), pp. 197, 198.

If reliance had been placed solely on data from personal interviews, weighting of the sample would have been necessary because young adults (16–25 age group) were greatly under-represented and elderly people (60+ age group) over-represented. The basis for analysis, however, was the sample data drawn from both the direct personal interview and the self-administered questionnaire, and the social profile of this combined sample is extremely close to the profile of the population as provided for in 1966 by the 10 per cent sample census, thus indicating the effectiveness of the self-administered questionnaire and the validity of the unweighted sample.

The questionnaire used in both studies in central Scotland was identical and had four major sections:

(1) investigation of a range of twenty-four active outdoor recreation pursuits, with particular attention to those activities that make demands on land and water resources;

(2) gathering of information on informal outdoor recreation, particularly the pattern of activities in the weekend before interview;

(3) investigation of the role of the motor vehicle in influencing outdoor recreation patterns;

(4) gathering of information on personal and social characteristics of the individual interviewed.

These surveys yield information of varying reliability at various scales and provide the basis for much of the analysis and comment in this book. They also underline the paucity and infrequency of data on outdoor recreation; the Government's decision to incorporate questions on recreation and leisure on a continuing basis in the household survey is particularly welcome. Neither research nor policy-making can proceed adequately in the absence of sound data, and a regular flow of information on participation in recreation, on the supply (actual and potential) of recreation resources, and on those recreational journeys that link areas of supply and demand, remains an urgent necessity.

# References

PREFACE

Duffield, B.S. (1973). *Outdoor Recreational Traffic Patterns in the Edinburgh Area, A Report on SSRC Research Project HR 1596,* University of Edinburgh.

Duffield, B.S., and Owen, M.L. (1970). *Leisure + Countryside =, A Geographical Appraisal of Countryside Recreation in Lanarkshire* (ed. J.T. Coppock), University of Edinburgh.

Duffield, B.S. , and Owen, M.L. (1971). *Leisure + Countryside =, A Geographical Appraisal of Countryside Recreation in the Edinburgh Area* (ed. J.T. Coppock), University of Edinburgh.

Owen, M.L., and Duffield, B.S. (1971). *The Touring Caravan in Scotland* (ed. J.T. Coppock), Scottish Tourist Board, Edinburgh.

Owen, M.L., and Duffield, B.S. (1972). *Summer Holiday Traffic,* University of Edinburgh.

Owen, M.L., and Duffield, B.S. (1973). *Self-Catering Accommodation in North East Scotland,* University of Edinburgh.

1  AIMS AND CONCEPTS

Coleman, A., and Maggs, K.R.A. (1965). *Land Use Survey Handbook,* 4th (Scottish) edn., Geographical Association, London.

Coppock, J.T. (1966). The recreational use of land and water in rural Britain. *Tijdschr. econ. soc. Geogr.,* **57**, 81–96.

Linton, D.L. (1968). The assessment of scenery as a natural resource. *Scott. geogr. Mag.,* **84**, 219–38.

Patmore, J.A. (1970). *Land and Leisure,* Problems in Modern Geography, David & Charles, Newton Abbot.

Select Committee of the House of Lords on Sport and Leisure (1973). *Second Report, Evidence, Appendices and Index,* H.M.S.O. London, Q. 1571.

Snaith, R. (1973). Submerged demand in a framework of recreation planning. Paper to P.T.R.C. Conference, Brighton, p.1.

Wolfe, R.I. (1964). Perspective on outdoor recreation: a bibliographical review. *Geogr. Rev.,* **54**, 203–38.

Zimmerman, E.W. (1951). *World Resources and Industries,* Harper & Brethen, New York, p.7.

2   THE LEISURE BUDGET AND PASSIVE RECREATION

British Travel Association–University of Keele (1967). *Pilot National Recreation Survey, Report No.1,* University of Keele, London.

Burton, T.L. (1971). *Experiments in Recreation Research, University of Birmingham Urban and Regional Studies* No. 1, George Allen & Unwin, London, chapter 7.

Duffield, B.S., and Owen, M.L. (1970). *Leisure + Countryside =, A Geographical Appraisal of Countryside Recreation in Lanarkshire* (ed. J.T. Coppock), University of Edinburgh.

Duffield, B.S., and Owen, M.L. (1971). *Leisure + Countryside =, A Geographical Appraisal of Countryside Recreation in the Edinburgh Area* (ed. J.T. Coppock). University of Edinburgh.

Maw, R. (1969). Construction of a leisure model. *Off. Archit. Plann.,* **32**, 924–35.

North Regional Planning Committee (1969). *Outdoor Leisure Activities in the Northern Region,* City Planning Office, Newcastle upon Tyne.

North West Sports Council (1972). *Leisure in the North West,* Deansgate Press, Salford.

Select Committee of the House of Lords on Sport and Leisure (1973). *Second Report,* together with the proceedings of the Committee, H.M.S.O., London.

Sillitoe, K.K. (1969). *Planning for Leisure,* H.M.S.O., London.

Young, M., and Willmott, P. (1973). *The Symmetrical Family,* Routledge & Kegan Paul, London.


3   PASSIVE RECREATION AND THE ROLE OF THE MOTOR CAR

Beaty, A.N.S., Pearson-Kirk, D., Cal, P.C., and Grieg, M.T. (1973). The recreational demand of an urban area. Paper to P.T.R.C. Conference, Brighton.

British Travel Association–University of Keele (1967). *Pilot National Recreation Survey, Report No. 1,* University of Keele, London.

Duffield, B.S., and Owen, M.L. (1970). *Leisure + Countryside =, A Geographical Appraisal of Countryside Recreation in Lanarkshire* (ed. J.T. Coppock), University of Edinburgh.

Duffield, B.S., and Owen, M.L., (1971a). *Leisure + Countryside =, A Geographical Appraisal of Countryside Recreation in the Edinburgh Area* (ed. J.T. Coppock), University of Edinburgh.

Duffield, B.S., and Owen, M.L. (1971b). *The Pentland Hills: A Research Study,* University of Edinburgh.

Law, S., and Perry, N.H. (1971). Countryside recreation for Londoners: a preliminary research approach. *G.L.C. Intell. Unit q. Bull.,* **14**.

Lindsey County Council–University of Nottingham (1967). *Lindsey Countryside Recreational Survey,* Lindsey.

Ministry of Land and Natural Resources (1966). *Leisure in the Countryside, England and Wales,* Cmnd 2928, H.M.S.O., London.

Mutch, W.E.S. (1968). *Public Recreation in National Forests: A Factual Survey,* Forestry Commission Booklet No. 21, H.M.S.O., London, pp. 24, 57.

North Regional Planning Committee (1969). *Outdoor Leisure Activities in the Northern Region,* City Planning Office, Newcastle upon Tyne, p. 43.

North West Sports Council (1972). *Leisure in the North West,* Deansgate Press, Salford.

Patmore, J.A. (1970). *Land and Leisure,* David & Charles, Newton Abbot, pp. 110–16.

Select Committee of the House of Lords on Sport and Leisure (1973). *Second Report,* together with the proceedings of the Committee, H.M.S.O., London, p. 466.

Sillitoe, K.K. (1969). *Planning for Leisure,* H.M.S.O., London, p.100.

Wager, J. (1967). Outdoor recreation on common land. *J. Tn. Plann. Inst., Lond.,* 53, 398–403.

Young, M., and Willmott, P. (1973). *The Symmetrical Family,* Routledge & Kegan Paul, London, p. 372.

Zetter, J.A. (1971). *The Evolution of Country Park Policy,* Countryside Commission, London.

## 4  THE DEMAND FOR ACTIVE RECREATION

Auto Cycle Union (1972). Private communication.

Baring, R., and Goodhead, N. (1964). Angling: sport of the three million. *Sport and Recreation,* 5, 9 and 10.

British Amateur Athletic Board (1972). Private communication.

British Automobile Club (1972). Private communication.

British Canoeing Union (1972). Private communication.

British Field Sports Society (1972). Unpublished paper for Working Party on Role of Voluntary Movements and Young in the Environment.

British Gliding Association (1972). Private communication.

British Horse Society (1972). Private communication.

British Light Aviation Centre (1972). Private communication.

British Mountaineering Council (1972). Private communication.

British Ski Federation (1972). Private communication.

British Sub-Aqua Club (1972). Private communication.

British Travel Association (1969). *Patterns in British Holiday-making 1951–68,* London, p.19.

British Travel Association–University of Keele (1967). *Pilot National Recreation Survey, Report No. 1,* University of Keele, London.

British Travel Association–University of Keele (1969). *Pilot National Recreation Survey, Report No. 2,* University of Keele, London.

Coppock, J.T. (1966). The recreational use of land and water in rural Britain. *Tijdschr. econ. soc. Geogr.*, **57**, 81–96.

Cyclists Touring Club (1972). Private communication.

Dower, M. (1964). Industrial Britain, the function of open country. *J. Tn. Plann. Inst., Lond.*, **50**, 136.

Dower, M. (1965). The fourth wave. *Architects' J.*, **141**, 123–90.

Duffield, B.S., and Owen, M.L. (1970). *Leisure + Countryside =, A Geographical Appraisal of Countryside Recreation in Lanarkshire* (ed. J.T. Coppock), University of Edinburgh.

Duffield, B.S., and Owen, M.L. (1971). *Leisure + Countryside =, A Geographical Appraisal of Countryside Recreation in the Edinburgh Area* (ed. J.T. Coppock), University of Edinburgh.

Football Association (1972). Private communication.

*Forestry Policy* (1972). Government White Paper, H.M.S.O., London.

Game Conservancy (1972). Private communication.

Gamekeepers Association (1972). Private communication.

Golf Development Council (1972). Private communication.

Horserace Betting Levy Board (1972). Private communication.

Institution of Water Engineers (1972). *Recreation on Reservoirs and Rivers*, London.

Lawn Tennis Association (1972). Private communication.

Masters of the Fox Hounds Association (1972). Private communication.

National Cricket Association (1972). Private communication.

Natural Environment Research Council (1971). *National Angling Survey 1970*, N.E.R.C., London.

North Regional Planning Committee (1969). *Outdoor Leisure Activities in the Northern Region*, City Planning Office, Newcastle upon Tyne.

North West Sports Council (1972). *Leisure in the North West*, Deansgate Press, Salford.

Opinion Research Centre (1973). *Sports Sponsorship Survey*, London.

Phillips, A.A.C. (1972). British outdoor recreation policies. Paper to Conference on Outdoor Recreation, Trent Polytechnic.

Ramblers Association (1972). Private communication.

*Recreation News* (1972). **44**, 1.

Red Deer Commission (1972a). Private communication.

Red Deer Commission (1972b). *Annual Report for 1971*, H.M.S.O., Edinburgh, p.12.

Royal Yachting Association (1972). Private communication.

Scottish Tourist Board (1972). *Third Report*, Edinburgh.

Scottish Youth Hostels Association (1972). Private communication.

Select Committee of the House of Lords on Sport and Leisure (1973). *Second Report,* H.M.S.O., London, p. 232.

Sillitoe, K.K. (1969). *Planning for Leisure,* H.M.S.O., London.

Sports Council (1972). Private communication.

Tanner, M.F. (1973). *Water Resources and Recreation,* Sports Council Water Recreation Series Study 3, London.

Warden, A.N. (1956). *The Rabbit,* Collins, London.

Wildfowlers' Association of Great Britain and Ireland (1972). *Annual Report and Year Book 1971-72.*

Wynne Edwards, V.C., Jenkins, D., and Watson, A. (1960). A population study of red grouse in Scotland. *New Scient.,* 8, 709-11.

Youth Hostels Association (1972). Private communication.

## 5   RECREATION, PARTICIPANTS AND FUTURE LEVELS OF DEMAND

British Travel Association-University of Keele (1967). *Pilot National Recreation Survey, Report No. 1,* University of Keele, London.

Burton, T.L. (1971). *Experiments in Recreation Research,* George Allen & Unwin, London.

Duffield, B.S., and Owen, M.L. (1970). *Leisure + Countryside =, A Geographical Appraisal of Countryside Recreation in Lanarkshire* (ed. J.T. Coppock), University of Edinburgh.

Duffield, B.S., and Owen, M.L. (1971). *Leisure + Countryside =, A Geographical Appraisal of Countryside Recreation in the Edinburgh Area* (ed. J.T. Coppock), University of Edinburgh.

North Regional Planning Committee (1969). *Outdoor Leisure Activities in the Northern Region,* City Planning Office, Newcastle upon Tyne.

North West Sports Council (1972). *Leisure in the North West,* Deansgate Press, Salford.

Proctor, C. (1962). *Dependence of Recreation Participation on Background Characteristics of Sample Persons in the Sept. 1960 National Recreation Survey,* Appendix A to O.R.R.R.C. Study Report, No. 19.

Rodgers, H.B. (1969). Leisure and recreation. *Urban Stud.,* 6, 368-84.

Select Committee of the House of Lords on Sport and Leisure (1973). *Second Report,* together with the proceedings of the Committee, H.M.S.O., London, p. xxii.

Sillitoe, K.K. (1969). *Planning for Leisure,* H.M.S.O., London.

Wolfe, R.I. (1969). Discussion of vacation homes, environmental preferences and spatial behaviour. *J. Leisure Research,* 1, 85-7.

Young, M., and Willmott, P. (1973). *The Symmetrical Family,* Routledge & Kegan Paul, London.

# 6 RECREATION RESOURCES: TOWARDS AN EVALUATION

An Foras Forbatha (1966). *Planning for Amenity and Tourism,* Specimen Development Plan Manual 2-3, Dublin.

An Foras Forbatha (1970). *Planning for Amenity, Recreation and Tourism,* vol. 2, Dublin.

Bayfield, N., and Moyes, S. (1972). Some automatic people-counters for gates and stiles. *Recreation News Supplement,* No. 6.

Bayfield, N., and Picknell, B. (1971). The construction and use of a photoflux people counter. *Recreation News Supplement,* No.5.

Blacksell, M. (1971). *Recreation and Land Use — A Study in the Dartmoor National Park,* Exeter Essays in Geography, Exeter.

British Travel Association-University of Keele, (1967). *Pilot National Recreation Survey, Report No.1,* University of Keele, London.

Buchanan, C., and Partners (1971). *South Hampshire Study,* supplementary vol. 2, H.M.S.O.. London.

Bungay, K. (1972). Monitoring changes in camping and caravanning. Paper to Conference on Use of Aerial Photography in Countryside Research, Countryside Commission, London.

Burbridge, V. (1971). Methods of evaluating rural resources: the Canadian experience. *J. r. Tn. Plann. Inst.,* **57,** 257–9.

Canada Land Inventory (1969). *Land Capability Classification for Outdoor Recreation,* Report No. 6, Department of Regional Economic Expansion, Ottawa.

Clark, D.S. (1970). Hertfordshire countryside plan — visual assessment. Paper to Landscape Research Group Seminar, York.

Clawson, M., and Knetsch, J.L. (1966). *Economics of Outdoor Recreation,* Johns Hopkins Press, Baltimore, p.36.

Coker, A.M., and Coker, P.D. (1972). Some practical details of the use of pressure sensitive counters. *Recreation News Supplement,* No.7.

Coppock, J.T. (1973a). In discussion on Symposium on Recreation and Resources. *Geogrl J,* **139,** 492-4.

Coppock, J.T. (1973b). The location of open-air museums, in *Country Life Museums,* Report of a conference in Stirling, Jan., 1972, by Countryside Commission for Scotland on the Scottish Country Life Museums Trust.

Countryside Commission for Scotland (1973). *A Policy for Country Parks,* information sheet no. 4, Countryside Commission for Scotland, Perth, p.3.

Countryside Recreation Research Advisory Group (1970–2). *Countryside Recreation Glossary,* Countryside Commission, London, p.2.

Coventry County Council, Solihull Borough Council, Warwickshire County Council (1971). *Coventry–Solihull–Warwickshire: A Strategy for the Sub-Region.*

Duffield, B.S. and Forsyth, J.F. (1972). Assessing the impact of recreational use on coastal sites in East Lothian. Paper to the Countryside Commission Conference on the Use of Aerial Photography in Countryside Research, London.

Duffield, B.S., and Owen, M.L. (1970). *Leisure + Countryside =, A Geographical Appraisal of Countryside Recreation in Lanarkshire* (ed. J.T. Coppock), University of Edinburgh.

Duffield, B.S., and Owen, M.L. (1971a). *Leisure + Countryside =, A Geographical Appraisal of Countryside Recreation in the Edinburgh Area* (ed. J.T. Coppock), University of Edinburgh.

Duffield, B.S., and Owen, M.L. (1971b). *The Touring Caravan in Scotland* (ed. J.T. Coppock), University of Edinburgh.

Fines, K.D. (1968). Landscape evaluation – a research project in East Sussex. *Reg. Stud.,* **2**, 41–55.

Forbes, J. (1969). A map analysis of potentially developable land. *Reg. Stud.,* **3**, 179–95.

Helliwell, D.R. (1969). *Survey of Severnside: A method of evaluating the conservation value of large areas.* Internal leaflet produced by the Land Use Section, Nature Conservancy, Shrewsbury.

Huxley, T., and Pratt, J. (1966). *Preliminary Survey of Holyrood Park,* Nature Conservancy, Edinburgh.

Kitching, L.C. (1969). *Hertfordshire Countryside Appraisal,* Hertfordshire County Council, Hertford.

Land Use Consultants (1971). *A Planning Classification of Scottish Landscape Resources,* C.C.S. Occasional Paper 1, Countryside Commission, Perth.

Lindsey County Council (1970). *Countryside Recreation: The Ecological Implications,* Lindsey County Council.

Linton, D.L. (1968). The assessment of scenery as a natural resource. *Scott. geogrl. Mag.,* **84**, 219–38.

Lopatina, Ye.R., and Nazarovskiy, O.R. (1967). *Experimental Compilation of a Map Evaluating the Natural Conditions of Human Living (with particular reference to the Kazakh S.S.R.).* Navka, Leningrad.

Murray, W.H. (1962). *Highland Landscape,* National Trust for Scotland, Aberdeen University Press.

National Playing Fields Association (1971). *Outdoor Playing Space Requirements,* London.

Nature Conservancy (1967). *The Biotic Effects of Public Pressures on the Environment.* Monkswood Experimental Station, Symposium No.3.

Outdoor Recreation Resources Review Commission (1962a). *The Quality of Outdoor Recreation: As Evidenced by User Satisfaction,* O.R.R.R.C. Study Report No. 5, Washington, D.C.

Outdoor Recreation Resources Review Commission (1962b). *Rockefeller Classification,* U. S. Govt Printing Office, Washington, D.C.

Priddle, G., Clark, C., and Douglas, L. (1973). The behavioural carrying capacity of primitive areas for Wilderness Travel. Mimeograph from Dept of Geography, University of Waterloo.

Scottish Development Department (1972). *Towards Cleaner Water,* H.M.S.O., Edinburgh.

Scottish Tourist Board (1970). *Recreation Planning for the Clyde,* Edinburgh.

Select Committee on Scottish Affairs (1972). *Land Resource Use in Scotland,* vol. 3, Evidence of Countryside Commission for Scotland, H.M.S.O., London, p.3.

Sidaway, R. (1972). Assessing day visitors and camping use in the New Forest. Paper to Recreational Economics Symposium, Dept of Environment, London.

South-east Joint Planning Study, Informal Working Party (1971). *Informal Countryside Recreation in the South-East Region,* Countryside Commission, London.

South Hampshire Plan Advisory Committee (1969). *South Hampshire Plan Study Report, Group A, Rural Conservation, No. 5, Rural Landscape.*

Standing Conference on Regional Planning in South Wales and Monmouthshire: Recreation Sub-Committee (1971). *Potential Surface Technique,* Glamorgan County Council.

Standing Conference on Regional Planning in South Wales and Monmouthshire: Recreation Sub-Committee (1973). *Recreation in South Wales,* Glamorgan County Council.

Thomas, D. (1963). *Agriculture in Wales during the Napoleonic Wars,* University of Wales Press, Cardiff.

Vedenin, Y.A., and Miroshnichenko, N.N. (1971). Evaluation of the natural environment for recreation purposes. *Ekistics,* **184**, 223-6.

Weaver, J. (1954). Crop combinations in the middle west. *Geogrl. Rev.,* **44**, 175-200.

Zetter, J., and Benyon, J. (1971). Sherwood Forest Study. Unpublished papers from the Countryside Commission.

Zobler, L. (1962). An economic–historical view of natural resource use and conservation. *Econ. Geogr.,* **38**, 189-94.

7 GOVERNMENT POLICIES AND THE ATTITUDES OF OTHER LAND USERS

Appleton, J.H. (1970). *Disused Railways in the Countryside of England and Wales,* Countryside Commission, H.M.S.O., London.

Best, R.H., and Coppock, J.T. (1962). *The Changing of Land Use in Britain,* Faber & Faber, London, p. 113.

British Travel Association (1969). *Patterns in British Holiday-making, 1951-1968,* London.

Coppock, J.T. (1968). The Countryside (Scotland) Act and the geographer. *Scott. geogrl Mag.,* **34**, 210.

Countryside Commission for Scotland (1973). Private communication.

Darling, F.F., and Morton-Boyd, J. (1964). *The Highlands and Islands,* Collins, London, p.112.

Davies, E.T. (1969). *Tourism and the Cornish Farmer,* University of Exeter.

Davies, E.T. (1971). *Farm Tourism in Cornwall and Devon,* University of Exeter.

Davies, E.T. (1973). *Tourism on Devon Farms, A Physical and Economic Appraisal,* Univeristy of Exeter.

Denman, D.R. (ed.) (1963). *Contemporary Problems of Land Ownership,* University Press, Cambridge, p.28.

Dower, M. (1965). The fourth wave. *Architects' J.,* **141**, 123-90.

Downing, P., and Dower, M. (1973). *Second Homes in England and Wales,* DART Publication No. 7, Countryside Commission, London.

Duffield, B.S., and Owen, M.L. (1970) *Leisure + Countryside =, A Geographical Appraisal of Countryside Recreation in Lanarkshire* (ed. J.T. Coppock), University of Edinburgh.

Duffield, B.S., and Owen, M.L. (1971). *Leisure + Countryside =, A Geographical Appraisal of Countryside Recreation in the Edinburgh Area* (ed. J.T. Coppock), University of Edinburgh.

Ferguson, C. (1972). Unpublished paper to Scottish Tourist Board's Conference on Tourism and the Environment in Scotland, Glasgow.

Forestry Commission (1972). *Fifty-second Annual Report and Accounts, 1971-2,* H.M.S.O., London.

*Forestry Policy* (1972). Government White Paper, H.M.S.O., London.

Frederick, Sir Charles *et al.* (1930). *Foxhunting,* Faber, London.

Gasson, R. (1966). *The Influence of Urbanization on Farm Ownership and Practice,* Studies in Rural Land Use No. 1, Wye College, London.

Harrison, A. (1966). *The Farms of Buckinghamshire,* Department of Agricultural Economics, University of Reading.

Institution of Water Engineers (1972). *Recreation on Reservoirs and Rivers,* London, p.6.

Ironside, R.G. (1971). Agricultural and recreational land use in Canada: Potential for conflict or benefit. *Can. J. agric. Econ.,* **19**, 3.

Irvine, R.M. (1966). *Amenity Agriculture,* British Columbia Geography Series No. 11, University of British Columbia.

Jacobs, C.A.J. (1973). *Farms and Tourism in Upland Denbighshire,* Denbigh County Council.

Linton, D.L. (1968). The assessment of scenery as a natural resource. *Scott. geogrl Mag.* **84**, 219-38.

Master of the Fox Hounds Association (1972). Private communication.

Ministry of Defence (1973). *Report of the Defence Lands Committee, 1971-3,* H.M.S.O., London, p.9.

Ministry of Land and Natural Resources (1966). *Leisure in the Countryside: England and Wales,* Cmnd 2928, H.M.S.O., London.

National Parks Commission (1955). *Sixth Report,* H.M.S.O., London, p.25.

National Parks Committee (1945). *National Parks in Scotland,* Cmnd 6631, H.M.S.O., Edinburgh.

Natural Environment Research Council (1973). *Report 1972-4*, H.M.S.O., London, p.132.

National Trust for Scotland (1964). *Countryside Conference*, Inverness, p.18.

Natural Resources (Technical) Committee (1957). *Forestry, Agriculture and Marginal Land*, H.M.S.O., London, p.20.

Nature Conservancy (1973). Private communication.

North of Scotland Hydro-Electric Board (1971). *Land Resource Use in Scotland*, Memorandum of Evidence for the Board, p.1.

*Parliamentary Debates* (1973). Vol. 861, no. 163, cols. 518-19.

*Parliamentary Papers* (1874). Vol. LXXII (III).

Phillips, A.A.C. (1972). British outdoor recreation policies. Paper to Conference on Outdoor Recreation, Trent Polytechnic.

Rew, R.H. (1895). *Report on the County of Norfolk*, Royal Commission on Agriculture, Cmnd 7915, H.M.S.O., London.

Select Committee on Scottish Affairs (1972). *Land Resource Use in Scotland*, vols. 1-5, H.M.S.O., London.

Select Committee of the House of Lords on Sport and Leisure (1973). *First and Second Reports, Evidence, Appendices and Index*, H.M.S.O., London.

Stamp, L.D., and Hoskins, W.G. (1963). *The Common Lands of England and Wales*, Collins, London, p.81.

Tanner, M.F. (1973). *Water Resources and Recreation, Sports Council Water Recreation Series Study 3*, Sports Council, London.

Verney, R.B. (1972). *Sinews for Survival*, H.M.S.O., London.

8 THE INTERACTION OF RECREATIONISTS AND RESOURCES

Archer, B. (1973). *The Impact of Domestic Tourism*, Bangor Occasional Papers in Economics, No. 2, University of Wales Press, Bangor, p.31.

Beaty, A.N.S., Pearson-Kirk, D., Cal. P.C., and Grieg, M.T. (1973). The recreational demand of an urban area, Paper to P.T.R.C. Conference, Brighton.

Bielckus, C.L., Rogers, A.W., and Wibberley, G.P. (1972). *Second Homes in England and Wales*, Wye College, University of London.

British Travel Association–University of Keele (1967). *Pilot National Recreation Survey, Report No. 1.*, University of Keele, London.

Burton, T.L. (1967). *Windsor Great Park: A Recreation Study*, Studies in Rural Land Use, Report No. 8, Wye College, Kent, p.30.

Burton, T.L. (1971). *Experiments in Recreation Research*, University of Birmingham, Urban and Regional Studies, No. 2, George Allen & Unwin, London.

Central Statistical Office (1972). *Social Trends No. 3*, H.M.S.O., London.

Clawson, M., Held, R. Burnell, and Stoddard, C.H. (1960). *Land for the Future*, Johns Hopkins Press, Baltimore.

Downing, P., and Dower, M. (1973). *Second Homes in England and Wales,* Countryside Commission, London, p.6.

Duffield, B.S., and Owen, M.L. (1970). *Leisure + Countryside =, A Geographical Appraisal of Countryside Recreation in Lanarkshire* (ed J.T. Coppock), University of Edinburgh, p.101.

Duffield, B.S., and Owen, M.L. (1971). *Leisure + Countryside =, A Geographical Appraisal of Countryside Recreation in the Edinburgh Area* (ed. J.T. Coppock), University of Edinburgh.

Duffield, B.S., and Owen, M.L. (1972). *Survey of Summer Holiday Traffic* (ed. J. T. Coppock), University of Edinburgh.

Law, S. (1967). Planning for outdoor recreation in the countryside. *J. Tn. Plann. Inst.,* 53, 383–6.

Law, S., and Perry, N.H. (1971). Countryside recreation for Londoners – a preliminary research approach. G.L.C. *Intell. Unit q. Bull.,* No. 14, 11–16.

Mackinlay, D.A. (1969). *Upper Speyside,* University of Edinburgh, p.32.

North West Sports Council (1972). *Leisure in the North West,* Deansgate Press, Salford.

Owen, M.L., and Duffield, B.S. (1971). *The Touring Caravan in Scotland* (ed. J.T. Coppock), Scottish Tourist Board, Edinburgh.

Patmore, J.A. (1970). *Land and Leisure in England and Wales,* Problems in Modern Geography, David & Charles, Newton Abbot, p.151.

Wager, J. (1967). Outdoor recreation on common land. *J. Tn. Plann. Inst., Lond.,* 53; 400.

9  PROSPECTS: A SYSTEMS APPROACH

Appleyard, D., Lynch, K., and Myer, J.R. (1964). *The View from the Road.* Community values as affected by transportation reports. *Highway Res.,* Record No. 2, National Research Council, Pub. 1065

Bonsey, C. (1968). The rising tide of outdoor recreation. *County Council Gazette,* 61, 306–9.

British Travel Association–University of Keele (1967). *Pilot National Recreation Survey, Report No. 1,* University of Keele, London, p.87.

Burke, H.D., Lewis, G.H., and Orr, H.R. (1968). *A Method of Classifying Scenery from a Roadway.* United States Forest Service, Park Practice Guideline, Development 3/68.

Burton, T.L. (1967). *Windsor Great Park: A Recreation Study, Studies in Rural Land Use, No. 8,* Wye College, Kent, p.8.

Carrothers, G.A.P. (1956). An historical review of the gravity and potential concepts of human interaction. *J. Am. Inst. Plann.,* 22. 97.

Colenutt, R.J. (1969). Modelling travel patterns of day visitors to the country-side. *Area,* no. 2.

Colenutt, R.J. (1970). *An Investigation into the Factors Affecting the Patterns*

*of Trip Generation and Route Choice of Day Visitors to the Countryside,*
Ph.D. thesis, University of Bristol.

Converse, P.D., Huegy, H.W., and Mitchell, R.V. (1930). *Elements of Marketing,*
Prentice Hall, Englewood Cliffs, N.J.

Countryside Commission (1970). *The Demand for Outdoor Recreation in the
Countryside,* Report of a seminar held in London, p.2.

Duffield, B.S. (1973). *Outdoor Recreation Traffic Patterns in the Edinburgh Area,
A Report on SSRC Research Project, HT 1596,* University of Edinburgh, pp. 21–7.

Duffield, B.S., and Owen, M.L. (1970). *Leisure + Countryside =, A Geographical
Appraisal of Countryside Recreation in Lanarkshire* (ed. J. T. Coppock), University
of Edinburgh.

Duffield, B.S., and Owen, M.L. (1971). *Leisure + Countryside =, A Geographical
Appraisal of Countryside Recreation in the Edinburgh Area* (ed. J.T. Coppock),
University of Edinburgh.

Ellis, J.B. (1966). *Outdoor Recreation Planning in Michigan, A Systems Approach;
Part I: A Manual for Programme Recsys,* Dept of Commerce, Lansing, Michigan.

Ellis, J.B. (1967). *A Systems Model for Recreational Travel in Ontario: A
Progress Report, Report RR 126,* Dept of Highways, Ontario.

Ellis, J.B., and Van Doren, C.S. (1966). A comparative evaluation of gravity and
system theory models for state-wide recreational traffic flow. *J. reg. Sci.,* 6, 57–70.

Hansen, W.G. (1959). How accessibility shapes land use. *J. Am. Inst. Plann.,*
25, 74.

McLaughlin, W.A. (1966). *Multi-Path Systems Traffic Assignment Logarithm,
Report RB 108,* Dept of Highways, Ontario.

Mansfield, N.W. (1968). Traffic policy in the Lake District National Park, *J. Tn.
Plann. Inst., Lond.,* 54, 265.

Milstein, D., and Reid, L. (1966). *Michigan Outdoor Recreation Demand Study:
Methods and Models,* vol. 1 Dept of Conservation, Michigan, chapter 6.

Morrill, R.L. (1963). The distribution of migration distances. *Pa. Proc. reg. Sci.
Ass.,* 11, 75.

Newton, I. (1687). *Philosophiae Naturalis Principia Mathematica.*

North Regional Planning Committee (1969). *Outdoor Leisure Activities in the
Northern Region,* City Planning Office, Newcastle upon Tyne, p. 43.

North West Sports Council (1972). *Leisure in the North West,* Deansgate Press,
Salford.

Reilly, W.J. (1929). *Methods for the Study of Retail Relationships,* Bulletin
N2 994, University of Texas.

Simpson, H.D., and Zetter, J.A. (1971). *West Cumberland Trunk Road Study,*
Countryside Commission, London.

Stewart, J.C. (1948). Demographic gravitation: evidence and application.
*Sociometry,* 11, 1–2.

Tourism and Recreation Research Unit (1974). TRIP *Series, No. 1, Systems*

*Description, TRRU Research Report No. 11.* University of Edinburgh.

Van Doren, C.S. (1967). *An Interaction Travel Model for Projecting Attendence of Campers at Michigan State Parks: A Study in Recreational Geography,* Ph.D. thesis, Michigan State University, p. 106.

Wall, G. (1972). Socio-economic variations in pleasure trip patterns: The case of Hull car-owners. *Trans. Inst. Brit. Geogr.,* **57**, 45–58.

Wennergren, E.B., and Nielsen, D.B. (1970). Probability estimates of recreation demands. *J. Leisure Research,* **2**, 114.

Wolfe, R.I. (1966). *Parameters of Recreational Travel in Ontario: A Progress Report, Report RB 111,* Dept of Highways, Ontario.

Yapp, W.B. (1969). *The Weekend Motorist in the Lake District,* Countryside Commission, London, p.17.

Zipf, G.K. (1949). *Human Behaviour and the Principal of Least Effort,* Addison-Wesley Press, Cambridge.


## POSTSCRIPT

Berry, B.J.L. (1970). The future geography of the United States in the year 2000. *Trans. Inst. Brit. Geogr.,* **51**, 21–50.

Coppock, J.T. (1973). The location of open-air museums, in *Country Life Museums,* Report of a Conference in Stirling, Jan. 1972, by Countryside Commission for Scotland and the Scottish Country Life Museum Trust.

Duffield, B.S., and Owen, M.L. (1970). *Leisure + Countryside =, A Geographical Appraisal of Countryside Recreation in Lanarkshire* (ed. J.T. Coppock), University of Edinburgh.

Duffield, B.S., Owen, M.L., Wright, W.D.C., and Walters, I.S. (1968). *Establishment of a Scottish Water Sports Centre: Report of the Research Team,* Confidential Report to the Sports Council for Scotland.

Emmett, I. (1973). Research into leisure. Paper to Symposium on Work and Leisure, University of Salford.

Owen, M.L., and Duffield B.S.(1971). *The Touring Caravan in Scotland* (ed. J.T. Coppock) Scottish Tourist Board, Edinburgh.

Parker, S.R. (1971). *The Future of Work and Leisure,* MacGibbon & Kee, London.

Scottish Development Department (1972). *Caravan and Camping Sites in Scotland, Town and Country Planning (Scotland) Acts, Development Plans Technical Advice Notes,* Ref. DP/TAN/10.

Select Committee of the House of Lords on Sport and Leisure (1973). *Evidence,* House of Lords Paper 193 (I–III).

Sewell, W.R.D. (1971). Environmental perception and attitudes of engineers and public health officials. *Environment and Behaviour,* **3**, 23–56.

Sewell, W.R.D., and Roston, J. (1970). *Recreational Fishing Evaluation,* Dept of Fisheries, Queen's Printer, Ottawa.

APPENDIX

British Travel Association-University of Keele (1967). *Pilot National Recreation Survey, Report No. 1,* University of Keele, London.

British Travel Association–University of Keele (1969). *Pilot National Recreation Survey, Report No. 2,* University of Keele, London.

Duffield, B.S., and Owen, M.L. (1970). *Leisure + Countryside = , A Geographical Appraisal of Countryside Recreation in the Edinburgh Area* (ed. J.T. Coppock), University of Edinburgh.

North Regional Planning Committee (1969). *Outdoor Leisure Activities in the Northern Region,* City Planning Office, Newcastle Upon Tyne.

North West Sports Council (1972). *Leisure in the North West,* Deansgate Press, Salford.

Opinion Research Centre (1973). *Sports Sponsorship Survey,* London.

Sillitoe, K.K. (1969). *Planning for Leisure,* H.M.S.O., London.

Young, M., and Willmott, P. (1973). *The Symmetrical Family,* Routledge & Kegan Paul, London.

# Index

258 INDEX

Holme Pierrepoint National Water Sports
Centre  138
Holyrood Park  97
Hookway, R.  1
Horse Riding Establishments Act  62
Horserace Betting Levy Board  44
horse-racing  44
Hotson, J.McG.  108
houses and gardens open to the public  147
Hull  197
Humber–Mersey  175
hunting  139
Huron, L.  223
Huxley, T., and Pratt, J.  97, 246

impact  225, 227
index, growth potential  83, 88–9
site attraction  213, 216
information system  227
Inner London Education Authority  230
Institute of Baths Management  54
Institute of Community Studies  39, 91
Institution of Water Engineers  45, 137
interaction  150–91, 200–2, 222
intervening opportunities  222
Inverness  136, 189
Ironside, R.G.  130, 248
Irvine, R.M.  147, 248

Jacobs, C.A.J.  144, 248
journeys, recreational  150–66
by caravan  166–91
in central Scotland  197–8
length of  195–9
modelling of  193
spatial distribution of  197–8
systems approach to  203–4
to play  156–7

Keele University  46–7, 229–30
Kilkerran Parklands  147
Kitching, L.C.  103, 246

Lake District, afforestation in  133
and M6  124
National Turst in  138
reservoirs in  44–5
seasonal pressure on  129
weekend motorist in  196
Lake District National Park  196

Lammermuirs  141
Lanark County Council  225
Lanarkshire  106, 112, 151, 153–4, 159–60,
163, 165, 190, 199, 208
land, derelict  99
developable  101, 104
private  139–47
acceptance of recreation on  148
commercial recreation on  147
recreational developments of  145
public recreational  123
land capability  100, 104
land use, and recreation  142, 147
Land Use Consultants  101
land users, attitudes of, to recreation  139–49
Land Utilisation Survey  1
landowners see land, private
landscapes  114
Law, S.  151, 250
Law, S., and Perry, N.H.  25, 241, 250
Lawn Tennis Association  44
leisure, and class  10, 13
and weather  17–19
attitudes to  15
recreational use of  16–17
weekend  20, 22
Leisure and the Countryside  34
Leisure in the North-West  55–6, 165, 197,
234
Leisure + Countryside =  225
life-space  5
Lindsey County Council  29
Linton, D.L.  6, 112, 125, 240, 246, 248
litter  144–5
Local Government (Scotland) Act  165
Loch Earn  189
Loch Lomond  189, 190
Loch Tay  189
lochs, Scottish  45
London  142
Greater  25, 235
Inner  235
long-distance footpaths  141
Longleat  147
Longniddry  18–19
Looe  46
Lopatina, Y.R., and Nazarovskiy, O.R.
104, 246

Mackinlay, D.A.  167, 250
McLaughlan, W.A.  221, 251
Mansfield, N.W.  196, 251
maps, automated  108, 120
environmental  120
land capability  104

# ECONOMIC LAWS, POLICY, PLANNING

BY

ISTVÁN FRISS

Member of the Hungarian Academy of Sciences

AKADÉMIAI KIADÓ, BUDAPEST 1971

Translated by
Gy. Hajdu, P. Morvay and J. Rácz


Translation revised by
M. H. Dobb, Ph. D.
Em. Reader in econ., Trinity College, Cambridge

# CONTENTS

# PREFACE

This volume of essays has, as a matter of course, to speak for itself, still I feel obliged to account for the reasons I had in mind when deciding upon just this selection. It seems all the more necessary to do this since the book, though based on a Hungarian collection of some of my papers published in autumn 1968, is not identical with the Hungarian one. Four of the studies have not been reproduced here, another one has been added instead, for the following considerations: some of the material had become more or less outdated; some of the essays originally meant mainly for Hungarian readers claimed broader clarification; something had to be omitted in order to open room for the study on Long-term National Economic Planning without making the book too voluminous.

In choosing the title "Economic Laws, Policy, Planning" I wished to indicate not only the main themes of the essays and the ideas that have most occupied my mind during the last years, but also problems on which, naturally and necessarily, economists of both socialist and capitalist countries have focussed lately. To this, I should like to add a few complementary remarks.

Taking part in the preparatory work of the economic reform that has been carried out in Hungary from January 1, 1968 on, I had the opportunity to contribute to bringing to light the reasons of some difficulties we had in the control of our economy and thus sketch the broad outlines of the necessary reform. Some of the papers in this book deal fully or partly with problems arising therefrom. But it has been perfectly clear to me right from the beginning that although the reform can and most probably will greatly enhance our possibilities, accelerate our economic development, by relieving us of so many brakes to an optimal, and sometimes even a normal, functioning of our economic life, yet it cannot and will not prove a panacea to all of our troubles. Notably: some of our inconveniences were obviously due to errors either in planning or economic policy-making and there could be no doubt that even the best and ever so efficient reform will not make correct economic decisions superfluous or a sensible and proper, and scientifically well-founded, economic policy something we can dispense with.

Some economists in Hungary and elsewhere cherish the illusion that methods more perfect than actually used in mathematical programming and optimization, by an extensive assistance of computers, will supply us with a key to the right economic policy, enabling us to make faultless economic decisions. Hungary may boast of having many excellent representatives of the mathematical school of economics, who have greatly contributed to improving our planning methods so far. But the problem involved in most economic decisions of real importance is a political rather than a mathematical one. A politically correct decision once found, mathematics is surely necessary to find the right way to carry it out. First the task must be clearly set by those whom society authorizes to do so, only thereafter will the problem of optimization arise.

In a socialist country like ours, the plans of the national economy adopted by the competent authorities, especially the medium- and long-term plans, are or should be the main tool of implementation, and a mirror, of the economic policy of the government. Precisely my search after the scientific foundation of national planning had induced me to investigate some problems of economic policy which in turn have led to a quest for the potentiality of a plan. In other words: how broad is the sphere of powers of governments or other decision makers, how ample are their possibilities of shaping economic events? To what limits can economic life and growth or development be moulded according to the ideas and intentions of a political-economic body or of a person?

The possibility of government intervention in economic matters, even of very powerful ones could, of course, not be questioned. But experience seems to speak not unambiguously of the beneficence and desirability of government actions. Apparently there has not always been perfect harmony between aims and effects. Having taken part in the planning of some very successful actions—as e.g. the stabilization of the Hungarian currency in 1946, after an inflation unparalleled in history—I have good reasons to believe that the results of such actions might fully correspond to the goals set forth. But how and when, under what conditions can such a correspondence be arrived at?

To put the answer briefly: it is by taking into account existing objective conditions of economic life and the postulates set by these, that the harmony between aims and effects can be safely established. So the nature of these objective economic laws had to be examined, too. In what does the objectivity and the significance of economic laws consist? In what manner do they work; in what ways are they connected with the activities of people; how can one get to know them? To clear up these questions involves already the answers to the question as to the power of the government to shape economic events and the feasibility of a plan.

The growing requirements of a scientific approach to planning, together with the scientific-technical revolution now in progress and the huge dimensions of modern means of production, have raised the demand for long-term, i. e. 15- or even 20-year plans of the national economy. Many countries have started already the elaboration of such plans. But here new doubts are added to the old ones. The greater the span of time we try to look over, the greater the uncertainties, the role of factors whose formation can hardly be influenced or whose occurrence cannot even be foreseen by us. Is there any sense in making such plans? Is there any reality in them? I have tried to prove that, in spite of all the incertitudes and difficulties, an answer in the affirmative can be given to these questions.

So much for the reasons of this selection.

The reader will notice that in treating the last-mentioned, as in discussing other problems of principle, I did not make any attempt to simplify the matter or to deny the difficulties that still are facing us and hamper us in finding the proper solution. I have emphasized it more than once, and say it here again, that there is no chance of finding proper solutions if not by a close collaboration of men of practice with the men of science; and only a perpetual confrontation of theory with experience can and will gradually and eventually give the satisfactory results.

It is needless perhaps to mention that the essays of this volume, as will be seen from their contents too, had grown out of similar confrontations. The first of them was written at the end of 1964, the one on Long-term National Economic Planning about a year ago, the rest in the years 1967–1968. Their sequence in the book is not a chronological one, but rather of a logical character.

My warm thanks are due to Maurice Dobb for his arduous work in correcting the English of the papers, and to Tamás Földi who took upon himself the laborious task of selecting them, omitting unnecessary repetitions and bringing the figures up to date.

Budapest, July 1970.

*ISTVÁN FRISS*

# ECONOMY AND IDEOLOGY

The relation between economy and ideology will be examined in this article mainly from the point of view of our ideological work.

"The mode of production of material life conditions the social, political and intellectual life process in general. It is not the consciousness of men that determines their being but, on the contrary, their social being that determines their consciousness".[1] This famous statement by *Marx*, to be found in the preface to his work: *A Critique of Political Economy* is an important, one could even say a decisive, constituent of Marxism. Its importance is somewhat illuminated by the fact that the idea formulated in it accompanies almost the whole work of *Marx* and *Engels*. It may be found in a somewhat similar wording in the *German Ideology* written 15 years earlier and reappears in the later works of these authors. It is difficult to overestimate its importance for those working in various fields of ideological activity. If they want to work effectively, they must always keep in mind that it is the social existence of people that determines their consciousness and thus they have to reckon with a consciousness that reflects actual social existence. A host of troubles follow from the unfortunately frequent fault of neglecting this fundamental interrelation.

Of course, this very important and irrefutable statement of *Marx*—verified by millions of facts in history and everyday life—must not be simplified or vulgarized. It would be a grave mistake to make efforts to deduce the entirety of ideological forms merely from material reality or, even more narrowly, from the economic basis. Already our classics emphatically warned us against this mistake. To refer to a single example only, the following may be quoted from Engels' letter to Starkenburg, dated January 25, 1894: "Political, juridical, philosophical, religious, literary, artistic, etc., development is based on economic development. But all these react upon one another and also on the economic basis. It is not that the economic condition is the *cause and alone active*, while everything else has only a passive effect. There is, rather, interaction on the basis of economic necessity, which *ultimately* always asserts itself".[2] Particularly those working in ideological fields, must, simultaneously, keep in view the similarly fundamental Marxian doctrine that the idea itself becomes a material force as soon as it penetrates the masses. This is the basis on which the entire ideological

[1] K. Marx and F. Engels: *Selected Works*, Vol. I. Preface to a contribution to the critique of Political Economy. Moscow, 1969. Progress Publishers. p. 503.
[2] K. Marx and F. Engels: *Selected Works*, Vol. II. Moscow, 1949. Foreign Languages Publishing House. p. 498.

11

educative work of our party is built. It is this to which the principle—which is a requirement and a statement as well—corresponds: the conscious element had and must have a great and growing role in building socialism and later in that of communism.

These two additions are necessary in order to interpret correctly and implement correctly every conclusion deriving from the fundamental fact that it is the material reality, social existence that determines the consciousness of people. Even ideological mistakes, errors and distortions, the various forms of false consciousness, are related by some threads to material reality. This can undoubtedly be proven with the aid of ideological phenomena of either the past or the present. In *Capital* Marx not only exposed those who praised capitalist society but demonstrated and deduced step by step, with scientific meticulousness and accuracy, why and how actual capitalist relations appear in a form belying their essence and how these phenomena constitute—as in a mirror turning reality upside down—the building stones of vulgar economics. But similar experience may be gained every day even in our own society in various fields. "... The life process of society, which is based on the process of material production, does not strip of its mystical veil until it is treated as production by freely associated men, and is consciously regulated by them in accordance with a settled plan".[3] And let us add: we have not yet attained this today.

Have we not attained it? Perhaps this statement will shock some readers and even evoke consternation. "How is it possible?"—they may ask. We have had a planned economy in Hungary for sixteen years. Can it be doubted then that the material productive process of our social life is under the deliberate and purposeful control of freely associated people? This cannot be doubted or we run into conflict with facts, and with our principles that have been adhered to up to now.

In fact, there exists no contradiction. It is with justification that we speak about our being a society of freely associated people and production in our country being subject to deliberate and planned control. But, as in general, reality is not so simple, here either, as to be squeezed into the formula "yes or no". In our society freely associated people control material production in a deliberate and planned manner; yet reality, in its extreme complexity, is full of all kinds of deficiencies and contradictions if seen from the standpoint of purposefulness or even of evident rationality.

It is, therefore, highly important for us and for all those working in ideological fields, to know the basic facts: and not only the results but also the deficiencies. This problem is so important that I feel I must point out a few of these fundamental facts, although, of course, it is by no means my task or purpose to give here an economic analysis of our society. To begin with, our results are substantial, indeed. It will suffice to glance at the *Statistical Pocket Book* of the Hungarian Central Statistical Office for 1964 to convince ourselves of this. (I refer to this publication because it has been published in many thousand copies and it is easily accessible to everybody.) Let us see, e.g., the development of production, productivity and employment. If we

---

[3] K. Marx: *Capital*, Vol. I. Moscow, 1966. Progress Publishers. p. 79–80.

take industrial production in 1938 as a hundred, it rose by 1949 to 128, and by 1963 to 533, that is to say more then fivefold. Total employment in industry increased to round twofold, and from this it already follows that production per person employed—what is generally called the productivity of labour—increased in industry to almost 2·6-fold in this quarter of a century.[4]

The number of gainfully occupied people decreased between 1949 and 1963 by more than half a million in agriculture, it increased at the same time in the other branches of the national economy by 1·25 million, meaning a net increase of three quarters of a million. Since in this period population increased by only a tenth, this development also meant that the greatest curse of capitalist Hungary, unemployment involving misery and uncertainty of existence, has been liquidated. Development of living standards is difficult to follow because of the changes in the pattern of consumption. It is, however, known that in 1949 we first surpassed the pre-war level in per capita consumption of the population—in so far as this consumption is comparable at all with the earlier one because of changes in pattern. This can be established with some reliability, in spite of the fact that in these comparisons there are many factors of uncertainty, including deficiencies of old statistical surveys. I may add that, knowing the extremely miserable pre-war living standards of the peasantry living on small or dwarf holdings as well as of the landless agricultural workers who constituted a large part of the pre-war population, the living standards of the majority of the rural population has considerably increased in absolute terms, as well as in comparison with other classes and strata of the population. The development of living standards may be studied with the aid of various data. From the relevant data of the Central Statistical Office there are particularly two indicators which characterize the situation of the two great classes of our population: namely, the per capita personal disposable real income of workers and employees and the per capita personal comsumption of the peasantry. In comparison with 1949 the first indicator rose by 1963 by 90·6 per cent, the second by 68·5 per cent.[5] However, statistical data do not show everywhere such favourable development. It is particularly conspicuous that the increase of agricultural production has not kept pace with that of industry at all. Though a comparison with pre-war years is rather uncertain, again because of deficiencies of earlier statistical surveys and structural shifts, it is probable that total of agricultural production in 1949—i. e., five years after the strong decline caused by the war—at least approached the average of the last ten pre-war years. I refer to a ten-year average since in agriculture—owing to strong fluctuations in output because of weather conditions—not much conclusion could be drawn from a comparison of a few selected years. For lack of a better one, 1949 can be taken as a basis for

[4] Since then we attained further results. By 1969, industrial production rose to 7·6-fold of that in 1938, employment to 3·5-fold. (*Statistical Pocket Book of Hungary*, 1970.)

[5] In 1969, the per capita real income of workers and employees was 146 per cent of that in 1960, and the same indicator for the per capita personal consumption of the peasantry was 141 per cent. (Ibid.)

13

further comparison because it was neither particularly good nor bad. The gross production value of that year was exceeded in 1960 by 35 per cent, in 1961 by 36, in 1962 by 38 and in 1963 by 44 per cent.[6]

Thus, gross agricultural production increased in comparison with 1949 not even by a half, and if we subtract from the gross (cumulated) production value the material inputs which also considerably increased, the whole increment will be around one sixth or one fifth. The very fact that gross output has been steadily increasing for some time is a significant success of our socialist agriculture. But the rate of growth is, as we have seen, rather modest. In the final analysis, while the production of total industry increased from 1949 to 1962 to three and a half-times and also the part of *national income* generated in industry rose almost proportionally, national income generated in agriculture increased by only 13 per cent, so that the total of national income rose two and a half-times.[7]

Nor are international comparisons based on other statistical figures completely reassuring. I wish to refer here only to some data published in the equally easily accessible International Statistical Pocket Book of our Statistical Office[8] adding that these data and the comparisons based on them contain (owing to differences in national surveys and methods, to unreliability of some data collections) much greater uncertainties than those quoted earlier and may be thus accepted only with some reservation. Even in view of this, it is worth while to consider the figures. It is particularly important to know how we stand in competition with capitalist countries. Most aggregate indicators testify to the great superiority of the socialist countries. The index number of industrial production for the socialist countries (taking the present area) was more than sevenfold of what it was in 1937, while that for the capitalist countries (equally for their present area) was only about 250. The average annual growth rate of industrial production between 1951–60 was 13·6 per cent in the socialist countries and 5 per cent in capitalist countries.[9]

In detail, however, differences are rather great. Considering, e. g., per capita national income, this rose from 1953 to 1960 by 72 per cent in the Soviet Union, by 56 in Romania, by 55 in Bulgaria, by 51 in Czechoslovakia, by 48 in Poland and by 38 per cent in Hungary. In the same period, the increase was 55 per cent in Austria, 48 per cent in the GFR and 44 per cent in

[6] Development in later years is indicated by the following figures: taking the average of 1951–55 as 100, the gross production value of agriculture was 138 in the average of 1966—1969. (Ibid.)

[7] Total industrial production rose by 1969 to 4·8-fold from 1950 and its contribution to national income to 4·3-fold, while national income generated in agriculture was lower in 1965 than in 1950 and exceeded it even in 1969 only by 16 per cent, while total national income increased in the meantime to almost 2·9-fold. (Ibid.)

[8] *Nemzetközi Statisztikai Zsebkönyv*, Budapest, 1962.

[9] The average annual growth rate of the industrial production of socialist countries between 1959 and 1969 was 10·8 per cent, that of non-socialist countries 5·5, of advanced capitalist countries 5·2 per cent. (*Nemzetközi Statisztikai Évkönyv* 1970. Budapest, 1970.)

14

Italy.[10] Thus, the rate of economic growth was greater in some capitalist countries than in some socialist countries. The same can be found in the field of total industrial production. We may add that these figures, since they refer only to a much narrower field, are more reliable than those for national income. If the data for 1953 are taken as 100, industrial production increased by 1960 as follows: Soviet Union 212, Bulgaria 252, Poland 198, Czechoslovakia 192, GDR 182, Romania 172, and Hungary 160. Index numbers for the same period were for some capitalist countries: Japan 261, GFR 180, Italy 180, France 174, Mexico 172.[11]

Thus, some capitalist countries have surpassed Hungary in this field. Of course, besides the reservations already mentioned, it must be taken into account that in the capitalist countries there are also business fluctuations. It would be a mistake, therefore, to draw far-reaching conclusions from these figures. But it remains a fact that the great superiority of socialist economy is not revealed in these figures. It follows, that we have not yet succeeded in exploiting all the possibilities inherent in socialist planned economy. As a matter of fact, to establish this — even if with less scientific foundation — we need not statistical comparisons. Our daily press and periodicals frequently treat the deficiencies of our economy. Our leaders have repeatedly warned that labour discipline was not satisfactory. This is known also from personal experience to all those who have been in close contact with our building trade on the occasion of building a home or asking for repair work. There are complaints to be read or heard about the quality of various goods. We cannot achieve a desirable concentration in investments, some projects get protracted, some are costing more than was originally planned, some are not as up-to-date as is desirable. The rate of technical progress is not satisfactory and this causes some difficulties also in foreign trade. Again, it is a frequent complaint that there is much rush-work at the end of each quarter and still more at the end of the year, resulting in poor quality and high costs of products. Obviously, the effects of these and similar deficiencies must eventually show also in the statistical figures. So, if we find any disquieting moments in the statistical figures we should not comfort ourselves by saying that the data are unreliable. Individual figures may be uncertain, but the global picture emerging from them certainly corresponds to reality.

Nor should we believe that our situation in this respect is much worse than that of other socialist countries. True, Hungary figures in some tables less favourably than other socialist countries, but this may be sufficiently explained by the fact that there was a counterrevolution in Hungary in 1956. This paralyzed industrial production for several months and threw back development. Nevertheless, development problems strongly engage eco-

[10] Between 1960 and 1968 national income increased in the Soviet Union by 73 per cent, in Romania by 95, in Bulgaria by 77, in Czechoslovakia by 38, in Poland by 66, in Hungary by 54 per cent. GNP increased in Austria by 37 per cent, in the GFR by 38, in Italy by 52 per cent. (Ibid.)

[11] To supplement these with some recent figures for some socialist and capitalist countries: if 1958 is taken as 100, by 1968 industrial production rose to 195 in the Soviet Union, 244 in Bulgaria, 190 in Poland, 156 in Czechoslovakia, 160 in the GDR, 269 in Romania, 177 in Hungary, 271 in Japan, 147 in the GFR, 177 in Italy, 144 in France, 183 in Mexico. (Ibid.)

nomic leaders and economists not only in Hungary but also in other socialist countries. For instance, in 1964. J. Goldman published an article in the periodical of the Czechoslovak Planning office, entitled: "Trends and fluctuations in the growth rates of some socialist countries".[12] In this he compared data from Czechoslovakia, Poland, Hungary and the GDR in various tables and called attention to strong fluctuations in development. In the last analysis he traced them back to certain deficiencies of the established system of economic planning and control, and in connection with these deficiencies he referred to the well-known Polish economist W. Brus, who thought to find the roots of these evils in rigidity, excessive material inputs, insufficient stimulation of technical progress, as well as in certain remnants of alienation and in a bureaucracy inherited from the past. We could amply quote also from the Soviet economic and daily press to prove how deeply these problems engage leaders of the economy and economists. Economists are haunted in every socialist country by the question why we cannot avail ourselves fully of the superiority of our socialist economic system, what we should do to eliminate present deficiencies, and to achieve thereby a considerable upswing of our economy. In Czechoslovakia there has been a very wide and vivid discussion about these problems. The central party newspapers published a voluminous document with the title: "Draft of the principles concerning the improvement of planned economic control."[13] The most important principles will be discussed in plenary session by the Central Committee of the Czechoslovak Communist Party and decision will be taken on improvement of economic control. In the Soviet Union there was a sharp discussion in 1962 in *Pravda* and it started again in 1964 about questions related to these we have mentioned. Here in Hungary a comprehensive inquiry was started in 1964 on the initiative of the Party to disclose the deficiencies and to work out possible ways of remedying them; but even earlier much was done by various economic bodies, as well as by the economic and daily press, to prepare for this work.

There was repeatedly discussed in this context the fact that economic science was lagging behind the requirements of the national economy. This is certainly true and the situation does not become more tolerable if we add that, according to what has been said, this is not an exclusively domestic phenomenon but one to be found in socialist countries in general. Research into the causes, explanation and origin of this phenomenon leads us unavoidably to circumstances in the period of the personality cult. Of course, a lagging behind of economic science from requirements cannot be directly traced back to these circumstances. But it was due to these circumstances that many promising research activities aimed at the improvement of economic planning and control, started in the Soviet Union in the twenties, were entirely buried by later events and their continuation or renewal became impossible. In the last two decades of Stalin's life it was not advis-

[12] J. Goldman: Tempo rustu a opakujici v ekonomice nekterych socialistickych zemi (Trends and fluctuations in the growth rates of some socialist countries). *Plánované Hospodárstvi*, 1964. No. 9. pp. 1–14.
[13] *Új Szó*. Bratislava, 20. Oct. 1964.

able to announce new discoveries in the social sciences. In this period a system of economic control and management comprising many bureaucratic elements developed, the activity of which it was difficult to criticise. Accordingly, there emerged the type of economic leader who did not demand or expect anything from science because they considered themselves to be high above science. Hardly twelve years have passed since the death of Stalin. We have succeeded in doing away with the personality cult and also in improving much in other fields, including economic control, but not yet enough. According to a statement at the Seventh Party Congress, "the methods of control must be improved and perfected, particularly in the planning and implementation of investment, as well as in the modernization of productive equipment and productive processes, where we can still find serious deficiencies".[14] And a resolution of the Eighth Congress has stated: "Improvement of economic control is a condition of further progress".[15] Economic science has also made great progress in these past years, but it has not yet succeeded in making up for its former backwardness. As a matter of fact, the two belong closely together. At the same time, it would be a mistake not to acknowledge the development achieved. In these last years we have understood much that we did not understand earlier, and in many fields we know how certain things could be done better. Whether we really do them better does not depend on science alone. In order to eliminate certain evils, it may be necessary to change some institutions or institutional measures. Not infrequently this is rather difficult, because people tend to stick to existing institutions and rules.

All that has been said in the foregoing referred to the social existence of our people. From it, we must draw the conclusion that our present socialist system and the economic relations on which it relies are not yet quite as they should be, they are still deficient in many respects, and we did not recognize quite clearly and in all cases what could serve as a remedy. Nevertheless, it is great progress against the past that we see the deficiencies and problems more clearly; that comprehensive deep-going scientific research has been started to reveal their causes; that wide and vivid discussions are going on about their substance and ways of improvement. This, however, does not change the fact: our whole society bears—although to a decreasing extent but still in many respects— the imprint and consequences of the past, including the capitalist past.

It may happen, therefore, that some of our measures do not lead to the desired results or involve many undesired effects beside the desired ones. We conduct a planned economy, but our economic activities are accompanied by a series of unplanned, even unforeseen and undesirable events. At the same time, it also happens that we cannot implement some of our plans and decisions quite according to our intentions. There exist certain deficiencies in relation to which we have repeatedly taken decisions without succeed-

[14] A Magyar Szocialista Munkáspárt VII. kongresszusának jegyzőkönyve (Proceedings of the 7th Congress of the HSWP). Budapest, 1960. Kossuth Könyvkiadó. p. 598.
[15] A Magyar Szocialista Munkáspárt VIII. kongresszusának jegyzőkönyve (Proceedings of the 8th Congress of the HSWP). Budapest, 1963. Kossuth Könyvkiadó. p. 448.

ing in eliminating them. In vain have we recognized some mistakes and evils; they continued to be repeated in the course of years; sometimes even their easing was hardly possible. Let us think, e. g. of rush-work at the end of each quarter. A hundred years ago, Marx wrote in *Capital:* "Let us now picture to ourselves, by way of change, a community of free individuals, carrying on their work with the means of production in common, in which the labour-power of all the different individuals is consciously applied as the combined labour-power of the community. The social relation of the individual producers, with regard both to their labour and to its products, are in this case perfectly simple and intelligible, and that with regard not only to production but also to distribution".[16]

When our economic activities are accompanied by a host of unwanted, unforeseen, unplanned, spontaneous phenomena and when we so often stand helpless or, at least, looking for advice before the phenomena and consequences we ourselves have called into being and which will not obey us, then, obviously, the association of human beings as this was envisaged by Marx has not, or not quite, materialized. Then, something must be still alive from what Marx described in 1844, in the *Economic-philosophical Manuscripts* in the following way: "The object turned out by labour, the product of labour confronts it as a *foreign substance*, as a *power foreign* to the producer".[17] We have not yet quite left behind us the historical development characterized in 1845 — 46 by Marx and Engels in the *German Ideology* as follows: ". . . this consolidation of what we ourselves produce into an objective power above us, growing out of our control, thwarting our expectations, bringing to naught our calculations, is one of the chief factors in historical development up till now".[18] Of course, this is no longer the main motive in our country. We have still to study and investigate in our own society what was illuminated by Marx in the third volume of *Capital*, written in 1863–67: ". . . how production relations are converted into entities and rendered independent in relation to the agents of production . . .",[19] and to which he referred by saying: ". . . appear to them as overwhelming natural laws that irresistibly enforce their will over them and confront them as blind necessity".[20] There are people in our country who very clearly see the various deficiencies in our society but who object to using the term "alienation" in connection with certain deficiencies. Their objection is explained and justified by the fact that the enemies of our people's democracy make efforts to forge a weapon from the concept of alienation for the fight against our system. But the use of a Marxian concept cannot be decided simply in this way. From certain phenomena indicating alienation our enemies wish perforce to deduce the impossible statement that the dictatorship of the proletariat was an alienated power and that the source of alienation was planned control of the national economy by the government and party. As

[16] K. Marx: *Capital*, Vol. I. ed. cited in Note 3. p. 78–79.
[17] K. Marx: *Economic-Philosophical Manuscripts of 1844*. Budapest, 1962. Kossuth Könyvkiadó. p. 45 (in Hungarian).
[18] K. Marx and F. Engels: *Selected Works*, Vol. I. Moscow 1969. Progress Publishers. p. 36.
[19] K. Marx: *Capital*, Vol. III. ed. cited in Note 3. p. 831.
[20] Ibidem.

against this, the truth which can and must be proved by millions of facts of everyday life is, that virtually our party and state—even if sometimes they comprise elements which do not entirely conform to their substance—represent the forces fighting *against* alienation, rather than being alienated from the people. It is, however, true, that they have still much to fight against in this field. Thus it is not allowable even in this field to think in rigid metaphysical terms of "yes and no". Above all we must not forget that the economic foundation of our present society is not yet the perfect form on a communist basis, where no kind of alienation can find a hold. The economic and social relations are not yet clearly intelligible, transparent or expedient. It follows that the present social consciousness of our people is not what the social consciousness of a people living under communism will be. Nor can we expect that deliberate will and decision will always have the desired results.

For our *ideological activity* this is of great importance because it makes clearer to us the medium in which we have to act. The purpose of this activity is the socialist education of the masses, the raising of their consciousness and, through this, a guidance of their actions. We have all learned from our classics that millions of instances of practical everyday experience are needed for forming and transforming the consciousness of the masses. Ideas will penetrate the everyday life of the masses, can seize them and guide their activities, if they correspond to the real needs of people stemming from everyday life or, at least, do not contradict these. Therefore, we must see clearly that our cultural and ideological work should not get into contradiction with the everyday facts of practical life.

I shall try to illuminate what has been said above with the aid of a few concrete examples. In Hungary one of the fields of our ideological activity which claims central attention is the countryside. Transforming the manner of thinking is here a particularly important task and also raises special problems, since it was only a few years ago that the overwhelming majority of the peasantry took the road from individual farming to collective production. Our comrades working in the ideological field have to perform the greater part of their task of rendering socialist consciousness dominant also among the rural population at a time when socialist production relations are becoming predominant in agriculture. These comrades must put up with rather complicated problems, and we are not allowed to simplify these problems—as is not infrequently done today—as though these consisted only of liquidating ideas inherited from an age of private ownership of land of individual small farms. As a matter of fact, such ideas are not simply survivals of the past which are now dying away; they receive day by day new stimuli from present economic phenomena and reality as, e. g., household-plot farming, market relations, etc. Not to take this into account, not to draw the consequences that follow from it, to believe that the sole task is to liquidate certain "remnants" would mean that our propaganda work would get into a vacuum and miss its aim. Should we fight perhaps for the liquidation of household farming or certain market relations, in order to make production relations more uniform, clear-cut and consequently more socialist? This would contradict the development of our economy, our

19

2*

economic policy which, for the time being, lays much weight on production conducted in household plots, and even on its further development. Those who work in ideological fields must thoroughly understand this problem. They must understand that it will still take considerable time before the development of productive forces, the strengthening of common farms, the predominance of such means of production as can be used only in common large-scale farming, make household farming obsolete and induce cooperative members to seek prosperity exclusively in the common farm. Clearly, under such conditions we could set quite different targets for our cultural and ideological work.

Again, let us look at participation of workers in the operation and control of state-owned enterprises. From the teaching of Marx and Lenin just mentioned, to the effect that the consciousness of the masses is formed mainly by their own everyday experience, there obviously follows the importance of such participation in shaping the consciousness of workers. It is a primary requirement for developing and improving our socialist democracy, for raising the whole level of society that the masses of working people should take part in the conduct of enterprises, above all in elaborating enterprise plans. Obviously this is the most efficient way of convincing workers by the practice of everyday life that they are the masters of this country. It is accordingly self-evident that we should strive towards making workers—all workers, if possible—participate in operating the plants they are working in. It is a fact, however, that even the appointed leaders of a plant have, in many cases, not much say in such matters. It happens that the plan of an enterprise is drawn up by the supervising ministry, and even its manager has hardly any role in this procedure. For some time now economic science has placed a considerable expansion of enterprise autonomy on the order of the day. For the time being, however, most of our firms are not "enterprises" in the sense that they could decide on what they are going to undertake. Our enterprise managers must frequently operate within very narrow limits. Does this alter our objective that workers should be drawn into the control of plants to a maximum extent, into drawing up their plants? Of course, it does not. But when setting our objectives we must start from the actual situation. Let us take into account present conditions when deciding on what conditions we are going to create. In other words, we must not consider our objective—as not infrequently happens today—as one for which all conditions are already given, and as if its realization depended only on the efforts of individual workers and organs of the enterprise, in other words, on how we are able to persuade them to make such efforts. In this case, our propaganda would become a voice calling in the wilderness; leaders and workers of enterprises would feel it to be detached from reality.

Let us take an example from a narrower field, from a branch of industry where labour discipline is conspicuously loose. Closer examination will show invariably that the production plan exceeds what could be performed with the given labour force under given conditions. In such a branch, every enterprise must suffer from labour shortage and make efforts to recruit its labour force, even at the cost of other enterprises, belonging to the same branch. Evidently, such a situation does not favour a strengthening of

20

labour discipline, since the leaders must be cautious in taking disciplinary measures if they do not want to be left without workers. True, a socially conscious minority of workers will continue to work in a disciplined manner even under such conditions. However, when we are in search of ideological arguments suitable for strengthening labour discipline in general, we cannot disregard—as we frequently disregard today—the situation created by an overstrained plan. Otherwise the danger persists that our propaganda will become empty preaching.

Or let us take a more general problem, the question of how conflicts between the interests of national economy and those of the enterprise, or between the individual enterprise and the general interest, can be eliminated. The fact itself that this problem is widely discussed proves that today the interests of the worker may conflict with those of the enterprise or of the economy as a whole. Is it possible to expect workers and managers to decide, as a rule, against their own individual or enterprise interests? It is always possible for an individual to rise above the ranks; but here we are concerned with the behaviour and reaction of the masses rather than with those of excellent individuals. We must also understand that, in the majority of cases, the worker or the leader of an enterprise does not do something conspicuously improper by following his own interest or that of the enterprise. In the majority of cases either it is not clear to him what action would be required by a more general interest, or he simply follows the way of least resistance that seems compatible with his moral principles and does not conflict with his ideas about human character, without requiring any particular risk or sacrifice. To avoid misunderstanding, I must emphasize, once more, that our objective is evidently correct and it should be sought after by all means; some material conditions, however, must be created in order to attain it. In the case in question it must obviously be achieved that the more general interest is enforced without major harm to the individual one. This is by no means an unrealistic requirement, even if it demands all kinds of changes being made in our system of planning and control.

The superiority of our system over capitalist society consists precisely in its serving the *maximum welfare of the whole working population*. As against this, capitalist society assures *maximum welfare for a minority*, so that the existence of the great majority — be it better or worse depending on circumstances, perhaps relatively good—is at any rate subordinated to this narrow objective. It follows from this fundamental property of our system that the participation of the broadest masses in managing the affairs of socialist economy, state and society depends not on some "concession" made by political and economic leaders; it is in the interest of us all. We must, therefore, endeavour to bring it about that every worker and employee should feel the interest of his plant, enterprise, institution to be his own and should feel concern for it, and similarly with cooperative members with regard to the interest of their cooperative. In addition, all workers must be made to feel the same with regard to the more general interests of the national economy, the country as a whole. This should be kept in view in our whole ideological work. At the same time, we should realize that our words will fall on fertile soil only if what we say is based on careful analysis

21

and profound knowledge of reality. We must never take for granted—as frequently happens—circumstances which do not yet exist, the material conditions of which will materialize only in the near or even the more distant future; in a word, which at present would contradict the everyday experience of the masses.

Let us summarize briefly some conclusions. First, our examination of the relation between economy and ideology has strengthened the well-known thesis that, from the point of view of the development of our society and of accelerating this development, it is of utmost importance to educate people in a socialist and communist spirit, to raise their socialist consciousness, as the main pledge of our victory. Second, if we wish our ideological work to be really effective, it must always remain in harmony with the facts of physical reality: it is only the unity of word and action that can ensure its efficiency. Third, we must recognize that there are still many deficiencies in economic processes, that we do not always succeed in finding the most expedient measures for improving things, that we must still work hard at the solution of certain problems. In case of deficiencies, no bigger mistake can be made than not to acknowledge them or even to try to embellish the real situation. If we build upon an imagined state of affairs that does not exist—at least not yet—our words will be mere incantation and exorcism. The task is here to fight against faults and deficiencies, a fight for their earliest possible elimination, for the creation of more favourable material conditions. This fight should be aided by ideological work that reveals reality without embellishing it, and deduces from it what should be done.

I have restricted myself to presenting only a few fundamental relations between economy and ideology. I thought it was necessary to point out these interrelations, since they are discussed comparatively rarely and too little, and mainly because unfortunately in everyday practice we frequently sin against them.

# SOME FUNDAMENTAL PROBLEMS IN THE POLITICAL ECONOMY OF SOCIALISM

## CONCEPT AND ROLE OF THE POLITICAL ECONOMY OF SOCIALISM

The political economy of socialism is the scientifically systematized summary of our knowledge, researches and theories regarding the internal relationships, laws, rules and movement of socialist economy.[1] It is thus the science on whose findings, teachings and rules we should rely when establishing socialist production relations, directing the development of our socialist economy in a planned manner and constructing the economic basis of a socialist society.

With these premises I wish to stress the important role of this discipline, whereas the word "should" is meant to delimit this to some extent. Such delimitation is necessary from two aspects. First, I wish to indicate that our science necessarily belongs to the young disciplines. Since its subject is the socialist economy, it can be hardly older than this economy itself, even if its roots reach farther back; namely, we knew certain features of socialist economy even before the first one came really into being. If, however, our discipline is young, presumably also its body of knowledge is narrower and maybe more open to argument than that of the older disciplines, its teachings and laws are more in need of further study and verification. I may add the limitations in question have, in addition to the youth of the discipline, also other historical reasons. On the other hand, with the word "should" I also wished to indicate that in the actual building of socialism we do not always or everywhere apply even the already recognized laws and rules, or verified theses. This, too, has its historical and political reasons.

The laws of every science express and reflect *objective* relationships. The term "objective" means that these relationships exist independently of whether or not they correspond to our wishes, ideas and efforts. But obviously, no science can strive to embrace *all* relations existing between the phenomena appearing in its field. This is an obvious absurdity. The innumerable multitude of phenomena are connected with each other by innumerable material relations. We make efforts at finding the most characteristic internal relationships of the phenomena in the field of socialist economy. We are looking for those relationships that enable us to systematize the infinitely complicated and diversified world of economic phenomena in a surveyable manner, to reveal what regulates the movements of this continuously moving world. In other words, we are looking for the

[1] Internal relationships, laws and rules are related concepts. Between the latter two I make the distinction that the essential and more stable internal relationships will be called laws, the other, however, rules.

law or laws of movement governing socialist economy. We are doing this not simply for the sake of knowing them; we want to apply this knowledge in the actual process of establishing the economic foundations of socialism. It is in this way that the engineer studies, in his own field, the laws of nature and technology, learning even some mathematics in order to formulate and describe them, because by their application he wants to build houses, railways, power plants, cars, sewing machines, microscopes and satellites.


POLITICAL ECONOMY, PLANNING, ECONOMIC POLICY

In his pamphlet against Dühring, Engels defined political economy as the science of the conditions and forms under which different human societies had turned out, exchanged and distributed products.[2] In the preface to his work "Contribution to the Critique of Political Economy", Marx wrote: "the anatomy of civil society is to be sought in political economy", further, that "the sum total of relations of production constitutes the economic structure of society".[3] In the preface to "Capital" (first edition), he writes about the "natural laws of capitalist production", and characterizes these laws by saying that "these tendencies are working with iron necessity towards inevitable results". In the same place, in connection with his book, he wrote: "It is the ultimate aim of this work to lay bare the economic law of motion of modern society".[4] As the reader will notice, it was essentially with these definitions and terms that I have introduced my statement about the political economy of socialism.

Here, however, we must face a problem. Stalin, in his work "Economic problems of socialism in the Soviet Union" wrote that "The rational organization of productive forces, of economic planning, etc. are not problems of the economic policy of directing bodies... Political economy investigates the laws of development of men's relations of production. Economic policy draws practical conclusions from this, gives them concrete shape, and builds its day-to-day work on them. To foist upon political economy problems of economic policy is to kill it as a science".[5] Here, I do not intend to argue with Stalin. What he says is correct. More exactly, it would be correct if it were true. From his statement it follows, namely, that in formulating economic policy and in the practice of planning the leading organs rely on the results of political economy. But at the time when this statement was written the actual situation had long been quite different. The leading bodies did not claim the help of science, and the men of science, research workers and teachers could not gain insight into the development of the economy as a whole, into the real problems of economic policy and of planning. By

[2] K. Marx and F. Engels: *Collected Works*, Vol. 20. Budapest 1963. Kossuth Könyvkiadó. p. 148.
[3] K. Marx and F. Engels: *Selected Works*, Vol. I, Moscow, 1969. Progress Publishers. p. 503.
[4] K. Marx: *Capital*, Vol. I. Moscow, 1961. Foreign Languages Publishing House. pp. 8-10.
[5] J. V. Stalin: *Economic Problems of Socialism in the U.S.S.R.* Moscow, 1952. Foreign Languages Publishing House. p. 81.

*separating economic science from the activity of the leading bodies*, the statement quoted has furnished pseudo-theoretical justification of this extremely harmful practice.

Evidently, economic policy and planning are in themselves not part of the science of political economy, no more than the technology of producing sulphuric acid is part of chemistry. But chemistry, in combination with some other disciplines, must enable us to find the rules according to which we can work out the technology of obtaining sulphuric acid, and organize its large-scale production. In the same manner, political economy must give an answer to the question *what laws and rules must be observed in planning and economic policy?* However, the political economy of socialism can solve this task only by proceeding hand in hand with practice, looking for an answer to its actual and ever renewed problems, by striking its roots into practice and feeding from it. Without such connection the political economy of socialism is destined to sterility and stagnation, but neither can economic policy or planning be founded on a really scientific basis.

Therefore, the concept according to which economic policy and planning belong to the scope of activity of the leading bodies that stand above criticism and, accordingly, political economy and science in general need not deal with these, was dominant also in Hungary for a long time and is sometimes haunting even today. However, the majority both of those engaged in the political economy of socialism and of our economic leaders have become aware that this concept was untenable. Their agreement on this question and their resulting cooperation has already yielded considerable results and promises for the future further progress in, and a higher level of, both science and practice.


## THE BASIC LAW OF SOCIALISM, AND THE LAW OF PLANNED PROPORTIONATE DEVELOPMENT

Thus, we want to know the objective economic laws of socialist society in order to utilize them in building socialism. But the deplorable situation reviewed, together with the correspondingly harmful concept, had prevailed for a long time and led to such an interpretation of the economic laws of socialism and to such teachings as were of little use in the building of socialism. In recent years considerable *changes and improvements* have taken place in this field. Those engaged in the political economy of socialism have been provided with sufficient statistical information regarding economic development to an increasing extent, they could get acquainted also with the topical, most urgent problems of this development of economic policy and planning. They have made and are making great and partly already successful efforts at solving the problems which have been put upon the order of the day by socialist construction and at making up for the lagging behind of their science. This has become possible because there is a growing recognition among the leading organs that economic policy and national economic planning can satisfy the requirements of socialism only by relying on science.

If, beside welcoming this fact, I add that we cannot rest satisfied with the results hitherto achieved, my purpose is by no means to find fault at any cost. I should like to make clearer the way that should be followed and thereby promote and accelerate the healthy development that has started. I have in view essentially the method of Marx, as it can and should be followed under our given conditions. This method is praised by many but followed by few. It is precisely its application that has to be learned. It is since *Marx* has revealed the economic laws of capitalism by analyzing the functioning of capitalist society that we understand why the law of capitalist accumulation is a law of capitalism, how it works and asserts itself, and what factors can diminish or counterbalance its effects. There are few laws of our own society of which we have as much knowledge as that.

Today we know that the formulation by Stalin of the *basic economic law of socialism* is not satisfactory. We say that in socialism the purpose of production is the fullest possible satisfaction of the needs of society. We also call attention to the fact that a production satisfying these needs will not be automatically attained and that fullest possible satisfaction is not identical with absolute satisfaction. With this, no doubt, we have come nearer to an undertsanding of the requirements raised by the law. Yet, neither from this, nor from an analysis of the notion of needs—by distinguishing, e. g., acknowledged and unacknowledged needs; primary, secondary and tertiary needs; full and adjusted needs; effective and latent needs, etc.—can we understand how the law concretely operates, how it makes its effects felt, how it asserts itself or what we should actually do, what measures we should apply to meet the requirements of this law or how we can utilize it in the building of socialism.

Today we also know that *the law of planned proportionate development*, instead of expressing a single major relationship prevailing in socialist society summarizes a multitude of important relationships. We conduct researches into the major problems of economic development, the necessary proportions of consumption and accumulation, of industry and agriculture, of the various branches of production, of the various forms of consumption, of productive and non-productive investments, etc. Of all these we know much more than even a few years ago, but not enough to serve as a firm and satisfactory foundation in formulating and implementing economic policy and planning. As a matter of fact, the level of development of our discipline can be measured essentially by its applicability. In practice, of course, not even applicability can be measured, we know only how far the law actually asserts itself. But we can assume that there is no essential difference between the two. At any rate, it will be worth while to investigate how the basic economic law of socialism and the law of planned proportionate development have asserted themselves in our country.

In fact, the material and cultural development of our society has been considerable and—apart from a single period of about two years—fairly regular since the year 1948 that we used to regard as the turning point, that is, since we have unequivocally chosen the road to building socialism. But we must also remember the well-known and frequently exposed deficiencies of our system of economic control, planning and management. We have to conclude that with better planning, management and control, with a better mechanism, we could have achieved a fuller assertion of the basic law.

Something similar may be said about the law of planned proportionate development. It may be assumed with some justification that if the above-mentioned, recognized and exposed deficiencies were smaller, it would occur less frequently that certain products were unsaleable while others were lacking; that some investments cost more time and money than planned; that shortages in materials or spare parts hindered production, that from time to time whole industries and even whole branches of the economy were found to be lagging behind the general rate of development. All such phenomena are, however, patent violations of the law of planned, proportional development.

In connection with both laws it seems justifiable to say that on the present level of development of our society, we must not expect their full or even approximately full implementation. After all, both are laws of the *socialist* economy; as long as the building of socialism is not completed, we cannot expect them to be fulfilled with maximum efficiency. Or, conversely, we could say that it will only be when both laws assert themselves with the minimum of obstacles that we shall be justified in regarding the building of socialism as complete.

With all this, however, we have not come nearer to answering the question how these laws should be applied in practice; instead, we have come back to where we have started from. What must we do in order that these laws should assert themselves more efficiently? How should the first one be applied and how the second? How can they be utilized in building socialism? It cannot be denied that up to now we have not succeeded in giving a satisfactory answer to either of these questions.

SOME OTHER LAWS OF THE POLITICAL ECONOMY OF SOCIALISM

The two great laws just discussed, which cover the whole of the economy, do not seem to be applicable in practice to the building of socialism in a really useful and successful manner. But, perhaps, the situation is better with respect to the application of certain other laws, whose scope is perhaps more restricted? Even this could hardly be supported. I do not want to say similar things about many laws and thus engage in repetition; I will, therefore, remain satisfied with touching briefly upon *three* laws which are frequently quoted. Though all three of them relate to highly important economic relationships, it was not in view of their importance that I selected precisely these three, but because one of them is valid in *all* socio-economic formations, the second in *several* but not in all, while the third prevails only in conditions of *socialist* economy.

*The first law requires mutual correspondence between productive forces and productive relations* or, more widely formulated: *their relation to each other.* Productive relations may furnish an adequate framework for the development of the productive forces, but they may also become fetters on development. In the words of Marx: "At a certain stage of their development, the

27

material productive forces of society come in conflict with the existing relations of production . . ."[6] and a collision between society's productive forces and the prevailing productive relations may lead to social revolution. We may add that, even if events do not take the form of a sharp collision and a revolution within the given social formation, usually the productive relations are less flexible and develop more slowly (even in socialism) than the productive forces. Thus, however adequately or perfectly the productive relations may have corresponded to the productive forces in a given period, after some longer time this correspondance will become insufficient and the productive relations have to be changed in order that they should become adequate again. *Such a change is now taking place in Hungary with the reform of the system of economic control and management.* But, as has been said, the law in itself does not tell us where, in what respect and how the productive relations should be changed.

*The law of value* is a law of several socio-economic formations, it prevails in a narrower or wider scope in every society where commodity production plays some smaller or greater role. It expresses the objective tendency for commodities to be exchanged for one another in proportion to the amounts of socially necessary labour used in their production; in other words, that their relative prices develop accordingly. Perhaps there is no other single issue of our discipline that could have provoked so many and fervent debates as the role of commodity production and value in a socialist economy. At present, nobody denies any longer that in socialism also a kind of commodity production is taking place and the law of value is at work. The effect of this law manifests itself, among other things, in the fact that if relative prices of many commodities deviate substantially and for long from what the proportions of socially necessary labour inputs would justify, harmful effects or disturbances will appear in the functioning of the economy. Opinions, however, differ as to *what should be considered in socialism as socially necessary labour*, how it can and should be accounted for, as well as how the law of value should or could be applied or used in the building of socialism.

The law of *distribution according to work performed* is a law only of the socialist economy. What do we mean by this? Essentially what Marx wrote (in the "Critique of the Gotha Program") about the distribution in socialism of consumer goods among individual producers. As is known, Marx here dissected that point in the program which demanded "cooperative regulation of the total labour with a fair distribution of the proceeds of labour". Marx pointed out that, to begin with, a certain part has to be deducted not from the "proceeds of labour" (the meaning of which is unclear) but from the aggregate social product, before distributing it in the form of consumer goods among individual producers of the collective. Then he shows that "the individual producer exactly receives back from society, after the deductions have been made, what he gives to it" and, accordingly, "the right of the producers is *proportional* to the labour they supply". He states that although here "no one can give anything except his labour" and . . . "nothing can

[6] K. Marx and F. Engels: op. cit. Vol. 13. p. 6.

28

pass into the ownership of individuals, except for individual means of consumption", "this *equal right* is still constantly stigmatized by bourgeois limitation"; this is unavoidable "in the first phase of communist society".[7] It is thus this equal right which is expressed by the law formulated either as "equal wages for equal work" or in the form that wages should be in proportion to the amount and quality of labour performed; or else, that he who works more or better should also earn more.

All that is undoubtedly interesting, important and instructive. Unfortunately, it has the same deficiency as we have met above: we can hardly draw a practical lesson from it for the building of socialism, particularly for the solution of our problems connected with wages policy. The problem generally arises not in the form of whether we should or should not pay more to A who performs more, or more valuable work for society than B does; the problem is how to decide whether A really performs more or more valuable work. Furthermore, for the purposes of practice we must also decide by how much the work performed by A is more or less valuable than that performed by B and by how much he should earn more. Unfortunately, none of the formulations of the law as quoted above can answer these questions.

Of course, the decisions of socialist wages policy cannot remain pending, even if we are not able to read an answer from the law of distribution. Evidently, the problem, as all other problems of practical life, has to be and will be somehow decided, whether science is or is not capable of providing a solution to them.

The practical achievements of the socialist countries—as the abolition of exploitation, hunger and misery, the ending of the education monopoly of well-to-do classes, the rapidly growing number of young people studying in secondary schools and institutions of higher education, the rising standards of living, the acceleration of social progress—sufficiently prove that *the laws of socialist society, as objective laws, assert themselves even if our knowledge of them is deficient.*

We have investigated above only how far we are able to utilize in practice certain well-known laws of the political economy of socialism. We have found that these laws do not suffice to orientate us with regard to the detailed problems we have to face in the process of building socialism.

REVEALING THE LAWS AND THE REQUIREMENT OF CONTINUITY

If the laws do not yield us an answer, then we must have posed the wrong question. Marx, in his *Critique of the Gotha Program* did not ask what followed from the law of distribution as regards practical wages policy. He only asked how a society whose means of production were in collective ownership and which, accordingly, was able to decide upon the distribution of the social product as a whole, would have to proceed. It was in this way that he could formulate the law of distribution according to work performed.

[7] K. Marx and F. Engels: *Selected Works*, Vol. II. Moscow, 1949. Foreign Languages Publishing House. pp. 21–23.

Let us, then, start questioning again. As I have mentioned, the task of political economy is to disclose the major interrelations and laws of motion of the socialist economy, or, in simpler words, to investigate how this economy works, what regulates its functions, what moves and propels it.

At first sight, everything seems to be extremely simple. The state owns the decisive part of the means of production; nothing could be more natural for the economy, its movement and development than to be regulated by the state plan.

This is a fact, and a very essential one at that, a characteristic feature of our economic and social system. The effects and influences of the national economic plan are really felt in every field of the socialist economy.

But, with this statement we have only circumvented the question we are concerned with. In order to know exactly how our economy functions, what regulates its operation, we have to ask: on what considerations and how does the state establish the plan regulating economic activities? Let us now disregard the closely related problem of what body or institution—planning office, ministry, etc.—prepares and elaborates the plan, or in what framework and according to what rules this body operates. Nor do we ask here who, or what body, is called upon to approve the plan, that is, how a document prepared by some persons will become the plan of the state. These are aspects of decisive importance but, for the time being, we are concerned solely with the economic laws on which the state plan is, or should be, based and with the conceptions the government is trying to serve by means of it. To what extent can conceptions and objectives be served by the plan? In other words, what is the degree of freedom in planning and what factors place limitations upon it?

Evidently, the state is free in establishing its plan within the limits set by objective necessities, that is, the essential economic interrelations, laws and rules that exist independently of human will and desire. A plan that does not take these into account—whether it covers the whole economy or only a part of it—is voluntaristic, neglecting science and running counter to life, and thus is doomed to failure. So we have again come back to our starting point. As soon as it comes to actual planning, we cannot circumvent the task of revealing the essential economic relationships, that is, the laws and rules of a socialist economy.

For the government, more exactly, for those engaged in drawing up plan proposals, the given amount of resources available to society mark the only possible starting point. The first and most important of the productive forces is man himself. Planners must take into account the present and the probable future number of people, their distribution by age, sex and geographical location, their physical and intellectual conditions, including education, abilities, experience, habits, aims and even their prejudices. Only in the knowledge of all these are we able to consider with sufficient scientific accuracy what our people are capable of and willing to do with the other resources and in the given conditions.

As regards these other resources and conditions we must take into account, first of all, the natural endowments, such as the geographical area, the configurations of the terrain, climate, water supply, mineral deposits, the composition and quality of the soil etc.; part of these exist in a form already more or less altered by man. Another set of material resources was created and can be further developed by man; but at a given point of time even these have to be considered as given. Here belong, first of all, productive plant and equipment, public and residential buildings, roads, railways, electric grids, gas and oil pipelines, warehouses, shops, banks, as well as stocks of materials, intermediate and finished goods. The decisive part of all these is owned by the state or the cooperatives. Finally, there are the things owned by individual people as personal property: clothing, furniture and other durable goods, a considerable part of residential buildings etc.

An overwhelming majority of these material resources is far from being quantitatively and qualitatively constant, or independent of human activity. Man is able to increase their quantity and to change their structure, thereby providing the material basis of his existence, the level of which, in turn, is determined by historically developed customs and ideas. Meanwhile, in addition even population is changing in number, qualitative composition and geographical location. As a consequence, even the most important of these productive forces, i. e., labour-power, changes as regards its quantity, quality and distribution. The development of social economy and of labour-power itself depends on human labour; and without continuously exerted labour no society could exist. Some plant or another may stop producing but the machinery of production as a whole cannot stop, practically not for a single day.

The first important conclusion to be drawn from all this is that without adequate preparation, no sudden and substantial change can be brought about in the sphere of material production. As a matter of fact, the given amount, structure and geographical location of human and material productive forces and the similarly given human and social customs determine to a great extent what can and must be done. With due preparation, by creating adequate conditions, even certain sudden and substantial changes can be achieved. For instance, the implementation of a large investment project requires preparatory work taking many years; then, suddenly, the putting of it into operation causes important changes. From what has been said it is possible to draw the conclusion—and this again has played a certain role when we elaborated our new economic system—that some of the functions of the economic mechanism require not much planning or even no planning at all. Namely, a preponderant part of production consists of what economists call simple reproduction, that is, the continuous repetition of earlier processes.

In order to avoid misunderstanding, I would warn against an oversimplified interpretation. What we call simple reproduction, does not really need much or even any planning *on a national level*. In reality, however, that is in the plant, shop, cooperative or mine, even simple reproduction almost always requires all sorts of new intellectual and physical efforts, among other reasons because in most cases it is not a mere repetition of earlier processes but involves changes in the performance required and in its conditions.

In our society as a whole, however, reproduction is extended rather than simple. True, frequently the conditions of extension are uncomplicated, requiring only quantitative change. Therefore, the *individual* cases of extension in themselves do not seem to constitute a difficult or complicated task for planning. The situation is, however, different when viewing extended reproduction on a *social scale*. Here we have to face more complicated problems, independently of whether there exists planning in a society or not. Let us remember that extended reproduction already existed on a large scale prior to the birth of socialist economy. In many capitalist countries extended reproduction is taking place even in our days without any planning at the social level. Nevertheless, it should be clear that extended reproduction on a social scale always assumes and postulates some specific proportions in the allocation of productive forces and conditions of production, the existence of certain mutual interdependence in their quantitative and qualitative development.

Marx was the first to show, starting from an analysis of the capitalist economy unique in its depth and versatility, that extended reproduction involved the creation and observance of a multitude of proportions both in physical and value terms and also to indicate some of the most important proportions, for instance the necessary correlation between the quantities of means of production and consumer goods produced.

We know that in a capitalist economy the proportionality postulated by extended reproduction—that is, such reallocation of productive forces and conditions of production as is needed to maintain this proportionality—is ensured by the assertion of the *law of value*, and with the aid of *the market mechanism*. It is similarly known that this holds only for the classical, free-competition capitalism, and that not even in this case does the law of value assert itself in all fields and without any restriction. In modern state monopoly capitalism which was born from a huge development in productive forces, this development itself necessitated the introduction or strengthening of government interference with the operation of the market mechanism and a planned influencing of important fields of the economy, in the interest of the capitalist class and, within it, mainly in that of big monopolies.

Whereas in capitalist countries it was economic development that brought about, in a more or less spontaneous manner, the phenomena of purposeful government intervention and planning, in socialist countries these have been characteristic features of the economy from the very outset, expressing the very essence of the socialist system. Purposefulness and the plan require from us also the creation and maintenance of proportionalities. Each individual productive unit is a link in a complicated chain of organizations. In order to expand production in any single unit, capacities must be increased in all preceding links of the chain and unless the product is destined for final consumption, also in all subsequent links. Since, however, owing to the different natural and physical properties of the various productive forces, production cannot expand simultaneously and evenly in all fields, every

extension involves smaller or major changes in the pattern of production and in the composition of productive forces. The rate of these changes in pattern and composition will differ in the various fields. All this leads to endless and complicated changes in proportions, and it is the task of the planners to ensure the desired proportions. As Lenin said, planning means deliberate efforts aimed at maintaining proportionality. (Of course, the national economic plan has to satisfy also other important requirements.)

In view of all these, let us examine what laws must be taken into account by the planners, what is the degree of their freedom, if they have freedom at all? The new value annually created by social production is the national income. The greater part of this—according to the practice developed over a long period in our country, about three-fourths—is destined for consumption, the rest is the basis of so-called social accumulation. This is the part that makes extended reproduction possible, over and above simple reproduction. The accumulated part of national income is added to the already existing amount of circulating and fixed capital engaged in production.

What rules and relationships must be taken into account in the planning of social accumulation, what restricts the freedom of planners in this respect? First of all, it should be obvious that a considerable part of what can be accumulated from the national income is already earmarked for completing those extension projects that were started, or at least decided upon, in earlier years. Investments aimed at extending production frequently take several years. Moreover, their putting into operation may raise special requirements in manpower that can be met only with the aid of special education and training; this, too, may take some time. But even allocation of the remaining part of social accumulation is strongly restricted. Present and even future limitations may be set by the supply of energy, raw materials and labour; most of these quantitative or qualitative limitations are such as cannot be eliminated overnight. It is evident, e. g., that it would make no sense to build manufacturing plants for which the supply of energy, water, etc. cannot yet be assured. A limitation of a more general character is set by the aggregate of material means that can be produced and set aside for investment purposes, and by the physical composition of this total (considering also possibilities of exchange and conversion by foreign trade). A further limitation consists in that, owing to technological considerations, most productive capacities are economically efficient only when they are built on a definite scale, and this holds also for an expansion of already existing capacities.

I believe what has been said here will make it sufficiently clear that the hands of government and planners are strongly tied in drawing up the plan, at least as regards the *near future*. But is also follows that, the farther we look ahead the greater is the possibility of substantial changes. Indeed, in most cases some modest change can be attained already in a single year, and if efforts serving the same purpose are continued in every subsequent year, the cumulated result may be a substantial change, e. g. the creation of a new industry, an improvement in the supply of raw materials, energy, etc. In order to avoid misunderstanding, this is far from meaning that, step by step, we could bring about any kind of major change at will, or that we

33

could arbitrarily choose the objectives of a long-term plan. Such voluntaristic experiments would be, again, doomed to failure. In order to choose long-term plan objectives correctly, the achievements of science and technology already attained and foreseeable must be conscientiously studied, together with the anticipated development of social needs as a whole. In other words, in all probability, any of these needs could be *fully* met only at the expense of other, equally important needs, so that none of them can fully assert itself, in the same manner as a body moves under the impact of different forces, i. e. in a direction conforming to the resultant of all forces.

A series of uncertainties will further complicate the task of developing proportions in a planned way. A plan must always start from the known endowments, but part of these can be assessed only by estimates, some of which are rather inaccurate. It may turn out that the quantity of crude oil that can be extracted in a given site is larger or smaller than was estimated in the course of planning. The weather conditions are uncertain and may cause large differences between planned and actual results in agricultural production and, as a consequence, in the economy as a whole. Developments in the international market may—in spite of the most careful surveys, studies and prognoses—essentially differ from what we have counted on in the plan. International progress in the field of science and technology may cause even greater surprises.

The law of planned proportionate development—in the sense roughly outlined here—is really a fundamentally important law of a socialist economy. Essentially, it requires us to take into consideration the mutual and multilateral interdependence of the various forces and conditions of production, postulating the existence of specific proportions among all these. What is more, the future changes in each individual factor are subject to a multitude of influences, some of which are proportions unknown or uncertain at the time of planning. All this, evidently, imposes a most difficult and responsible task on the planners.

## PLANNING AND CONSUMPTION: NEW ASPECTS OF THE LAW OF DISTRIBUTION ACCORDING TO WORK PERFORMED

Let us revert to the three-fourths of national income destined for consumption. The planners must decide how a given aggregate value of consumption is likely to materialize in quantities of individual goods. Knowledge of the pattern of consumption in the preceding years generally provides a reliable basis; but also the more or less foreseeable changes in tastes, demand, fashion, habits of consumption etc. must be considered. In the framework of extended reproduction, however, the total of national income destined for consumption is also bound to grow. Here, we have to deal with two questions: in what products will this increment be embodied, and how will this additional mass of products be distributed among the various layers and members of society? The two questions are closely interrelated. Society, more exactly its bodies controlling economic development, have a free hand inasmuch as they can—at least partly—decide among whom and in what

proportions the incremental income should be distributed. This freedom, however, is not unrestricted, as a portion of incremental income is going to be distributed automatically among the various layers and members of society, without any intervention by government and planners, in conformity with the prevailing regulations affecting wages, salaries, pensions, etc. As regards the rest of incremental income, society, or its bodies entrusted with economic management, may decide in what form and to whom it should be allocated. Obviously, some rules must be observed here also. These may often take the form of demands raised by some social strata or occupational groups backed up by public opinion. Such "tensions" or "pressures" will indicate, e. g., that the salaries of the teachers, or certain pensions, etc. are too low, or that it is necessary to increase family allowances, university scholarships, state subsidies granted to nurseries or theatres, and so on.

Depending partly on who are going to obtain the *automatically* distributed part of the increment of national income destined for consumption (owing to prevailing regulations of wages, salaries, pensions, etc.), and partly on to whom the "disposable" part of this increment will be allocated, the structure of consumer demand, as well as the required physical composition of the consumption fund may change very differently. (It may, of course, happen that part of the consumer goods wanted must be imported from abroad. This does not cause any change in principle, it only means that part of the national income produced at home has to be exchanged for foreign products.)

Above we have said that planners must take into account certain rules which frequently make themselves felt in the form of "tensions". It is important to know what rules must be taken into account, partly because if they are accounted for in time, perhaps the tensions themselves can be avoided, and partly because the justification for apparent tensions can be checked precisely by investigating whether they conform to the rules or not.

We have seen that in socialism the law of distribution according to work performed governs the distribution of consumer goods among producers. When discussing this law, we have found that hardly any practical conclusion can be drawn from it for comparing quantities and qualities of productive work performed by different people. In reality, however, not only the various kinds of *productive* labour must be compared. When distributing the total of consumer goods, also those have to be supplied who do not perform any "productive" work but whose labour is also necessary for society, as e. g. those employed in the health service, the state administration or the army; finally, some part is due to the old and disabled who do not work. Thus, the law of distribution according to work performed does not provide satisfactory orientation, even apart from the practical difficulties of its application.

There is a further law which must be taken into account: the law of social equality. Evidently, the law of distribution according to work and the law of social equality, though complementary in a sense, contradict each other. Everyday experience has proved that, in the course of the development of socialist economy, of extended reproduction, both laws assert themselves. This phenomenon is similar to the one observed in allocations serving the development of various productive forces under the impact of partly contradictory needs and requirements. Most frequently, one or the other law comes to the foreground, depending on the given level of development of society and on its actual objectives; but sometimes a combined effect of the two may be observed. Thus, e. g., measures of wage policy implemented in 1966 served to effect partly a differentiation of incomes according to work performed (by introducing various wage supplements for productive plants) and partly their equalization (by raising the contribution to social insurance in the higher wage and salary brackets).

Thus, also in planning the distribution of consumer goods, planners must observe certain laws and rules, among them the law of distribution according to work performed. The same relates, of course, to planning the output of consumer goods. The question, however, in what manner and to what extent the different and often conflicting requirements following from the laws and rules of socialist economy, within the framework of given possibilities should be met must be decided by the competent social bodies, usually by weighing political considerations. By this we mean that the decision must follow the political line adopted by the party in respect of its allies, as well as of its cultural, social, etc. policies, as determined by resolutions taken by its Congress and other bodies.

## IMPLEMENTATION OF THE PLAN WITH REGARD TO PRODUCTIVE RELATIONS

The objective requirements of the laws of socialist economy must be taken into consideration by the planners: they must allocate labour and material resources of production available to society in conformity with these requirements, otherwise they will arrive at a voluntaristic conception detached from reality and impossible to implement, instead of a plan conforming to the requirements of a socialist economy. But even the best plan is but a plan, that is, a summary of ideas and intentions existing in the minds of its authors. Its implementation requires a complicated series of human actions and these, in turn, assume the existence of a specific set of social productive relations.

As is known, in any society there exist some specific productive relations, relations between people, governing the output, exchange and distribution of the social product. It is also known that the given productive relations may or may not correspond to the existing level of productive forces and, accordingly, they may facilitate or hinder the further development of the latter. In general, the ownership of the means of production decisively characterizes the productive relations and together with these, the economic foundations of a society.

What are the productive relations that would correspond on the one hand, to the socialist ownership relations (i. e., the social ownership of the decisive part of the means of production) and, on the other hand, to the present degree of development of productive forces? When, after the victory of the proletarian revolution in Russia, the key positions of production had been taken over by the state, most communists believed, as did Lenin himself, that the productive relations will be decisively characterized by direct instructions issued by the government. But Lenin soon recognized the error of this. In an article written in autumn 1921, on the fourth anniversary of the October Revolution, he wrote: " . . . without sufficient calculation we assumed that state production and state distribution of products could be organized in our small-peasant country according to communistic principles, by direct command of the proletarian state. Life has shown that we made an error. Several degrees of transition: state capitalism and socialism are needed *to prepare*—by working through long years—the transition to communism".[8]

It would be pointless to digress here on what we can say about productive relations under communism on the basis of our present knowledge. At present and even in the foreseeable future, our task is to complete the building of socialism. In fact, the productive relations of socialism have developed according to an essentially similar pattern in Soviet Russia after 1921, later in the Soviet Union, and more recently in all countries which turned socialist around the end of the forties. Of course, in some respects productive relations may differ in each socialist country. They cannot be quite uniform, among other reasons, because, at the time of taking the road towards socialism, the level of development of productive forces was different in each country and is still different today, although to a decreasing extent. But, owing to the fact that a decisive part of the means of production is in social ownership in all these countries, the productive relations are similar in many respects, and they even agree in the most important features. The same holds also for productive relations in Hungary.

From the sentences of Lenin just quoted, we should by no means conclude that, according to him, under socialist conditions the ideal productive relations conforming to production and distribution would be those based on central instructions emanating from a national economic plan. Such a view cannot be attributed to Lenin, for the simple reason that up to 1921 when the GOELRO (the national plan of electrification) was initiated there had been no national economic plan whatever, so that production and distribution within the state-owned sector could not have been regulated according to a plan. It was only much later that the system of central instructions derived from the breakdown of a national economic plan was developed in the Soviet Union, and the same system was adopted even much later by the European socialist countries.

A survey of the historical development of our socio-economic relations would lead me too far from my proper subject and could not be fitted into the framework of the present study. Besides, these relations have been widely discussed in our press during the debates preceding the introduction of the new economic mechanism. These publications have extensively dealt with the system of central instructions emanating from a national economic plan which had prevailed in our country until the end of 1967. There is, accordingly, no need here to review either the old economic mechanism or the new one that will supplant it. I would emphasize here only that commodity and

[8] V. I. Lenin: *Selected Works*, Vol. III. Budapest, 1967. Kossuth Könyvkiadó. p. 358.

money relations have existed, and have played an important role, in the socialist countries even before the new economic reforms. All products had prices at which they were sold to intermediate or final users. The workers and employees obtained their wages and salaries in the form of money and it was for money that they bought all that they needed. Even the cooperative peasants obtained a major (and increasing) part of their income in money and covered an increasing part of their needs by purchases with money. In addition to purchases in cash, certain goods could be also bought on credit. On credits an interest had to be paid, and interest was paid to those who had deposited money with the saving banks. This general feature of socialist productive relations can be observed in all socialist countries: it corresponds to the present level of development of productive forces, independently of the differences existing between various socialist countries.

Since the over-centralization of economic management and the concomitant system of centrally issued plan instructions and breakdown have been, though in different forms, common features of all European socialist countries, they may be considered as being in harmony with some earlier level of development of the productive forces. From the fact, however, that the reform of this system has everywhere been put on the order of the day, the conclusion must be drawn that what has been adequate not long ago is regarded as outdated in our days. This is how the relations of production gradually adjust themselves to the requirements raised by the development of productive forces.

### NEW ASPECTS OF THE LAW OF VALUE

From their researches relating to capitalism, Marx, Engels and Lenin drew the conclusion that after the socialization of the means of production producers would cease to exchange their products, and the amount of labour necessary for turning out the different products would cease to express their values, moreover, the individual labour would become part of social labour in an immediate way, instead of the former round-about way leading through the act of exchange. These ideas have not been confirmed by factual development. Even today our society is not able to assess its present and future needs with sufficient accuracy. It is not able to assess with satisfactory accuracy the total of disposable labour power, nor can it distribute this in perfect harmony with social needs; and the same applies to the total of embodied labour that can be set in motion by live labour.

Thus, no central plan could be perfect, and the economic mechanism that has hitherto served to implement it has even increased the difference between the actual distribution of total labour power and the one that would have been required by social needs. Accordingly, a considerable part of the products was, from the outset, obliged to take the form of commodities, in order to verify the social necessity of the labour embodied in them. As a result, it has happened that even under socialist conditions the labour embodied in a product could turn out to be more (or, in some cases, less) than the socially necessary labour. If this occurs under capitalism, most frequently, though not always, it causes the price of the commodity in question to rise or fall, and this change leads its producers to expand or reduce its output. In our country such adjustment of prices to the market situation was possible only to a very small extent (even today it is limited). Thus, the fact that a product embodied more or less labour than the socially necessary amount tended to produce effects and consequences different from what would happen under capitalism. One of the consequences used to be, e.g., that the commodity could not be sold at its fixed price, and large stocks of it were piled up or, inversely, it could not be had at the fixed price at all or only by privileged buyers. All this goes to prove that the law of value has always existed and operated in our economy. True, it hardly affected the prices directly—with the exception of the seasonal products of agriculture and a few fields accessible to the private sector. Our economic reform makes the effect of the law of value on prices more conspicuous. (Let me remark in parenthesis, that this effect is generally not very quick or immediate in modern capitalism either.) But in the long run the law of value has made its effect felt even before this, mainly in the form of distortions in production and distribution caused by prices standing opposed to the law becoming more and more intolerable. The law has made its effects felt also in the form of "seasonal sales" when formerly unsaleable products have been offered for sale at substantially reduced prices. Sooner or later, prices contradicting the law had to be adjusted. And, evidently, even without a price change, the growing stocks of some commodities and the shortage of others were, in themselves, bound to cause sooner or later some changes in their production.

As soon as it had been generally recognized that commodity production was taking place also under socialism, the operation of the law of value under socialist conditions was no more contested. But the exact place of the law in the socialist economy is still uncertain and vividly discussed. Without dwelling upon this debate and its uncertainties, it may be stated on the basis of what has been said that, in addition, the law of value is an expression of objective relationships that assert themselves in our economy, whether we notice them or not. As matters stand, it will be obviously more favourable, if, instead of keeping our eyes shut to the effects of the law of value, we take them into consideration and draw from them the proper conclusions as regards production, planning, pricing and in every other respect.

*

I started by stating that our endeavours aimed at deducing, from the political economy of socialism, the laws governing our present economic life serve more than the mere extension of our body of scientific knowledge: we wish to utilize our results in the practical building of socialism. I have tried to show that no practical conclusions can be drawn from these economic laws if we separate them from the actual problems of economic policy. I have made efforts to given an inkling of these problems and thereby *to characterize the nature and contents of the laws of socialist economy.*

I believe, that from what has been said here, some important inferences may also be drawn in relation to other problems not mentioned in this study. Thus, e.g., the question whether under socialism the character of labour is directly social, or whether its social character must still be verified indirectly, cannot be answered unless it is made unequivocally clear in what fields and in what manner the law of value asserts itself in our economy.

The discussions preceding the reform of our economic mechanism have acted as a ferment also in scientific research engaged in the political economy of socialism. Vivid debates have started around notions thought for a long time to be clear—and this is an unmistakable sign of a scientific advance. But, as in the discussions of economic policy many views rooted in prejudice had to be cleared away by arduous work before the new views could force their way, in the field of political economy also many an old and familiar thesis must be subjected to thorough criticism before notions more exactly reflecting reality can take their place. In my study I have tried to show how, in my opinion, this work should proceed. Its main objective should be to investigate the laws of the political economy of socialism in real life, in close connection with their practical application. Instead of restricting ourselves to registering how they appeared in past economic events as shown by statistics, we should also keep in mind how their manifestation and deliberate application present themselves as problems to be solved by economic policy and planning, in their efforts at controlling a socialist economy.

# LAWS AND CONTROL OF SOCIALIST ECONOMY

For several reasons it seems convenient to examine the laws of socialist economy by starting from the laws of capitalism. First, the long history of capitalism furnishes many a useful experience. Second, in our days capitalism prevails on a considerable part of the earth in various forms, from its more primitive types to the most advanced ones, so that the different stages of its development may be studied simultaneously. Third, we have in our hands the analysis of capitalism by Marx. Finally, it is a relevant fact that most of the now existing socialist societies had started to develop as heirs to capitalist societies and still bear certain features reminiscent of those of their ancestors, not only as regards the level of productive forces, but, as a consequence, also in their formal productive relations, as e.g., the organizational forms of wage-payments, of retail trade, of institutions, as well as in the formal expression of many other production relations.

## THE CLASSICS OF MARXISM ON THE CONTROL OF ECONOMY UNDER CAPITALISM AND SOCIALISM

Marx's presentation of the economic laws of capitalism is unique in its system, appositeness, wealth and versatility. According to him, the individual capitalist who, by his ownership of the means of production, is called upon to make economic decisions, is being led by the aim of maximizing his profits. This is the prime mover of his economic activities. But his efforts for this purpose necessarily conflict with similar efforts of other capitalists. The theatre of these conflicts is the market where their competition takes place and capitalist economy is regulated. Although capitalist production, as any other social production, has to meet also some needs of society as a whole, the individual capitalist is interested in meeting these needs only in so far as this will influence his profits.

Thus, in this system the decisive influences on production emanate, instead of from society itself or from any elected (or otherwise appointed) body, from individual capitalists whose leading motive is profit-making as opposed to meeting the needs of society. In other words, these needs are being met in a spontaneous way, independently of the will and consciousness of individuals, or at any rate not exactly in the way intended by them. The major internal relationships, that is the objective laws of capitalism, are not only independent of the aims and decisions of those active in the economy — this being a feature of all objective laws — but they usually assert themselves with a blind, elementary force, as a natural necessity. For us,

41

however, the relevant fact is that they unavoidably assert themselves and create certain equilibrium situations, proportions, etc. that are necessary from the point of view of society. In the words of Marx: ". . . the masses of products corresponding to the different needs require different and quantitatively determined masses of the total labour of society. That this *necessity* of the *distribution* of social labour in definite proportions cannot possibly be done away with by a *particular form* of social production but can only change the *form* in which it *appears*, is self-evident. No natural laws can be done away with. What can change, in historically different circumstances, is only the *form* in which these laws operate. And the form in which this proportional distribution of labour operates, in a state of society where the interconnection of social labour is manifested in the *private exchange* of the individual products of labour, is precisely the *exchange value* of these products."[1]

Thus, it is the assertion—through a multitude of individual exchanges— of the *value*, i.e. of the socially necessary amount of labour input incorporated in products, that regulates production and channels it into directions conforming to social needs. To quote Marx again: "If this division is proportional, then the products of various groups are sold at their values (at a later stage of development at their prices of production), or at prices which are certain modifications of these values or prices of production determined by general laws" . . . "so that not only is no more than the necessary labour-time used up for each specific commodity, but only the necessary proportional quantity of the total social labour-time is used up in the various groups." . . . "*The social need*, that is, the use-value on a social scale, appears here as a determining factor in the amount of total social labour-time which is expended in various specific spheres of production."[2] (*Italics are mine. I. F.*)

The situation here described is an ideal case of capitalism, that is, one which does not and cannot occur in reality. In fact, it assumes that social labour is being distributed among and within various branches of the economy in perfect conformity with social needs, and that, accordingly, the prices at which the products are sold exactly correspond to the value (or to some form of value modified by an economic law). This ideal situation never occurs, but the laws of capitalism, being tendencies asserting themselves like a natural force, work in the direction of creating a situation approaching it. Thus, *equilibrium* asserts itself as a constant fluctuation around an ideal equilibrium situation, and *proportionality* as a continuous change (and violation) of proportions.

But competition between producers—more exactly, the efforts of capitalists aimed at maximizing their individual profits leading to competition—not only ensures the assertion of value, but also involves a continuous expansion of production, its becoming cheaper, its improvement, as well as a continuous increase in labour productivity and in the technological level; in short, an upswing of productive forces unprecedented before the

[1] K. Marx and F. Engels: *Selected Works*, Vol. II. Moscow, 1954. Foreign Languages Publishing House. pp. 418–419.
[2] K. Marx: *Capital*, Vol. III. Moscow, 1966. Progress Publishers. pp. 635–636.

coming of capitalism. As Marx has shown, the development of productive forces leads to an increasing socialization of production. This again, increasingly postulates social interference with, and social control of economic activities. We have to face here an objective law, a commanding necessity, which has led in our days—among other things—to a situation where developed and developing capitalist countries experiment with methods aimed at a planned influencing and control of the economy by society. These experiments are, however, limited by capitalist private ownership extending over the best part of the means of production.

Before proceeding any further, let us take a glance at the laws of capitalist economy, some of which have been already mentioned. It should be clear from what has been said that although the value of commodities asserts itself through competition, this happens under the ever-changing conditions created by technological progress, the growing productivity of labour and the increasingly social character of production. All these are important and general processes asserting themselves as necessities, or rules. Therefore, one is justified in referring not only to the law of value, but also to the law of competition, to the law of increasing labour productivity and to other laws as well. Only we must never forget that these processes are not phenomena having an autonomous existence but necessarily deriving from certain relations characteristic of modern societies. The main features of these social relations are that, on the one hand, the means of production are the private property of certain individuals and, on the other hand, those who with their live labour actually convert these means of production into things useful and necessary for society do not own the means of production. This description of the relations existing in capitalist society is far from being complete, but it emphasises the most fundamental relations which exert the greatest influence on human activities and thus essentially determine the behaviour of social classes, movements within society. Economic laws assert themselves through human activity and this, in turn, depends on the given social relations. In a society where social relations are such that a small minority owns the means of production whereas the majority is deprived of these means, a deliberate social control of the national economy, that is, a fully conscious utilization of economic laws to the benefit of the community, is impossible.

Only a socialist revolution is able to make possible a deliberate social control of the economy. By taking the means of production into social ownership, society becomes able to weigh up objective social interrelations and rules, existing needs and disposable resources, to decide what needs shall be met and to what extent, in short, to direct social development in a planned way. The ideal case of capitalism described above can be confronted with the ideal case of socialism. To quote Marx again: "It is only where production is under the actual, predetermining control of society that the latter establishes a relation between the volume of social labour-time applied in producing definite articles, and the volume of the social want to be satisfied by these articles."[3]

[3] K. Marx: *Capital*, ibid. p. 187.

I wish to add that though achievement of the ideal case of socialism raises difficulties different from those that arise in approaching the ideal case of capitalism, *up to now* we have not succeeded in attaining the ideal situation in our society. Already, in our classical writings references may be found that such a situation can be attained only through gradual evolution, through deliberate, planned control. As Engels wrote, "with the seizing of the means of production by society, commodity production is done away with, and simultaneously, the mastery of the product over the producer. Anarchy in social production is replaced by systematic, definite organization" . . . "The whole sphere of the conditions of life which environ man, and which have hitherto ruled man, now comes under the dominion and control of man," . . . "only from that time will the social causes set in movement by him have, in the main and in a constantly growing measure, the results intended by him. It is the ascent of man from the kingdom of necessity to the kingdom of freedom."[4] And Lenin, referring to this statement of Engels, wrote in 1918 the following: ". . . by "leap" the teachers of socialism meant turning-points on a world-historical scale, and that leaps of this kind extended over decades and even longer periods."[5]

According to these teachings, after the victory of socialist revolution society will be able—in possession of the conditions of production, of the means of production—to record the social needs and the resources available for meeting these, first of all the available manpower, in order to use the latter in the most rational way. It follows that statistics, national accounting and checking will become much more important than they were earlier and the most important requirement will be to register the amount of available manpower and to allocate it most economically and rationally. From what has been said above, our classics also derived the conclusion that after the victory of socialist revolution, after the socialization of the means of production, there will be no need for labour to assert its usefulness through exchange value, as it will be allocated by society in a planned way, according to social needs. They were of the opinion—and I shall revert to this problem later—that the categories of commodity and money will cease to exist and that society will, of necessity, do its best to secure for its members the highest possible level of material and cultural welfare, together with the maximum possibility of developing and utilizing their capabilities.

From the substance of the Marxian approach it also followed that our classics did not forecast *in concreto* events subsequent to the victory of a socialist revolution. Neither could they foresee where and under what conditions would the proletarian revolution gain its first victory. From their observations they drew the conclusion that, most likely, this was bound to occur in the industrially advanced countries, and that its occurrence would be more or less simultaneous.

History has taught us a different lesson. Instead of a simultaneous victory in the industrially advanced countries of the world, proletarian revolution has seized power in a single country which was at a relatively low

[4] K. Marx and F. Engels: op. cit. pp. 140–141.
[5] V. I. Lenin: *Selected Works*, Vol. II. Moscow, 1949. Foreign Languages Publishing House. p. 729.

level of capitalist development and, at the same time, burdened with significant remnants of feudalism. And although—conforming to the Marxian teachings and their own programs — the leaders of this revolution have made efforts in order to introduce a planned control and management of social production and, accordingly, the socially organized distribution of products, it soon turned out that, under the given conditions, this could not be achieved. After the victory of the proletarian revolution in Russia society came, in fact, into possession of the means of production which had been at a relatively high level of development in industry and transport; it also nationalized the banks and landed property. But all this could not alter the fact that the great majority of the population was engaged in small-scale farming and was connected with capitalism only through the liens of trade and credit rather than of production. Under such conditions the assessing of social needs and allocation of resources, a planned organization of production and distribution proved to be impossible.

When preparing the October revolution, and particularly after it, Lenin —in conformity with the principles expounded here—emphasized the necessity of building up a system of national accounting and distribution. He had thought that, although the preponderant part of the economy consisted of small peasant farms, the weight and influence of the proletarian state would promote a relatively quick transition to socialist distribution that would take over the functions of trade.

But then came the 1921 Kronstadt mutiny and many visible manifestations of dissatisfaction among the peasantry. It was not scientific reasoning or discussion but the facts of life, the growing contradiction of interest between the working class and the peasantry which signalized that something was wrong. These facts postulated a change in production relations, and this change came about, putting the categories of money, commodity and trade in their rightful place again.

Since then, nobody has denied that the categories of commodity, money and trade existed—in a certain framework, in certain forms and having a certain content—in the Soviet Union and in the socialist countries in general. But vivid debates started, already in the early 1920's, in order to clear up the role, character and development trends of these categories in socialism. These debates are still going on after all these forty years. All the time they were connected with the actual requirements of economic development. There is no need to follow here the history of these discussions. Suffice to mention that, about 12–14 years ago they entered a new phase which has not yet been concluded. It was about this time that new views regarding the role and importance of the categories of value, commodity and money were expounded in various socialist countries. Let me remind the reader that the articles of Professor Liberman of Kharkov and those by Gy. Péter and others in our own country were published in these years, dealing with the necessity and expediency of certain changes in the system of economic control. It is not difficult to recognize, in the debates about the economic mechanism started a few years ago, a continuation of these earlier ideas.

In order to understand this debate I have to add something to what has been said above. In the *Critique of the Gotha Program* Marx wrote—and though differently worded, this corresponds to the above statements—that in a society relying on the common ownership of the means of production producers would not exchange their products, the labour spent on a product *would not appear in the form of value*, individual labour would immediately become part of social labour, instead of the former roundabout way. We have seen, however, that commodities and money exist even in a socialist society. Thus the question of how this practice can be reconciled with theory emerges with justification. But the problem of value involves more than this. Does the law of value exist and operate or not? Does it not follow from the existence of commodity, money and trade that it is the socially necessary labour embodied in the commodity that asserts itself in the price, developing in trade? Or does it assert itself in unsaleable stocks of some goods and in a shortage of others? Even in this case the law of value operates in some way, although further investigation is necessary to reveal how it works and, particularly, how it affects the allocation of social labour? Or is the situation such that society (or some body appointed for this purpose) regulates all economic activities according to the plan and also all prices are fixed in this way, having no effect on the allocation of labour? If so, the law of value does not operate.

Planning gradually gained ground in Soviet society and enabled the transition to the five-year plans. Collectivization of agriculture was practically completed in the years of the first five-year plan. The Soviet Union achieved brilliant economic victories and an unprecedented rate of growth. But planning could not be a substitute for organized distribution through trade. Instead, a complicated network of state-owned retail trade came into being. Nor were money or commodities abolished. Somehow the contradiction between Marxian theory and practical life, the everyday experience of the Soviet economy had to be cleared up. There was a national economic plan covering all major economic processes that could be successfully implemented; but at the same time, the categories of commodity, money and market have continued to exist; there was even a free market where peasants could sell what produce was left to them after compulsory deliveries. But, if production and the allocation of labour had been already drawn into the scope of planned control and organization by society, why and how did the categories of commodity, money and market continue to exist? And, conversely, did they not, by their very existence, affect production and the allocation of manpower, by asserting the law of value?

Long before World War II the idea emerged that a central plan was also able to allocate labour and other resources and to regulate production in this manner. In other words: by taking into account the productive forces available and the development objectives of society, such dynamic equilibrium situations and such proportions could be established by plan-instructions as would have developed if the law of value had been in operation, i.e., if prices corresponded to values. It is necessary to deal with this view because it has not yet been struck from the agenda and it emerged even in the form that it is consequently only in a planned economy that the law of value can be enforced.

However, the contradiction outlined cannot be solved in this manner,

capitalist conditions. What they called value cannot be determined by a central organ, starting from the average labour actually used; it can develop only in the market. If, in other words, we accept that the average labour used is identical with value, then we must also take it for granted that social labour has been globally allocated in accordance with social needs, But if such allocation can be attained, then the insertion of value, price and money is superfluous and senseless. Thus, the eclectic concept that became dominant did not correspond to the Marxian concept.

This concept has been shaken by the facts themselves. The economies of socialist countries developed, the living standards of their population steadily increased from year to year — apart from a very few exceptional periods—but at the back of this development, in general very successful, convincingly proving the superiority of socialist economy, there were phenomena that caused concern because they seemed to indicate that social control was not quite perfect. Such phenomena were to be found in almost all socialist countries, but let us deal here only with those observed in Hungary. (As a further restriction, we leave out of account the years before the counter-revolution when, as is known, we made great mistakes also in economic policy.)

First: after the counter-revolution of 1956 national income has been growing steadily but this growth has been far less even than could have been expected under conditions of planned development. In 1960 the growth rate was more than 10 per cent, but it was less than 2 per cent in 1965. Second: the part of national income used for accumulation showed even greater fluctuations: in 1960 it rose from the previous year by 35 per cent, while in 1965 it declined by 15 per cent. Third: in general, the part of accumulation appearing as the increment of circulating assets (essentially stocks of finished goods) was greater (often by very much) than was planned. For example, in each year between 1961 and 1964, the annual increment of circulating assets amounted to more than 50 per cent of the increase in fixed assets. Fourth: it happened repeatedly that the total of annual consumption and accumulation exceeded the national income generated in the same year, i.e., that the foreign indebtedness of the country increased. Fifth: although the technological level of production, as well as the productivity of industrial labour, increased from year to year, our lag behind several advanced countries, among them many socialist ones, seemed to increase instead of diminishing. Sixth: we generally fulfilled and even over-fulfilled our production plans, but some, often extremely important, parts of the plans remained unfulfilled. Seventh: the efficiency of our economic activity has diminished in recent years, i.e. the volume of means used in production has grown at a higher rate than the volume of national income produced.

These are the facts characteristic of our whole economy which have shaken the dominant view. If we look at the details of the economy instead of the whole, we will find many irrationalities, waste, deficiencies and phenomena which run counter to the plans. The quality of our products, either investment goods or consumer goods, is often not satisfactory. It happens that important goods which are in demand and are or can be produced in our country, cannot be found on the market and also that such goods are turned out which are not needed by anybody. It can be not infrequently shown that production is badly organized and costly. From all this it follows that although production is carried on in this country in a socially controlled manner relying on a central plan, both the plan and the social control are far from being perfect.

Nor is the picture satisfactory that emerges if the results in economic and technological development are compared with those in some advanced capitalist countries. And this is not only of theoretical interest but—in view of the competition between the two systems—of great political and practical importance.

But the facts, experiences as well as considerations and investigations associated with them, did not call attention only to these deficiencies. They indicated unequivocally that the prevailing system of planning and management itself diminishes the efficiency of the economy and the rate of growth. This system was born under such domestic and international political and economic conditions – analysis of which would not be in place here – which, by their nature, have favoured overcentralization and bureaucratism. Overcentralization hindered local initiative, thus weakening one of the most important motive forces of society. With this situation, once recognized, we could not remain satisfied. The movement for the reform of the economic mechanism has started, as it did in some other socialist countries as well. The slogan of this movement was everywhere that centralization must be diminished and greater autonomy of local authorities and enterprises, providing favourable conditions for individual initiative, must be substituted for central plan-instructions.

### REFORM OF THE ECONOMIC MECHANISM AND THE LAWS OF SOCIALIST ECONOMY

Initially it seemed that the reform of the economic mechanism would not touch the theoretical problems of a socialist economy. It turned out, however, that a revision of practice necessitates also revision of its theoretical foundations. We have seen that, in relation to our present society theory partly accepted, partly discarded what Marx had said about a socialist society. According to this concept, socially necessary labour equalled the average labour spent on turning out a product; in other words, the total labour used for turning out the total quantity of a product was regarded as *necessary labour*. From this, theory has concluded that planned social control, in short, the national economic plan, allocates total labour exactly in harmony with social needs, as Marx said about socialism.

But already Andersen has written the story of how the nakedness of the emperor became revealed, in vain did the host of courtiers allege he had beautiful clothes on. Similarly, the shortcomings of our plans have become manifest. As a matter of fact, reform of the economic mechanism is necessary also because in our country some products are being turned out—mostly without violating the plan—that are superfluous, are unsaleable (unsaleable at least at their production costs); because it happens again here that labour, raw materials or other resources of society are wasted; because there are innumerable examples of the fact that social control of the economy is not yet sufficiently effective in our country, that much of what is planned does not materialize, whereas things happen that were not planned.

Thus, we have to abandon the tacitly or expressly accepted view that the definition by Marx, which we called above the ideal case of socialism, is *fully applicable* to our present society. It would be absurd to say that in this country planned control of production is not asserted, but it would be equally absurd to say that our plans secure complete harmony between social needs and the amount of social labour spent on their satisfaction. On the whole, development has been good and satisfactory, but many objectives which we set ourselves have not been attained. We still cannot measure or assess scientifically what social needs really exist, nor the social labour really necessary and available for their satisfaction, nor can we scientifically allocate social labour in perfect harmony with social needs. In other words, although in this country there is planned control of economy, this is not quite identical with what Marx meant by the term.

We cannot avoid the conclusion that planned control of production and other processes embracing the whole economy are an extremely difficult and complicated task, the solution of which assumes a vast body of knowledge. Since we are not in possession of this knowledge to the required extent, we can not yet solve the task in a satisfactory way. Thus, in the sense in which the term was used by Marx, production is *not* under the planned control of society. True, we might say that the building of socialism has not yet been completed; even if we did not yet clarify what is still lacking, it is fairly obvious that our society, including its system of economic control, must be raised to a higher level. And Marx, when forecasting the situation in a socialist economy, generally assumed a higher level of development than our present one. To this higher level relates also his statement that in a society based on social ownership of the means of production the labour spent on products will not take the form of value, i.e., an objective property of these products, since individual labour will immediately become part of total labour. It is this higher level of development that the quoted statement of Engels refers to, and so do some similar statements of Lenin. True, the wording Marx and Engels have used several times may make us believe that planned control in its perfect state can be achieved at one stroke, as a sudden leap, with the socialization of the means of production. But already Lenin taught, as we have seen, that this leap might take a long time.

The leap, indeed, must take at least several decades. Once this has been understood, there is no more need to invest societies with phantastic properties. On the contrary, strengthened by the reassuring consciousness of our really great achievements, we must be able to put up with some unsavoury facts. In our present society not all production serves the most efficient satisfaction of social needs. The domination of products over producers has not yet completely ceased. Not all kinds of anarchy and spontaneity have been as yet supplanted by planned, organized rational activity. Not every kind of individual labour is immediately becoming part of total social labour. We are not yet in a position to apply the laws of our own social activity with full competence.

Does this mean that what Marx, Engels and Lenin said about socialism must be discarded? Evidently not. Our classics have deduced from the development trends known to them some, not too many, well-founded and scientifically justified general theses about what a "mature" socialist society would look like. They cannot be blamed if, in the past decades, we prematurely tried to apply *all* these theses simultanously, that is, partly in an incorrect manner, to our own society. Instead, we should draw from this experience the conclusion that the laws of our present socialist economy must be established by ourselves, relying on the analysis of our own observations. At what stage are we now in recognizing these laws and in applying them to the control of our economy?

Our textbooks enumerate a considerable number of laws of socialist economy. To mention only the most important ones: the fundamental economic law of socialism, the law of planned proportionate development, the law of distribution according to work performed, the law of the continuous increase of labour productivity. To these the same applies as to the laws of capitalism mentioned above. We saw that the latter were not phenomena having an autonomous existence, they were derived necessarily from capitalist social relations. Similarly, the laws of socialist economy derive from socialist social relations. They constitute an interdependent system since they all spring from the same soil. They indicate important, general processes which assert themselves of necessity and, therefore, they justly bear the name of a law. From these laws, however, we can learn only how the processes are being *regularly* reproduced. We cannot reveal new interrelations by attributing to some law or other, or to a system of laws, a more or less independent existence, e.g., by alleging that production in our country is regulated by the law of the planned proportionate development of the socialist economy, or by the system of economic laws of socialism. No conclusion whatever can be deduced from the names or the wording of these laws as to the mode of their application and utilization, that is, as to what *we* have really to do. We have to remember that even in socialism economic laws assert themselves through the activities of men, of the masses; and that these activities are also here rooted in social and economic relations. Accordingly, it is these relations that must be studied extensively and from different aspects, in order to be able to find out what objectives can be correctly set for ourselves and with what measures these can be attained. It is a merit of our Party that, when preparing the reform of the economic mechanism, it proceeded precisely in this manner. The existing relations were subjected to analysis and lessons were drawn from the analysis. The most important of these conclusions provide certain orientation as to the *laws and the control* of our socialist economy at the present level of its development.

First, it can be stated that according to all experience hitherto gained, the activity of all units of economic activity *cannot be rationally regulated from a single centre*. Economic decisions can be correctly taken only where the needed *local and professional knowledge* is greatest. Thus, there are economic decisions which should be taken in a workshop and others which must be taken in the Central Committee of the Party. We have overcentralized our economic management, now we have to *decentralize* it. As a matter of fact, the attempt to regulate everything from a single centre—quite apart from its practical impossibility—is not only irrational from an economic point of view but also violates the political principle of *democratic centralism*. Central regulation frequently interferes with the autonomy of enterprises and local bodies in an irrational and incorrect manner, limiting their initiative and braking their development. It may be expected with some justification that the reform, by changing these circumstances, will accelerate economic growth.

Second, it may be stated that *certain decisions must be taken centrally*. This is in harmony with the recognition formulated in the preceding paragraph. As soon as the decisive part of the means of production is in public ownership, there must be a body to direct development according to these interests. (It must be noted that all means of production have not been socialized at a single stroke; neither here nor elsewhere.) Amidst our efforts to direct everything from the centre, we have neglected the scientific investigation of the most important problem, namely, how can we decide *what* is required by the interests of society as a whole, how should central decisions be prepared, what decisions should be centrally taken and how should these decisions be implemented. To some extent, even the role in economic control of the body representing the universal interests of society, i.e. the Party, was weakened. Now we must make amends for having violated this law. The law must be utilized by improving the preparation of decisions and the process of decision-making as regards the most important problems of economic control.

Thirdly, central economic decisions must be enforced upon enterprises and local bodies in such a way as to interfere least with their autonomy and initiative, that is, *by means of economic regulators indirectly influencing their activities*, rather than by direct instructions. A wide range of experience proves in the most varied fields of the economy—most conspicuously perhaps in agricultural production and in the labour supply of coal mining—that our aims can be much more efficiently attained by economic measures than by instructions or any number of plan indicators issued to enterprises. There is a whole armoury available to society for influencing the economy. This does not, of course, preclude that some central decisions should be enforced by decrees—where careful consideration shows that this is the most expedient or perhaps the only possible way. The activity of our governmental bodies connected with the reform is aimed today at a correct application of this rule.

Fourthly, it can be stated that a substitution of economic methods for control by central plan or central instructions assumes, or rather requires, an *expansion of commodity and money relations*. If, in other words, the plan instructions cease to link the activities of individual enterprises, they must be connected with one another by means of a *market* where they appear as buyers and sellers, as contracting parties; a market where they can sell their products as commodities and buy the necessary goods as commodities. Central control must and can assert itself on the market with the aid of various economic measures in the sphere of price policy, credit policy, taxes, customs duties, etc. The government decrees falling within the scope of the reform of economic mechanism issued to-date show that our competent bodies make efforts to apply also this rule in a correct manner.

Fifthly, a system of economic mechanism built upon a decentralization of economic decisions, a substitution of indirect influencing for direct instructions, an expansion of commodity and money relations, and the regulative functions of the market, necessarily assumes also that some of the *prices* should depend on the market, on free agreement of buyers and sellers. Certain prices can, and, owing to various circumstances must, be centrally regulated, but central regulation of all prices—unless we assume such perfect information of the central organ as has been proved impossible—would in practice determine the amount of demand for each individual product and thereby prevent production from adapting itself to demand. Such rigidity of prices would inevitably lead to disturbances. It would involve —despite contrary intentions—the central authority deciding questions where correct decision cannot be taken centrally. After all, if the distribution of global social labour is not in harmony with social needs and adjustments become necessary, then either the price changes will readjust production (provided prices are permitted to change according to the market situation) or some other processes will take over this function. This means that the labour spent on products appears also in our society in the form of value and, as a tendency, also the law of value asserts itself. At the present stage of development this is the situation and the same tendency seems to emerge as a factor in further development. This law must and can partly be taken into account in the course of price regulation connected with the reform; its further application raises many, as yet unsolved, problems and requires much study and work.

These are the most important conclusions concerning the laws and control of socialist economy that can be drawn from the reform of the economic mechanism and related considerations. Of course, I could not deal with many important problems and with many important aspects of the problems here discussed. That would have gone beyond the scope of this study. Finally, I should like to draw some futher conclusions from what has been presented.

For the time being and in the foreseeable future we shall not be in a position to create, exclusively by means of planned social control, a full harmony between the quantities of social labour used for the production of the various products and the volume of social needs to be satisfied by these products. Nor is there any proof that development would proceed in this direction. We are compelled and, as far as we can judge today, we shall be compelled for some time to avail ourselves of the help of commodity, money and market relations in order to ensure a correct distribution of the resources available to society. Therefore, we must study and improve the application of these means and of the law of value.

But in the meantime we must make every effort to develop and improve planned social control of production. By relying on an improved system of statistics, national accounting and information, by using contemporary mathematical methods and other scientific devices, we must closely follow the progress of science and technology and the possibilities and requirements deriving from them in connection with raising production, national income and the general welfare of our society, as well as with the development of international relations in the fields of politics, economy, technology and general education, together with the most important implications of these. It is on these grounds that social needs and the possibilities of meeting them must be assessed, confronted and ranked. But to meet this challenge, the system and methods of social decision-making must be raised to a higher level.

With the reform of our economic mechanism we have started on the way of improving the system of economic control and management. Indefatigably developing and improving the elements and the whole system of this control, we shall apply it with growing competence. It is in this way that we can master the application of the laws governing our social development, and become more and more capable of deliberately controlling our own fate.

# PRINCIPAL FEATURES OF THE NEW ECONOMIC MECHANISM IN HUNGARY

## ON SOME BASIC FEATURES OF THE NEW SYSTEM

When elaborating our new system, we were led by the endeavour, similarly to other socialist countries, to increase the efficiency of our planning and of our economic activities, with a view to accelerating the rate of development. The measures we have taken or are planning to take for that purpose are, in part, similar to those in other socialist countries; in part, however, they are characteristic of our reform only.

Our decisions had been preceded by research studies, detailed and comprehensive discussions regarding several not quite satisfactory aspects and phenomena of our economic development. These studies and discussions revealed a number of causes of these deficiencies and threw up many reasonable propositions for their elimination. From all these efforts, *some generally accepted conclusions* have resulted, which have supplied a *basis for our decisions*: the most important ones may be summarized as follows.

1. In the system of planning and economic control that we have hitherto applied, industrial, commercial, etc. enterprises were obliged to observe a larger or smaller number of so-called *plan indicators*, each setting some target to be attained or a limit to be observed. These indicators were, in some way or other, derived from the national economic plan but were mostly, from the nature of things, only indirectly related to the latter. They limited the scope of decision of enterprise leaders, restricted their chances of, and their inclination to, initiative, their ambitions and sense of responsibility. The indicators did not and, in fact, could not reckon with the local endowments and requirements of the enterprises and, therefore, did not help and often even hindered the choice of the most favourable, economically most efficient solutions, i.e. the most rational utilization of available resources.

2. The *essential task* of a national economic plan is to provide, for a given society, the quickest and most favourable material and cultural development attainable under prevailing conditions. Now, such a course of development is only realizable if there are wide paths open for developing initiative, for carrying out rational local decisions. Therefore we need not, and even must not, give enterprises and other local organs any particularly detailed prescriptions concerning their activities. The national economic plan must provide for such main proportions as would permit the most favourable development, whereas the system of economic control and management has to ensure, first, the realization of these proportions, second, complete freedom and responsibility of decisions—in a framework of legal rules—on the part of competent leaders who are sufficiently aware of the

local possibilities and conditions, third, that a market controlled mainly, though not exclusively, by means of economic regulators and a system of incentives acting on individuals should correctly orientate those leaders towards the genuine needs of society as a whole.

3. The national economic plan establishes the main objectives of the national economy ensuring the most favourable material and cultural development of society, and determines the allocation of resources available for their realization. In the new system of national economic control *this function of the plan is combined with the function of the socialist market.* This combination makes it possible to obtain a truer picture of the partial processes going on in the economy, about the perpetually changing needs of society and, especially, of individal consumers, than we were able to obtain in the past. This market will not be simply the theatre for an unlimited assertion of spontaneous processes; it will be affected by economic and administrative regulators serving to realize the major objectives laid down in the national economic plan. A more extensive reliance on the market within the system of economic control does not contradict the basic principle of central planning and control; on the contrary, it enhances the efficiency of the latter.

Adequate operation of such a market mechanism presupposes among other things, the creation of a *price system* where the relative prices of products and services are roughly proportionate to the amounts of socially necessary labour embodied in them. At the same time, however, prices must adapt themselves to the domestic, or, in some cases, even to the international market situation much more flexibly than they did in the past. In other words, prices have not only to *influence* the market situation, but also to *reflect*—at least to a limited extent—the conditions prevailing on the market, the relation of supply and demand and, in the last resort, the requirements of society. This latter function of prices, as an impulse emanating from the market, should be strong enough to induce, when necessary, deliberate deviations from the plan in certain respects. This market will be correctly orientated only when producers and sellers do not hold monopolistic positions or if they cannot use such positions for eliminating the regulatory function that has to be exerted by the needs of society.

Another important precondition for creating such a market is the elaboration of a system of partly economic, partly administrative *regulators* (with a preponderance of the former), that would channel the activity of all economic units in such directions of development and towards such proportions in the allocation of resources as are favourable for implementing the national economic plan. This system of regulators must orientate economic units in any new situation on what they have to do in conformity with what society expects from them. The national economic plan, the economic regulators, the central measures and legal rules issued by the state, the ways of utilizing centralized financial means as prescribed by the state: all these together create the economic environment in which enterprises have to operate. Contrary to the former situation where it was, in the main, by the plan indicators that enterprises had been informed on what they had to do, and unlike the economic reforms introduced or under implementation in some socialist countries, in our new system the enterprises are no longer given any numerically determined plan targets, tasks or indicators whatever. To this, exceptions occur only in cases where exceptional circumstances justify them.

4. We hope to achieve the objective of using the system of personal incentives preponderantly in the service of meeting the needs of society by relying mainly on the *interests associated with the enterprise profits*. By this we mean that the leaders and the whole collective of each enterprise will be interested in attaining the highest possible profit. If domestic and international competition prevents producers and sellers from exploiting monopolistic positions in the market, they will not be able to raise prices and obtain higher profits in this way. They must then attempt to reduce their costs, improve the quality of products, develop new processes of manufacturing and new kinds of manufactures, improve their organization and their product pattern, and so on. Whichever of these methods they apply—alone or in combination · they will simultaneously promote improved or more efficient ways of meeting the needs of society.

From the foregoing it also follows that the economic reforms undertaken in various socialist countries, though having related features, do rather differ in a number of others. Differences between the various national systems of economic control are likely to grow as a result of the reforms. We attach special importance to preventing such differences from reacting, in any field or in any form, unfavourably on the vigorous development of our economic relations with these countries.

*Our reform was introduced on January 1st, 1968.* Some steps in the direction of the new system were made earlier but they were only of a preparatory character. We were of the opinion that practically all major changes had to be introduced simultaneously, in order to attain the combined effect expected from them. It has been already said that enterprises are informed about their tasks by the market, by the economic regulators and by government decrees. All these had, accordingly, to be inaugurated simultaneously, and the preparation of all this could not be finished before the date mentioned. Also the various related tasks of organization, information and professional training required time.

Even so, the simultaneous introduction of all elements of the system in January, 1968, does not and, obviously, cannot mean that the effects of the reform will present themselves at once or even in a short time. Thus, for instance, the sum of the profits attained by a given enterprise in 1968 will be known only at the beginning of 1969, so that decisions on their utilization cannot be made before this. Moreover, 1968 is the third year of our current five-year plan; this also indicates that we could not begin all things afresh. The years 1968–1970 we consider as a period of introduction that will permit the consequences of the new system gradually to unfold.

In what follows I shall attempt to describe this new system, not in its totality (e.g., I do not deal with agriculture or certain other questions) but in its larger context, with respect to the major objectives to be attained and the intended functioning of the system, in the hope of being able to give a picture of such of its features as we consider most important.

The leading party and state bodies called upon to control the national economy in a planned way must evidently, also under the new system, rely on a national economic plan as the basis for control, and they must be able to have at their disposal the means necessary for the plan's implementation. These requirements, however, will be modified with regard to certain features.

1. In the future the national economic plan will contain *considerably fewer details* than before. It must contain, however, also in the future the major social, economic and technological objectives of development, the progressive tendencies of economic growth, the rate of this growth, the main structural proportions of the national economy and their planned changes. Moreover, the plan must establish, in conformity with its objectives, the major economic regulators and the guiding principles of their application.

National economic plans cover *periods of various length*: generally they are elaborated for one year, five and fifteen years. Of these, the first type was formerly preponderant in economic control and management; the five-year plan had mainly informative functions. In the future, *the five-year plan will be the decisive tool* of central economic control; most economic regulators being directly associated with it. In order to increase their reliability, we want our national economic plans to have a more sound foundation than they used to have. One of the methods applied for this purpose consists in giving a greater role to the long-term (15–20 year) plans; this involves the necessity of elaborating their methodology in time, in order to be able to establish our next five-year plan within the perspective of some long-term plan. Five-year plans must, also in the future, be approved by Parliament. Annual plans are approved by the government; they serve mainly as a basis for the operative economic control exerted by the latter. The national economic plan is broken down only by branches: it does not contain targets for any individual organization.

2. The five-year and long-term plans will increasingly rely on *economic and technical conceptions* elaborated by scientific methods. Such conceptions must generally rely on knowledge of the most up-to-date technology, and must take into consideration the endowments of our country as well as the requirements of economic efficiency.

Economic and technical conceptions are elaborated for development tasks of various scope and importance, at correspondingly higher or lower levels of various organizations. Such conceptions must then be brought into relation with one another and coordinated accordingly. Conceptions relating to a branch of national economy must, in general, be elaborated by the competent ministry or some other national authority; conceptions of national importance and those covering several branches belong to the competence of the National Board of Technical Development. (The latter is a consultative organ of the government, participating in the preparation of decisions of economic policy.)

3. Also *the role and tasks of the ministries and other national authorities are modified* by the new system. Formerly, their function consisted mainly

in giving concrete instructions to the branches and enterprises under their supervision. In the future their tasks will be considerably shifted towards general economic control. They will take part, mainly in respect of the fields supervised by them, in the preparation of decision of central economic policy, of the national economic plan and of the means necessary for its implementation; of course, they will continue their administrative functions connected with supervising enterprises belonging to their sphere of competence.

Accordingly, government decrees issued on the tasks and competence of the various ministries prescribe, as a rule—apart from participation in the preparation of economico-political decisions, of the plan and of the economic regulators—also some special tasks in connection with the fields to be supervised. Thus, for instance, the minister of construction and urban development has to assert the particular points of view connected with architecture, construction, production of building materials, and is responsible for working out the national policies on urban development, housing and communal services. The minister of home trade takes part in the preparation of decisions regarding the price system and consumer prices, maintains the unity of home trade policy extending to both state-owned and cooperative trading units. The National Office of Materials and Prices elaborates the propositions and guiding principles in the field of price policy and implements measures concerning the regulation of trade in certain production goods. The minister of foreign trade is responsible for elaborating and declaring foreign-trade policy and for coordinating all foreign-trade activities. The minister of labour elaborates, among other things, the wage rates, proposals concerning wage policy aimed at raising the standard of living, directs and assists the activity of local councils in the field of labour supply and employment. The minister of finance prepares proposals regarding the state budget and the system of financial regulators with the aim of achieving the objectives of economic policy. The president of the National Planning Office elaborates proposals regarding the national economic plan, coordinates the work of all planning agencies and deals with the international coordination of plans between socialist countries.

Since the new type of economic control requires a smaller staff, the ministries are able to fulfil their tasks with the aid of a personnel reduced by 30 per cent (i.e. by about 2,000 persons).

4. Evidently, *the considerable increase in enterprise autonomy* and the wider competence of enterprise executives *do not interfere with their dependence on the state as the owner of enterprises*. The autonomy is expressed, among other things, in the right of disposition of the enterprises over their assets (within the limits set by legal rules); in that they are responsible for their obligations up to the amount of these assets, and in that their assets cannot be withdrawn from them. On the other hand, their dependence on the state is reflected in principles which stipulate that enterprises can be founded only by a minister or leader of a national authority or by the executive committee of a local council, and that the founder has the right to determine the sphere of activity of the enterprise, as well as to appoint and discharge its director and deputy director(s). Moreover, the founder may

liquidate the enterprise if its activity is no longer needed by the national economy, if its profitable operation cannot be continued, or if the activity in question can be pursued more economically by another enterprise. Exceptionally, when national economic interests make it necessary, the founder may also order the reorganization of an enterprise. The founder may link up several enterprises under a trust. A trust can issue instructions to the enterprises belonging to it, but the latter have their own accountancy. (The number of trusts remaining in existence after January 1st, 1968, is very small.) The founder has also the right and obligation critically to evaluate activities of the enterprise as a whole and the work performed by the manager and his deputies, as well as to take decisions regarding their salaries and premia. The Council of Ministers may rule that certain activities can be pursued only with special permission. Thus, permission of the minister of foreign trade is necessary for foreign-trade activities.

Apart from these expressions of dependence, *the director decides autonomously in matters concerning the enterprise on his own personal responsibility.* Thus, he approves the plan of the enterprise, the measures aimed at technological development, he decides on the product pattern, on the introduction of new articles, on the utilization of the enterprise's own resources for development purposes, on investments, on the raising of credits, etc. Several enterprises may form, under a special contract, a union in the framework of which the participants preserve full autonomy; an enterprise may belong to several unions. Enterprises can found common undertakings.

The autonomy of the director is emphasized also by a principle which stipulates that the founder can instruct an enterprise to pursue a determined kind of activity only in those exceptional cases when this is required in order to achieve a task connected with national defence or to meet a foreign-trade obligation undertaken by the government. In such cases, however, the founder must take care that obeying such instructions should not cause economic damage to the enterprise; and eventual damage must be compensated in some way or another.

5. We have seen that the direct, administrative control of enterprises by plan indicators and plan directives issued by the ministries has ceased after January 1st, 1968. Some other kinds of administrative regulators, however, will play a certain role in economic control. These were referred to already above, but later on we shall deal with them in the context of, e.g. trade in production goods and foreign trade. Still, basically the tools applied by the party and state leadership in order to control the economy in the interest of the national plan will be *economic regulators acting either directly or, in most cases, indirectly.* These economic regulators are extremely diversified, and may be classified variously according to their nature, field of application or other points of view. If we keep in view the main tools for realizing the objectives of economic policy, it is convenient to distinguish the following six groups.

To the *first* group belong the means of *price policy.* These are applied by the government with reference to both producer and consumer prices, although the ways of application are different, since also the objectives to be achieved in these fields differ in most respects. As regards *prices of consumer goods and services*, it is absolutely necessary to ensure a high degree of general stability, in spite of changes, in both directions, of the prices affecting a not unimportant group of commodities. The requirement of general stability evidently puts a limit upon the extent to which such prices can be expected to affect demand and supply. The situation is different with *producer prices* which have to play, according to our intentions, an important role in economic control. Even in their case there will be fixed maximum prices or such as can move only between fixed upper and lower limits; and the prices of the most important raw materials will be fixed or regulated centrally. On the other hand, however, our intention is to let the conditions of the market, of supply and demand or, more precisely, the factors affecting these to assert themselves to a wide extent; accordingly, the price movements affecting a great part of production goods will be left to free agreement between sellers and purchasers. By these measures, prices are intended to influence enterprises in such a way that the latter—in attempting to maximize their profits—shall act rationally also from the point of view of society, i.e., employ social labour economically and turn out commodities meeting genuine social needs. Here, however, so many contradictory points of view and interest emerge that we can only hope for a complete achievement of, or even a satisfactory approach to, this objective as a result of further development and improvement in the price mechanism that may take a couple of years. We intend to elaborate also a long-term plan of price development in harmony with, and as a part of, the national economic plan. This price plan would serve both as a prognosis and as a basis for future price measures.

The *second* important group comprises tools serving *policy regarding the development of personal incomes*. These extend to the working people as a whole, i.e., not only to workers and employees of enterprises, but also to cooperative members and to those employed by public (budgetary) bodies and institutions. Though the enterprises have, within the general regulations, considerable freedom to determine individual incomes, the state provides that the aggregate of personal incomes should not increase abruptly and unexpectedly. This will be ensured partly with the aid of regulators influencing the utilization of enterprise incomes and partly by appropriations of the state budget limiting the expenditure of each body and institution.

The *third* group belongs to the field of *investment policy*. In the new system a considerable and increasing part of investments will be realized as a result of autonomous enterprise decisions. In this field the state will assert its own point of view on investment policy mainly by means of credit policy. But, in addition, the state has also other means of influencing decisively the main tendencies of development, namely, by centrally taken decisions regarding the largest investment projects, by the determination of a set of lump sums, each of which will be used for investments serving a special purpose[1] and, finally, by financing certain investments out of the state budget.

[1] Cf. p. 71.

The *fourth* group covers the means of *credit policy*. By the granting of credits, banks influence production, turnover, consumption, investments and foreign trade. *Short-term* credits may be granted, as a rule, to every creditworthy enterprise, on any kind of saleable production and for any other purpose of normal, justifiable utilization, including the financing of any circulation proceeding at a normal pace. Before granting *medium-term* credits, however, the expected income of the development fund of the enterprise (fed by parts of profits and depreciation allowances serving this purpose), and also the interests of the national economy as a whole are taken into account. The condition for granting *long-term* credits is that production expected from the investment in question must ensure at least the amount of profits (and their ratio to invested means) prescribed by the "Directives of Credit Policy". The banks pursue a selective credit policy by varying credit conditions; they promote certain enterprise activities which they deem useful and hinder others which they deem inexpedient. They make efforts to promote improvements in the supply offered by producers, e.g., the supply of such consumer goods as are most in demand, the extension of services offered to the population, etc. They give preference to investments promising highest efficiency and quickest returns. In its turn, however, the credit policy of the banks is, in its main features, prescribed by the government and thus becomes another tool of planned economic control.

The *fifth* group includes the means of *foreign-trade policy*. Here belong measures determining the foreign-exchange multiplier, customs duties, the deposits to be made in certain cases when an enterprise imports investment goods for its own use, state refunds on exports, etc. As regards their operation and effects, these economic regulators are difficult to separate from other forms of state control. They are, in other words, more or less interwoven with measures of an administrative nature as, e.g., the issuing of permits regarding foreign-trade transactions, or the fixing of export and import quotas in the framework of regulating trade in production goods. All these together enable the state to control the commodity pattern and direction of foreign trade.

Finally, the *sixth* group includes the means of *fiscal and budgetary policy* of the state, such as taxes, fees, charges, etc. It is through them that the state ensures the flow of a definite part of net social income into the state budget in such a way that their total amount should cover expenditures incurred by the state (in respect of national defence, salaries of state employees, pensions, family allowances, maternity and other assistance as well as payments made on investments, refunds, subsidies, and so on). With the aid of this group of measures the state can stimulate economic units to increase efficiency, to use their capacities to an optimum extent, etc. By means of them the state can thus influence and direct the national economy in various ways and in many fields; in the first place, however, they act most efficaciously on the distribution of incomes and on the development of consumption.

With the aid of instruments applied in the fields of price and wage policies and of investment, foreign-trade, credit and budgetary policies, the state is in a position to regulate effectively the inflow of money into the national economy and the utilization of all available resources. It can ensure the undisturbed continuity of extended reproduction and, in some decisive respects, creates and maintains equilibrium situations important for the national economy. Among the latter, especially important are: equilibrium between the purchasing power of the population and the supply of commodities and services, equilibrium of the country's balance of payments, and equilibrium of the state budget.


## ENSURING CONTINUITY OF EXTENDED REPRODUCTION

**1.** One of the decisive conditions for continuous production is its undisturbed supply with raw materials, fuel, power, intermediate goods, equipment or, in a word, with production goods. In this field, a radical change has come about by substituting for the former system of *allocations* based on the so-called "plan of supply with materials and technological equipment" (and on its breakdown by enterprises) *trade* in production goods relying on direct market relations between enterprises. The officially regulated procedures and deadlines for giving and accepting orders by enterprises are no longer valid. The producing enterprise can freely decide on whether it will sell its products to a processing enterprise or to a trading company or to final consumers. Of course, the users are similarly free to choose between the possibilities of purchasing from a home producer, from the trade or, eventually—within the regulations concerning foreign trade and the allocation of foreign exchange—from abroad. Also administrative prescriptions regarding purchases made by budgetary organs have been cancelled; of course, such expenditure will continue to be limited by budget appropriations.

*Certain administrative regulations will continue to exist*, affecting a few products specially important for domestic supply or for foreign trade, or in cases where market tensions must be mitigated. One type of such regulation more or less corresponds to the former system of centralized stocks and allocations (at present, this is applied only to meat and grain), another consists in establishing quotas (most of these are import or export quotas affecting, at present, about 20 commodities on both sides). The sphere of commodities affected by such regulations is likely to be reduced after some time.

As far as can be judged from various preliminary estimates and random samples, it seems that, at least in respect of the first quarter of 1968, enterprises had no difficulties about the supply of production goods. True, they attempted to accumulate as early as 1967, some reserves in certain goods difficult to obtain; other needs were ensured by giving orders covering a shorter or longer period, according to the nature of their production, but at least for the first quarter of 1968.

Surveys made in various industrial enterprises seem to suggest that, in spite of the transitional character of this year, industrial output in 1968 will grow at a fairly normal rate, by about five per cent on the average.

2. Another decisive condition for undisturbed continuity of production is an adequate *supply of labour*. The present situation may be characterized by a scarcity (especially in Budapest) of certain kinds of qualified labour as well as unskilled workers, and by minor surpluses in other kinds, especially in the countryside. Radical changes are not likely to occur even under the new system, at least not in the near future. The new Code of Labour approved by Parliament in September, 1967, facilitated the termination of employment on the part of either the employee or the employer. On the basis of analyses so far made it seems that for enterprises, especially those operating in Budapest, to produce the required supply of labour causes far more difficulty than to find employment for redundant labour. Accordingly, many enterprises show, in comparison with the past, greater interest in improving social facilities, e.g. dressing-rooms, baths and showers, dining-rooms etc., in order to increase their power of attracting workers also in this way. It seems likely that industrial employment will increase in 1968 by 2–3 per cent, i.e., by about 30,000 to 40,000 people.

3. Extended reproduction means by definition an expansion of output, the *development of enterprises* in a certain respect. Greater autonomy of enterprises involves most questions connected with their own development being decided upon by themselves. For this, however, they must have access to all necessary means. The new mechanism, in fact, makes this possible for them. In general, enterprises may retain 60 per cent of all depreciation allowances (sometimes even 100 per cent, e.g., in the case of state-owned farms), and also a part of their profits considerably exceeding the amounts they were formerly permitted to retain. In addition, they can raise bank credits for development purposes. At the outset, of course, most of the means available to them will be used partly to complete investments that had been started before the introduction of the new system, and partly to meet the daily need for current renewals and replacement.

4. Even for purposes of simple reproduction, and to a greater extent for those of extended reproduction, enterprises periodically obtain *credits*. In order to widen their autonomy, the state has ordered *a general reshaping* by January 1st, 1968, *of the funds devoted to financing circulating capital*. As a result, the average enterprise is now able to cover about 60 to 70 per cent of the necessary circulating capital out of its own funds. Over and above this, creditworthy enterprises may raise short- and medium-term credits in order to meet circulating capital requirements. According to a decision of the Economic Committee (the economic cabinet of the government) an enterprise is considered as creditworthy when it regularly sells its products on the market, meets its payment obligations in time and is able to ensure a timely repayment of the credit in question.

5. As also follows from the foregoing, the *continuous marketing* of the commodities that are produced become an *important condition of undisturbed continuity* of production. Since the introduction of the new economic control system did not involve any radical or sudden change in either consumption by the population or in demand by the producers, investors and foreign trade, continuous sale of at least the bulk of the goods produced

seems to be ensured. Surveys covering many enterprises of various types in the first quarter of 1968 suggest that we do not have to reckon with the prospect of any serious difficulty with regard to marketing.

## EQUILIBRIUM BETWEEN THE POPULATION'S PURCHASING POWER AND THE SUPPLY OF COMMODITIES

1. One of the decisive factors in the purchasing power of the population is the *rate of employment*. In another context we have shown in the previous chapter that no considerable changes in this field had to be reckoned with after January 1st, 1968.

2. The other decisive factor in purchasing power is the growth of *money incomes*, i.e., the level of wages, salaries and cooperative incomes earned by the working population, and of pensions, family allowances, sickness benefits and other non-wage incomes. As regards wages, it may be supposed that a greater differentiation and perhaps also a more rapid increase will take place. As a result of this, within a given enterprise or institution some individual wages may rise considerably. The rise of aggregate incomes, however, will be restricted by the principle stipulating that the limit for increasing the level of average wages within an enterprise must depend on the increase in its profits, and that in 1968 the annual rise in average wages must not exceed 4 per cent; for budgetary bodies and institutions generally an annual rise of 2 per cent is planned. As regards non-wage incomes, their rise in 1968 will in most cases be governed by prevailing legal regulations.

3. The supply of commodities or the *"commodity fund"* (this term means the aggregate value of all commodities and services available to the population in a year) must be in equilibrium with the purchasing power of the population. Seen from the commodity side, the factors in equilibrium are the structure of the commodity fund and the quantities of the individual commodities included in it, on the one hand, and their prices, on the other. The size of the stocks of consumer goods has been increased and at present these are relatively large. Measures were taken also to improve the pattern of the commodity fund, that is, to adapt it better to present and expected future demand of the population. Thus, in general the situation seems very reassuring. In some special fields, however, it is not yet satisfactory, and it seems that we cannot improve it completely within a short time, because domestic production does not meet demand whereas imports are limited by considerations affecting the balance of payments, and a rise of the prices in question cannot be permitted, since broad layers of the population would be affected thereby. Nevertheless, we repeat that the general situation is characterized by favourable symptoms rather than by still existing partial scarcities.

4. As has been said, equilibrium between purchasing power and the commodity fund depends in part on the prices of consumer goods. On January 1st, 1968, an *overall revision of producer prices* took place. The main aim was to bring price relations much nearer to the prevailing proportions of social inputs (with the exception of certain deviations indicated by consid-

erations of economic policy). *One of the long-term objectives of the price reform is that the relative prices of consumer goods and services also should correspond more or less to the relations existing between their prime costs,* so that approximately the same economic considerations could govern the decisions of both consumers and producers. This, however, cannot be attained within the next few years, not even in the course of one or two five-year plans, because it requires such a comprehensive transformation of the whole consumption pattern of the population as would prove economically and politically unbearable without a corresponding transformation of the income pattern, and this latter requires much time. As a result of such considerations, although the *consumer prices of a very large number of articles were changed by January 1st, 1968,* these changes were arranged in such a way that they mostly compensated each other's effects. Nevertheless, the relations between consumer prices tend to approach those existing between producer prices and to reflect more truly international price relations. Moreover, prices have become more flexible.

When establishing the new prices, the government made efforts to ensure that *the real purchasing power of the population as a whole, and even of any important layer taken separately, should not decrease:* on the contrary, it was intended that the combined effects of price reductions should slightly overcompensate those of price rises. All this, of course, refers to the initial price situation of January 1st, 1968. Part of the consumer prices (e.g. those of most seasonal articles) were even formerly more or less free to develop according to market conditions. But whereas formerly the sphere of free prices amounted to about 14 per cent of the total turnover of consumer goods, in 1968 the scope of free prices has been widened (by some fashion articles, cosmetics and other goods) so that it now amounts to about 23 per cent of total turnover. Around 50 per cent of the turnover continues to be sold to consumers at prices officially limited from above, so that only downward changes in their prices can occur. Finally, for the remaining 27 per cent of turnover prices are permitted to rise in comparison to the initial level, according to market conditions but within determined limits. In most such cases the limit of price rise is 5 per cent; for a few commodity groups it amounts to 10 per cent. Prices subject to such limitation can be reduced without official permission. In the final analysis, considerable changes in the general level of consumer prices are not likely to occur—mainly because, as has been shown, the rise in purchasing power is rather limited—and thus equilibrium between purchasing power and the commodity fund may be considered as safe.


BALANCE OF TRADE AND OF INTERNATIONAL PAYMENTS

1. One of the most important requirements for undisturbed and expanding economic activity is *equilibrium in the country's balance of international payments,* taking some fairly long period into account. Thus, payments connected with commodity imports and other kinds of obligation must not exceed the aggregate income resulting from exports and other claims.

In some countries a considerable part of all income from abroad consists of payment other than for exports (40 per cent in Great Britain and Italy, 25 per cent in Austria etc.). In Hungary, 90 per cent of all income from abroad arises from commodity exports. Hence, equilibrium in our balance of payments depends mainly on an appropriate development of our foreign trade.

2. The new system introduced on January 1st, 1968, has involved changes in the field of foreign trade primarily by having *bridged the abyss that formerly separated inland producers and consumers from foreign markets.* Importers and users of foreign production goods now pay the actual foreign purchase prices, converted into forints with the aid of an officially established uniform multiplier. Exporters and producers receive the prices actually obtained for their products, converted into forints in the same way. Thus, international prices will affect our home market, and from this influence we hope for favourable results, in the first place for our technological progress. (The multiplier corresponds to the average cost of obtaining foreign exchange through exports. Thus, it overwhelmingly depends on the commodity pattern of our exports destined for the various foreign countries. In no way can it be considered either as an exchange rate, or as the expression of the parity of purchasing power.) In harmony with the main features of the new economic system, changes came about also in the relations between enterprises producing export goods or using imported commodities, on the one hand, and the specialized foreign-trade enterprises, on the other. (Though the latter are often called in English also "companies", the principles and forms of their organization and operation are exactly the same as in the case of every other state-owned enterprise, and differ widely from those prevailing in the case of the few genuine joint-stock corporations and limited companies existing in our country.) These relations vary according to the different types of contract that can now be applied. The most common form, however, will be the one under which the foreign-trade enterprise acts as a commission agent for the enterprise producing export goods or using imported goods.

3. Of course, these changes do not and cannot mean the abandonment or loosening, on the part of the government, of control of foreign trade. In order to ensure such control, export and import activities may be conducted only on the basis of *permits issued by the minister of foreign trade.* The main object of the licensing is to influence the development of foreign trade by countries. Permits can be applied for only by enterprises or other organizations entitled to engage in foreign-trade transactions; their number has increased considerably. According to the regulations, the permit entitles its holder also to purchase the kind and amount of foreign currency necessary for the transaction; such purchases, of course, must be made according to the rules of the prevailing foreign exchange regulations. The minister of foreign trade, when deciding on applications for permits, does not investigate the necessity or the commercial conditions of the transaction in question, with the exception of cases where the equilibrium of the inland market or other interests of the national economy need to be safeguarded.

4. In order to ensure equilibrium in the balance of payments it is absolutely necessary *to follow up and to influence, according to central plans, the*

*development of foreign trade separately by countries,* i.e. the import and export flows from and to each individual country, and certain major country groups. An analysis of our balance of payments according to the three main groups consisting of the socialist, developed capitalist and developing countries shows that difficulties present themselves only with respect to the second group. In this case our balance of payments was passive in the preceding years (though the deficit was not too great), and it is likely to be passive also in 1968. According to our conceptions of economic policy and plans we want to develop our economic connections with each of these three major groups of countries. But if we want to eliminate the payments deficit in the case of the developed capitalist countries—and in the foregoing we have already referred to the great importance of this objective—then our economic connections with these countries must develop in such a way that our aggregate returns in convertible currencies deriving from exports and other claims (as, e.g., tourism) must increase more rapidly than our similar expenditure on imports and other liabilities (e.g., interest).

5. For a time after introducing the reform, certain enterprises would have suffered losses as a result of the uniform exchange multiplier. Such enterprises now receive *state refunds* if the national economy is significantly interested in the continuation of their production or their exports and, accordingly, also in their being adequately supplied with materials (e.g. in order to fulfil some interstate obligation or to safeguard some other national interest). In cases of emergency, the state refunds will make possible, e.g. the fulfilment of an export obligation arising from an interstate agreement; it would however, not be in the interest of the national economy to perpetuate such losses by always refunding them. Accordingly, the payment of such refunds is restricted to a definite period of time. Sometimes, their rates will be gradually reduced, in order to urge enterprises to eliminate the causes of losses.

6. Also the *customs tariff* belongs to the instruments used in controlling the national economy and especially foreign trade. In 1968 a new, three-column customs tariff was introduced, containing three kinds of customs duties: (a) those of the autonomous tariff, (b) the customs duties applied on the ground of the most-favoured-nation clause, and (c) preferential duties. In international relations, i.e. in negotiations with capitalist countries or with international organizations consisting wholly or mainly of such countries (EEC or GATT), customs policy may serve as a means for obtaining reductions in foreign customs duties or other advantages. The preferential tariff is applied to developing countries. In addition, customs duties may also serve to protect the home producer when it would be inexpedient to expose him to the full effect of international competition (e.g., when a new product is introduced, or a new branch is created). In such cases, the customs duty restricts competition and protects the home industry.

7. A further possibility of influencing foreign trade in relations with individual countries consists in establishing *import quotas* for certain products. Such measures can be taken by the government only according to the provisions contained in the national economic plan. In 1968, import quotas cover about 10–15 per cent of the estimated total of imported mate-

rials. Consumer goods from capitalist countries can be imported only within the limits of lump sums reserved for such purposes. Enterprises investing from their own resources can purchase equipment from capitalist countries when they deposit, for a term of two years, a sum in forints equal to the foreign-exchange price, multiplied by a special coefficient fixed for these obligatory deposits. This restriction is, however, not in perfect harmony with the spirit of the new system of economic control; it certainly acts to some extent against technological progress and, therefore, its application is planned only for a fairly short transitional period.

In order to eliminate the deficit in the turnover with developed capitalist countries we must, in the first place, carry out *changes in the commodity pattern of our exports*. By this we mean primarily a strong increase in export of machinery that amounted in 1967 only to little more than 3 per cent of all exports going to these countries. Experience shows, however, that such changes require at least a couple of years. In these years of transition the deficit must be gradually reduced, i.e. the regulators available must help in approaching equilibrium.


## EQUILIBRIUM OF THE STATE BUDGET

1. Evidently, any normal development of economic activities requires, under the new control system also, equilibrium in the state budget, i.e., the state must possess the means necessary to maintain such equilibrium. The new mechanism has, however, brought about rather important changes in the structure of the budget. As a result, *the share of net social income withdrawn for central purposes has decreased*, since state-owned enterprises and cooperatives will retain for their own purposes almost 40 per cent of all profits realized by them, as against 15 per cent in 1967. Nevertheless, more than 80 per cent of all revenues of the 1968 state budget will be paid by enterprises and cooperatives. Out of the revenues coming from them, more than 31 per cent will consist of taxes on profits; 22 per cent are charges paid on fixed and circulating capital (amounting to 5 per cent p.a. of its value); nearly 13 per cent is furnished by non-deductible taxes on wages and salaries and social insurance contributions (amounting on an average to 25 per cent of the wage expenditure). The importance of turnover taxes considerably decreases as a result of the price reform, but they still amount to 18 per cent of the budget revenues collected from enterprises. Production tax, depreciation allowances, customs duties and other revenues amount to more than 16 per cent. Budget revenues stemming from sources other than enterprises and cooperatives represent less than 20 per cent of the total.

2. The *subsidies* paid to enterprises absorb almost 37 per cent of all budget revenues collected from enterprises; these amount to more than one-fifth of all budget expenditure. Of this sum, more than a third is spent in state refunds on exports which we have dealt with above though most of this expenditure is compensated by various budget revenues deriving from foreign trade. Not much less is the share of expenditure needed for sup-

porting consumer prices. This kind of expenditure has considerably increased under the new system although it would perhaps be more correct to say that in the new structure its real size appears more clearly. Also subsidies paid to producers and in supporting producer prices have still some importance. The spending of the budgetary organs amounts to slightly less than two-fifths of total budget expenditure; finally, investments and increases in the stock of circulating capital financed by the state amount to less than one-fifth.

## INVESTMENTS, TECHNOLOGICAL PROGRESS, TRANSFORMATION OF THE PRODUCTION PATTERN

1. One of the aims of the reform is to create a more favourable economic (in the first place productive) structure. Structural transformation can, of course, take place only step by step, mainly—though not exclusively—as a result of continued investments and other measures serving technological progress.

An important new feature of the investment system is *the increased role of enterprises and local councils as regards investments falling within their competence*. In 1968, 40 per cent of all investments will be realized on the basis of enterprise decisions; the investments financed by the state—including centrally approved investments as well as those made by local councils—amount to 60 per cent. (For the time being, the share of previously started investments still being implemented is in both spheres considerable.)

2. State investments are (a) individual large projects approved by the government; (b) "investments grouped according to objectives" which have to be implemented on account of lump sums reserved by the national economic plan for the realization of various determined development objectives (here, only proposals generally describing the purpose and type of investments and the aggregate sum to be spent on them are approved by the government, without deciding on the individual projects); (c) certain other investments which are, as a rule, decided on by the supervisory organs.

(a) *Individual large projects* liable to government decision are those creating new factories or large plants, as well as such extension and reconstruction projects as will increase the output of an industrial branch by at least 25–30 per cent. The investment cost of these projects must amount to at least 300 million forints in mining, in the production of electric power and in the chemical industry, 200 million in metallurgy, heating plants, engineering, construction, production of building materials, 100 million in the light industries, in agriculture and forestry, in the food industry, in water supplies, transport and communication, in trade and in the sphere of non-productive investments. Proposals regarding these investments are submitted to the government by the minister (or leader of a national office) supervising the field in question, or by the president of the executive committee of the competent local council. When the proposal is approved by the government, it is incorporated in the national economic plan.

(b) The term *"investments grouped according to objectives"* means investments that will be implemented as a series of more or less homogeneous objects, each of which serves the same purpose, e.g., the development of a network under a uniform plan, or the purchase of equipment serving technological development of a determined nature. Among these there are both productive and non-productive investments. The common objective of such investments may be, e.g., the development of sources of energy, the creation of a network of power lines, railroads, highways, the purchase of rolling stock for transport, the establishment of sewage-systems, etc. Regarding such investments—except for those made by local councils—the minister supervising the branch submits a proposal to the government; after approval they are incorporated in the national economic plan. Proposals regarding investments of a similar kind to be made by local councils are summarized by the president of the National Planning Office; they are submitted to, and approved by, the government together with the national economic plan.

(c) The so-called *"other state investments"* (generally of a non-productive character) are approved individually by the competent supervisory organ (within the financial limits set by the budget), or by the organs disposing of their own resources.

3. In contrast with the former system, even state investments will not be covered always or exclusively out of the state budget. *Nor will the contributions made from the state budget be necessarily free of charge.* Most of them will be made available to the future user under an obligation of partial or total repayment. Regarding the method of financing, large individual investment projects and the "investments grouped according to objectives", the government takes its decisions at the time when the investment proposals are approved; in other cases, this decision is taken at the time when the permit for implementation is issued. The large investment projects are financed by the state budget; but when the resulting object will be operated by an enterprise, the latter can be obliged to finance all or a part of the investment cost from a *loan granted by the state.* The "investments grouped according to objectives" may be financed either from the budget or from loans granted by the state or from the investor's own resources. (State loans differ from bank credits in that their periods of amortization and rates of interest are established by special central decisions.)

4. As has been said, a considerable part of investment will be realized on the basis of autonomous decisions made by enterprises, cooperatives and local councils. To the sphere of enterprise and cooperative investment belong those involving replacement, current modernization and adaptation to market requirements, improvement of product quality and extension of output. The financial source of such investment is the *development fund.* In addition, enterprises and cooperatives can raise bank credits in order to finance investments (and the complementary increase of their stock of circulating capital); such credits must be repaid from the development fund.

5. *In 1968,* enterprises and cooperatives will dispose (for the implementation of investments depending on their own decisions) of a sum equalling about 40 per cent of all planned investments. In the current year, however,

relatively few new investments can be started, because some of the previously started investments must also be continued and finished at the expense of the enterprise development fund. The new situation, however, has made it possible for enterprises and cooperatives to undertake immediately certain minor investments that had frequently been much neglected in the past, and thereby to eliminate some of their bottlenecks, improve working conditions, introduce new technological processes, and so on. Surveys made in this connection show that enterprises, in fact, avail themselves of such opportunities.

According to estimates concerning industry and construction, the share of investments to be made out of enterprise funds will, by 1970, rise to about 50 per cent, against 40 per cent in 1968.

As regards investments made directly by the state, in 1968 a relatively large part of the means available for such purposes will be absorbed in the completion of previously started investment projects. Since, in addition, so-called "other state investments" require considerable expenditure, only a relatively small number of new large investment projects will be started this year.

6. Under the new mechanism, initiatives aiming at an *improvement of quality and the introduction of new products* will be taken mainly by producing enterprises. They may finance such development measures (as part of their costs) either from their own resources or by raising credits. They are free to decide whether to undertake the necessary work of preparation themselves or through another enterprise, a special research institute, etc., or else to buy the licence of an already known procedure. The supervisory organs may assert their own ideas mainly by consultation and by forwarding information to the enterprises; sometimes they may commission an enterprise or a group of enterprises to undertake development work of a specific kind.

The prices of certain products and services contain, among the cost factors, an *"allowance for technological innovation"* expressed in percentage of the sales price. These allowances feed the enterprise's "innovation fund" (which must be distinguished from the "development fund of the enterprise" formed out of that part of profits which remain for the disposition of the enterprise). Such a fund existed even before introducing the new economic system. But whereas in the past its value was considered as the upper limit of enterprise expenditure aimed at technological development, now it marks rather the *minimum*. (The cost of technological development can be charged against production costs in all enterprises, whether a technological innovation fund is formed or not.) Out of the fund a certain charge has to be paid to the supervisory ministry where this serves as a basis for covering risks which may arise in connection with development measures (when they exceed the limit of what a single enterprise may be expected to take), as well as for the costs of purchasing technological information and documentation, of elaborating and introducing new standards, etc. Apart from this charge, the enterprise is free to avail itself of its technological innovation fund.

1. We have seen that, according to the budget estimates for 1968, more than 80 per cent of all state revenues will be furnished by enterprises and cooperatives. The main channels of income collection are: the charge on assets, the tax on wages and salaries, the social insurance contributions and the turnover tax (all these were applied even before 1968) and, *from 1968 on, the production tax and the tax on profits.*

The production tax of enterprises serves mainly to collect incomes having the nature of a rent, i. e., depending on exceptionally favourable natural or other endowments.

The taxation of enterprise profits is associated with the system of enterprise funds. Each enterprise has to form its sharing, development and reserve funds.

The initial size of the *sharing fund* on January 1st, 1968 equalled the amount accounted for in the balance sheet of 1967 *plus* eventual balances from preceding years, both having the character of being owed to the sharing fund according to the new regulations.

As regards the enterprise *development fund*, its initial value on January 1st, 1968, equalled 40 per cent of the development fund available on the basis of the balance sheet of 1967, *plus* the balance of the former "own investment fund of the enterprise".

The initial value of the *reserve fund* had to be taken as equal to 60 per cent of the development fund that could have been formed on the basis of the 1967 balance sheet. If, however, this sum did not attain an amount equal to 0·5 percent of the 1967 wage bill, the reserve fund had to be supplemented up to this amount, on account of the part of 1967 profits that would otherwise have been owing to the state budget.

Enterprise profits liable to taxation must be divided into parts to be used to supplement personal incomes (that is, to feed the sharing fund) and to add to enterprise assets (that is, to feed the development fund). In principle, this division should rest on the proportion of the wage bill to the value of (fixed and circulating) capital constantly employed by the enterprise. The direct assertion of this proportion would, however, result in a too low share of income supplementation, in comparison with the share destined for development. Therefore, before calculating proportions, the wage bill is multiplied by a factor varying by branches, and profits are divided according to the proportion between the "weighted" wage bill and the value of assets. At present, a multiplier of two is generally applied, but higher multipliers are employed in branches where the proportion of fixed and circulating capital deviates considerably from the average. Thus, e. g., wage expenditure in iron metallurgy, aluminium and paper industry have to be multiplied by 4; in coal mining and forestry the multiplier is 6.

After dividing profits into two parts, each part is taxed differently. The part of profits payable into the sharing fund is taxed progressively, at rates extending from 0 to 70 per cent (above the tax-free part, the lowest tax rate is 20 per cent and this rate increases by grades of 10 per cent, up to 70 per cent, according to the proportion existing between the amount of profits destined for this purpose and the amount of the wage bill). The part of profits payable into the development fund is taxed, as a rule, at a uniform rate of 60 per cent, but the tax rate of certain branches is different (e. g., it amounts to 70 per cent in trade and to 45 per cent in agriculture).

2. The *sharing fund, designed to supplement the incomes of workers and employees of the enterprise,* is divided into three parts, serving (a) payments in money, (b) benefits in kind, (c) the part serving as a reserve for the next year. Supplements to income paid in money include premia, rewards, innovation fees, housing contributions, scholarships, aids and the annual profit-shares. Benefits in kind include those granted by the enterprise in order to reduce the prices of catering, kindergarten fees, recreation costs, as well as enterprise contributions to the costs of social, cultural and sports facilities. From the sharing fund payments may be made not only to workers and employees of the enterprise but also to home workers, apprentices, and to persons rendering continuous services to the enterprise as doctors, teachers of professional training courses, etc.

Before calculating the amount due to the sharing fund, the profit tax must be deducted. Moreover, *wage expenditures caused by an eventual rise in the level of average wages against the "basic" level of 1967 must be deducted* from the part of profits due to the sharing fund and, at the same time, be added to the amount of taxable profits. This rule serves to deter enterprises from excessively raising the level of average wages which could result in tensions between various enterprises. Under the present system any rise in the level of average wages necessarily reduces the possibility of supplementing individual incomes. Moreover, for the year 1968, the additional requirement applies that the level of average wages within an enterprise cannot rise by more than 4 per cent. This restriction, however, does not apply to the supplementation of personal incomes paid from the sharing fund under other headings.

Any increase of average wages against their basic (1967) level must be covered also in the years after 1968, from the sharing fund. Thus, an increase in the level of average wages involves also an increased burden on the sharing fund. In view of this, the tax-free part of the profits due to the sharing fund will be increased each year by 2 per cent of the annual wage bill. The tax-free part of profits due to the sharing fund is 3 per cent of the wage-bill in 1968; it will amount to 5 per cent in 1969, and to 7 per cent in 1970. Also the progression in the tax rate will be shifted upwards accordingly.

*The workers and employees* of an enterprise, *from the point of view of profit-sharing, are classed as follows.*

(a) The first category includes the general managers, directors and deputy directors appointed by the supervisory organ as well as the persons appointed by the director, as leaders and deputy leaders of sections, plants, major workshops, other employees having similar responsibilities, as well as the technological and economic advisers. According to estimates, the number of such persons will amount to 0·5–1·0 per cent of the whole personnel, depending on the particular conditions of each enterprise. Persons belonging to this group are permitted to receive profit shares, as a group average, up to 80 per cent of their fixed salaries.

(b) To the second category belong the leaders of sections and subsections not figuring in the first category, the leaders of workshops, senior foremen, foremen, projectors, constructors, technologists, economists, etc. Their total number is estimated at 4·5–12 per cent; their profit shares may attain, as a group average, 50 per cent of their salaries.

(c) To the third category belong all other employees and workers, i. e. 87–95 per cent of the staff. Profit shares of this group may amount to 15 per cent of wages and salaries as a group average.

The division of the sharing fund among these three groups takes place according to the proportions between the respective products obtained when multiplying their aggregate annual salaries by the sharing rates enumerated above. The sharing rates established for each group (80, 50, and 15 per cent) mean that *aggregate* profit shares exceeding these rates cannot be paid; the eventual surplus will serve as a reserve. Within a category, however, the amounts of *individual* shares are not limited.

*When the annual balance sheet of the enterprise shows a loss*, and this loss cannot be compensated from the reserve funds, only 75 per cent of the salaries of employees belonging to the first group, and 85 per cent of the salaries of these belonging to the second may be paid. The salaries and wages of employees and workers belonging to the third group must be paid, even in this case, without deduction.

A certain part of *the major benefits independent of wages* (e. g. the allotments of working and protective clothing, uniforms, enterprise expenditures on the maintenance of workers' hostels, on the transport of workers, etc.) are, as a rule, covered on the account of overall enterprise costs. Contributions actually made by an enterprise in 1967 to catering at reduced prices, and the amount that could have been spent—according to the prevailing norms—on the maintenance of children's institutions in 1967 can be deducted from the 1968 profits before taxation. The enterprise is free to increase (out of its sharing fund) as well as to reduce, or eventually to cease, its contributions to catering at reduced prices, and to use the amounts saved either for paying the staff an indemnity, or for increasing its expenditure on other social purposes. The enterprise may also improve the services of its kindergarten and similar institutions on account of its sharing funds.

## THE DEVELOPMENT OF SOCIALIST DEMOCRACY

We consider as one of the main features of our new system the extension and strengthening of our socialist democracy. This reform intends, both in its main principles and in its partial rules, to eliminate or at least alleviate bureaucratic restrictions and prescriptions, to widen the number of persons interested in economic decisions, to create economic incentives acting on the masses and to extend the possibilities of economic control being exercised by them.

Within the enterprise, the tendencies enhancing democracy assert themselves primarily in the increased role of *the competent trade union and of its local organization*. Before nominating the director and the deputy director of an enterprise, the supervisory organ is obliged to hear the opinion of the competent trade union. Trade unions have not the formal right of vetoing a nomination, but under our conditions it is hardly possible for the supervisory organ to neglect an emphatic opinion of the trade union.

*The distribution of the sharing fund takes place according to a collective agreement* concluded by the director and the trade union committee of the enterprise. Within the limits set by this agreement the director decides, after considering the opinion of the trade union committee, on the distribution of the fund serving directly to supplement personal incomes. Collective agreements determine also the classification of the jobs existing in the enterprise and, thereby also the grouping of individuals, for the purposes of profit-sharing, in the first, second or third category mentioned above. The trade union committee of the enterprise decides — after hearing the director's opinion — on questions regarding the utilization of enterprise contributions to the recreation fund, the granting of assistance, the operation of cultural centres and libraries of the enterprise, expenditures of the sports club, and minor purchases for social welfare.

Before taking decisions affecting living and working conditions, the competent ministers are obliged to ask for the *opinion of the competent trade union* or — in cases affecting several branches — that of the National Council of Trade Unions. The latter has the right to express its opinion on any labour and wage question of national importance.

In addition, the competence of *local councils* is widened. In spending their own resources, they are able to decide autonomously on most questions of development and investment.

All these changes necessarily tend to increase the interest of the wide masses in all matters concerning the enterprises they are working in and the communities they belong to. At the same time, the sphere of those entitled to take decisions is considerably widened, so that the spheres of the decision-makers and of those affected by the decisions tend to overlap. Relations between leaders and the people led by them are becoming more direct, with the result that the masses may review, understand and influence the activity of their leaders to a greater extent than they were able to in the past.

In its final outcome, the new system of economic control must contribute towards raising *social consciousness* to a higher level, towards enhancing the features of our society.[2]

[2] With a view to a better putting into practice the principles outlined above, some modification in the system of regulators has been effectuated after the manuscript of this book was closed.

# IDEAS ON THE IMPROVEMENT OF NATIONAL
ECONOMIC PLANNING

The development of production relations and of productive forces is essentially a continuous process in our society, still, production relations will, as a rule, lag behind the rapidly developing forces of production. Thus, from time to time, a major adjustment of production relations, a reform of economic management, becomes necessary. This course of development will also explain, why in the history of economic theory, discussion on certain questions which were thought to have been settled is revived time and again. The discussions now going on about commodity and money relationships, value, economic planning, etc., seem to repeat much of what had been said about them in the Soviet Union thirty or even fourty years ago, but the present discussion unfolds at a higher stage of development, takes a more concrete form and leads to other conclusions.

In our days a major adjustment of production relations is taking place in several of the socialist countries. This is one of the circumstances which makes it timely and even unavoidable for us to improve the plan and planning, particularly *the central, national economic plan and planning*, and this will be the subject of our present paper. The different parts of the economic mechanism and the various fields of the economy are, in other words, intricately interrelated. It may be easily seen that changes in the system of prices, investment, taxation, credit, etc., will involve changes in production, investment, foreign and domestic trade, etc., and thus also in the *planning* of these. At the same time, the changes impending or in part already introduced in the economic mechanism alter the *relationship between the central plan and the enterprises*. The independence of enterprises, their scope of decision, is being increased, and their obligations arising from the plan are being reduced. In some countries the opinion prevails that enterprises should not be given any kind of obligatory plan indicators. In general, it is intended to increase the role of the market and of money and commodity relations, that is, to orientate enterprises increasingly by means of the market, profits, profitability, etc. rather than by direct instructions.

These tendencies are often being deliberately misinterpreted in the capitalist world, in the sense that the communists themselves have come to recognize the market as a better institution for controlling the economy than are plans. Socialists, however, emphasize that they have no intention of abandoning central planning or even reducing its importance. This is another reason why the improvement of the plan and of planning should be put upon the order of the day. A great or perhaps the greatest *advantage of socialist economy* over capitalism consists in the possibility of a *deliberate harmoni-*

*zation, on the basis of a common plan, of the economic activities performed by
its members.* Even some bourgeois economists have come to recognize this
advantage. The reform of the "economic mechanism" requires us to make
the most of this advantage, to improve planning.

There is, however, even a third reason. In recent years *the growth of our
economy has slowed down, the efficiency of our efforts has diminished.* No doubt,
we are able to explain in many ways why that should have happened, e. g.
because of a shift in the structure of the economy towards more capital
intensive branches, and with many other arguments. But all these arguments can only *describe* the change from certain aspects. They do not offer
convincing proof that it was an unavoidable necessity for development to
slow down or for efficiency to diminish. On the contrary, knowing certain
deficiencies of our planning and management methods, we can take it as
certain that these deficiencies had some role in the unfavourable development.

There are numerous differences between the various socialist countries
regarding the contents, the methods of elaboration, implementation, as well
as with respect to a possible modification of the national economic plans.
Still, there is a general consensus among them that *the institution which
serves for the deliberate control of society* — and within that, of the economy — is
the Party, *the leading political body,* acting on behalf of the working class and
the working population in general. Thus, it is usually the Party that,
through its highest organs, the Congress or the Central Committee, *takes
decisions on the major trends and problems of social and economic development.*
Usually, there exists also a central agency engaged in planning, in preparing
the materials necessary for the Party to take decisions on the major problems. The same agency will elaborate the plan in detail after the decision has
been taken, and deals also with any modifications which may prove to be
necessary during implementation. One of the principal means for deliberately
controlling the economy and society is in all socialist countries the plan.

It is undoubted, however, that this field still needs improvement in several
socialist countries. In order that the Party should be indeed in a position to
decide on the major problems and development trends, it is necessary first
of all that the central agency engaged in planning should submit such
material to the Party as will enable the decision-making body — Congress
or the Central Committee — *to make its choice among different alternatives,
i. e. it should really have something to decide upon.* Second, the decision-
taking Party body must deal only with questions for the decision of which it
is competent, that is, with such *matters as need political consideration,* and
can be judged by the members of Congress or the Central Committee, rather
than with problems for which only a few specialists are really competent.
Today this double requirement is often not met. It frequently occurs that
the proposal submitted by the central planning agency does not offer any
choice of alternatives, and thus it can be either accepted or rejected only
in its entirety. As a rule, it must be accepted, for the simple reason that in
case it were rejected the economy would be left for some time without a
central plan and thus exposed to disturbances. On the other hand, it also
happens that such specialized questions are often submitted as would

require, from their nature, decision by a competent body of specialists. In all these cases a Party decision cannot but be formal.

True, we have above assumed certain postulates which are not self-evident and need further argument. Is it really necessary to offer a choice to the decision-making body? Is it not conceivable to submit for approval immediately the plan which is likely to be the best? Is it always possible to submit a proposal which the highest Party organ is really competent to decide upon and not some narrower circle of specialists? What problems, then, would be left to be covered in this document? In short: can the above-mentioned two requirements be met in reality?

Obviously, in this paper only a theoretical, general answer can be given. But even this theoretical statement must be rather sketchy and restricted to a few major problems deemed particularly important and timely. The set of problems touched upon here is so complicated and diversified that its detailed discussion would require many times the space available for this study.

At the end of these introductory remarks it should be added that, although the following are general statements, not restricted to any country, they are supported mainly by Hungarian experience.

## CAN AN OPTIMUM PLAN BE ESTABLISHED WITHOUT A POLITICAL DECISION? THE TASKS OF THE PLANNING BODY IN THE PREPARATION OF DECISION-MAKING

Obviously, it would be superfluous to offer to the leading political body the possibilities of choice if the central planning agency were able to elaborate what was unquestionably the best plan alternative. But then the planning agency itself would be in a position deliberately to control the development of society. It may be easily seen, however, that plan-decisions must be taken on a set of major problems which the planning agency cannot, or is not called upon to, decide. Such a question is, e. g., how much should be used by society from the global social product for consumption and how should this be allocated; how much should be used for defence purposes, and so on? It is not possible first to draw up a plan and subsequently deduce from it the answers to these question. Quite the converse: these problems and some others of similar importance must be decided first, and only afterwards can and must the central planning agency be given the task of elaborating the best possible plan on the basis of the decisions already taken.

The planning agency, however, has also an important role in the preliminaries of decision-making. It has to elaborate the possible consequences of each alternative decision. What can be said in favour of using such and such an amount of the social product for consumption and of allocating it in such and such a way? What problems arise in this connection, what difficulties, advantages, disadvantages or dangers should be expected? What would be the advantages, disadvantages and possible dangers if somewhat more (or less) were used for consumption, or its allocation pattern were more or less different?

80

In the case referred to and in general with problems requiring a political decision, the various possible solutions involve different advantages and disadvantages. These cannot be simply reduced to a common denominator, be rendered homogeneous and added or subtracted. And even if this were possible, the advantages and disadvantages would not be comparable because in most cases *they do not affect, or not to the same extent, the same persons or economic units*. Thus, no correct solution can be found by applying purely mathematical methods. It is necessary that—after having analyzed the material (information and proposals) available to them—those elected and invested by society with authority to do so, should consider, discuss and, finally, decide on the problem.

But a decision based on weighing and discussion is needed not only because often an uneven distribution of advantages and disadvantages, and, thus, a collision of interests is involved, or because the problems cannot—in most cases—be translated into mathematical equations, but also because decisions generally involve the taking of risks and responsibilities. *Our knowledge and information are limited* and thus we are able to foresee the future only with an approximate exactness. Only a leading body chosen by society is authorized and also obliged to take such decisions as well as the risks and responsibilities involved in them.

What, then, is the task of the central planning agency?

I have already referred to that above. First it prepares the information and proposal to be submitted to the leading political body for decision and, when the latter is taken, it draws up the plan proper. The material to be submitted by the planners to the competent body consists of several plan-variants which, starting from the given situation, set different objectives or compute different growth paths in a consistent manner. Each of the *plan-variants* comprises only the major objectives and the main features and interrelations of a plan corresponding to these. I will later point out what I mean by this. The *basic conceptions* and major objectives of the variants will be called *plan-conceptions*. Thus, the decision-making body selects a conception—to which again, there may belong several variants differing only in some details—and then the planning body will draw up, on the basis of the selected variant or variants, the plan, but now already in considerable detail.

Now, how is the planning organ capable of elaborating conceptions or plan-variants?

It can do so because it need not start from a vacuum but *from a given society*. We have always to deal with a given situation, with a society of a given composition, at a given stage of economic, cultural and political development and disposing of productive forces of a given level of development, structure and allocation. Knowing these endowments and the various trends of development, the planners are able to elaborate proposals for the major objectives they consider advisable to be set for the next five years, and in many fields even for longer periods than this. These objectives relate to the raising of social welfare, to the development of individual abilities of the members of society, as well as to development of productive forces and of production. The basic conception of the plan combines these major objectives.

81

The factors mentioned, which characterize a given society—i. e. the living and cultural standards of society and its members, the level of development of productive forces and of production, as well as the structure and allocation of the latter—are in close connection and interaction, they constitute an organic whole. All these factors belong together, assume each other's existence, and correspond to each other even if there are also *contradictions* between them—as is usual between the whole and its parts. The planning agency must, of course, pay attention to this. It has to draw up conceptions and plan-variants of such a kind that the relation of the parts to each other, their mutual correspondence and mutual determination will not get dissolved in the course of development, that is, development of the parts will take place *proportionally to each other*.

Speaking of the relation between the planning agency and the decision-making body, it must, however, be remarked that *certain important elements of decision cannot be entirely eliminated from the work of the planning agency*, due to the particular character of its tasks. A plan can represent a vast number of infinitely complicated economic processes only in rough outlines, as does a model. Even if it is bound by certain directives, it will be fundamentally the planners who decide on what to select from the multitude of social processes and how to classify and insert them into a conception in the course of compiling and elaborating a conception and its variants. This is unavoidable. Similarly, estimations regarding the final results of each variant (which are likely to influence the decision) are also made by them alone.

All these taken together will have an important bearing on what proposals are submitted to the competent party body. Thus, although the deliberate shaping of the development of society is the task of the Party which also takes the responsibility, both are, to a certain extent, shared by the planning agency.

## PROBLEMS REQUIRING POLITICAL DECISION

It has been mentioned that the planning agency having knowledge of the given situation, of some major factors and the tendencies of development, will elaborate conceptions and variants which correspond to certain selected objectives. For this purpose it must establish what objectives it is advisable to set, partly in order to raise the welfare of people and to unfold their abilities and partly to increase productive forces and production. This distinction and double classification of objectives is applied to stress the double role of *man* played in society. Man, as a producer *brings about social progress*; on the other hand, he is *the objective of social progress*. Accordingly, when planners address themselves to the task of establishing advisable *objectives*, they have to start from *two major groups* of needs, endowments and possibilities. The first will comprise the bodily and intellectual needs of man, the other the productive forces called upon to meet these needs. From both groups there follow certain implications with regard to the allocation and pattern of resources available to society. (There is also a third group of needs arising from the maintenance and security of the state.) In the course of elaborating the conception these requirements stemming from different categories of needs, will get intertwined, and so their origin need not be distinguished any further.

But for the time being, we are still at the beginning. It stands to reason that the planners should begin their work with *the fundamental requirement of socialism*, i. e. with raising the welfare of society to the maximum possible extent and with the development of every member of society into a fully diversified personality. This objective, however, is so general and equivocal that it affords very little help or support for elaborating any plan or conception. First, we must get closer to the contents of this requirement and render it more concrete.

The first decision to be taken—and one that transcends the competence of the planning agency—is about the *time horizon* (period or date) to which the raising of welfare should relate. Obviously, we must arrive at a different plan variant if our aim is to increase the per capita volume of products evenly through five years, to the maximum possible extent and then to keep it at an unchanged level for several years, from what we should do if the objective was to maintain an even development, for, say, 25 years.

In addition, the *objectives* to be attained in respect of welfare have to be determined in their main outlines. It is generally accepted that a certain minimum of nutrition, housing and clothing must precede other needs. But how can we establish the *ranking of preferences for the others?* A given pattern of needs is everywhere the product of a long spontaneous development. When elaborating the plan-variants the planners must, however, take into account also the scientifically assessed or estimated development of needs in order to be able correctly to plan production and investment. To be able to do so, first the *political body* commissioned by society has to decide on the objectives of *income distribution policies*. What should be the *proportion* of the lowest earnings to the highest, or between the earnings of unskilled and skilled workers, or those of a foreman and an engineer, or between *wages and fringe benefits* over and above wages? Obviously, the task is also in this respect to solve contradictions, to reconcile *conflicting interests*, since from the sum of personal incomes of a given magnitude some persons may be allotted a bigger sum only if others get less. In the same way, if a decision has been taken on the combined expenditure on health and educational purposes, the outlays of the first field can be increased only at the expense of the second. And the same applies for smaller fields within any other aggregate.

In our above considerations we started from the first group of objectives. The conception will be enriched by other points of view, partly of a different nature, if we start from the requirement of the development of productive forces and of production. They are only partly different since some of the requirements coincide with those arising from the development of human needs. As a matter of fact, the most important one of productive forces is man himself. Therefore, the development of production, its improvement and diversification goes hand in hand with the mass development of human capacities, the expansion of human knowledge, the growing mastery over nature surrounding man and with a gradual re-allocation of manpower between various productive and non-productive occupations, assuming their existence and building upon them. At the same time man, by continually developing *science and technology* and relying on their results, is continually *regrouping and renewing production and changing its pattern* by introducing new means of production and processes, new products, and by developing new branches of production and abandoning some old ones.

All this demands investments of a defined nature and order of magnitude, raising, at the same time, certain requirements affecting educational objectives and institutions, as well as the trends of scientific and technological research. But it would be a mistake to believe that all the requirements we have mentioned can be quite unequivocally and exactly defined. First, the development of science and technology *can be foreseen only in broad outline*. A considerable part of new discoveries and inventions occurs as a surprise, unexpectedly, and may revolutionize production in an incalculable manner and extent. But even in the case of expected and foreseeable discoveries and inventions one cannot tell exactly when they will materialize. Second, owing to the limited amount of available resources, in any period, only a part even of the desired development and investment targets can be realized. Thus, in this respect also several variants have to be elaborated, by simultaneously working out, as exactly as possible, the *advantages and disadvantages and the possible dangers and risks to be expected*. The choice must be left to the decision-making body because, again, there are several different and conflicting interests.

Consideration of the ideas mentioned up to now is, however, not sufficient for drawing up the main outlines, the conception of a national economic plan. We are part of a *world economy*, maintaining exchange relations with about a hundred countries, each at a different stage of economic and technical development. Therefore, in decisions on production, and particularly in those on development, we have to weigh in the most circumspect manner how we can *accelerate our own development* with the aid of foreign economic, technical and scientific relations. Since here we have to conform to events or series of events which are going to take place mostly beyond our borders, entirely or partly independently of our decisions, and influenced by us only to a limited extent or not at all, the role of unknown or uncertain elements is particularly great. Here belong business fluctuations occurring in capitalist markets, which can turn a purchase or a sale that is advantageous today into a disadvantageous one by tomorrow, and conversely. It can and must be ensured that *our own development shall not be at the mercy of developments in capitalist markets,* it should not be a function of the latter. This is secured not only by our own strength, which is fundamentally relied upon, but also by the fact that we are part of the broad camp of socialist countries adhering to identical political ideas and willing to offer economic, technological and scientific assistance to each other. On the other hand, a development of our relations with other countries may be useful to other nations, among them to those of the socialist camp. Thus, risks which—as we have seen—are in any case inseparable from planning, must be taken to a reasonable extent in this field as well. But taking them is the prime obligation of the decision-making political body.

Finally, another field remains where developments beyond our borders must be duly taken into account. And this is *defence*. Only the body deliberately directing the entire development of society can take decision on what part of the resources available to the country be used for defence, as well as on the allocation and mode of utilization of this sum. For this purpose an extraordinarily intensive, diversified and profound analysis of the *international political* situation is necessary. It should be, however, obvious that no study, however perfect, enables us to foresee future development with full accuracy. Any decision to be taken will affect wide and very different sections of society. Such decisions determine what part of the population should serve in the army or be employed in the war industries; they influence the volume of investments and the pattern of industrial and agricultural production, as well as transport to a considerable extent and through all these, of course, they determine also the extent and pattern of employment, the trends of development for educational institutions, science and technology and the allocation of investment.

In broad outlines, these are the most important initial assumptions and ideas which may serve to guide the central planning agency when elaborating proposals for the leading political body and in which the planning agency has to ask the political body for objectives to be set and decisions to be made.

As we have seen, all the various viewpoints and all interests conflict as to *how the resources available to society shall be allocated.*

In order to avoid any mistaken interpretation, it should be pointed out that the freedom and scope of any such decision is strongly limited by existing endowments, by the past and by all that is already going on. No abrupt or fundamental changes can be planned to take place by tomorrow. But in a few years, changes may become already significant. This is why decisions on the trends of development are particularly important.


OVERALL PLAN-CONCEPTION *VERSUS* "SECTORAL APPROACH"

When speaking about the preparation for decision-taking, we have established that the planning agency has to submit to the political body the conceptions comprising the major objectives, the fundamental ideas involved in the plan and the plan-variants conforming to the former. As for the process of elaborating the conceptions and plan-variants we have found that the consistency and mutual determination of the parts and considerations affecting the national economy require certain proportions to be observed in the course of planned development. Finally, when dealing with problems requiring political decisions, we have stressed some important major considerations. We have, however, not yet mentioned a further essential feature of plan-variants. Any plan-variant must comprise those main factors and interrelations of the national economy which, in their combination, determine the entire development of the economy. Thus, when the political body chooses the conception or variant of economic development valid for five years or some longer period, it simultaneously takes a decision about all these major issues.

These features, however, do not yet distinguish plan-variants from a plan without alternatives, a type which may be and frequently is submitted by the planners to the decision-making body. The main difference consists, evidently, in the existence or absence of *alternatives*. Further, a "single" plan does not betray its inherent *contradictions, difficulties and problems* while plan-variants must necessarily disclose them. A "single" plan inadvertently gives the impression that things will develop as prescribed in it and there are no other ways and trends available. Plan-variants, however, emphasize the fact that society has a certain *freedom of choice*, particularly in establishing the trend of future development, and can also take into account the danger that unplanned, unwanted, or unforeseen processes might *divert development* from the way that is deemed desirable.

*Hungary's first five-year plan*, launched in 1950, was an instance when the planning agency worked on the basis of fundamental ideas received from above, that is, in a sense, on the basis of a conception. This conception, however, turned out to be a wrong one and the result was bad, too. The basic conception was an *extremely rapid development* of the whole economy, *particularly of heavy industry*. Plan-variants had not been drawn up and, particularly, it had not been planned what should be done in case of something developing differently from what had been provided for. When it turned out that the various objectives of the plan could not be simultaneously realized, the leadership—in spite of danger signals—doggedly insisted on carrying out the rapid development of heavy industry which was the essence of the basic conception. It followed that the development of the economy became one-sided, disproportionate and *distorted*, the standard of living declined and finally, in the fourth year of the plan, even the leadership was compelled to abandon the planned development of heavy industry and the realization of the entire plan. This was a glaring example of what harm can be done to society as a whole if the decision is not preceded by an all-round weighing of processes to be anticipated and if the leadership rigidly reject criticism.

Nor can we accept as satisfactory the rather widespread practice which, in the absence of a basic conception, tries to compile a national economic plan by simply putting together such elements as seem to be best. It is, of course, good if each branch, field and every economic and administrative unit draw up their own optimum plans. Who should know better their endowments, possibilities or needs? But, by simply putting them together, these partial plans cannot be integrated into a national economic plan. Those who draw up the plans of individual branches know their own needs and the requirements involved in them, but they do not know the *possibilities* and available resources *of the economy* as a whole, their needs and requirements do not fit exactly together, do not exactly complement each other. Thus, even in the best case, some patchwork is needed to fit them together. But there is also a greater possible evil. What should happen if—as is inevitable in our existing mechanism, but may occur in any other one—the combined development requirements of the branches are greater, maybe much greater than the resources available to society make possible? Should the planning agency cut all claims by the same percentage? This is surely not workable since, however correct each of the objectives may be by itself, they cannot be *equally* important for society. But who should decide? Presumably, all claims can be convincingly justified by those who advance them. There is nothing to do but *bargain*. He who is clever at bargaining is likely to fare better. There is, however, wide experience to show that the inevitable result is a *fragmentation of resources, a slowing down of development, a diminished efficiency*. This is what a sectoral approach leads to.

All this becomes unavoidable when, from time to time the leading political bodies pass a *decision* on the development in a *definite plan period, say five years*, of a major productive field of the economy, or an important branch, maybe a non-productive social field, taken out of context, without taking account of its interrelations with the economy at large. Such a decision should not be made since the given field is an integral, inseparable part of society, of the economy as a whole, having complicated interrelations with the various parts of the former and its development partly depends on developments going on elsewhere and partly influences such development. A decision that seemingly relates only to a single branch or field does, in reality, affect the whole of the national economy. More often than not it cannot be implemented or, if it is still enforced, it will lead to unwanted results and distortions somewhere else.

Thus, our general statement seems justified that, in order to maintain correct proportions, *decision on major questions of development must be taken simultaneously*.

Some people defend the compromise emerging as a result of bargaining between branches by saying that situations are frequent where, in the final analysis, not much else could be done. According to this argument, the freedom of choice and decision is, as a rule, strictly limited and, within these limits, no major blunders can be committed in this manner. Material resources are scarce and most of them are engaged by pre-determined objectives of development, by investment projects begun or already accepted. If the objectives and targets comprised in the final plan are each correct by themselves, and if also the requirements of quality and technological development are being observed what can be wrong in such a plan?

Our answer must be that a plan drawn up in the way described cannot be very good even if each of the tasks set in it is correct in itself. Scarcity of material resources is a relative term. By "scarcity" we generally mean that they are insufficient relative to the claims. But, as we have already mentioned, the mechanism of planning may be such that the needs will, of necessity, by far surpass the possibilities. But this can be only an additional reason why the available means and resources should be used in the most rational way, instead of being fragmented. The greatest shortcoming of the procedure we have criticized is precisely that, by trying to give something to everyone, nobody is given enough, *none of the objectives obtains as much as would be needed for its most rational realization*. Thus, the means which, had they been used in a concentrated manner, could have brought about substantial progress, are used inefficiently because of their fragmentation.

It will be surely better than the above procedure if the body called upon to make decision selects—after careful consideration—from the proposals submitted a basic conception which seems to be the best and the variant comprising the main objectives. We have already referred to the fact that with reference to the immediate future the given situation, current economic activities or those already decided upon put strong limitations in actual fact on freedom of choice and decision. But we have likewise stressed that the decision will strongly influence, or even determine, the main trends of future economic development. Presumably, both planners and leaders would have more *favourable opportunities for realizing quickly and efficiently* desired changes if they worked out the plan on the basis of a conception chosen after careful consideration and by using a plan-variant which ensured the most harmonious development of the major components of the economy, than if they had to work by way of bargaining. Presumably, by starting from such a general conception and a complex plan-variant best corresponding to it, investments and other economic efforts could be much better coordinated and *concentrated*, and the resources of the economy could be *more rationally used*, than would be suggested by any sectoral approach. It is likely, therefore, that in this way there will be larger scope for new technical solutions, and it will become easier to dispense with everything that is antiquated or obsolete. Thus, it will become possible to accelerate both technical progress and economic growth, to improve economic efficiency. A clear and convincing conception might become an extremely important catalytic for mobilizing the masses, for awakening their interest, it might greatly contribute to make the workers feel the plan their own and put all their efforts into its best possible implementation. Thus, it may be justly assumed that in this manner the progress of socialist society and economy can be accelerated.

We certainly do not intend to give the impression of having discovered some panacea. What we propose here is not an elaborated solution or a recipe to be immediately applied, only the outline of a vast, complicated, fastidious task, that will still take much time to elaborate. If it is successfully carried out, it will lead to the solution. But I hope to have succeeded in proving what I have said that it is not only worth while but absolutely necessary and, therefore essential to undertake this task.

## RELIABILITY OF INITIAL DATA

In all developed economies innumerable and widely differentiated productive activities are going on. They are interrelated with each other, they assume each other's existence and depend on each other. Accordingly, as we have already pointed out, the normal existence and development of such economies require that this vast diversity of productive activities should be maintained and developed in a co-ordinated, harmonious and proportionate manner. In capitalism this many-sided interrelation, harmony and proportionality is expected to be provided for by the market. But, as is known, the market achieves this only through smaller or bigger shocks, through losses inflicted upon society and, especially upon the working masses. This type of regulation takes place *ex post*; a continuous disturbance of interrelations, harmony and proportions is followed by sudden repercussions which reestablish them for some time. One of the decisive advantages of the *national economic* plan over the market should consist precisely in *protecting both individuals and society from the losses* involved in such repercussions.

This advantage of the plan over the market can be fully realized only if the plan takes correctly into account the real factors which exercise an influence on the market, that is, on the relation of demand to supply. It is, therefore, a fundamental requirement of any scientifically founded planning that the data necessary for the elaboration of the plan should be checked for their reliability, on the basis of information by scientists and other specialists. Undoubtedly, there is still much to improve in our planning in this respect.

The scope of data *relating to the past*, i. e. those which can be more or less exactly established by observations, statistical surveys, accounting, computations or in any other way, should be extended and their evaluation, analysis and classification improved. Similarly, the scope of data *indicating expected development*, and by all means to be taken into account in planning, should be extended and their processing improved. These should include the opinions of specialists, international experience, estimating, extrapolation and prognoses.

To the first group belong all kinds of coefficients applied in planning which relate to the use of materials, energy, working time, as well as the most diverse norms used in the planning of social, cultural, health and educational fields, the data relating to the number, distribution by age and sex of the population, its territorial location, data on natural resources, on the productive capacity of enterprises, etc., etc. Although there is plenty of data available, *there are still many blank areas.*

It is equally important to consider the change of interrelations involved, or made necessary, by progress. To this end, relying on a wide panel of specialists, first the major trends of *scientific, technical and economic development* at home and in the most advanced industrial countries should be discovered and evaluated. All this has to be done in a better way than it has been done hitherto. Second, the development trends of the *population's needs, demands and consumption* in our country and in the most developed economies should also be analyzed and evaluated in a better manner. Third, the realized and expected development of our *international economic relations* should be studied and estimated partly on the basis of our own development and partly against the international background of technological development and business fluctuations.

I cannot expound here the tasks that are set by these requirements to our existing planning, economic, local council and scientific apparatus, etc., nor what new institutions or organizations it is advisable to create. It remains true that, particularly in some fields, much work left undone must now be performed, and that for this purpose men and machines are needed. But if our plans become better and more reliable, this will sufficiently make up for the additional work to be done.

## THE PLAN SHOULD BE CONSISTENT AND FREE FROM CONTRADICTION

The plan, of course, cannot provide for an unsurveyable mass of interrelations and much less for their expected changes. It must, however, comprise the major proportions that characterize the whole economy, their expected changes and the major objectives of development. It is a fundamental requirement that all these should be in harmony with each other. It is a decisive criterion of a scientifically founded plan that it is internally consistent and free from contradiction. In other words: the assertion of some objective specified in the plan must not come into conflict with the realization of some other objective or objectives and much less exclude it.

From the requirement of consistency and harmony it similarly follows that we are not at liberty to plan a higher utilization of any of the resources than is allowed by the existing ones or those to be created in the plan period; indeed, somewhat less than this should be planned. This applies to all resources to be employed, inclusive of imports. The insufficiency of a single condition might render it impossible to reach some important objective. This is why we should remain somewhat below the limit of possibilities when planning the utilization of resources. To what extent this should be done will be decided by practical experience and other considerations.

Does this mean that we must not draw up a "strained" plan, i. e. one aimed at the maximum utilization of all resources? It seems that the question should be formulated more precisely. From what has been said it follows that a scientifically founded plan requires us absolutely to observe the reality of the plan, its consistency, i. e. that it should be realizable. If, e. g., we plan more investment than can be realized either because labour or building material, machinery or any other essential factor is in short supply, the result will be not more investment but less and, in addition, we will have much trouble. This would be an inadmissible over-straining of the plan. It leads to a similar over-straining, equally inadmissible, if the plan assumes the most favourable development of all or of too many factors necessary for its implementation. That is to say, it is practically impossible that all of the many factors should develop most favourably.

One cannot complain if the *production* of certain scarce materials or goods is planned in a "strained" manner, i. e. that the fulfilment of the plan can be realized only if various factors simultaneously develop in a favourable direction. However, the *utilization* of such products must not be planned on the same basis but only to the extent of an amount whose production can be safely reckoned with.

In our first five-year plan — as has been mentioned in another context — we prescribed extremely high growth rates. In reality, we could not even approach them. From this, some drew the conclusion that only low growth rates can be planned. This conclusion is not supported either by science, or by experience. The high or low value of the growth rate is in itself no scientific proof of its being either unrealistic or realizable.

The requirement of internal consistency has not been fully met in our plans. One of the reasons was our own fault. But it also contributed to the mistakes made that *no adequate methods* existed for checking the harmony and consistency of the plan. *Even today these methods are not perfectly adequate.* In our traditional system of balances we cannot check, or only by very laborious methods and even then not quite sufficiently, whether the plans of production, investment, material supply, foreign trade, supply of the population's consumption, education, health, manpower, etc. are fully consistent with each other, in the sense that each of their mutual requirements can be fully met. Even the much less complicated task of checking the mutual consistency of the production plans of the various industries is but insufficiently accomplished.

This is partly connected with the fact that the plan, by its very nature, cannot fully or even approximately embrace the entirety of even the *direct* inter-industry relations. The system of balances serving this purpose covers only the factors deemed most important and even these only in necessarily rough outlines looked at from certain points of view or by stressing some of them. It is still more difficult to follow the reverberations of the effects, that is, the *indirect* inter-industry interrelations.

Thus, efforts at consistency, as a corollary of the scientific character of planning, oblige us first, not to make any concessions by tolerating any of the contradictions which can be traced to the present state of the arts and, second, to do everything in our power to improve the methods which would serve to check whether the plans are free from contradiction. In recent years we have made considerable progress in this field. By means of the *balance of inter-industry relations* (input-output table) we are in a position to check the plan for consistency—if only to the modest extent allowed by the sector-breakdown actually employed. It has been ascertained that the system of tables offered by the input-output method is suited for disclosing and checking such internal relationships of the plan as are hardly accessible to the traditional system of balances. Thus, e. g. the indirect effects of planned structural changes can be followed to a satisfactory extent in the system of input-output tables, far beyond the directly related productive branches; in the system of traditional balances this cannot be done or only with difficulty and at most imperfectly. Incidentally, by using modern computation techniques even the traditional methods could be made to serve the scientific requirements in an improved manner. Of course, everything must be done to take further steps forward.

## THE PLAN AND THE ECONOMIC MECHANISM. CENTRALIZATION *VERSUS* DECENTRALIZATION. THE PLAN AND THE MARKET

At the beginning of this paper I have already mentioned the connection between the plan and the economic mechanism. Now I must return to the problem because of the intricate and fundamentally important connections between the two. With any kind of economic mechanism, it is one of the decisive questions of socialist society: *What is or what should be the role of the plan in controlling the national economy?*

To put it more concretely: the primary problem, which arises in all socialist countries when establishing a planned economy is what degree of *centralization* should be introduced? What is it possible and worth-while centrally to decide, determine, control, prescribe by instructions, i. e. to insert into the central national economic plan? Though this is not identical with the problem of what should be prescribed for the enterprise, to what extent is the enterprise independent - it is easy to see that it is a closely related one.

The various socialist countries have attempted to solve this problem at different times and in different ways. In the course of historical development, however, partly owing to the international situation, partly due to other factors, strong centralization came generally into the foreground, in the sense that *the operation of enterprises was regulated by the plan in detail.* There are considerable differences between countries and there may be some even within the same country, with regard to what is compulsory for the enterprises. It has become general, however, that by deducing the tasks from the central plan, there is prescribed for the enterprises in their plans— though there may be important differences in detail— what goods and how much to produce, what materials and how much of them to use, how much to invest and for what purpose, how many workers and employees to engage, what wages and salaries to pay, what prime costs should be and to whom and for how much to sell the products. Even further requirements are likely to be imposed upon the enterprise and the material incentives are usually coupled with implementation of the detailed plan indicators.

Under such conditions the enterprise has hardly any independence. This has a most unfavourable effect *on the ability and propensity* of the enterprise's collective and leadership *to take initiative*. Their initiative is generally limited to a narrow sphere, despite the fact that to evoke it would ensure that the best opportunities were discovered and most of the utilized reserves, thereby promoting and greatly *accelerating* the progress of both the collective and leadership in question and of society as a whole. They are interested not in the most rational solution but in just meeting the plan indicators and, at the same time, in meeting them easily, thus also in hiding their reserves from the eyes of the supervising authorities. This often leads to the creation of an atmosphere of mistrust between the enterprise and its supervising authorities.

It was partly the recognition of these drawbacks that started the reform of the economic mechanism. One of the important requirements of the reform is to relegate decision-making to the body which has the best local and special information. The reform means *decentralization* in the sense that enterprises are given greater *independence*, that they are controlled with the aid of fewer instructions or none at all. In addition, a system of economic incentives is introduced, aimed at making both the collective and the leadership of enterprises interested in the most rational decision. It is, however, *not* enough to abstain from prescribing what the enterprise should turn out or how much material and wages can be used. It is also necessary to enable the enterprise to produce what it deems most rational, with inputs of such volume and composition as it considers expedient, and to be able to sell its product in the best possible way. This will all become possible, and, with it, the desired greater independence of the enterprise can be brought about, only if *market relations* expand and such categories as *price*, money, etc., gain in importance.

The necessity of the reform can be deduced also from a recognition that *commodity production* is a much more general and lasting feature of socialist society than was thought earlier. Although *socialist commodity production* considerably differs from the capitalist one, from the fact that commodity production is carried on in both systems, there follow also similar features. The case is similar with the *socialist market*, which fundamentally differs from the capitalist one and still shows some analogous features. It differs mainly in its conditions which are decisively determined by the socialist state and also in the fact that the majority of sellers are state enterprises (and the rest mostly cooperatives), and that even among buyers the state enterprises and cooperatives have a considerable weight. The independent movement of enterprises must be secured on *this* particular market.

But if enterprises make decisions themselves and if the plan is not passed down to enterprises in the form of instructions and plan-indicators, *how will the plan be realized?*

At first sight it seems there is no problem whatsoever. The state has a rich arsenal of economic measures at its disposal to prompt and impel the enterprises to fulfil the plan. *Price policy, credit and interest rate policy* and several other measures are indeed not only suitable for stimulating the enterprises in the direction of some desired activity but may be even more efficient than instructions because they are capable of moving people through their material interests. Thus, there is really no problem in this sense. We could ensure the implementation of the plan but that would not be sufficient. The real question is still left open: for the realization of *what objectives* and *to what extent* should the state use the economic measures available in order to influence activities? Does the plan in itself yield sufficient orientation for that? In our opninion, barely enough.

It is well known that *the scientific basis of our plans is insufficient* and recent party decisions in most countries demanded precisely on this account that planning should be improved. But even with a scientifically well founded method, the natural limits of information and human foresight will always introduce—as we have mentioned—*uncertainties* into the plan. It might always happen that unforeseen bad harvest—either at home or abroad—or the unexpected emergence of some new product and, due to this, a change in consumers' needs or the development of trade cycles in capitalist countries demanded a modification of our original plan. It is mostly *the market which first issues such warnings.* It would be a mistake *not* to take notice of such warnings and, by applying economic measures, *rigidly* to enforce implementation of the original plan.

Does it, however, follow from all we have said that control of the economy should be ceded to *market forces?* This cannot be done because it is generally known (and we have ourselves stated) that the market regulates economic processes only *ex post* and with great losses. Further, though it is in our interest that the capitalist world market should make its influence felt even on our market, e. g., by accelerating technical development, we *cannot throw our economy on the mercy* of these effects. True, we have here to deal with a market regulated by the socialist state, where demand and supply work under conditions strongly influenced by the state. But in regulating the market, the state was led by objectives laid down in the plan. If it were a mistake rigidly to enforce the plan in case of deviations between the plan and the market, it would not be satisfactory either to rely completely on the market. It is highly improbable that we could ensure in this way a favourable economic development, least of all a most favourable one.

What then, are we to do? It is now clear that we cannot *blindly* rely either on the plan or on the market. This means, however, what we should consider *both*, and weigh them carefully. True, we have to deal with a complicated problem and there are many details needing analysis and elaborations. Still, even if maximum caution is fully observed, we may state that we should seek for a solution by *simultaneously developing the contradictory aspects*. We must partly improve planning and partly develop also the socialist market and the information system for transmitting market impulses. In this manner the supervisory body will be in a position to confront the information available with the development concept of the economy and accordingly to take a decision either to modify the plan—and in this case all necessary changes should be made simultaneously—or to change the system of indirect economic measures of influence for asserting the superiority of the plan; or to change both. Depending on the importance of the problems involved, this body may be either the central bank, or the central planning agency, or the government.

*

Disclosure of the scientific laws of planning, similarly to the economic laws of society, is a process aimed at improving our knowledge and methods. Thus, the task has no perfect or final solution. We must, however, make efforts to ensure that our planning practice should not lag behind the level already attained by science.

We have established that neither the practice of our planning agency, nor the manner in which we at present decide on planning problems meet the scientific standars required of them.

In this paper I have tried to point out the actual content of the requirements for an improvement of planning and to outline the tasks following from these. But on whom do these requirements lay a charge? On the planners? On the scientists and specialists? On the leaders, the politicians? Obviously, on all of them. It is in the interest of all of us, and of society as a whole to realize the unity of theory and practice in this field.

# ROLE OF THE NATIONAL ECONOMIC PLAN IN DIRECTING THE PROGRESS OF SOCIETY

Both the state, and the dictatorship of the proletariat can be established, and the means of production can be nationalized only when and where *the level of productive forces* is relatively high and a substantial *part of production is already of a social character.* Even the Russia of 1917, an economically underdeveloped country as a whole, had some highly concentrated large-scale industry in several branches. But as soon as such a level of productive forces and such a social character of production are given, the shortest road whereby social progress can lead to material and cultural wellbeing of society and the widest possibility of activating the capabilities of all its members can be secured by means of central control of the economy, by relying on some plans. The birth of a proletarian state and the subsequent nationalization of the means of production (or at least the decisive part of them) renders this planned central control both possible and necessary.

Here lies one of the most decisive advantages of the socialist countries over capitalism. In the leading Western capitalist countries the level of productive forces and the overwhelming social character of production also require economic planning and central control, and to a certain extent their governments are forced to take some measures to this effect. The scope and efficiency of such measures are, however, limited by the private ownership of a decisive part of the means of production, and also because the state is ruled by the minority of capitalists. These two facts alone necessarily prevent central economic control and the plan from serving genuine interests and the most favourable development of society as a whole.

In a class society central control of social development — if it exists at all — necessarily serves the interests of the ruling class or classes. The socialist countries are not excepted from this rule. But here the interests of the ruling class is, at the same time, the interest of everybody, or at least of the vast majority of society. Differences between classes and contradictions deriving from these have not yet ceased to exist, but they ceased to be antagonistic contradictions. The ruling class, the workers, exercise their power in alliance with all other working classes. One of the major tasks in directing social progress consists precisely in solving class contradiction peacefully, in avoiding sharp conflicts and in gradually eliminating class differences. Another major task in directing social development is to enable the country as a whole to take an active part in the class struggle going on in the international arena. Everyday experience shows that this struggle is carried on by all kinds of means, partly by economic and cultural methods of a more civilized character but also by the most bloody, cruel and inhuman methods, amounting even to genocide.

Thus, control of social development is primarily a *political task*. The policy of the ruling class will serve the interest of all working classes only where the ruling class are the workers. Therefore it is only in socialist countries that the national economic plan—the scope of which by far transcends, from the nature of things, the economic sphere taken in the strict sense—can become an important and efficient tool of planned central control operated in the interest of society as a whole.

By saying that it may become such a tool I mean that it will not become necessarily, immediately or completely. Planning and planned central economic control are extremely complicated affairs. They are a science which does not come as a gift to the proletarian state, to its planning and leading bodies by the mere fact of establishing the dictatorship of the proletariat and by owning the decisive part of the means of production. Even today, this young science cannot compete with her older sisters, and at the time when the first dictatorship of the proletariat was born, only some of its general principles were known. To learn and acquire the art of leading society and the actual leading and controlling of society had to be accomplished simultaneously, in one and the same process, and all this at a time when social development and transformation were particularly rapid. The immensity of these tasks should be evident.

Obviously, there are limits to the possible influence of a national economic plan. There is no panacea that could replace deficiency of natural endowments or could automatically ward off elementary disasters or war. Neither can it relieve—if this were thought desirable—the national economy of the influence of the external world. But on the national economic plan may depend the extent to which a *socialist society utilizes the totality of resources at its disposal*, in the first place the main factors of its progress: the faculties and labour power of its people. In the socialist countries the five-year plan is a programme for the whole of society, embracing production, social and defensive tasks. Its effect can be felt in almost every field of social activity. Therefore, it is a pivotal problem in the whole progress of society that the plan should be sound and correct.


THE PLAN AND THE ACTUAL MECHANISM OF THE ECONOMY

Whether the plan is sound and correct will be decided, of course, only by practice. But, in order to implement a plan existing on paper and in the minds of people, some mechanism connecting the plan with practice is needed. And the role of this mechanism is never confined to the mere transmission of central decisions: it may strengthen or weaken the effect of what is being transmitted or may even produce quite different effects.

In our previous economic mechanism that we are now going to change, the plan is connected with practice by means of a system of obligatory plan indicators each of which represent some part of the national economic plan to be implemented by an individual unit of economic activity. This system restricts—independently of whether the contents of the national economic plan is correct or not—the initiative and freedom of decision of local and enterprise executives, by preventing them from solving such problems of production, wages, utilization of resources etc., for which only they can find the optimum solution. On the contrary, the system frequently induces them to choose solutions which involve a less than optimum utilization of the available resources, or even waste.

There were, of course, historical reasons why and how this system of plan indicators and its breakdown came into being. This does not, however, alter the fact that the system is no longer any good. First, it does not always influence local and enterprise executives in the right direction (sometimes it has even misled them), and it does not leave enough room for their capabilities and performance to develop. Thereby, it tends to hinder the progress of society which it should promote. It must be liquidated and replaced by a new mechanism.

Still, even with this imperfect mechanism the Hungarian economy and society attained a much faster development than we ever dreamed of before the liberation of our country. On the whole, the same is true of all socialist countries. This goes to prove that the socialist system involving planned central control of the economy has its favourable effects despite certain handicaps. It may be assumed with some justification that without these handicaps our development would have been even faster. Of course, we do not assert that our plans were always perfect, or that a more favourable development was hindered only by an obsolete mechanism. On the contrary: it may be taken as certain that even our plans were not the best possible. In all probability, a higher rate of growth could have been achieved even with these primitive methods of planning if we had had a better mechanism. But it is equally justifiable to assume that, with better planning, even the old mechanism could have produced better results. Of course, any improvement in planning would also have needed a better mechanism. The existing mechanism, in other words, had not only a breaking effect on the implementation of our plans, but affected unfavourably the planning process itself. It did not, e.g., provide all the information necessary for realistic planning. But it is no use wasting our time with speculations of the "what, if" type.

Instead, let us consider *the role of the plan* under the new mechanism *and some problems in improving it*. This is all the more necessary since, in connection with the reform or our economic system, it has been frequently stated—without any further qualification – that we are going to maintain a planned economy, and that the influence of the central economic plan must be even enhanced in the future. Such general statements, in the absence of further explanation, are not very convincing. The aim of the present article is to outline the concrete meaning of these statements and make some hints as to how planning, this most important tool for directing social development can and should be improved.

Since the national economic plan is an instrument for directing our social development, its effectiveness has to be measured by the extent to which it serves the objectives that have been set by society or, more exactly, by the leaders appointed and controlled by society. We have seen that the setting of these objectives—though inseparable from planning—belongs to the sphere of general politics rather than to national economic planning and has to be decided by the competent political bodies; the decisios of these serving as a basis and starting point for planning. (In the previons study of mine in this volume these problems were extensively dealt with.) Here I have to deal with another complex task which is rather scientific in character. This is the drawing up of the draft plan to be submitted by the central planning agency —in Hungary the *National Planning Office*—to the highest political bodies, namely, the *Congress or the Central Committee of the Party*. It is in this context that I have to deal with improvement of the plan and of the procedure of planning. It evidently follows from the complicated nature of the task itself that we have not yet succeeded in finding a satisfactory solution. The deficiencies of our plan and of our planning methods are, however, due also to other causes and it is important to identify these.

To begin with, for a long time we have neglected *thorough scientific analysis of our plans* on the basis of their factual implementation. The reports on the fulfilment of our annual and five-year plans generally do not raise the question whether the plan itself was correct, whether it contained errors or not, where and what kind of errors and mistakes have been committed. These reports state only which of the plan objectives have been attained or remained unfulfilled, and try to explain what happened. In other words, *the subject of investigation is not the plan but its fulfilment*. But since the only real proof of a plan is practice, the most important and most reliable way of improving our plans and planning methods is to reveal such deficiencies and errors of our former plans as were shown up by practice. Therefore, all our plans should be subject after their implementation to an *ex post* revision, in order to draw conclusions for future planning. This type of *ex post* analysis has not yet been performed by anybody. And we are likely to commit even graver mistakes in future planning if we are not aware of our former mistakes that have contributed to the occurrence of present disturbances and disproportions. We can reveal these mistakes and their effects only by analyzing the practical implementation of our plans. It would take us too far a field to search for reasons why this type of analysis has not been undertaken up to now. But this neglected work must be undertaken sooner or later, not only for its historical interest and importance, but primarily because it may substantially contribute to improving our plans and economic activity as a whole.

As a matter of fact, not only the *ex post* analysis of plan implementation was neglected; but also the scientific analysis of the plans *prior* to their implementation was lacking. This is the second reason for deficiencies in our planning. To begin with, the national economic plan is not submitted to the legislative bodies, to the press, to politicians, scientists and economists in such a form as would lend itself to a thorough analysis. The plan may call forth enthusiasm from the public and the experts or leave them cool; anyhow, it does not make them acquainted with its problematics, with the way in which and with what margin of error the expected results have been calculated. Such a plan does not solicit *criticism;* it does not even allow a *contribution* to be made. The statement by Tinbergen, the well-known author of *Econometrics* relating to published plans in general may just as well fit our own: "The published plans are books of which the number of pages vary from a few tens to a few thousands . . . especially the more elaborate plans are dull texts of which the reader feels that the most important information is withheld from him. In order to bring the information the policy-maker really needs for his decisions, more must be said about the methods used, the possible margins of error in the figures used, the available tools of policy and alternative solutions. As a rule, only scanty indications about these four subjects will be found in the published plans".[1]

This situation must be also changed, otherwise we lose a valuable chance for improving the plan.

As a third reason, it may be mentioned that those engaged in central planning could not, of course, simply abandon the system of control and management of the economy that had been applied in our country over a period of two decades. This system was characterized, among other things, by an extremely hard, sometimes irresistible pressure on leaders of needs to be satisfied, needs that were always greater and growing quicker than the resources available. Generally these needs were almost equally justified. Independently of other sources of error, this pressure in addition often caused economic leaders to make certain mistakes.

In addition to the difficulties in improving the system of planning, the task itself is very complicated. The major obstacles are: the vast number of *internal* factors constituting the economy and influencing its development, the great diversity of their interrelations which are difficult to account for, difficulty of forecasting the development of such unknown or insufficiently known factors as *scientific and technological progress* and, finally, the development of those *political and economic factors* which have to be considered as *external* to our economy and society. Some of these are not even sufficiently known to us, but they exert great influence on our development. These latter factors are hardly quantifiable or capable of being influenced. It is, obviously, quite impossible to account for all factors that may affect the development of our economy. Aggregation and choice of points of emphasis are unavoidable in planning. The plan, even the most detailed one, is necessarily only an outline, a simplified model of what will happen to the economy. Planners must neglect many things but they must take care not to neglect factors that might influence development in a way entirely different from what they have planned.

In our recent literature several economists—they may be a dozen—made attempts to approach the problem of drawing up the plan from several

---

[1] J. Tinbergen: *Central Planning.* New Haven–London, 1964. Yale University Press. p. 47.

7*

aspects. The diversity of the problem necessitates this many-sided approach. A solution of the problem is, of course, still far away and it may be only relative and temporary since, with the development of society, *the methods of central control and planning must also develop and improve*. The approaches mentioned have contributed to clearing-up the whole problem and thus we have certainly come nearer to a solution. In what follows I shall, therefore, try also to take into account the results of the attempts in question.

## PLAN, SOCIAL WELFARE AND SOCIAL PROGRESS

The *socialist character* of centrally controlling social progress becomes manifest primarily in the fact that the main problem, the leading motive of the plan, is: an all-round development of the faculties of citizens, a rapid raising of their welfare in every field, including cultural fields. The primacy of this problem should be correctly interpreted in the sense that all other problems are, in the final analysis, subordinated to this one, this being the measure of social progress. The safety of the socialist state, its defence against all enemies, stands, of course, in the first place on the list of problems to be solved by central control. But, on the one hand, defence of the socialist country is at the same time a prime condition of the welfare of citizens and, on the other hand, also defence requirements must be met in view of the other interests of citizens, in harmony with them as far as possible.

For some time, about three-quarters of our annual national income have been *consumed*, directly or indirectly, *by the population*. Evidently, when we speak about the welfare of society, it is mainly the utilization of this part that has to be considered. But it would be altogether too narrow an interpretation of the problem to restrict ourselves to this part. As a matter of fact, the remaining quarter, destined for accumulation, must also serve towards raising social welfare, both as regards that part of it which serves to extend production and that part which is used for other public needs. The latter will be indeed used for the most part directly in raising welfare of the population—e. g. in the form of residential construction, drainage, etc. Also in deciding on problems of accumulation the starting point should be social development and progress.

Accordingly, the plan must deal comprehensively with all major problems falling within the scope of this, if only to the extent of their fundamental, determinant features. The most important among these are:

1. Directions in the development of income distribution. The first question is how much should be spent by society in the form of wages or in related forms from the annually available *increment* of the consumption fund and how much in other forms; and also, how should the lower and upper limits of wages be changed and how are the two related requirements of socialist wage policy—differentiation according to performance and social equality—to be met, since these two requirements, partly complementing, partly contradicting each other, act as a tendency, side by side.

2. How should allocation from the *social fund*, i. e., means used in forms other than wages, grow and in what proportions should they be distributed

among the population under and over working age (children and old people), and allocated for improving the health service, education, the arts and other activities.

3. How should the means destined for education, vocational training and re-training be distributed, that is, in what directions should education and training be developed in order to meet requirements as they arise on a social scale today, as well as in the near and distant future.

4. How should the material needs of the population, including their expected development estimated on the basis of forecasts, be accounted for in planning and in controlling production? Obviously, this is not the only aspect of the problem of deciding about production, since foreign trade plays a great and ever increasing role in supplying the population. There are, however, many products which do not appear in foreign trade at all, and also the majority of others come from domestic sources.

All these are such substantial problems of social progress that their solution cannot be left to specialists alone. For, as has been shown, decisions about them will influence, among other things, the growth of productive investments and even more those directly affecting the material and cultural welfare of the population, changes in the structure of the economy, indeed, almost every problem of importance for economic development. The population itself must take part in such decisions to the greatest possible extent. In some cases extensive inquiries must be made to discover public opinion. It follows that decisions on such questions cannot be made by the specialized ministries (such as the Ministry of Labour, the Ministry of Education or the Ministry of Health), they fall within the competence of the leading political bodies of society.


PLANNING AND AGRICULTURE

In directing and planning social progress, agriculture demands particular attention in our country. Its weight and importance is determined by the fact that the number of people employed, or rather engaged in it, amounts even today to *one-third of the country's population*—although the flow of labour from agriculture to the other branches has continued already for some years. Very likely, the reduction of manpower in agriculture will continue for a long time, but we hope, it will not interfere with agricultural production in the manner in which it did some time in the past. Migration from agriculture is, in itself, a world-wide phenomenon, a natural consequence of the industrialization of agriculture and the growing productivity of labour; and this process is as yet far from being concluded. This fact does not, however, diminish but rather increases the importance of the agricultural aspects of social control and planning. It is even possible that it will become expedient temporarily to increase the number of those engaged in agriculture, namely when a greater raising of output is desirable than can be secured by technological progress and a growing productivity of labour.

Since the war Hungary's *agricultural production* has risen by about a quarter in comparison with the pre-war level if we take the average of several years, in view of the fluctuation in the production due to natural conditions. This increase is rather small, particularly when compared with the industry, the output of which is now many times greater than before the war. The comparison is more favourable if, instead of total production, output per worker is contrasted with that of industry. While, in other words, industrial employment substantially increased, agricultural employment fell *by one-third* in the same period. The relative contribution of agriculture to the national income has diminished. If we take 1949 as 100, the total of national income was 282 in 1965, while the net contribution of agriculture was only 113.

Of course, the problem is not simply that agriculture is lagging behind. For a correct judgement several factors must be considered. First, agricultural population fell during this period from half of the total to one-third. Then the contribution of agriculture to national income fluctuates rather sharply, as its output still depends to a great extent on the weather. For instance, in 1964 it was greater by 12 per cent than in 1965. Further, owing to industrialization, part of the value that appeared earlier as a contribution of agriculture to national income now appears in the output of industry. In addition, the great social transformation that has taken place with the collectivization of agriculture was unavoidably accompained by repercussions that acted against the growth of production. Finally, *too little has been invested* in agriculture by comparison with other branches of the economy; the ratio of investments to employment, to the quantity of capital engaged, or to the desired increment of production was lower than in other branches of the national economy.

This latter mistake was a direct consequence of the forced rate of industrialization which, at the beginning of the fifties, sharpened the disproportion in the development of industry and agriculture. And although we succeeded in mitigating the exaggerations of our industrialization policy, in relation to agriculture a certain kind of subjective approach continued to prevail. Year by year a considerable growth of agricultural output was planned without sufficiently supporting it with adequate investments. A certain "ideological" justification for the relative backwardness of agricultural investment was provided by the—not long ago still widespread—view that although the ownership of the agricultural cooperatives is of a socialist nature, still as group-ownership, it is of lower grade than ownership by the state where the owner is the nation as a whole. There were even people who went as far as to propose that farming cooperatives should be transformed into state farms as soon as possible. This view has almost disappeared, thanks to the discussions of the last two or three years. The opinion has become general that we have no reason to consider cooperative ownership as a lower grade of socialist ownership compared with ownership by the state. Let us remember that the indicators of economic efficiency are generally not worse in cooperatives than in state farms, frequently they are even better. Some role is certainly played by the fact that in the management of cooperatives we find fewer bureaucratic elements and that a greater role is played by local initiative and local decisions, i. e. by the elements intended to be rendered general in the new mechanism. One might say that with the implementation of the new economic mechanism the state farms will have to develop, in certain respects, in the direction shown by the cooperatives. Even up to now, central planning affected the cooperatives generally not by means of direct instructions but much more with the aid of economic measures of influence. It is perhaps agriculture that proves most convincingly the effectiveness of economic regulators. Let us only remember how many people were afraid of, and warned us against the abolition of compulsory delivery of agricultural products in 1957. They thought that without compulsory delivery the urban population could not be supplied with food. But compulsory delivery disappeared and our food supply improved instead of deteriorating.

On the other hand, owing to the new economic mechanism, the agricultural cooperatives will, as regards their methods of management, approach the state farms in many respects. But, obviously, farming cooperatives will not become state farms on this account, nor will state farms become cooperatives.

Thus, there is no obstacle—either inherent in the form of owernship or otherwise—to the plan efficiently serving the social control of agricultural development. With proper instruments, our agricultural plans can be implemented with the same efficiency as those concerning any other branch of the economy. As in other branches, in agriculture also it will depend on whether the plans are correct. This again, depends fundamentally on the decisions directing agricultural development.

Decision, and a more unequivocal and definite decision than hitherto, must be taken above all on *the main direction of agricultural development*. In deciding this problem, both the expected development of domestic needs and possibilities of exporting agricultural produce and foodstuffs must be taken into account, with the aid of market research and prognosis. The latter are of particular importance since our exports of agricultural produce and foodstuffs are and will remain for some years a substantial part of our exports to developed capitalist countries, and cannot be replaced by other items.

Decision must be taken on several problems, arising partly from the collectivization of agriculture completed only a few years ago, partly from the industrialization process that has taken place and is still going on in agriculture, and partly from earlier or forthcoming social changes affecting agriculture. Here belong several problems connected with the social care of the agricultural population, with industrial location, with the relations between town and countryside and those affecting detached farmsteads, finally questions concerning the relations between agriculture and industry, particularly the food industry.

Decision has been already taken that the *earnings of and the social benefits for* those engaged in agriculture must be gradually raised to the level of industrial workers, but this refers only to the *averages* of earnings and of benefits. There remains still to be decided how and by what means—presumably by a combination of prices and taxes—an exaggerated dispersion of incomes can be diminished; if not to equalize incomes, at any rate to make the living standards of low-income rural strata approach those of the best-earning strata of the peasantry.

Thus, again, the future development of agriculture will be a proof of whether the direction of social progress is correct. This is all the more so since, as has been shown, agricultural development is most closely connected with that in industry, investments, foreign trade and general welfare. Changes in agriculture affect almost every field of the economy.

## PLAN, TECHNOLOGICAL DEVELOPMENT AND INVESTMENT

One of the most important and most difficult problems of planned control is accounting for, estimating and planning technical progress. This is important mainly because it is most closely connected with the *productivity of labour*; only a rise in productivity makes possible the raising of social welfare. It is important also because science and technical progress widen our knowledge of our natural environment and enable us to improve it, they create new needs together with the means to satisfy them, and make possible the elimination of the most heavy, tedious or dangerous sorts of physical labour. It is important, again, because only by keeping pace with technical development in advanced countries can we successfully participate in competition on the world market by producing commodities in such quality and volume as will enable us to buy abroad from the proceeds of their sale what we are in need of.

At the same time, *the planning* of technical progress sets very difficult tasks for planners. At the head of development we find such countries whose material and intellectual power and resources available for research and innovation are of such an order of magnitude as seem unattainable for us. We hardly know anything about the research and experimental activities going on in their workshops, laboratories and scientific institutes until they come forward with their results. Still, it is this kind of work that we must somehow keep pace with.

Thus, on the one hand, we must make efforts—by highly diversified and as extensive as possible scientific and technological activity—to obtain the most diversified information and be in a position to make well-founded decisions. On the other hand, we must definitely liquidate the practice according to which all those putting up claims that seem justified are allocated material and intellectual resources in proportion to their claims.

Even in our own past few decades some examples may be found to prove in a convincing manner that even scarce resources may yield substantial results if they are well used. We can still remember that in the backward agrarian Hungary before World War II, whose industrial output was only a fraction of what it is today, such important and even pioneering products could be turned out as, e. g., the electrical engine of Kandó or the engine of Jendrassik. There were also some enterprises the products of which had reached the world level at the time. This should serve as a lesson; and we have to select on the basis of circumspect scientific investigation some—not too many—fields where even with our limited material and human resources substantial results can be achieved, even by international standards, if we take into account a rational international division of labour in research and developmental activity and some other important points of view. In all other fields we should strive to maintain the position we have already reached, relying mainly not on our own research bases but on adaptation of foreign results, either in the form of scientific and technical cooperation between socialist countries or by buying licences from industrially developed capitalist countries. It may and, obviously, it will occur that owing to our limited resources we must abandon development projects even in fields where some results had been achieved earlier. In some cases, even our actual output may have to be reduced; this is what is now being done in coal mining.

In this connection it is of decisive importance that at present we have more favourable possibilities for shaping our production pattern and for utilizing our resources rationally, since we belong to the system of the socialist world economy and take part in the *socialist international division of labour*. However, we have not yet succeeded in utilizing these possibilities to the necessary extent, so that not only our technical progress but also the necessary structural transformation of our production has proceeded more slowly than was desirable. Of course, the structural transformation of an economy cannot be performed overnight and it is also obvious that the necessary transformation is bound to take place in any case, by dint of the laws of nature. But this will be a rather slow process if our plans do not sufficiently channel our development in this direction, as was the case in the past; precisely *because they did not secure the most rational allocation of resources*. The emphasis we had placed on some major branches of industry, such as telecommunication, precision engineering, machine tools, electrical engineering or the chemical industry, could not be considered as constituting such a rational allocation of resources, since any of these fields alone is larger than could be fully covered even if we had concentrated all our human and material resources upon it. Our resources should be allocated perhaps to more, perhaps to fewer special fields, but at any rate to much *narrower* ones. Let us add, that even the industries mentioned above could not obtain specially earmarked allocations from our resources—at least as regards scientific and technological research and, particularly, investment.

True, the mistakes we have committed were connected not only with the deficiencies of planning, they were also aggravated by the prevailing economic mechanism. The main deficiency of the latter is not that it transmits the plan to practice poorly and in a distorted way, but that it influences planning incorrectly, against the national economic interest, in the direction of fragmentation of resources instead of concentrating them. The pressure on planners to meet requirements that are growing faster than the resources has already been mentioned. And claims upon investment have no practical limit since investments are allocated to the enterprises free of charge. Our whole system of investment decision works in such a way that it tries to satisfy all claims to the same extent, as if all of them were equally justified. But almost all claims can be shown to be justified if sufficiently good arguments are put forward. No wonder that planners became overwhelmed by a feeling of frustration, by the conviction that "poverty is our main evil", since we can never satisfy all justifiable claims. As a consequence, not even the most justifiable investment projects are supplied to the extent that would be necessary for their speediest, cheapest and most efficient realization; development programmes become protracted in time, *investment resources are fragmented*. The result is that new projects have to be implemented in a too slow and too expensive way, so that when they are put into operation, they often are already obsolete or, at least, not the most up-to-date ones.

The reform of our system of economic control and management promises to cure this situation radically by abolishing the free-of-charge allocation of investment resources. It will put an end to the great pressure which has led to the consequences described above. But this change in itself cannot ensure a correct allocation of investment resources, nor can this be expected from the greater autonomy of enterprises enabling them to decide on a considerable part of investment. It is necessary that *a national economic plan and a central control of economic development* should influence their investment decisions by economic regulators. Further, the national economic plan establishes the main directions for centralized investments (i. e., those falling outside the scope of enterprises); it contains even individual data for certain major investment projects. In the final analysis, national economic planning is responsible for the correct allocation of all resources available for investment purposes. Thus, here we have to do not with some detailed problems but with the very *fundaments* of social progress. In these, scientific and technical development, rational allocation of investment, structural changes of production and foreign trade, improvement of labour productivity, adequate relations between town and countryside, the rise in the material and cultural well-being of society become intertwined.


PLAN AND FOREIGN TRADE

No planned central control of the economy is conceivable without a central *control of foreign trade;* this is also a condition of planned social progress. Foreign trade is the field where even under non-socialist conditions state interference has a long history, justifying its necessity. But, although the necessity for interference is testified by history, the *planning* of foreign trade is very difficult since the role of factors that escape the planners, because they are entirely or partly independent of them, is here at its greatest. Interference is perhaps most frequent in this field precisely because foresight and scope for preventive influencing are here most limited.

These statements hold for Hungary to an increased extent. If a country having a relatively small area and a dense population attains a certain level of industrial development, foreign trade will have an important role in supplying its industry with raw materials. This is the situation also in our country, with the result that foreign trade has a relatively great importance in its economic relations with the rest of the world. Most of the raw materials and other commodities purchased from abroad are financed from the sales-receipts of goods sold there. In this respect there are significant differences between various countries. There are countries which obtain substantial sums of foreign exchange from sources other than the export of commodities: from transport, tourism and other services, from transfers coming from citizens of the country (or their relatives) living abroad, from interest and amortization of credits granted to foreigners, or from profit on investments made abroad. In Hungary the majority of the commodity purchases made in each year have to be paid for from the commodity exports of the same year. Thus, for our country *foreign trade is almost the only and at any rate the most important means* of securing balanced economic relations with the rest of the world, that is, equilibrium in our balance of international payments. There are few fields of the economy where such importance would be attached to equilibrium as in the case of the balance of international payments. A lasting disequilibrium in this balance may endanger economic development as a whole.

In consideration of all these, it may be stated that foreign trade is a pivotal factor in the Hungarian economy, so that it has to be given a *central position* also in planning. This means not only that foreign trade must be planned most carefully but also that the plans for every major field of the economy must be drafted with due consideration for the possible, or probable or desirable development of foreign trade. Thus, the essential problems of industrial or agricultural development must be decided — among others — by calculating whether, instead of producing some necessary product at home, it would not be more advantageous to produce and export *something else* and buy with the foreign exchange earned in this way the product which is necessary. This is always worthwhile considering if it is intended to introduce some new product in the production of which we have no experience. Nor can the scale of production be correctly planned and unit costs calculated without reliably assessing import and export possibilities.

But if this is true of production, it must be true of productive investment as well. It is no doubt a deficiency of our planning practice that this principle has not been consistently applied. Generally, when deciding on the inclusion in the plan of some investment project, the possibility of attaining an export surplus or a saving in imports was always an important argument. Nevertheless, several major investment projects have been proposed and decided upon *without carefully assessing and weighing* their effects on foreign trade and the balance of payments. No doubt, this is partly due to the lack of a sufficiently elaborated method for such assessment and also necessary information is scarce.

We have seen that central planning and control of foreign trade is inseparable from that of production. Thus, it is inseparable also from planning and control of investment. Only a small step forward is needed to acknowledge that in Hungarian national planning and control foreign trade is closely connected with technical development and with structural transformation of the economy. This is comprehensively expressed in the statement that foreign trade has a substantial weight in controlling the development of our whole economy.

Up to this point I have dealt with some questions and with some major components of development that have central importance for the control of social progress, I have tried to show that the four major fields, the four major complexes which are for various reasons in the foreground of Hungarian planning, are closely interrelated and that they are of decisive importance for planned control. Our research workers who touched upon the problems of planning have raised these problems from various aspects.

The same problems are being dealt with in another way by other workers who are engaged in the *application and applicability of mathematical methods in economics*, or in applying mathematics to the analysis of the economy and to the control of economic development. With the aid of new methods they have tried to introduce some principle of systematization in the mass of economic phenomena, which are difficult to survey, facilitating thereby orientation and foresight and thus also rational decision. With their help we are more and more in a position to follow up the direct and indirect effects of economic actions, those which appear quickly and are easy to see as well as those which have reverberating and long-term effects. Their results, coupled with modern, high-efficiency computer techniques enable us to elaborate and analyze any number of partial plan variants, each satisfying a given set of requirements, and to solve quickly such planning tasks as — owing to the huge amount of labour and time they used to require — were earlier not even attempted or the deficient and roughly approximate solution of which we had to put up with. As everywhere in the world, in this country as well several research workers are engaged in extending these mathematical methods to ever newer fields and problems of the economy and development and — though practical applications are relatively scarce and even these generally lag behind the possibilities disclosed and worked out — the use and importance of these methods is beyond discussion. With their aid it can be assured that the plans become scientifically better founded than previously, consistently satisfying the requirements of practice, and also that they become free from contradictions.

## TRANSITION TO THE NEW SYSTEM OF CONTROL

In some fields the reform of our economic mechanism has begun earlier, but its general implementation from the 1st of January, 1968, has set new problems and tasks to the political body that controls social and economic development as well as to planners. We are in the middle of our third five-year plan period. The results achieved in the course of these two years are satisfactory. Not as if the many problems engaging us in connection with our development had all been solved. Neither our balance of payments, nor our production pattern, nor agricultural development, nor our investment policy are satisfactory. And there are numerous other tasks awaiting solution. But, after a period of healthy development, our problems have not been aggravated, they may be said *to have eased*. The real income of the population has risen at a higher rate than was expected, its growth in the first two years of our five-year plan being more than 10 per cent. The growth of the national income was similarly favourable; whereas in 1965 it rose by only one per cent, it increased by 6 per cent in 1966, that is, by as much as in 1963 or 1961. We expect from the reform of economic control and management above all a healthier development of the economy, the elimination of phenomena that hitherto had accompanied our economic growth and gave rise to anxieties. We hope that this can be achieved by means of scientific and technical progress, by transforming the pattern of production and by accelerating the growth of national income and the welfare of the population.

But what conclusions follow from this for the plan and the planning procedure?

Sound deliberation suggests that we should by no means become overconfident. According to the resolution taken by the Central Committee of our Party in 1967, therefore, we did not plan an *acceleration of the rate of growth*. We did not want to increase the requirements raised against ourselves earlier, and thereby to augment the troubles connected with transition to the new system of planning. Unless we have an important reason for a change, the wisest course is to stick to our original plan.

Even so, there is sufficient food for thought. Under the new conditions, the role of commodity and money relations will grow substantially, and so will their influence on production and turnover. We must be prepared – as has been pointed out by several Hungarian economists – for the market frequently to require something else than the plan. What should be done in such cases? The lack of plan indicators must not in the least hinder us in setting ourselves all objectives that we deem necessary; we have abundant experience that most objectives can be more efficiently reached with economic regulators than with direct plan instructions. Difficulties arise if we do not know *what objectives* should be striven for with the aid of economic regulators. In this case we cannot be guided by general considerations, or statements asserting that in a socialist country the plan is the fundamental factor and its supremacy over the market has to be safeguarded. Such statements provide no help if, in some concrete case, it turns out that, at prevailing prices, market demand for TV sets, or leather shoes or tractors is smaller than what we had planned. Decision can be taken only with knowledge of the factors that influence and determine the plan and the market. The domestic and the foreign market situation, prices and their tendencies, our needs and their expected changes, our production facilities and costs, the position of our balance of trade and payments in relation to various countries must be known. Expert decision on what should be done can be taken only on such a basis.

But possible conflicts of the plan and the market are only one kind of contradiction to be expected. In the new system of economic control and management, namely, *contradictory effects* must assert themselves, precisely in order that the system should operate efficiently. If there are factors which induce enterprise managers to raise a greater demand for import goods, there must be some other factors which prevent them from wanting too much. Some incentives will promote the expansion of enterprise investments, others tend to curb investment activity. The situation will be similar in almost every field. So long as this applies only to enterprise decisions, this does not affect the central planning agency, nor the political body responsible for the control of social development. The situation is, however, different when such effects appear on a national scale. Both the central planning agency and the responsible political body are most closely interested in the levels of investment, foreign trade, prices and the balance of payments. But changes in all these cannot be precisely known in advance, however circumspect previous regulation has been; at most they can be predicted with greater or less probability. The aim of previous circumspect regulation is precisely that we should not be exposed to disagreable surprises. Now what should happen if things still take a course deviating from what has been planned, expected or desired? If we wish to avoid that uncertainty, and even confusion should become prevalent in such cases, we must prepare ourselves also for such occurrences.

It seems expedient to establish, for the initial period of the new system of economic control and management, a special board from the representatives of the economy, certain governmental agencies and of the party leadership, with a triple task: to follow with attention the *development of the situation;* to *decide* on economic measures to be taken should differences of opinion arise between the leading government bodies; and to *work out proposals* should the situation deviate in some important field from the desired one to any considerable extent. The attention of this body should be focussed exclusively on the following major fields: *(1) real wages and real incomes; (2) employment; (3) foreign trade; (4) investment and (5) prices.* With its tasks limited to these problems, this body could provide effective help to the responsible political leadership in keeping under control the progress of social development on decisive points even in the case of an unexpected development of events.


SOME ADDITIONAL STATEMENTS

Our study requires some additional statements. The first: all major problems of society and economy are *so closely interrelated* that decision on any of them cannot be taken without this decision influencing also the others. Once we have decided in what fields and how the welfare of society should be raised, many things have been already implicitly decided, e. g., as regards investment, production, location of plants, foreign trade, health, education, etc. Similarly, if a decision has been taken on the major problems of agriculture, this decision automatically includes a set of decisions regarding many questions of industrial development, location, foreign trade and living standards. The list need not be continued. After what has been said there is need of no further proof to show that the more important fields are all closely interrelated, they mutually influence and determine each other, not only at the moment but regarding their future trends. Decision must, therefore, be such as to make possible and secure a development of the various fields that mutually complement each other and are in harmony with each other.

*Second*: it must be emphasized that there are no economic decisions that are *merely economic*, that is, which do not touch upon other fields of social life as well. Decisions taken on economic problems of major importance will, in most cases, deeply influence the various factors of living conditions, the present and future situation of people. But the problems influencing the life of people or even influencing them decisively—whether of an economic or some other character—are never problems purely for specialists, but in every case social problems, political problems. It would be wrong, therefore, to trust economic specialists with decision of these problems, however well trained they may be. It would be wrong for two reasons. First, because even the best economic experts do not necessarily have *outstanding political judgement*. Second, since we have to deal with political problems, the decision requires a *social standpoint, a political standpoint*, one determined and conditioned by class points of view, rather than by mere expert knowledge. It goes without saying that expert knowledge of highest standard is an indispensable condition for drawing up the national economic plan before it is submitted for political decision. A correct political decision can be taken only on the basis of such a plan as satisfies the requirements raised in this article in every respect, and only if those who take the decision have sufficient economic horizon to survey the subject they decide upon.

The *third* additional remark derives from the complexity and diversity of the questions and decisions connected with the plan, which I have tried to make plain. This suggests that we should not only endeavour to improve planning but also make efforts to work out adequate methods and procedures for the *decisions*. From the experience gained up to now and relying on the considerations and discussions of the former it seems expedient to decide, on the five-year plan of the economy or on a plan covering an even longer period, *in several stages*. In the course of drawing up the plan proposal, the central planning agency should consult, and ask for the decision of, the leading political body several times. As a first step it should make a proposal only on the major features of the plan; at that time, only these would be approved by the political body. This would be followed by the elaboration of somewhat more detailed plan variants, each based on the decisions that had been taken in the first stage. These variants would be submitted again to the political body for choice and decision. It may happen that the work carried out on the basis of the decision taken will reveal such problems as again necessitate a decision to be taken by the leading political body.

All our efforts aimed at the development and improvement of these methods and procedures must be based on a recognition that only the continuous checking of our plans in practice, combined with permanent criticism of ourselves and correction of the mistakes committed and gradual improvement of our work are capable of raising planning, the planned central control of social progress, to a level that corresponds to the requirements of science.

# ON LONG-TERM NATIONAL ECONOMIC PLANNING

Let us start at the beginning. Is it possible to draw up a realistic long-term economic plan, i.e. one covering at least 10, but, preferably even 15 or 20 years? If so, is it needed and what is its use? It is not quite easy to answer these questions; I will, however, try.

Let us take the first question. Is it possible? We are now engaged in drawing up a 15-year plan for 1971–85. We trust we can manage, but many things we do not see clearly as yet. We try to learn from our earlier experiences and partly also from those of others. Unfortunately, these are not too heartening.

It was about ten years ago that we first experimented with long-term planning. We tried to prepare a plan for the period 1960–80. The National Planning Office, more than a dozen committees and a host of specialists were working on it. In 1961 a summary was achieved, then a more detailed version became ready by 1962 and a modified one in 1963, since it was found that the growth rates planned had been too high. Then, partly because of the doubts that had arisen, the project was abandoned.

In the meantime almost half of the period 1960–1980 has elapsed. What does the comparison of the targets then planned with actual reality show? I will quote only a few examples. According to the plan made at that time, coal production should have been increased to a rather considerable extent. Much higher energy consumption had been planned than proved to be necessary. The plan for metallurgy stood the test in relative terms, that for engineering did not at all. Development of agriculture lagged far behind the planned level.

This is certainly not too reassuring. Nor can other CMEA countries which simultaneously experimented with long-term planning boast much better results. A great part of the data relating to 1970 in the 1961–81 plan of the Soviet Union, accepted at the 22nd Party Congress in October 1961, proved also to be untenable. (According to these, e.g., "By 1970 the Soviet Union will exceed the United States in terms of per capita production, including that of the major agricultural products, and everybody will have plenty of material goods at their disposal.")

It cannot be denied that our first attempt ended in mixed and by no means satisfactory results. And for what reasons? We have not analyzed them, at least not in a scientific manner. But I believe I have succeeded in convincingly proving one of the greatest weaknesses in Hungarian planning, mainly in our five-year planning, to lie in two interrelated features of the method employed, namely, in the sectoral approach and in the lack of a general conception.[1] But we tried to draw up the twenty-year plan on the basis of the same methods. Obviously, it is here that at least one cause of the failure must lie.

It is also obvious that with the mistake once recognized the possibility of avoiding it the next time is greatly increased. I am speaking only of the possibility, not of a certainty. According to historical experience both individuals and collectives are inclined to repeat even an error that has been recognized as such. Now that committees have once again been formed around the Planning Office to carry out the preparations for the long-term plan—and we shall revert to these committees below—there has been a deliberate effort to break with the sectoral approach. This was not quite successful, but it can still be remedied. We have not yet reached the stage of working out a general conception, but we are already on the way to it. Observance of these two points is surely not enough for surmounting easily the obstacles in the way of long-term planning (of the obstacles themselves we shall speak later) but it affords a promising chance for compiling a realistic plan. We shall see that this promise is supported also by other arguments.

Thus, to our first question we may answer with some optimism—and at the present stage of development of human society we can hardly do without optimism—that in all probability we will succeed in drawing up a realistic 15-year economic plan. Let us now turn to the second question: is it needed and what will be its use?

To this question, more or less identical and more or less convincing answers have already been given by several specialists. Examining them carefully, some duplicities in approach will be observed. The harmony is not complete. Let us see. G. Kovács says: "The long-term plan is the strategic program of the general and economic policy of the party and the government. The purpose of its elaboration is to provide a clear perspective as well as proper orientation in drawing up the medium-term plans."[2] According to T. Morva: "The purpose of a fifteen or twenty-year plan is to work out the long-term directions of development and to point out the firm corner stones which decisively determine the direction and character of progress in the development of production."[3] I. Hetényi puts it this way: "There are some processes of great importance which can be assessed and their directions of development and their order of importance established only on the basis of harmonized long-term tendencies (plans)."[4] J. Drecin, again, says: "The long-term plan gives a comprehensive and harmonized (consistent) idea of the tendencies and prospects of social, political and economic progress; it is destined to provide orientation for deliberate social actions (decisions) to be made in the near future in order to satisfy the objective

[1] I. Friss: *Ideas on the Improvement of National Economic Planning*, in this volume. Similar problems presented themselves in the Soviet Union in the second half of the fifties in connection with planning practice. See T. Morva's article in *Népgazdasági tervezés és irányítás* (National economic planning and control). Budapest, 1968. Közgazdasági és Jogi Könyvkiadó. pp. 246–247.

[2] *Népgazdasági tervezés és irányítás*, p. 36.

[3] Ibid. p. 238.

[4] *Gazdaság*, 1968, No. 4.

requirements of a more distant future and to reach the social objectives relating to that more distant future."[5]

It is not opposed concepts that I have confronted here with one another. The duplicity of approach emerges here and there from the same statement although with varying emphasis: political programme and orientation, plan and tendency. Behind them there loom two questions. One is, whether it is possible to draw up a clear perspective with such a large number of unknown factors influencing development. The second is, to what extent are we capable of influencing this development under the conditions of so great uncertainty.

The two questions arise from the same underlying doubts. Where is the limit between the objective factors external to us which can not, or can hardly, be influenced by higher central control, on the one hand, and the effects on the economy of social forces and deliberate central control, on the other. In other words: to what extent are we active agents and to what extent passive spectators of the development of our economic—and, of course, also of our non-economic—destinies? Again differently formulated: where is the boundary between social development taking place under the effect of spontaneous forces and that brought about by the plan? This is a fundamental question and one which finds wide reflection in international, mainly economic, philosophical and sociological literature.[6]

Considering all this, the answer to the first question is given by two peculiar features of the long-term plan. One consists in the fact that a

[5] From a memorandum of the Long-term Planning Department of the National Planning Office to the Consultative Committee.

[6] This is no place, nor is there any need to dwell here at length on this literature. It is still worth while to mention some of its features related to planning. Since planning has only a comparatively low and only recently established standing in bourgeois literature, a passive approach has been characteristic up to recent times. In some countries the justification of planning was denied and only forecasting or prognosis acknowledged. In socialist economics, again, prognosis was regarded only as an important tool and complementary to directive planning. "The prognosis answers the question: what can be expected from the future? What is it that will certainly materialize, independently of the will of the decision-makers? . . . The system of indicators that does not meet the requirement (of being addressed to someone) is no plan, no program of activity, only a prognosis." [J. Kornai: A többszintű népgazdasági programozás alkalmazásáról (On the application of multi-level national economic programming), Közgazdasági Szemle, 1968, No. 2.] or: ". . . the prognosis determines what can happen and under what conditions, while the plan determines what should happen and who must do what in order that this should happen". (N. Lebedinskiy, Long-term plans and prognoses. Kommunist, 1968, No. 9.). Recently, however, owing to causes which I will mention later in this article, another view has also been spreading in socialist economies. According to an article by V. Trapeznikov, Member of the Academy of Sciences of the Soviet Union, in Izvestiya on May 17th, 1967, "It is not only interesting but indispensable to see the future directions of scientific and technical progress . . . the GOELRO Plan, the development plans of our country, beginning with the first five-year plan—were all development prognoses of the most important branches of our economy." Yu. Belik, I. Konnig and others sharply attacked this conception of which Trapeznikov is not the only exponent. In an article by the Czech economist O. Lacina (Long-term prognosis of the Czechoslovak economy, Czechoslovak Economic Papers, 1969. No. 11.) and in publications of some other Czech and Slovak economists, the terms "long-term plan" and "long-term forecast" are used in a more or less similar sense.

fifteen-year plan cannot be as detailed and definite as a five-year plan. We knew this already when preparing our first long-term plan. At that time I wrote that ". . . the fifteen-year plan, much more than the five-year plan, must take into account not only the given results of technical progress but also the *trends* of scientific and technological development and the *expected* results of that development. However, the obvious fact that the progress of science and technology and the rate of this development can be foreseen only approximately or imagined for fifteen years ahead and can be outlined only roughly, leads to the equally obvious conclusion that the fifteen-year plans cannot be so directive in character as are the five-year plans and much less so than the annual ones. They must reserve much more freedom for later changes, possible transfers, and must be exceedingly flexible."[7]

The second feature consists in the fact that the fifteen-year plan offers greater possibilities for asserting a general conception of economic policy (if there exists any—we shall revert to the problem of general conception later on), than do the plans covering shorter periods. The existing situation, the projects in train or those just started or even those only decided upon would tie the hands of those in control. Of course, with the passing of time, the relative weight of these limitations will decrease. One great Soviet pioneer of scientific planning G. A. Feldman wrote already more than forty years ago: "The longer the time horizon for which we plan the development of the economy, the more independent of the initial situation shall we become."[8]

The second question—as already pointed out and as it also emerges from what was said above—is closely related to the first one. The answer was long ago given by science. We are able deliberately to influence development to the extent that we know its internal relationships and laws, the springs of motion as well as the possibilities and methods of influencing them. To find out about this is the task of science, a scientific achievement. To realize this scientific achievement, to disclose the internal relationships of the movement of our society and, relying on the laws recognized, deliberately to direct the movement—this is our task. "The chief defect of all hitherto existing materialism"—wrote Marx in 1845—"is that the thing (*Gegenstand*), reality, sensousness, is conceived only in the form of . . . *contemplation* (*Anschauung*); but not as *human* . . . *practice* . . . In practice man must prove the truth, . . . the reality and power, . . . of his reasoning . . . The coincidence of the changing of circumstances and of human activity can be conceived and rationally understood only as *revolutionizing practice*."[9]

[7] I. Friss: Az MSZMP VII. kongresszusa és a közgazdaságtudomány feladata (7th Congress of the HSWP and the tasks of economics). *Közgazdasági Szemle*, 1960, No. 5, p. 532.

[8] G. A. Feldman: On the theory of the growth rate of national income. *Planovoe Khoziaistvo*, 1928. No. 11. (In Hungarian: Közgazdasági Szemle, 1967, No. 11, p. 1352).

[9] K. Marx: Theses on Feuerbach, in: K. Marx and F. Engels: *Selected Works*, Vol. II. Moscow, 1949. Foreign Languages Publishing House. pp. 365–366.

What have these two notions to do with each other?

The long-term plan is our own internal affair, a matter of high public importance. It is an important affair also in other socialist countries. And the theory of convergence?

"It is one of our new important tasks to fight tendencies towards "breaking-up"—e.g. the theories of convergence—and ideas aimed at a deliberate subversion of Marxism." Thus the recently published scientific directives of the Hungarian Socialist Workers Party.[10]

Why do I then mix these two highly different things?

I am doing so because one of the fundamental questions in long-term planning is whether we can take as an example the most advanced capitalist countries? Can we set in some field—and if so, in which one—as the objective of a long-term plan to achieve a state which has already been attained in some, or, maybe in all highly advanced capitalist countries?

It is not my intention, however, to mislead the reader—who would never forgive me if he saw any such intention—and I will not try to make him believe that anybody, be it the planner or the man in the street, had any doubt that, at least in some fields, we indeed want to achieve things that exist in the most advanced capitalist countries. And in those particular fields it would be fine to achieve it as early as possible. But if we want to remain on earth, on the basis of realities and not walk in the clouds, we shall have to put up with the idea that only in the framework of a long-term plan can we reach the level of supply in motor-cars—true I could have mentioned also a less ambitious example—that exists now in the United States of America.

But are we not, in this way, selling our souls to the devil, that is, to the theory of convergence? As a matter of fact, the advocates of the theory of convergence would allege that the developed capitalist and the developed socialist countries are of a related nature and advancing in the same direction. What is the difference between them and ourselves and what is the correct standpoint?

Let us examine this point somewhat more closely.

W. W. Rostow, one of the originators of the theory of convergence, the discoverer of the stages of economic growth makes no secret of the fact that the purpose of his discovery is to confront the Marxian interpretation of historical development, which he does not like, with an alternative theory which he likes.[11] Every country, he would explain, has to go through five stages of economic development which regularly follow upon each other. He is not boasting of the fact, but his book proves it convincingly, that he has never read and does not know Marx. But, obviously, this is not important to him. What is important is to prove that the socialist revolution did not bring any essential new momentum into the economic development of Russia, that the Russian take-off—the beginning of modern economic

[10] *Társadalmi Szemle*, 1969, Nos 7–8, p. 62.
[11] W. W. Rostow: *The stages of economic growth*. London–New York, 1960. Cambridge University Press. pp. IX, 2 and 106.

development in Rostow's terms — took place similarly to and simultaneously with the Canadian one; the five-year plans have to be interpreted as a later stage of development and the Russian affair, the Russian case, fits as well into the lose framework of his development-stage analysis as does the American one.[12] In other words: It was quite superfluous to make such a fierce and bloody performance as the socialist revolution since economic development would occur in the same way with or without revolution and would proceed in the same direction in both socialist and capitalist countries.

It would be meaningless to criticize here Rostow's theory which is based on impressions and similarities rather than on intensive research; this has been done by distinguished bourgeois economists such as e.g. F. Perroux, M. Shinohara, S. Kuznets.[13] This kind of convergence theory is rather transparent and it is not difficult to show the flaws in it. If it still had success also, and even great success, with others than arch-enemies of communism, this can be explained by at least three major causes. First of all, it is captivating; whith its simplicity, its lack of scientific pretensions, it yielded a theory which, although in dim colours, has thrown a new light on many things. Secondly, for the petty bourgeois it has furnished a reassuring refutation of that rascal Karl Marx. Thirdly, this theory has found believers also because it has some true foundations which present-day experience has proved to be right. It speaks of the leading sectors of economic take-off, distinguishing primary, main growth sectors, complementary growth sectors and derived ones. Indeed, in certain phases of development individual economic sectors played an outstanding role in the development of some country. Then he goes on: "Like the take-off, long-term growth requires that the society not only generate vast quantities of capital for depreciation and maintenance, for housing and for a balanced complement of utilities and other overheads, but also a sequence of highly productive primary sectors, growing rapidly, based on new production functions."[14]

It is true, indeed; let us think only of the sudden growth of the modern motor car industry, or of the chemical industry with its production of plastics and man-made fibres, or of telecommunication techniques and electronics. These findings are correct and appropriate, in spite of the fact that Rostow puts his whole theory at the service of anti-communism and anti-sovietism, of the cold war and armaments. In fact, from the point of view of our subject it is worth noting that this correct and appropriate findings should be taken into account also in long-term planning.

One of the outstanding advocates of the theory of convergence is J. K. Galbraith. He says: "Among the least enchanting words in the business lexicon are planning, government control, state support and socialism. To consider the likelihood of these in the future would be to bring home the appalling extent to which they are already a fact."[15]

[12] Ibid. pp. 66 and 93.
[13] On the same critiques, see G. Ripp: *A gazdasági növekedés szakaszai és az ipari társadalom elmélete* (The stages of economic growth and the theory of the industrial state). Budapest, 1967. Kossuth Könyvkiadó. pp. 165 ff.
[14] W. W. Rostow: op. cit. p. 53.
[15] J. K. Galbraith: *The new industrial state.* London, 1967. Hamilton. p. 389.

Unlike Rostow, Galbraith does not preach anti-Soviet propaganda, cold war or armaments. He finds that a convergence of the two systems can be observed in the field of modern large-scale production requiring big capital, complicated production processes and organization. From this he draws the conclusion that in capitalist countries also there is a need for price control and the elimination of the market, for planning and for full autonomy for large-scale enterprises, that it is necessary for the government to regulate the volume of total demand, to provide for adequante education and training of manpower, etc. "Thus convergence between the two ostensibly different industrial systems occurs at all fundametal points. This is an exceedingly fortunate thing . . . it will dispose of the notion of inevitable conflict based in irreconcilable difference."[16]

The political views of Galbraith are much more progressive than those of Rostow—but his theory may nonetheless, or accordingly, actually serve the policy of "breaking-up". And is he right? Certainly not, when he comes near to putting the sign of equality between the socialist and the advanced capitalist countries. But he is undoubtedly right in stating that large-scale capitalist enterprises as well as governments must, absolutely must, plan their economic activities. (As a matter of fact this had already been stated by Lenin with respect to the biggest capitalist monopolies more than fifty years ago—although not with respect to state-monopoly capitalism which existed at the time in its infancy only.) He is also right when he finds many similar traits in organizational forms, in pricing, the organization of supply and demand and other things.

Thus, we need not accept the theory of convergence to recognize what otherwise unequivocally emerges from the data and figures about the socio-economic development of the advanced capitalist and advanced socialist countries, namely, that there is really much similarity between the two. How could it be otherwise? For producing material wealth, the same, or more or less similar, means are available to both. "With productive forces roughly on the same level of development, the material-technical aspects of the process of economic development must necessarily have common features even in the case of deviating production relations"—says Ripp.[17] In addition, there must be similarities also with respect to production relations in the two systems, even if the fundamental relations of production, those of ownership, are radically different. In the US, productive forces could not have reached their present extraordinarily high level, had not proper organizational, control, planning, recording, selling, information-technical etc. methods and means been developed simultaneously. These are partly inseparable from capitalist ownership relations and exploitation, but partly they constitute, separated from the latter, the most suitable carriers of the development of widely socialized and advanced forces of production. Therefore, Marx's statement that "The country that is more developed industrially only shows to the less developed the image of its own future"[18] is—*mutatis mutandis*—true also if the more developed country is a capital-

[16] Ibid. p. 391.
[17] G. Ripp: op. cit. p. 99.
[18] K. Marx: *Capital*, Vol. 1. Moscow, 1949. Foreign Languages Publishing House. 19 p.

ist and the less developed a socialist one. The United States is the most aggressive state of the world, the ally and supporter of the most reactionary and corrupt systems, which is financing and organizing *coups d'état* all over the world and carrying on genocidal wars.[19] It is not by coincidence that she is at the same time the wealthiest state of the world; nor do the above facts exclude the possibility that American methods should serve, in several respects, as an orientation in working out our long-term plans.

If as early as fifteen years ago large-scale capitalist monopolies could not do without planning, with the emergence of state-monopoly capitalism planning had to come to embrace the whole of the national economy.[20] With this step also the activities of the state, which had grown together with the monopolies, will come to embrace new fields—planning and what is necessary for implementing the plan.[21] It is, however, worth noting that at the present stage of their organization the capitalist countries are generally unsuited for preparing comprehensive long-term national plans, and some of them (such as England, France, Norway, The Netherlands, the United States, Japan) are drawing up forecasts and prognoses only.[22]

[19] J. M. Gillman, a Marxist analyst of American capitalism pointed already in 1964 to the close connection between prosperity, armaments and war: "In the years following the Korean war, ... large and increasing amounts of government spending were necessary to prop up production and employment ... Now we cannot relax these expenditures ... Indeed, the very viability of the system now seems suspended on the brink of war." (Quoted from J. M. Gillman: *Prosperity in Crisis*. New York, 1965. Marzani and Munsell. p. 162.

[20] Galbraith wrote already some years ago that: "The difference between modern national communities is not in having a plan, but in the degree to which the existence of the plan is avowed, in the formality with which the goals are spelled out, and in the particular techniques used to achieve the goals of the plan." "... two closely interrelated and much debated questions: first, the extent of state initiative, as opposed to market incentive, that is required for reaching planning goals; and second, the extent to which state initiative requires public ownership of productive facilities." (*Economic Development in Perspective*. Harvard Univ. Press, Cambridge, Mass. 1964, p. 62.)

[21] Here are two illustrative examples to characterize the spread of government activity: (1) "In the United States, it is no longer necessary to find an appropriate doctrinal justification for a very extensive exercise of government initiative. One measure of the scope of this initiative is the proportion of the Gross National Product controlled and disposed of by the State. In the United States, this is approximately 20 per cent of the total ..." (J. K. Galbraith: *Economic Development*. p. 69.) (2) "The Japanese Five-Year Plan is based on the private enterprise system ..." "However, it is stated that there is a limit to the voluntary adjustment power of private enterprise, and that, therefore, it is necessary for the government to take appropriate measures to realize the plan. This is particularly the case: (a) for basic industries, (b) for those things which are difficult for private enterprise to carry out, such as the building of roads, railways, port facilities for industrial centers, etc., (c) for improvements of the sewage system, parks, and other environmental services as well as construction of homes for those in low income brackets, (d) for promotion of education, especially scientific education, and compilation of elaborate economic statistics." Economic Planning Agency, Japanese Government, New Long Range Economic Plan of Japan, 1958–61. pp. 18, 19. (Quoted by Rudolf Bićanić in: Problems of Planning East and West. The Hague. 1969. Mouton. p. 25. from a publication of the Economic Planning Bureau of the Japanese Government.)

[22] According to P. de Wolff, Director of the Netherlands Central Plan Bureau: "... the Netherlands does not pay much attention to long-term planning and there are no overall long-term plans." Further: "At present long-term planning is mainly

Thus, to select development objectives and the methods and measures necessary for their attainment, a study of the developed capitalist countries may offer great help; but as regards the secret of preparing a long-term plan we can draw but very little on the experience of these countries.

## PAST AND FUTURE—THE TREND LINE

In the book entitled „National economic planning and control" containing 18 studies by distinguished Hungarian economists, we can read the following remark by G. Kovács: "In the field of long-term planning we have as yet no sufficient experience. This, in itself, is enough for very deviating views to emerge from the debate."[23] Kovács is alluding here to the studies in the 1965 and 1966 volumes of the *Közgazdasági Szemle* on long-range planning in an open economy.

The debate has been going on ever since, with the participation of those mentioned above and of others of whom Ferenc Jánossy should be specially mentioned, but the remark of Kovács on the whole still holds. Yet, in the last two years a considerable change has been taking place in Hungary in the field of long-term economic planning. In 1967, extensive activities were unfolding, aimed at preparing the 1971–85 national economic plan. A considerable part of this work, of course, is being carried out by the National Planning Office within the scope of its regular activities. But what distinguishes it from routine planning work is precisely the participation of a wide circle of specialists from outside the Planning Office. To support and check its own activity, the Planning Office has set up nine committees. The task of these is to prepare and work out important component parts, essential questions of the fifteen-year plan. The first committee deals with living conditions and social reproduction of manpower, the second with industry, the third with the building materials industry and construction, the fourth with agriculture and the food industry, the fifth with transport and communication, the sixth with international relations and foreign trade, the seventh with the regional allocation of productive forces. The activities of these committees are synthetized and assisted by the eighth, the Economic Committee which also deals with analytical and methodological prob-

restricted to the governmental sector and to subjects requiring long preparation." (*The scope, methods and tools of planning*. The Hague. 1965. pp. 9, and 13.) —Leif Johansen, on the basis of whose model—published in 1960— forecasts are made about the future economic development of Norway up to 1990, reported last year on the work which was performed in order to compare actual development with that worked out with the aid of the model and established: ". . . there is as yet no question of having a final and definitive projection of the Norwegian economy up to 1990. Nor is it likely that such a thing will be worked out." (Leif Johansen, in co-operation with H. Alstadheim and A. Langsether: Explorations in long-term projections for the Norwegian economy. *Economics of Planning*, Nos. 1–2. 1968, p. 116.) The model serves to provide basic points for the government to take decisions on the economic problems and for the drawing up of four-year plans.

[23] *Népgazdasági tervezés és irányítás*. p. 75.

lems. Finally, the chairmen of the eight committees, together with some theoretical economists and leading personalities of economic life, form the ninth, the Consultative Committee headed by the President of the Planning Office.

Those participating in this work had set themselves as their first objective to analyze the past. Reaching partly back to 1949 and partly also forward to 1967–68, they surveyed primarily the 17 years from 1950 to 1966. Relying on many partial studies, a comprehensive study was prepared by the spring of 1969. This contains many lessons to be observed in drawing up the long-term plan. It is difficult to find from the many conclusions one that could be termed the most important. I still believe that the following should be particularly remembered: "A higher growth rate *in terms of magnitude* was realistically not possible. Still, with more prudent economic policies and more purposeful economic control and management, with a more circumspect utilization of possibilities, above all by increasing efficiency to the fullest possible extent in the activity of production and development, even a considerably higher rate of development could have been secured."[24]

This summary of the lessons of the past raises three major requirements as regards the future: (1) more purposeful and scientifically founded economic policies are needed; (2) the methods of economic control and management must be improved; (3) the efficiency of the economic, especially of production and development activities, must be increased. Thus we shall be able to attain considerably faster development than in the past. At least the first and the third requirement should be considered as directly referring to long-term planning. As regards the second requirement, at the beginning of last year, an essential step was made towards improving economic control and management, and the fourth five-year plan, starting in 1971, will constitute a further step in this direction.

The fifties, especially 1951, 1952 and the first half of 1953 constituted the darkest period of our economic history. It has been said many times already that in the period subjective and voluntaristic ideas prevailed and tasks had been set which far exceeded our forces and possibilities in the fields both of investment and of production, and of raising the standard of living. Even when it became clear that a simultaneous realization of all our objectives was entirely impossible, we stubbornly adhered particularly to the attainment of the investment tasks, unrealistic in themselves, and this led to a declining standard of living of workers, undermining the confidence of the working class in the policy of the Party. Forced collectivization and anti-kulak campaigns roused the resistance of wide masses of the peasantry and weakened the firm alliance between the latter and the working class. For all this the country had to pay years later, during the counter-revolution.

The termination of this stage at the end of June 1953 was not followed by a correct economic policy but by a faltering one which was part of the

[24] *A népgazdaság fejlődésének fő vonásai 1950–67 években* (Main features of development of the national economy between 1950–67). Mimeographed, March 31, 1969, p. 4.

wire-pulling characteristic of the whole political life.[25] The conditions of a scientifically based economic policy began to ripen only after July 1956 and came to be realized in 1957. But the policy could not be asserted any more. As a reaction to the earlier failure and as a result of the subsequent disillusionment, an economic policy followed which is described in the above-mentioned summary of the Planning Office as one characterized by the setting of manifold tasks, and by the vague defining of the order and extent of objectives, an intermittent weakening of the forces of central control and exaggerated autonomistic tendencies of particular forces.[26]

Unquestionably, all this must have unfavourably affected the progress of the Hungarian economy and under more favourable conditions the growth rate could have been higher. How much higher? This is a difficult question. "Considerably higher" as can be read in the passage we have quoted. But in the preceding sentence we have also read that "a higher growth rate in terms of magnitude was not possible". And the text refers to undoubtedly existing objective causes braking progress, both external and internal ones, to the insufficiency of international cooperation, to the country's relative scarcity of raw materials and to the adverse conditions of their extraction. (The problem of the attainable growth rate will have to be dealt with separately; here I wish to mention only a few lessons to be drawn from the past with a bearing on the future.) This again raises the question touched upon at the beginning of this article; to what extent are we passive spectators and to what extent active agents shaping our destinies? There I referred to the answer given by science, that "We are able deliberately to influence development to the extent that we know its internal relationships and laws, the springs of motion as well as the possibilities and methods of influencing them". But now we need a more concrete answer. The really concrete and irrefutable answer can, of course, be given only by pratice. We must prove in practice whether we can accelerate the rate of economic growth and, if so, to what extent. However, even pending success or failure in proving this in practice, the problem deserves theoretical consideration.

Ferenc Jánossy's thought provoking book, *A gazdasági fejlődés trendvonala és a helyreállítási periódusok* (The trendline of economic development and the reconstruction periods), published in Hungarian 1966 and in German in 1969 (Frankfurt a.M. Verlag Neue Kritik) is an outstanding work in recent Hungarian economic literature. The problems dealt with in this work are closely related to those of long-term planning. The author starts from a phenomenon which, although conspicuous, has been noticed only by a few before him and examined or taken into consideration by even

[25] I. Friss: Az MDP gazdaságpolitikája (Economic Policy of the Hungarian Workers' Party). *A Magyar Tudományos Akadémia Társadalmi-történeti tudományok osztályának közleményei*, Nos. 1–3. 1961. pp. 45–69.

[26] Cf., essentially on the same subject, pages 85—88 of this volume. I may add, that this is not an exclusively Hungarian phenomenon. As regards its Soviet counterpart, I have already referred to T. Morva's article (see Note 1.). But it has its counterpart also under capitalist conditions: "The standard modern development plan is an investment plan." . . . "There is a grave danger, however, that such a plan will present all things as equally important. They are not. . . . Strong forces work against strategic concentration." (J. K. Galbraith: *Economic Development.* p. 73.)

fewer—namely, from the existence of trend lines characteristic of economic development which have proved to be surprisingly stable. The trend lines are, of course, of approximate character only, but Jánossy convincingly proves that they do exist at least in the economic development of some countries. Nor does he rest satisfied with proving the existence of this phenomenon which has been essentially discovered by him.[27] Constructing a model which convincingly illustrates not only the stability of the trend line but also deviations from the latter, he gives an interpretation and explanation of this strange phenomenon. And even if his interpretation and explanation are not above criticism, they undoubtedly contain correct ideas and statements which are worth attention.

The extraordinarily rapid development experienced at times in some capitalist as well as socialist countries, "the economic miracles", can be explained by the fact that the breaks caused by war or economic crises are or may be followed by a period of very rapid development until the country in question has reached the development level it would have attained without a break, according to the trend line characteristic of its development. Then the rapid development, as if hitting a wall, suddenly loses momentum and slows down to the level which conforms to the trend line.

Jánossy believes that the economic development of a country depends in the long run on how the capacities inherent in its manpower can unfold. The economic development level will depend primarily on the professional structure or the total labour force, on the distribution of skill. The stability of the trend line of economic development is fundamentally determined by the inertia which has a stabilizing effect on the change in the professional structure. Changes in this structure are, on the other hand, the precondition for a quicker economic growth. How is it possible to attain the former or the latter? By accelerating the training of manpower. This again can be achieved only with the aid of "inefficient" investment; inefficient in the sense that, owing to the relative underdevelopment of manpower, it can be utilized only with a low degree of efficiency and will be prematurely worn out. Such investment can be made only or mainly in a planned economy when inefficiency can deliberately be underwritten in order to accelerate progress. Beyond a certain limit, the acceleration of economic growth can be made possible only with the aid of "inefficient" investments.

Jánossy is no economic historian, but his conception outlined above is, evidently, in contradiction with the views predominant in economic history about the "period of post-war reconstruction". Prior to the publication of Jánossy's book we had attributed the rapid development of those times

[27] In the latest book of Eric Lundberg there is a remark which supports Jánossy's theory on trend lines and reconstruction periods. He makes the following comment on a graph which shows the growth of *Japanese* GNP after the war and the projection of the trend in the inter-war period (1930–63): "In 1953 GNP had about reached the maximum prewar level. But with regard to an extrapolation of the interwar trend of 4·6 per cent a year, the actual 1953 figure was about 50 per cent below the trend level. The graph gives a strong impression of a tremendous "room for expansion", or a gap that in some mysterious way seems to be pulling up the GNP curve to its explosive postwar growth rate." (*Instability and economic growth.* 1968. p. 320.) But Lundberg does not follow up this train of thought.

exclusively to the superiority of the socialist order of production. The coming into power of the working classes, the penetration of their organizations into the leading bodies of society, the socialization of mines, factories and banks, as well as the central leading role of the state have enabled, on the one hand, the bringing of the enthusiasm and creative will of the masses, liberated from oppression, terror, and the horrors of war, into harmony with productive possibilities and, on the other hand, the rationalization of the productive profile of enterprises, their amalgamation, their supply with raw materials, the liquidation of bottlenecks and the utilization of capacities created earlier but left idle, a previously unattained level of employment for those capable of and willing to work, and, together with all this, a sudden increase in industrial output. Presumably, these facts were not doubted by Jánossy, but he would believe that the essence of the matter lies not here but in the fact that both in socialist and capitalist countries the development interrupted by war or other causes will rapidly gain momentum as soon as obstacles cease to exist and that this rapid development will come to a halt on reaching the trend line, slowing down according to the slope of the latter. Reconstruction periods and trend lines in several countries have proved Jánossy to be right, rendering it probable that this theory contained some truth and has a general validity extending beyond his examples.

Yes, but—from the nature of things—Jánossy's statements about the development trend line of socialist Hungary are based on too few data and on too short a period. If war or an economic crisis can for a shorter or longer period deflect development from its trend line, why could not a possible "critical" period of economic policy have a similar effect? And if we add that in 1947–1948 new production relations became predominant—that is, also the slope of the trend line had to change—how can we claim with conviction that in the break in economic growth experienced in 1952 "undoubtedly the objective rules of economic development were manifesting themselves" or that it was in this year that the reconstruction period came to an end?

Further, where is the limit beyond which an acceleration of development can be made possible only by "inefficient" investments? Is it not possible, perhaps, to attain considerable acceleration by other means? Jánossy is stating with emphasis that the trend line is not identical with fate. He also writes that "the trend line of capitalist Hungary is flatter than that of other capitalist economies . . . nor does the trend line of socialist Hungary rise as steeply as it could have risen in a better organized planned economy, in one more satisfactorily answering the requirements of economic development."[28] This latter statement is sufficiently self-explanatory. And it implies that by deliberate action there is a possibility of increasing the upward slope of the trend line.

We have started from objective laws and have arrived at the necessity for deliberate human action. And it is the plan that offers a tool for harmonizing and deliberately directing massive human activities on a national

[28] Jánossy: op. cit. p. 86. (Quotation refers to the Hungarian edition.)

124

scale. The longer the period of planning, the less are we bound by the conditions of the present situation, the greater our freedom. It is, accordingly, the long-term plan which offers true possibilities of realistically influencing the trend line in the desired sense and at the same time of carrying into effect correct and audaciously bold conceptions of a better economic policy —if we have any. We must also utilize the plan to improve the efficiency of economic activities, above all in production and development.

G. A. Feldman's already quoted article "On the theory of the growth rate of national income" is based on such a concept of the plan. This ingenious piece of writing is perhaps unique in the whole literature on planning. "*Scientific* planning of the developing social, economic and technical aggregate that the Soviet country is to become within the next decades is generally inconceivable without a proper scientific method"—he wrote. And: "It is inconceivable that the plans for a *complicated apparatus* like the national economy could be drawn up on the basis of an *uncomplicated planning method*". And since "the theory of national economic planning does not as yet exist, has not as yet been worked out", he set himself the task of promoting it, in the belief that "a more or less perfect planning of the national economy can be realized only on the basis of a succinctly, mathematically formulated theory; only then can the arguments about the plan be restricted to theoretical statements and the setting of objectives with full confidence in the accuracy of the calculations."[29]

How much did this man know nearly forty years ago; we, even if we had known it, had forgotten it, partly rediscovered it only recently and part of his ideas is still not yet generally known. He knew that an exact mathematical expression can be found for many fundamental, important economic relationships and laws. He was searching for these without mathematics becoming an end in itself in the course of his research work: he never lost connection with Soviet reality or the experience of advanced capitalist countries.[30] He pointed to the importance of the percentage rate of capital to be replaced on account of moral depreciation and also pointed out that even if continuous replacement of the fixed capital cannot be realized in each enterprise, an order of renewals can be established within the framework of *planned* regulation for both industries and enterprises.[31] He called attention to such indicators as "the efficiency of capital utilization" (the ratio of newly produced value to capital), and the ability of the productive apparatus to expand reproduction (the ratio between capital necessary for simple and that needed for extended reproduction) and was of the opinion that the main task of the planning agencies was precisely to regulate the growth of these.[32] He disclosed that "the greater the efficiency of capital used in the production of export goods in comparison with the efficiency of

[29] G. A. Feldman: op. cit. (in Hungarian), pp. 1379 and 1382.
[30] "Only the study of the development of industrialized countries and of our own experiences can decide the correct size of $V_p$ (the share of workers within total consumption—I. F.). For similar understandable reasons, the size of necessary defense expenditure cannot be established by mathematical methods." (Ibid. p. 1376.)
[31] Ibid. p. 1351.
[32] Ibid. p. 1379.

capital serving domestic consumption, the greater will be the growth in consumption."[33]

Thus Feldman keeps in view both "a well founded economic policy, purposeful economic control and efficiency in both productive and development activities". But, in all likelihood, the true importance of his work lies not in his findings or theses, but—at least to no lesser degree—in that he recognized and emphasized the fact that it was possible to develop planning on scientific basis and, together with this, to work out a better scientific foundation for directing and controlling society and the economy, to shape our fate ever more consciously. And if we are listening to the most important lesson to be derived from over 17 years of economic development, we may realize that the past has also this message for the present: we have the possibility of acting in a better way than hitherto and of accelerating progress. Let us avail ourselves of this possibility.


## HOW RAPIDLY CAN WELFARE GROW?

This question is closely related to the one, how quick can be the rate of economic development? I have cursorily touched upon this problem above and indicated that I intended to return to it. Indeed, this is one of the fundamental problems in long-term planning.

It must be explained—and it has been said already by many of those engaged in the problem—that what we mean here is not growth or development in the usual sense. It is easy to state the percentage increase in steel production or milk consumption from one year to the next or over several years. It is also easy to state the change in the number of motorcars in use. Here, however, a possible change in the composition by quality of the cars may be of some importance and, therefore, the figure obtained will perhaps reflect this change less truly than the ones in our earlier examples. If, however, we are considering the output of a whole country, the millions of products whose production has changed in varying degrees—including the fact that production of some may have been abandoned and new ones been introduced—it becomes obvious that the measurement of change is a complicated task which can be solved only on certain assumptions. This truth will hold the more, the longer the period over which the change should be measured. But, instead of going into the details of difficulties and the possible methods of surmounting them, let me state that there exist solutions acceptable as approximations from the point of view of planning, and we call as witness one of the outstanding bourgeois experts on economic growth. S. Kuznets: "These problems of comparability, either in space or in time, should not overwhelm us to the point of our despairing of the possibility of meaningful and objectively testable measures of national product in relation to the population. There is, after all, a strong element of

[33] Ibid. p. 1376.

126

community of human wants and needs translatable in the modern sense of means, ends, and values of economic activity."[34]

Of course, economic development can be measured by means of several types of indicators and, because of the problems of interpretation already mentioned, it is even expedient to use several indicators. The most widespread measure is the change in productivity or, what is related to this, in per capita national income (or GNP or NNP).

Jánossy states most interestingly that "if we calculate the average growth in productivity for periods, at the beginning and at the end of which production reaches the trend line, we shall obtain, almost in every case, an average growth rate that lies *within relatively narrow limits, i.e. between the annual rates of 1·7 and 2 per cent.* For example, between 1913 and 1963 the annual growth rate in productivity was 1·7 per cent for Great Britain, 1·8 per cent for Sweden and Belgium, 1·9 per cent for France and Norway and 2 per cent for Japan and the USA.[35] In some contrast with this statement, Jánossy also states that between 1900 and 1960 the productivity of labour increased in Japan at an annual rate of 2·5 per cent and that in the United State "the productivity of labour . . . increased from 1870 to the present day, that is, over almost a whole century, at an almost steady rate of yearly 2 per cent."[36] In connection with an example worked out for the sake of illustration where it is assumed that labour productivity "increases at an annual rate of 4 per cent, that is, doubles in 18 years", he remarks that "economic growth of such dazzling rapidity has in the long run never been experienced in any country."[37]

I have quoted Jánossy at such length because he would consider the maximum rate of growth to be more moderate than is the view of most other bourgeois and socialist economists who presumably started from the experience of shorter periods with a relatively more favourable economic development. The director of the Dutch Central Plan Bureau, P. de Wolff, already quoted above, writes: "The question of an optimal rate of growth has been much debated by theoreticians, but so far these efforts have remained without practical results." . . . "it is perhaps safe to put the maximum level for productivity at 5% . . ."[38]

Clopper Almon has prepared, with the aid of a dynamic input-output model, a forecast for the American economy up to 1975 and in this he envisages an economic growth rate of above 5 per cent p.a.[39] According to the Czech economist Otakar Lacina, the studies prepared with the aim of forecasting long-term trends in the Czechoslovak economy "have yielded the result that in the future the Czechoslovak economy may attain an annual average 5 per cent growth rate in national income."[40]

[34] S. Kuznets: *Modern economic growth.* New-Haven–London, 1966. Yale Univ. Press. p. 24.

[35] Jánossy: op. cit. p. 54.

[36] Ibid. pp. 54. and 101.

[37] Ibid. p. 206.

[38] de Wolff: op. cit. p. 11.

[39] See a review of Clopper Almon's book by A. Bródy in *Közgazdasági Szemle,* 1967, Nos. 7–8.

[40] Lacina: op. cit. p. 16.

In the course of preparation for long-term planning in Hungary, the Committees mentioned above have analyzed development in various fields of the economy over 17 years (1950–66). The summary of the analysis prepared by the National Planning Office states that "the objectives of *rapid economic growth* have materialized under conspicuous contradictions ... per capita national income in 1967 exceeded about 2·3-fold that in 1950, which means an annual average growth rate of 5·2 per cent over 17 years. This substantially exceeds the rate of about 1·5 to 2 per cent in the inter-war years but—in comparison with the boom in developed countries after the Second World War—this does not count as outstanding and lags behind the average of the CMEA countries. (Between 1950 and 1967 per capita national income in the CMEA countries increased at the annual rate of 7 per cent and GNP per head in the Common Market countries at a rate of about 4·5 per cent. According to another analysis, on the basis of the growth in per capita national income between 1937 and 1960, this country occupies the ninth place among 24 European countries.) It was, however, a favourable sign that the growth rate has accelerated. In the past ten years the annual average growth rate was 5·7 per cent, while in the period between 1950 and 1958 it was only 4·6 per cent."[41]

Between 2 per cent, 4 per cent and 5 per cent there are, undoubtedly, considerable differences. And let us remember that these are compound rates of growth. At the rate of 2 per cent per capita national income will rise in 20 years to about 1·5-fold, at 4 per cent to 2·2-fold and at 5 per cent to more than 2·6-fold. Let us assume that a socialist country can attain an annual growth rate of 8 per cent, then we have already a 4·7-fold increase. Projecting these percentages to a period of 100 years, per capita national income would rise to 7·25-fold, 50-fold, 131-fold and 2,200-fold respectively, of the present level. It follows that it makes no sense to project higher percentages to a hundred years because the results cannot be sensibly interpreted at all. It is, however, also obvious, that to draw up a 100-year plan would not make sense, either, because—owing to uncertainties—even for much shorter periods it is impossible to foresee the basic features and to trace their development. This is why we should draw up plans for 15 years and not for 100, not even for 30. With an annual growth rate of 8 per cent in per capita national income we would not grow in the 15 years indefinitely, only to threefold and would thus approach the North-American level in terms of magnitude. On the basis of our present knowledge even this would be conceivable only with utmost efforts.

We have to build our 15-year plan not on fanciful ideas but on calculations. No such calculations have as yet been carried out; which is strange enough even if we know that such calculations have not occurred as yet in the planning practice of other socialist countries, either.[42] I believe we can

---

[41] *Népgazdaságunk fejlődésének fő vonásai*, p. 30.

[42] This is, unfortunately, a bottleneck in the planning practice of socialist countries, even in advanced Soviet planning. "Deficiencies of the plan can delay the attainment of the desired objectives to no smaller extent than non-fulfilment by some enterprises" wrote B. P. Kolpakov, President of the Statistical Office of the RSSR and S. Kamaletdinov, President of the Computation Centre of the Statistical Office of the RFSR in *Pravda*, on 18. Feb. 1967. In his latest book, Academician Fedorenko devotes greater

set ourselves the task of carrying them out and this may even be approached in several ways. From among the factors influencing the changes in productivity performance many important ones, if not all, can be quantified and calculated *at the national level*, together with their secondary effects, with the aid of data perhaps difficult to obtain but still obtainable and by relying on proper computing techniques. Such factors are, *e.g.* the bottlenecks whose liquidation is important from the national economic standpoint; the mechanization of working processes such as transportation and inter-factory transport with high labour requirements on a national scale; the introduction of technologies involving great savings in materials, etc. Similarly, the effects on productivity of particularly large investment projects may be also quantified and calculated on a national scale. The same applies to production techniques and licences to be procured from abroad. If correctly applied, they may greatly contribute to accelerating the rise in the productivity of labour.[43] It should also be remembered and taken into account that skilled labour contributes even without investment to a large extent to raising productivity. Kenneth J. Arrow emphasized this already many years ago.[44] The effect of foreign trade and some other factors on productivity can and should also be taken into account and even calculated.

---

space to the critique of economics; I quote from him the following words: "Planning practice and those in control of economic development have to this day not received an answer to the following questions: can we draw up an optimal central plan, compare the plan variants and select from among them the best ones? . . . objective economic phenomena had often been neglected, a scientific approach to solving national economic tasks has been replaced with a merely empirical approach." Further: "An intuitive approach to elaborating economic decisions, which had been predominant in the past, . . . is becoming increasingly useless." (N. P. Fedorenko, On the elaboration of a system of optimum functioning of the national economy —In Russian —1968. pp. 8. and 21.)

[43] Remembering, of course that utilization of a license requires, beyond its purchase, the meeting of several requirements. ". . . to take over and adapt the most advanced technologies, its not only necessary that the country handing them over should willingly provide all the help needed —also the country taking them over must meet some personal and material conditions. Although the taking over of finished technical solutions can be attained generally more quickly and at lower cost than if we had to discover everything ourselves, it would nonetheless be ridiculous to believe that adaptation can be effected without any difficulty, trouble, or at one stroke. There may be machines, equipment, instruments, perhaps buildings, perhaps even materials needed that may not exist in our country. To procure them, of course, puts a burden on the economy and requires time and effort. Problems of personnel can usually be overcome, even with greater difficulty or will take, at least, a much longer time. Nor can experiments be entirely dispensed with, and also diseases of infancy will occur . . . Various factors . . . have various characteristics. The problems of personnel may prove to constitute the most rigid factor. Skilled workers, engineers and other specialists cannot be trained overnight —not to speak of scientists." (I. Friss, A XXIII. kongresszus és a magyar közgazdaságtudomány (The 23rd Congress of CPSU and the Hungarian economic science) *Közgazdasági Szemle*, 1962, No. 7, pp. 779 and 780.)

[44] E. Lundberg has established that "The Horndal iron works in Sweden had no new investment . . . for a period of fifteen years, yet productivity . . . rose on the average close to 2 per cent per annum . . . I advance the hypothesis here that technical change in general can be ascribed to experience, that it is the very activity of production which gives rise to problems for which favourable responses are selected over time . . ." (K. J. Arrow: The economic implications of learning by doing. *The Review of Economic Studies*. 1962, June. p. 156.)

All this certainly requires hard thinking, much time, work and fatigue. To raise planning to a really scientific level is a great and difficult task. Nor do I cherish the illusion that this can be attained within one year. Now, that hundreds of specialists and advisers have been working and pondering for two years already on the preparation of a long-term plan without any spectacular results, this fact has come to be increasingly understood. Advanced societies are the most complicated formations brought about so far by earthly development. Already Feldman indicated that we could not expect to solve the problems of planning with simple tools. But who should solve these problems if not those whose lot it is to participate in building a new society which should, if possible, be better than the existing ones? Who, if not those whose very social survival is dependent on raising the productivity of labour and increasing social welfare at a more rapid rate than has ever before been experienced in history?

## WHY DID THE SOVIET UNION WIN THE WAR?

I am aware that a scientifically founded answer to this question could not fail to be a very long one. And if we wanted to give a brief answer, we should simply say that it was because she was defending a just cause. However, all this has no (or at least no immediate) bearing on long-term planning. But there is a part of the full answer from which important lessons can also be drawn for long-term planning.

What I mean is that the technical superiority of the Soviet Union over the Germans achieved in the course of the war was an important, I may say decisive factor in the victory. There are some people who believe that in this superiority American aid played an important part. Statistical data, however, show that the considerable American technical aid was negligible in comparison to the technical equipment of Soviet origin and that in the concluding stages of the war Soviet technical equipment was of overpowering superiority over that of the Germans even after allowing for the aircraft, tanks, lorries and arms of foreign origin, and that the monthly output of war material by far exceeded that turned out by Germany.

Based on actual figures, Marshal Zhukov shows in his memoirs how enormous Soviet power already was at Kursk and how annihilating it became in the last battle fought for Berlin. As a matter of fact, the war started under very different conditions. In June 1941 the Germans attacked with many thousands of modern aircraft and tanks while the Red Army had hardly any modern tanks or modern aeroplanes.

General Yakovlev, the Soviet aircraft construction engineer gives in his book a colourful and highly illustrative account of how this change had come about in the air force. The aircraft industry practically enjoyed priority over almost all other branches of production, but together with the other war industries it certainly enjoyed one over all civilian production. The government and the leaders of the defence forces raised enormous demands on the aircraft industry, not only in quantitative but also in qualitative terms. But the Soviet government secured everything needed to meet these demands that was possible from the human aspect, even some-what more, in terms of labour, materials, money, advice.

What is the lesson of this for planning in general, and for long-term planning in particular? It is this: if there is a clearly defined objective and a decision has been taken that many other objectives should be subordinated to this objective, and if the necessary forces are concentrated on attaining this objective and if there exists the power to implement this decision —great, sometimes surprisingly great successes can be achieved. For this it is not absolutely necessary to have a rigid, warlike system of priorities and subordination—as the one set up in our example under conditions of war—but it is absolutely necessary to have some ordering principle, some *conception*, which assigns their place to the various activities, distinguishes the important and highly important tasks from the unimportant ones, establishes an order, or makes it possible that such an order be established.

The first plan of the Soviet Union, the GOELRO plan drawn up in 1920 to electrify the Soviet Union and to explore its raw material resources has remained to this day an example of long-term planning with a conception. True, Rudolf Bicanić interprets this conception in a way that: "Not all economic activities are equally suitable for planning." ..."It is not accidental that in the Soviet Union general planning started first in electricity (GOEL-RO plan for the electrification of the Soviet Union in 1920)" ... "Natural resources were to follow."[45]

The description by Günther Kohlmey seems to be more correct: "Already before the operative plans . . . a long-term plan is worked out. This is . . . an historical event . . . a basic foundation for economic processes to remain lastingly and wholly efficient: it is the long-term planning of the whole of social life."[46] According to the opinion of István Hetényi "this plan (the GOELRO) was up to the present best suited adequately to answer international, political, social and technical tendencies".[47] In what respect was this plan superior to many later ones? Its makers had no possibility of studying any science of national economic planning, could not know or apply any, for none at the time existed. But they appreciated and elaborated some problems of fundamental importance. Thus, first they had a general plan upon which the others could be built. As Kohlmey writes in the passage quoted: "Since all planning means unity not only of long-term and operative planning, but also of planning on national, industrial, plant and regional levels, on the basis of the GOELRO plan they proceeded to work out long-term plans for the various branches of the economy and industry."

Those who drew up this first big plan could not make the mistake which their followers—including ourselves—did make one after the other, namely, to construct the national economic plan by fitting together partial plans. Nor would this in itself be a mistake if the ordering principle, the conception, did not become lost in the process.

[45] R. Bicanić: *Problems of planning East and West.* 1967. p. 21.
[46] G. Kohlmey, *Zur Entstehung der Theorie von der sozialistischen Wirtschaft.* Berlin. 1967. p. 39.
[47] Gazdasági fejlődés és hosszútávú tervezés (Economic development and long-term planning). *Gazdaság,* 1968, No. 4, p. 7.

Conception presupposes an order of importance, it will thus guard also against the mistakes of taking decisions on important major problems *separately, independently of each other*, and partly or in their details or in their consequences contradicting each other. All major problems of society and the economy are so *closely interrelated* that we cannot take a decision on any of them without this decision affecting also the others. If we decide to raise the welfare of society and its directions, many other things will already have been decided upon, such as investments, production, location, foreign trade, education and cultural affairs. Similarly, if we take a decision on the major problems of agricultural development, many question of industrial development, location, foreign trade, the raising of living level, will have been simultaneously decided.[48]

The acceptance of a conception which comprises ordering and preferences relating to things which are not commensurable, or only partly or from certain aspects commensurable, is obviously not a simple planning problem but at the same time a primary political question. It could be relegated to the domain of planning if the undoubtedly best solution could be found merely with scientific methods, deductions and calculations, and a decision could be taken on this basis, without taking a political stand. In the case of a conception, however, which may affect the fate of a whole country, this cannot be done.

It is thus all the more important that the political decision be scientifically founded. The acceptance of the conception and the political decision will determine the direction of future work for planners and establish the major features of the plan. To aim at providing the best scientific foundation and construction of a plan, or at its optimization, at finding the most favourable variant, without analyzing the scientific bases of the ideas and decisions serving as a background to the plan, would mean only half the work being done or even less. Although even a plan based upon incorrect conceptions can be correctly drawn up from the point of view of planning techniques, it will never be a good plan and even less an optimal one.

How can the scientific foundation and the soundness of the basic idea, the conception, the ordering principle be secured? In the first place, the decision-making body must have the confidence of society, must act on its behalf, empowered by society, since it is the fate of society that is involved. Secondly, the greatest possible number of competent people, specialists, scientists, members of Parliament must be drawn into the scope of elaborating the conception, into the work of preparing the decision. Thirdly, efforts should be made to bring the plan's implementation under wide democratic control with the participation of the masses.

If it can thus be ensured that the resources of an economy are concentrated on and used for the proper purposes, then the most important conditions for favourable development obtainable by our own efforts would be provided.

[48] See the previous study in this volume.

Up to now we have been dealing only with general questions of long-term planning and were reflecting on these. Can we plan the future or can we prepare only forecasts; can we use the examples of developed capitalist countries for setting long-term objectives; what conclusions can we draw from our socialist development up to now; what can be the rate of growth; why is a conception necessary—these and other general questions of this type have been discussed, but our own long-term plan has hardly been mentioned. It is time now to turn to this subject.

The planners and specialists—there are many hundreds—who are working on the preparation of the long-term plan, partly in the nine committees partly in the apparatus of the Planning Office, have carried out up to now a many-sided and extensive work. If, in spite of the many tasks performed, we are still in the preparatory stage and, apart from a few building stones, have nothing from the building of the fifteen-year plan itself, this is a consequence of the novelty and extreme complexity of the task. True, as has been mentioned, an analysis of Hungarian economic development over 17 years has been prepared and there are some hypotheses, ideas, assumptions available for certain parts of the plan. It is, perhaps, of even greater importance that those participating in the work are beginning to form certain ideas about the possible ways of drawing up the long-term plan and about the possible methods of harmonizing and directing the work going on in the committees and in other places. Here I wish to deal less with what is ready than rather with what I am beginning to realize about the possible and desirable methods of continuing the work, relying on the material worked out and already discussed.

I will not deal here with the division of labour established between the Planning Office and the committees, nor with the working phases which follow partly from the nature of the work and partly from that division of labour. Instead, I will start from the fact that in the whole planning process there will be certain peaks and nodal points where some political decision will sum up the work performed and draw its balance, starting thereby a new phase of the work. On the basis of what has been said hitherto I cannot imagine—and I shall try to explain why—that we could arrive at the finished plan in a single working phase, without intermediate political decisions.

Thus, we are now in the phase of preparing the first political decision and, most likely, at the beginning rather than in the middle of that phase. We have some knowledge and certain assumptions, on the basis of which we can sketch the rough outlines of our long-term plan, without planning work in the stricter sense or without scientifically founded calculations. What do we know and what are we assuming? We know that in the last 17 years, per capita national income in Hungary increased by an annual average of 5·3 per cent—within that by an annual average of 5·7 per cent in the past ten years—and also that although this exceeds by 1 per cent the average growth rate in the Common Market countries, it is 1·5 per cent less than that of the CMEA countries and much less than in capitalist Japan. We know that the pattern of employment is rapidly changing: the share of those working in agriculture has fallen from the 50 per cent level in 1945 to 30 per cent and diminished also in absolute terms, while both the number and share of industrially employed has greatly increased, and that in recent years employment has grown also in the servicing branches (e.g. trade, transport etc.) both in absolute and relative terms. We also know, both from our own experiences and the example of more advanced countries that this process is far from coming to an end. Urbanization, migration from the countryside to the towns, is similarly going on at a fairly rapid rate. We can tell with relatively high accuracy how the number as well as the age and sex distribution of the population of working age is likely to develop. We know that it is justifiable to reckon with a decrease in working hours and with longer paid holidays. We know, both from our own experience and from the example of more advanced countries, quite a lot about future trends of personal consumption, about energy consumption, transport, etc., etc. We can rely on examples furnished by the most developed countries especially as regards production (industries, technology, organization and scale), the pattern of consumption, the organization and the bearing on production of science and scientific research — carefully weighing, of course, the differences.

As I have said, on the basis of such knowledge and assumption we can, even without scientifically founded plan calculations, draw the rough outlines of a long-term plan. We know how much, what types of and how many hours of labour and its output will be available over the 15 years in question for the production of material goods. Since under the not too favourable conditions of the past 20 years the productivity of labour increased by more than 5 per cent as an annual average, it will not be too bold to reckon with at least a similar growth rate over the next 15 years and to assume that, accordingly, society will have to decide each year on the utilization of an increased volume of products. We may also with a certain probability expect an annual 5 per cent growth in per capita national income over the next 15 years. Since for some longer period we have consumed about 75 per cent of our national income and accumulated 25 per cent, this ratio can also be projected into the 1971–85 period. Needless to say, this is not a scientifically founded or elaborated plan. *In the plan* itself, it must be proved that the productivity of labour, production in the various industries and branches of the economy, national income etc. will develop in such and such a way under the influence of such and such factors and that we can choose from among such and such further measures. The plan will contain such or similar arguments. But, as has been shown, a draft plan to provide a starting point for planning can be prepared even with our present knowledge.

Work of this type has been performed already in the National Planning Office and, as a result, a small table has been presented containing the expected investment data of the 15 years. Accordingly, as calculated at 1968 prices, the estimated minimum investment volumes to serve as a basis for planning are Ft 430–450 billion (one billion = a thousand million) for 1971–75, Ft 540–560 billion for 1976–80 and Ft 650–700 billion for 1981–85, as against Ft 336 billion investment foreseen in the current five-year plan. The sums have been distributed among three investment groups: industry and construction, agriculture and forestry, and non-industrial infrastructure (water economy, transport, communication, trade and non-productive branches). In this distribution they started from the assumption that the shares of industrial and agricultural investment would somewhat decrease and that of infrastructural investment would grow, and for the possible extent of decrease and growth two variants have been worked out both for the second and the third five-year period. As can be seen, we are approaching what may be termed draft plan variants.

This is enough to start with, though two objections may be justified. One is that there are few variants and that the differences between them are small. The second, that the breakdown into three groups is insufficient and does not throw the problems into suitable relief. For example, each individual would accept in industry the fact that the share of industry and construction should decrease from the present 48 per cent to 40 or 45, with the second thought that this decrease should take place at the expense of the others. Taking this train of thought as a basis, it could perhaps be continued in the following or in some similar manner.

The allocation of investments should be worked out for each of the three plan periods in three different ways, assuming, e.g., a 5, 6 or 7 per cent annual growth rate of national income. Knowing that in this country the share of so-called non-productive investments within total investment is low in comparison with the more developed countries, in the distribution we could start from the fact that their share will grow by 3 per cent in each five-year plan period against that in the 1971–75 plan period—where no major change can presumably be made. In this part, first priority should be given to residential construction, providing e.g. for 450,000, 550,000 or 650,000 dwelling units to be built in consecutive five-year periods. But, in order to be able to build these homes, those industries must be developed which produce the material, component parts and equipment etc. necessary for building. These will, most likely, require further investment allocations, to the detriment of the industrial and construction sectors. At any rate, all the economic effects of residential construction must be followed up with all their consequences. Then other possible items of non-productive investments should be taken in turn, judging them and comparing them according to their importance. First would come health, education and science. Of course, the effects here must also be traced through the whole economy, and then many production and investment problems of the plan—or rather, the draft plan—will have been decided upon also in other fields, observing, however, the priorities of health and education.

Next, those investment sums should be allocated from the global fund which can be planned with relatively great safety. Such are, e.g., road construction, energy, electricity, water, steam, oil and gas networks, transport and, perhaps, also metallurgy. Then the shares of at least 15–20 industries should be allocated, to avoid a too high degree of aggregation which would blur the outlines of problems. Here, maybe, further preferences could be asserted and what we know about the advanced, developing or backward character of some industries on a world scale, should be taken into account, and also the domestic and international market situation and needs. Beyond this, to approach a correct distribution, those interested should be made to compete with each other for investment allocation. Let us e.g. assume that in the first distribution industrial branches A, B, C, D and E received a total of Ft 50 billion in a breakdown of 13·8, 15·9 and 5 billion, and that the representatives of some or all other industries find their allocations insufficient. We may then say: well, let us see what you offer to the economy in exchange for the investment funds. Their offers and proposals would then be thoroughly examined. Presumably the decisions taken on this basis would fundamentally change the original distribution. Thus, investment and partly also production tasks become gradually settled and the outline of a conception will emerge.

Of course, after these steps we have only a simplified rough estimate in our hands, more exactly three variants of estimates for each of the three plan periods, or at least for the last two, should the elaboration of the first one be in a too advanced stage by then. From the standpoint of a proper *scientifically founded plan* this is still very little: loose ideas, with a kernel of distant reality. As a matter of fact, let us remember that our initial assumptions were far from having a scientifically exact character. From the moment that we leave reliable and accurate data concerning the amount of labour time available to society, we are treading on marshy soil. We have, e.g., assumed a certain development in per capita industrial production deviating not too much from that prevailing hitherto. It is known, however, that what we mean by growth in industrial production is actually the increase in money terms, by which we express—for lack of a better solution—industrial production in an aggregate form. Value in money terms, however, depends on many different factors; its trend deviates in several respects from the trends in production. Why should this sum change over the next 15 years in the same way or almost in the same way as in the 17 years analyzed? This would be mere coincidence. History offers only the comfort that the "growth in industrial production" in various countries and periods—as measured by similar methods—has moved between relatively close limits. Let us add that there are many such factors in economic development the future trends of which we can at best guess. Two of these are particularly important. One is the fluctuation of prices in foreign capitalist markets. This affects selling and purchasing possibilities abroad in a far-reaching manner. The other is technical progress. This also influences the market to a large extent but may also radically change the pattern of production.

But what follows from all this? We have started from certain empirical facts and indicators based on the generalization of experience. From these the following seemed to be of particular importance: the growth rates in productivity of labour, in industrial and agricultural production as well as in national income, the changes in the pattern of employment, the ratio between consumption and accumulation in the allocation of national income, urbanization and demographical changes. We also called to our aid international experience and examples of countries industrially more developed than our own. Observing these, as well as other facts and assumptions, we have estimated the investment possibilities of the fifteen-year

136

plan period in terms of current prices and have worked out variants regarding their allocation. The circumstance that these variants are in harmony with certain experience and foreign examples, though lending them considerable weight, does not raise them to the rank of a scientifically based plan, does not prove their realistic character or consistency. Planning work proper, the efficiency and productivity calculations, the consistency analyses are still to come.

The first political decision relating to the long-term plan is shortly due. Has work started along correct lines; are the plan-variants as outlined correct; which should be preferred from among the various possibilities; what risks can or cannot be taken; should not also other possibilities be considered; should not other objectives also be set or given different weights? All these questions require many-sided political consideration and discussion, a decision to be taken with political responsibility. We have here—if not yet in its final form—the 15 year programme of the Party, so that a flashlight illuminates already for the whole people the major objectives and possibilities for the next fifteen years—how they will be living and what will be worth-while working for throughout these fifteen years. At the same time also the fourth five-year plan for 1971–75 is on the agenda; it should be checked from the perspective of the 15 years: what will be reaped from the efforts of these five years?

From among the committees, the one dealing with Manpower and Living Standards has also prepared—after having concluded its part of the analytical work covering the development of 17 years—what is called in long-term planning terminology a "hypothesis", but what the committee has termed explanatorily "the first draft of the conception of economic and social policy concerning employment and the standard of living". I cannot undertake to give here even the most summary extract of this extremely rich and interesting material; but I wish to call attention to two important and generally valid lessons that can be drawn from it.

One is that even in such a comparatively small collective of but a few dozen specialists, planners, senior executives and scientists, it was not possible to come to a uniform standpoint on all major questions, although the problems could and were indeed thoroughly and repeatedly discussed. For example, some were of the opinion that the rate of accumulation should be increased in order to accelerate development; others thought that it should be diminished in order to increase efficiency. (In parenthesis, I would like to remark that neither of these two statements expresses eternal rules, the question cannot be decided in such general terms.)

Another important lesson of general validity finds its expression in the correct presentation of the fact recognized earlier and also repeatedly stressed by myself, that important problems are usually complex, affecting many fields, and that, as a consequence, decisions on any problem will influence or delimit decisions to be taken on many other questions. Decisions aimed at shaping the standard of living and employment extensively affect urbanization and settlement conditions, a major group of investments—primarily residential construction, road building, extension of drainage and water conduits, the number of new hospital beds, the building of nurseries

137

and kindergartens, primary schools, the expansion of higher education and the purchase of instruments, foreign trade, home trade, the food and clothing industries, the whole system of education, the system of social insurance (health service), etc., etc.

In planning work proper, which, as we have seen, is still before us, there are great problems awaiting the application of mathematics. The various efficiency calculations, as well as those relating to labour productivity and changes in structure, must play an important role. The multi-level national economic programming work of János Kornai has brought the actual introduction of mathematical programming and optimization into planning nearer than anything previously known. He has presented us at last with a programming method that has been developed in close connection with practical planning work and can, therefore, also be applied in planning. In the words of the author, it makes it possible *"as related to our information, that is in relative terms*, by minimizing potential equilibrium disturbances, for every interrelation of the plan to be brought into equilibrium". It enables, again in the words of the author, "the planning agencies to submit political plan variants prepared for decision to those bodies which are called upon to take political decisions . . . showing the different consequences o these variants."[49]

Hungary's economic development—similarly to that of other small countries which have reached a certain level of economic development—is greatly affected by international economic relations, above all by foreign trade. It was possible to allow for this fact in the preparatory work of long-term planning. The single major deficiency is that we have no chance (or hardly any) to weigh up and, particularly, to quantify the effects of the growing integration of CMEA countries upon our economic development. Our relations with the CMEA countries, of course, do figure in our long-term ideas with considerable weight but we should reckon only with such a degree of development and expansion in this connection as can be inferred from the results of past years and can be supported by a projection into the future of recent discussion. If in these 15 years a qualitative change can be achieved in the integration and economic cooperation of the CMEA countries, this, of course, may greatly accelerate progress and shorten by several years the time needed to attain our objectives.

## BRIEF SUMMARY AND SOME ADDITIONAL REMARKS

We can become not only onlookers but active contributors in shaping our economic destinies.

With the unselfish efforts of the best sons and daughters of the nation (and with external help) we have created a system where the possibility exists for rationality and the interests of society to prevail.

[49] J. Kornai: A többszintű népgazdasági programozás modellje (Model of multi-level programming). *Közgazdasági Szemle*, 1968, No. 1, and A többszintű népgazdasági programozás gyakorlati alkalmazásáról (On the practical application of multi-level national economic planning). *Közgazdasági Szemle*, 1968, No. 2, pp. 181 and 183.

However, for this purpose an adequate political decision system must be created so that the most important questions of economic development could—on the basis of conscientious scientific preparation—be decided, and not only formally, by the social-political body which is exclusively competent to take such a decision.

There exists a possibility to select by means of this decision from among the various possibilities the most favourable one, considered as such by the competent social-political body since

— we can regulate the growth rate with acceptable accuracy by influencing the factors affecting it;
— we can calculate with satisfactory exactness how the capital/output ratio will develop in the case of different variants and how the indicators of national economic efficiency will develop in general;
— we can calculate with sufficient accuracy the cost of the major productive investment projects planned, the value of their output, their results and efficiency at the national economic level, when confronted with other possible investments;
— we can calculate with reliable accuracy future trends in the productivity of labour, depending on changes in the pattern of manpower and on its allocation to works of different productivity in the case of different variants;
— there exists the possibility of submitting equally consistent plan variants to the body taking the decision, and deviations in the consequences of decisions about different variants can be assessed.

But we have created not only a social system which enables rationality and the interests of society to prevail; we have also created a vast apparatus which can successfully defy the requirements of rationality and social interest.

For some time now, we have been deciding from year to year to carry out a greater volume of investments than is possible with the available resources of labour, building materials, fittings, etc. We know that this will not result in more investment than could be realized with available capacities in the case of a correct decision; but, on the contrary, it will result in less investment because labour discipline cannot be maintained, resources cannot be concentrated and utilized with greatest relative efficiency. Still, we take each year the wrong decision, handling the problem as if it were a natural calamity, something external to us, as if some power above us hindered us from "harmonizing needs with possibilities".

But we should not extrapolate, however usual and useful this may be in long-term planning, we should not project the deficiencies of the past into the future. Instead, let us do everything to change the situation, to bring it about that proper decisions are taken within the framework of an adequate decision-system, and that, on the basis of a suitable long-term plan, development is substantially accelerated.

# ECONOMIC RESEARCH IN THE SERVICE OF NATIONAL
# ECONOMIC PLANNING

Our investigations will deal mainly with the nature and character of the research projects related to the plan and the planning activity which covers the whole of the country's economy, in short, to the national economic plan and economy-wide planning.

National economic plans can be drawn up—as is well known—for the long term (ten, fifteen or even twenty years), five-year and annual plans are regularly drawn up, and sometimes, in some countries, plans are made even for six months or shorter terms. There are features characteristic of all these economy-wide plans which are, therefore, common and, accordingly, these plans have also some problems in common. In addition, however, the plans covering different periods have also their own special problems. In the following mainly the requirements of five-year planning will be kept in view but the majority of my statements holds not only for these plans.

Central planning, covering the whole economy of a country, is going on today in many countries which are on various levels of socio-economic development. National economic planning in our country and in the other *socialist countries* is of a particular nature and importance because the plan serves as a basis for the deliberate central control of socio-economic development and is also an important tool of this control. Thus the question to which we have to seek an answer is not what should a national economic plan cover in general but the question *what requirements should be met by a plan serving the economic control of society* and this fundamental objective must be kept in view also in the course of research into these problems.

With a certain simplification of the actual situation we may say that in our country the *Hungarian Socialist Workers' Party* (its Congress, or between two Congresses, the Central Committee)—as a representative of the whole society and as a central body—takes the decisions on the deliberate control of socio-economic development, and the *National Planning Office*, being the central planning agency, partly prepares the decisions, or rather their economic part, and partly draws up the plan based on the decisions taken. The problems subject to research should be all those which are accessible for research activity and which can strengthen the scientific foundations of planning in connection with either the decisions or the drawing up of the plan itself.

The following few statements can be laid down as more or less self-explanatory and may serve as general starting points in national economic planning:

140

1. We can and, therefore, must start only from the given potentialities and conditions. Thus, a broad assessment of these must precede planning.

2. The conditions of the tasks to be set must be given or created on the basis of the potentialities before or in the course of carrying out the taks.

3. The national economic plan can be of varying dimensions, more or less detailed, but it must absolutely comprise the provisions for the most important activities (groups or series of activities) complementing and determining each other and those for the main processes taking place and the major economic proportions coming about under the effect of the former. The national economic plan is, as a matter of fact, the coordinated plan of the economic activities of the social units. Such activities, however, are carried out every day by millions. Thus, the plan has to *select*, to choose the most important ones and it also has to aggregate the units to be classified into some group on the basis of some important characteristics or criteria. Similarly, a legion of problems can be found which may or must be subject to research. Here, I can draw attention only to the most important research subjects, more exactly, only to directions and groups of research subjects, not to individual research projects.

4. The activities and processes which may be considered as the most important ones since they determine the development of the economy as a whole, interact and mutually influence one another to such an extent that no group can be planned separately, detached from the others and taken out of its context. To avoid misunderstanding, I add that, obviously, one or several important objectives to be attained can be set in any field if the conclusions are subsequently drawn for all other fields concerned and this does not lead to contradictions. But it must be clear that any major group or series of activities will reverberate throughout the economy—whether we start from agriculture, or foreign trade, or investments etc. From this it follows that any attempt to prepare the five-year agricultural (or industrial or foreign trade etc.) plan of a country in any other form than as part of the whole national economic plan, will miss its aim. The stressing of some objectives means giving them preference over others, i.e. that from the resources available under the plan the attainment of this objective must first be secured—and it can be only attained if resources are sufficient for this purpose—other objectives can be set and planned only to the extent made possible by the remaining resources. It should be clear that it is impossible to select in this manner an entire major field—e.g. agriculture—or rather, if we make such an attempt, the following up and analysis of all consequences, all mutual and feedback effects will amount almost to the drawing up of the entire plan of the national economy; thus the complex plan of such a major field will be no longer the plan of a *single* field but will decide that of the others also.

It follows from the nature of things that decision about the national economic plan cannot, as a rule, be a single act. First, decision must be taken on the main ideas of development, on the basic directions of the plan. This means that the central political body takes a stand with respect to a few most important objectives of economic development, stating that all other objectives of development can be ranked only after these. How can the political body reach such a decision? On a scientific foundation only in case this first decision has already been preceded by adequate preparation. Generally, it will be in this way that the planning agency will make a proposal about the basic conception. This proposal, however, cannot yet be called a plan in the usual sense, i.e. it is not a plan consisting of harmonized parts and covering all important fields of the economy, nor is it a rough picture or outline of such a plan. In the first approximation the basic conception will resemble rather a working hypothesis, a proposal supported by undeniable facts, sober arguments and many-sided considerations about the advisable direction of development. If then the political body takes its decision, this will entail many important consequences in the most diverse fields of the economy, among others because it will be necessary to secure certain qualified specialists, a certain development of investments, transport and foreign trade, since—owing to the interdependence of the various branches of production and consumption—it will affect every field of the national economy. At the same time, however, it also leaves open a whole series of questions. These can be solved in several ways and in several combinations.

Thus, on the basis of the first draft of the basic conception, the first decision has been taken. The planning agency must, for the time being, continue to work on this basic conception. Now, however, starting from the basic conception, it has to work out such drafts as will approach the actual plan in the sense that they cover every important field of the national economy and present variants and alternative solutions for various important problems, showing the consequences, merits and drawbacks of each. It may, of course, happen that these drafts will bring to the surface such a contradiction or contradictions in the basic conception as will make necessary or justify the choice of another conception. In such cases, the whole work must be started afresh. But if this does not happen, the central political body will choose, by a new decision, one of the variants submitted. From now on, the basic conception will be the guiding principle of the actual plan. Obviously, it many happen that the political body, before sanctioning the basic conception in this way, puts new questions and orders further drafts to be worked out. Accordingly, before becoming final, the basic conception may travel several times between the central political body and the central planning agency, each time in a more concrete and fuller form.

It may be seen from the above that decision-taking is a complicated process. In fact, the technical and the political problems are rather interwoven in the planning process since what and in what form is presented to those called upon to decide already influences the decision to be taken to some extent. Some research is, therefore, needed to work out the problems which really demand a political decision.[1]

In the past, the connections between decisions and planning were far from developing as described above. We have, therefore, no practical experience of the method described. For the time being, it is just an idea. But this idea seems to be reasonable and expedient. The solutions to such problems must, however, be submitted to the test of experience. Our present ideas cannot be really confronted even with actual practice or with that of the past, for the simple reason that not even this practice is sufficiently known. To be able to introduce a better system, therefore, scientific research is needed which will critically analyze the history of our planning and decision system up to the recent past.

The connection between planning and decision-taking has been pushed into the foreground by the introduction of the new economic mechanism. This fact itself makes it probable that there exists a close connection between decision-taking, planning, the plan and the mechanism. Very likely the old—insufficiently known—system of decision-taking was related to the old mechanism. Surely, the new mechanism imperatively requires that planning and decision-taking be raised to a scientific level. At the same time, it necessarily involves increased democratization since: (a) it calls for central control to be based on local autonomy and initiative; (b) it draws into the work of planning a wider range of organs, specialists and other interested persons; (c) it renders decisions clear, accessible, criticizable and controllable as opposed to earlier practice when decisions were often taken without sufficiently known justification. All these statements are, however, not fully proven. Scientific research is needed to disclose the connections between decisions, planning, the plan and the mechanism. *The plan is, above all, a plan of resource allocation.* Under the new mechanism, the market can be a preliminary basis for this allocation but later on it is, by all means, its tool, its superviser and its correcting medium. It is necessary to investigate, among other things, how the market mechanism asserts itself under the conditions of modern monopoly capitalism which are, in a sense, comparable with our conditions, what differences there are from this point of view between the various fields of the economy, what mutual effects prevail between the market and the efforts of the monopolies in respect of economic policy, etc.


### THE METHOD

In connection with long-term planning of the national economy there are a great many methodological problems waiting for solution. In most cases, their clarification is possible only on the basis of scientific research of a high standard. At the beginning of this study it has been pointed out that in planning we can and must start only from existing potentialities and

[1] Problems of the implications of political decisions are discussed in detail in the study "Ideas on the Improvement of National Economic Planning" in this Volume.

conditions. Their extensive assessment must, therefore, always precede planning. Even the solution of this single task requires research. The field has to be surveyed: what conditions must or should be known to the planners, on which of these is information available, and what other conditions should be taken into account, in what manner can they be recognized or approached? Where are the major white spots, and where are only some minor modifications needed for the sake of accuracy. The problems of market (demand) research, the various information systems should be studied and partly also the problem of the extent to which it is worth while to examine these. One must also clarify—with the aid of mathematical-statistical methods—what dangers are inherent in the unknown or uncertain factors, to what extent might they distort the drawing up of a plan. One must know which circumstances should be given greater than average attention because of the approximative estimates used in planning them.

A highly important and as yet unsatisfactorily solved problem of long-term planning is how to ensure the internal consistency of the plan, to make it free from contradictions. We are not thinking here of the cases—not infrequent in the past—where competent bodies accepted and enacted a plan whose internal contradictions had been known; what we have in mind is the *theoretical problem of ensuring the fullest possible consistency of the plan*. As a matter of fact, the problem is created mainly by the circumstance—mentioned in the introduction—that any national economic plan can be only a highly simplified reflection of reality. The simpler the model used for representing the whole economy, the easier it will be to ensure—on the basis of this model—full internal consistency and to eliminate the contradictions, but the less can we be sure that there will be no contradictions in reality. We should, therefore, work with such models as will offer the best possible guarantees against any uncomfortable surprise. The method of balances as worked out in the Soviet Union with prolonged effort solved this problem only in rough outline. The input-output table raised the solution to a higher level and enabled its handling with the aid of mathematics. Modern computation techniques rendered great help to planners also in this field, they facilitated—among other things—the drawing up of variants. Research workers have, however, to face further tasks also in this respect; they have to study, among other things, how the possible sources of error can be discovered, eliminated and prevented.

It is, indeed, part of the problem discussed—but owing to its importance a question to be studied separately—how to secure a mutual harmony and correspondence between the value relations expressed in terms of money and the material (physical) relations. In vain have either the traditional method of balances or the input-output tables been used both for value expressions and for quantities of material goods, the difficulties and problems due to their different natures cannot be fully eliminated. The greatest difficulty will remain concealed, if planning in value terms assumes constant prices or assumes that the value of the goods remains constant, and also if changes in physical connections (input coefficients) are disregarded in planning. In reality, both do change and, in addition, often not only in different degrees but in different directions. Research must disclose whether such

144

possible but uncertain changes can be taken into account at all in planning; if so, in what manner and to what extent can this be done or, rather, where can this be done and where not.

In the various fields of planning and in various connections, *models are of great importance.* It is an important task of research to seek and find models truly representing either the whole of the economy or some major or minor part of it, or some of its processes. Whether a model is adequate or not can, of course, be decided only by confronting it with practice, with experience. Thus, the adequate character of a model must be proved by a number of cases corresponding to the nature of the phenomenon in question. Even if the models are not sufficient to draw up a plan of the economy, or some partial field of it, they are indispensable for working out plan variants, and can do good service in checking the consistency of the plan.

It has been mentioned that the national economic plan must cover the most important series of actions and processes that complement and determine one another. We do not know as yet, however, which these are, which of their details should be covered by the plan, which of them can be neglected without endangering the reliability of the plan and which cannot. To find out is a separate task of research.

Extremely important are the research activities aimed at finding the most favourable solution of some planning task, that is, some *optimum.* An optimum solution can be sought, of course, only if we know the problem whose optimum solution we are looking for, i. e. if the objective (objective function) can be determined with sufficient accuracy and if the conditions (constraints) are known or can be determined. Up to now we could not yet attain such an unequivocal determination of the objective and the conditions of the national economy as a whole. This does not mean that research aimed at this target should be abandoned. With regard to more modest but still considerably important tasks, optimization has already brought partly satisfactory results and partly pointed to certain directions which provide food for thought and deserve further research (e.g. the two-level planning work going on in the Planning Office and aimed at the improvement of partial plans which had been worked out earlier with traditional methods). New research may yield further valuable results.

An important part of research work into planning methodology consist of the regular and intensive investigation of the planning methods used in the developed capitalist countries and of the study of the material collected by international organizations. In certain capitalist countries—such as France, Norway, the Netherlands etc.—several methods of measurement, estimation, error finding etc. have been worked out by planners which, with minor or major modifications, may be used also in this country. It may also be instructive to know how planning is related to economic policy in the advanced capitalist countries or how the preparation of decisions on economic policy and their influence figures in the planning methods worked out for the underdeveloped countries.

145

## RESEARCH CONNECTED WITH THE FUNDAMENTAL DIRECTION
## AND BASIC CONCEPTIONS OF THE PLAN

The elaboration of a national economic plan starts with laying down the bas directions of the plan, more exactly with the preparation of proposals to l submitted by the central planning agency to the central political body co cerning the basic conceptions of the plan. It follows that the basic concept tions and thus also the preparation of the proposal on the basic dire tions are of great importance. In popular language it could be said the this is the first occasion for blunders—though there will be several othe later on.

In spite of its high importance, the problem of elaborating the basic co ceptions has no scientific past or basis whatsoever. True, not even the bas directions have been accorded the importance due to them in drawing u the plan. The causes are rooted in the past, they are mainly historical an many be found in the bad experiences of "plan conceptions" lacking an scientific foundation. It is unnecessary to deal with them here. But one c the causes is also the fact that a completed plan no longer shows, in genera whether it rests on carefully worked out basic directions or not. (This aspect will be dealt with below.)

The basic directions of the plan can by no means be identified with th main lines of development of the national economy, nor with its main objec tive of securing the most favourable development of society and its members This is a general and broadly formulated objective which allows hardly an concrete conclusions to be drawn with respect to the national economic plan In itself, it cannot yield an answer even to the obvious question, when o over what period can this most favourable development be attained? Quit obviously, other conclusions will be drawn if this requirement is interpreted as meaning that society should reach a maximum level of development, say in ten years, independently of the standard of living of society during the period up to then, and a different answer must be given if it means that society must develop evenly, to the greatest possible extent throughout the ten years. It should be also clear that the requirement can be given other interpretations also.

But let us go further. It is also not clear what should be understood by development or development level. To take a simplified example: which society is more developed, the one in which each member of the society enjoys an average daily 3,000 calories of food consumption and two persons share a room, or the society where per capita food consumption is only 2,500 calories but every person has a room to himself? Clearly, there are many variations of the question. But let us assume that the competent political body has already decided what should be understood by development and level of development and also that by most favourable development an approximately even and maximum development through some longer period should be meant. These decisions do not yet tell us anything about the rate of development to be attained or its level. Nor can they really say anything since the level and rate of development cannot be predetermined magnitudes, independent of the conditions, circumstances and forms of

development but will result only from the concrete conditions and facts of development itself.

Accordingly, the task of the central planning agency in the field of working out the basic directions consists precisely in submitting to the political body such a basic conception, such an outline of the plan as will yield the most favourable development in the accepted sense of raising the standard of living. But it follows already from the uncertain formulation of the task that no single solution exists. Thus, the planners must submit the outlines of at least two, possibly more, variants which would be of approximately the same value, that is, which would enable roughly the same rate of growth. But how, and on what basis should planners draw up such variants? Neither the practice of planning nor the scientific research work carried out up to now have provided a sufficient basis for working out adequate basic directions. There were, however, several attempts made and by improving them one can hope to approach the problem in a scientific manner.

The first method which offers itself for this purpose is an analysis of the country's natural endowments, economic, historical, etc. conditions. It has often been said that one of the greatest deficiencies of our plans drawn up in the late forties and the early fifties was that they did not properly take into account the potentialities and special conditions of the country. But even apart from the mistakes made, it is obvious that our plans should be based mainly on these characteristics. It has, however, not been clarified as yet how this requirement should be met. In recent years it has often been emphasized that our foreign economic relations have a great and increasing importance for the economy. Does this not reduce the importance of starting from the potentialities? This is by no means the case. The role of foreign economic relations is, indeed, outstanding and it is already a commonplace that the efficiency of our economy can be considerably increased if we do not endeavour to turn out every possible product at home but import part of them in exchange for goods that can be produced in excess of domestic demand. Obviously, this does not reduce the importance of our potentialities and special conditions since it is only on the basis of these that it can be decided what to produce and what to import. There are many goods which scarcely enter into international trade because of the high transportation costs involved. We posses, however, natural deposits which can be extracted in our country under conditions that are, in general, not worse than in other countries, or, at least, in some countries. Such are e.g. bauxite, manganese ore, oil, natural gas, uranium and even part of our coal deposits. Soil and climatic conditions in this country enable us to work in several branches of plant cultivation and animal husbandry under conditions not worse than the European average, and in some branches even under better conditions. These products are, at the same time, raw materials for the food industry. As for the example of foreign countries with more developed raw material extraction or agricultural and food-production: this can be extensively studied in detail as to what development and what profitability can be achieved in various branches of production with different investments and current inputs. In this way some foothold can be established for working out the basic directions or at least part of them.

Another such approximative method may be an analysis of historically given examples, such as:

1. first of all the various stages in our own past, mainly those where development was satisfactory or even outstandingly rapid, with periods of a proper length (at least five years) to be investigated, in order to make it worth-while to draw some lessons therefrom;

2. the economically most advanced countries;

3. countries which have reached a particularly rapid development over at least one longer period of their history; and

4. countries which are in a similar position to this country with respect to area, population, natural conditions, and the level of cultural and economic development.

Beyond a general analysis of the past, efforts should be directed mainly to obtaining an answer — as reliable scientifically as possible — to the question as to what was in the given case the source or the main source of the achievement, under what effects it came about; what were its human, natural and historical conditions or what changes occurred in these; and which of the factors that contributed to the most favourable development in the given case are available or can be created in this country. A clarification of these problems will also yield some guiding principles for working out some (perhaps several) basic directions.

For a third possible method of scientific approach foreign trade may provide some starting points. By starting from the volume of trade that is transacted with some countries or groups of countries and by examining the commodity pattern of this trade, one can select the branches of engineering, light industry or agriculture which should be mainly developed. It is thus not the commodities to be traded abroad under the given conditions that we are looking for. In the latter case we should take into account the comparative advantages to be derived from given conditions. Now a starting point must be found in foreign trade for working out the conception of the national economic plan. Such a starting point offers itself in the trade transacted with the Soviet Union, which constitutes a considerable part of our total foreign trade and provides long-term agreements relating to sizeable volumes of certain commodities. In two or three industries — as e.g. the vehicle-building industry, the electronics of long-distance networks, some food-producing equipment; and also in some branches of agriculture, certain fruits and vegetables — these agreements can be of such a magnitude as to determine the outlines of a basic conception. But in some fields and in respect of certain articles, great possibilities — e.g. of cooperation — may arise with other socialist and also with non-socialist countries. The research task is here to analyze on the basis of foreign and domestic examples, the experiences gained in some of the branches or in connection with products and articles where growth was conspicuous, to investigate the capital, material and labour intensities of their production (inclusive of the requirements in highly qualified manpower and managers), the time necessary for the introduction and the running-in, the consequences due to obsolescence and the requirements of maintaining the technological level, and relying on all these, to examine the prospects of profitable production to be developed

148

on the basis of the given conception, its expected contribution to economic development as a whole and the part it may play in the latter.

All these researches may partly provide ideas and food for thought for the planners, and partly support and verify their assumptions and conclusions. They will make it possible to propose in a well-founded manner two or three development schemes (basic directions) which seem most advantageous, to take into account realistically whether the necessary conditions and possibilities exist for each of the schemes, and what advantages and difficulties are entailed by the acceptance of this or that conception. On the basis of these directions the allocation of all resources can be drawn up in rough outline. The "skeleton" of the plan must thus be prepared in such detail as will enable the approximate setting of the rate of growth and thus the comparability and comparative evaluation of several draft plans prepared in the same manner. It is the task of economico-mathematical research to construct and to test a model which satisfies the requirements of such a "skeleton" plan.

## RELATIONS BETWEEN THE BASIC CONCEPTION AND THE PLAN

In view of the complexity and uncertainty of the process outlined, the question arises whether it is really necessary to work out several schemes and leave it to the political body to choose one from among them. No historical example can be quoted. But there are several examples of a national economic plan being drawn up on the basis of directives considered to be fundamental. Such a basic directive was, e.g., the development of coal mining and of ferrous metallurgy in Hungary at the beginning of the fifties. Of course, there existed some ideas and motivations to justify this directive, but they were without any scientific foundation. It can be assumed that whenever and wherever some basic conception provided the basis of a national economic plan, good arguments could be listed in support of the idea even if these did not rest on scientific research. *Scientific foundation of the plan does, however, imperatively require that the submitting and approval of the basic conception should be preceded by scientific examination and weighing.*

Secondly, the question arises: is there any real need for some basic conception? As a matter of fact, even at present we are not starting out from any basic conception in the above sense, and we seem to be able to manage without any. Moreover—as has been mentioned—a five-year national economic plan, once ready, no longer shows whether scientifically elaborated basic directions served as its basis or not. Of course, with some knowledge of the subject, this can be found out by studying the plan. If the plan relies on one or more basic conceptions, this can be gauged from the plan, one can establish which is the single or which are the major conceptions that dominate, as it were, the plan, to which the other parts of the plan are subordinated. If, however, such basic ideas cannot be gauged from the plan, if the plan comprises many correct objectives of the same or almost the same rank, then the plan has no basic conception. In such cases, therefore, if the planners do not have any basic conception as a compass, it is difficult to draw

149

up the plan in any other way than by putting together the ideas which seem the best and trying to fit them into a uniform plan. Some difficulties must, however, be reckoned with in such cases. And these difficulties do not derive from abstract speculation, they are very real and unavoidable difficulties as have been experienced and paid for dearly in this country. In almost all fields of material production, as well as in other fields requiring economic inputs, there are good, rational, well founded and justified ideas, perhaps worked out in detail, about development. These ideas are, of course, best known to the specialists of the field in question, who are thus most competent to work out and represent these plans and ideas. But, precisely because there are reasonable development requirements in all—or almost all—fields, and the specialists of the respective fields represent them and defend them with conviction, the claims that can be listed on this basis in all cases surpass by far the potentialities.

It should accordingly be clear that part of the claims cannot be met at all, or only in part, or only in a longer period than is desirable. There can be no question of comparing these claims on the ground of the economic advantages their satisfaction would offer. First, part of these claims is of a nature that in meeting them economic viewpoints play only a secondary role or none at all. On the other hand, even development requirements of an economic character can be compared only with difficulty if they arise in different fields. Their utility on the national economic level depends, in fact, not only and not even mainly on the time of realization—which can be easily calculated—nor on some other, equally computable, indicator but on the combined final results they are able to yield, through an intricate network of transmissions, to the economy. This fact puts some limitation on economic calculation in general.

For lack of a proper scale of measurement, the planners can do nothing but try to reduce all claims to some extent until their sum equals the amount that can be satisfied with the aid of the resources available. (Experience has shown, however, that planners do not even go as far as this, but often leave some claims open in the hope that in the course of the planning period some solution can be found.) Thus, nobody receives as much as would be needed to satisfy his claims in a reasonable way and, in addition, resources become diluted and progress is slower than is possible. It is then alleged that the reason lies in the scarcity of capital, since everybody may see that we have not enough to satisfy all justified claims. But obviously, as long as we proceed in the manner described we shall always remain short of capital. As a matter of fact, scarcity of capital—if we do not simply mean that capital has to be dealt with in the same manner as all resources in limited supply—is obviously a relative concept, to be compared with capital requirements. With business fluctuations, there may be alternative shortages and abundance of capital even in the same rich capitalist country. Now, in our country, if we proceed in the way described, there may always come forward more justifiable needs than we are ever able to meet. The method described (which is just a symptom of the harmful disease called, for lack of a better term, "sectoral approach" of the economy) occasions not only the fragmentation of productive resources but also has the result that in

150

case of a collision between the interests of producers and consumers it is usually the consumers who fare worse since they are the last to announce their needs.

The basic conception is important since with its aid we want to come nearer to discovering the most advantageous development and in the course of searching we discover that we can never attain this objective by putting together the most favourable development of the parts. *The question is, how to allocate the basic factors of production, manpower and means of production to achieve an enduring most favourable development?* In other words: man and his natural as well as man-made conditions should be combined in the productive process in such a way as to bring about an ever higher degree of satisfaction for society as a result and simultaneously create also the conditions for further advance to a still higher level.

No more can be distributed than is available. This is true for the allocation of both consumer goods and forces of production. But productive forces can be distributed in many different ways and different distributions will lead to highly different results.

All these are obvious truths. Still, there are some who would see, feel and perceive primarily that our freedom of action in directing the economy is a minimum. A given population will—they believe—decide with its given requirements, purchasing power and habits, without our interference, what and how much it should be supplied with; the manpower and the means of production available will, on the other hand, fundamentally determine by their composition and distribution and in view of foreign trading and credit possibilities what and how much can be produced and even in what direction the economy should be expanded and to what extent. Those who see matters in this way, are inclined to exaggerate the importance of potentialities in delimiting our freedom of action and to belittle the weight, role and importance of deliberate control in the formulation of our future. Indeed, even if they are not completely aware of it, the advocates of the undoubtedly still dominant sectoral approach are devoted to the above ideas.

To avoid any misunderstanding, I must add two remarks. First: the potentialities—and I will revert to this question below—must be taken into account most thoroughly, in a manysided way, and their role must not be neglected or left out of account. Second: what should be meant by deliberate control is a general control of the major outlines, as necessitated by the social interest. Not only can this be reconciled with freedom of decision of individuals in their own personal affairs—in so far as they do not interfere with the freedom of others—but is precisely built upon their freedom of decision.

The grain of truth in the fundamentally fatalistic conception criticized here is that the potentialities and conditions have, indeed, a decisive weight and importance, and we cannot detach ourselves from them, nor jump over them. Every attempt in economic policy or planning which does not fully account for potentialities is harmful and dangerous voluntarism. But from the point of view of economic policy and planning how we utilize our potentialities is even more important since on this will depend how we are able to accelerate our progress.

Experience has shown that without any planning or deliberate direction or, if you like, with the minimum of planning and economic control that can be shown to exist to various extents even in advanced capitalist countries, it was possible to achieve over some longer period—several decades before 1960—e.g. in Sweden an annual growth rate in national income of nearly 4 per cent, in Great Britain one of about 2 per cent and in the USA one of about 3 per cent.

The results achieved by the socialist countries which are deliberately planning and controlling their economy are much more favourable, but they show great differences and variations. Of ourselves we know that we committed numerous mistakes of several kinds in the planning and control of the economy and thus we may safely venture the statement that the most favourable level of growth rate has not yet been attained in this country. Nor can the other socialist countries be assumed to be completely free from some of the mistakes committed in this country. It does not seem to be too bold an assumption, therefore, that the whole socialist world system as well as each of the socialist countries taken separately, is capable of achieving a growth rate much higher than the actual one and one surpassing by far that of the capitalist countries. To achieve this, however, the mistakes and deficiencies experienced must be gradually corrected or abolished. With the reform of the control and management of the economy in Hungary we have taken the road towards this goal. The next step should be to raise decisions concerning the development of the economy to a higher level so that these are scientifically well-founded and correspond to the interests of a socialist society.

CONSUMPTION, NEEDS, INCOMES

After a decision has been taken regarding the basic conception, the central planning agency starts planning work, that is, to draw up the plan in greater detail. It is not, of course, our task to deal with the method of drawing up the plan or with planning itself. Suffice here to mention that it is, obviously, by no means necessary or useful to go beyond certain limits as regards detail in planning. Where this limit should be drawn is—as I mentioned earlier—a separate problem for research. In general, the tasks should be set in such detail as is needed partly to assess the most important effects, links and interrelations as well as the necessary conditions—to be created accordingly—of the activities planned, simultaneously with a disclosure of the still hidden contradictions inherent in the basic directions selected and probably needing new political decision. On the other hand, details are needed in order that the leaders and to some extent the staff in certain fields can see what contribution society expects from them in the interest of economic development. The plan should be worked out in that degree of detail and not further. To what this amounts in practice can be decided only by long experience as well as on the basis of research based on this experience.

As mentioned above, the problem of the basic directions is only the first but by no means the only important one among those needing political

152

decision. With the decision about the basic conception—even if it does not need any revision in the light of further work—only the basic direction of development has been marked out. Knowledge of it gives no information as to the concrete methods of realizing it or about the concrete measures to be taken. There are further important political and technical problems awaiting decision to be thus taken partly by the political bodies and partly by the planning agency. A major part of both, however, requires a scientifically supported decision and thus necessitates in most cases scientific investigation and research. The most important research projects that can be thought of will now be treated—noting, however, that no attempt is made at completeness—for the sake of easier survey, i.e. for practical reasons and not on the basis of a classification of scientific standards, in two groups. First the problems connected with the level of living (needs) and then those connected with the forces of production will be dealt with. It should be mentioned that these two groups are linked to one another and even overlap to some extent.

In connection with the *level of living* the problem of the time horizon should be mentioned in the first place, mainly to clarify some aspects of the problem. In a socialist economy as has been mentioned, it is natural that planning and central control should be directed towards the most favourable development of the economy and of its individual members. But as regards the concrete content of all this, no conclusions can be drawn from the general statement made above. To be able to plan further political decisions are necessary, first of all to decide the period to which the most favourable development should be related.

As an example of this the possibility has already been mentioned of providing for an approximately even favourable development over some longer period. This assumption may be justified by certain considerations. Let us start from the assumption—generally in agreement with reality—that extended reproduction takes place in society, that is, in any given period the global social product is somewhat higher than in the preceding one. In the next period the volume of production will lie between two theoretically possible extremes. The first extreme is where society puts an end to extended reproduction, consumes the quantity produced in excess of the level of the preceding period and does not produce any more in the next. In this case economic development, the growth of national wealth ceases. In the period in question the consumption of society—identified here, for the sake of simplicity, with the level of living—has grown to the greatest possible extent, but in the next period it cannot rise at all since production is not expanding. Thus we have come into contradiction with the objective that we declared to be fundamental.

In the case of the theoretically possible other extreme, society will use for the expansion of production the total increment or surplus of the global social product in the period in question. In this case the wealth of society would increase to the greatest possible extent, but the level of living would not rise at all. This would also contradict our basic objective. The correct solution obviously must lie between the two extremes. In an abstract sense, in general terms which can be modified in reality by various factors—development can be accelerated by increasing accumulation. From this it also follows that a higher future level of living (consumption) will compensate for the lower level of living (consumption) of the present.

It is possible for a decision to be made according to which consumption is kept low for five, ten or even twenty years while maintaining simultaneously a high rate of accumulation after which the proportion is modified in favour of consumption. Obviously, the general rate of growth will differ according to whether the relatively low rate of growth in consumption and the accompanying high rate of accumulation is provided for five, ten or twenty years. But it is equally obvious that the members of society pay in the first case with five, in the second with ten and in the third with twenty years of low living standards for a later rapid rise in the level of living. In the meantime, however, people are born and die and society partly changes. With some simplification: the present generation pays with its lower level of living for a more rapidly rising level in the next generation. There are some scientists who propose on certain grounds a time horizon of twenty years (Strumilin) or one of 12 and a half years (Minc) or one of 8 — 9 years (Notkin), but none of these can be convincingly supported. This proves that *under normal conditions* the political authority should make a choice from among variants each of which would ensure reproduction on an increasing scale to such an extent that an approximately steady year to year rise in living standards could be guaranteed over some longer period. As has also been pointed out, even development refers to measurable, quantifiable development — the national level to total utilization and total inputs — and even to these only under certain conditions, assumptions and with some simplification. In connection with the problem of the time horizon, research should be aimed at disclosing — taking at least 15 years but possibly 20 years and even longer periods — to what extent and for what reasons development in the socialist countries with the most rapid progress has deviated from an approximatively even one and what positive or negative effects these deviations have on development itself.

In connection with the level of living, research projects should be mentioned which are aimed at one of the major problems of economic control and planning, that is, the assessment of social needs. A particularly important field of research is that of the expected, probable, plannable development of consumption. It is a remarkable feature of these researches that — apart from their general connections with socialist planning — they do not much differ from research with a similar purpose in advanced capitalist countries. The essential difference lies in the fact that with us the plan is the major means for deliberately controlling social development while in non-socialist countries these projects are — even in their most developed form — at best a means of orientating the economic policies of a narrower or broader ruling class.

In our country the planning and forecasting of consumption needs can serve — if it can be raised to a level considerably higher than at present — among other things, to influence consumption from the centre so far as this is possible and desirable at all. In non-socialist countries this influence is exerted — in a direction considerably deviating from public interests — by advertising and propaganda machinery, mainly by the great monopolies. Of course, this difference will affect the results of research in various ways.

But the methods themselves are—as has been mentioned—identical in substance. These researches are aimed partly at carefully studying the consumption pattern in the most advanced countries and how these patterns have come about, and partly consist—with the application of modern mathematical methods and computation techniques—in establishing income distribution, demand functions, longer time series, consumption cross-sections, etc. The same difficulty arises in all countries of whatever social system in connection with the study of expected consumption, due to the factor of uncertainty, i.e. to the fact that there is little chance of foreseeing the emergence of new products and new consumption habits.

Another broad field of investigation is concerned with social (public) needs. Part of these, namely those connected with education, will be dealt with in the next section, when treating questions related to forces of production. But apart from these, there are problems of social supply, social care, special problems related to children and old people as well as those emerging in various cultural fields. All these need also highly diversified and intensive research of a non-economic character. But all of them have economic effects as well, material requirements which have to be reckoned with in the various aspects of planning. It should be mentioned that in this field deliberate control by society is much more marked than in connection with the consumption problems treated above. The allocation of available means to the various useful and necessary objectives requires that social decisions should to be taken. Since these decisions will affect different strata of society from important material and cultural points of view, they are of necessity not technical but political in character. Thus, the research mentioned above will serve not only the drawing up of the plan itself but also the preparation of political decisions.

Similarly, research connected with income distribution serves not only planning but the preparation of political decisions also. In this field the number of problems requiring a political decision is extremely high. To mention but a few: how much of the increment of national income in five or more years and in individual years should be spent on accumulation and how much on consumption; of the increment falling to consumption, how much should be paid out in the form of wages and pensions, how much should be spent on child welfare institutions, etc. What part of wages should be paid out to those engaged in production and how much to those employed in other fields. Should the previously lower and/or upper limit of wage rates be changed and if so, should the ratio of the two also change and in what direction.

The research necessary for the preparation of decisions is partly of an historical character, investigating how these problems have been solved in practice in our country or in other—socialist and non-socialist—countries in the course of development, and what conclusions can be drawn from history in this respect, what rules could be established. Another part of the research work is theoretical, partly statistical and even speculative in character. These deal with such questions as the relations between income distribution and the level of living, between income distribution and technological development, the conclusions that can be drawn regarding income

155

distribution from modern directions of technological development and, particularly, from automation; the conclusions that follow from the socialist ownership of the means of production and its two forms; the implications of socialist ethics, etc.

## THE FORCES OF PRODUCTION

Among the research tasks connected with planning, those related to the development of productive forces and, particularly, to *labour* and *manpower planning* play a highly important role. Their importance is due partly to the fact that manpower is the most important of productive forces, whose quantitative and qualitative development decisively influences the possible rate of growth of the economy. On the other hand, part of the related problems requires the longest horizon of planning. In society, and particularly in the productive fields, a constantly greater number—both in absolute and relative terms—of highly qualified manpower is needed; technicians, engineers, specialists and scientists whose training requires 4, 8, 10 or even more years beyond the basic education. But even basic education has to be organized according to the type and requirements of further training. Beside the claims that are raised by the material and intellectual needs of society upon manpower (in the broadest sense), also account should be taken of the fact that an overall development of the capacities of every individual member of society is an important social objective in itself. Here scientific research has to employ, in addition to the comparative and historical methods, also mathematical ones: model-building, efficiency computations, etc.

In connection with research related to planning the development of productive forces, there are also comprehensive projects embracing the whole of the economy. An outstanding place is occupied by those aimed at comparing the development and the level of development of socialist and non-socialist countries. This group of research projects includes investigations aimed at establishing indicators for gauging the level of economic development by selecting some indicators of production and consumption and designed to analyze the problems involved. They include the deduction of various possible main or major development trends from historical examples, comparison of the economic patterns of advanced and less developed, socialist and non-socialist countries, their classification according to types and other characteristics as well as the study and analysis of the relationship between the various types of development and their changes on the one hand and the natural endowments, the development of productive forces, the international division of labour, etc. on the other.

Similar comparative and analytical studies can and should be undertaken separately for each of the main branches of the economy, particularly for the most important ones but even for smaller fields. It is certainly worth while to investigate—from the point of view of conclusions to be drawn for planning—for example the development of steel production in the countries leading in this field, its material basis, technological directions, productivity, equipment and choice of products; or the development of motor car

156

production, or that of machine tools; the place of plastics in the production pattern of advanced countries, changes in their ratio to natural materials, trends of development, etc.

Particularly intensive studies are needed in the fields connected with *technological development*, research, designing and construction. The fields of analysis should be: technological development in the most advanced countries, their material and intellectual basis, methods and mechanism, the length and duration of research from basic research to implementation, the relative proportion of the various stages, distribution and concentration of research, its organizational forms, methods of production and product development, purchase of production processes and licences from abroad, cooperation possibilities with socialist and non-socialist countries, etc. Of course, here we are thinking only of economic research projects connected with the planning of technical development. These can say very little or nothing about the concrete aims of technical development, about the immediate tasks to be solved. The uncertainties arising here—caused by the fact that the rate and contents of technical development are controlled by the world powers richer in intellectual and material wealth, which carefully guard their secrets while we have still to aim at world standards—belong to the gravest problems of national economic planning. Economic research cannot solve these problems but, by disclosing the economic aspects of technical work, it can yield useful information on what is worth while to investigate with our own forces; on the economic ramifications and reverberations of certain developments; on the allocation of the available material resources to various purposes, etc.

Another important research task connected with these problems is to trace the causes that have retarded and hindered technical progress or rendered it difficult up to the present; to establish the connections between these phenomena and the mistakes or deficiencies of planning; to find out what can and should be done to attain the most favourable technical development in reality, and how and in what manner this can be promoted from the aspect of planning. Similarly to the subject mentioned earlier, here too, part of the studies is historical in character, relating to the development of Hungary and the foreign countries most interesting from the point of view of this comparison, while another part is connected with economic efficiency calculations. Some of these projects cannot be carried out without the construction of a model, etc.

A further important subject of research into the planning of the allocation of productive forces is the *territorial location of the forces of production*. This requires a political decision, since it affects broad masses of the population in their most important interests, to determine where, what and to what extent development should take place. Economic research is needed to establish the economic advantages or drawbacks of some solution, and to work out the total economic costs, taking into account the "consequential" investments, manpower supply and transport. On the basis of the political decision it is a further task for research to find the optimum proportion in the territorial distribution of the branches of production.

The problem of the external, international relations of the economy has an important role in long-term national economic planning. As mentioned in connection with the question of main directions, the desirable, possible and expected development of our international relations has to be weighed when setting the direction of production. From this task derive the research projects connected with the development of international relations. In this field, too, comparative, historical and mathematical research is equally needed. The latter is aimed mainly at the efficiency problems of foreign trade, at the optimization of trade under certain conditions. These questions cannot, however, be separated from the problems of the production pattern, that is, neither from investment problems nor from those of technical development. For the preparation of political decisions a combined and complex investigation of these problems is needed, based, in turn, also on such decisions.

It has been repeatedly mentioned that it is necessary to analyze progress in other socialist as well as in advanced capitalist countries from some points of view—e.g. from that of consumption or technological progress. But these countries have also to be studied in themselves, in their historical development and thus we shall have to study the developing countries with which we maintain trading connections or shall enter into trade in the future—from the point of view of our international, foreign trade relations.

It is a characteristic feature of the planning of our international relations that they involve greater than average uncertainties since the development of these relations depends not only on ourselves but also on our partners. In this field it is, therefore, particularly justified to reckon with various possibilities, to draw up different plan variants. These relations can be influenced to a greater extent than is usual by political and even defence considerations. And conversely, these connections can greatly influence the development of our policies and even our defence. All this will affect planning and the research work connected with planning.

## SOME FURTHER PROBLEMS

Up to now we have spoken about the tasks of economic research connected with national economic planning which are related either to planning methods or basic conceptions of the plan, or some major, important groups of planning problems (social needs, productive forces, etc.). There may arise innumerable other research problems connected in concrete form with the immediate tasks facing the economy. As a matter of fact, if the plan is actually the basis of central economic control and an important means to this end, it is obvious that the major objectives to be realized in the course of economic development deserve special attention and demand special solutions in planning as well. Other special research problems may arise in connection with the planning of these objectives. As an example, let me quote just two problems of this type.

It is a fact that, not only in Hungary but also in the USSR and other European socialist countries, the development of agriculture usually falls behind both the plan and the general growth of the economy. In the majority of the countries the plans—also the five-year plans of Hungary—have provided for an essentially quicker development of agriculture, which would have been more in harmony with the overall growth of the economy. However, while in the other branches of the economy it was possible in most cases to fulfil and even overfulfil the plan, the actual development of agriculture always lagged behind to some extent, sometimes even considerably. Research workers should be given the task of investigating and disclosing the causes of this occurence, the mistakes committed and the ways to avoid them in the future; to work out the highest attainable growth rate in agricultural production and the conditions for achieving it; to ascertain what rate of agricultural production should be aimed at in order to ensure the most favourable development of the economy as a whole, and what kind of plan should be drawn up to serve the realization of this development most effectively.

The even, fluctuating or cyclical character of economic growth constitutes a special problem for planning. It is only in recent years that greater attention has been paid to this aspect of the question. On the basis of general consideration it was, of course, known that even in the best case development could be only approximatively even. This follows, among other things, from the strong effect of fluctuating weather conditions on agriculture and through this on the economy as a whole. It also follows, among other things, from the variations in the rate of return of investments. Even if accumulation and, particularly, investment inputs rose evenly year by year, because of differences in the period of completion and the rate of return, capacities with a different output volume and value will enter the production process each year. We know that in Hungary economic progress has been far from even; it has shown great fluctuations ever since the introduction of a planned economy, throughout the period of laying the foundations of socialism and in the latter stage of efforts aimed at accomplishing the construction of a socialist economy. We also know that the situation is similar in the majority of socialist countries. We were, however, generally inclined to consider this an abnormal situation, the result of the voluntarism that had dominated the economy in the earlier period, on the one hand, and the counter-revolution later on, on the other.

Since it has been established, however, that this uneven development is characteristic of all European socialist countries, research workers should be set the task to work out the origins of the major fluctuations in various fields of the economy or in general, and to clarify the question whether these were due to the mistakes or, rather, only to the mistakes made. If so, to what extent can these deficiencies be shown also in planning and to what extent were they the consequences which could not, or only partly, be accounted for in planning; what are the chances that development should be more even in the future and what implications has this for planning, etc; It goes without saying that in this field, too, historical, comparative, mathematical and speculative methods of research should equally be employed.